The Effective Reader/Writer

Annotated Instructor's Edition

D.J. Henry

Daytona State College

PEARSON

Boston Columbus Indianapolis New York San Francisco Upper Saddle River
Amsterdam Cape Town Dubai London Madrid Milan Munich Paris Montréal Toronto
Delhi Mexico City São Paulo Sydney Hong Kong Seoul Singapore Taipei Tokyo

Executive Editor: Matt Wright
Editorial Assistant: Laura Marenghi
Development Editor: Erin Dye
Marketing Manager: Jennifer Edwards
Production Manager: Ellen MacElree
Senior Supplements Editor: Donna Campion
Executive Digital Producer: Stefanie A. Snajder
Digital Editor: Sara Gordus
Digital Content Specialist: Anne Leung
Project Coordination: Cenveo© Publisher Services
Cover Designer/Manager: Wendy Ann Fredericks
Cover Photos: © Shutterstock/Rangizz; Fotolia/Marzanna Syncerz; Shutterstock/Paul Michael Hughes
Senior Manufacturing Buyer: Roy L. Pickering, Jr.
Printer/Binder: R. R. Donnelley & Sons/Willard
Cover Printer: Phoenix Color/Hagerstown

Designer: Anthony Limerick
Design Director: Stuart Jackman
Publisher Sophie Mitchell

Credits and acknowledgments for material borrowed from other sources and reproduced, with permission, in this textbook appear on pages 754–756.

Library of Congress Control Number: 2014942284

10 9 8 7 6 5 4 3 2 1—DOW—17 16 15 14

Student ISBN-13: 978-0-205-89095-8
Student ISBN-10: 0-205-89095-4
Instructor's Review Copy ISBN-13: 978-0-321-82964-1
Instructor's Review Copy ISBN-10: 0-321-82964-6

www.pearsonhighered.com

Brief Contents

Detailed Contents

MODULE 4

Word Choice, Tone, and Purpose 122

UNIT 3 Reading and Writing Paragraphs and Essays

MODULE 5

Stated Main Ideas in Reading and Writing Paragraphs 162

MODULE 6

Supporting Details in Reading and Writing Paragraphs 196

UNIT 5 Critical Thinking and Argument

UNIT 6 Mastering Grammar, Punctuation, and Mechanics with MySkillsLab

Preface

The Effective Reader/Writer offers a balanced approach to literacy by bringing instruction for reading and writing together in one textbook.

Research indicates that when reading and writing are taught together, students achieve better in both areas (Tierney & Shanahan, 1991). Although reading and writing are not identical, they are similar, complementary developmental processes. They both have recursive before, during, and after phases, and the outcome of both is that the individual constructs his or her own meaning. *The Effective Reader/Writer* builds on these similarities.

How Does *The Effective Reader/Writer* Emphasize Process?

Emphasis on reading and writing as processes is embedded in instruction throughout the textbook. The reading, writing, and reading/writing processes are introduced and illustrated in Unit 1 with two-page four-color graphics that explain these processes individually and then show how they work together.

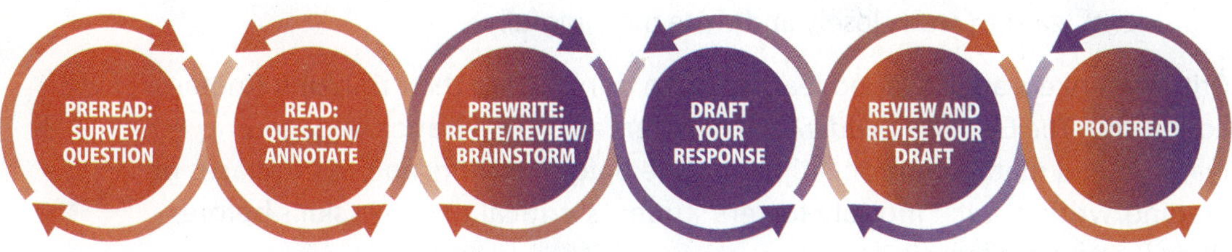

Appropriate process icons appear throughout the textbook as signals to guide students through the reading and writing process of particular assignments.

How Does *The Effective Reader/ Writer* Help Students Think Critically?

One of the most significant benefits of teaching reading and writing together is that students become better critical thinkers (Langer & Applebee, 1987). A critical thinker raises questions; considers multiple perspectives; gathers, analyzes, and assesses information; applies new knowledge; and reflects to self-improve. While Unit 5 offers extensive direct instruction for the high-level critical thinking skills, *The Effective Reader/Writer* deepens critical thinking by asking students to assume the role of both readers and writers within each and every module. For example,

- Students learn to clarify an author's purpose when they read and their own purposes when they write.
- Students learn to ask questions to comprehend and compose texts.
- Students learn to assess supporting details in what they read and in preparation for what they write.
- Students learn to evaluate the impact of word choices made by authors in what they read and as they prepare to write for a specific audience.
- Students learn to develop logical inferences and conclusions based on what they read and in preparation for what they write.
- Students learn to identify and analyze sources in what they read and in preparation for what they write.
- Students learn to read closely and write meaningfully.

Critical thinkers are engaged learners who think about their thinking (metacognition). *The Effective Reader/Writer* fosters and encourages engaged learning and metacognition. Mirroring the before, during, and after phases of reading/writing, each module fosters students' critical thinking skills before, during, and after learning.

Before Learning:

In each module opener, the photographic organizer introduces the concept or main topic of the module and guides students to think critically about the concept. To prepare to learn, students . . .

- **Call up prior knowledge:** Students analyze the engaging set of photographs to compose captions that state how each photograph represents or relates to the topic of the module.
- **Make predictions:** By answering the question "What's the point of…?", students make written predictions about the significance of the topic and how it applies to everyday, college, and working life.
- **Engage visual and tactile learning modes:** Students consider photographs to call up their prior knowledge, analyze what the images represent, and respond with written predictions about the importance of the concept.
- **Utilize writing-to-learn:** Students reflect in writing about their level of understanding and the need to know/learn more about the topic of the module.

During Learning:

Throughout each module, examples and explanations engage students as active learners; then practices offer opportunities for students to apply what they learn and test their understanding. To learn, students . . .

- **Engage with examples:** Examples are designed as directed thinking activities that reinforce instruction by guiding students to complete an exercise that applies the instruction to a specific situation. Explanations follow immediately.
- **Model think-alouds:** Each think-aloud records one student's answer to the example and explains the thought process or decisions he or she made as he or she completed the example. Students are encouraged to use writing-to-learn to record their own think-alouds about what and how they are learning.
- **Apply core concepts to specific situations:** Practices guide students to apply what they are learning to situations or content encountered in everyday, college, or working life.

After Learning:

Each module ends with a series of after learning activities, such as Workshops; Reading/Writing Assignments for Everyday, College, and Working Life; Review Tests; and an Academic Learning Log. These varied activities reinforce learning and offer students the opportunity to track and reflect upon their mastery of the concepts studied in the module. To think critically after learning, students . . .

- **Apply concepts:** The module Workshop guides students to apply the concepts they have learned in the module as a strategy throughout the reading/writing process. The Reading/Writing Assignments are designed as choices students can select to apply what they have learned in the Workshop.
- **Review concepts and test ongoing mastery:** Each module offers two Review Tests (one in print and one in MySkillsLab). Students read a passage and answer objective reading comprehension questions. These questions also cover concepts taught in previous modules.
- **Respond to reading passages:** Most Review Tests ask students to think critically to summarize the passage. All Review Tests conclude with a writing prompt, "What Do You Think?" Students think critically to use information from the reading passage to address a specific writing situation.
- **Reflect upon learning:** In the Academic Learning Logs students recall key vocabulary and concepts for each learning outcome. Students use their own words or create concept maps to call up what they have learned. Students also analyze their level of mastery, identify what they still need to study, and explain how they plan to continue their studies.

How Does *The Effective Reader/Writer* Provide Students with Purpose and Self-Assessment Tools?

Learning Outcomes

Each module in Units 1–6 begins by stating student learning outcomes and offering pre-learning activities called "What's the Point?" that guide students in the use of predicting, questioning, and setting a purpose for learning. Throughout the modules, students learn by applying core concepts to meaningful reading and writing situations, thereby developing and internalizing reading and writing processes. Modules end with after learning summaries and applications tied to the module's student learning outcomes so students may self-assess, monitor progress, and address individual needs. Each module is also aligned to an additional Review Test in MySkillsLab.

6

LEARNING OUTCOMES

Supporting Details in Reading and Writing Paragraphs

To better understand the purpose of supporting details, compare a paragraph to a well-planned house of ideas. The *topic* or general subject matter is the roof. The roof covers all the rooms of the house, just like the topic covers all the details in a paragraph. The main idea determines the frame of the house, and the *supporting details* are the studs and beams that give shape to the different rooms. The frame is made up of *major* supports that bear the weight of the building and smaller *minor* supports that give shape and form to the different rooms in the house. Just as pieces of wood, steel, or blocks support and shape the house, specific and well-chosen details give strength and shape to a writer's ideas.

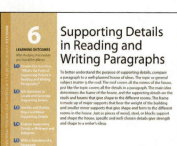

Levels of Learning

The best way *to learn* is *to do*. Thus, one of the primary aims of this text is to give students plentiful opportunities to apply what they are learning. Every concept introduced in the book is accompanied by an **explanation** of the concept, an **example** with explanation of the example, and one or more **practice** exercises.

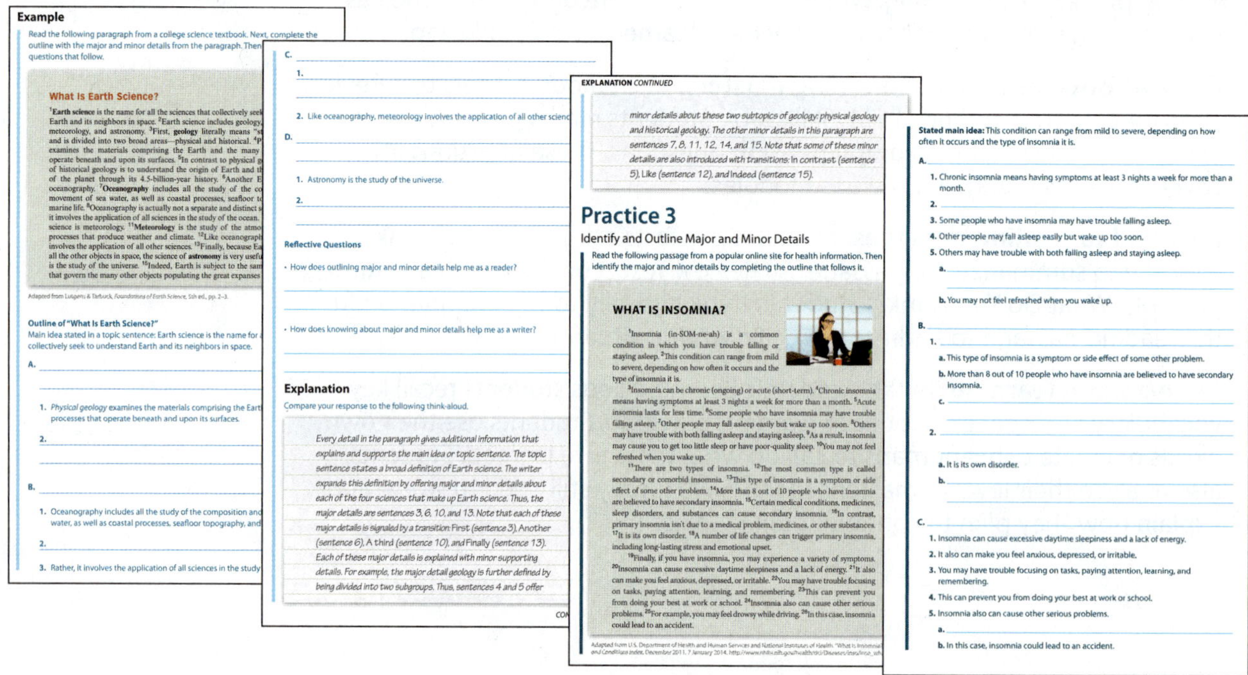

Example

Read the following paragraph from a college science textbook. Next, complete the outline with the major and minor details from the paragraph. Then questions that follow.

What Is Earth Science?

Adapted from Lutgens & Tarbuck, *Foundations of Earth Science*, 5th ed., pp. 2–3.

Outline of "What Is Earth Science?"

Main idea stated in a topic sentence: Earth science is the name for collectively seek to understand Earth and its neighbors in space.

A. ______

1. *Physical geology* examines the materials comprising the Eart processes that operate beneath and upon its surfaces.
2. ______

B. ______

1. Oceanography includes all the study of the composition and water, as well as coastal processes, seafloor topography, and
2. ______
3. Rather, it involves the application of all sciences in the study

C. ______

1. ______
2. Like oceanography, meteorology involves the application of all other scienc

D. ______

1. Astronomy is the study of the universe.
2. ______

Reflective Questions

- How does outlining major and minor details help me as a reader?
- How does knowing about major and minor details help me as a writer?

Explanation

Compare your response to the following think-aloud.

Every detail in the paragraph gives additional information that explains and supports the main idea or topic sentence. The topic sentence states a broad definition of Earth science. The writer expands this definition by offering major and minor details about each of the four sciences that make up Earth science. Thus, the major details are sentences 3, 6, 10, and 13. Note that each of these major details is signaled by a transition: First *(sentence 3),* Another *(sentence 6),* A third *(sentence 10), and* Finally *(sentence 13). Each of these major details is explained with minor supporting details. For example, the major detail geology is further defined by being divided into two subgroups. Thus, sentences 4 and 5 offer*

EXPLANATION *CONTINUED*

minor details about these two subtopics of geology: physical geology and historical geology. The other minor details in this paragraph are sentences 7, 8, 11, 12, 14, and 15. Note that some of these minor details are also introduced with transitions: In contrast *(sentence 5),* Like *(sentence 12), and* Indeed *(sentence 15).*

Practice 3

Identify and Outline Major and Minor Details

Read the following passage from a popular online site for health information. Then identify the major and minor details by completing the outline that follows it.

WHAT IS INSOMNIA?

[1]Insomnia (in-SOM-ne-ah) is a common condition in which you have trouble falling or staying asleep. [2]This condition can range from mild to severe, depending on how often it occurs and the type of insomnia it is.

[3]Insomnia can be chronic (ongoing) or acute (short-term). [4]Chronic insomnia means having symptoms at least 3 nights a week for more than a month. [5]Acute insomnia lasts for less time. [6]Some people who have insomnia may have trouble falling asleep. [7]Other people may fall asleep easily but wake up too soon. [8]Others may have trouble with both falling asleep and staying asleep. [9]As a result, insomnia may cause you to get too little sleep or have poor-quality sleep. [10]You may not feel refreshed when you wake up.

[11]There are two types of insomnia. [12]The most common type is called secondary or comorbid insomnia. [13]This type of insomnia is a symptom or side effect of some other problem. [14]More than 8 out of 10 people who have insomnia are believed to have secondary insomnia. [15]Certain medical conditions, medicines, sleep disorders, and substances can cause secondary insomnia. [16]In contrast, primary insomnia isn't due to a medical problem, medicines, or other substances. [17]It is its own disorder. [18]A number of life changes can trigger primary insomnia, including long-lasting stress and emotional upset.

[19]Finally, if you have insomnia, you may experience a variety of symptoms. [20]Insomnia can cause excessive daytime sleepiness and a lack of energy. [21]It also can make you feel anxious, depressed, or irritable. [22]You may have trouble focusing on tasks, paying attention, learning, and remembering. [23]This can prevent you from doing your best at work or school. [24]Insomnia also can cause other serious problems. [25]For example, you may feel drowsy while driving. [26]In this case, insomnia could lead to an accident.

Stated main idea: This condition can range from mild to severe, depending on how often it occurs and the type of insomnia it is.

A. ______

1. Chronic insomnia means having symptoms at least 3 nights a week for more than a month.
2. ______
3. Some people who have insomnia may have trouble falling asleep.
4. Other people may fall asleep easily but wake up too soon.
5. Others may have trouble with both falling asleep and staying asleep.
   a. ______
   b. You may not feel refreshed when you wake up.

B. ______

1. ______
   a. This type of insomnia is a symptom or side effect of some other problem.
   b. More than 8 out of 10 people who have insomnia are believed to have secondary insomnia.
   c. ______
2. ______
   a. It is its own disorder.
   b. ______

C. ______

1. Insomnia can cause excessive daytime sleepiness and a lack of energy.
2. It also can make you feel anxious, depressed, or irritable.
3. You may have trouble focusing on tasks, paying attention, learning, and remembering.
4. This can prevent you from doing your best at work or school.
5. Insomnia also can cause other serious problems.
   a. ______
   b. In this case, insomnia could lead to an accident.

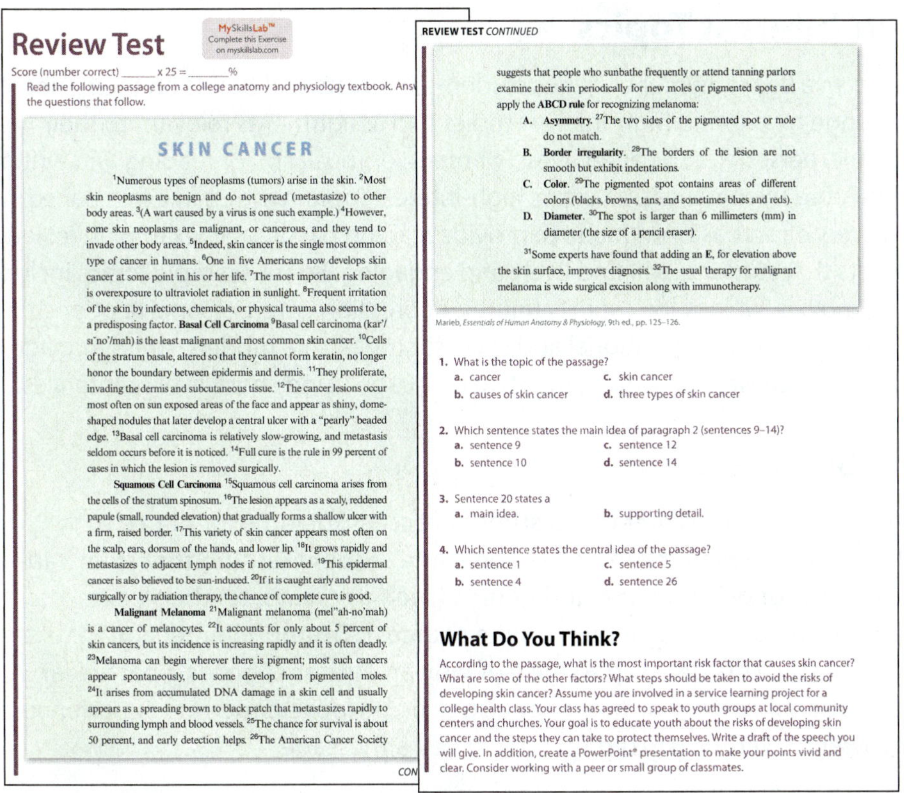

Review Test

MySkillsLab™ Complete this Exercise on myskillslab.com

Score (number correct) ______ x 25 = ______%

Read the following passage from a college anatomy and physiology textbook. Answer the questions that follow.

SKIN CANCER

[1]Numerous types of neoplasms (tumors) arise in the skin. [2]Most skin neoplasms are benign and do not spread (metastasize) to other body areas. [3](A wart caused by a virus is one such example.) [4]However, some skin neoplasms are malignant, or cancerous, and they tend to invade other body areas. [5]Indeed, skin cancer is the single most common type of cancer in humans. [6]One in five Americans now develops skin cancer at some point in his or her life. [7]The most important risk factor is overexposure to ultraviolet radiation in sunlight. [8]Frequent irritation of the skin by infections, chemicals, or physical trauma also seems to be a predisposing factor. **Basal Cell Carcinoma** [9]Basal cell carcinoma (kar'/sı˝no'/mah) is the least malignant and most common skin cancer. [10]Cells of the stratum basale, altered so that they cannot form keratin, no longer honor the boundary between epidermis and dermis. [11]They proliferate, invading the dermis and subcutaneous tissue. [12]The cancer lesions occur most often on sun exposed areas of the face and appear as shiny, dome-shaped nodules that later develop a central ulcer with a "pearly" beaded edge. [13]Basal cell carcinoma is relatively slow-growing, and metastasis seldom occurs before it is noticed. [14]Full cure is the rule in 99 percent of cases in which the lesion is removed surgically.

Squamous Cell Carcinoma [15]Squamous cell carcinoma arises from the cells of the stratum spinosum. [16]The lesion appears as a scaly, reddened papule (small, rounded elevation) that gradually forms a shallow ulcer with a firm, raised border. [17]This variety of skin cancer appears most often on the scalp, ears, dorsum of the hands, and lower lip. [18]It grows rapidly and metastasizes to adjacent lymph nodes if not removed. [19]This epidermal cancer is also believed to be sun-induced. [20]If it is caught early and removed surgically or by radiation therapy, the chance of complete cure is good.

Malignant Melanoma [21]Malignant melanoma (mel"ah-no'mah) is a cancer of melanocytes. [22]It accounts for only about 5 percent of skin cancers, but its incidence is increasing rapidly and it is often deadly. [23]Melanoma can begin wherever there is pigment; most such cancers appear spontaneously, but some develop from pigmented moles. [24]It arises from accumulated DNA damage in a skin cell and usually appears as a spreading brown to black patch that metastasizes rapidly to surrounding lymph and blood vessels. [25]The chance for survival is about 50 percent, and early detection helps. [26]The American Cancer Society

CON

REVIEW TEST *CONTINUED*

suggests that people who sunbathe frequently or attend tanning parlors examine their skin periodically for new moles or pigmented spots and apply the **ABCD rule** for recognizing melanoma:

A. **Asymmetry.** [27]The two sides of the pigmented spot or mole do not match.
B. **Border irregularity.** [28]The borders of the lesion are not smooth but exhibit indentations.
C. **Color.** [29]The pigmented spot contains areas of different colors (blacks, browns, tans, and sometimes blues and reds).
D. **Diameter.** [30]The spot is larger than 6 millimeters (mm) in diameter (the size of a pencil eraser).

[31]Some experts have found that adding an **E**, for elevation above the skin surface, improves diagnosis. [32]The usual therapy for malignant melanoma is wide surgical excision along with immunotherapy.

Marieb, *Essentials of Human Anatomy & Physiology*, 9th ed., pp. 125–126.

1. What is the topic of the passage?
   a. cancer c. skin cancer
   b. causes of skin cancer d. three types of skin cancer
2. Which sentence states the main idea of paragraph 2 (sentences 9–14)?
   a. sentence 9 c. sentence 12
   b. sentence 10 d. sentence 14
3. Sentence 20 states a
   a. main idea. b. supporting detail.
4. Which sentence states the central idea of the passage?
   a. sentence 1 c. sentence 5
   b. sentence 4 d. sentence 26

What Do You Think?

According to the passage, what is the most important risk factor that causes skin cancer? What are some of the other factors? What steps should be taken to avoid the risks of developing skin cancer? Assume you are involved in a service learning project for a college health class. Your class has agreed to speak to youth groups at local community centers and churches. Your goal is to educate youth about the risks of developing skin cancer and the steps they can take to protect themselves. Write a draft of the speech you will give. In addition, create a PowerPoint® presentation to make your points vivid and clear. Consider working with a peer or small group of classmates.

Each module also contains **two review tests**, one in print and one in MySkillsLab, in which students read passages to practice their reading skills and then respond to the passage in writing based on a *What Do You Think?* writing prompt. Finally, each module closes with a **review**. Each module also features a section of **reading and writing assignments**. These assignments create realistic writing situations that direct students to consider audience and purpose as they respond to topics and situations relevant to "Everyday Life," "College Life," and "Working Life." Thus, the text offers several levels of learning. Not only are students given an abundance of practice so that they focus on individual skills, but they are also provided with challenging writing situations in which to employ their reading/writing process.

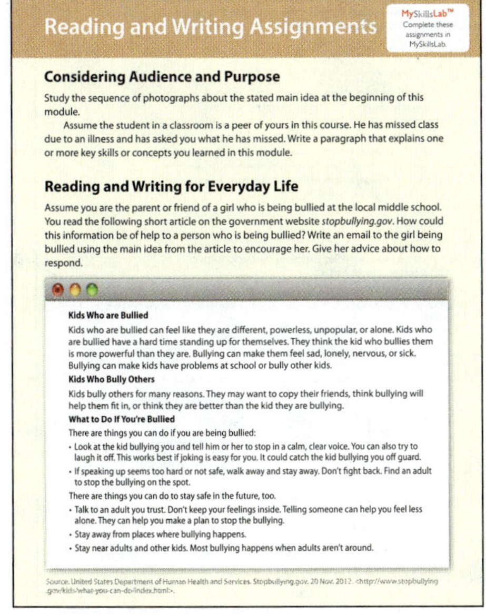

Reading and Writing Assignments

MySkillsLab™ Complete these assignments in MySkillsLab.

Considering Audience and Purpose

Study the sequence of photographs about the stated main idea at the beginning of this module.

Assume the student in a classroom is a peer of yours in this course. He has missed class due to an illness and has asked you what he has missed. Write a paragraph that explains one or more key skills or concepts you learned in this module.

Reading and Writing for Everyday Life

Assume you are the parent or friend of a girl who is being bullied at the local middle school. You read the following short article on the government website *stopbullying.gov*. How could this information be of help to a person who is being bullied? Write an email to the girl being bullied using the main idea from the article to encourage her. Give her advice about how to respond.

Kids Who are Bullied

Kids who are bullied can feel like they are different, powerless, unpopular, or alone. Kids who are bullied have a hard time standing up for themselves. They think the kid who bullies them is more powerful than they are. Bullying can make them feel sad, lonely, nervous, or sick. Bullying can make kids have problems at school or bully other kids.

Kids Who Bully Others

Kids bully others for many reasons. They may want to copy their friends, think bullying will help them fit in, or think they are better than the kid they are bullying.

What to Do If You're Bullied

There are things you can do if you are being bullied:

- Look at the kid bullying you and tell him or her to stop in a calm, clear voice. You can also try to laugh it off. This works best if joking is easy for you. It could catch the kid bullying you off guard.
- If speaking up seems too hard or not safe, walk away and stay away. Don't fight back. Find an adult to stop the bullying on the spot.

There are things you can do to stay safe in the future, too.

- Talk to an adult you trust. Don't keep your feelings inside. Telling someone can help you feel less alone. They can help you make a plan to stop the bullying.
- Stay away from places where bullying happens.
- Stay near adults and other kids. Most bullying happens when adults aren't around.

Source: United States Department of Human Health and Services. Stopbullying.gov. 20 Nov. 2012. <http://www.stopbullying.gov/kids/what-you-can-do/index.html>.

Academic Learning Log: Module Review

Summary of Key Concepts of Time Order and Space Order

Assess your comprehension of time order and space order patterns.

LO1

1. The two time order patterns of organization are ______ and ______.
2. ______ is the time order pattern used to show a series of events by describing ______ things occurred and in ______.
3. ______ is the time order pattern used to show ______, ______, or ______ that can be repeated at any time with similar results.
4. Space order is ______.

LO1 LO2 LO3 LO4 LO5

6. Sensory details are ______, ______, ______, ______, and ______.

LO1 LO2 LO3 LO4

7. Readers and writers ask the reporter's questions ______, ______, ______, and ______ to identify and generate relevant details using time order and space order.

High-Interest Topics

The Effective Reader/Writer engages students' interests and builds on their prior knowledge by offering high-interest topics and assignments relevant to their academic, personal, and career lives. For many, enthusiasm for reading and writing is stimulated by material that offers high-interest topics written in a fast-paced style. Every effort has been made to provide reading passages in examples, reviews, and tests that students will find lively and engaging. Some example topics include gangs, movies, weight loss, sports figures, depression, interpersonal relationships, drug use, nutrition, inspirational and success stories, role models, stress management, and exercise—all written in active language using short, lively sentences.

Text Structure

The Effective Reader/Writer offers students access to and experience with materials that present both professional and student writing that span various patterns of organization and genres (such as essays, textbook excerpts, articles from books, magazines, online sources). Through immersion in text structure, students develop a sense of why an author chooses a particular organizational pattern or genre for a specific purpose. Students experience the power of well-organized text to convey a message.

Visual Instruction and Learning Activities

The Effective Reader/Writer uses photographs, graphics, and annotation of instructional examples to reach visual learners and drive concepts home. For example, each module opens with a photographic organizer that activates the thinking process by introducing and illustrating the skill in question, and stimulating prewriting activities. As another example, visual learning activities introduce and facilitate writing assignments; concept maps, charts, graphs, and annotated examples enable students to "see" the concept clearly.

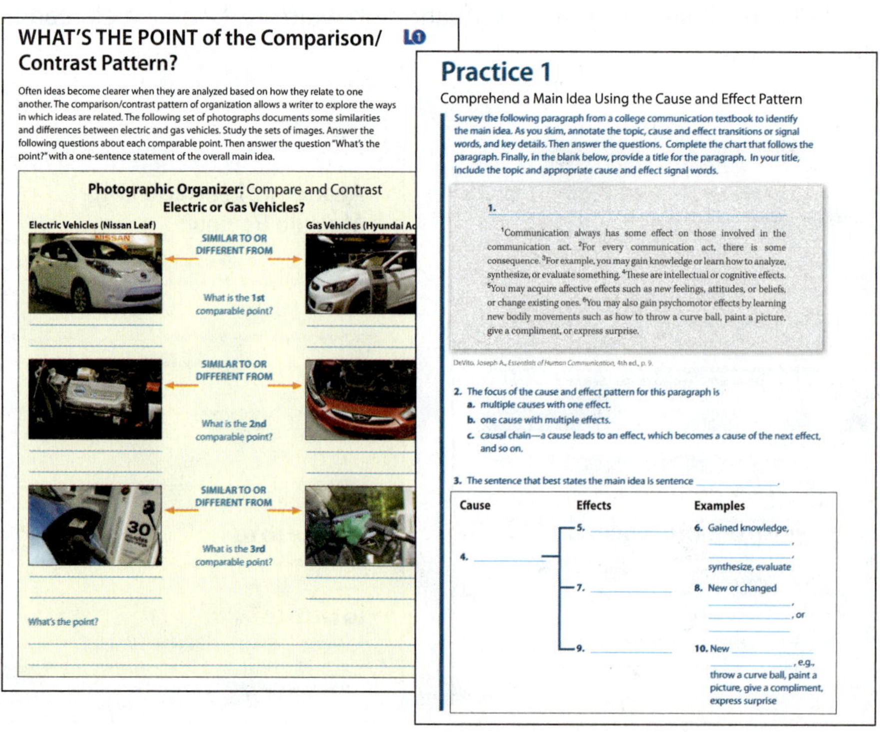

WHAT'S THE POINT of the Comparison/Contrast Pattern? LO1

Often ideas become clearer when they are analyzed based on how they relate to one another. The comparison/contrast pattern of organization allows a writer to explore the ways in which ideas are related. The following set of photographs documents some similarities and differences between electric and gas vehicles. Study the sets of images. Answer the following questions about each comparable point. Then answer the question "What's the point?" with a one-sentence statement of the overall main idea.

Photographic Organizer: Compare and Contrast
Electric or Gas Vehicles?

Electric Vehicles (Nissan Leaf) | Gas Vehicles (Hyundai Ac

SIMILAR TO OR DIFFERENT FROM
What is the **1st** comparable point?

SIMILAR TO OR DIFFERENT FROM
What is the **2nd** comparable point?

SIMILAR TO OR DIFFERENT FROM
What is the **3rd** comparable point?

What's the point?

Practice 1

Comprehend a Main Idea Using the Cause and Effect Pattern

Survey the following paragraph from a college communication textbook to identify the main idea. As you skim, annotate the topic, cause and effect transitions or signal words, and key details. Then answer the questions. Complete the chart that follows the paragraph. Finally, in the blank below, provide a title for the paragraph. In your title, include the topic and appropriate cause and effect signal words.

1. ____________

[1]Communication always has some effect on those involved in the communication act. [2]For every communication act, there is some consequence. [3]For example, you may gain knowledge or learn how to analyze, synthesize, or evaluate something. [4]These are intellectual or cognitive effects. [5]You may acquire affective effects such as new feelings, attitudes, or beliefs, or change existing ones. [6]You may also gain psychomotor effects by learning new bodily movements such as how to throw a curve ball, paint a picture, give a compliment, or express surprise.

DeVito, Joseph A., *Essentials of Human Communication*, 4th ed., p. 9.

2. The focus of the cause and effect pattern for this paragraph is
   a. multiple causes with one effect.
   b. one cause with multiple effects.
   c. causal chain—a cause leads to an effect, which becomes a cause of the next effect, and so on.

3. The sentence that best states the main idea is sentence ________.

Cause	Effects	Examples
4. ________	5. ________	6. Gained knowledge, ________, ________, synthesize, evaluate
	7. ________	8. New or changed ________, ________, or ________
	9. ________	10. New ________ ________, e.g., throw a curve ball, paint a picture, give a compliment, express surprise

How Is *The Effective Reader/Writer* Organized?

The Effective Reader/Writer's structure taps into the similarities between reading and writing by systematically correlating reading and writing skills and concepts into units/modules of instruction. The sequence of units is designed to offer comprehensive coverage of the reading/writing processes and skills while at the same time providing distinct modules that allow for individualization of instruction based on the needs of specific teaching-learning situations. For example, Unit 1, "The Reading and Writing Process," is composed of two modules, and the flow of instruction begins with an introduction to the key concepts common to reading and writing in Module 1. Then, Module 2 integrates those two processes in a reading/writing strategy. Each subsequent unit offers a logical presentation of key concepts and skills for the development of effective readers and writers moving from vocabulary and word choice to paragraph and essay structure and then focusing on strategic skills such as patterns of organization, inferences, argument, and research. In addition, the instruction moves from foundational skills to higher-level skills. For example, Unit 2, "Vocabulary," first guides students to learn and use new words based on context clues and word parts in Module 3; then Module 4 teaches the students to consider the impact of word choice, tone, and purpose as they read what others have written and compose their own writings. Finally, Unit 6, "Mastering Grammar, Punctuation, and Mechanics with MySkillsLab," offers an extensive handbook with in-depth practice online.

Research indicates that teaching reading and writing together reduces the need for direct instruction in grammar and increases a student's sense of effective organization, argument, and various other writing skills. Combined reading/writing instruction develops a "sentence sense" that serves as the foundation of grammatical awareness (Haussamen, NCTE, 2004).

Thus, Unit 6, "Mastering Grammar, Punctuation, and Mechanics with MySkillsLab," supports individualized grammar instruction. As student and teacher partner together to identify specific patterns of a student's needs, Unit 6 serves as a quick hard-copy reference handbook that defines and illustrates the rules for the most common grammatical errors committed by students. In addition, each grammar lesson is amplified by and supplemented with access to MySkillsLab for in-depth practice and assessment of specific skills. Furthermore, as students discover additional needs, individualized study plans can be created in MySkillsLab.

Unit 7, "Reading Selections," offers students rich opportunities to interact with text as both readers and writers—applying the literacy skills attained as they progress through instruction. Selections are published pieces that reflect diverse voices addressing high-interest cultural topics. Each selection features a vocabulary prompt and after reading activities that include objective reading comprehension items, after reading discussion questions, and reader response prompts.

How Does *The Effective Reader/ Writer* Prepare Students for Success?

Perhaps one of the greatest motivations and underlying goal of *The Effective Reader/Writer* is to offer an opportunity to develop the literacy skills of our students as quickly as possible. To do so, *The Effective Reader/Writer* taps into brain-based learning, fosters metacognition, places instruction in meaningful contexts, and engages students with high-interest content and visual presentation. Your work as a classroom instructor is of the utmost value; the opportunity to partner with you to nurture student success is a great honor. My hope is that *The Effective Reader/Writer* complements your aspirations as a teacher and inspires your students to realize their full potential.

Instructor Support and Professional Development

Pearson is pleased to offer a variety of support materials to help make teaching reading and writing easier for teachers and to help students excel in their coursework. Many of our student supplements are available free or at a greatly reduced price when packaged with *The Effective Reader/Writer.* Visit www.pearsonhighereducation.com, contact your local Pearson sales representative, or review a detailed listing of the full supplements package in the *Instructor's Resource Manual* for more information.

Book-Specific Ancillary Material
Annotated Instructor's Edition for *The Effective Reader/Writer*
ISBN 0-321-82964-6/978-0-321-82964-1
The *AIE* offers in-text answers to all exercises, practice sets, and reading/writing assignments. It also indicates which activities are offered simultaneously in MySkillsLab. It is a valuable resource for experienced and first-time instructors alike.

Instructor's Resource Manual for *The Effective Reader/Writer*
ISBN 0-321-82965-4/978-0-321-82965-8
The material in the *IRM,* written by Loretta Rodgers of Eastfield College, is designed to save instructors time and provide them with effective options for teaching the integrated reading/writing course. It offers suggestions for setting up their course; provides sample syllabus models; provides lots of extra practice for students who need it; and offers quizzes and grammar tests, including unit tests. This valuable resource is exceptionally useful for adjuncts who might need advice in setting up their initial classes or who might be teaching a variety of courses with too many students and not enough time.

Test Bank for The Effective Reader/Writer
ISBN 0-321-82965-4/978-0-321-82965-8
An abundance of extra practice exercises are included in the *Test Bank for The Effective Reader/Writer*. The *Test Bank*, created by Sandra Chumchal of Blinn College, can also be used to create tests in Pearson's MyTest test creation tool.

PowerPoint Presentation for The Effective Reader/Writer
ISBN 0-321-82963-8/978-0-321-82963-4
Kim Koledoye, Houston Community College, has created PowerPoint presentations to accompany each module of *The Effective Reader/Writer*, which consist of classroom-ready lecture outline slides, lecture tips and classroom activities, and module review questions. It is available for download from the Instructor Resource Center.

Answer Key for The Effective Reader/Writer
ISBN 0-321-95600-1/978-0-321-95600-2
The Answer Key contains the solutions to the exercises in the student edition of the text. It is available for download from the Instructor Resource Center.

Professional Development
Pearson offers a variety of professional development programs and resources to support full- and part-time instructors. These include Pedagogy & Practice, an open-access digital resource gallery [http://pedagogyandpractice.pearsonhighered.com/], and our Speaking About English online conference series, featuring scholar/educators addressing pedagogical topics via web-based presentations. These conferences are held twice a year and are free of cost to attend. Information about future conferences, as well as archives of past sessions, can be found on the conference website [http://www.pearsonhighered.com/speakingabout/english/]. Updated information about any and all of these Partnership Programs can always be found on our catalog page [http://www.pearsonhighered.com/english/].

Looking for more Grammar coverage? Here are some options that are FREE when bundled with *The Effective Reader/Writer!*
The Prentice Hall Grammar Workbook 3e by Jeanette Adkins, Tarrant County CC
ISBN: **0-205-73907-5**
This workbook is a comprehensive source of instruction for students who need additional grammar, punctuation, and mechanics assistance. Covering such topics as subject-verb agreement, conjunctions, modifiers, capital letters, and vocabulary, each chapter provides helpful explanations, examples, and exercises.

The Pearson Lab Manual for Developing Writers by Linda Copeland, St. Louis CC-Merramac
This three-volume workbook is an ideal supplement for any developmental writing sequence.

1. **Volume A: Sentences (0-205-63409-5)**

At this level, exercises and applications of grammar, punctuation and mechanics stress rules rather than simply skill and drill. There are many composing exercises that apply sentence skills explained in the students' primary textbook.

1. **Volume B: Paragraphs (0-205-69341-5) & Volume C: Essays (0-205-69340-7)**

The exercises encourage students to apply key concepts covered in most writing classes—i.e. topic sentences, thesis statements, coherence, unity, and levels of development. *Analysis* exercises give further illustration of concepts explained in class and in the primary textbook; *Building* exercises give students the "raw materials" to develop paragraphs and/or essays along the various modes. Revision prompts encourage students to look at specific key elements of their own writing and assess whether they have met the needs of their reading audience.

MySkillsLab™ www.myskillslab.com

Efficiently blending the market-leading and proven practice from MyWritingLab and MyReadingLab into a single application and learning path, MySkillsLab offers a wealth of practice opportunity, additional instruction/content support, and extensive progress tracking for integrated reading/writing courses. For more than half a decade, MySkillsLab has been the most widely used online learning application for the integrated reading/writing course across two- and four-year institutions. We have published case studies demonstrating how MySkillsLab (or, individually, MyReadingLab and MyWritingLab) consistently benefits students' mastery of key reading skills, reading comprehension, writing skills, and critical thinking.

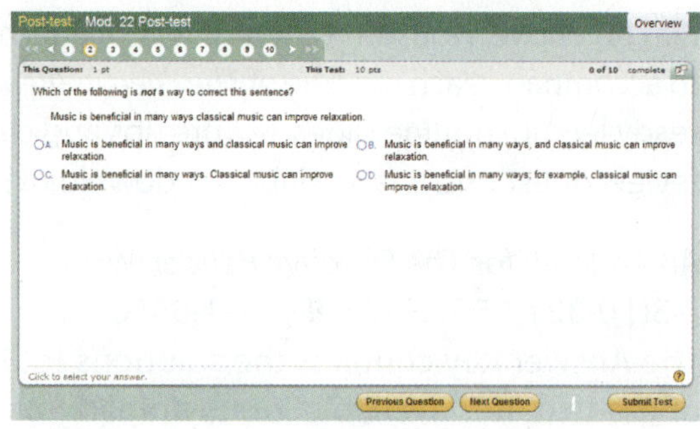

Reading MySkillsLab improves students' mastery of 26 reading skills across four levels of difficulty via mastery-based skill practice, and improves students' reading levels with the Lexile® framework (www.Lexile.com) to measure both reader ability and text difficulty on the same scale and pair students with readings within their Lexile range.

Writing MySkillsLab offers skill remediation in grammar and punctuation, paragraph development, essay development, and research, and improves students' overall writing through automatic scoring by Pearson's proven Intelligent Essay Assessor (IEA).

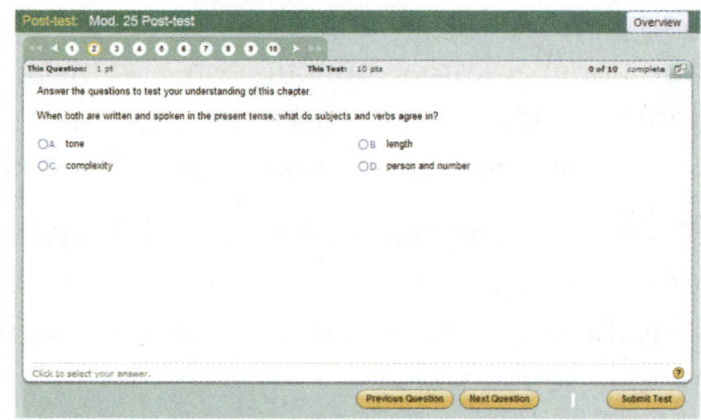

A Deeper Connection Between Print and Media

Pearson's MySkillsLab (www.myskillslab.com) is deeply integrated into the assignments and activities in *The Effective Reader/Writer*. Students can complete and submit various exercises and activities within the eText/MySkillsLab course and some of the results flow right to the Instructor Gradebook. Additionally, there are specific D. J. Henry–authored videos that expand upon the reading, writing, and thinking processes outlined in the modules.

Acknowledgments

I would like to gratefully recognize the invaluable insights provided by the following colleagues who served as reviewers. I deeply appreciate their investment of time, energy, and wisdom.

Tia Adger, Piedmont Technical College
Stephanie Alexander, Mountwest Community & Technical College
Elizabeth Andrews, South Florida State College
Wes Anthony, Cleveland Community College
Holly Baker, Arkansas State University, Heber Springs
Lisa Barnes, Delaware County Community College
Andrea Berta, The University of Texas at El Paso
Tracie Bohl, North Central Texas College
Susan E. Bowling, University of Arkansas at Little Rock
Leslie Brian, Houston Community College; Lonestar College System: Atascocita and Kingwood Campus
Teresa Carrillo, Joliet Junior College
Sandra Chumchal, Blinn College
Peggy E. Coleman, Mountwest Community & Technical College
Vivian Corll, Broward College
Karen Cowden, Valencia College
Wendy Crader, Northeast Lakeview College
Kathi Crowe, Bluegrass Community and Technical College
Deborah Davis, Richland College
JoAnn Davis, St. Philip's College
Patricia Davis, Houston Community College
Brian Dickson, Community College of Denver
Barbara Doyle, Arkansas State University
Curt Duffy, Los Angeles Pierce College
Kelly Edmondson, Cincinnati State Technical & Community College
Adam Floridia, Middlesex Community College (CT)
Mindy Flowers, Midland College
Dwedor Morais Ford, Winston-Salem State University
Paul Gallagher, Red Rocks Community College
Susannah M. Givens, Northern Virginia Community College
Cynthia M. Gomez, Hodges University
Sharon Green, Niagara University
Anthony Halderman, Allan Hancock College
Eric Hibbison, J. Sargeant Reynolds Community College
Deanna S. Highe, Central Piedmont Community College
Lori Hughes, Lone Star College-Montgomery
Pam Hunt, Paris Junior College
Janis Innis, Houston Community College
Diana Jividen, Southern West Virginia Community & Technical College
Leslie G. Johnson, North Central Texas College
Julie Kelly, St. Johns River State College
Ali Khalil, Arkansas State University
Kimberly Koledoye, Houston Community College
Vicky Krug, Westmoreland County Community College
Patty Kunkel, Santa Fe College
James F. Lanfrey, Blinn College
Judith L. Lanfrey, Blinn College
Charlotte Laughlin, McLennan Community College
Debra F. Lee, Nash Community College
Brian Longacre, Asheville Buncombe Technical College
Leslie J. Lovenstein, Pulaski Technical College
Caroline Mains, Palo Alto College
Patricia A. Malinowski, Finger Lakes Community College
David Maslanne, Lone Star College—Cy Fair
Janet Matthews, Odessa College
Brook Mayo, Asheville Buncombe Technical College
Ed McCourt, Jacksonville University
Patrick McMahon, Marymount California University
April Mitchell, Johnston Community College
Lance Morita, Leeward Community College
Nancy S. Morrison, J. Sargeant Reynolds Community College
Robbi Muckenfuss, Durham Technical Community College
Carol Murphy, Barton Community College
Lana Myers, Lone Star College—Montgomery
Laura Myers, Hawkeye Community College
Donna Brumback Nalley, South University Online
Margot Nasti, Kingsborough Community College
Meridith M. Nelson, Des Moines Area Community College
Nicole Oechslin, Piedmont Virginia Community College
Ray Orkwis, Northern Virginia Community College
Calisa A. Pierce, Kanawha Valley Community & Technical College
Tiffany Porter, Coastal Bend College
Elizabeth Price, Ranger College
Sonya Prince, San Jacinto College
Loretta Ramirez, Marymount California University
Adalia Reyna, South Texas College
Carole Roper, San Bernardino Valley College
Vanessa L. Ruccolo, Virginia Tech
Anna Schmidt, Lone Star College—Cy Fair
Ryan S. Shadle, Cincinnati State
Dixie Shaw-Tillmon, The University of Texas at San Antonio
Susan Silva, El Paso Community College
Kina Siriphant-Lara, San Jacinto College
Debra Slaton, Cisco College
Deanna D. Spring, Somerset Community College
Kathy K. Stein, Sul Ross State University
Karen Tanguma, Coastal Bend College
Sanci Teague, West Kentucky Community and Technical College
Kim G. Thomas, Polk State College
Alexandr Tolj, John Tyler Community College
Priscilla Underwood, Quinsigamond Community College
Maria C. Villar-Smith, Miami Dade College
Julie Voss, Front Range Community College
Vivian Walters, Arkansas State University—Beebe
Matthew F. Wegener, Olympic College

1

LEARNING OUTCOMES

After studying this module you should be able to:

- LO 1 Answer the Question "What's the Point of Reading and Writing?"
- LO 2 Connect Reading and Writing
- LO 3 Activate Prior Knowledge During Reading and Writing
- LO 4 Assess the Reading Situation and the Writing Situation

An Introduction to Reading and Writing

Reading and writing are active processes in which we make and express meaning through our interaction with text. During the reading process, we draw information from a text to create meaning. Effective readers create meaning by seeking to comprehend a writer's ideas. When what you've read makes sense, you've achieved **comprehension**, an understanding of the material. Effective readers rely on the reading process to ask questions, find answers, and react to a writer's ideas.

Comprehension is an understanding of the material you've read.

Writing is an active process during which you express information in text form to create meaning. Writers create meaning by developing, organizing, and communicating ideas to other people. Effective writers rely on the writing process to discover, organize, and express information as clearly as possible. Effective writers seek to build comprehension in readers.

WHAT'S THE POINT of Reading and Writing? 

Good reading and writing skills are not only the foundation for your college success, but also the cornerstone for your success in your career and in your everyday life.

Photographic Organizer: Reasons to Read and Write

Before you study this module, predict why it is important to become an effective reader and writer. The following photographs illustrate some of the reading and writing situations we experience in our everyday, college, and working lives. Write a caption for each photograph that states a reason or benefit of reading and writing in each situation. Then state the point of becoming an effective reader and writer.

READING

This young woman is reading for pleasure. She is entertained.

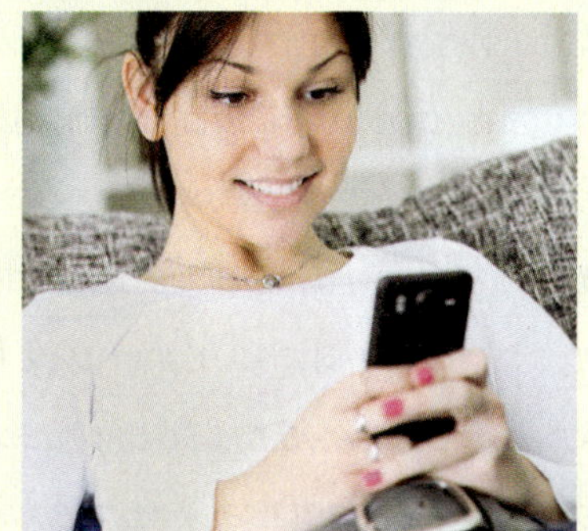

WRITING

She is communicating with friends or family through e-mail or social networks.

READING

These are college students reading to learn new ideas.

WRITING

Students write to explore, question, or demonstrate what they have learned.

READING

This is a businessman reading for information related to his job. He is gaining expertise.

WRITING

A businessperson often writes reports, letters, and e-mails to bosses, colleagues, and customers.

What's the point of becoming an effective reader and writer?

It's important to become an effective reader in order to read for pleasure, learn in college, and be informed on the job. Being an effective writer increases personal expression, academic success, and economic potential.

What's the Point? One Student's Response

The following paragraph is one student's response to the question "What's the point of reading and writing?"

If I improve my reading and writing I will have more success in college, in my personal life, and in my career. Of course, both reading and writing are necessary to succeed in college. When we read in college, we learn new ideas. When we write in college, we explore and respond to ideas. But reading and writing are also important outside the classroom. For example, if I have strong reading and writing skills, I am much more likely to get a job, promotions, and higher pay. In addition, reading and writing well allows me to express myself in everyday life. For example, I am really worried about forest fires started by careless campers. So I have read about what causes these fires and how to prevent them. A well-written letter to the editor of a newspaper might make just one person think about campfire safety. Reading is listening to the thoughts of other people, and writing is thinking out loud on paper. Reading and writing allow me to gather, think about, record, organize, learn about, remember, and share ideas.

Connect Reading and Writing

Reading and writing are closely related thinking processes. **Reading** is the process of getting meaning from written symbols. **Writing** is the process of expressing meaning with written symbols. A writer (author) sends a message, and a reader (audience) receives a message. An effective writer thinks about what the reader needs to know. An effective reader thinks about the writer's purpose. Thus, writing and reading rely on and strengthen each other.

Reading is the process of getting meaning from written symbols.

Writing is the process of expressing meaning with written symbols.

Remember, reading and writing is a conversation between the writer and the reader. One writes; the other reads. But the conversation often doesn't end there. A reader's response to a piece of writing keeps the dialogue going. When you write a summary, your response is to restate the author's ideas. It's like saying to the author, "If I understood you correctly, you said . . ." When you offer your own views about the author's ideas, you are answering the author's implied question, "What do you think?" An effective reader draws conclusions, or **inferences**, about what the writer meant in the passage.

An **inference** is an idea that is based on given details.

In your reading and writing classes, your professor often steps into the conversation. He or she stands in for the author and becomes the reader of your written response. In this case, your professor evaluates both your reading and your writing abilities. Your professor checks your response for comprehension of the author's message as well as the development of your writing ability. The following chart illustrates this exchange of ideas.

The Reading/Writing Cycle: Exchange of Information

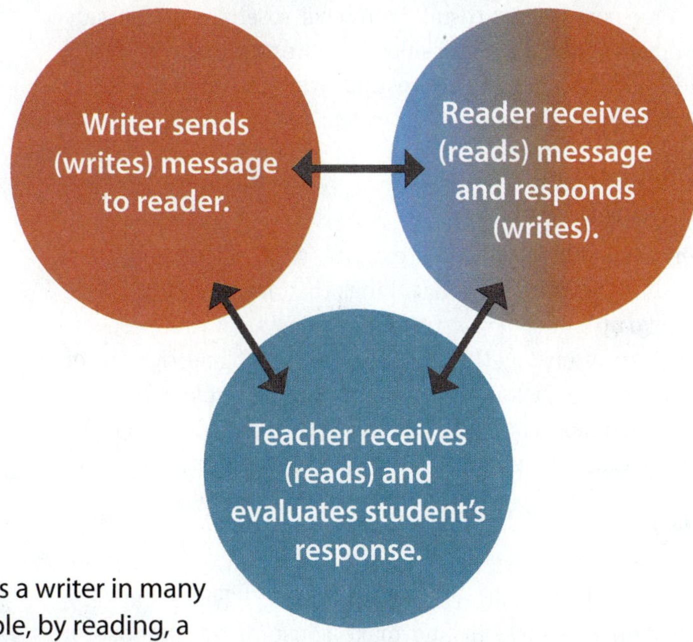

Reading benefits a writer in many ways. For example, by reading, a writer gains the following:

- New vocabulary
- Different opinions on a topic
- Additional facts about a topic
- Details that support an opinion
- Connections between prior knowledge and new ideas
- Varying ways to apply writing techniques
  - Ways to use punctuation
  - Ways to use fresh or creative expressions
  - Ways to write sentences
  - Ways to organize ideas
  - Ways to open and close an essay

The more you read, the more you know and the more you have to write about. Likewise, writing benefits a reader in many ways. By writing, a reader gains a deeper understanding of how to reach an audience, how to organize and connect ideas, and how to respond to the ideas of other people. Writing also helps a reader to learn. **Writing to learn** is a powerful way to connect reading and writing. Writing to learn activities use questions and written responses to focus attention on an important concept, idea, or task. At times, you may write to learn about a specific concept or idea. At other times, you may write to learn more about how you think or approach a reading or writing task.

Writing to learn is the use of short, informal writing activities to deepen the understanding of a key concept, idea, or passage.

Example

Assume you are taking a college course in communication. The following text is an excerpt from your weekly reading assignments. Your professor expects you to respond in writing and share your response in class. To prepare your response, answer the questions that appear after the selection.

THE ESSENTIALS OF HUMAN COMMUNICATION

Three Ways to Organize Perception

[1]Perception is the process by which you become aware of objects, events, and, especially, people through your senses: sight, smell, taste, touch, and hearing. [2]Perception is an active, not passive, process. [3]Your perceptions result from what exists in the outside world and from your own experiences, desires, needs and wants, loves and hatreds. [4]Three interesting ways in which people organize their perceptions are by rules, by schemata, and by scripts.

ORGANIZATION BY RULES

[5]One often used rule is that of proximity, or physical closeness. [6]The rule, simply stated, says that things that are physically close together make up a unit. [7]Thus, using this rule, you would perceive people who are often together, or messages sent one right after the other, as units, as belonging together. [8]For example, when you see a person nod her head and at the same time say yes, you think of the two messages (the nod and the yes) as one unit.

ORGANIZATION BY SCHEMATA

[9]Another way you organize material is by creating schemata. [10]Schemata are mental patterns or structures. [11]These patterns of thought help you sort out and make sense of the millions of items of information you come into contact with every day as well as those you already have in memory. [12]Schemata may thus be viewed as general ideas about people, yourself, or social roles. [13]You develop schemata from your own experiences. [14]These experiences include actual as well as vicarious experience gained from television, reading, and hearsay. [15]For example, you may have developed schemata about college athletes, and this might include that they are strong and ambitious.

THE ESSENTIALS OF HUMAN COMMUNICATION

ORGANIZATION BY SCRIPTS

[16]A script is really a type of schema. [17]Like a schema, a script is an organized body of information about some action, event, or procedure. [18]It's a general idea of how some event should play out or unfold; it's the rules governing the events and their sequence. [19]For example, you probably have a script for how you do laundry.

Adapted from De Vito, Joseph A., *Essentials of Human Communication*, 4th ed., pp. 55–57.

1. What new or important vocabulary did I learn?

Answers will vary. See explanations.

2. What are the most important facts?

3. What idea(s) do I need to clarify? What confused me?

4. What have I seen or experienced in life that relates to the ideas in the passage?

Explanation

Compare your questions and answers to the ones given here.

1. *What new or important vocabulary did I learn?*

I learned new meanings for the words perception, rule, *and* scripts, *but* proximity *and* schemata *were new words to me.*

2. *What are the most important facts?*

Perception is an active use of the senses of sight, smell, taste, touch, and hearing to become aware of objects, events, and people. Three ways people organize their perceptions are by rules, by schemata, and by

CONTINUED

EXPLANATION *CONTINUED*

scripts. The rule of proximity or physical closeness is that things close together make up one object or unit, such as nodding and saying yes sends one message.

Schemata are mental patterns or structures—patterns of thought, such as general ideas about what athletes are like. A script is a general idea of how some event should play out—the rules governing the events and their sequence, such as how one does laundry.

3. *What idea(s) do I need to clarify? What confused me?*

I need to clarify the meaning of two words. They are schemata and vicarious.

4. *What have I seen or experienced in life that relates to the ideas in the passage?*

I see the rule of proximity in food dishes such as bacon and eggs or spaghetti and meatballs. My schemata for firefighters are that they are strong, brave, and selfless. I also have a script I act out every morning. I have a certain routine for making coffee and reading the paper.

Practice 1

Connect Reading and Writing

Assume you are taking a college course in psychology. The following text is an excerpt from your weekly reading assignments. Your professor had indicated that this topic may be an essay question on the unit exam. To prepare for the exam, answer the questions that appear after the selection.

NEURONS

Answers will vary.

[1]Every thought you think, every emotion you feel, every sensation you experience, every decision you reach, every move you make—in short, all of human behavior—is rooted in a biological event. [2]The story begins where the action begins, in the smallest unit of the brain—the nerve cell, or neuron.

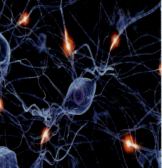

The Structure of the Neuron

[3]All of our thoughts, feelings, and behaviors can ultimately be traced to the activity of neurons—the specialized cells that conduct impulses through the nervous system. [4]Neurons perform several important tasks. [5]First, afferent (sensory) neurons relay messages from the sense organs and receptors—

eyes, ears, nose, mouth, and skin—to the brain or spinal cord. [6]Second, efferent (motor) neurons convey signals from the central nervous system to the glands and the muscles, enabling the body to move. [7]And third, interneurons carry information between neurons in the brain and between neurons in the spinal cord.

[8]Although no two neurons are exactly alike, nearly all are made up of three important parts: the cell body, the dendrites, and the axon. [9]The cell body, or soma, contains the nucleus; the cell body carries out the metabolic, or life-sustaining, functions of a neuron. [10]Branching out from the cell body are the dendrites; they look much like the leafless branches of a tree (dendrite comes from the Greek word for "tree"). [11]The dendrites are the primary receivers of signals from other neurons, but the cell body can also receive signals directly. [12]Dendrites also do more than just receive signals from other neurons and relay them to the cell body.

[13]The axon is the slender, tail-like extension of the neuron that sprouts into many branches, each ending in a bulbous axon terminal. [14]Signals move from the axon terminals to the dendrites or cell bodies of other neurons and to muscles, glands, and other parts of the body.

Adapted from Wood, et al., *Mastering the World of Psychology*, 3rd ed., pp. 39-40.

1. What new or important vocabulary did I learn?

afferent, efferent, soma, dendrites, axon

2. What are the most important facts?

Afferent (sensory) neurons relay messages from the sense organs and receptors—eyes, ears, nose, mouth, and skin—to the brain or spinal cord. Efferent (motor) neurons convey signals from the central nervous system to the glands and the muscles, enabling the body to move. Neurons have three important parts: the cell body, the dendrites, and the axon.

3. What idea(s) do I need to clarify? What confused me?

Answers will vary.

4. What have I seen or experienced in life that relates to the ideas in the passage?

Neurons remind me of a call center. So when I eat my favorite salty foods, afferent neurons send the taste to my brain. Or when I need to get up off the couch, the efferent neurons tell my brain to move my muscles.

L3 Activate Prior Knowledge During Reading and Writing

We all have learned a great deal of information from our experiences throughout our lives. This body of information is called **prior knowledge**.

Prior knowledge is the large body of information that is learned throughout a lifetime of experience.

Knowledge is gained from experience and stored in memory. Every day, our prior knowledge is expanded by what we experience. For example, a small child hears the word *hot* as her father blows on a spoonful of steaming soup. The hungry child grabs for the bowl and cries as some of the hot liquid spills on her hand. The child has learned and will remember the meaning of *hot*.

Both readers and writers activate prior knowledge. Readers reflect on what they already know about a topic before reading. Then, during reading, they constantly compare new ideas with what they already know as they try to infer what the writer means. After reading, they note what they have learned and how the new information has changed their understanding of the topic. Likewise, just like readers, writers activate their own prior knowledge before they write. They call up what they already know about a topic and think about what they need to know to clearly communicate an idea to their readers. Writers use prewriting techniques such as brainstorming, freewriting, listing, or mapping to call up their prior knowledge. You will learn more about these techniques later in this unit. The following graphic illustrates specific ways to connect to prior knowledge in each phase of the reading and writing processes. Connecting to prior knowledge increases comprehension and links the reader, writer, and topic.

Activate Prior Knowledge

The Body of Knowledge Learned Throughout a Lifetime of Experience

Call up prior knowledge	Check new information against prior knowledge	Expect growth or change of knowledge
BEFORE READING	**DURING READING**	**AFTER READING**
What do I already know? What do I need to know?	Does this idea/detail make sense based on what I already know?	What did I learn?
BEFORE WRITING	**DURING WRITING**	**AFTER WRITING**
What does my reader already know? What does my reader need to know?	Does this idea/detail make sense based on what my reader already knows?	What did my reader learn?

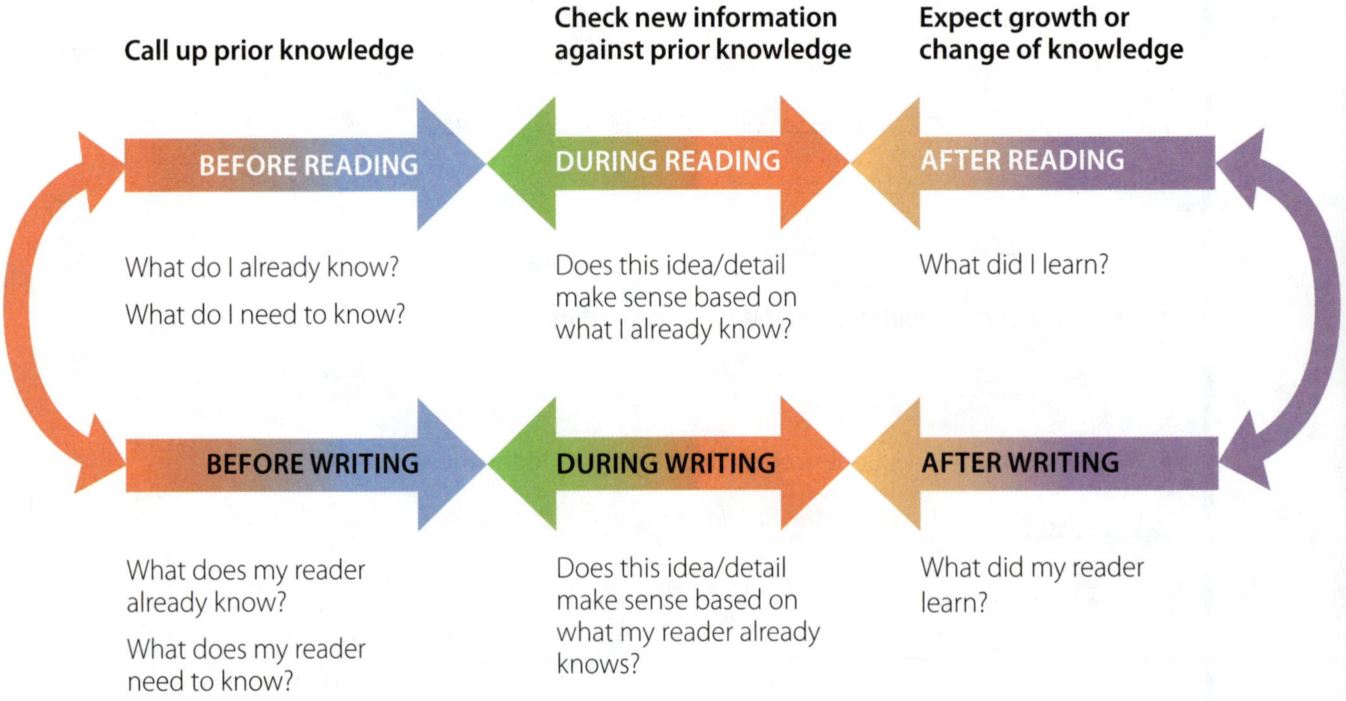

Example

Assume you are the parent of a teenager who has started smoking and you want to convince her to stop. Quickly look over the following passage. Complete the form that follows to activate your prior knowledge about the topic. Remember that your teenage daughter is your reader. *Answers will vary.*

Toxic Fumes: Cigarette Smoke

[1]Most of the compounds in cigarette smoke are gaseous, and many of them are toxic. [2]By far the most hazardous of these gases is carbon monoxide, the same gas that is emitted from the exhaust pipe of a car. [3]The difference is that there are community or statewide standards to keep carbon monoxide auto emissions within a safe level, whereas no standards exist for cigarette smoke. [4]The amount of carbon monoxide that stays in a smoker's blood is related to activity levels. [5]During the day, carbon monoxide remains in the blood for two to four hours; during sleep, however, it remains for up to eight hours.

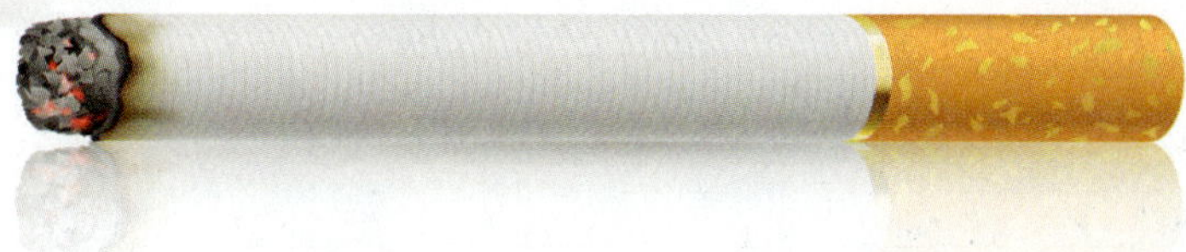

Adapted from Pruitt B. E, & Stein, Jane J., *Health Styles*, 2nd ed., p. 183.

1. What do I already know?

____

____

2. What do I need to know?

____

____

3. What does my audience already know?

____

____

4. What does my audience need to know?

____

____

Explanation

A common strategy used by an effective reader/writer is the "think-aloud." A think-aloud identifies the thought processes a person uses during reading or writing. Compare your responses to the following student's think-aloud about her responses to the questions to call up prior knowledge of the topic:

I smoked for years and ended up with COPD, a lung disease, so I know I really don't want my daughter to smoke. While I knew that cigarette smoke was toxic, I didn't know what kinds of chemicals were in cigarettes. I am alarmed that we breathe in carbon monoxide when we inhale smoke. I want to learn more about the other harmful chemicals in cigarette smoke. I am sure my daughter doesn't know about the carbon monoxide she is inhaling, and I think she would also be interested in knowing about the other harmful chemicals, too. She definitely needs to know how harmful smoking is.

The more prior knowledge we have about a topic, the more likely we are to understand that topic. The more you know, the easier it is to learn. This is why effective readers build their knowledge base by reading often! Likewise, effective writers tap into their own prior knowledge and assess the prior knowledge of their audience.

Active readers and writers call up prior knowledge by using questions. The following practice will prepare you to use questions before you read and write. You will study this skill in more depth in the next sections.

Practice 2

Activate Prior Knowledge

Assume you are tutoring at-risk students at a local middle school. You want to teach them how to improve their memory of what they learn. Quickly look over the following passage. Complete the form that follows to activate your prior knowledge about mnemonic devices. Remember that your students are your readers. *Answers will vary.*

MNEMONIC DEVICES

[1]**Mnemonic devices** are strategies that improve memory. [2]Mnemonics can easily double your recall and are well worth the effort of learning. [3]Mnemonic devices not only help you learn something in the first place, but should you forget it, you will be able to relearn it more effectively.

[4]Probably the single most effective mnemonic device is the use of **interactive images**. [5]Forming images of objects interacting will improve memory even without any effort to learn the material. [6]For example, if you want to learn someone's first name, visualize someone else you already know who has the same first name. [7]Then imagine that person interacting with your new acquaintance in some way. [8]You might envision them fighting or hugging.

[9]Another effective mnemonic device is the use of *acronyms*. [10]Acronyms are words made from the first letters of the important words in a phrase. [11]Acronyms can be pronounced. [12]One example is NOW, for the National Organization for Women. [13]Initialisms are simply the initial letters of words in a phrase that probably do not combine to make a word, such as DNA for deoxyribonucleic acid. [14]**Initialisms** may be easier to make up. [15]The idea of using both acronyms and initialisms is to create a single unit that can be "unpacked" as a set of cues for something more complicated.

Adapted from Kosslyn Stephen M., and Rosenberg, Robin S., *Psychology: The Brain, The Person, The World*, pp. 228–229.

1. What do I already know?

2. What do I need to know?

3. What does my audience already know?

4. What does my audience need to know?

L4 Assess the Reading Situation and the Writing Situation

Although reading and writing are closely related and interact in the communication process, usually you are mainly doing one or the other. A reading session occurs as a specific **reading situation** in which there is a purpose or goal for reading, the topic about which you are reading, and you, the reader or audience. Likewise, a piece of writing develops in response to a specific **writing situation** that is composed of the topic (your subject), the purpose for writing (your goal), and the audience (your reader).

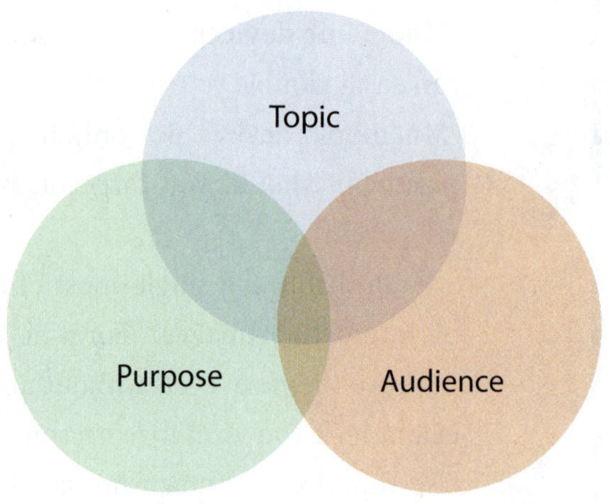

A **reading situation** is the time in which a reader (or audience) has a purpose or goal for reading about a specific topic.

A **writing situation** is the time in which a writer has a goal for writing about a specific topic for a specific audience.

The Topic: What You Read or Write

A **topic** is the subject matter dealt with in a piece of text. As readers, we are, at times, drawn to topics that are of interest in our personal lives. Other times, we read about topics that are assigned to us in college or those that enable us to perform well at work. Effective readers immediately identify the topic of a passage to better understand the writer's point about the topic. As writers, often our topic naturally emerges from our need to communicate. For example, we may choose to compose a letter of complaint to a business or an e-mail to a friend. In college, we are often assigned a topic; however, there are also many times when we are encouraged to choose our own topics for college writing assignments. Thus, many of us face writer's block in our search for a topic. You can break through writer's block by building a topic bank for college writing. Writers often skim newspapers, magazines, textbooks, and the Internet to look for interesting or significant topics. By building a bank of writing topics, you also become more adept as a reader at identifying another writer's topic.

A **topic** is the subject matter dealt with in a piece of text.

Example

Skim a newspaper, a magazine, and a textbook and write a list of five topics from each one. Then, share your list with your class or in a small group. *Answers will vary.*

1. Topics from a newspaper:

2. Topics from a magazine:

3. Topics from a book:

Explanation

Compare your responses to the following student response.

1. *Topics from a newspaper:*
Single-Gender Classes in Schools; Jobless Rates; New York Fashion Week; Tornado Destruction; Tim Tebow
2. *Topics from a magazine:*
Welfare Reform; Caring for Tattoos; Taylor Swift; Gay Marriage; MTV Awards
3. *Topics from a book:*
Self-Disclosure; Elements of Human Communication; Types of Families; Principles of Conflict; Listening Barriers

Practice 3

Assess the Reading and Writing Situation: The Topic

Build a bank of topics for reading or writing by listing ideas in a special section in your notebook. Complete the following thinking guide to create, discuss, review, and expand several lists.

1. Write down the major topics of importance in a specific course (such as biology, psychology, or history).
2. Find interesting or important current events about which to read or write.
   a. Topics most often covered in magazines and newspapers
   b. Controversial topics from television (such as news and talk shows)
   c. Topics about which you want to learn more
   d. Topics about which you feel deeply
   e. Hobbies and personal interests
3. Share your lists with your classmates; use class discussion to identify more topics for reading or writing.
4. Review and expand your list on a regular basis.

The Purpose: Why You Read and Write

Effective reading and writing focuses on a goal or **purpose**. Your comprehension improves when you have a specific purpose for reading. Likewise, your writing will flow much more easily when you write with purpose. The following chart presents three basic purposes for reading and writing.

Purpose is the goal or reason, such as to inform, to entertain, or to persuade, for reading or writing.

To Inform

READING
When reading for information, your purpose is to read for understanding, to acquire knowledge, gather facts, or apply information. You read to gather information that you can apply to achieve a goal.

WRITING
When writing informatively, your purpose is to share, explain, or demonstrate understanding of information.

Example:
An informative text explains the steps of photosynthesis, gives instructions about how to use a new piece of software, or explains the major causes of stress.

To Entertain or to Be Expressive

READING
When reading for entertainment, your purpose is to find pleasure and to broaden your own experiences and imagination. When reading expressive text, you may analyze the ideas to achieve a level of understanding that goes beyond basic recall of information.

WRITING
When writing to be entertaining or expressive, your purpose is to share with or to amuse the reader with your personal opinions, feelings, or reactions to a topic.

Example:
An entertaining or expressive piece—a poem, short story, or personal essay, for example—that expresses a personal view. For example, you may write a personal essay that explores your experience with a social problem, such as poverty or drug abuse.

To Argue

READING
When reading an argumentative text, your purpose is to evaluate the ideas critically. You read with an open mind, yet you examine the logic and trustworthiness of the writer's ideas.

WRITING
When writing an argument, your purpose is to change your reader's opinion or call your reader to take action.

Example:
An argumentative essay that convinces a reader to change his or her opinion or to take action. For example, a lawyer makes closing remarks insisting that the jury must see that his client is innocent and vote "not guilty."

Example

State the purpose of each of the following topic sentences. Discuss with your class or in a small group how a writer's purposes may be combined in certain situations. Remember the three basic purposes of reading and writing. *Answers will vary.*

1. My experience and education make me an excellent candidate for this job.

2. Adult stem cell research should be funded by the government.

3. The gentle breeze, the lapping water, and the dappled shade soothe the human soul.

4. Eating disorders fall into several categories based on their symptoms.

Explanation

Compare your responses to the following student response.

1. My experience and education make me an excellent candidate for this job.

to present a viable argument to a prospective employer to hire the writer

2. Adult stem cell research should be funded by the government.

to argue in support of government funding for stem cell research

3. The gentle breeze, the lapping water, and the dappled shade soothe the human soul.

to express the power of the beauty in nature

4. Eating disorders fall into several categories based on their symptoms.

to inform the reader about the types and traits of eating disorders

Practice 4

Assess the Reading and Writing Situation: The Purpose

Complete the following thinking guide in your notebook to identify purposes for reading or writing. *Answers will vary.*

1. Annotate, or mark, the lists of topics in your topic bank to indicate possible purposes for writing about each one. Beside each topic write **I** for informative, **P** for persuasive, or **E** for expressive.
2. Generate three sets of topics based on different purposes for reading and writing.
3. Select one topic from each of the three purposes and complete the following statements:
   a. This topic will inform the reader about . . .
   b. This topic will argue for or against . . .
   c. This topic will express . . .

The Audience: Who You Are as a Reader and Who Reads Your Writing

When we take part in a conversation, we know exactly to whom we are speaking and we adjust our tone, word choice, and examples to match the situation. For example, contrast how you talk with a friend with the way you talk to the dean of your college. **Audience** has the same impact in reading and writing situations. An effective writer chooses topics, words, and details that are best suited to a specific audience. An effective reader takes into consideration the audience the writer intended to reach and becomes a member of that audience.

An **audience** is the intended reader of a piece of text.

To appreciate the role of audience in reading and writing situations, assume that you have chosen to write about the topic of marijuana. What main points do you want each of the following audiences to read about this drug? Use the blanks below each picture to record your ideas.

Example

Based on your first thoughts about the audiences represented by the four pictures on page 19, write a brief response to the following questions. Then, discuss your answers with your class or in a small group. *Answers will vary.*

- What are the most important traits of each audience represented by the pictures?
- Did your main points differ based on the audience? Why or why not?
- Will your word choice or examples differ based on the audience? Why or why not?

Explanation

Compare your responses to the following student's think-aloud about her responses to the questions about audience.

The first picture shows an audience of elementary school students of the same age. They look innocent. The second picture shows a group of young men and women in a classroom, probably a college class. They probably come from different levels of income. The third picture shows a group of businesswomen. These women are probably well educated. The last picture shows elected officials in a session. This group is made up of different aged adults. Most are probably well educated. The four pictures show audiences that differ in life experiences. My main point would differ based on the audience. For example, I would warn the children about the peer pressure to use marijuana and give them tips about how to resist. I would tell the college students about the harmful effects of the drug on their brains and bodies. I would warn the women about how to identify if a family member were using marijuana and what kind of help is available. Finally, I would try to persuade the elected officials to keep marijuana illegal. Yes, my word choice would differ for each audience. You just can't talk to children the same way you talk to adults.

Practice 5

Assess the Reading and Writing Situation: The Audience

Complete the following thinking guide in your notebook to identify the audience of a reading or writing situation.

1. Locate a short passage to read. You may choose a passage from any of the example exercises or practices in this module. Complete steps 3 through 6.
2. Choose a specific topic and purpose to write about. You may choose to respond to one of the passages in any of the example exercises or practices in this module. Complete steps 3 through 6.
3. List the traits of the audience that are relevant to the topic and purpose:
   a. age
   b. gender
   c. education level
4. If the intended audience is a general audience of mixed traits, identify the main traits most relevant to the topic and purpose.
5. Identify three or four points about the topic of most interest to a specific audience.
6. Identify several key words to describe the topic and hook the interest of the specific audience of the reading passage. Search the Internet to find key words best suited for the audience of your writing. Open your Internet browser (Google.com, Bing.com, etc.). Type in "Thesaurus.com." When the page opens, type a key word in the search box and click "Enter."

Reading and Writing Assignments

MySkillsLab™
Complete these assignments in MySkillsLab.

Considering Audience and Purpose

Study the set of photographs about the reading process at the beginning of this module. Assume you keep a journal and are writing an entry about your thoughts on this course and your reading and writing skills. Explain your use of reading and writing in your personal life, college life, and work life—and how you think this course will affect your reading and writing skills in each area of your life.

Reading and Writing for Everyday Life

Assume the Parent-Teacher Association of your child's school sent a letter to you with the following information about a proposed federal law affecting the school's lunch program. Read the information. Then, write a letter to your congressional representative to support or oppose the proposed law. Explain your reasons for your position.

Oak Street School PTA
57 Oak Street
Belmont, MA 01923

A Senate bill is being considered that if passed would provide $5 billion for healthier school lunch programs. The bill would require schools to eliminate all junk foods, including vending machines that dispense soft drinks and candy. It would also require schools to serve healthier foods. While students would still be served foods such as pizza and sloppy joes, the ingredients would change to low-fat dairy products and whole grains. Schools would also offer fruits and vegetables that many kids don't get at home. The money to pay for the program will be taken from the Federal Food Stamps Program.

Jamal Owens

Jamal Owens,
President, Oak Street School PTA

Reading and Writing for College Life

Assume you are taking a college course in sociology and your instructor has assigned the chapter on culture for this week's reading assignment. In addition to reading the chapter, your professor also requires each student to identify and respond to a topic of importance or interest in the chapter. You are to explain the topic and why it is of interest and then post your response on the course website. Assume you have chosen the following paragraphs to respond to. Read the paragraphs. Restate the main point and explain why it is an important or interesting point to consider.

SUBCULTURES

Groups of people who focus on some activity or who occupy some small corner in life tend to develop specialized ways to communicate with one another. To outsiders, their talk, even if it is in English, can seem like a foreign language. People who specialize in some occupation—from cabbies to politicians—tend to develop a subculture, a world within the larger world of the dominant culture. Subcultures are not limited to occupations, for they include any corner in life in which people's experiences lead them to have distinctive ways of looking at life or some aspect of it.

U.S. society contains thousands of subcultures. Some are as broad as the way of life we associate with teenagers, others as narrow as those we associate with bodybuilders—or with politicians. Some U.S. ethnic groups also form subcultures: Their values, norms, and foods set them apart. So might their religion, music, language, and clothing. Even sociologists form a subculture. As you are learning, they also use a unique language in their efforts to understand the world.

Adapted from Henslin, James M., *Essentials of Sociology: A Down-to-Earth Approach*, 8th ed., p. 48.

Reading and Writing for Working Life

Assume you work for a clothing retail store in the customer service department and you received the following letter detailing a customer's complaint. Read the letter. Then, write a response that offers a solution to the problem.

Dear Sir or Madam:

I recently bought a pair of running shoes (item #34561) from your website on January 13 and received the order on January 20. Unfortunately, upon opening the package, I saw that a pair of used shoes had been shipped. Dirt was in the ridges of the soles, and the top part of the left shoe was also dirty. My order number is AZ0919.

To resolve the problem, I would like you to credit my account for the amount charged for the shoes. While I have been a satisfied customer in the past, I no longer wish to do business with your company, so a new pair of shoes is unacceptable.

Thank you for your prompt attention to this matter. If you need to contact me, you can reach me at (444) 444-4444.

Sincerely,

Joe Smith

Workshop: Write to Learn

Writing about what you have read deepens your understanding. Compose a paragraph that explains what you have learned about reading and writing based on your study of this module. Use the following questions to guide your thinking and to outline a written response about what you have learned. Turn the questions into statements and give supporting reasons and examples.

I. What is the connection between reading and writing?
II. Why is it important to activate prior knowledge during reading and writing?
III. Why should one assess the reading situation and the writing situation?

Review Test

MySkillsLab™
Complete this Review Test in MySkillsLab.

Read the following passage from the college textbook *Introduction to Hospitality Management*. Then, complete the study chart.

1170L/11.9 GE/559 words

Decision-Making Styles

[1]Decision makers differ in their way of thinking; some are rational and logical, whereas others are intuitive and creative. [2]Rational decision makers look at the information in order. [3]They organize the information and make sure it is logical and consistent. [4]Only after carefully studying all of the given options do they finally make the decision. [5]Intuitive thinkers, on the other hand, can look at information that is not necessarily in order. [6]They can make quick decisions based on their spontaneous creativity and intuition. [7]Although a careful analysis is still required, these types of people are comfortable looking at all solutions as a whole as opposed to studying each option separately.

[8]The second dimension in which people differ is each individual's tolerance for ambiguity. [9]Managers who have a high tolerance for ambiguity are lucky in that they save a lot of time while making a decision. [10]These individuals can process many thoughts at the same time. [11]Unfortunately, some managers have a low tolerance for ambiguity. [12]These individuals must have order and consistency in the way they organize and process the information so as to minimize ambiguity.

[13]Upon review of the two dimensions of decision making, ways of thinking and tolerance for ambiguity, and their subdivisions, four major decision-making styles become evident:

1. [14]The directive style entails having a low tolerance for ambiguity as well as being a rational thinker. [15]Individuals who fall into the category of having a directive decision-making style are usually logical and very efficient. [16]They also have a primary focus on the short run and are relatively quick decision makers. [17]Directive decision makers value speed and efficiency, which can cause them to be remiss in assessing all alternatives, such that decisions are often made with minimal information.

2. [18]Decision makers who have an analytic style of decision making have a large tolerance for ambiguity. [19]Compared to directive decision makers, these people require more information before making their decisions and, consequently, they consider more alternatives. [20]Individuals with an analytic style are careful

CONTINUED

decision makers, which gives them leeway to adapt or cope with unique situations.

3. [21]Decision makers who have a conceptual style of decision making look at numerous alternatives and are typically very broad in their outlook. [22]Their focus is on the long run of the decision made. [23]These individuals are typically creative and often find creative solutions to the problem with which they are dealing.

4. [24]Decision makers who work well with others are said to have a behavioral style of decision making. [25]This entails being receptive to suggestions and ideas from others as well as being concerned about the achievements of their employees. [26]They commonly communicate with their coworkers through meetings. [27]These individuals try to avoid conflict as often as possible, because acceptance by others is very important to them.

[28]At least one of these decision-making styles is always used by managers. [29]However, decision makers often combine two or more styles to make a decision. [30]Most often a manager will have one dominant decision-making style and use one or more other styles as alternates. [31]Flexible individuals vary their decision-making styles according to each unique situation. [32]If the style is to consider riskier options (analytic style) or if the decision is made based on suggestions from subordinates (behavioral style), each style will eventually bring the decision maker to the optimal solution for the unique problem he or she is facing.

Walker, John R., *Introduction to Hospitality Management*, 3rd ed., pp. 565-567.

1. What is the topic of the passage?

decision-making styles

2. What is the purpose of the passage?

to inform

3. Who is the intended audience of the passage?

educated adults

4. What are the seven key terms and their definitions?

Term	Definition
a. *Rational decision makers*	*look at the information in order, organize information, make sure it is logical and consistent, and after careful consideration make a decision*
b. *Intuitive thinkers*	*make quick decisions based on their spontaneous creativity and intuition looking at all solutions*
c. *Tolerance for ambiguity*	*can process many thoughts at the same time*
d. *Directive style*	*has low tolerance for ambiguity, is a rational thinker, values speed and efficiency, does not assess all alternatives, makes decisions with minimal information*
e. *Analytical style*	*requires more information, considers more alternatives, makes careful decisions, is able to adapt*
f. *Conceptual style*	*looks at many options, focuses on the long run, is creative*
g. *Behavioral style*	*is receptive of input from others, is concerned about achievement of coworkers, communicates with coworkers, avoids conflict, needs acceptance*

What Do You Think?

Assume you are applying for a job as a manager at a local retail clothing store. As a manager, you will have to make many decisions such as hiring employees, giving promotions, stocking and displaying merchandise, and solving customer problems. Write a paragraph to be included in your letter of application that describes your decision-making style. Be sure to give examples.

Academic Learning Log: Module Review

Summary of Key Concepts of an Introduction to Reading and Writing

Assess your comprehension of the introduction to reading and writing.

LO1 **1.** Comprehension is *the process of getting meaning from written symbols*.

LO1 **2.** Reading is *the understanding of information*.

LO1 **3.** Writing is *the process of expressing meaning with written symbols*.

LO2 **4.** The reading/writing cycle is *an exchange of information between a reader and a writer*.

LO2 **5.** Writing to learn is *the use of short, informal writing activities to deepen the understanding of a key concept, idea, or passage*.

LO3 **6.** Prior knowledge is *the large body of information that is learned throughout a lifetime of experience*.

LO3 **7.** Use prior knowledge to *increase comprehension*.

a. *Activate prior knowledge* by asking "What do I already know about this topic?"

b. Check *new information* against your prior knowledge by asking, "Does this make sense based on what I know?"

c. Check for *growth or change* in the knowledge base by asking, "What did I learn?"

LO4 **8.** A reading or writing situation is composed of a *topic*, the *purpose* for reading or writing, and the *audience*.

LO4 **9.** A **topic** is *the subject matter dealt with in a piece of text*.
Purpose is *the goal or reason for reading or writing*.
An **audience** is *the intended reader of a piece of text.*.

LO4 **10.** The three basic purposes for reading and writing are *to inform*, *to entertain or to be expressive*, and *to argue*.

Test Your Comprehension of an Introduction to Reading and Writing

Respond in your own words to the following questions and prompts.

L3 What is prior knowledge?

Prior knowledge is all the information you already know about a topic.

L2 What is the reading/writing cycle?

The reading/writing cycle is an exchange of information. The writer sends a message, and a reader receives and responds to the message.

L2 In what way does reading benefit a writer?

A writer gains new vocabulary, different opinions and additional facts about a topic, ways to use punctuation, ways to use fresh or creative expressions, ways to write sentences, ways to organize ideas, and ways to open and close an essay.

L3 Draw a graph that illustrates specific ways to connect to prior knowledge in each phase of the reading and writing process.

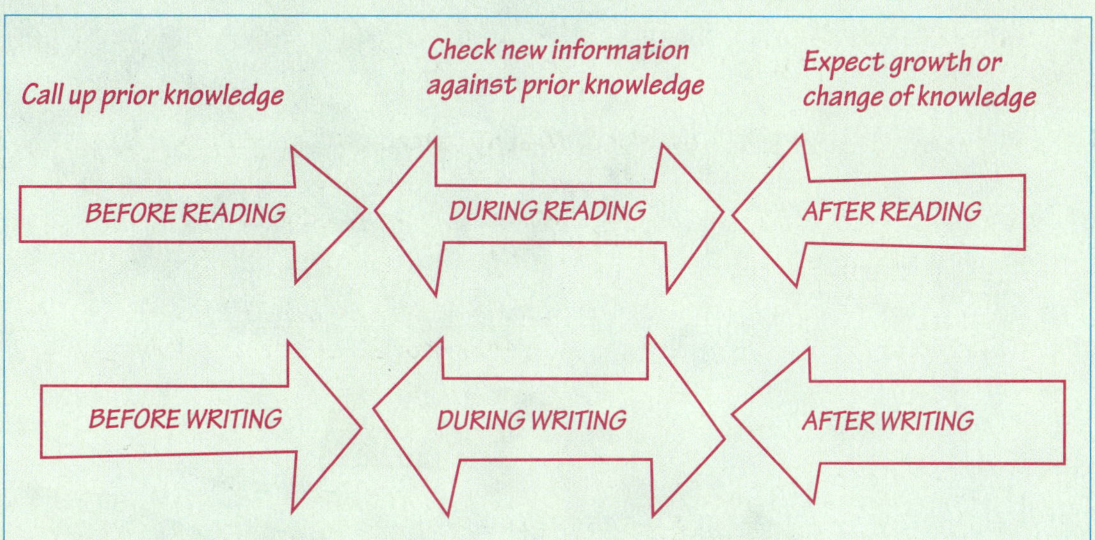

L4 How does one assess the reading or writing situation?

To assess a reading or writing situation, identify the topic, the purpose, and the audience of the piece of text.

> **MySkillsLab™**
> Complete the Post-test for Module 1 in MySkillsLab.

2

LEARNING OUTCOMES

After studying this module you should be able to:

- **LO 1** Answer the Question "What's the Point of Developing a Reading/Writing Strategy?"
- **LO 2** Develop a Reading/Writing Strategy
- **LO 3** Apply the Reading/Writing Strategy: Before, During, and After Reading
- **LO 4** Apply the Reading/Writing Strategy: After Reading, Write a Draft
- **LO 5** Apply the Reading/Writing Strategy: After Writing, Review, Revise, and Proofread Your Draft

Develop a Reading/Writing Strategy

When we tap into the power of the reading/writing cycle as an exchange of information, we build both our knowledge and our communication skills.

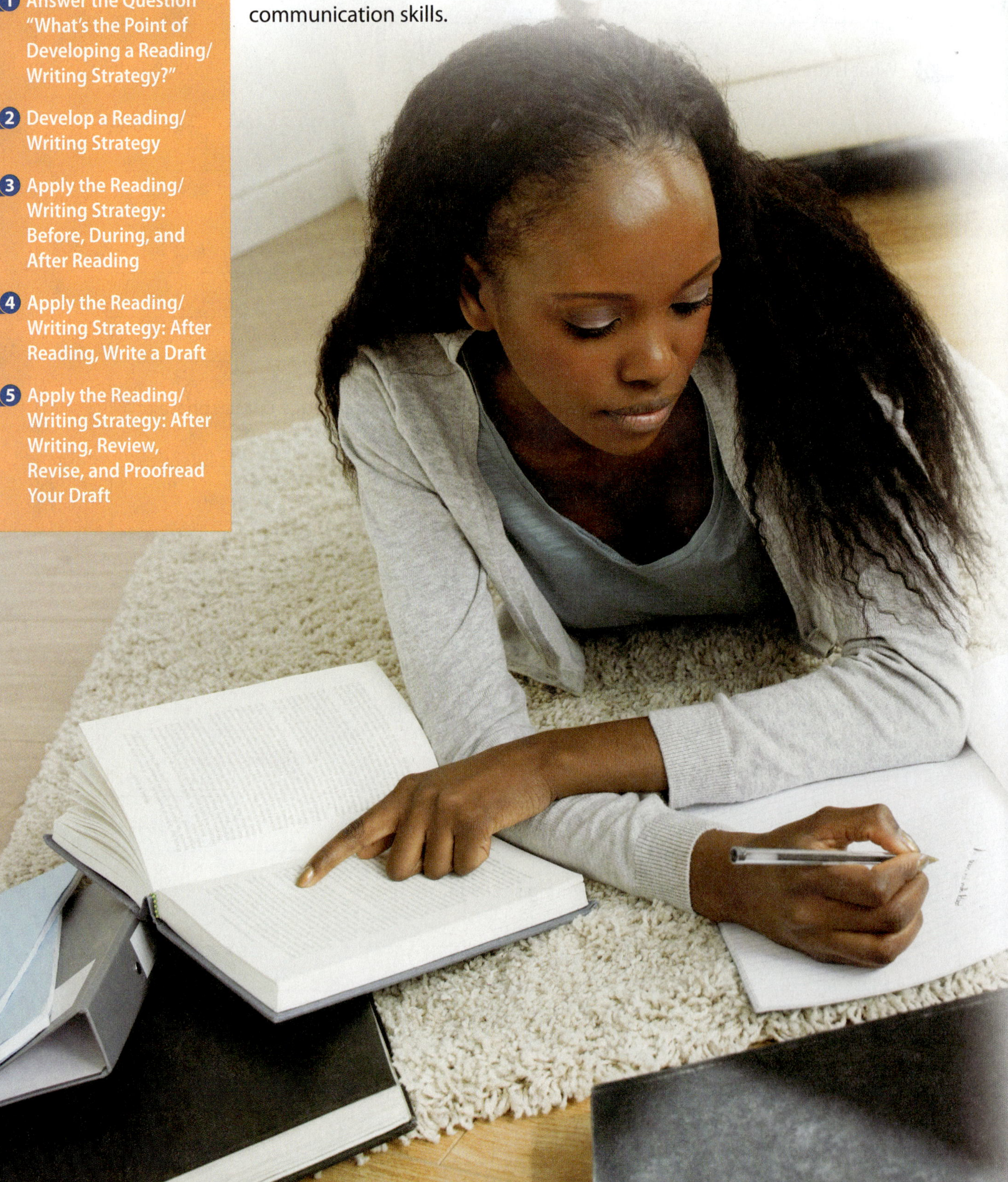

WHAT'S THE POINT of Developing a Reading/Writing Strategy?

Written language allows an exchange of ideas between a writer and a reader. An effective writer makes every effort to make ideas clear so the reader can understand and respond to them. Likewise, an effective reader makes every effort to understand and respond to the ideas of the writer. As two equal parts of the communication process, writing and reading are essential to your success in your everyday life, your college life, and your work life.

Photographic Organizer: Develop a Reading/Writing Strategy

Before you study this module, predict the importance of developing a reading/writing strategy. For each of the photographs below, write a caption that identifies the reading/writing situation as everyday life, college life, and work life. Also, predict the type of reading and writing required for each situation. Finally, state the point of developing a reading/writing strategy.

College life—reading and writing about course material

Work life—reading and writing reports, memos, and e-mails

Everyday life—reading and writing mail about bills and other personal matters

What's the point of developing a reading/writing strategy?

Developing a reading/writing strategy increases comprehension and strengthens writing skills in everyday life, college life, and work life.

What's the Point? One Student's Response

The following paragraph is one student's response to the question "What's the point of developing a reading/writing strategy?"

Having a strategy will make it easier to read and write in any situation. For example, in college, one of the main ways you learn is by reading, taking notes, and then writing papers, reports, and exams. I am studying business so I can start my own fitness company. Running a business means you have to read and write legal documents. And in everyday life, reading and writing can be a real strength. For example, my phone company overcharged me on my cell phone bill. I had to read the company's complaint policy guidelines to write an e-mail to get my bill corrected.

L2 Develop a Reading/Writing Strategy

Often, we find it necessary to read something and then respond to it in writing. This creates a reading/writing situation. A **reading/writing situation** occurs when a person reads text and responds in writing to what was read. For example, in everyday life, we read and respond to e-mails, letters to editors, or postings on blogs or social networks. In college life, we read textbooks and articles, along with a wide variety of other material across the curriculum. Then, we respond to what we have read by composing essays and reports. In working life, we read and respond in writing to e-mails, memos, reports, training materials, company policies, and other reading material.

A **reading/writing situation** occurs when a person reads text and responds in writing to what was read.

As we learned in Module 1, reading and writing are closely related and use similar thinking processes. By coordinating these two types of processes, you can improve both your reading and your writing. A **reading/writing strategy** is a series of

A Reading/Writing Strategy

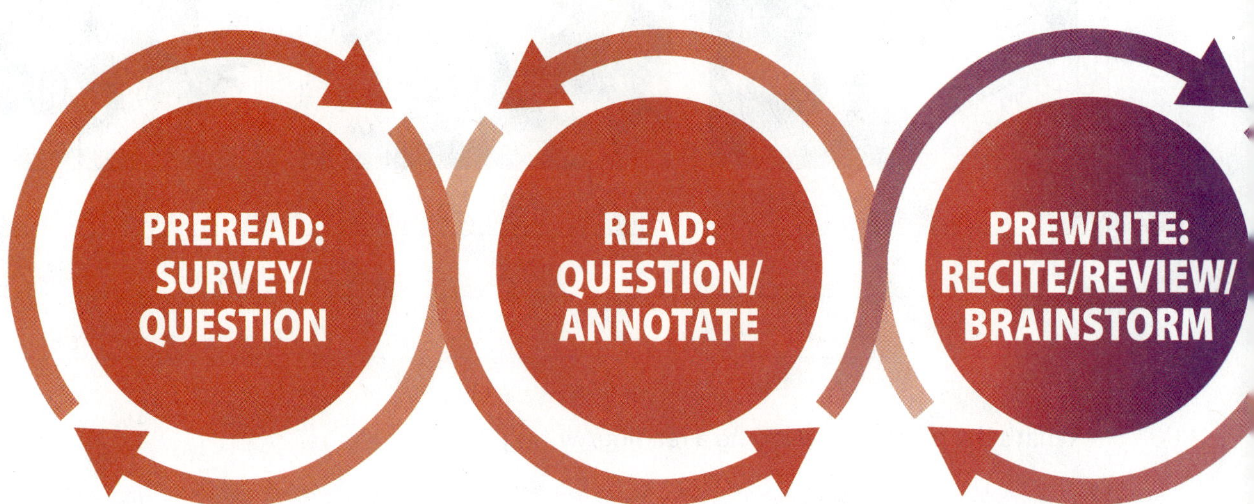

Preread: Survey/Question

- Create questions based on a survey of titles, headings, bold/italic terms, and visuals.

Ask:

- What is my prior knowledge of this topic?
- What is my purpose for reading?
- Who is the intended audience?

Read: Question/Annotate

- Continue to ask/record questions.
- Underline main ideas.
- Circle new or key words.
- Highlight key supporting details.
- Restate ideas out loud.

Ask:

- What prior knowledge can I use to make inferences about the text's meaning?
- What evidence allows me to make those inferences?

Prewrite: Recite/Review/Brainstorm

List, cluster, or outline topics based on your survey; leave room to fill in details during reading. Record predicted answers.

- Freewrite to analyze prior knowledge, purpose for reading, and audience.
- Freewrite a first response to the text.
- Take notes/Recite ideas: Record main ideas in your own words.
- Add supporting details from the reading to the list, cluster, or outline of key topics.
- Brainstorm/list topics from the reading to respond to in writing.
- Identify the intended audience of your writing.
- Compose an outline of ideas for your written response.

steps that coordinates the reading process with the writing process to help you comprehend and respond to text. The following graphic offers a reading/writing strategy.

A **reading/writing strategy** is a series of steps that coordinates the reading process with the writing process to comprehend and respond to text.

Your purpose in any reading/writing situation is to respond to what you are reading. Your response may vary. At times, you may only restate or summarize the writer's main point. At other times, you may analyze the writer's logic or expressions, agree or disagree with particular points, or explore your own treatment of the particular topic. The close relationship and similarities between reading and writing can be developed into a reading/writing strategy that you can use in your everyday life, college life, and work life.

Draft

- Read your annotated text.
- Freewrite a response based on the completed list, cluster, or outline of key topics and details.
- Compose a thesis statement for your response.
- Compose an introduction, body, and conclusion of your response to the reading.

Review and Revise Your Draft

- Review your draft for clear use of wording, details, and organization.
- Annotate your draft with needed revisions.
- Rewrite your draft based on your review and annotations.

Proofread

- Reread your draft to identify/correct errors.
- Annotate your draft with needed corrections.
- Create and publish a polished draft.

L3 Apply the Reading/Writing Strategy: Before, During, and After Reading

Before Reading/Writing: Survey and Ask Questions

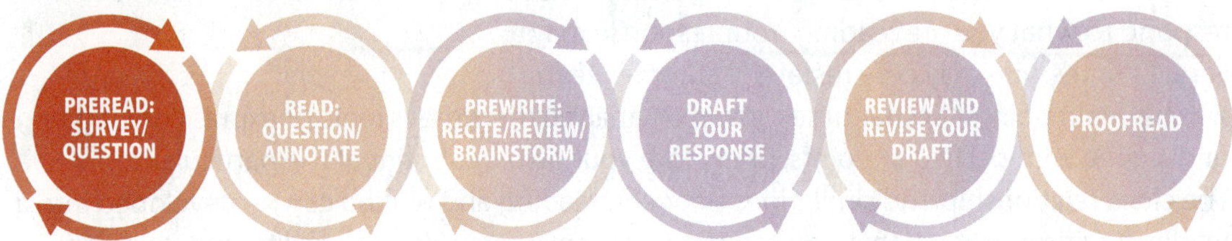

Before reading strategies are vital steps to take *as your prewriting process* in any reading/writing situation. Survey the passage and form questions that will prompt written responses from you. Answer these questions during and after reading.

PREREAD TO SURVEY

Quickly look over, or skim, the reading to activate prior knowledge and clarify your purpose for reading and writing. As you skim, note the special features of the text that highlight the writer's key points: key terms in *italic* and **bold** type, titles and headings, pictures and graphs, introductions, conclusions, summaries, and, in textbooks, end-of-chapter questions.

QUESTION

To aid in comprehension and to prewrite your response, ask questions before you read. Turn the key features of the text into questions. Use the reporter's questions—*who, what, when, where, why,* and *how*—to turn key terms and headings into questions. Use reflective questions to activate prior knowledge and track any changes in your own views as you read.

The following thinking guide can help you preread, survey, and question as a reading/writing strategy.

Step by Step: Survey and Question

- ☐ **Survey** a reading passage to find out how it is organized and what it is going to talk about or teach you by creating questions based on the following text features: *Italics*, **Bold type**, Titles, Introduction, Headings, Pictures, and Graphics. Read the first paragraph, summaries, and questions.
- ☐ **Ask questions** before you read as a prewriting step for your written response. First, record your questions based on text features to be answered during and after reading.

  Ask questions based on the text features:

  What is the passage about?

  How is the material organized?

  What do I already know about this idea? (What is my prior knowledge?)

  What is my purpose for reading/writing?

  What points may I want to address or include in my written response?

Example

Assume you are taking a college course in sociology, and the following section from the textbook is part of your required reading for the week. Begin the process of understanding and responding to the ideas. Use the "Step by Step: Survey and Question" thinking guide.

68 ***SOCIOLOGY: A DOWN-TO-EARTH APPROACH***

SOCIALIZATION INTO THE SELF AND MIND

[1]When you were born, you had no ideas. [2]You didn't know that you were a son or daughter. [3]You didn't even know that you were a he or she. [4]How did you develop a self, your image of who you are? [5]How did you develop your ability to reason? [6]Let's find out.

COOLEY AND THE LOOKING-GLASS SELF

[7]About a hundred years ago, Charles Horton Cooley (1864–1929), a symbolic interactionist who taught at the University of Michigan, concluded that the self is part of how *society* makes us human. [8]He said that *our sense of self develops from interaction with others*. [9]To describe the process by which this unique aspect of "humanness" develops, Cooley (1902) coined the term *looking-glass self*. [10]He summarized this idea in the following couplet:

> [11]*Each to each a looking-glass*
> *Reflects the other that doth pass.*

[12]The looking-glass self contains three elements:

1. [13]***We imagine how we appear to those around us.*** [14]For example, we may think that others perceive us as witty or dull.
2. [15]***We interpret others' reactions.*** [16]We come to conclusions about how others evaluate us. [17]Do they like us for being witty? [18]Do they dislike us for being dull?
3. [19]***We develop a self-concept.*** [20]How we interpret others' reactions to us frames our feelings and ideas about ourselves. [21]A favorable reflection in this *social mirror* leads to a positive self-concept; a negative reflection leads to a negative self-concept.

[22]Note that the development of the self does *not* depend on accurate evaluations. [23]Even if we grossly misinterpret how others think about us, those misjudgments become part of our self-concept. [24]Note also that *although the self-concept begins in childhood, its development is an ongoing, lifelong process.* [25]During our everyday lives, we monitor how others react to us. [26]As we do so, we continually modify the self. [27]The self, then, is never a finished product—it is always in process, even into our old age.

MEAD AND ROLE TAKING

[28]Another symbolic interactionist, George Herbert Mead (1863–1931), who taught at the University of Chicago, pointed out how important play is as we develop a self. [29]As we play with others, we learn to **take the role of the other.** [30]That is, we learn to put ourselves in someone else's shoes—to understand how someone else feels and thinks and to anticipate how that person will act.

CONTINUED

EXAMPLE *CONTINUED*

[31]This doesn't happen overnight. [32]We develop this ability over a period of years (Mead 1934; Denzin 2007). [33]Psychologist John Plavel (1968) asked 8- and 14-year-olds to explain a board game to children who were blindfolded and to others who were not. [34]The 14-year-olds gave more detailed instructions to those who were blindfolded, but the 8-year-olds gave the same instructions to everyone. [35]The younger children could not yet take the role of the other, while the older children could.

Mead analyzed taking ***the role of the other*** as an essential part of learning to be a full-fledged member of society. At first, we are able to take the role only of ***significant others***, as this child is doing. Later we develop the capacity to take the role of ***the generalized other***, which is essential not only for cooperation but also for the control of antisocial desires.

[36]As we develop this ability, at first we can take only the role of **significant others,** individuals who significantly influence our lives, such as parents or siblings. [37]By assuming their roles during play, such as dressing up in our parents' clothing, we cultivate the ability to put ourselves in the place of significant others.

[38]As our self gradually develops, we internalize the expectations of more and more people. [39]Our ability to take the role of others eventually extends to being able to take the role of "the group as a whole." [40]Mead used the term **generalized other** to refer to our perception of how people in general think of us.

[41]Taking the role of others is essential if we are to become cooperative members of human groups—whether they be our family, friends, or co-workers. [42]This ability allows us to modify our behavior by anticipating how others will react—something Genie never learned.

[43]As Figure 3.1 illustrates, we go through three stages as we learn to take the role of the other:

1. ***Imitation.*** [44]Under the age of 3, we can only mimic others. [45]We do not yet have a sense of self separate from others, and we can only imitate people's gestures and words. [46](This stage is actually not role taking, but it prepares us for it.)
2. ***Play.*** [47]During the second stage, from the ages of about 3 to 6, we pretend to take the roles of specific people. [48]We might pretend that we are a firefighter, a wrestler, a nurse, Supergirl, Spiderman, a princess, and so on. [49]We also like costumes at this stage and enjoy dressing up in our parents' clothing, or tying a towel around our neck to "become" Superman or Wonder Woman.
3. ***Team Games.*** [50]This third stage, organized play, or team games, begins roughly when we enter school. [51]The significance for the self is that to play these games we must be able to take multiple roles. [52]One of Mead's favorite examples was that of a baseball game, in which each player must be able to take the role of all the other players. [53]To play baseball, it isn't

enough that we know our own role; we also must be able to anticipate what everyone else on the field will do when the ball is hit or thrown.

FIGURE 3.1 – How We Learn to Take the Role of the Other: Mead's Three Stages

To help his students understand the term ***generalized other***, Mead used baseball as an illustration. Why are team sports and organized games excellent examples ***to*** use in explaining this concept?

Stage 1: Imitation	**Stage 2: Play**	**Stage 3: Team Games**
Children under age 3 No sense of self Imitate others	Ages 3 to 6 Play "pretend" others (princess, Spiderman, etc.)	After about age 6 or 7 Team games ("organized play") Learn to take multiple roles

[54]Mead also said there were two parts of the self, the "I" and the "me." [55]The "I" is *the self as subject*, the active, spontaneous, creative part of the self. [56]In contrast, the "me" is *the self as object*. [57]It is made up of attitudes we internalize from our interactions with others. [58]Mead chose these pronouns because in English "I" is the active agent, as in "I shoved him," while "me" is the object of action, as in "He shoved me." [59]Mead stressed that we are not passive in the socialization process. [60]We are not like robots, with programmed software shoved into us. [61]Rather, our "I" is active. [62]It evaluates the reactions of others and organizes them into a unified whole.

[63]Mead added that the "I" even monitors the "me," fine tuning our ideas and attitudes to help us better meet what others expect of us.

[64]**In Sum**—In studying the details, you don't want to miss the main point, which some find startling: *Both our self and our mind are social products*. [65]Mead stressed that we cannot think without symbols. [66]But where do these symbols come from? [67]Only from society, which gives us our symbols by giving us language. [68]If society did not provide the symbols, we would not be able to think and so would not possess a self-concept or that entity we call the mind. [69]The self and mind, then, like language, are products of society.

Henslin, James M., *Sociology: A Down-to-Earth Approach*, 10th ed., pp. 68-70.

Before Reading/Writing: Survey and Question

Questions based on text features:

____

____

____

____

____

____

Standard prereading questions:

1. What is the passage about? ______________________

2. How is the material organized? ______________________

3. What do I already know about this idea? (What is my prior knowledge?)

____

4. What is my purpose for reading/writing? ______________________

5. What points may I want to address or include in my written response? ______________________

Explanation

Compare your responses to the following student think-aloud about his before reading/writing strategy.

As I surveyed this textbook section, I created the following questions to answer as I read. I will set up these in my notebook as two-column questions and answers. I will write the questions on the left side of the paper. Then, I will write the answers on the right side of the paper. That way, I can cover up the answers and quiz myself after reading.

Questions based on text features:

What is the definition of self?

Who is Cooley? What is the looking-glass self?

What are the three dimensions to the looking-glass self?

Who is Mead? What is role taking?

How do we take the role of the other?

What are significant others?

What are generalized others?

What are imitation, play, and team games, and how do they relate to self-concept?

Standard prereading questions:

1. *What is the passage about? The topic is about self-concept.*
2. *How is the material organized? The material has several lists of ideas. And it gives definitions for the key terms.*
3. *What do I already know about this idea? (What is my prior knowledge?) I have a really good friend who struggles with low self-esteem. He is always worried about what other people think of him. He never feels like he can live up to his parents' expectations, and he was bullied all through public school.*
4. *What is my purpose for reading/writing? I want to understand how society affects a person's self-concept so I can be stronger as a person and understand and maybe help people like my friend.*
5. *What points may I want to address or include in my written response? I need to be able to restate the points Cooley and Mead make about the self. But I also would like to make the connection between what I learn about the self to low self-esteem. I would like to be able to share helpful information with my friend.*

Practice 1

Before Reading/Writing: Survey and Question

Assume you are a member of the organization Students against Destructive Decisions (SADD). You have been asked to write an article about some of the dangers of college drinking for the upcoming newsletter that will go out to all students on your campus. You have found the following information on a government site on the Internet. Apply before reading/writing strategies as you prepare to write your article for the newsletter.

Reading/Writing Questions based on text features:

____

____

____

____

____

Standard prereading-prewriting questions:

What is the passage about? ____

How is the material organized? ____

What do I already know about this idea? (What is my prior knowledge?) ____________

____

What is my purpose for reading/writing?

____

What points may I want to address or include in my written response? ____________

____

Beyond Hangovers: Effects of Alcohol on the Brain

[1]You're chatting with friends at a party and a waitress comes around with glasses of champagne. [2]You drink one, then another, maybe even a few more. [3]Before you realize it, you are laughing more loudly than usual and swaying as you walk. [4]By the end of the evening, you are too slow to move out of the way of a waiter with a dessert tray and have trouble speaking clearly. [5]The next morning, you wake

up feeling dizzy and your head hurts. [6]You may have a hard time remembering everything you did the night before.

[7]These reactions illustrate how quickly and dramatically alcohol affects the brain. [8]The brain is an intricate maze of connections that keeps our physical and psychological processes running smoothly. [9]Disruption of any of these connections can affect how the brain works. [10]Alcohol also can have longer-lasting consequences for the brain—changing the way it looks and works and resulting in a range of problems.

[11]Most people do not realize how extensively alcohol can affect the brain. [12]But recognizing these potential consequences will help you make better decisions about what amount of alcohol is appropriate for you.

What Happens Inside the Brain?

[13]The brain's structure is complex. [14]It includes multiple systems that interact to support all of your body's functions—from thinking to breathing to moving.

[15]These multiple brain systems communicate with each other through about a trillion tiny nerve cells called *neurons.* [16]Neurons in the brain translate information into electrical and chemical signals the brain can understand. [17]They also send messages from the brain to the rest of the body.

[18]Chemicals called *neurotransmitters* carry messages between the neurons. [19]Neurotransmitters can be very powerful. [20]Depending on the type and the amount of neurotransmitter, these chemicals can either intensify or minimize your body's responses, your feelings, and your mood. [21]The brain works to balance the neurotransmitters that speed things up with the ones that slow things down to keep your body operating at the right pace.

[22]Alcohol can slow the pace of communication between neurotransmitters in the brain.

Alcohol Shrinks and Disturbs Brain Tissue

[23]Heavy alcohol consumption—even on a single occasion—can throw the delicate balance of neurotransmitters off course. [24]Alcohol can cause your neurotransmitters to relay information too slowly, so you feel extremely drowsy. [25]Alcohol-related disruptions to the neurotransmitter balance also can trigger mood and behavioral changes, including depression, agitation, memory loss, and even seizures.

[26]Long-term, heavy drinking causes alterations in the neurons, such as reductions in the size of brain cells. [27]As a result of these and other changes, brain mass shrinks and the brain's inner cavity grows bigger. [28]These changes may affect a wide range of abilities, including motor coordination; temperature regulation; sleep; mood; and various cognitive functions, including learning and memory.

[29]One neurotransmitter particularly susceptible to even small amounts of alcohol is called *glutamate.* [30]Among other things, glutamate affects memory. [31]Researchers believe that alcohol interferes with glutamate action, and this

CONTINUED

PRACTICE 1 *CONTINUED*

may be what causes some people to temporarily "black out," or forget much of what happened during a night of heavy drinking. [32]Alcohol also causes an increased release of *serotonin*, another neurotransmitter, which helps regulate emotional expression, and *endorphins*, which are natural substances that may spark feelings of relaxation and euphoria as intoxication sets in. [33]Researchers now understand that the brain tries to compensate for these disruptions. [34]Neurotransmitters adapt to create balance in the brain despite the presence of alcohol. [35]But making these adaptations can have negative results, including building alcohol tolerance, developing alcohol dependence, and experiencing alcohol withdrawal symptoms.

What Factors Make a Difference?

[36]Different people react differently to alcohol. [37]That is because a variety of factors can influence your brain's response to alcohol. [38]These factors include:

- [39]**How much and how often you drink—**The more you drink, the more vulnerable your brain is.
- [40]**Your genetic background and family history of alcoholism—** Certain ethnic populations can have stronger reactions to alcohol, and children of alcoholics are more likely to become alcoholics themselves.
- [41]**Your physical health—**If you have liver or nutrition problems, the effects of alcohol will take longer to wear off.

Are Brain Problems Reversible?

[42]Abstaining from alcohol over several months to a year may allow structural brain changes to partially correct. [43]Abstinence also can help reverse negative effects on thinking skills, including problem solving, memory, and attention.

During Reading: Read, Question, Annotate

During reading strategies are also vital steps to take as part of your prewriting process in any reading/writing situation. As you read, annotate ideas that answer the questions you formed before reading.

READ AND QUESTION

As you read, *continue to ask questions* about what you are reading. Compare new ideas to your prior knowledge. Repair confusion. Stay focused and alert.

ANNOTATE

Annotation is marking the text to highlight key ideas or add your own margin notes. Annotations may include underlining, circling, numbering, using color highlights, and drawing pictures or restating ideas in the margin. Annotations draw key information from the text for use in your written response.

The following thinking guide can help you read, question, and annotate as a reading/writing strategy.

Step by Step: Read, Question, and Annotate

❑ **Read** and think about the importance of the information by continuing to ask questions:

- Does this new information agree with what I already know?
- Do I need to change what I thought I knew?
- What is the significance of this information?
- What information provided allows me to infer, or draw conclusions, about the text?

❑ **Question**, acknowledge, and resolve any confusion as it occurs.

- Create questions based on the headings, subheadings, and words in **bold** type and *italics*.
- Reread the parts you don't understand.
- Reread when your mind drifts during reading.
- Read ahead to see if the idea becomes clearer.
- Determine the meaning of words from the context. Look up new or different words.
- Think about ideas even when they differ from your own.

❑ **Annotate** to make the material your own. Make sure you understand by marking the text or adding notes in the margins.

- Create a picture in the margin.
- Mark your text by underlining, circling, or otherwise highlighting topics, key terms, and main ideas.
- Rephrase an idea in the margin.
- Answer questions that were created based on the headings and subheadings.
- Write a brief summary of the section or passage.

Example

Assume you are taking a college course in health. First, preread the following passage from the textbook *Access to Health* by surveying and questioning. Then, read and annotate the key ideas in the passage. Use the thinking guide "Step by Step: Read, Question, and Annotate." *Student responses may vary.*

Interpersonal Relationship Types

[1]Each relationship, whether friendship or love, a primary relationship or a work relationship, is unique. [2]Yet there are general types that research has identified—and these categories will offer considerable insight into your own interpersonal relationships.

FRIENDSHIP

[3]One theory of **friendship** identifies three major types: friendships of reciprocity, receptivity, and association. [4]The *friendship of reciprocity*, the ideal type, is characterized by loyalty, self-sacrifice, mutual affection, and generosity. [5]A friendship of reciprocity is based on equality. [6]Each individual shares equally in giving and receiving the benefits and rewards of the relationship.

[7]In the *friendship of receptivity*, in contrast, there is an imbalance in giving and receiving; one person is the primary giver and the other the primary receiver. [8]This is a positive imbalance, however, because each person gains something from the relationship. [9]The different needs of both the person who receives affection and the person who gives it are satisfied. [10]This is the friendship that may develop between a teacher and a student or between a doctor and a patient. [11]In fact, a difference in status is essential for the friendship of receptivity to develop.

[12]The *friendship of association* is transitory; it might be described as a friendly relationship rather than a true friendship. [13]Associative friendships are the kind you have with classmates, neighbors, or coworkers. [14]There is no great loyalty, no great trust, no great giving or receiving. [15]The association is cordial but not intense.

LOVE

[16]Like friendships, romantic partnerships come in different styles as well.

[17]**Eros love** seeks beauty and sensuality and focuses on physical attractiveness, sometimes to the exclusion of qualities others might consider more important and more lasting. [18]The erotic lover has an idealized image of beauty that is unattainable in reality. [19]Consequently, the erotic lover often feels unfulfilled.

[20]**Ludic love** seeks entertainment and excitement and sees love as fun, a game. [21]To the ludic lover, love is not to be taken too seriously; emotions are to be held in check lest they get out of hand and make trouble. [22]The ludic lover retains a partner only so long as the partner is interesting and amusing. [23]When the partner is no longer interesting enough, it's time to change.

[24]**Storge love** is a peaceful and tranquil love. [25]Like ludus, storge lacks passion and intensity. [26]Storgic lovers set out not to find a lover but to establish a companionable relationship with someone they know and with whom they can share interests and activities. [27]Storgic love is a gradual process of unfolding thoughts and feelings and is sometimes difficult to distinguish from friendship.

[28]**Pragma love** is practical and traditional and seeks compatibility and a relationship in which important needs and desires will be satisfied. [29]The pragma lover is concerned with the social qualifications of a potential mate even more than with personal qualities; family and background are extremely important to the pragma lover, who relies not so much on feelings as on logic.

[30]**Manic love** is an obsessive love that needs to give and receive constant attention and affection. [31]When attention and affection are not constant, or when an expression of increased commitment is not returned, reactions such as depression, jealousy, and self-doubt can lead to extreme lows.

[32]**Agapic love** is compassionate and selfless. [33]The agapic lover loves both the stranger on the road and the annoying neighbor. [34]Jesus, Buddha, and Gandhi practiced and preached this unqualified spiritual love—a love that is offered without concern for personal reward or gain and without any expectation that the love will be reciprocated.

Donatelle, Rebecca J., and Ketcham, Patricia, *Access to Health*, 12th ed., pp. 104–106.

Explanation

Compare your responses to the following student think-aloud about how she used questions and annotations as a reading/writing strategy.

I completed the survey and question stage before I began reading. The questions I created before reading helped me annotate during reading, I asked "What are the types of interpersonal relationships discussed in this passage? What are the three types of friendship? What are the six types of love? To answer these questions, I annotated the passage by circling all the words in bold and italic print throughout the passage. I also underlined their definitions. Then I wrote the following summary to answer my prereading questions. "The two types of interpersonal relationships discussed in this passage are friendship and love. Research has identified three major types of friendship. They are friendship of reciprocity, receptivity, and association. The passage also identified six types of love. They are eros, ludic, storge, pragma, manic, and agapic love."

After Reading–Prewriting: Recite, Review, Brainstorm

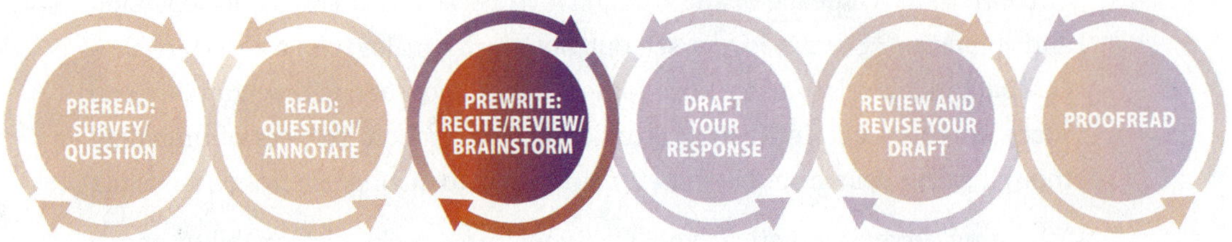

Effective reader/writers use the *after reading steps* recite *and* review *as prewriting steps* to help brainstorm their written responses to the text. Prewriting includes reading and thinking about your topic before you write a rough draft, and capturing your prewriting thinking on paper. Prewriting allows you to explore ideas without worrying about polishing them. Therefore, your prewrite has been going on as you surveyed, questioned, read, and annotated a passage.

At this point, it is also important to know the type of response you will write. Basically, there are two general types of response. The first type is a summary in which you only restate the writer's ideas. You will learn in depth about the summary response in Module 8. The second type is a personal response, in which you agree or disagree with the writer's ideas, or you explain the significance of the ideas or how to apply the information. You are now ready to use your questions and annotations to brainstorm ideas for your written response to the passage.

RECITE

Writing annotations, summaries, notes, and questions/answers are all different ways to recite what you read. Reciting ideas during and after reading deepens comprehension. And the deeper your comprehension, the better your written response will be.

REVIEW

Review of a passage includes rereading and recalling ideas. For example, effective reader/writers set their prereading questions up as two-column notes with the questions on the left side and the answers on the right. Then, to review, they cover up the answers and try to answer the questions as a self-test. However, review also includes connecting new information to your prior knowledge and thinking about how new ideas may have changed the way you think about a topic. When you review, you often form opinions and think about how to use or apply the information.

BRAINSTORM

After you have read, recited, and reviewed the ideas in a passage, you are ready to respond in writing. Use the words in bold and italics, headings, subheadings, and your annotations as the focus of your brainstorming. Freewrite a personal reaction to record your opinion or what you have learned. Create a concept map or outline of the major details in the passage based on key terms or ideas. Generate minor details that explain the importance of each term or idea or how the concept can be applied. A major detail explains your main idea; a minor detail explains a major detail.

The following thinking guide can help you prewrite, recite, review, and brainstorm ideas as a reading/writing strategy.

Step by Step: Recite, Review, Brainstorm

❑ **Recite** the information. Think about what you have read, and write about it in your notebook.

- Summarize the most important parts.
- Answer your prereading questions.
- Rephrase ideas into your own words.
- Record changes in your opinions based on the new information.

❑ **Review** the information.

- Connect new information to your prior knowledge about the topic.
- Form opinions about the material and the author.
- Revisit your answers to the prereading questions.
- Review new words and their meanings based on the way they were used in the passage.
- Think of ways to use or apply new information.

❑ **Brainstorm** ideas for your written response to the passage.

- **Freewrite** a response to what you have read by answering the following questions:
  - What have I learned?
  - What is the most important idea?
  - What is the significance of the idea?
  - How can this idea be used or applied?
  - With which ideas do I agree?
  - With which ideas do I disagree?
- **Map** the relationship among ideas you have annotated in the text.
  - Draw a circle on your page and write a key word or phrase in the circle.
  - Write a word that relates to the topic, circle the word, and connect it to the topic circle with a line.
  - Repeat this process so a set of major supports radiates out from the topic circle.
  - Write a word that relates to one of the major supports, circle it, and connect it to that major support circle.
  - Repeat this process for each of the major supports to create clusters of minor supports.
- **Outline** or list key ideas and details in blocks of thought.
  - Label each major idea with the capital letters A, B, C, and so on.
  - Under each major idea, list and label its supports with the numbers 1, 2, 3, and so on.

Example

Assume you are a concerned citizen who wants to address the problem of graffiti in your town. You recently attended a training seminar for community organizers and received the following guidelines about how to organize a graffiti cleanup day. You are in the process of following the steps in the guidelines and are ready to write a letter to the public announcing the event and calling for volunteers. Prewrite a draft of your letter. First, preread by surveying and questioning the guidelines "How to Organize a Graffiti Cleanup." Then, read and annotate the key ideas in the guidelines. Finally, on your own paper, brainstorm details for your letter based on the guidelines. Use the thinking guide "Step by Step: Recite, Review, Brainstorm."

Ask questions based on the text features.

What areas need a graffiti cleanup day?

How do I organize a cleanup day?

How do I recruit volunteers?

How do I advertise the event?

What is the passage about?

how to organize a graffiti cleanup day

How is the material organized?

a series of steps

What do I already know about this idea? (What is my prior knowledge?)

Answers may vary.

What is my purpose for reading/writing?

to learn how to organize a cleanup day in my community

What points may I want to address or include in my written response?

the location and time of the cleanup, how many people are needed, the refreshments that will be provided, why it's important to remove graffiti

HOW TO ORGANIZE A GRAFFITI CLEANUP

To eradicate graffiti, the entire community must work together. Businesses, religious groups, youth clubs, public and private schools, neighborhood associations, local newspapers and radio stations, all need to be involved to eliminate graffiti. The nonprofit organization GraffitiGone, which has helped hundreds of communities eradicate graffiti, offers the following guidelines to clean up graffiti in your neighborhood.

1. IDENTIFY AREAS TO BE CLEANED OF GRAFFITI.

- Identify locations that are disfigured by graffiti and select the method of removal. Paint and solvent, or other cleaning solutions, may be necessary to remove graffiti (including markers) from surfaces such as concrete walls, fences, utility boxes, signs, etc.
- Predict the number of workers and the materials needed to remove or paint over graffiti.
- Take a picture of the graffiti before it is removed to assist law enforcement in the investigation of the vandalism.
- Obtain written permission from property owners prior to the cleanup.

2. ORGANIZE AN EVENT.

- Select a date. Most volunteers prefer Saturday mornings.
- Determine how and when materials and equipment will arrive. Plan for safe storage and disposal of paint and cleaning compounds before, during, and after the cleanup.
- Identify sources for materials. Ask the owner of the property, local paint suppliers, or other businesses to donate paint and other equipment.

3. IDENTIFY AND RECRUIT VOLUNTEERS.

- Identify and involve people who can provide pickup trucks or vans to help transport equipment and volunteers and for trash collection at the end of the event.
- Invite residents of the targeted neighborhood.
- Enlist volunteers specifically for cleanup after the event.
- Determine how volunteers will be assigned and the sequencing of tasks.
- Provide refreshments such as coffee, water, snacks, etc.

4. ADVERTISE THE EVENT.

- Notify and involve the local law enforcement. Consider having a police officer on-site at your event.
- Create flyers and posters to advertise the cleanup. Remove all posters and flyers immediately after the event!
- Contact the local media (newspapers, radio stations, and local TV news shows).
- Contact local church, school, civic, and business groups.

CONTINUED

EXAMPLE *CONTINUED*

Use this space to brainstorm details for your letter. Use the thinking guide "Step by Step: Recite, Review, Brainstorm" to review brainstorming strategies.

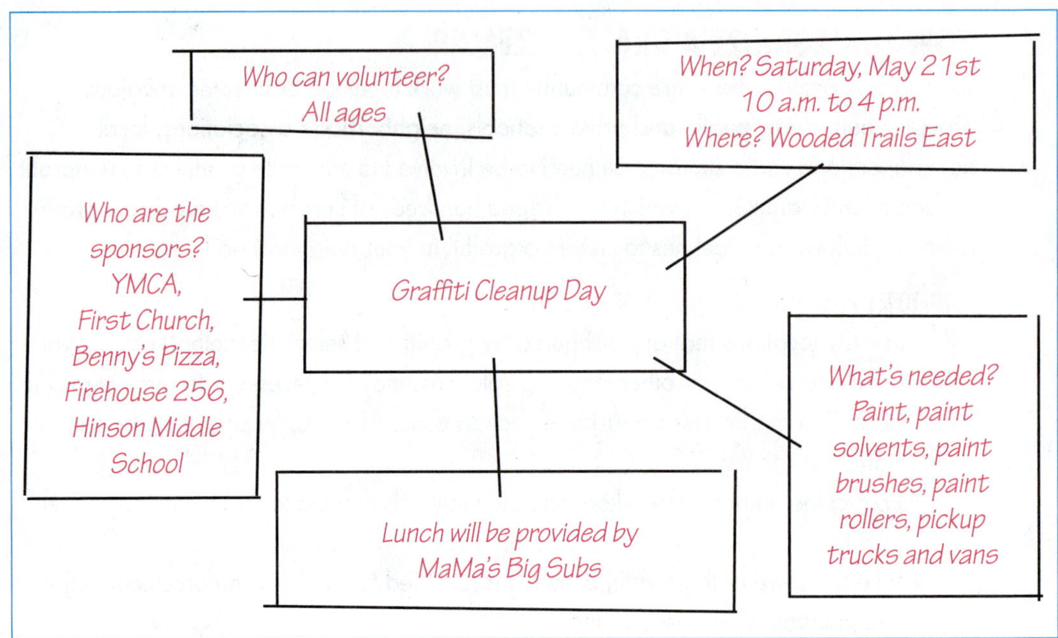

Who can volunteer? All ages
When? Saturday, May 21st
10 a.m. to 4 p.m.
Where? Wooded Trails East
Who are the sponsors? YMCA, First Church, Benny's Pizza, Firehouse 256, Hinson Middle School
Graffiti Cleanup Day
What's needed? Paint, paint solvents, paint brushes, paint rollers, pickup trucks and vans
Lunch will be provided by MaMa's Big Subs

Explanation

Compare your responses to the following student think-aloud about how he recited and reviewed the passage, and then brainstormed his written response.

Before I read, I surveyed the headings, skimmed the bulleted lists, and came up with the following questions.

Ask questions based on the text features.

What areas need a graffiti cleanup day? How do I organize a cleanup day? How do I recruit volunteers? How do I advertise the event?

What is the passage about?

how to organize a graffiti cleanup day

How is the material organized?

a series of steps

What do I already know about this idea? (What is my prior knowledge?)

Our neighborhood has got graffiti on the side walls of businesses and on private fences. It is very ugly. Some people think graffiti is art, but I think it's wrong to mess up somebody else's stuff.

What is my purpose for reading/writing?

to learn how to organize a cleanup day in my community

What points may I want to address or include in my written response?

the location and time of the cleanup, how many people are needed, the refreshments that will be provided, why it's important to remove graffiti

HOW TO ORGANIZE A GRAFFITI CLEANUP

To eradicate graffiti, the entire community must work together. Businesses, religious groups, youth clubs, public and private schools, neighborhood associations, local newspapers and radio stations, all need to be involved to eliminate graffiti. The nonprofit organization GraffitiGone, which has helped hundreds of communities eradicate graffiti, offers the following guidelines to clean up graffiti in your neighborhood.

1. IDENTIFY AREAS TO BE CLEANED OF GRAFFITI.

- Identify locations that are disfigured by graffiti and select the method of removal. Paint and solvent, or other cleaning solutions, may be necessary to remove graffiti (including markers) from surfaces such as concrete walls, fences, utility boxes, signs, etc.
- Predict the number of workers and the materials needed to remove or paint over graffiti.
- Take a picture of the graffiti before it is removed to assist law enforcement in the investigation of the vandalism.
- Obtain written permission from property owners prior to the cleanup.

2. ORGANIZE AN EVENT.

- Select a date. Most volunteers prefer Saturday mornings.
- Determine how and when materials and equipment will arrive. Plan for safe storage and disposal of paint and cleaning compounds before, during, and after the cleanup.
- Identify sources for materials. Ask the owner of the property, local paint suppliers, or other businesses to donate paint and other equipment.

3. IDENTIFY AND RECRUIT VOLUNTEERS.

- Identify and involve people who can provide pickup trucks or vans to help transport equipment and volunteers and for trash collection at the end of the event.
- Invite residents of targeted neighborhood.
- Enlist volunteers specifically for cleanup after the event.
- Determine how volunteers will be assigned and the sequencing of tasks.
- Provide refreshments such as coffee, water, snacks, etc.

4. ADVERTISE THE EVENT.

- Notify and involve the local law enforcement. Consider having a police officer on-site at your event.
- Create flyers and posters to advertise the cleanup. Remove all posters and flyers immediately after the event!
- Contact the local media (newspapers, radio stations, and local TV news shows).
- Contact local church, school, civic, and businesses groups.

CONTINUED

EXPLANATION *CONTINUED*

During reading, I kept in mind that I need to write a letter to announce the event and ask for volunteers. So, I underlined the following ideas so I would remember to put them in my letter: identify location, predict number of workers and materials needed, date, Saturday, who has pickup trucks or vans, volunteers after event, and refreshments. After readings, needed I studied the underlined ideas and organized them into the following concept map. The reporter's questions helped me think up and organize the details.

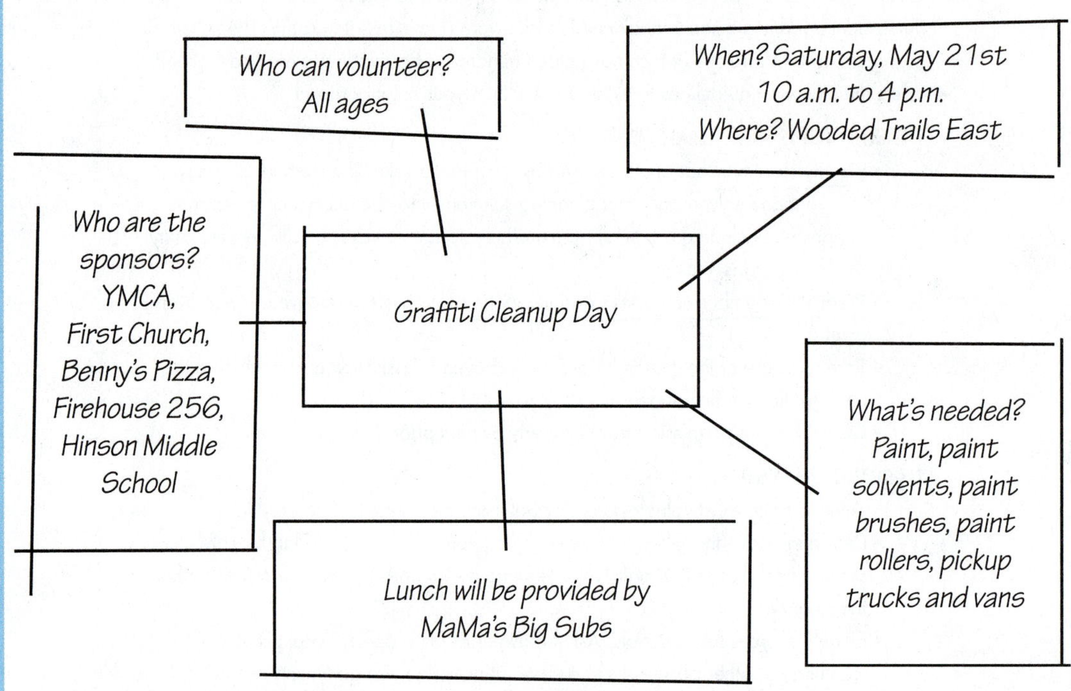
Who can volunteer? All ages
When? Saturday, May 21st
10 a.m. to 4 p.m.
Where? Wooded Trails East
Who are the sponsors? YMCA, First Church, Benny's Pizza, Firehouse 256, Hinson Middle School
Graffiti Cleanup Day
What's needed? Paint, paint solvents, paint brushes, paint rollers, pickup trucks and vans
Lunch will be provided by MaMa's Big Subs

Practice 2

Apply the After Reading–Prewriting Strategy: Before, During, and After Reading

Assume you are taking a college course in the basics of technology. Every week you are assigned specific readings to respond to in writing. Prewrite a draft of your response to an assigned reading. First, preread by surveying and questioning the following passage from the textbook *Introductory Technology in Action*. Then, read and annotate the key ideas in the passage. Finally, on your own paper, brainstorm your response to what you have read. Use the before, during, and after thinking guides on pages 34, 43, and 47.

Student responses may vary.

Ask questions based on the text features.

What is relativism?

What is situational ethics?

What are societal ethics?

What is rule utilitarianism?

What is the difference between unethical behavior and amoral behavior?

What is the passage about?

ethics in computing

How is the material organized?

as a series of questions and answers

What do I already know about this idea? (What is my prior knowledge?)

Answers may vary.

What is my purpose for reading/writing?

Answers may vary.

What points may I want to address or include in my written response?

Answers may vary.

ETHICS IN COMPUTING

[1]You just bought a new notebook computer. [2]You know you can go to BitTorrent or LimeWire to download the latest summer blockbuster movie and its soundtrack. [3]You also probably know this is unethical. [4]Although pirating music and videos is a valid example of unethical behavior, it has been overused as an illustration of the ethical challenges of technology. [5]There is a vast range of ethical issues surrounding technology, several of which we will discuss in this section. [6]Many other issues are discussed in the Ethics in IT sections of each chapter throughout the book.

Difference between ethics and morals?

WHAT IS ETHICS?

[7]Ethics is the study of the general nature of morals and of the specific moral choices made by individuals. [8]Morals involve conforming to established or accepted ideas of right and wrong (as generally dictated by society), and are usually viewed as black and white. [9]Ethical issues often involve subtle distinctions, such as the difference between fairness and equity.

[10]Ethical values are the guidelines you use to make decisions each day. [11]For example, the person in front of you at the coffee shop drops a dollar on the floor and doesn't notice it. [12]Do you tell him or her about it, or do you pick up the dollar and use it to pay for your coffee?

[13]**Doesn't everyone have the same basic ethics?** [14]There are many systems of ethical conduct. [15]***Relativism*** is a theory that holds that there is no universal moral truth and that instead there are only beliefs, perspectives, and values. [16]Everyone has his or her own ideas of right and wrong, and so who are we to judge anyone else? [17]Another ethical philosophy is ***situational ethics***, which states that decision making should be based on the circumstances of a particular situation and not on fixed laws.

[18]Many other ethical systems have been proposed over time, some of which are defined by religious traditions. [19]For example, the expression "Judeo-Christian ethics" refers to the common set of basic values shared across the Jewish and Christian religious traditions. [20]These include behaviors such as respecting property and relationships, honoring one's parents, and being kind to others.

[21]**Are laws established to guide people's ethical actions?** [22]Laws are formal, written standards designed to apply to everyone. [23]Laws are enforced by government agencies (such as the police, the Federal Bureau of Investigation, the Food and Drug Administration, and so on) and interpreted by the courts.

276 ***INTRODUCTORY TECHNOLOGY IN ACTION***

[24]It is not possible to pass laws that cover every possible behavior that human beings can engage in. [25]Therefore, ***societal ethics*** provides a general set of unwritten guidelines for people to follow.

[26]***Rule utilitarianism*** is an ethical theory that espouses establishing moral guidelines through specific rules. [27]The idea behind this system is that if everyone adheres to the same moral code, society as a whole will improve and people will be happier. [28]Many societies follow this system in general terms, including the United States. [29]For instance, laws against nudity in public places (except for a few nude beaches) in the United States help define public nudity as immoral.

[30]**Don't some people behave unethically?** [31]Although many valid systems of ethical conduct exist, sometimes people act in a manner that violates the beliefs they hold or the beliefs of the ethical system they say they follow. [32]***Unethical behavior*** can be defined as not conforming to a set of approved standards of social or professional behavior. [33]For instance, using your phone to text message your friends during an exam is prohibited by most colleges' rules of student conduct. [34]This behavior is different from ***amoral behavior***, in which a person has no sense of right and wrong and no interest in the moral consequences of his or her actions.

difference between unethical and amoral behavior?

[35]**Is unethical behavior a euphemism for illegal activity?** [36]Unethical behavior does not have to be illegal. [37]An example of an unethical but not illegal practice is supermarket slotting fees. [38]These are fees that some supermarkets charge to produce companies and product manufacturers for the privilege of having their products placed on store shelves. [39]This is considered unethical by many people because it puts smaller companies, which often don't have the financial resources to pay these fees, at a disadvantage. [40]Not all illegal behavior is unethical. [41]Civil disobedience, which is manifested by intentionally refusing to obey certain laws, is used as a form of protest to effect change in extreme situations. [42]Gandhi's nonviolent resistance to the British rule of India, which led to India's establishment as an independent country, is an example of civil disobedience. [43]Although the British were ruling India, is it ever ethical for one country to control another country's people?

[44]**Which system of ethics works best?** [45]There is no universal agreement on which is the best system of ethics. [46]Most societies use a blend of different systems. [47]Regardless of the ethical system of the society in which you live, all ethical decisions are greatly influenced by personal ethics.

Evans, Alan, Martin, Kendall, and Poatsy, Mary Anne, *Technology in Action, Introductory Version*, 7th ed., pp. 142–143.

L4 Apply the Reading/Writing Strategy: After Prewriting, Write a Draft

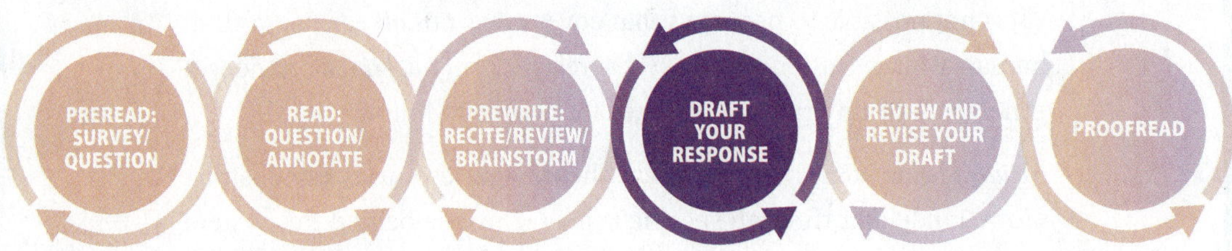

The drafting stage of the reading/writing process takes the ideas generated during prewriting and develops them into an initial version of your written response to what you have read. This first draft may be revised several times during the next phases of the reading/writing process. This phase may also include several tasks, depending on the reading/writing situation. An essay or letter may require the drafting of an introduction, a main idea (such as a topic sentence or thesis statement), supporting details, and a conclusion. A stand-alone paragraph, such as a summary, may require only the main idea and major supporting details.

The following thinking guide can help you draft your written response as a reading/writing strategy.

Step by Step: Drafting

- ☐ Write your main idea in a complete sentence.
- ☐ As you write a thesis statement or topic sentence, assert an idea instead of announcing your topic. Avoid the following announcements:
  - "I am going to write about…"
  - "My paragraph (or essay) is about…"
  - "My topic is…"
- ☐ As you write your first draft, do not worry about issues such as spelling and grammar.
- ☐ Generate major and minor details to support your main idea.
- ☐ As you write, include new ideas as they occur to you without self-criticism or editing before you have a complete draft; this first draft does not need to be perfect. You will use the revision process to evaluate details for logic and relevance once your draft is complete.
- ☐ Use the first draft to discover how your ideas flow and fit together.
- ☐ Resolve to write multiple drafts to produce your best work.

Example

Assume you are continuing your work as a concerned citizen to organize a graffiti cleanup day. You have carefully read the guidelines about how to organize a cleanup day.

(See last example, p. 48.) You have also brainstormed ideas for a letter you are writing to the public announcing the event and calling for volunteers. Based on your prewrite, write a draft of your letter. Use the thinking guide "Step by Step: Drafting."

Explanation

Compare your use of the reading/writing process and your draft to the following student think-aloud about how she drafted her written response to the passage.

The concept map I brainstormed after I read the guidelines really made it easy to write a first draft of my letter. As I drafted, the concept map even made me think of additional details that needed to be included. My goal for my first draft was to get all my thoughts written out sentence by sentence in a way that made sense. In this first draft, I didn't take time to choose exactly the best words or to check spelling or punctuation. Instead I focused on being detailed and logical. I also drafted an introduction and conclusion for my letter. In the introduction, I wanted to really get my readers' interest and let them know how important the cause is. Then, the conclusion is a strong call to come and get involved. Here is what I wrote.

<u>*Graffiti Cleanup Day: Make Wooded Trails Beautiful Again*</u>

Graffiti hurts, ,scares people, graffiti hurts property, graffiti is vandalism. Right now, right here in Wooded Trails, graffiti blihts our fences, trafic signs, sidewalks, the outside walls of businesses. Our community needs to be cleaned up. And we can do it. Come join in and make Wooded Trails beautiful again. All ages welcome. Graffiti Cleanup Day is Saturday May 21st, 10 a.m. to 4 p.m. The event will kick off in the parking lot of First National Bank at 33 Wilshire Blvd. Paint, paint solvents, rubber gloves, paint rollers, brushes, and ladders being provided by the YMCA, First Church, Benny's Pizza, Firehouse 256 and Hinson Middle School. Lunch will be provided by MaMa's Big Subs. Get your family and friend together bring your pick up trucks and vans (we can use em) and let's take back Wooded Trails from vandals.

Practice 3

Apply the Reading/Writing Strategy: After Prewriting, Write a Draft

Assume you are continuing your work as a college student in a course in the basics of technology. Based on the prewrite you created in Practice 2, draft your written response to the passage from the textbook *Introductory Technology in Action*. Use your own paper. Use the thinking guide "Step by Step: Drafting."

Student responses may vary.

L5 Apply the Reading/Writing Strategy: After Writing, Review, Revise, and Proofread Your Draft

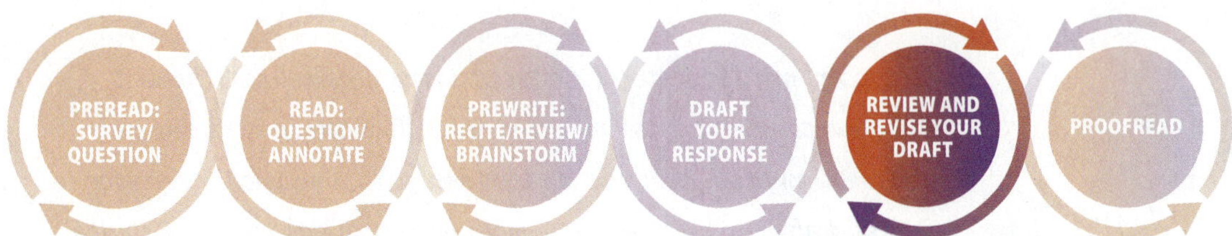

Now that you have gotten your ideas on paper, you can review your work to make sure your paragraph offers a focused, unified, well-supported, and coherent chunk of information. As you revise your draft, review and apply what you have learned.

REVIEW

Take another look at what you have written. Ask questions that your reader would ask. Think about the flow of your ideas and how easily a reader can follow your thoughts. Annotate your own writing with the revisions you think will improve the writing.

REVISE

Revising is re-seeing your work through the eyes of your reader. Revising is reworking your draft for clarity, logic, interest, and believability.

Step by Step: Review and Revise

- ❑ Read your draft out loud (either on your own or to a peer). This is an easy way to identify parts of your draft that may be unclear or awkward.
- ❑ Annotate your draft, as needed, with the revisions you will make.
- ❑ Make sure you properly refer to the author and title of the passage to which you are responding as needed.
- ❑ Make sure your main idea is stated clearly in a topic sentence or thesis statement.
- ❑ Make sure that the details in the body of your paragraph or essay fully support your topic sentence or thesis statement.
- ❑ Make sure every sentence in a paragraph relates to your main idea so that a reader can easily follow the logic of your ideas.
- ❑ Move information as needed into the most logical order.
- ❑ Add transitions as needed to clarify the relationship between ideas.
- ❑ Add details and examples as needed to strengthen or clarify the main idea and supporting points.
- ❑ Delete irrelevant details.

- [ ] If your paragraph or essay draft seems to end abruptly, add a concluding sentence (or paragraph, if you are writing an essay), restating and summing up your main points.
- [ ] Replace vague words and details with vivid and precise expressions.

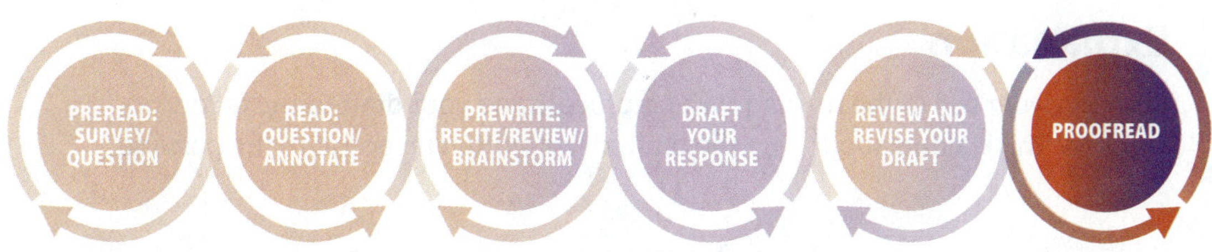

PROOFREAD

Once you have revised your paragraph, take time to carefully proofread your work. Proofreading is correcting errors in punctuation, capitalization, mechanics, grammar, and spelling. When you proofread, you are both a reader looking for errors that need correction and a writer creating a clean, polished copy. Publishing a clean, error-free draft proves you are committed to excellence and that you take pride in your work. Many student writers struggle with common errors, and every writer has her or his own pattern or habit of careless errors. To create a polished draft, a writer masters the rules of writing and edits to eliminate careless errors.

The following thinking guide can help you review, revise, and proofread your written response as a reading/writing strategy.

Step by Step: Proofread

Allow some time to pass between revising and proofreading.

- [ ] Read your work one sentence at a time from the end to the beginning. Reading your work from the end to the beginning allows you to focus on each sentence.
- [ ] Read again from the beginning with a cover sheet of paper that you slide down the page as you read so that you focus on one sentence at a time.
- [ ] Use a highlighter to mark mistakes.
- [ ] Proofread more than once; focus on one type of error at a time.
- [ ] Proofread for the types of errors you commonly make.
- [ ] Use word processing spell checkers carefully (they don't know the difference between words such as *there, their,* or *they're*).
- [ ] Use a dictionary to double check your spelling.

Example

Assume you are continuing your work as a concerned citizen to organize a graffiti cleanup day. Revise the draft of your letter to announce Graffiti Cleanup Day. Use the thinking guides "Step by Step: Review and Revise" and "Step by Step: Proofread."

Explanation

Compare your use of the reading/writing process and your draft to the following student's think-aloud about how she drafted her written response to the passage.

By brainstorming ideas with a concept map, I didn't have to add any details, and all the details related to my main point. However, I did move the information about where and when to appear earlier in the letter. Where and when are really the most important details, so they should be closer to the beginning. I also revised some words and phrases to make the details more vivid and smooth sounding when I read the letter out loud.

Graffiti Cleanup Day: Make Wooded Trails Beautiful Again

scars neighborhoods / sinks / values

Graffiti ~~hurts~~, graffiti scares people, graffiti ~~hurts~~ property . Graffiti is

mars

vandalism. Right now, right here in Wooded Trails, graffiti ~~blihts~~ our fences, trafic

outside

signs, sidewalks, the walls of businesses. Our community needs to be cleaned up. And we can do it by following the guidelines of the nonprofit organization GraffitiGone. Come join in and make Wooded Trails beautiful again.

move this sentence to

All ages welcome. [Graffiti Cleanup Day is Saturday May 21st, 10 a.m. to 4 p.m. The event will kick off in the parking lot of First National Bank at 33 Wilshire Blvd.] Paint, paint solvents, rubber gloves, paint rollers, brushes, and ladders are being provided by the YMCA, First Church, Benny's Pizza, Firehouse 256 and Hinson Middle School. Lunch will be provided by MaMas Big Subs. Get your family and friends together bring your pick up trucks and vans (we can use em) and let's take

the

[back] Wooded Trails from vandals. Let's cleanup together.

move word

After I finished revising, I took a break. Then, I asked a couple of people to help me proofread. My brother and a classmate read my letter and pointed out a few comma errors and run-on sentences. The spell check on my computer also pointed out misspelled words and an apostrophe error. I decided to end the letter with an exclamation point for emphasis. It was very helpful to revise for wording and then to proofread to polish.

Graffiti Cleanup Day: Make Wooded Trails Beautiful Again

Graffiti scars neighborhoods ^ graffiti scares people ^ graffiti sinks property values ^; Graffiti is vandalism. ^ Right now, right here in Wooded Trails, graffiti mars our fences, ~~trafic~~ traffic signs, sidewalks, and the outside walls of businesses. Graffiti Cleanup Day is Saturday ^, May 21st, 10 a.m. to 4 p.m. The event will kick off in the parking lot of First National Bank at 33 Wilshire Blvd. Our community needs to be cleaned up. ~~And~~ , and we can do it by following the guidelines of the nonprofit organization GraffitiGone.

Come join in and make Wooded Trails beautiful again. All ages welcome. Paint, paint solvents, rubber gloves, paint rollers, brushes, and ladders are being provided by the YMCA, First Church, Benny's Pizza, Firehouse 25 ^, and Hinson Middle School. Lunch will be provided by MaMa^'s Big Subs. Get your family and friends together ^, bring your ~~pick up~~ pickup trucks and vans (we can use em) ^, and let's take Wooded Trails back from the vandals. Let's ~~cleanup~~ clean up together. ^!

Practice 4

Apply the Reading/Writing Strategy: After Writing, Review and Revise Your Draft

Assume you are continuing your work as a college student in a course in the basics of technology. Review and revise the draft you wrote in Practice 3 in response to the passage from the textbook *Introductory Technology in Action*. Use your own paper. Use the thinking guides "Step by Step: Review and Revise" and "Step by Step: Proofread."

Answers may vary.

Practice 5

Applying the Reading/Writing Strategy: After Writing, Proofread Your Draft

Assume you are continuing your work as a college student in a course in the basics of technology. Proofread the revised draft you wrote in response to the passage from the textbook *Introductory Technology in Action* in Practice 4. Use the thinking guides "Step by Step: Review and Revise " and "Step by Step: Proofread." *Answers may vary.*

Reading and Writing Assignments

MySkillsLab™
Complete these assignments in MySkillsLab.

Considering Audience and Purpose

Study the sequence of photographs about the reading/writing process at the beginning of this module. Assume you are working with the businesspeople in the work group in the second photograph to respond to a report from the main office that offers several suggested actions to take to increase sales. Write an e-mail to the group suggesting a reading/writing strategy to respond to the report.

Reading and Writing for Everyday Life

Assume you received the following letter from a debt collection agency. However, this is not your debt. In the past, you have received similar notices that were meant for a person who has the same name as you and lives in your town. Write a response to the debt collection agency to dispute the debt.

RE: Central Debt Collection Agency

ACCOUNT NO: 76549

Total Due: $1,100.00

This is a demand for payment. Your past due account has been referred for collection. In an effort to give you an opportunity to resolve this delinquency, please send your payment or explanation of non-payment. As required by law, you are hereby notified that a negative credit report reflecting your credit record may be submitted to a reporting agency if you fail to fulfill the term of your debt.

Unless you notify Central Debt Collections directly within 30 days after receiving this notice that you dispute the validity of this debt, Central Debt Collections will assume the debt is valid.

Reading and Writing for College Life

Assume you are taking the college course Introduction to Literature. Your professor has given you a study guide for an upcoming exam. One of the questions is: "What is the difference between hyperbole and understatement?" You have located the following passage in your textbook. Read the passage and answer the study question.

Hyperbole and Understatement

Most of us, from time to time, emphasize a point with a statement containing an exaggeration: "Faster than greased lightning," "I've told him a thousand times." We speak, then, not literal truth but use a figure of speech called **overstatement** or **hyperbole**. Poets, too, being fond of emphasis, often exaggerate for effect. Instances are Marvell's claim of a love that should grow "vaster than empires and more slow." Another is John Burgon's description of Petra: "A rose-red city, half as old as time." Overstatement can also be used for humor. Take, for instance, the fat woman's boast (from a blues song): "Every time I shake, some skinny gal loses her home." The opposite is **understatement**, which is a figure of speech that implies more than is said. For example, Robert Frost's line "One could do worse than be a swinger of birches" uses understatement. All through the poem, he has suggested that to swing on a birch tree is one of the most deeply satisfying activities in the world.

Adapted from Kennedy, X. J., and Gioia, Dana, *Literature: An Introduction to Fiction, Poetry, and Drama*, 8th ed., p. 867.

Reading and Writing for Working Life

Assume you are an assistant manager at a local grocery store. The manager sent you the following e-mail, identifying several complaints filed by customers and asking you to compose and send a memo to all employees that addresses these problems. Read the manager's e-mail and compose a memo that includes actions employees must take to eliminate the complaints.

To: Assistant Manager

RE: Customer Complaints

Over the course of the past several months, a number of customers have registered complaints at the customer service counter. It is imperative that we educate our employees about the impact of their behavior and offer guidelines and training sessions to improve customer service. Please identify and schedule the training sessions that are needed. In addition, note that some complaints come from improper employee behavior, not a lack of training. In these instances, provide guidelines to employees to reduce those complaints. The complaints are as follows:

- Employees smoking on sidewalks by the front doors instead of in designated smoking areas
- Damaged food from improper bagging techniques
- Rude behavior and remarks from the associates in the deli department
- Personal discussions among employees in front of customers at the checkout counters

Workshop: Develop a Reading/ Writing Strategy

Developing a reading/writing strategy deepens your understanding of what you read and strengthens your skills as a writer. Choose a passage to read and respond to in writing. You may select a passage in an example, practice, or writing assignment within this module. Or you may select a passage of your own choosing. Use the following guide to comprehend and respond to the passage.

PREREAD: SURVEY/ QUESTION

Ask questions about the text's features.

____

____

What is the passage about?

____

____

PREREAD: SURVEY/ QUESTION

How is the material organized?

____

____

What do I already know about this idea? (What is my prior knowledge?)

____

____

What is my purpose for reading/writing?

____

____

What points may I want to address or include in my written response?

____

____

Read and Annotate

As you read, annotate key ideas, particularly those details that answer your prereading questions.

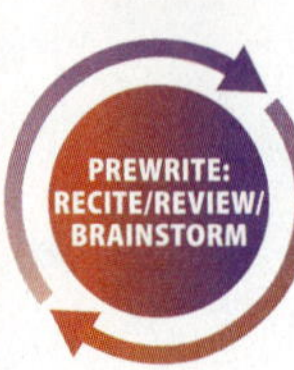

Step by Step: Recite, Review, and Brainstorm

Recite the information. Summarize the most important parts. Answer your prereading questions. Rephrase ideas into your own words. Record changes in your opinions based on the new information. **Review** the information. **Brainstorm** ideas for your written response to the passage. Freewrite a response to what you have read. **Map** the relationships among ideas you have annotated in the text. **Outline** or list key ideas and details in blocks of thought. Use your own paper.

Write a Draft of Your Response

Using the ideas you generated by brainstorming, compose a draft of your response. Use your own paper.

Revise Your Draft

Once you have created a draft of your paragraph, read the draft and answer the questions in the "Questions for Revising a Paragraph" box that follows. Indicate your answers by annotating your paper. If you answer "yes" to a question, underline, check, or circle examples. If you answer "no" to a question, write additional details in the margins and draw lines to indicate their placement. Revise your paragraph based on your reflection. (*Hint:* Experienced writers create several drafts as they focus on one or two questions per draft.)

Step by Step: Questions for Revising a Paragraph

- ❑ Have I stated or implied a focused main idea?
- ❑ Is the logical order of the ideas clear? Have I used specific words to guide my reader, such as *first, second, next,* etc.?
- ❑ Have I made my point with adequate details?
- ❑ Do all the details support my point?
- ❑ What impact will my paragraph have on my reader?

Proofread Your Draft

Once you have made any revisions to your paragraph that may be needed, proofread your paragraph to eliminate careless errors. Work with a classmate to give and receive feedback about your paragraphs.

Review Test

MySkillsLab™
Complete this Review Test in MySkillsLab.

Use the reading/writing strategy to comprehend and respond to the following article about credit cards from a government website. Before reading, survey the article. Use the ideas in **bold** print to create five questions to guide your reading. During reading, annotate the key ideas in the text. Answer the questions you asked before reading. Finally, use the writing process to respond to the ideas in the passage by answering the *What Do You Think?* prompt.

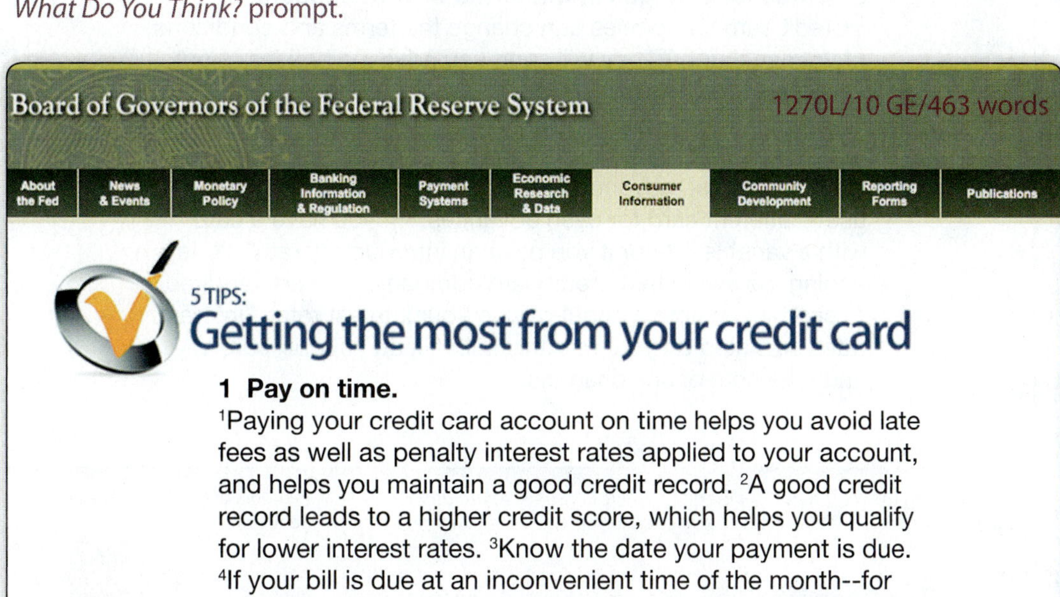

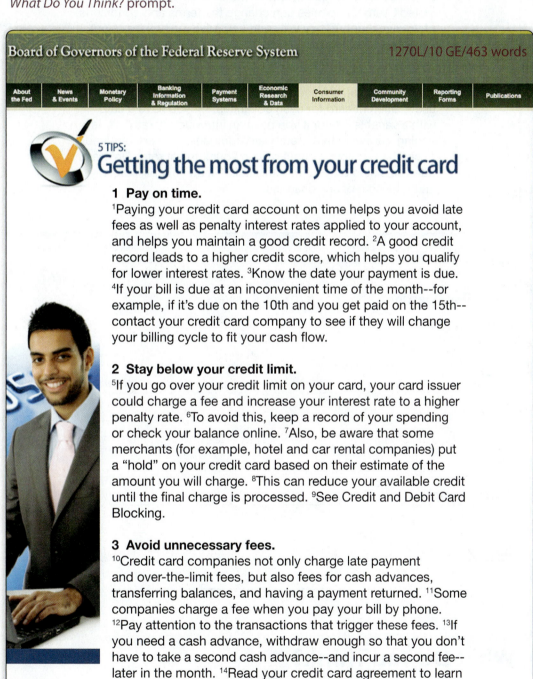

Board of Governors of the Federal Reserve System

1270L/10 GE/463 words

About the Fed | News & Events | Monetary Policy | Banking Information & Regulation | Payment Systems | Economic Research & Data | Consumer Information | Community Development | Reporting Forms | Publications

5 TIPS:

Getting the most from your credit card

1 Pay on time.

[1]Paying your credit card account on time helps you avoid late fees as well as penalty interest rates applied to your account, and helps you maintain a good credit record. [2]A good credit record leads to a higher credit score, which helps you qualify for lower interest rates. [3]Know the date your payment is due. [4]If your bill is due at an inconvenient time of the month--for example, if it's due on the 10th and you get paid on the 15th--contact your credit card company to see if they will change your billing cycle to fit your cash flow.

2 Stay below your credit limit.

[5]If you go over your credit limit on your card, your card issuer could charge a fee and increase your interest rate to a higher penalty rate. [6]To avoid this, keep a record of your spending or check your balance online. [7]Also, be aware that some merchants (for example, hotel and car rental companies) put a "hold" on your credit card based on their estimate of the amount you will charge. [8]This can reduce your available credit until the final charge is processed. [9]See Credit and Debit Card Blocking.

3 Avoid unnecessary fees.

[10]Credit card companies not only charge late payment and over-the-limit fees, but also fees for cash advances, transferring balances, and having a payment returned. [11]Some companies charge a fee when you pay your bill by phone. [12]Pay attention to the transactions that trigger these fees. [13]If you need a cash advance, withdraw enough so that you don't have to take a second cash advance--and incur a second fee--later in the month. [14]Read your credit card agreement to learn more about the fees that your credit card company charges.

4 Pay more than the minimum payment.

[15]If you can't pay your balance in full each month, try to pay as much of the total as you can. [16]Over time, you'll pay less

in interest charges--money that you will be able to spend on other things, and you'll pay off your balance sooner. [17]See the Federal Reserve's Credit Card Repayment Calculator to determine possible repayment timelines.

5 Watch for changes in the terms of your account. [18]Credit card companies can change the terms and conditions of your account. [19]They will send you advance notices about changes in fees, interest rates, billing, and other features. [20]By reading these "change in terms" notices, you can decide whether you want to change the way you use the card. [21]For example, if cash advance fees increase, you may decide to use a different card for cash advances. [22]If you have a card with a variable rate or if you have an introductory rate that is ending, be aware that credit card companies are not required to send you a notice about raising your interest rate. [23]Interest rates are listed on your monthly bill. [24]Read your bill carefully and take note of any changes.

"5 Tips: Getting the Most from Your Credit Card," *FR: Consumer Information*. Board of Governors of the Federal Reserve System. 17 June 2010. Web. <http://www.federalreserve.gov/consumerinfo/fivetips_creditcard.htm>.

Prereading Questions	Answers
1. *Why pay on time?*	*to avoid late fees, gain higher credit score, get lower rates*
2. *How do you stay below your credit limit?*	*keep good records, check balance*
3. *How can you avoid unnecessary fees?*	*pay attention to transactions that trigger fees*
4. *Why pay more than the minimum payment?*	*to pay less interest and pay off sooner*
5. *Why watch for changes in account terms?*	*To decide how to use the card*

What Do You Think?

Do you have a credit card? Why or why not? What are some of the dangers of using a credit card? What are some advantages? Assume you are related to or are friends with someone who is applying for a credit card for the first time. Write a message to advise this person about how to get the most out of a credit card.

Academic Learning Log: Module Review

Summary of Key Concepts of Developing a Reading/Writing Strategy

Assess your comprehension of the reading/writing strategy.

LO2 **1.** A reading/writing situation is the occurrence of a person *reading text and responding in writing to what was read*.

LO2 **2.** Reading is *an active process during which the reader makes meaning of the text*.

LO2 **3.** Writing is *the process of creating text*.

LO2 **4.** A reading/writing strategy is *a series of steps that coordinates the reading process with the writing process in order to comprehend and respond to text*.

LO2 **5.** The six basic phases of the reading/writing strategy are *preread*, *read*, *prewrite*, *draft*, *review*, and *proofread*.

LO3 **6.** Before reading/writing, preread, *survey*, and *question*.

LO3 **7.** Survey is *a quick look through a piece of text to activate prior knowledge and clarify a purpose for reading and writing*.

LO3 **8.** During reading/before writing, read, *question*, and *annotate*.

LO3 **9.** Annotation is *marking text to highlight key ideas or add margin notes.*

LO3 **10.** After reading/ *prewriting*, recite, review, and *brainstorm*.

LO3 **11.** Prewriting is *reading, thinking, and capturing ideas about a topic before writing a rough draft*.

LO3 **12.** Three ways to brainstorm are to *freewrite*, *map*, and *outline*.

LO3 **13.** A major detail explains or supports a *main idea*.

LO3 **14.** A minor detail explains or supports a *major detail*.

LO4 **15.** Drafting *is the process of taking the ideas generated during prewriting and developing them into an initial version of a written response to a reading passage*.

LO4 **16.** A topic sentence is a sentence that *states the main idea of a paragraph*.

LO4 **17.** A thesis statement is a sentence that *states the main or central idea of a longer passage of two or more paragraphs*.

LO5 **18.** After reading/writing, *review* and *revise* your draft.

LO5 **19.** Revising is reworking your draft for clarity, *logic*, *interest*, and believability.

LO5 **20.** After reading/writing, *proofread* your draft. Proofreading is preparing your work for *publication*. Proofreading is *correcting errors in a piece of writing*.

Test Your Comprehension of Developing a Reading/Writing Strategy

Respond to the following prompts and questions.

LO1 LO2 LO3 LO4 LO5

In your own words, explain the point of developing a reading/writing strategy.

L1 L2 L3 L4 L5

Create a graph or concept map to illustrate the reading/writing strategy.

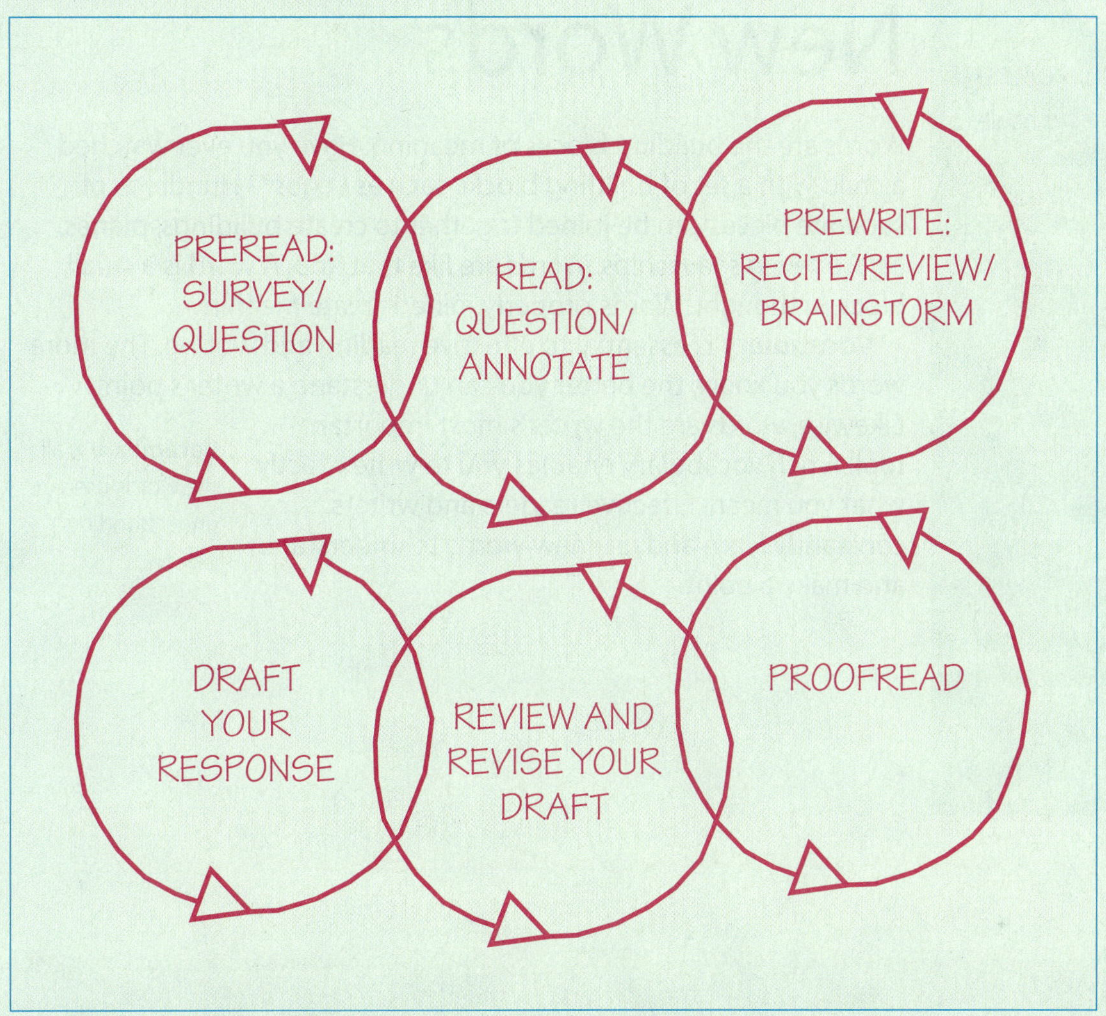

L1 L2 L3 L4 L5

1. **How will I use what I have learned?** In your notebook, discuss how you will apply what you have learned about the reading/writing strategy. When will you apply this knowledge?

2. **What do I still need to study about the reading/writing strategy?** In your notebook, discuss your ongoing study needs. Describe what, when, and how you will continue studying and using the reading/writing strategy.

MySkillsLab™
Complete the Post-test for Module 2 in MySkillsLab.

3

LEARNING OUTCOMES

After studying this module you should be able to:

- **LO 1** Answer the Question "What's the Point of Learning and Using New Words?"
- **LO 2** Use Context Clues to Comprehend and Make a Point
- **LO 3** Use a Dictionary to Comprehend and Make a Point
- **LO 4** Use Vocabulary Resources in Textbooks to Comprehend and Make a Point

Learning and Using New Words

Words are the building blocks of meaning. Have you ever watched a child with a set of building blocks such as Legos®? Hundreds of separate pieces can be joined together to create buildings, planes, cars, or even spaceships. Words are like that, too. A word is a small block of thought. Words properly joined create meaning.

Vocabulary is essential to effective reading and writing. The more words you know, the better you can understand a writer's point. Likewise, words are the writer's most important tool. A rich vocabulary enables you to write exactly what you mean. Effective readers and writers constantly learn and use new words to understand and make a point.

Vocabulary is all the words used or understood by a person.

WHAT'S THE POINT of Learning and Using New Words?

How many words do you have in your vocabulary? If you are like most people, you know about 60,000 words by the time you are 18 years old. During your college studies, you will most likely learn an additional 20,000 words. Each subject you study will have its own set of words that you will be expected to read, comprehend, and use in writing. In everyday life, you are exposed to new words as you engage in hobbies, read and negotiate legal contracts, and purchase products and services. In working life, each job or career brings with it a specialized set of words that you will be expected to use in your communications with supervisors, coworkers, and the public. In all areas of our lives, we are exposed to new words we need to learn and use.

Photographic Organizer: Learning and Using New Words

Before you study this module, predict the importance of vocabulary. Consider the following images and captions. Next to each photograph, predict how learning new words relates to reading and writing in academic life, everyday life, and working life. Finally, answer the question "What's the point of learning and using new words?"

When a student adds words to her vocabulary, she increases her prior knowledge, raises her comprehension, and improves her ability to write clearly.

A person must understand medical terms in order to communicate with a physician about personal health issues.

Vocabulary is a key aspect of success in working life. A businessperson must choose the best words to make a sale, get a loan, or earn a promotion.

What's the point of learning and using new words?

Learning and using new words will increase a person's ability to understand and share ideas in academic classes, increase enjoyment of words in everyday life, and increase success in working life.

What's the Point? One Writer's Response

The following paragraph offers one writer's response to the question: What's the point of learning and using new words?

A large vocabulary helps us get our point across in all areas of our lives. And when we don't know a word, a dictionary gives us the information we need to add the new word to our vocabulary. In our college life, every course has its own set of vocabulary to learn. For example, I am struggling with the terms in my algebra class. It's like a foreign language to me. However, as I learn new algebra terms, I get better at solving algebra problems. In everyday life, a good vocabulary allows us to communicate with others about important issues. For example, we need to know medical terms that doctors use so we can share and understand information about our health. In working life, our use of words can help or hurt our chances of being hired. And once hired, an employer or employee sends or receives instructions, directives, memos, manuals, and other materials that must be understood to be effective. A good vocabulary helps us understand and share what we know.

To learn and use words appropriately, effective readers and writers apply a variety of vocabulary strategies throughout the reading/writing process. These strategies include using context clues, analyzing word parts, using a dictionary, and using textbook resources. The following sections guide you into use of context clues, a dictionary, and textbook resources.

Use Context Clues to Comprehend and Make a Point

Effective readers and writers interact with new words in a number of ways. One way is to use **context clues**. The meaning of a word is shaped by its context. The word *context* means "surroundings." The meaning of a word is shaped by the words surrounding it. Effective readers use context clues to learn new words or new uses for known words. Effective writers employ context clues to communicate clearly and effectively to their readers.

A **context clue** is the information that surrounds a new word and is used to understand its meaning.

There are four types of context clues:

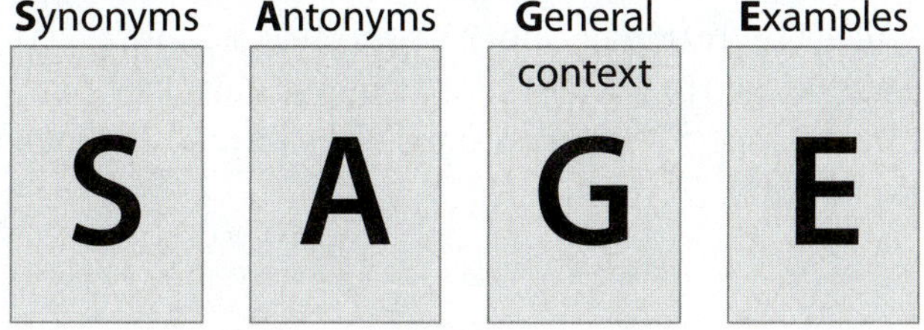

Notice that when the first letters of each type of context clue are put together, they spell the word **SAGE**. The word *sage* means "wise." Using context clues throughout the reading/writing process is a wise—SAGE—strategy.

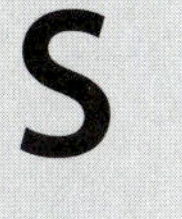

Synonyms

A **synonym** is a word that has the same or nearly the same meaning as another word. Many times, a writer will place a synonym near a new or difficult word or term as a context clue to the word's meaning. Usually, a synonym is set off with a pair of commas, a pair of dashes, or a pair of parentheses before and after it.

Synonym Signal Words

or *that* *is*

A **synonym** is a word that has the same or nearly the same meaning as another word.

Example

Assume you have been assigned to read the following information for your college psychology class. Before reading, skim the paragraph and underline the key terms in **bold** print. During reading, circle the signal words for each synonym and underline the synonym for the word in **bold**. After reading, complete the Write to Learn Vocabulary: Synonyms as Context Clues graphic organizer. Fill in the chart with the key terms and their synonyms from the paragraph. Then link each term to your prior knowledge by giving an example that you have observed or experienced.

[1]**Motivation**, that is the reason or the reward, accounts for why we start, continue, and complete activities. [2]At times, we pursue an activity as an end in itself, simply because it is enjoyable, not because of an attached award. [3]In these instances, we are pulled by **intrinsic motivation**, that is, internal (inside) rewards. [4]Other times, we act to gain a reward outside ourselves or to avoid some undesirable consequence. [5]Then, we are pulled by **extrinsic motivation** or external (outside) rewards.

Write to Learn Vocabulary: Synonyms as Context Clues		
Key Term	**Synonym**	**My Example**
motivation	*reason or reward*	*a college degree*
intrinsic motivation	*internal, inside rewards*	*enjoy learning about new ideas and being with people*
extrinsic motivation	*external, outside rewards*	*earn more money with a college degree*

Explanations

Compare your responses to the following student's think-aloud.

The signal words that is *in sentences 1 and 3 and* or *in sentences 1 and 5 helped me identify the synonyms. It was also helpful that the writer gave additional synonyms in parentheses for the terms* intrinsic *and* extrinsic *in sentences 3 and 5. These were new terms for me. So the synonyms really made the meanings clear. I like underlining the words or terms during reading and filling in the chart after reading. I also like coming up with my own examples. It made me really think about how the words apply to the real world. The first term I underlined and wrote in the chart was* motivation. *It had two synonyms:* reason *or* reward. *I used the example of a college degree because that is my reason for being in this class. The second term I underlined and recorded was* intrinsic motivation *and its synonym* internal rewards. *My example for intrinsic motivation is that I enjoy learning new ideas, and I also enjoy being with people like my teachers and classmates. The third term I underlined and wrote in the chart was* extrinsic motivation *and its synonym* external rewards. *My example for an extrinsic reward is that I can earn more money with a college degree.*

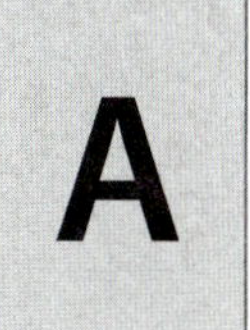

Antonyms

An **antonym** is a word that has the opposite meaning of another word. Antonyms help you see the shade of a word's meaning by showing you what the original word is *not*. Writers use antonyms to make a point more vivid or powerful and to guide the reader into a deeper meaning. The following contrast words often act as signals that an antonym is being used.

An **antonym** is a word that has the opposite meaning of another word.

Antonym Signal Words

but	*however*	*in contrast*	*instead*
unlike	*not yet*	*on the other hand*	

Sometimes antonyms appear next to the new word. In those cases, commas, dashes, or parentheses set them off. At other times, writers place antonyms in other parts of the sentence to emphasize the contrast between the ideas.

When writers use an antonym to clarify the meaning of a word, they assume that the reader knows the meaning of the antonym. However, if you are not sure of the meaning of the antonym, you can use two steps to understand the key term based on its antonym. First, identify the antonym given for the key term. Second, supply a word that means the opposite of the antonym used in the sentence.

Examples

Before reading, skim the paragraph to find and circle signal words for the antonyms of three key words. During reading, underline the key words and their antonyms. After reading, answer the questions to define each key word. Complete the Write to Learn Vocabulary: Antonyms as Context Clues graphic organizer. Fill in the chart with the key terms and their antonyms from the paragraph. Give a definition of each key term.

[1]During dinner, Anne Marie let out a long, loud burp that mortified her mother but delighted her friends. [2]Her mother's reaction was surprisingly dismissive, in contrast to her usual deep concern for her daughter's misbehavior. [3]Anne Marie expected a garrulous lecture, not silent acceptance, from her mother.

1. Which word best defines **mortified**?
   a. horrified
   b. killed
   c. silenced
   d. delighted

2. Which word best defines **dismissive**?
   a. polite
   b. indifferent
   c. funny
   d. angry

2. Which word best defines **garrulous**?
   a. calm
   b. angry
   c. silly
   d. long-winded

Write to Learn Vocabulary: Antonyms as Context Clues		
Key Term	**Antonym**	**My Example**
mortified	delighted	Mortified means horrified.
dismissive	concerned	Dismissive means indifferent.
garrulous	silent	Garrulous means long-winded.

Explanations

Compare your responses to the following student's think-aloud.

Before reading, I circled but *in sentence 1,* in contrast *in sentence 2, and* not *in sentence 3. Circling these signal words for antonyms helped me identify the three key terms and their antonyms as I read. It was obvious that* delighted *was the antonym for* mortified. Concerned *was the antonym for* dismissive. Silent *was the antonym for* garrulous. *The answer to question 1 is (a)* horrified. Horrified *is another antonym for* delighted, *and it was the only word that made sense in the sentence. It helped for me to plug in each choice and read it out loud to see if it made sense. The answer to question 2 is (b)* indifferent*—the opposite of* concerned. *The answer to question 3 is (d)* long-winded, *which is the opposite of* silent. *I noticed that thinking of an antonym for the antonym used by the writer actually gives a synonym, or the real meaning of the key word. I used these definitions in the chart. Underlining these words and their antonyms during reading and thinking about the meaning of the antonyms after reading made filling in the chart easy and quick. I filled in the chart with the following information.*

Key Term	*Antonym*	*Definition*
mortified	*delighted*	Mortified *means* horrified.
dismissive	*concerned*	Dismissive *means* indifferent.
garrulous	*silent*	Garrulous *means* long-winded.

G

General Context

Often you will find that the writer has chosen not to provide either a synonym clue or an antonym clue. In that case, the writer expects the reader to rely on the **general context** of the passage to understand the meaning of the unfamiliar word. This requires a reader to read the entire sentence, or to read ahead for a few sentences, for information that will help clarify the meaning of the new word.

General context is the information (words and sentences) that surrounds a word and influences its meaning.

Information about the word can be included in the passage in several ways. Sometimes, a writer gives a definition. Other times, a writer uses vivid word pictures or descriptions of a situation to convey the word's meaning. Writers may also include information about a term that describes certain aspects of its meaning, such as traits or benefits. Thus, a reader may need to figure out the meaning of a key word by using logic and reasoning skills.

Example

Read the following paragraph from a college communication textbook. Before reading, circle the key term in **bold** print. Then skim the paragraph to underline each time the term is repeated. During reading, underline details that explain an aspect of the key term. After reading, complete the Write to Learn Vocabulary: General Sense of the Passage as a Context Clue graphic organizer and answer the comprehension questions.

Student responses may vary.

NONVERBAL COMMUNICATION

[1]**Nonverbal communication** is communication without words. [2]You communicate nonverbally when you gesture, smile or frown, widen your eyes, move your chair closer to someone, wear jewelry, touch someone, raise your vocal volume, or even say nothing. [3]The crucial aspect of nonverbal communication is that the message you send is in some way received by one or more other people. [4]If you gesture while alone in your room and no one is there to see you, then most theorists would argue that communication has not taken place. [5]The same, of course, is true of verbal messages; if you recite a speech and no one hears it, then communication has not taken place. [6]Using nonverbal communication effectively can yield two major benefits. [7]First, the greater your ability to send and receive nonverbal signals, the higher your attractiveness, popularity, and psychosocial well-being are likely to be. [8]Second, the greater your nonverbal skills, the more successful you're likely to be at communicating information and influencing others.

DeVito, Joseph A., *Human Communication: The Basic Course*, 12th ed., p. 117.

Mark each of the following statements as T for true or F for false.

__F__ **1.** Nonverbal communication is a form of verbal communication.

__F__ **2.** Nonverbal communication may occur when you are alone.

__T__ **3.** Silence is a type of nonverbal communication.

__T__ **4.** Nonverbal communication affects one's ability to succeed.

Write to Learn:
General Sense of the Passage as a Context Clue

What It Is Like

Verbal communication—a message must be received by one or more people

What It Is Not

A gesture you make while alone that no one sees or receives

Key Term

Nonverbal communication

Types

Gesture, smile, or frown, widen your eyes, move your chair closer to someone, wear jewelry, touch someone, raise vocal volume, say nothing

Traits (Descriptions, Causes, Benefits, etc.)

Communication without words can increase attractiveness, popularity, psychosocial well-being, ability to communicate information and influence others.

Explanations

Compare your responses to the following student's think-aloud.

Annotating the text helped me fill in the chart, and filling in the chart helped me answer the questions. I had to think about where to put certain ideas from the paragraph into the chart. For example, at first, I thought to fill in the box labeled "traits" with "The crucial aspect of nonverbal communication is that the message you send is in some way received by one or more other people." But that is a "trait" that makes nonverbal communication like verbal communication. So I put that idea in the "What It Is Like" box. Here is how I completed the chart and answered the questions.

What It Is Like. Verbal communication—a message must be received by one or more people. Sentence 5 makes the similarity between nonverbal messages and verbal messages by saying, "The same, of course, is true of verbal messages . . ."

What It Is Not. A gesture you make while alone that no one sees or receives.

Types. Gesture, smile, or frown, widen your eyes, move your chair closer to someone, wear jewelry, touch someone, raise vocal volume, say nothing.

Traits. Communication without words can increase attractiveness, popularity, psychosocial well-being, ability to communicate information and influence others.

1. F. Nonverbal communication (without words) is the exact opposite of verbal communication (with words). Both are forms of communication.
2. F. This idea is stated in sentences 3 through 5.
3. T. This idea is stated in 2.
4. T. This idea is explained in sentences 7 and 8.

Examples

Many times a writer will show the meaning of a new or difficult word by providing one or more examples. The following signal words often introduce an example.

Example Signal Words

consists of *for example* *for instance* *including* *such as*

Colons and dashes can also indicate examples.

Example

Read the following paragraph from a college health textbook. Before reading, circle key terms in **bold** or *italic* print. Then skim the paragraph to underline each time the terms are repeated. During reading, underline examples of each key term. After reading, complete the Write to Learn Vocabulary: Examples as Context Clues graphic organizer. Then, answer the questions that follow. *Student responses may vary.*

Designing Your Exercise Program: Selecting Activities

[1]For each individual, there is a correct "dose" of exercise to effectively promote physical fitness. [2]Every exercise prescription includes at least one **mode of exercise**—that is, a specific type of exercise or physical activity to be performed. [3]For example, to improve cardiorespiratory fitness, you could select from a wide variety of activities, such as running, swimming, or cycling. [4]To ensure that you'll engage in the exercise regularly, you should choose activities that you will enjoy doing, that are available to you, and that carry little risk of injury. [5]For example, physical activities can be classified as being either *high-impact* or *low-impact*, based on the amount of stress placed on joints during the activity. [6]Low-impact activities put

CONTINUED

EXAMPLE *CONTINUED*

less stress on the joints than high-impact activities. [7]Because of the strong correlation between high-impact activities and injuries, many fitness experts recommend low-impact activities for fitness beginners or for people susceptible to injury (such as people who are older or overweight). [8]Examples of low-impact activities include walking, cycling, swimming, and low-impact dance activities. [9]High-impact activities consist of running, basketball, and high-impact dance.

--Adapted from Powers, Scott K., Dodd, Stephen L., and Jackson, Erica M., *Total Fitness & Wellness*, 6th ed., pp. 29-30.

Write to Learn:
Examples as Context Clues

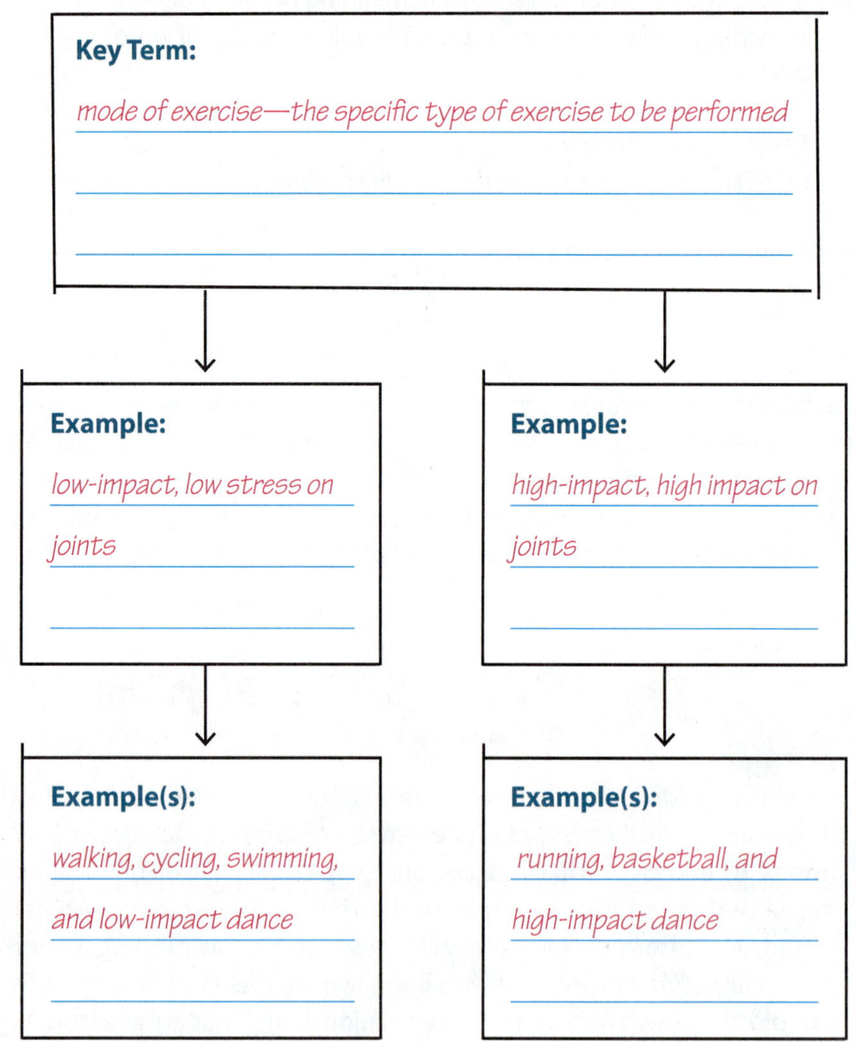

Key Term:
mode of exercise—the specific type of exercise to be performed
Example:
low-impact, low stress on
joints
Example:
high-impact, high impact on
joints
Example(s):
walking, cycling, swimming,
and low-impact dance
Example(s):
running, basketball, and
high-impact dance

1. The best meaning of the word **mode** as used in sentence 1 is

a. dose.
(c.) type.
b. activity.
d. performance.

2. The best meaning of the word **impact** as used in sentence 5 is

(a.) force.
c. speed.
b. injury.
d. fitness.

3. Which of the following is an example of low-impact exercise?

a. running
c. basketball
(b.) swimming

Explanations

Compare your responses to the following student's think-aloud.

The example signal words helped me find the examples for each key term, such as sentences 5, 8, and 9 used the word example *and the signal words* for example, include, *and* consists of. *I gave the following information in the chart and answers for the questions.*

Key Term	*Example*	*Examples*
mode of exercise, specific type of exercise to be performed	*low-impact*	*walking, cycling, swimming, low-impact dance*
	high-impact	*running, basketball, high-impact dance*

Practice 1

Use Context Clues to Comprehend a Point

Read the following paragraph from the college textbook *America and Its Peoples*. Answer the questions that follow the paragraph.

THE FIRST DISCOVERY OF AMERICA

[1]The world was a much colder place 75,000 years ago. [2]The Wisconsin **glaciation**, a great ice age, had begun. [3]Year after year, water being drawn from the oceans formed into mighty ice caps, which in turn spread over vast reaches of land. [4]This process dramatically lowered ocean levels. In the area of the Bering Straits, where today 56 miles of ocean separate Siberia from Alaska, a land bridge emerged. [5]At times this link between Asia and America, *Beringia*, may have been 1000 miles wide. [6]Most experts believe it provided the pathway used by early humans to enter a new world. [7]These people, known as **Paleo-Indians**, were **nomads** and **predators**, not settlers and farmers. [8]With stone-tipped spears, they hunted mastodons, woolly mammoths, giant beavers, giant sloths, and bighorn bison, as well as many smaller animals. [9]The mammals led prehistoric men and women to America up to 30,000 or more years ago. [10]For generations, these humans roamed Alaska in small bands, gathering seeds and berries when not hunting the big game or attacking and killing one another. [11]Eventually, corridors opened through the Rocky Mountains as the ice started to recede. [12]The **migratory** cycle began anew. [13]Animals and humans trekked southward and eastward, reaching the bottom of South America and the east coast of North America by about 8000 B.C. [14]This long journey covered thousands of miles and took several centuries to complete. [15]In the process Paleo-Indians had become Native Americans.

Martin, James Kirby, Roberts, Randy J., Mintz, Steven, McMurry, Linda O., and Jones, James H., *America and Its Peoples: Volume 1 to 1877*, 5th ed., p. 5.

1. The best meaning of the word **glaciation** as used in sentence 2 is

a. freeze. (circled)
b. thaw.
c. move.
d. era.

2. The best meaning of the word **Paleo-Indians** as used in sentence 7 is

a. local Americans.
b. official Americans.
c. ancient Americans. (circled)
d. present-day Americans.

3. The best meaning of the word **nomad** as used in sentence 7 is

a. invader.
b. traveler. (circled)
c. outcast.
d. planter.

4. The best meaning of the word **predator** as used in sentence 7 is
   a. herder.
   b. warrior.
   c. murderer.
   d. hunter.

5. The best meaning of the word **migratory** as used in sentence 12 is
   a. moving.
   b. freezing.
   c. building.
   d. settling.

So far, you have used context clues as a reader to learn new words before, during, and after reading a paragraph. However, context clues are also tools used by writers to make a particular point or detail clear to the reader. Just as readers use graphic organizers like the Write to Learn Vocabulary charts, writers use similar charts or graphics to generate and organize ideas before writing.

Example

Assume you are taking a college health course. Your professor has asked you to read a section in your textbook and respond in writing. During the prewriting phase of your reading/writing strategy, you created the following word-concept chart to generate and organize details based on your annotations of the passage. Based on the words and ideas in the word-concept map, write a one-paragraph rough draft. In your paragraph, define wellness, discuss causes, and give examples. Use context clues to clarify key terms. Introduce context clues with appropriate signal words and/or punctuation such as commas, parentheses, or dashes.

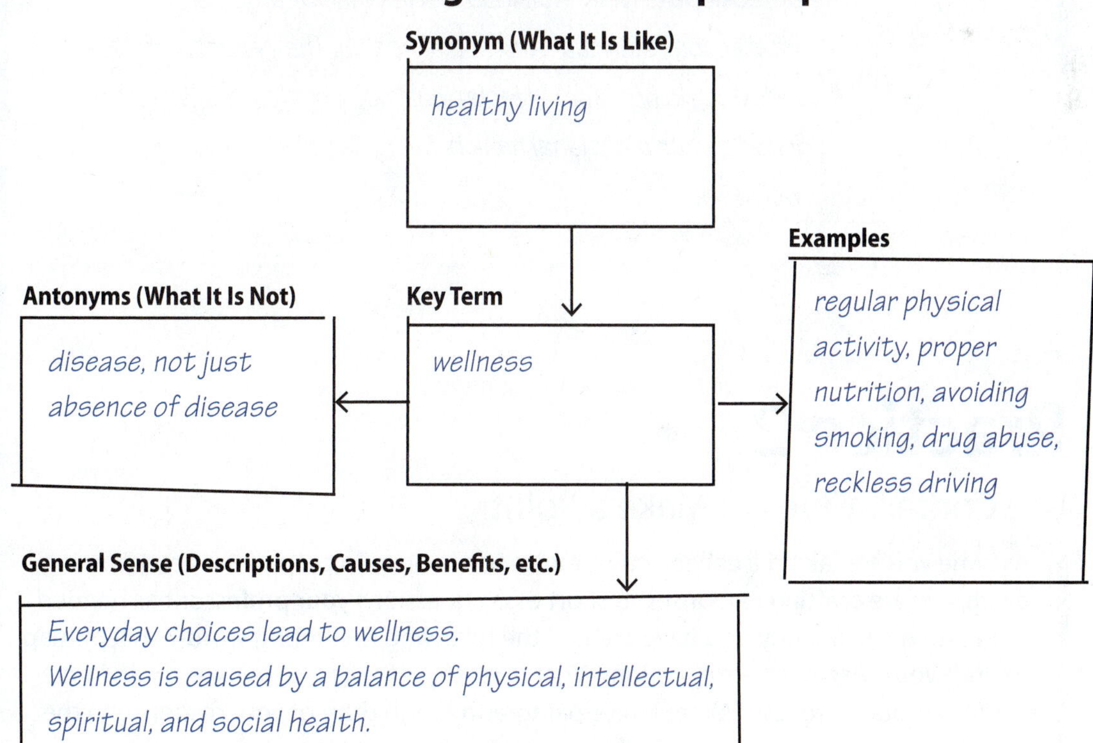
Prewriting Word-Concept Map
Synonym (What It Is Like)
healthy living
Antonyms (What It Is Not)
disease, not just absence of disease
Key Term
wellness
Examples
regular physical activity, proper nutrition, avoiding smoking, drug abuse, reckless driving
General Sense (Descriptions, Causes, Benefits, etc.)
Everyday choices lead to wellness.
Wellness is caused by a balance of physical, intellectual, spiritual, and social health.
The aspects of wellness do not work in isolation. Poor physical health can lead to poor emotional health.

--Adapted from Powers, Scott K., Dodd, Stephen L., and Jackson , Erica M., *Total Fitness & Wellness*, 6th ed., pp. 2,16.

EXAMPLE *CONTINUED*

Rough Draft:

Student responses may vary.

Explanation

Compare your responses to the following rough draft.

Wellness, or healthy living, is achieved by practicing a healthy lifestyle, which includes regular physical activity and proper nutrition. Wellness is not just the absence of disease. It is also eliminating unhealthy behaviors such as high-risk activities including smoking, drug abuse, or reckless driving. Wellness is a balance of physical, intellectual, spiritual, and social health. The aspects of wellness do not work in isolation. Poor physical health can lead to poor emotional health. Everyday choices lead to wellness.

Practice 2

Use Context Clues to Make a Point

Assume you are taking a college communication course. To prepare for an upcoming exam, you are drafting responses to short essay questions your professor has handed out to guide your study. You have created the following prewriting word-concept map to draft your answer to the question "What does the term *source-receiver* mean in the communication process?" Write a one-paragraph rough draft of your response to the question. Use context clues to clarify key terms. Introduce context clues with appropriate signal words and/or punctuation such as commas, parentheses, or dashes.

Prewriting Word-Concept Map

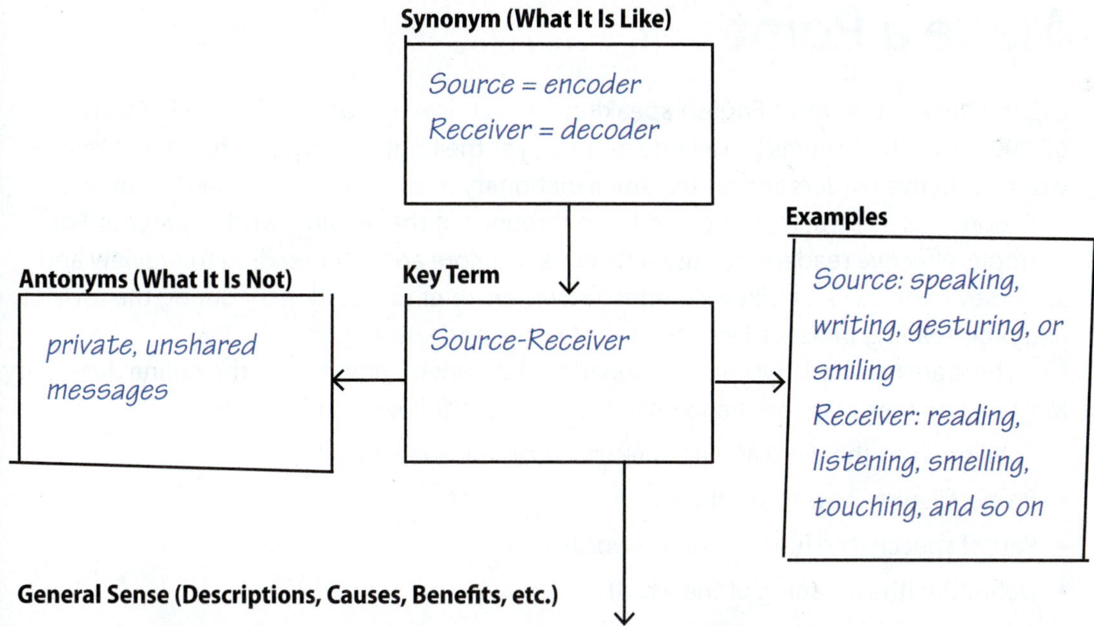

General Sense (Descriptions, Causes, Benefits, etc.)

Each person is involved in the communication process as both a source and a receiver.
A source sends a message. A receiver takes in a message.
A sender also receives messages—when you send a message, you receive your own message (you hear yourself, see your gestures, etc.), and you receive messages from the other person through your senses of sight, sound, touch, and smell.

--Adapted from DeVito, Joseph, A. *Human Communication: The Basic Course,* pp. 9–10.

Rough Draft:

Student responses may vary. The term source-receiver means that each person involved in the communication process is both a source (or encoder) and a receiver (or decoder). For example, speaking, writing, gesturing, and smiling are sources of messages. Reading, listening, touching, and smelling are examples of receiving messages. As you send messages, you're also receiving messages. You're receiving your own messages (for example, you hear yourself and you see your own gestures). You're also receiving messages from the other person through your senses of sight, sound, touch, and smell.

L3 Use a Dictionary to Comprehend and Make a Point

Experts believe that most English-speaking adults know and use between 25,000 and 50,000 words. That seems like a large number, yet the English language has over a million words. Effective readers and writers use a dictionary to understand new or difficult words. A dictionary is a useful resource to refer to throughout the reading/writing process. For example, effective readers may use a dictionary before and after reading to preview and study key or new words. Likewise, effective writers refer to a dictionary during the revision and proofreading phases to ensure correct usage and spelling.

There are two basic types of dictionaries: the print dictionary and the online dictionary. Most dictionaries, both print and online, provide the following information:

- Spelling (how the word and its different forms are spelled)
- Pronunciation (how to say the word)
- Part of speech (the function of the word)
- Definition (the meaning of the word)
- Synonyms (words that have similar meanings)
- Etymology (the history of the word)

Print dictionaries have a feature that sets them apart from online dictionaries. To help you find a word, print dictionaries offer guide words at the top of each page. These guide words indicate words that appear on the specific page based on their alphabetical order.

Example

Study the following portion of a page from the *Merriam-Webster Collegiate Dictionary,* 11th Edition. Only the words that alphabetically fall between the two guide words appear on this page. Analyze the list of words that follow. Mark **Y** for Yes or **N** for No to indicate if each word appears on this page of the dictionary.

aged \ˈā-jəd, ˈājd; ˈājd *for 1b*\ *adj* (15c) **1 :** grown old: as **a :** of an advanced age ⟨an ~ man⟩ **b :** having attained a specified age ⟨a man ~ 40 years⟩ **2 :** typical of old age — **ag·ed·ness** \ˈā-jəd-nəs\ *n*

age–group \ˈāj-ˌgrüp\ *n* (1904) : a segment of a population that is of approximately the same age or is within a specified range of ages

age·ism *also* **ag·ism** \ˈā-(ˌ)ji-zəm\ *n* (1969) : prejudice or discrimination against a particular age-group and esp. the elderly — **age·ist** *also* **ag·ist** \-jist\ *adj*

age·less \ˈāj-ləs\ *adj* (1651) **1 :** not growing old or showing the effects of age **2 :** TIMELESS, ETERNAL ⟨~ truths⟩ — **age·less·ly** *adv* — **age·less·ness** *n*

age·long \ˈāj-ˌlȯŋ\ *adj* (1810) : lasting for an age : EVERLASTING

age–mate \-ˌmāt\ *n* (1583) : one who is of about the same age as another

agen·cy \ˈā-jən(t)-sē\ *n, pl* **-cies** (1640) **1 a :** the office or function of an agent **b :** the relationship between a principal and that person's agent **2 :** the capacity, condition, or state of acting or of exerting power : OPERATION **3 :** a person or thing through which power is exerted or an end is achieved : INSTRUMENTALITY ⟨communicated through the ~ of the ambassador⟩ **4 :** an establishment engaged in doing business for another ⟨an advertising ~⟩ **5 :** an administrative division (as of a government) ⟨the ~ for consumer protection⟩

[1]**ag·glu·ti·nate** \ə-ˈglü-tᵊn-ˌāt\ *vb* **-nat·ed; -nat·ing** [L *agglutinatus,* pp. of *agglutinare* to glue to, fr. *ad-* + *glutinare* to glue, fr. *glutin-, gluten* glue — more at CLAY] *vt* (1586) **1 :** to cause to adhere : FASTEN **2 :** to combine into a compound : attach to a base as an affix **3 :** to cause to undergo agglutination ~ *vi* **1 :** to unite or combine into a group or mass **2 :** to form words by agglutination

[2]**ag·glu·ti·nate** \-tᵊn-ət, -tᵊn-ˌāt\ *n* (1952) : a clump of agglutinated material (as blood cells or mineral particles in soil)

ag·glu·ti·na·tion \ə-ˌglü-tᵊn-ˈā-shən\ *n* (1541) **1 :** the action or process of agglutinating **2 :** a mass or group formed by the union of separate elements **3 :** the formation of derivational or inflectional words by putting together constituents of which each expresses a single definite meaning **4 :** a reaction in which particles (as red blood cells or bacteria) suspended in a liquid collect into clumps and which occurs esp. as a serologic response to a specific antibody

ag·glu·ti·na·tive \ə-ˈglü-tᵊn-ˌā-tiv, -ə-tiv\ *adj* (1634) **1 :** ADHESIVE **2 :** characterized by linguistic agglutination

ag·glu·ti·nin \ə-ˈglü-tᵊn-ən\ *n* [ISV *agglutin*ation + *-in*] (1902) : a substance (as an antibody) producing agglutination

ag·glu·ti·no·gen \ə-ˈglü-tᵊn-ə-jən\ *n* [*agglutin*in + *-o-* + *-gen*] (1904) : an antigen whose presence results in the formation of an agglutinin — **ag·glu·ti·no·gen·ic** \-ˌglü-tᵊn-ə-ˈje-nik\ *adj*

Y 1. agent N 2. agrarian N 3. agree N 4. age

N 5. aggressor Y 6. aggravate Y 7. aggregate Y 8. aggie

N 9. agile N 10. aft

Explanations

Compare your responses to the following think-aloud.

The guide words aged and aggressive have the same first two letters ag. So I was able to look at the third letters of agent, agrarian, agree, age, agile, and aft to figure out if they appeared on the page. The longer words had more of the same letters as the guide word aggressive. So I had to look at the fourth letter of aggie, the fifth letter of aggravate, and the eighth letter of aggressor to see if each one of them appears on this page of the dictionary. Here is my list of answers.

(1) Y. (2) N. (3) N. (4) N. (5) N. (6) Y. (7). Y. (8) Y. (9) N. (10) N.

Most dictionaries differ from each other in the way they give other information about words. Each dictionary will explain how to use its resources in its introductory material.

How to Access and Read an Online Dictionary Entry

Online dictionaries are easy to access and easy to use, and all offer a wide range of similar learning resources. Each online dictionary varies in ways to access its resources. Preview several online dictionaries. Browse their sites to see which resources seem most helpful to you. Two highly popular, free online dictionaries are Merriam-Webster.com and Dictionary .com. The examples in this guide are taken from Merriam-Webster.com.

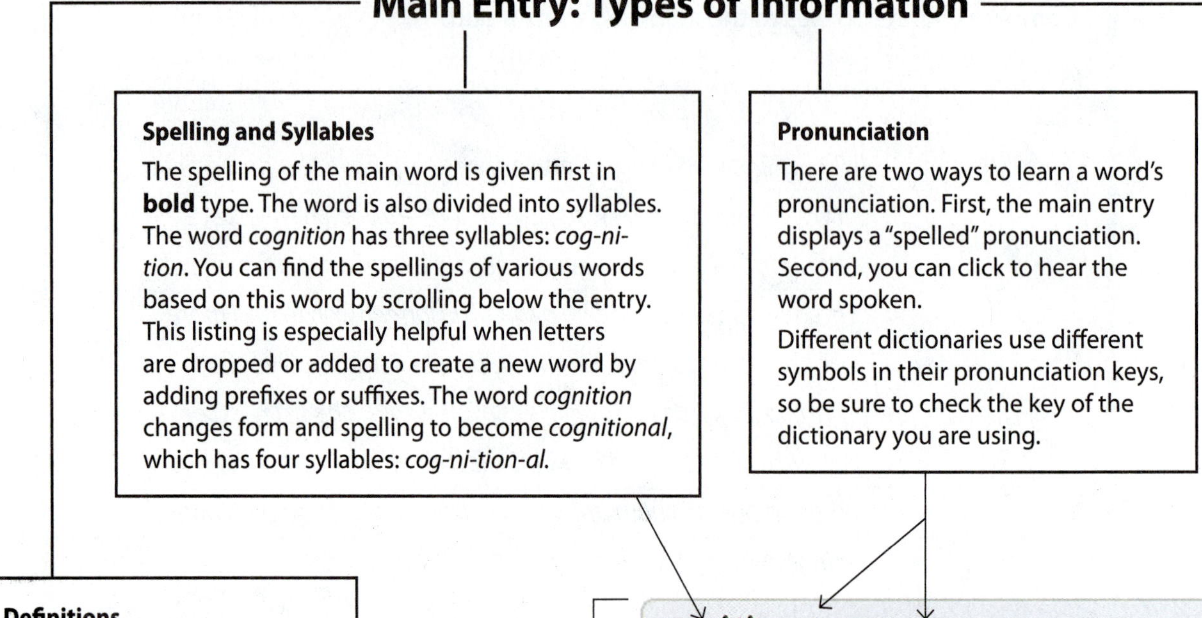

Main Entry: Types of Information
Spelling and Syllables
The spelling of the main word is given first in **bold** type. The word is also divided into syllables. The word *cognition* has three syllables: *cog-ni-tion*. You can find the spellings of various words based on this word by scrolling below the entry. This listing is especially helpful when letters are dropped or added to create a new word by adding prefixes or suffixes. The word *cognition* changes form and spelling to become *cognitional*, which has four syllables: *cog-ni-tion-al*.
Pronunciation
There are two ways to learn a word's pronunciation. First, the main entry displays a "spelled" pronunciation. Second, you can click to hear the word spoken.
Different dictionaries use different symbols in their pronunciation keys, so be sure to check the key of the dictionary you are using.

Definitions

Merriam-Webster.com provides a basic definition at the top of the entry followed by a full definition of the word below. Many words have more than one meaning. When there is more than one definition, each meaning is numbered. Many times the dictionary will also provide examples of sentences in which the word is used.

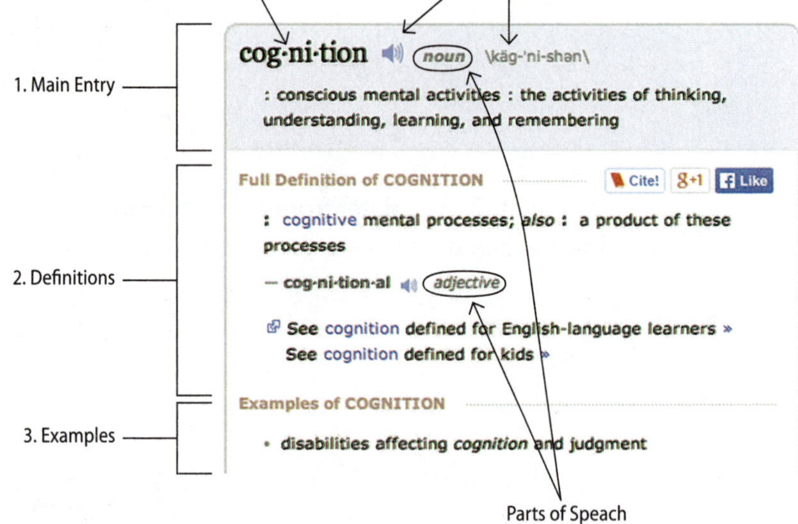

: conscious mental activities : the activities of thinking, understanding, learning, and remembering

--By permission. From *Merriam-Webster's Collegiate® Dictionary*, 11th Edition © 2014 by Merriam-Webster Inc. (www.Merriam-Webster.com).

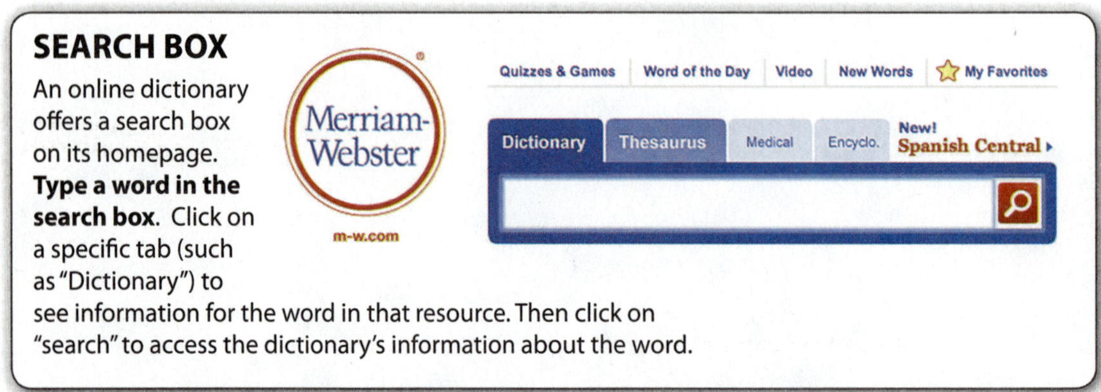

An online dictionary offers a search box on its homepage. **Type a word in the search box**. Click on a specific tab (such as "Dictionary") to see information for the word in that resource. Then click on "search" to access the dictionary's information about the word.

--By permission. From *Merriam-Webster's Collegiate® Dictionary*, 11th Edition © 2014 by Merriam-Webster Inc. (www.Merriam-Webster.com).

Parts of Speech

Parts of speech indicate how a word functions in a sentence. Dictionary entries tell you what part of speech a word is—noun, verb, adjective, and so on. The part of speech is abbreviated and printed in italics. Your dictionary provides a full list of abbreviations. At right are the most common abbreviations for the parts of speech.

adj	adjective
n	noun
adv	adverb
prep	preposition
conj	conjunction
pron	pronoun
interj	interjection
v, vi, vt	verb

[1]talk *verb* \ˈtȯk\

: to say words in order to express your thoughts, feelings, opinions, etc., to someone

: to have a conversation or discussion with someone

: to have a conversation about (something)

Full Definition of TALK

Cite! 8+1 Like

transitive verb

1 : to deliver or express in speech : UTTER

2 : to make the subject of conversation or discourse : DISCUSS <*talk* business>

3 : to influence, affect, or cause by talking <*talked* them into going>

4 : to use (a language) for conversing or communicating : SPEAK

intransitive verb

1 a : to express or exchange ideas by means of spoken words

b : to convey information or communicate in any way (as with signs or sounds) <can make a trumpet *talk*> <make the computer *talk* to the printer>

2 : to use speech : SPEAK

3 a : to speak idly : PRATE

b : GOSSIP

c : to reveal secret or confidential

4 : to give a talk : LECTURE

— talk·er *noun*

— talk back

: to answer impertinently

"Talk" verb and noun definitions

[2]talk *noun*

: an occurrence in which one person talks about something with another person : a conversation or discussion

: the act of talking formally about something before a group of people : a speech or lecture

: a formal discussion between two or more groups that are trying to reach an agreement about something

Full Definition of TALK

1 : the act or an instance of talking : SPEECH

2 : a way of speaking : LANGUAGE

3 : pointless or fruitless discussion : VERBIAGE

4 : a formal discussion, negotiation, or exchange of views — often used in plural

5 a : MENTION, REPORT

b : RUMOR, GOSSIP

6 : the topic of interested comment, conversation, or gossip <it's the *talk* of the town>

7 a : ADDRESS, LECTURE

b : written analysis or discussion presented in an informal or conversational manner

8 : communicative sounds or signs resembling or functioning as talk <bird *talk*>

Online dictionaries state the part of speech or function of a word in various ways.

First, the part of speech always appears in the [1]main entry.

Second, the part of speech is also stated for each of the various forms of a given word. In Merriam-Webster.com, the related forms of the word are shown under the [2]"Full Definition" heading. The entry for "cognition" provides one related form of the word. Notice that as the word changes in its function or part of speech, it also varies in the number of its syllables.

Third, some online dictionaries list definitions based on the parts of speech. For example, Merriam-Webster.com lists 16 different definitions of the word *talk*. The list is organized by part of speech starting with 8 definitions of its verb form and 8 definitions of its noun form.

Readers and writers may use a dictionary several times throughout the reading/writing process. An effective reader may choose to skim a passage for new or difficult words to look up before reading to better understand the writer's point during reading. At other times, a reader may choose to do an in-depth study of a word or set of words after reading as a way to review ideas and deepen understanding.

Example

Assume you are taking a college course in biology, and the chapter review has listed the key words you need to know to understand the concepts in the chapter. You have chosen the following word to study by using a dictionary. Find the word in a dictionary and complete the Vocabulary Study Card.

Vocabulary Study Card	
Word	*atom*
Spelling	*at•om*
Pronunciation	'a-təm
Part of Speech	*noun*
Definition	*1. one of the minute indivisible particles of which according to ancient materialism the universe is composed* *2. a tiny particle* *3. the smallest particle of an element that can exist either alone or in combination* *4. the atom considered as a source of vast potential energy*
Synonyms	*bit, crumb, dribble, fleck, flyspeck, grain, granule, molecule, morsel, mote, nubbin, nugget, particle, patch, scrap, scruple, snip, snippet, speck, tittle*
Etymology	*15th century, Middle English, from Latin atomos, from Greek atomos from atomos indivisible, from a- + temnein (to cut)*
Sentence	*The smallest possible particle of an element is the atom.*

Explanations

Compare your responses to the following student's think-aloud.

As I completed this vocabulary card for the word atom, I came across other words in the definition that I also need to learn such as nucleus, neutrons, protons, electrons. So I could see making up a set of vocabulary cards to learn how the words are related. I will use vocabulary cards before and after reading to learn new words in my college courses. I completed the card using the following information from Merriam-Webster.com.

Vocabulary Study Card
Word, atom
Spelling, at•om
Pronunciation, 'a-təm
Part of Speech, noun
Definition, 1. one of the minute indivisible particles of which according to ancient materialism the universe is composed
2. a tiny particle
3. the smallest particle of an element that can exist either alone or in combination
4. the atom considered as a source of vast potential energy
Synonyms: bit, crumb, dribble, fleck, flyspeck, grain, granule, molecule, morsel, mote, nubbin, nugget, particle, patch, scrap, scruple, snip, snippet, speck, tittle
Etymology: 15th century, Middle English, from Latin atomos, from Greek atomos from atomos indivisible, from a- + temnein (to cut)
Sentence: The smallest possible particle of an element is the atom.

Often, readers discover new or difficult words during reading that they then choose to look up after reading.

Practice 3

Use a Dictionary to Comprehend a Point

Assume you are taking a college course in earth science. Read the following passage from the textbook for the course. Skim and annotate the text for new or difficult words. Then either before or after reading, choose one new or difficult word you underlined and complete the Vocabulary Study Card with information from a dictionary.

IGNEOUS ROCKS: FORMED BY FIRE

[1]Igneous rocks form as magma cools and crystallizes. [2]But what is magma and what is its source? [3]Magma is molten rock generated by partial melting of rocks in Earth's mantle and in the lower crust in smaller amounts. [4]This molten material consists mainly of the elements found in silicate minerals. [5]Silicon and oxygen are the main constituents in magma, with lesser amounts of aluminum, iron, calcium, sodium, potassium, magnesium, and others. [6]Magma also contains some gases, particularly water vapor, which are confined within the magma body by the weight (pressure) of the overlying rocks. [7]Once formed, a magma body buoyantly rises to the surface because it is less dense than the surrounding rocks. [8]Occasionally molten rock reaches the surface, where it is called lava.

Lutgens, Frederick K., Tarbuck, Edward J., and Tasa, Dennis G., *Foundations of Earth Science,* 6th ed., p. 46.

Vocabulary Study Card	
Word	
Spelling	
Pronunciation	
Part of Speech	
Definition	
Synonyms	
Etymology	
Sentence	

One of the most common ways writers use a dictionary is during the proofreading phase of the writing process to check words for their correct spelling.

Example

Assume you wrote the following paragraph for a college humanities class, and a peer editor underlined words he thought might be misspelled. Use a dictionary to look up the underlined words. Edit the words to correct their spelling as needed.

Plato's Alegory of the Cave

[1]Plato was a Greek philosopher who lived from 427 BC to 347 BC. [2]He was a student of Socrates, who was a profound and controversial thinker of his time. [3]Socretes refused to desecreate his own beliefs; therefore, he was executed. [4]As a result of Socretes' death, Plato became more firmly entrencthed as one who publically taught truth as he understood it. [5]Plato recorded his teachings in his book *The Republic*. [6]In this book, Plato wrote an alegory called "The Alegory of the Cave." [7]In the alegory, Plato has Socretes tell a tale of men shackled in a cave. [8]They wore blinders and could only look at a blank wall of the cave. [9]The cave wall was illuminated by natural sun-light pouring in from the mouth of the cave, and a man-made fire behind and slightly above the chained men. [10]These two sources of light cast shadows on the wall. [11]These shadows were all that the men could see. [12]These shadows became reality for the men. [13]One man was unshackled and permitted to go into the light. [14]He then became aware that the shadows were not reality. [15]With his new conciousness of reality, the man returned to the cave. [16]Once there, he tried to teach the other chained men that the shadows were not realty. [17]The shadows were a distoration of reality. [18]His fellow prisoners mocked him. [19]They who had never seen the light did not believe him.

Explanations

Compare your responses to the following student's think-aloud.

The first thing I noticed was that 10 misspellings were underlined. However, there were only 6 words misspelled. Some of the words like "Socrates" and "allegory" were repeatedly misspelled. At first, I tried to look up the words in a print dictionary. But it was hard to find some of the words because the pages are based on guide words

CONTINUED

and all I had were misspelled words. It was much easier to use an online dictionary. For example, when I typed in the misspelled word conciousness and pressed enter, the next screen asked me if I meant consciousness. I had to click on the suggested word to see if the definition explained the way the word was used in the paragraph. Here are the correct spellings of the underlined words.

Socrates, desecrate, entrenched, allegory, consciousness, distortion

Practice 4

Use a Dictionary to Make a Point

Assume you are applying for a job as a manager at a local retail store. You asked a friend to proofread your letter of application. She underlined the words she thinks are misspelled. Use a dictionary to look up and correct the spelling of the words she underlined.

Dear Ms. Riley:
Store Manager Position at New Look

After reading the advertizment for the position of store manager at Macmo Store, I am submitting my application for this position. I am well suited to make a significant contribution to the company in this capacity. As you review my resume, you will see that my experience has allowed me to develop a strong set of skills. My collegues see me as a strong team member and leader. I have the following qualifications to offer:

- Experience as an inovative problem solver
- Hard worker who ably identifies problems and solutions
- Experiance in sales and customer service

During my role as an assistant manager for 5 years, I developed skill in recruiting, training, and managing a store team.
I am excited about the prospect of joining the Macmo team. I can be reached at 999-999-9999.

Yours sincerly,

Use Vocabulary Resources in Textbooks to Comprehend and Make a Point 

Writers and publishers offer a wide range of vocabulary resources in textbooks to support learning and deepen understanding. Effective readers and writers use vocabulary resources in textbooks as part of their reading/writing strategy. Before, during, and after reading, you may identify and define key terms you need to know and use as a reader and writer of content in this subject area. Before writing, you may use content words to brainstorm ideas to draft into a response to what you have read. After composing your first draft, you may revise and proofread your writing for clear and accurate use of the new or key words you have learned.

Be Aware of Content (Subject Area) Words

Many students think they should be able to pick up a textbook and simply read it. However, a textbook is written for a content or subject area, such as math, history, or English. Each content area has its own vocabulary. For example, a history textbook takes a different approach from that of a literature textbook. Different courses may use the same words, but the words often take on a new or different meaning in the context of the content area.

Examples

The following sentences all use the word *parallel*. Circle the letter of the course that would use the word in the context in which it appears.

1. The brain appears to be a parallel processor, in which many different groups of neuron circuits work on different tasks at the same time.

a. mathematics **c.** history
b. English **(d.)** psychology

2. Some writers use parallel structure of words and phrases for a balanced and smooth flow of ideas.

a. mathematics **c.** history
(b.) English **d.** psychology

3. Parallel lines never intersect.

(a.) mathematics **c.** history
b. English **d.** psychology

CONTINUED

Explanations

Compare your responses to the following student's think-aloud.

Context clues helped me figure out the correct definitions for each word. In item 1, the context of the sentence states that the word parallel *is used to describe the brain. A class that would study the brain is (d) psychology. In item 2, the word* parallel *is used to describe writing, so the course of study is (b) English. In item 3, the word* parallel *describes lines, so the word is used in a (a) mathematics course. I have a new appreciation for the ways a word can be used in so many different ways to talk about a wide range of topics. A basic idea takes on new meaning.*

Look for Textbook Definitions

You do not always need to use the dictionary to find the meaning of a word. In fact, many textbooks contain words or word groups that you cannot find in a dictionary. The content word is usually typed in **bold** or *italic* print. The definition follows, and many times an example is given. Context clues are helpful. As you read, annotate key terms, definitions, and examples.

Examples

Read the following passage from a psychology textbook. Annotate the text. Then answer the questions that follow. *Student annotations may vary.*

[1]**Disconfirmation** is a communication pattern in which you ignore a person's presence as well as that person's communications. [2]You say, in effect, that the person and what she or he has to say aren't worth serious attention. [3]Disconfirming responses often lead to loss of self-esteem. [4]Note that disconfirmation is not the same as rejection. [5]In **rejection**, you disagree with the person; you indicate your unwillingness to accept something the other person says or does. [6]In disconfirming someone, however, you deny that person's significance; you claim that what this person says or does simply does not count.

DeVito, Joseph A., *Interpersonal Communication Book*, p. 171.

1. A communication pattern in which you ignore a person's presence as well as that person's communications is *disconfirmation*.

2. An unwillingness to accept something the other person says or does is *rejection*.

Explanations

Compare your response to the following student's think-aloud.

This example showed me a way to take notes and learn special words in a textbook. First, I double underlined all the words in bold print. The bold print indicates that these words are key vocabulary terms. Next, I single underlined the definitions for each word in bold print. Item 1 defines the term disconfirmation. *Item 2 defines the term* rejection. *I also used an antonym and word parts to help me remember the term* disconfirmation. *The root word is* confirm, *which is an antonym of* rejection. *And the prefix* dis *makes me think of "not" like in* dislike. *So this is a way of saying "not confirming." It was helpful to have the difference between* rejection *and* disconfirmation *pointed out, too. Disconfirmation is worse than rejection. To be rejected, you at least have to be noticed. With disconfirmation, it's like you don't even exist.*

Practice 5

Use Vocabulary Resources in Textbooks to Comprehend a Point

Read each of the following textbook passages. Then write the definition for each of the words in **bold** print.

1. To say that $x + 4 <$ (is less than) 10 and $x <$ (is less than) 6 are **equivalent** is to say that they have the same solution set. For example, the number 3 is a solution to $x + 4 < 10$. It is also a solution for $x < 6$. The number -2 is a solution of $x < 6$. It is also a solution of $x + 4 < 10$. Any solution of one is a solution of the other; they are equivalent.

Bittinger, Marvin L., and Beecher, Judith A., *Introductory and Intermediate Algebra: Combined Approach*, p. 143.

Equivalent means having the same solution set.

2. To borrow the useful terms of the English novelist E. M. Forster, characters may seem **flat** or round. A **flat** character has only one outstanding trait or feature: for example, the stock character of the mad scientist, with his lust for absolute power and his crazily gleaming eyes.

Adapted from Kennedy, X. J., and Gioia, Dana, *Literature*, 8th ed., p. 78.

Flat means having only one outstanding trait or feature.

3. **Codependence** refers to a self-defeating relationship pattern in which a person is "addicted to the addict."

Donatelle, Rebecca J., *Access to Health*, 7th ed., p. 321.

Codependence means a self-defeating relationship pattern in which a person is "addicted to the addict."

Use a Glossary

Since each subject or content area has its own specific vocabulary, some textbooks provide an extra section in the back of the book called a **glossary** that alphabetically lists all the specialized terms with their definitions as they were used throughout the textbook. Other textbooks may provide short glossaries within each chapter; in these cases, the glossaries may appear in the margins or in highlighted boxes where the words first appear, or they may appear at the end of each chapter. The meanings given in a glossary are limited to the way in which the word or term is used in that content area.

A **glossary** is a list of selected terms with their definitions as used in a specific area of study.

Glossaries provide excellent opportunities for use in a reading/writing strategy. Before reading, skim the section for specialized terms (usually these words are in **bold** or *italic* print). Call up prior knowledge, what you already know about the terms. During reading, annotate the glossary words where they appear in the text. After reading, write vocabulary review lists using glossary terms by paraphrasing or restating the definitions in your own words. Before writing, use words from the glossary to brainstorm ideas for a draft. During revision and proofreading, check your usage and spelling against the glossary.

Example

The following selection is from a college psychology textbook. Before reading, use the glossary to survey the text and call up your prior knowledge. Use the rating scale below to evaluate your prior knowledge of the words in the glossary. Then read the passage. During reading, annotate the terms where they appear in the text. After reading, answer the questions and respond in writing.

Vocabulary Knowledge Rating Scale				
Word	**1** I don't know the word.	**2** I know a little. I have heard the word before.	**3** I know a fair amount. I know what it means, but am not sure how to use it.	**4** I know a lot. I can explain it to others and use it in writing.
algorithm				
heuristic				
representation				
strategy				

ALGORITHMS AND HEURISTICS: GETTING FROM HERE TO THERE

[1]To solve a problem you need a **strategy**, an approach to solving a problem determined by the type of **representation** used and the processing steps to be tried. [2]There are two types of strategies: algorithms and heuristics. [3]Let's say you heard about a fantastic price being offered on a hit alternative music CD by an independent record store, but you don't know the name of the store. [4]You could try to find it by calling every relevant listing in the yellow pages. [5]This process involves using an **algorithm**, a set of steps that if followed methodically will guarantee the right answer. [6]But you may not have time to call every store. [7]Instead, you might guess that the record store is in a part of town where many students live. [8]In this case, having reduced the list of candidates to those located near the campus, you might find the store after calling only a few. [9]This process reflects use of a **heuristic**, a rule of thumb that does not guarantee the correct answer but offers a likely shortcut to it. [10]One common heuristic is to divide a big problem into parts and solve them one at a time.

Glossary

algorithm a set of steps that, if followed methodically, will guarantee the solution to a problem.

heuristic a rule of thumb that does not guarantee the correct answer to a problem but offers a likely shortcut to it.

representation a way of looking at a problem.

strategy an approach to solving a problem, determined by the type of representation used and the processing steps to be tried.

Adapted from Kosslyn, Stephen M., *Psychology: The Brain, the Person, the World*, p. 206.

CONTINUED

EXAMPLE *CONTINUED*

Complete the Vocabulary Review List with information from the passage. Restate ideas in your own words. *Student responses may vary.*

Vocabulary Review List		
Word	**Definition**	**Example**
algorithm	a set of steps that, if followed methodically, will guarantee the solution to a problem	*Call every single listing in the yellow pages to find a specific item.*
heuristic	a rule of thumb that does not guarantee the correct answer to a problem but offers a likely shortcut to it	*Predict the area where it makes sense to sell the product and call stores in that area only.*
representation	a way of looking at a problem	*none given*
strategy	an approach to solving a problem, determined by the type of representation used and the processing steps to be tried	*algorithms and heuristics*

Write

Use key words from the passage to describe the way you solve a problem. Give examples, such as which strategy you used to enroll in this class or to buy a cell phone, car, appliance, etc.

I used the algorithm strategy to buy my big-screen, high-definition television. First, I went to Consumer Reports online and researched all the models so I had an idea about what was out there. I even did some comparison shopping online. But I still had to go to every store in the county. I even drove to the biggest city in the next county. Finally, I happened onto a great sale, and I was able to get exactly what I wanted for a really low price.

Explanation

Compare your response to the following student's think-aloud.

Before reading, I gave the following ratings: algorithm 1, heuristic 1, representation 3, strategy 4.

During reading, I double underlined each bold word, and I underlined each of their definitions. I noticed that the word representation didn't have a definition. It was part of the definition of strategy. I think representation is a synonym for type.

After reading, I filled in the Vocabulary Review List with the following examples. Algorithm example is calling every single listing in the yellow pages to find a specific item. Heuristic example is predicting where it makes sense to sell a product and then call stores in only that area. There weren't any examples given for representation. But I think algorithms and heuristics are the two examples of representations (types). Strategy examples are algorithms or heuristics.

Write: I used the algorithm strategy to buy my big-screen, high-definition television. First, I went to Consumer Reports online and researched all the models so I had an idea about what was out there. I even did some comparison shopping online. But I still had to go to every store in the county. I even drove to the biggest city in the next county. Finally, I happened onto a great sale, and I was able to get exactly what I wanted for a really low price.

Practice 6

Use Vocabulary Resources in Textbooks to Make a Point

The following selection is from a college anatomy and physiology textbook. Before reading, use the glossary to survey the text and call up your prior knowledge. Use the rating scale below to evaluate your prior knowledge of the words in the glossary. Then read the passage. During reading, annotate the terms where they appear in the text. After reading, answer the questions and respond in writing. *Student responses may vary.*

Vocabulary Knowledge Rating Scale

Word	1 I don't know the word.	2 I know a little. I have heard the word before.	3 I know a fair amount. I know what it means, but am not sure how to use it.	4 I know a lot. I can explain it to others and use it in writing.
energy				
chemical energy				
electrical energy				
kinetic energy				
mechanical energy				
potential energy				
radiant energy				

ENERGY

[1]In contrast to matter, energy is massless and does not take up space. [2]It can be measured only by its effects on matter. [3]Energy is commonly defined as the ability to do work or to put matter into motion. [4]When energy is actually doing work (moving objects), it is referred to as kinetic (kĭ-neh'tik) energy. [5]Kinetic energy is displayed in the constant movement of the tiniest particles of matter (atoms) as well as in larger objects, such as a bouncing ball. [6]When energy is inactive or stored (as in the batteries of an unused toy), it is called potential energy. [7]All forms of energy exhibit both kinetic and potential work capacities.

[8]Actually, energy is a physics topic, but it is difficult to separate matter and energy. [9]All living things are built of matter, and to grow and function they require a continuous supply of energy. [10]Thus, matter is the substance, and energy is the mover of the substance. [11]Because this is so, it is worth taking a brief detour to introduce the forms of energy the body uses as it does its work.

Forms of Energy

- [12]**Chemical energy** is stored in the bonds of chemical substances. [13]When the bonds are broken, the (potential) stored energy is unleashed and becomes kinetic energy (energy in action). [14]For example, when gasoline molecules are broken apart in your automobile engine, the energy released powers your car. [15]In like manner, all body activities are "run" by the chemical energy harvested from the foods we eat.
- [16]**Electrical energy** results from the movement of charged particles. [17]In your house, electrical energy is the flow of electrons along the wiring. [18]In your body, an electrical current is generated when charged particles (called ions) move across cell membranes. [19]The nervous system uses electrical currents called nerve impulses to transmit messages from one part of the body to another.
- [20]**Mechanical energy** is energy directly involved in moving matter. [21]When you ride a bicycle, your legs provide the mechanical energy that moves the pedals. [22]We can take this example one step further back: As the muscles in your legs shorten, they pull on your bones, causing your limbs to move (so that you can pedal the bike).
- [23]**Radiant energy** travels in waves; that is, it is the energy of the electromagnetic spectrum, which includes X rays, infrared radiation (heat energy), visible light, radio, and ultraviolet waves. [24]Light energy, which stimulates the retinas of your eyes, is important in vision. [25]Ultraviolet waves cause sunburn, but they also stimulate our bodies to make vitamin D.

Marieb, Elaine N., *Essentials of Human Anatomy and Physiology,* 9th ed., pp. 27–28.

Glossary

energy: the ability to do work

chemical energy: energy form stored in chemical bonds that hold atoms together

electrical energy: energy form resulting from the movement of charged particles

kinetic energy: energy of motion

mechanical energy: energy form directly involved with putting matter into motion

potential energy: stored energy

radiant energy: energy of the electromagnetic spectrum, which includes heat, light, ultraviolet waves, infrared waves, and other forms

PRACTICE 6 *CONTINUED*

Complete the Vocabulary Review List with information from the passage.

Vocabulary Review List		
Word	**Definition**	**Example**
energy	*the ability to do work*	*chemical, electrical, kinetic, mechanical, potential, radiant*
chemical energy	*energy form stored in chemical bonds that hold atoms together*	*gasoline molecules are broken apart in your automobile engine*
electrical energy	*energy form resulting from the movement of charged particles*	*the flow of electrons along wiring; the nervous system*
kinetic energy	*energy of motion*	*a bouncing ball*
mechanical energy	*energy form directly involved with putting matter into motion*	*legs provide the mechanical energy that moves the pedals; muscles pull the leg bones*
potential energy	*stored energy*	*the batteries of an unused toy*
radiant energy	*energy of the electromagnetic spectrum, which includes heat, light, ultraviolet waves, infrared waves, and other forms*	*ultraviolet waves cause sunburn*

Write

Identify and describe the different types of energy at work in the human body.

Five types of energy are at work in the human body. Chemical energy is harvested from the foods we eat and fuels our body. The nervous system uses electrical currents called nerve impulses to transmit messages from one part of the body to another. The muscles in your legs use mechanical energy as they shorten; they pull on your bones, causing your limbs to move and result in kinetic energy such as pedaling a bike. When the body is at rest, it has potential energy. Radiant energy, light energy, stimulates the retinas of your eyes and is key to vision. Ultraviolet waves cause sunburn, but they also stimulate our bodies to make vitamin D.

Reading and Writing Assignments

MySkillsLab™ Complete these assignments in MySkillsLab.

Considering Audience and Purpose

Study the sequence of photographs about vocabulary at the beginning of this module. Assume you are a classmate of the student in the first photograph. You and she have agreed to form a study group for your biology class. She has asked for advice from you about how to study. Write a note to her suggesting a reading/writing strategy to learn the vocabulary in the biology textbook.

Reading and Writing for Everyday Life

Assume you are buying a car from an individual rather than a car lot. The owner has presented you with a bill of sale. The following is an excerpt from the document.

- **Before Reading/Writing:** Skim the passage and underline at last three key terms that you need to know. Use an online dictionary to look up the meaning of these words.
- **During Reading:** Highlight details related to the key terms you identified before reading.
- **After Reading, Write:** In the space following the passage, use your own words to state the meaning of the key words you identified before reading. Write a response to the question: What is the most important idea to remember?

J. Smith
3 Home Lane
Lake View
Texas

Vehicle Bill of Sale

[1]I, J. Smith of 3 Home Lane, Lake View, Texas, hereby certify that I am the lawful owner of this vehicle and have the authority to sell it. [2]I hereby acknowledge the receipt of $3,000 in the form of cash, from Lola Reed, as full payment for the purchase of said vehicle, which is sold "AS IS." [3]I do hereby grant, sell and transfer full ownership of this vehicle to the buyer. [4]I certify that this vehicle, at the time of sale, is free from all encumbrances, taxes, fees and liens except as those specified on the Title or listed below; and that I (Seller) will defend and be held fully responsible for such lawful claims and demands with respect to the vehicle, if any.

Key Terms and Definitions:

Selection of words and statements of definitions may vary.

What is the most important idea to remember?

Answers may vary.

Reading and Writing for College Life

Assume you are taking a college biology course. Your textbook provides three vocabulary resources. (1) Key terms are highlighted in bold print and defined in the text. (2) Each chapter summary lists key vocabulary and identifies the page number where the term appears in text. (3) The last section of the textbook is a glossary of all key terms highlighted in bold in text.

- **Before Reading/Writing:** (1) Skim the passage. Note the "Chapter Summary: Key Terms." (2) Identify three key terms to learn. (3) List the three terms in the vocabulary review list to be completed during and after reading.
- **During Reading:** Annotate information in the text that you can use to complete the vocabulary review list.
- **After Reading, Write:** Complete the vocabulary review list with details from the passage and a dictionary. Write a response to the question: What is the most important idea to remember?

Chapter Summary: Key Terms

aerobic *(71)*
cytoplasmic fluid *(60)*
metabolically *(105)*
molecule *(2, 3)*
anaerobic *(71)*
enzymes *(104)*
metabolism *(105)*
ATP *(103)*
eukaryotic *(62)*
mitochondrion *(71)*

Mitochondria Use Energy Stored in Food Molecules to Produce ATP

[1]All eukaryotic cells contain **mitochondria** (singular, *mitochondrion*), which are sometimes called the "powerhouses of the cell." [2]These powerhouses extract energy from food molecules and store it in the high-energy bonds of ATP. [3]Different amounts of energy can be released from a food molecule, depending on how it is broken down. [4]The breakdown of food molecules begins with enzymes in the cytoplasmic fluid. [5]This process does not use oxygen. [6]This **anaerobic** ("without oxygen") breakdown does not convert much food energy into ATP energy. [7]Mitochondria enable a eukaryotic cell to use oxygen to break down high-energy molecules even further. [8]These **aerobic** ("with oxygen") reactions generate energy much more effectively. [9]About 16 times as much ATP is generated by aerobic metabolism in the mitochondria than by anaerobic metabolism in the cytoplasmic fluid. [10]Not surprisingly, mitochondria are found in large numbers in metabolically active cells, such as muscle. [11]And they are less abundant in cells that are less active, such as those of cartilage.

Adapted from Audesirk, Gerald, Audesirk, Teresa, and Byers, Bruce E., *Biology: Life on Earth,* 9th ed., p. 71.

After Reading

Complete the following chart with three key terms identified before reading. List the resources you used to complete the chart. *Responses may vary.*

Term	Part of Speech	Definition	Use in Sentence
aerobic	*adj*	*an organism or process dependent on oxygen*	*Aerobic reactions generate more energy.*
anaerobic	*adj*	*in the absence of air or oxygen*	*The anaerobic breakdown of food does not produce much energy.*
mitochondria	*noun*	*small organs in cells that help energy production*	*Mitochondria extract energy from food molecules.*

What is the most important idea to remember?

Answers may vary.

Reading and Writing for Working Life

Assume you have decided to start your own small business. You want to deduct business expenses from your income tax. Read the following section from an online document provided by the Internal Revenue Service.

- **Before Reading/Writing:** Skim the text and underline the key terms you need to know. Use an online dictionary to look up the meanings of these words.
- **During Reading:** Highlight details related to the key terms you identified before reading.
- **After Reading, Write:** In the space following the passage, use your own words to state the meaning of the key words you identified before reading. Write a response to the question: What is the most important idea to remember?

COST RECOVERY

[1]You can elect to deduct or amortize certain business start-up costs. [2]Although you generally cannot take a current deduction for a capital expense, you may be able to recover the amount you spend through depreciation, amortization, or depletion. [3]These recovery methods allow you to deduct part of your cost each year. [4]In this way, you are able to recover your capital expense.

Internal Revenue Service. "What Can I Deduct?" *Publication 535 (2010), Business Expenses*. Department of Treasury. <http://www.irs.gov/publications/p535/index.html>.

Key Terms and Definitions:

Selection of words and statements of definitions may vary.

What is the most important idea to remember?

Answers may vary.

Workshop: Write to Learn

Review and respond to the ideas you have learned in this module. Compose a paragraph that explains what you have learned about vocabulary based on your study of this module. Use the following steps to guide you as you draft your paragraph.

Prewrite a Draft of Your Paragraph

Use the questions in the blank outline below as a model to generate and organize your answers to the following questions. Turn the questions into statements and give supporting reasons and examples. Add items if needed.

I. What was my process for learning new or difficult words before studying this module?
   A.
   B.

II. What are the vocabulary strategies and resources available for readers and writers to learn and use new words?
   A.
   B.

III. How will my process for learning new or difficult words change now that I know about vocabulary strategies and resources?
   A.
   B.

Write a Draft of Your Paragraph

Using the ideas you generated during the prewriting phase, compose a draft of your paragraph. Return to the prewriting process at any time to generate additional details as needed. Use your own paper.

Revise Your Draft

Read your draft and respond to the questions in the following box. If you answer "yes" to a question, underline, check, or circle examples. If you answer "no" to a question, write additional details in the margins and draw lines to indicate their placement. Revise your paragraph based on your reflection.

Step by Step: Questions for Revising a Paragraph

- [ ] Have I stated or implied a focused main idea?
- [ ] Is the logical order of the ideas clear? Have I clearly guided my reader through the paragraph with words such as first, second, next, etc.?
- [ ] Have I made my point with adequate details?
- [ ] Do all the details support my point?
- [ ] What impact will my paragraph make on my reader?

Proofread Your Draft

Once you have made any revisions to your paragraph that may be needed, proofread your paragraph to eliminate careless errors. Work with a classmate to give and receive feedback about your paragraphs.

Review Test

MySkillsLab™
Complete this Review Test in MySkillsLab.

Score (number correct) ______ x 20 = ______%

The following selection is from a college film studies textbook. Before reading, survey the text and call up your prior knowledge. Then read and annotate the passage. After reading, answer the questions and respond in writing to the prompt "What Do You Think?"

1280L/12.1 GE/665 words

SPECIAL EFFECTS

[1]If William Shakespeare were alive today, he would be **enthralled** by the ability of computer-generated imagery (CGI) to create fantastic, brave new worlds, where the magical is commonplace. [2]This digital technology, perfected in the 1990s, revolutionized special effects. [3]Although it's very expensive, costing hundreds of thousands of dollars for only a few minutes of screen time, eventually CGI will save film producers millions.

[4]In the past, whole scenes often had to be reshot because of technical glitches. [5]For example, if a modern building or auto appeared in a period film, the scene had to be recut or even rephotographed. [6]Today, such details can be removed digitally. [7]So can a microphone that accidentally dips into the frame. [8]Even sweat on an actor's face can be **effaced** by an F/X technician.

[9]Computer-generated images can be stored for future use, when they can be digitally altered with new costumes, new backgrounds or foregrounds, or with a totally different atmosphere, as in the magical landscapes in *The Lord of the Rings* trilogy. [10]In fact, physical sets don't even have to be constructed in some instances, since images containing the sets can be created on a computer.

[11]Even realistic movies can benefit from this technology. [12]In *Forrest Gump*, a handful of extras were digitally expanded into a cast of thousands. [13]In the ultrarealistic Holocaust drama, *The Pianist*, the events take place during the World War II era, yet director Roman Polanski used CGI for several scenes—the bombed-out ruins of a city street, a character falling from a tall building, aircraft streaking across the skies.

[14]Traditional animation, with its time-consuming, hand-drawn cell images, is being replaced by computers, which produce images that are created digitally, not *a mano*. [15]CGI has produced a new "look" in animation, less detailed, more sculptural, more plastique—like the streamlined images of *Shrek*, *The Polar Express*, and *The Incredibles*.

[16]Acting has also been affected by this technology, though not usually in a positive way. [17]In *Star Wars,* for example, actors often performed in front of F/X bluescreens rather than with other actors, who were later digitally added to the shot by computer technicians. [18]Some critics have complained that such acting is often cold and mechanical, with none of the human subtleties that can be found in scenes where performers are actually interacting.

[19]Digital editing is also much easier than traditional methods. [20]Instead of handling a physical filmstrip and making actual cuts, modern editors need only to press a button to cut from one shot to another.

[21]In addition, CGI technology will eventually make film distribution and exhibition cheaper. [22]Today, film prints can cost up to $2,000 apiece. [23]A mainstream

American movie can be shown simultaneously on 2,000 screens, costing $4 million just for the cost of prints. [24]In the future, movies will be stored on digital disks, like a DVD, and will cost only a few dollars to manufacture. [25]Distributors will also save on shipping fees. Instead of the heavy reels of traditional movies, costing thousands of dollars to ship by bus, plane, or rail, in the future, a lightweight disk will be sent to movie theaters for only a few dollars. [26]Projection equipment will basically consist of a commercial DVD machine, not the **cumbersome**, expensive, mechanical projectors that have dominated film exhibition for over 100 years.

[27]The biggest danger of this technology, of course, is that it will fall into the hands of moneygrubbing hacks with the artistic sensibilities of gnats. [28]It's already happened. [29]The world's screens are dominated by soulless movies full of sound and fury, signifying nothing: pointless chases, explosions, **gratuitous** violence, explosions, lots of speed, explosions, and just for good measure, more explosions. [30]The story is usually predictable, the acting bereft of nuance, the sentiments banal. [31]But the special effects are **impeccable**. [32]In short, film artists interested in F/X materials need to be just as talented as artists in any other style or genre or technology. [33]It's what they do with the technology artistically that counts, not the technology per se.

Giannetti, Louis D., *Understanding Movies*, 12th ed., pp. 33–34.

1. The best meaning of **enthralled** in sentence 1 is

a. puzzled. **c.** frustrated.
b. upset. **(d.)** fascinated.

2. The best meaning of **effaced** in sentence 8 is

(a.) erased. **c.** monitored.
b. produced. **d.** increased.

3. The best meaning of **cumbersome** in sentence 26 is

a. easy to operate. **c.** modern.
(b.) hard to handle. **d.** noisy.

4. The best meaning of **gratuitous** in sentence 29 is

a. frightening. **(c.)** unnecessary.
b. exciting. **d.** extraordinary.

5. The best meaning of **impeccable** in sentence 31 is

a. ordinary. **(c.)** perfect.
b. visual. **d.** interesting.

What Do You Think?

Assume you write a film column for your college newspaper. Write a column agreeing or disagreeing with the author's point of view. State your opinion and explain why you think the way you do. Cite examples.

Academic Learning Log: Module Review

Summary of Key Concepts of Learning and Using New Words

Assess your comprehension of learning and using new words.

LO1 **1.** Vocabulary is *all the words used or understood by a person*.

LO1 **2.** SAGE stands for the four context clues: *synonym, antonym, general context, example*.

LO2 **3.** A synonym is *a word that has the same or nearly the same meaning as another word*.

LO2 **4.** Signal words for synonyms include *or*, *that,*, and *is*.

LO2 **5.** An antonym is a *word that has the opposite meaning of another word*.

LO2 **6.** Two examples of signal words for antonyms are *but* and *unlike*.

LO2 **7.** General context is *the information (words and sentences) that surround a word and influence its meaning*.

LO2 **8.** A reader *infers* the meaning of a word based on the general context of a passage.

LO2 **9.** A writer *implies* the meaning of a word using the general context of a passage.

LO2 **10.** The general context clue requires that you read *the entire sentence, or read ahead a few sentences to infer the meaning of a new or unfamiliar word*.

LO2 **11.** Many times a writer will show the meaning of a word by providing one or more

examples.

LO2 **12.** Example clues are often introduced with the signal words *consisting of*,

for example, *for instance*, *including*,

like, and *such as*.

LO3 **13.** *Colons* and *dashes* can also signal examples.

LO3 **14.** There are two basic types of dictionaries: the *print* dictionary and the *online* dictionary and both provide information about spelling, pronunciation, part of speech, definitions, synonyms, and etymology.

LO3 **15.** *Pronunciation* is how to say a word.

LO3 **16.** *Part of speech* is the function of a word.

LO3 **17.** *Etymology* gives the history or origin of a word.

LO4 **18.** Print dictionaries offer *guide words* at the top of each page to indicate the words that appear on the specific page based on their *alphabetical* order.

LO4 **19.** Each *content* or subject area, such as mathematics, history, and biology, has its own vocabulary.

LO4 **20.** A *glossary* is a list of selected terms with their definitions as used in a specific area of study.

Test Your Comprehension of Developing a Reading/Writing Strategy

Respond to the following questions and prompts. *Answers may vary.*

In your own words, what is vocabulary? Identify the most helpful skill you have learned.

Vocabulary is all the words used to share information. Each language has its own set of words, and each subject has its own set of words.

Demonstrate your use of context clues. Complete the chart based on the four types of context clues with three new words you have come across recently as you read and write for this class, another class, or any reading/writing situation.

New Word	
Context Clue	
Meaning of Word	
Source Sentence of Word	
New Word	
Context Clue	
Meaning of Word	
Source Sentence of Word	
New Word	
Context Clue	
Meaning of Word	
Source Sentence of Word	

Demonstrate your use of the dictionary. Use a dictionary to complete the chart with four new words you have come across recently as you read for this class, another class, or any reading situation.

Word	Etymology	Part of Speech	Definition	Sentence with Word

L1 L2 L3 L4

1. **How will I use what I have learned?** In your notebook, discuss how you will apply learning and using new words to your reading/writing strategy. When will you apply this knowledge to your reading/writing strategy?
2. **What do I still need to study about learning and using new words?** In your notebook, discuss your ongoing study needs. Describe what, when, and how you will continue learning and using new words.

Complete the Post-test for Module 3 in MySkillsLab.

4

LEARNING OUTCOMES

After studying this module you should be able to

- LO 1 Answer the question "What's the Point of Word Choice, Tone, and Purpose?"
- LO 2 Connect Topic, Audience, Word Choice, Tone, and Purpose
- LO 3 Use Tone to Comprehend and Make a Point
- LO 4 Use Subjective and Objective Words to Comprehend and Make a Point
- LO 5 Use Formal and Informal Words to Comprehend and Make a Point
- LO 6 Determine the General Purpose to Comprehend and Make a Point
- LO 7 Determine the Primary Purpose to Comprehend and Make a Point

Word Choice, Tone, and Purpose

Every piece of text is created by a writer who has a specific attitude or opinion about the chosen topic and a specific reason for sharing the information with a particular audience. Consider the following two thesis statements about the topic *distracted driving*. As you read these sentences, predict each writer's attitude and reason for writing and the intended audience for the message.

> Three types of distracted driving activities include visual, physical, and mental.
>
> I will never forget the nightmarish moment when my entire world shattered—the moment the police told me my son died due to distracted driving.

The contrast between these two sentences is vivid. The first lacks emotion. The writer's reason for writing seems to be simply to inform the public about the nature of distracted driving. However, the second sentence is heart wrenching. Perhaps this writer's reason for sharing is to convince the public to avoid the terrible tragedy caused by distracted driving. These sentences illustrate that writers carefully choose their words to make a specific point. Thus, readers thoughtfully consider the words a writer chooses to comprehend his or her point.

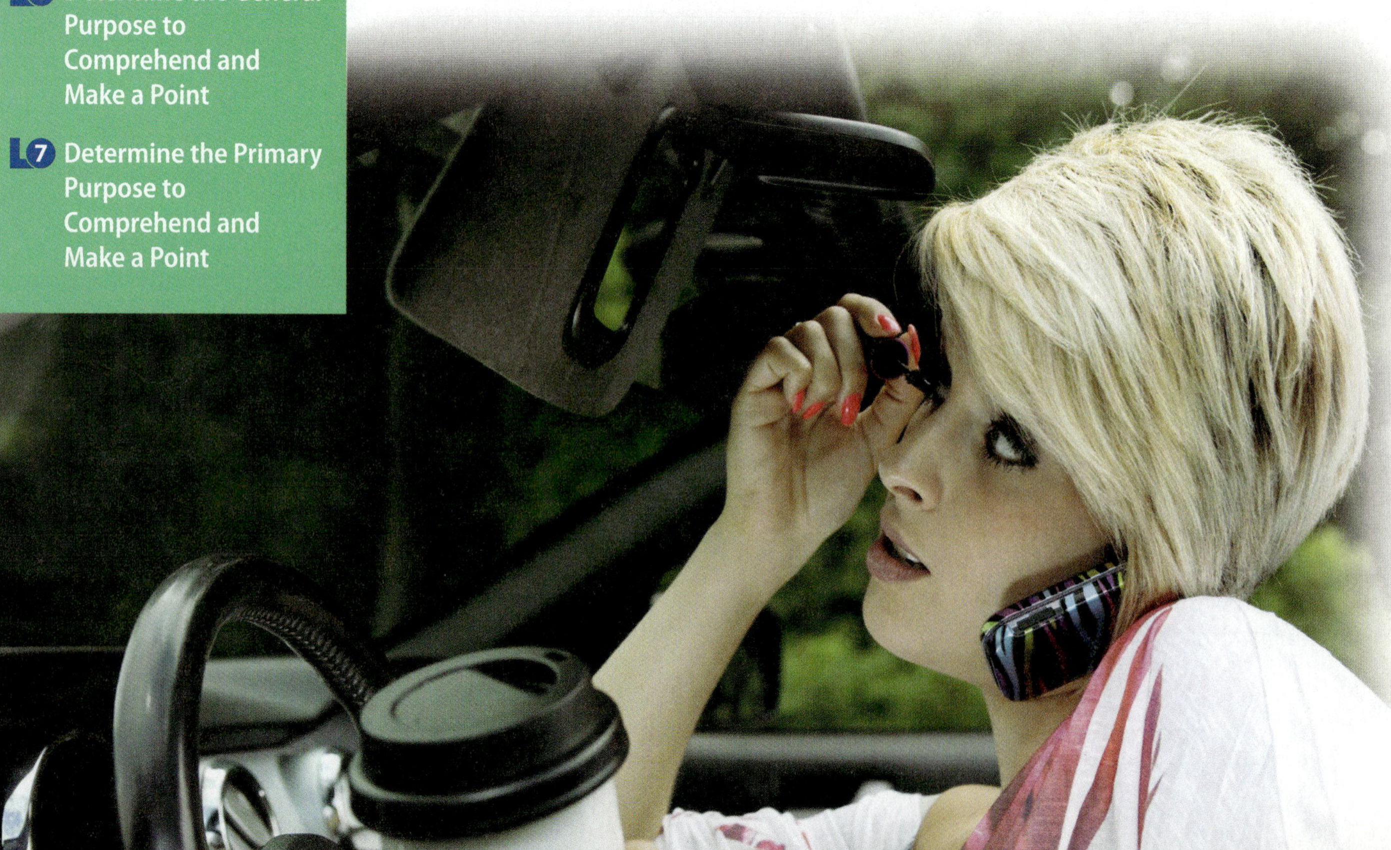

WHAT'S THE POINT of Word Choice, Tone, and Purpose? LO1

Word choice, tone, and purpose work together as we communicate with each other. Think about when you are really angry and you want to express how you feel. Which words pop into your mind first? Would you say those words to anyone at any time, or would you choose different words depending on who is with you and where you are? Tone is the emotion or attitude we express. Purpose is our reason for communicating. The words we choose help us communicate emotion or tone and purpose.

Photographic Organizer: Word Choice, Tone, and Purpose

Before you study this module, predict the relationship between purpose and tone. Consider the following images and captions. Each person represents a role or job. Next to each photograph, predict the following based on each person's role: the purpose for communicating and the emotion or tone likely used to communicate. Finally, answer the question "What's the point of word choice, tone, and purpose?"

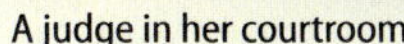

A judge in her courtroom

Purpose (reason to communicate): *to hand down a verdict or sentence*

Tone (emotion): *non-emotional, objective, factual*

A sales team waiting to make a sales presentation

Purpose (reason to communicate): *to convince someone to buy their product*

Tone (emotion): *excited, persuasive*

A professor in his classroom

Purpose (reason to communicate): *to teach a lesson, explain an idea*

Tone (emotion): *patient, enthusiastic, scholarly*

What's the point of word choice, tone, and purpose?

Your purpose for communicating affects your tone and the kinds of words you use.

What's the Point? One Student's Response

The following paragraph is one student's response to the question "What's the point of word choice, tone, and purpose?"

The words we choose are directly related to what we want to communicate. If we want to be critical of someone we choose completely different words than if we want to encourage or praise someone. Also, we choose words based on to whom we are talking. For example, I use a respectful tone and larger words when I talk to my teachers.

L2 Connect Topic, Audience, Word Choice, Tone, and Purpose

Words are power tools with which readers and writers create meaning. Words are what we say, but words are also how we say it. Take a moment to reflect: Compare what you talk about and how you speak to your friends to what you say and how you say it to a teacher, coach, or employer. If you are like most people, you choose your words based on to whom you are speaking––your audience. Think about the different impacts of the following three words: *crib*, *house*, *home*. All three words have the same basic meaning—a dwelling, a building in which people live. However, each word reveals a different attitude toward "a dwelling." Why use the word *crib* instead of *house* or *home*? Who is the most likely audience for the word *crib*—friend or employer? The words you choose, your **word choice**, reveal your attitude and purpose for communicating, whether in conversation or in writing. Thus, when we study how others use words to reveal **tone** and purpose, we deepen our understanding of what they are saying.

Word choice is the writer's selection of words based on meaning.

Tone is a manner of expression that communicates emotion or lack of emotion.

It is important to keep in mind that reading and writing is an exchange of information, a written conversation between the writer and the reader. The writer sends a message; the reader receives the message. An effective writer carefully chooses words to imply or suggest a point or to support a point. An effective reader thoughtfully analyzes the writer's word choice to infer the appropriate meaning suggested by the writer. In this communication cycle, the writer thinks about the effect of word choice on the reader, and the reader seeks to comprehend the writer's point based on the meaning suggested by the writer's chosen words. The following graphic illustrates this exchange of information.

Inferring and Implying Meaning as Readers and Writers

Writer Chooses Words to Imply Ideas

Writer Sends Message

Reader Analyzes Words to Infer Ideas

Reader Receives Message

To imply a point, a writer chooses words that set a tone to suggest a strong attitude or emotion. To comprehend the writer's point, a reader analyzes the tone of words chosen by the writer. This exchange relies on the reader's and the writer's prior knowledge of the literal definition and emotional meaning of words. Consider the following sentence.

Message Implied by Writer's Word Choice

Dictionary definition: Extremely angry **Tone:** Violently angry
Implication: Dangerous situation

The driver of the rear-ended vehicle was irate about the damage to his car.

Inference drawn: This driver may be yelling or threatening the driver who hit his car.

Message Inferred by Reader's Analysis of Writer's Word Choice

For this sentence to be effective, the writer had to consider the audience's prior knowledge of the word *irate* and if this word was the best choice to fulfill the purpose of communicating. To comprehend the writer's point, a reader may need to look up the definition of the word and think about the emotions associated with it and how the writer's use of the word supports the purpose of the point being made. Effective readers and writers connect topic, purpose, and audience to make and comprehend a point.

Survey the graphic on the next pages. You may recognize the similarities between it and the graphic in Module 1 that introduced and defined three key elements of reading and writing: Topic, Audience, and Purpose. This graphic builds on the prior knowledge established by your study in Module 1 and illustrates the relationship among topic, audience, word choice, tone, and purpose.

Reading/Writing: Connect Topic, Audience, Word Choice, Tone, and Purpose

As you may have noticed, word choice is a key tool for comprehending and making a point. A reader analyzes the writer's chosen words to identify the intended audience and to understand the writer's tone and purpose. A writer chooses words to establish a clear tone to reach a specific audience of readers for a particular purpose.

TOPIC: What You Read or Write

A topic is the subject matter dealt with in a piece of text. A topic is stated as a word or phrase. Thus, the word a writer chooses to state the topic often reflects the tone and purpose of the text. For example, *crib* focuses a writer's and a reader's attention one way while the word *home* suggests another focus.

THE AUDIENCE: Who Reads the Text

The audience is the individual or group of people for whom the text is written. A writer chooses words appropriate for the age and education of the audience. The writer who chooses to use the word *crib* for *house* is most likely writing to an audience of peers.

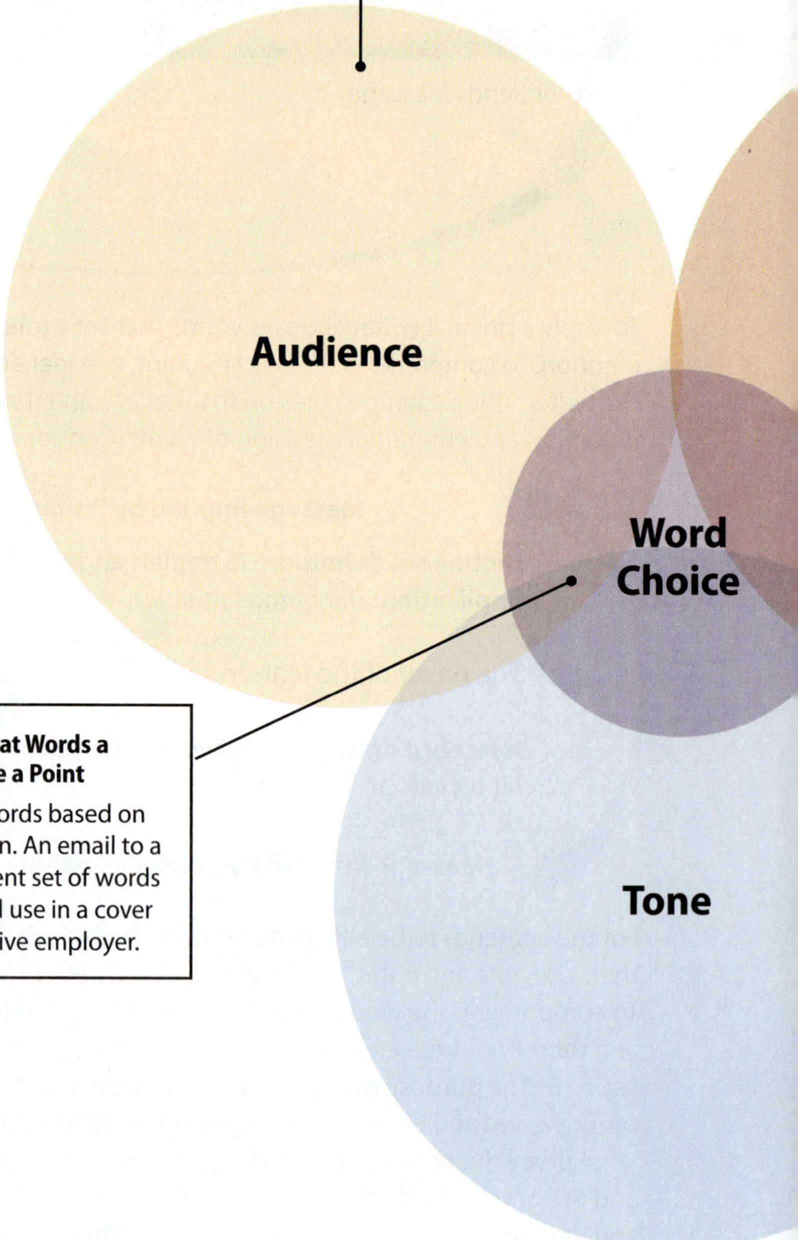

Audience

Word Choice

Tone

WORD CHOICE: What Words a Writer Uses to Make a Point

A writer chooses words based on the writing situation. An email to a friend uses a different set of words than a writer would use in a cover letter to a prospective employer.

Purpose

THE PURPOSE: Why You Read or Write

Purpose is the reason a writer writes about a topic. A reader seeks to understand and respond to a writer's purpose. Three general purposes are to inform, to entertain, and to argue. Word choice establishes purpose. The applicant writing a cover letter to apply for a job describes work experiences as having "worked from my *house*" rather than "worked from my *crib*." A neighbor inviting friends over for a visit may say, "Drop by my *crib* around 6 p.m."

THE TONE: How You Write—How You Are Influenced by What You Read

Tone is the writer's attitude toward a topic. The word *crib* suggests a casual, informal attitude. In contrast, *house* suggests a professional, formal attitude. The writer who chooses the word *crib* also taps into positive or negative emotions based on the experience of the reader. Writers choose words that will have the greatest impact on the audience. Word choice establishes tone.

Example

Each of the following four pieces of writing appeals to one of the audiences depicted by the following photos. All of the statements are about the same topic: Marijuana. Write the letter of the piece of writing next to the picture that shows its audience. Share your responses with a peer or small group. Discuss how word choice, tone, and purpose helped you identify the audience for each piece.

A. Scientists funded by the National Institute on Drug Abuse (NIDA), a federal government agency, have found that the damage to the brain's thinking abilities that results from smoking marijuana can last up to 28 days after an individual last smoked the drug.

B. Marijuana use today starts at a young age for many—and today stronger forms of the drug are offered to kids like you. Marijuana use is a serious threat—don't even think about it!

C. Under the influence of marijuana, you can forget your best friend's phone number, watch your grade point average drop like a stone, or get into a car accident.

D. Welcome to the Mothers Against Drugs speaker series. During today's speaker panel, we'll learn key facts about marijuana. You may have heard it called *pot*, *weed*, *grass*, *ganja*, or *skunk*, but marijuana by any other name is still a drug that damages our children's brains.

1. B

3. D

2. C

4. A

Explanation

Compare your responses to the following student's think-aloud.

For the audience shown in picture 1, I was torn between B and C. Both of these statements were aimed at young people. But phrases like "kids like you" and "don't even think about it" made statement B more appropriate for elementary students. I matched picture 2 with statement C. Statement C has a dark humor that teenagers can relate to and refers to issues and events common to teenagers. Picture 3 and statement D go together. This seemed obvious to me; the mothers want to know about the dangerous effects of drugs on their children. Picture 4 matches statement A. The audience of the information is made up of elected officials who make the laws concerning marijuana. Statement A sounded formal, like a report.

Practice 1

Connect Topic, Audience, Word Choice, Tone, and Purpose

The following list describes the purpose and audience of two common writing situations. Choose one of the situations and write a response. Choose words you think are most appropriate for the situation. Exchange your writing with a peer or share with a small group of classmates. Discuss the words you chose based on the audience and purpose of each writing situation. *Student responses may vary.*

- A thank you letter to Ms. Jones, Manager of La Fiesta restaurant, for the job interview you just had with her for the position of server.
- A posting on Facebook (or a specific social networking site) about a party you recently attended.

An effective reader thoughtfully notes the word choices the writer makes to grasp the writer's tone, purpose, and point. An effective writer carefully chooses words to set a tone and reveal a purpose to make a point to a specific audience. An effective reader/writer analyzes words in the text to determine the writer's tone and purpose and then establishes the tone and purpose of his or her response to the text.

L3 Use Tone to Comprehend and Make a Point

A writer's attitude is expressed by the tone of voice he or she assumes in the passage. A writer carefully chooses words for a specific impact on the reader.

For example, in an effort to share reliable information, textbooks strive for an objective tone. An **objective tone** includes facts and reasonable explanations. It is matter-of-fact and neutral. In contrast, a writer sharing a personal worldview through fiction and personal essays often uses a subjective tone. A **subjective tone** uses words that describe feelings, judgments, or opinions. The details given in a subjective tone are likely to include experiences, senses, feelings, and thoughts. Study the following table of words that describe the characteristics of tone. To grasp tone, a reader needs to carefully note the choice of vocabulary and details.

An **objective tone** is a neutral or unbiased expression of ideas.

A **subjective tone** is a personal expression of ideas.

Word Choice: Subjective and Objective Tone

Objective Tone	Characteristics	Subjective Tone	Characteristics
Impartial	An *impartial* tone is fair, not for or against an idea, person, place, thing, or event.	Personal	A *personal* tone expresses an individual's own views about an idea, person, place, thing, or event.
Unbiased	An *unbiased* tone does not show any feelings for or against a topic. Instead, it focuses on facts.	Biased	A *biased* tone expresses favor for or against a particular topic.
Neutral	A *neutral* tone does not show any feelings for or against a topic. Instead, it focuses on facts.	Emotional	*Emotional* words focus on feelings and reveal bias.
Formal	A *formal* tone chooses higher-level words and avoids using the pronouns *I* and *you*, thereby creating a sense of distance between the writer and the reader.	Informal	An *informal* tone uses the pronouns *I* and *you* to create a connection between the writer and the reader.
Literal	A *literal* tone is unbiased, neutral, or factual.	Figurative	A *figurative* tone is symbolic and poetic and uses one idea to represent another, such as using a white dove to represent hope or a dark cloud to represent grief.

Example

Analyze words for tone to comprehend a point.

A. Read the following list of statements. Based on word choice, choose the tone word that best describes each statement.

1. In January of 2010, an earthquake destroyed Port-au-Prince, Haiti.
a. biased (**b.**) unbiased

2. The magnitude-7 quake killed an estimated 200,000, left 250,000 injured, and made 1.5 million homeless.
(**a.**) literal **b.** figurative

3. Unless you saw it for yourself, you can't imagine the horror caused by the earthquake.
a. formal (**b.**) informal

4. Reports of children crying for parents and parents digging with their fingers for children are heart-rending images of human suffering caused by the quake.
a. neutral (**b.**) emotional

5. The United States government mobilized resources and manpower to aid in the relief effort.
(**a.**) objective **b.** subjective

B. Use tone words to make a point. Think of a significant natural disaster, such as Hurricane Sandy that hit the Northeast in 2012. Write five statements to describe the event. Choose words that establish the tone indicated before each blank. *Student responses may vary.*

6. (biased) *Hurricane Sandy is disturbing evidence of climate change due to human greed.*

7. (unbiased) *A number of people died during Hurricane Sandy.*

8. (emotional) *We lost everything but our lives!*

9. (formal) *President Obama pledged federal support for the restoration of communities affected by Hurricane Sandy.*

10. (informal) *You wouldn't believe the damage caused by Hurricane Sandy.*

Explanation

Compare your answers to the following student's think-aloud.

1. *The word* destroyed *is a factual description of the damage the earthquake caused, so the correct answer is (b)* unbiased **2.** *This sentence states facts so the answer is (a) literal.* **3.** *The use of* you *is informal and is used to state an opinion so the answer is (b) informal.* **4.** *The sentence creates a vivid image that taps into human emotions so the answer is (b) emotional.* **5.** *The sentence states facts and does not evaluate or judge the government's effort, so the answer is (a). I wrote the following sentences using tone words:* **6.** *(biased) "Hurricane Sandy is disturbing evidence of climate change due to human greed." I used biased words such as* disturbing *and* greed *to state a personal opinion.* **7.** *(unbiased) "A number of people died during Hurricane Sandy." This sentence just states facts.* **8.** *(emotional) "We lost everything but our lives!" I inserted an exclamation point to show emotion.* **9.** *(formal) "President Obama pledged federal support for the restoration of communities affected by Hurricane Sandy." I thought the tone words* pledged, restoration, *and* communities *sounded more formal than words like* promise, rebuild, *and* neighborhoods. **10.** *(informal) "You wouldn't believe the damage caused by Hurricane Sandy." The use of the pronoun* you *is informal.*

Practice 2

Use Tone to Comprehend and Make a Point

A. Read the followings statements about the dangers of sitting too much. Based on word choice, choose a tone word that best describes each statement.

1. Hey, don't just sit there, get up and move!
a. objective **(b.)** subjective

2. According to experts, sitting for long periods of time puts one at risk for heart disease, diabetes, and death, even for those who exercise daily.
(a.) objective **b.** biased

3. You just can't afford to be lazy when it comes to your health.
a. formal **(b.)** informal

4. To avoid the negative health effects of sitting for long periods of time, one may work at computer stations that require one to stand and walk during lunch and breaks.
(a.) neutral **b.** emotional

B. Assume you are the office manager of a local accounting firm. Concerned about the health of the office staff, upper management has decided to replace all desks with standing workstations. Write an explanation of the change to the office staff. Use a professional and positive tone. *Student responses may vary.*

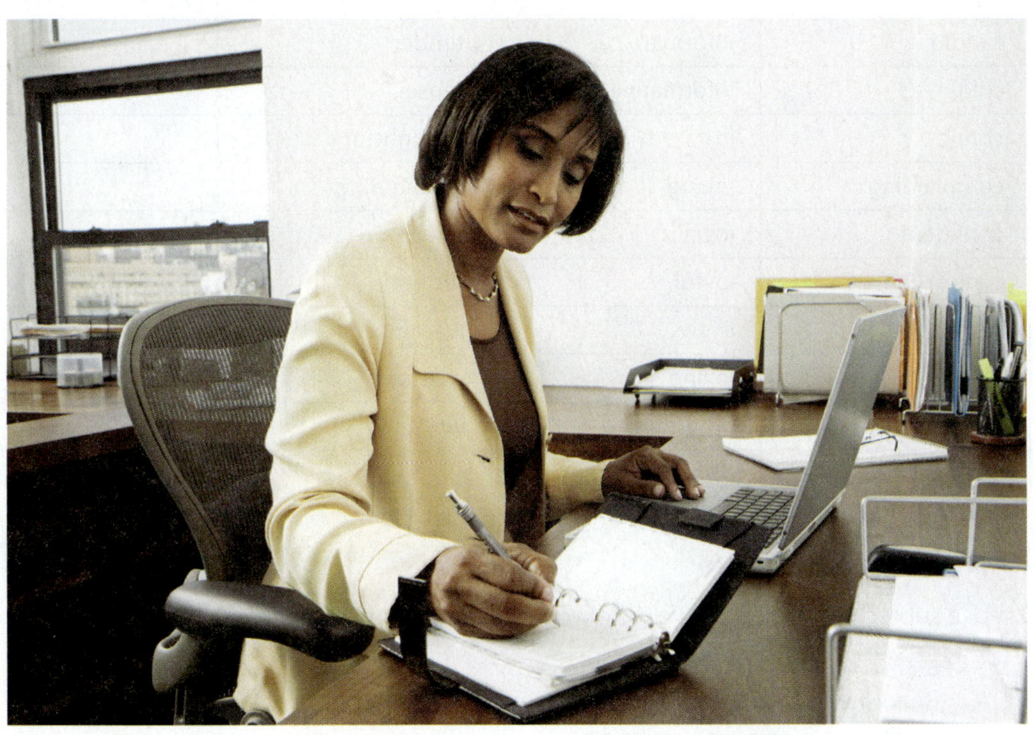

LO4 Use Subjective and Objective Words to Comprehend and Make a Point

Remember that just as tone can set the feeling for a conversation, it can also establish a feeling for a piece of writing. A small sample of words used to describe tone is listed here. Look up the meanings of any words you do not know. Developing your vocabulary helps you better understand a writer's word choice to establish tone.

Subjective Words			Objective Words
admiring	discouraged	odd	accurate
angry	disdainful	persuasive	factual
annoyed	dramatic	pleading	impartial
anxious	earnest	poetic	matter-of-fact
approving	elated	reverent	straightforward
arrogant	entertaining	rude	truthful
argumentative	fearful	sad	
assured	friendly	sarcastic	
belligerent	funny	self-pitying	
biting	gloomy	serious	
bitter	happy	sincere	
bored	hostile	supportive	
bubbly	humorous	suspenseful	
calm	idealistic	sympathetic	
candid	informal	tender	
cold	informative	tense	
comic	irritated	thoughtful	
complaining	joking	threatening	
confident	jovial	timid	
cynical	joyful	urgent	
demanding	lively	warning	
direct	loving	wistful	
disappointed	mournful	wry	
disbelieving	nice		

Example

Use subjective and objective tone words to comprehend and make a point.

A. Read the following items. Choose a word that best describes the tone of each statement. Use each word once.

anxious	encouraging	gloomy
elated	factual	persuasive

1. "If you care about saving lives, you should vote for gun control."

Tone: *persuasive*

2. "You can do anything if you put your mind to it. Come on! You can do it!"

Tone: *encouraging*

3. "I hope I do all right on this test. Even though I studied all night, I might forget important information."

Tone: *anxious*

4. "I won! I won!" Snively shouted as he realized he held the winning lottery ticket.

Tone: *elated*

5. Thick, heavy clouds hung low in the sky, like a soggy gray blanket. The trees were winter bare, and the ground was brown and wet. Though it was only 2 o'clock in the afternoon, a dusky shroud covered the neighborhood.

Tone: *gloomy*

6. A standard drink is defined as 12 ounces of beer, 5 ounces of wine, or 1.5 ounces of 72-proof distilled spirits, all of which contain the same amount of alcohol—about .54 ounces.

Tone: *factual*

B. Assume someone you know, such as a friend or family member, has just graduated from college with a degree in secondary education and is qualified to teach math and science at the middle and high school levels. The new graduate is nervous about finding a teaching position. Write a note to this person to congratulate him or her for graduating from college. Also include some encouraging words about his or her future as a teacher. Share your note with a peer or small group of classmates. Discuss the words you chose to achieve the tone of your note.
Student responses may vary.

Explanations

Compare your answers to the following student's think-aloud.

A. 1. *Persuasive. The words* if *and* should *sound persuasive to me. I looked up the meaning of* should*, and it points out something that is the right thing to do. But not everyone agrees about voting for gun control.*

CONTINUED

EXPLANATIONS *CONTINUED*

So this is a persuasive statement. **2.** *Encouraging.* **3.** *Anxious. The words* hope, even though, *and* might forget *state this person's text anxiety.* **4.** *Elated. The words* won, shouted, *and* winning *state good news. The way the writer repeated "I won!" really shows excitement.* **5.** *Gloomy. So many words that are negative such as* heavy, soggy gray blanket, winter bare, brown and wet, dusky shroud. *The whole picture is gloomy.* **6.** *Factual. This sentence just offers the facts that define a standard drink.*

B. *I pretended the college graduate was my cousin Nathan. First, I congratulated him; then I concluded with some encouraging words. Here is what I wrote: Dear Nathan, Congratulations on graduating from college with a degree in secondary education. I greatly admire your determination to finish your degree. I also admire your desire to teach young people. You will be an excellent teacher. You are patient and knowledgeable. Your students will be fortunate to have you as their teacher. Again, congratulations and best wishes.*

Practice 3

Use Subjective and Objective Words to Comprehend and Make a Point

A. Read the following items. Based on word choice, choose a word from the box that best describes the tone of each statement. Use each word once.

admiring	arrogant	factual	informative	warm
angry	bitter	happy	sad	wistful

1. "It is with sorrow that I must submit my resignation."

Tone: *sad*

2. "The best days were growing up on the farm before life became so fast paced."

Tone: *wistful*

3. "It is so good to see you again after such a long time. How is your wonderful family?"

Tone: *warm*

4. Manny shoots for the basket at an awkward angle. He hesitates. The ball is knocked out of his hands. The lost points may have just cost his team the win.

Tone: *informative*

5. "Animals can be divided into three groups based on the way they maintain body temperature."

Tone: *factual*

6. A quiet yet thrilling feeling of peace swept over her. Her children were healthy, she was successful in her job, and she was in love with her husband. It seemed she had all a person could want.

Tone: *happy*

7. "It isn't enough to say you are sorry after years of doing wrong. You just can't say you are sorry! How dare you think you can! Don't expect forgiveness, either!"

Tone: *bitter*

8. "It is with pleasure and pride that I offer this recommendation on behalf of Kareem Smith. He is hardworking, intelligent, and honest."

Tone: *admiring*

9. "Who broke the vase in the foyer? When I find out who did it, that person is going to be so sorry. Do you know how much that vase cost?"

Tone: *angry*

10. "I am the best there is, and don't you forget it. There is no one who beats me."

Tone: *arrogant*

B. Assume you live in a neighborhood that is governed by a board elected by the neighborhood. Recently, a group of preteens have been riding their skateboards in the middle of the busy main road through the neighborhood. When approached by you to warn them of the danger and to ask them to be more careful, they were disrespectful. Write a short letter to the president of the board about the dangerous behavior of this group. Explain the problem and offer a solution.

L5 Use Formal and Informal Words to Comprehend and Make a Point

The words we choose range in levels of tone from formal to informal. Writers choose the level of words based on their audience and purpose. Basically, tone words are in one of three levels: formal, standard, or informal. The following chart explains each level based on its audience, traits, uses, and examples.

Levels of Word Choice

Level	**Formal**	**Standard**	**Informal**
Audience	highly educated, specific	well-educated, general	familiar, specific
Traits	Uses third person *(he/she/they)*; no contractions as in *cannot* and *did not*; uses "learned" words; uses longer, more complicated words and sentences.	Follows correct usage in grammar, spelling, vocabulary, and punctuation; is considered acceptable by most people.	Uses personal first and second person pronouns (*I, me, we, us, you, your*); contractions as in *can't* and *didn't*; slang words; uses short, simple words and sentences.
Uses	a sermon, political speech, lecture, official letter, poetry	textbooks, mass media, college essays, business documents and communications	personal journals, letters, or emails, entertainment publications, everyday conversation
Examples	cerebral unparalleled	intelligent excellent	geek cool
Summary	Formal and standard levels of word choice are similar to each other. The difference is the degree of formality.		Informal language is how we usually talk in casual conversations with our friends and family. Informal language uses slang not acceptable in the standard or formal levels.

Effective readers skim a passage to determine the level of word choice to predict the writer's audience and purpose for writing. Effective writers choose the level of words most likely to reach a specific audience and fulfill a specific purpose. Most writers focus on word choice during the revision phase of the writing process.

Example

Read and identify the tone of each statement based on the following scale. In the space before each item, write 3 = Formal; 2 = Standard; 1 = Informal. Then revise each statement to reach the audience indicated in parentheses. *Student answers may vary.*

3 **1.** Democratic ideals and civic duty assert certain actions as essential and undeniable: Citizens must vote.

Revised (Audience: your best friend) *You gotta vote. It's your duty, the price you pay for living in a free country.*

1 **2.** I ain't getting this problem. Like, I ain't never been no good at math.

Revised (Audience: your teacher) *I don't understand this problem. Math is not my strongest subject.*

1 **3.** Hey, Ms. Taylor, you want us to work hard, then you ought to show us some respect. We have some cool suggestions to make workflow better.

Revised (Audience: your boss) *Ms. Taylor, may I respectfully suggest that we employees have several suggestions to improve our work process?*

2 **4.** My mom, Martha Elway, has earned the Woman of the Year award. She always gives to others. She never gets angry, even when others would. Also, she never gives up or turns her back on others.

Revised (Audience: community leaders at a public awards banquet) *My mother, Martha Elway, a generous, patient, and loyal friend to her family and community, well deserves the distinction of Woman of the Year.*

Explanations

Compare your answers to the following student's think-aloud.

1. *The tone is (3) formal because it uses longer words like* essential *and* undeniable. *I revised it to say, "You gotta vote. It's your duty, the price you pay for living in a free country."*

CONTINUED

2. The tone is (1) informal because it uses slang words and contractions such as ain't and like. I revised it to say, "I don't understand this problem. Math is not my strongest subject."

3. The tone is (1) informal. It even seems disrespectful, too familiar, and it uses slang such as cool. I revised it to say "Ms. Taylor, may I respectfully suggest that we employees have several suggestions to improve our work process?"

4. The tone is (2) standard. The writer follows the rules for writing but uses a tone that is less than formal and more like everyday conversation. I revised using longer, more complicated words that seem to give more weight to the occasion. "My mother, Martha Elway, a generous, patient, and loyal friend to her family and community, well deserves the distinction of Woman of the Year."

Practice 4

Use Formal and Informal Language

1. Choose one of the following reading/writing situations. Do not share your choice with your classmates.
   - **a.** a complaint letter to the manager of your favorite restaurant about poor service
   - **b.** an email to a friend who missed class, informing him or her about the most important point of today's lesson
   - **c.** a paragraph for the college's student newspaper, announcing a new tutoring service in the Learning Lab for math
   - **d.** a reading/writing situation of your own creation
2. Draft a piece of writing appropriate in tone based on audience and purpose as stated in the reading/writing situation you chose.
3. Next, exchange your work with a peer or small group of classmates. Then, as a reader, answer the following questions:
   Who is the audience for this writing? How do you know?

   What is the purpose of this writing? How do you know?

   What is the tone of this writing? How do you know?

Determine the General Purpose to Comprehend and Make a Point

LO6

As you learned in Module 1, three general purposes usually drive a main idea: to inform, to entertain, and to argue. The following graphic is designed to deepen your understanding of the relationship between tone and purpose. Study each of the situations represented by the photographs. Think about the purpose of each and how writers may use word choice to create a tone to achieve that purpose.

Three General Purposes: To Inform, To Argue, and To Entertain

- **To inform**. When a writer sets out to inform, he or she shares knowledge and information or offers instruction about a particular topic. A few of the tone words often used to describe this purpose include *objective*, *matter-of-fact*, and *straightforward*. Writers use facts to explain or describe the main idea to readers. Most textbook passages are written to inform. The following topic sentences reflect the writer's desire to inform.

1. The main causes of road rage are stress and anxiety.

2. A healthful diet includes several daily servings from each of the major food groups.

- **To argue**. A writer uses a logical argument to bring the reader into agreement with his or her view on the topic. A few of the tone words often used to describe this purpose include *argumentative, persuasive, forceful, controversial, positive, supportive, negative*, and *critical*. Writers assert a claim or a strong stand and offer convincing supports to sway the reader to their point of view. Politicians and advertisers often use argumentation to win support for their ideas and products. The following topic sentences reflect arguments posed by a writer.

3. Violence that arises from road rage must be harshly and swiftly punished.

4. How to achieve this should be a part of public school education from elementary through high school.

- **To entertain**. A writer whose purpose is to entertain sets out to captivate or interest the audience. A few of the tone words often used to describe this purpose include *amusing, entertaining, lively, humorous,* and *suspenseful*. Writers frequently use expressive language, vivid images, strong feelings, or sensory details (such as sights, sounds, tastes, textures, and smells). The following topic sentences reflect the writer's desire to entertain.

5. Think of our highways as a place to study how operating a powerful machine can turn normal people into four types of maniacs: the bully, the loudmouth, the speed-demon, and the exterminator.

6. I am zealously committed to eating a balanced diet from the four basic food groups: low-calorie, low-carbohydrate, low-fat, and low-taste.

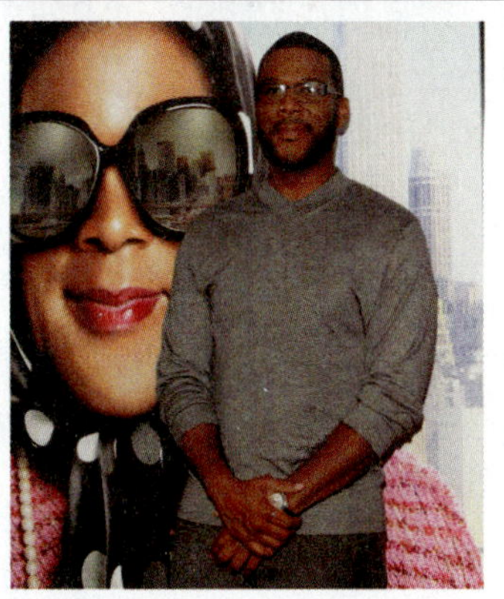

An effective reader notes a writer's choice of words and tone to determine the writer's purpose and point or main idea. An effective writer chooses words and establishes a tone for a specific purpose to make a point. An effective reader/writer studies the ways other writers use word choice, tone, and purpose to reach an audience and make a point about a topic.

Example

Determine the general purpose to comprehend and make a point.

A. Read each of the following paragraphs. Label each according to its purpose.
I = to inform **A** = to argue **E** = to entertain

E **1.** A young woman suffering from anxiety was constantly biting her nails. Worried about her habit of biting her fingernails down to the quick, she asked her doctor for some advice. To her surprise, her doctor advised her to take up yoga. She did, and soon her fingernails were growing normally. During her next scheduled appointment, her doctor noticed her healthy nails asked her if yoga had totally cured her nervousness. "No," she replied, "but now I can reach my toenails so I bite them instead."

I **2.** Yoga exercises benefit a person in three ways. Yoga leads to physical balance, mental alertness, and fewer injuries. The practice of yoga uses slow, steady motions to enter and hold poses that stretch and strengthen the body's muscles. Because each pose is held for at least 10 seconds, the body learns to adjust and find its natural balance. To find this balance, the mind must be actively involved. And as the muscles are stretched and strengthened, injuries are less likely to occur.

A **3.** Yoga is a much healthier practice than simple stretching. Stretching relies on a jerky movement that forces the body into a certain position. Often stretching is dynamic, using a bouncing motion, and the stretch is only held for a moment or two. Such stretching can lead to injuries. In contrast, yoga uses a static stretch that relies on inner balance to hold the pose for at least 10 to 15 seconds. To successfully enter and hold a yoga pose, the mind must focus on what the body needs to stay balanced. By holding a stretch, the body becomes strong and flexible, and the connection between the mind and body is strengthened more than with simple stretching.

B. Think of a product or behavior. The product or behavior may be either helpful or harmful. Assume someone you know is thinking about buying the product or participating in the behavior. Write an email to this person advising him or her about the product or the behavior. Choose a purpose and tone appropriate for your audience and the point you want to make.

Explanations

Compare your answers to the following student's think-aloud.

A. 1. *The writer uses vivid details, descriptions, and a surprise ending—a punch line—(E) to entertain the reader.*

2. *The writer's purpose here is simply (I) to inform the reader about three benefits of yoga.*

3. *The writer clearly believes that yoga is better than*

simple stretching and gives details (A) to argue that this view is correct.

B. I chose to write about chewing tobacco because most of the men in my family chew tobacco, and I do not want my little brother to start this nasty habit. My purpose was to make an argument against chewing tobacco, and my tone was informal. I wrote the following: "Dear Nate, I know Dad, Uncle Robert, and most of the guys in our family chew tobacco, but I am begging you not to even start! Chewing tobacco is a nasty habit that is hard to break once you are hooked. Chewing tobacco may make you feel like one of the guys, but I promise you, girls will be grossed out and turned off once they see you spit tobacco juice. The most important reason not to chew is because chewing tobacco can kill you. It causes cancer! So please, Nate, don't even think about chewing tobacco."

Practice 5

Determine the General Purpose

A. Read the following topic sentences. Label each according to its purpose.

I = to inform A = to argue E = to entertain

__A__ **1.** Cloning human beings should be banned.

__I__ **2.** The National Hurricane Center predicts a record number of hurricanes in the upcoming months.

__A__ **3.** Friends don't let friends drive drunk.

__I__ **4.** Bulimia and anorexia are two serious eating disorders.

__E__ **5.** A celebrity is a person who works hard all his life to become well known, then wears dark glasses to avoid being recognized. James B. Simpson

CONTINUED

PRACTICE 5 *CONTINUED*

___I___ **6.** Spanking as a way to discipline a child has a long history in many cultures.

___E___ **7.** Age is strictly a case of mind over matter. If you don't mind, it doesn't matter. Jack Benny

___I___ **8.** Kwanzaa is an African American tradition that is based on the African celebration of the "first fruits" of the harvest.

___E___ **9.** When I was a boy of fourteen, my father was so ignorant I could hardly stand to have the old man around. But when I got to be twenty-one, I was astonished at how much he had learned in seven years. Mark Twain

___A___ **10.** Rely on Denta-Fresh toothpaste to stop bad breath just as millions of others have.

B. Choose one of the topic sentences in part A of this practice. Draft an explanation that supports the topic sentence of your choice. Choose words appropriate for the purpose and tone of the topic sentence. Use your own paper.

LO7 Determine the Primary Purpose to Comprehend and Make a Point

In addition to the three general purposes, writers often write to fulfill a more specific purpose. The following table offers several examples of specific purposes within the three general purposes.

General and Specific Purposes		
To Inform	**To Entertain**	**To Argue**
to analyze	to amuse	to argue against
to clarify	to delight	to argue for
to discuss	to frighten	to convince
to establish	to interest	to criticize
to explain		to inspire (motivate a change)

Often a writer has two or more purposes in one piece of writing. Blending purposes adds interest and power to a piece of writing. Take, for example, the award-winning documentary *Fahrenheit 9/11*. This film attempts to inform and entertain, but its primary purpose is to argue. The film uses facts, personal bias, and humor to take a strong stand against President George W. Bush. Comics like Jon Stewart and Stephen Colbert use facts from daily events to entertain their audiences, but they are also giving information to their audiences. In these

Primary purpose is the writer's main reason for writing the passage.

cases, when a writer has more than one purpose, only one purpose is in control overall. This controlling purpose is called the **primary purpose.**

Consider the following statement that reflects two purposes—to argue and to inform.

> Spanking must be avoided as a way to discipline due to its long-term negative effects on the child.

The writer used the tone words *must be avoided* and *negative* to argue against spanking as a way to discipline. However, the writer also intends to inform the reader about the *long-term effects of spanking*. Based on the tone word *negative*, we know that the writer's main purpose is not to inform us with facts from both sides of the issue. The writer's primary purpose is to argue against spanking as a means of discipline.

You should also consider titles, headings, and prior knowledge about the writer. For example, it's easy to see that Jay Leno's primary purpose is to entertain us with his book *If Roast Beef Could Fly*. The title is funny, and we know Jay Leno is a comedian. An effective reader studies the general context of the passage to find out the writer's primary purpose. An effective writer makes his or her primary purpose clear in a tone established by word choice.

Example

Determine the primary purpose to comprehend and make a point.

A. Read the following paragraphs. Identify the primary purpose of each paragraph.

1.

On the Decay of the Art of Lying

By Mark Twain [Samuel Clemens]

[1]Observe, I do not mean to suggest that the "custom" of lying has suffered any decay or interruption—no, for the Lie, as a Virtue, A Principle, is eternal; the Lie, as a recreation, a solace, a refuge in time of need, the fourth Grace, the tenth Muse, man's best and surest friend, is immortal, and cannot perish from the earth while this club remains. [2]My complaint simply concerns the decay of the "art" of lying. [3]No high-minded man, no man of right feeling, can contemplate the lumbering and slovenly lying of the present day without grieving to see a noble art so prostituted. . . . No fact is more firmly established than that lying is a necessity of our circumstances—the deduction that it is then a Virtue goes without saying. [4]No virtue can reach its highest usefulness without careful and diligent cultivation—therefore, it goes without saying that this one ought to be taught in the public schools—even in the newspapers. [5]What chance has the ignorant uncultivated liar against the educated expert? [6]What chance have I against Mr. Per—against a lawyer?

Excerpt from Mark Twain, "On the Decay of the Art of Lying." *Classic Literature Library.* http://mark-twain.classic-literature.co.uk/on-the-decay-of-the-art-of-lying/.

The primary purpose of this passage is to

a. explain the virtue of lying.

(b.) amuse the reader by poking fun at the human act of lying.

c. convince the reader that lying is a virtue.

CONTINUED

EXAMPLES *CONTINUED*

2.

Long-Term Memory

[1]Think of long-term memory as a "data bank" or warehouse for all of your feelings and ideas. [2]Information you heard hours, days, weeks, even years ago is stored in long-term memory. [3]Long-term memory differs from short-term memory in several ways. [4]Long-term memory can handle large amounts of information; short-term memory has less space for storage. [5]Putting information in and getting it out again is a slow process in long-term memory. [6]On the other hand, short-term memory is a rapid process.

Adapted from Brownell, Judi, *Listening: Attitudes, Principles, and Skills*, p. 150.

The main purpose of this paragraph is to

a. argue against poor memory skills.

b. amuse the reader with humorous details about long-term memory.

c. inform the reader about the differences between long-term and short-term memory.

B. Write to learn or deepen your understanding about a writer's primary purpose. Choose one of the two paragraphs in Part A. Underline words and phrases that influence you. Write responses to the following questions: What impact did the words or phrases you underlined have on you? What other purpose(s) did the writer accomplish in the piece? Share and discuss your paragraph with a peer or small group of classmates.

Explanations

Compare your answers to the following student's think-aloud.

1. *Mark Twain is a well-known American humorist. I expect his primary purpose to be (b) to amuse the reader by poking fun at the human act of lying. His use of formal tone words makes this piece amusing. For example, he says lying is an "art" and he is "grieving to see a noble art so prostituted." His surprising praise of a dishonest behavior is what makes this funny.*

2. *The source note reveals that this paragraph comes from a textbook, and the primary purpose of a textbook is to inform. In addition, the tone of the title and details is factual and objective. Its main purpose is (c) to inform* *the reader about the differences between long-term and short-term memory.*

B. *I chose to reread Mark Twain's paragraph. In fact, I read it several times. The more times I read it the more I understood his humor. He is so sarcastic. He pokes fun at the fact that humans have always been and still are prone to lie. I like the way he describes "lying" as "the fourth Grace," and "man's best and surest friend." His suggestion that "the art of lying" should be taught in public schools is sadly ironic, as honest people need to learn how to defend themselves against effective liars.*

Practice 6

Determine the Primary Purpose to Comprehend and Make a Point

A. Read the following paragraphs. Identify the primary purpose of each.

1.

DIFFERENT WORDS, DIFFERENT WORLDS

by Deborah Tannen

[1]Many years ago, I was married to a man who shouted at me, "I do not give you the right to raise your voice to me, because you are a woman and I am a man." [2]This was frustrating because I knew it was unfair. [3]But I also knew just what was going on. [4]I ascribed his unfairness to his having grown up in a country where few people thought women and men have equal rights. [5]Now I am married to a man who is a partner and friend. [6]We come from similar backgrounds and share values and interests. [7]It is a continual source of pleasure to talk to him. [8]It is wonderful to have someone I can tell everything to, someone who understands. [9]But he doesn't always see things as I do, doesn't always react to things as I expect him to. [10]And I often don't understand why he says what he does.

—Tannen, Deborah, *You Just Don't Understand*, p. 23.

The primary purpose of this paragraph is to

a. entertain with amusing details about marriage.

(b.) explain that men and women often perceive things differently.

c. argue against the idea that men are superior to women.

CONTINUED

PRACTICE 6 *CONTINUED*

2.

HUMAN IMPACT ON LAKES

[1]Wakes created by motorboating disturb vegetation and the birds that nest in it. [2]Motorboats discharge an oily mixture with gas exhausts beneath the surface of the water. [3]This mixture escapes notice. [4]One gallon of oil per million gallons of water imparts an odor to lake water. [5]Eight gallons per million taints fish. [6]These oily discharges can lower oxygen levels and hurt the growth and life span of fish.

Adapted from Smith, Robert, and Smith, Thomas, *Elements of Ecology*, 4th ed., p. 462.

The primary purpose of this paragraph is to

- **a.** inform the reader about the impact of human motorboating activity on lakes.
- **b.** argue against the use of boats in lakes.
- **c.** entertain the reader with interesting details about boating.

3.

from METAMORPHOSIS

BY FRANZ KAFKA

[1]As Gregor Samsa awoke one morning from uneasy dreams he found himself transformed in his bed into a gigantic insect. [2]He was lying on his hard, as it were armor-plated, back and when he lifted his head a little he could see his dome-like brown belly divided into stiff arched segments on top of which the bed quilt could hardly keep in position and was about to slide off completely. [3]His numerous legs, which were pitifully thin compared to the rest of his bulk, waved helplessly before his eyes.

Source: The Literature Network. http://www.online-literature.com/franz-kafka/metamorphosis/1/

The main purpose of this paragraph is to

- **a.** explain to the reader that a human has turned into a bug.
- **b.** convince the reader that a human has turned into a bug.
- **c.** engage the reader with an absurd story.

B. Choose a paragraph from the paragraphs used in the Examples or Part A of this practice. Use your paragraph of choice as a model for your writing by following these steps. *Student responses may vary.*

1. Reread the paragraph: Look for topics for your writing. Note the writer's use of words and phrases.

2. Prewrite by completing the following statements:

a. My topic is ______________________________

____

b. My primary purpose is to ______________________________

____

c. My tone is ______________________________

____

3. Write a draft of your ideas.

____

____

____

____

____

____

____

____

____

____

4. Revise for tone.

____

____

____

____

____

____

____

____

____

____

Reading and Writing Assignments

MySkillsLab™
Complete these assignments in MySkillsLab.

Considering Audience and Purpose

Study the sequence of photographs about word choice, tone, and purpose at the beginning of this module. Assume the professor in the last photograph is your teacher for this course. He requires each student to share with the class an important lesson learned in the class. He also requires a written copy of the lesson. Write a paragraph that explains the most helpful skill or concept you learned in this module.

Reading and Writing for Everyday Life

Assume you have been in a longstanding dispute with someone you once thought of as a trusted friend. You have received a package with an apology letter from this person.

- **Before Reading/Writing**: Skim the letter for its primary purpose and tone.
- **During Reading**: Note details to which you want to respond.
- **After Reading**: Write a letter in response. Use a clear and distinctive tone to make your point.

Dear Friend,

I have long wanted to write to you to express my deep regret about our disagreement. When we argued, I said some hurtful things about you and your family. I was wrong to accuse you of lying. In an attempt to make you feel as bad as I did, I'm the one who took your mother's ring. I knew how much that ring meant to you, and I just wanted you to know what it felt like to lose something you really care about. I never meant for your son to take the blame. Though it will never be enough, I am returning your mother's ring to you. Hopefully, you will be able to forgive me. I am deeply sorry to have hurt you and your family.

Reading and Writing for College Life

Assume you are taking a college course in American History. Your professor has just handed you the following two paragraphs and a set of instructions.

- **Before Reading/Writing**: (1) Carefully read the professor's instructions. (2) Skim the paragraphs for tone and purpose. Note the word choice.
- **During Reading**: Annotate information in the text that you can use to write in response to the professor's instructions.
- **After Reading, Write**: Draft a response to the professor's question about the text. Adopt a clear tone such as formal, inspiring, or one of your choosing based on your purpose and the audience.

Instructions:

The following two paragraphs are the opening statements of the Declaration of Independence in Congress, July 4, 1776. Read the paragraphs. What do you think the writers mean by the phrase "unalienable Rights, that among these are Life, Liberty, and the pursuit of Happiness"? Write a paragraph that explains the meaning of this phrase. Give examples. Be prepared to share your thoughts with the class.

> When in the Course of human events, it becomes necessary for one people to dissolve the political bands which have connected them with another, and to assume among the powers of the earth, the separate and equal station to which the Laws of Nature and of Nature's God entitle them, a decent respect to the opinions of mankind requires that they should declare the causes which impel them to the separation.
>
> We hold these truths to be self-evident, that all men are created equal, that they are endowed by their Creator with certain unalienable Rights, that among these are Life, Liberty and the pursuit of Happiness.—That to secure these rights, Governments are instituted among Men, deriving their just powers from the consent of the governed,—That whenever any Form of Government becomes destructive of these ends, it is the Right of the People to alter or to abolish it, and to institute new Government, laying its foundation on such principles and organizing its powers in such form, as to them shall seem most likely to effect their Safety and Happiness.

Reading and Writing for Working Life

Assume you are an intern working in a small advertising firm known as Key Image. One of the firm's clients is Heavy Metal Fitness, a local gym. You have been asked to work on the advertising campaign for the gym. Read the following memo from the owner. Use the information to create a sales brochure for the gym. Follow the steps given below to read and write about the gym for the brochure.

- **Before Reading/Writing**: Skim the text and underline key words to use in the brochure.
- **During Reading**: Highlight details related to the key terms you identified before reading.
- **After Reading, Write**: In 75 words or less, state the best aspects of the gym. Include details to draw new clients.

To: Key Image
From: Henry Roberts, Owner Heavy Metal Fitness
RE: Information about Heavy Metal Fitness for Sales Brochure

The information you requested for the sales brochure follows:
Heavy Metal Fitness is a core and strength conditioning program based on functional training and movements, done over various times (short to long workouts) and Modes (types of exercises: Olympic lifts, power lifts, gymnastics, running, etc.). The workouts are universally scalable based on individual fitness levels. Everything is tailored to the individual. We train in a group dynamic. This allows for people to learn from, and push each other, while a certified trainer is present overseeing the entire workout stressing form, efficacy, and efficiency. Heavy Metal Fitness is not a boot camp for a month meeting in a park. It is not a Globo Gym that locks members into ridiculous contracts with no regard to fitness, health and wellness, or sense of community. This is our life. This is our passion. This is our love. We put everything we have into our programming, training environment, and those who commit to training with us. First visit is free.

Workshop: Respond to What You've Read

Choose a passage to read and respond to in writing. You may select a passage in an example, practice, or writing assignment within this module, or you may select a passage of your own choosing. Use the following guide to comprehend and respond to the passage. Apply what you have learned about word choice, tone, and purpose to your reading/writing strategy.

Preread: Survey and Question

Prereading/Writing questions based on text features (vocabulary):

____

____

____

____

____

Standard prereading/writing questions:

What is the passage about?

____

How is the material organized?

____

What do I already know about this idea? (What is my prior knowledge about the vocabulary?)

____

What is my purpose for reading/writing?

____

What is the writer's purpose and tone?

____

What points (vocabulary) may I want to address or include in my written response?

____

Read and Annotate

As you read, annotate key ideas, particularly those details that answer your prereading questions.

Recite, Review, and Brainstorm

Recite the information. Summarize the most important parts. Answer your prereading questions.

Rephrase ideas into your own words. Record changes in your opinions based on the new information. **Review** the information. **Brainstorm** ideas for your written response to the passage. **Freewrite** a response to what you have read. **Map** the relationship among ideas you have annotated in the text. **Outline** or list key ideas and details in blocks of thought.

Write a Draft of Your Response

Using the ideas you generated by brainstorming, compose a draft of your response. Use your own paper.

Revise Your Draft

Once you have created a draft of your writing, read the draft and answer the questions in the Questions for Revising box that follows. Indicate your answers by annotating your paper. If you answer "yes" to a question, underline, check, or circle examples. If you answer "no" to a question, write additional details in the margins and draw lines to indicate their placement. Revise your paragraph based on your reflection. (*Hint:* Experienced writers create several drafts as they focus on one or two questions per draft.)

Step by Step: Questions for Revising

- ☐ Have I stated or implied my overall point?
- ☐ Have I made my purpose clear?
- ☐ Is my tone appropriate for my audience and purpose?
- ☐ Is the logical order of the ideas clear? Have I used words to clearly guide my reader, such as *first*, *second*, *next*, etc.?
- ☐ Have I made my point with adequate details?
- ☐ Do all the details support my point?
- ☐ What impact will my paragraph make on my reader?

Proofread Your Draft

Once you have made any revisions to your writing that may be needed, proofread to eliminate careless errors. Work with a classmate to give and receive feedback about your writing.

Review Test

MySkillsLab™
Complete this Review Test in MySkillsLab.

Score (number correct) ______ x 5 = _______%

Word Choice, Tone, and Purpose

Read the following passage from a college health textbook. Answer the questions that follow.

1170L/10.9 GE/1012 words

BODY COMPOSITION

[1]Many people worry about their body weight. [2]However, how much you weigh is not always a good index of whether your body composition is healthy. [3]In fact, based on height and weight charts, some athletes appear to be 25 pounds overweight but really have very little body fat. [4]How is this possible?

What Is Body Composition and What Does It Tell Us?

[5]Body composition refers to the relative amounts of fat and fat-free tissues (e.g., bone, muscle, and internal organs) in the body. [6]Body composition is typically expressed as a percentage of fat in the body. [7]So if a person has 20% body fat, 20% of her body weight is fat mass. [8]The remaining 80% of her body weight is fat free or lean body mass. [9]Having a high percentage of body fat is associated with an increased risk of heart disease, diabetes, and other disorders. [10]However, having too low a percentage can also be linked to health problems, such as osteoporosis.

[11]Measuring percentage of body fat can help determine whether a person is at a healthy weight, overweight, or obese. [12]Someone who is "overweight" has a body fat percentage above the level that is considered to be "healthy," based on research examining the relationship between body fatness and rates of disease. [13]A person classified as obese has a very high percentage of body fat, generally over 25% for men and over 35% for women.

How Is Body Composition Related to Health?

[14]Maintaining a healthy body composition is an important goal to achieve a lifetime of wellness. [15]To determine a healthy body weight, you need to consider percentage of body fat.

[16]The human body contains two major types of fat: (1) essential fat and (2) storage fat. [17]Essential fat is necessary for body functions such as facilitating nerve impulses. [18]Locations of this fat include nerves and cell membranes. [19]Men have approximately 3% of their body weight as essential fat. In contrast, women—who carry more fat in their breasts, uterus, and other sex-specific sites—have approximately 12%.

[20]The second type of body fat is called storage fat, which is contained within adipose tissue (i.e., fat cells) in the body. [21]This fat may be visceral fat, which is located around internal organs, or subcutaneous fat, which is located just below the skin. [22]Storage fat provides energy for activity, insulates the body to retain

CONTINUED

heat, and protects against trauma to the body. [23]However, high levels of storage fat, particularly in the visceral region of the body, increase the risk of numerous diseases including cardiovascular disease, diabetes, and cancer. [24]Thus, maintaining a healthy body composition is such an important goal.

[25]In general, a healthy percentage of body fat for young men (20–39 years) can range from 8% to 19%, and for young women (20–39 years), from 21% to 32%. [26]However, many public health experts recommend levels at the lower end of these ranges for young adults, 12%–15% and 21%–25% for men and women, respectively. [27]For most people, a body fat percentage outside these ranges indicates an unhealthy body weight. [28]However, athletes or very active individuals might have lower values. [29]Some athletic men have as little as 5%–13% fat. [30]Likewise, athletic women can have as little as 12%–22%. [31]Keep in mind that these values are not recommended for the general population and that you can be healthy if your body fat percentage falls within the ranges mentioned.

[32]It is not just how much body fat a person carries that can greatly affect his risk for several chronic diseases; where he carries it also matters. [33]Fat cells are unequally distributed throughout the body, and the distribution of body fat is determined largely by genetics. [34]We inherit specific fat storage traits that determine the regional distribution of fat. [35]For example, many men have a high number of fat cells in the upper body and as a result store more fat within the abdominal area (e.g., around the waist). [36]This is referred to as the android pattern of obesity. [37]In contrast, women tend to carry more fat cells in the waist, hips, and thighs of the lower body. [38]This is called the gynoid pattern of obesity. [39]People who carry body fat primarily in the abdominal or waist area are at greater risk of developing heart disease and diabetes than are those who store body fat in the hips or lower part of the body.

Overweight and Obesity in the United States

[40]Obesity is often defined as a percentage of body fat greater than 25% for men and greater than 35% for women. [41]Current estimates for the United States suggest that nearly 34% of adults and approximately 17% of children and adolescents (ages 2–19) meet the criteria for obesity. [42]Obesity is a major health problem in the United States. [43]Numerous diseases have been linked to being too fat. [44]Because of a strong link between obesity and disease, the National Institutes of Health has estimated that obesity directly contributes to 15%–20% of the deaths in the United States.

[45]The burden of obesity has also had a significant effect on health-care costs. [46]Currently, an estimated 10% of all medical costs in the United States are attributed to overweight- and obesity-related health problems. [47]This adds up to the hefty price tag of $147 billion per year in direct medical costs. [48]This number is predicted to rise sharply in the future. [49]The World Health Organization reports that the obesity rates in the United States are the highest in the world and are continuing to climb. [50]The reports are based on studies indicating that the number of obese or overweight people in the United States has increased rapidly during the past 20 years. [51]In 2010, no state had a prevalence of obesity less than 20%; 36 states had a prevalence of 25% or more, and 12 states had a prevalence of 30% or more. [52]The good news is that the increase in adult obesity in the United States is leveling off. [53]The bad news

is that 67% of all Americans are either obese or overweight. [54]Furthermore, there is no evidence of a decrease in the rate of obesity among children. [55]Thus, obesity continues to be a major threat to wellness in the United States.

Adapted from Powers, Scott K., Dodd, Stephen L., and Jackson, Erica M., *Total Fitness & Wellness*, 6th ed., pp. 144-147.

Vocabulary in Context

1. What does the word **facilitating** in sentence 17 mean?

a. stopping
(b.) enabling
c. showing
d. slowing

2. What does the word **insulates** in sentence 22 mean?

a. warms
(b.) protects
c. controls
d. harms

Tone

3. The overall tone of the passage is

(a.) standard.
b. informal.
c. formal.

Purpose

4. The general purpose of this essay is to

(a.) explain the relationship between body composition and wellness.
b. amuse the reader with details about body composition.
c. argue that body composition is the most important factor in wellness.

5. Which of the following sentences best states the primary purpose of the essay?

a. sentence 2
b. sentence 5
(c.) sentence 14
d. sentence 16

What Do You Think?

Assume you are taking a college health course. Your professor has asked you to prove your understanding of the passage by writing a paragraph that discusses the following points:

- Define body composition, overweight, and obesity.
- Discuss the potential health consequences of not maintaining a healthy body composition.
- Discuss the public health impact of overweight and obesity in the United States.

Academic Learning Log: Module Review

Summary of Key Concepts of Word Choice, Tone, and Purpose

Assess your comprehension of word choice, tone, and purpose.

LO1 LO3

1. Tone is *a manner of expression that communicates emotion or lack of emotion* ____.

LO2 LO3

2. Word choice is *the writer's selection of words based on meaning* ____.

LO2 LO3

3. Effective readers and writers connect *topic*, *audience,*, purpose, and *word choice*.

LO2 LO3

4. A *reader* analyzes the writer's chosen words to identify the writer's *audience* and understand the writer's *tone* and *purpose.*. A *writer* chooses *words* to establish a clear *tone* to reach a specific *audience* of readers for a particular *purpose*.

LO4

5. Objective tone is *a neutral or unbiased expression of ideas*.

LO4

6. Subjective tone is a personal expression of ideas.

LO5

7. Formal language is elevated; standard language, while always correct, has a greater range and may at times have a less formal tone; informal language is how we talk in casual conversation and often includes slang words.

LO6

8. The writer's purpose is his or her reason for writing about a topic.

LO7

9. The primary purpose is the main reason the writer writes the passage.

LO7

10. A writer whose purpose is to inform often uses facts to teach or explain a main idea. A writer whose purpose is to entertain frequently uses expressive language, vivid images, strong feelings, or sensory details to be amusing, humorous, or suspenseful. A writer whose purpose is to argue asserts a claim, or strong stand, and offers convincing supports to sway readers to a particular point of view.

Test Your Comprehension of Tone and Purpose

Respond to the following questions and prompts. *Answers may vary.*

LO1 LO2

In your own words, what is the relationship between tone and purpose?

Tone reveals a writer's purpose. For example, to inform, a writer usually uses unbiased, neutral words. To entertain, a writer may use vivid, exaggerated, or surprising details and descriptions. To argue, a writer takes a strong stand with words like should *and* must.

LO2 LO3 LO4 LO5

How does word choice relate to tone and purpose for a reader and a writer?

The words a writer chooses reveal his or her attitude about and reason for writing. A reader determines a writer's tone and purpose based on the words the writer chose to use to express his or her ideas.

LO1 LO2 LO3 LO4 LO5 LO6 LO7

In your own words, describe how to determine tone and purpose. Describe how a writer establishes tone and purpose.

To determine tone and purpose, a reader studies the words the writer uses to make a point. A reader identifies the specific uses of facts and/or biased words. A reader uses these specific details to answer questions such as the following: Is the writer's purpose to inform, argue, or entertain? Is the writer's attitude toward the topic neutral or emotional? What effect does the writer want to have on the reader? To establish tone and purpose, a writer considers his or her audience and chooses a purpose and tone most appropriate for the audience. A writer carefully chooses words that reveal his or her attitude about a topic and purpose for writing.

L1 L2 L3 L4 L5 L6 L7

Use a checklist to help determine the tone and purpose of passages. Select a passage to analyze; then complete the following checklist with information from the passage.

Title of Passage:			
	Yes	**No**	**Examples (words or phrases)/Explanations**
Subjective Tone			
Objective Tone			
Formal Tone			
Informal Tone			
Primary Purpose			
To Inform			
To Argue			
To Entertain			

Summarize the two most important ideas in this module that will help you improve your reading/writing strategy.

L1 L2 L3 L4 L5 L6 L7

1. **How will I use what I have learned?** In your notebook, discuss how you will apply your own reading/writing strategy to what you have learned about word choice, tone, and purpose. When will you apply this knowledge to your reading/writing strategy?
2. **What do I still need to study about word choice, tone, and purpose?** In your notebook, discuss your ongoing study needs. Describe what, when, and how you will continue to study word choice, tone, and purpose.

Complete the Post-test for Module 4 in MySkillsLab.

5

LEARNING OUTCOMES

After studying this module you should be able to:

- LO 1 Answer the Question "What's the Point of Stated Main Ideas in Reading and Writing Paragraphs?"
- LO 2 Identify the Parts of a Paragraph and Levels of Information
- LO 3 Identify the Elements of a Main Idea
- LO 4 Before Reading, Skim and Annotate to Identify the Topic of a Paragraph
- LO 5 During Reading, Question and Annotate to Identify the Topic Sentence
- LO 6 Prewrite to Brainstorm and Draft a Topic Sentence
- LO 7 Identify the Central Idea and Thesis Statement of a Longer Passage

Stated Main Ideas in Reading and Writing Paragraphs

Have you ever listened to a speaker ramble on and on and wondered what point he or she was trying to make? If you have, then you already understand the value of a **main idea** in the reading/writing process.

A **main idea** connects all the information or details in a passage to form the key point a writer shares about a specific topic.

WHAT'S THE POINT of Stated Main Ideas in Reading and Writing Paragraphs? 

In the exchange of information between writers and readers, a stated main idea is an important tool that supports communication. An effective writer often states the main ideas so the reader can clearly understand the point of all the supporting details.

Photographic Organizer: Stated Main Ideas

Before you study this module, predict why it is important to become an effective reader and writer. The following photographs illustrate some of the reading and writing situations we experience in our everyday, college, and working lives. Write a caption for each photograph that states a reason or benefit of reading and writing in each situation. Then state the point of becoming an effective reader and writer.

Student in classroom

Stated main ideas help a student understand the main point of a lesson in a lecture or in a book.

Boy carrying recycling bin

A stated main idea motivates us to take action in our everyday lives.

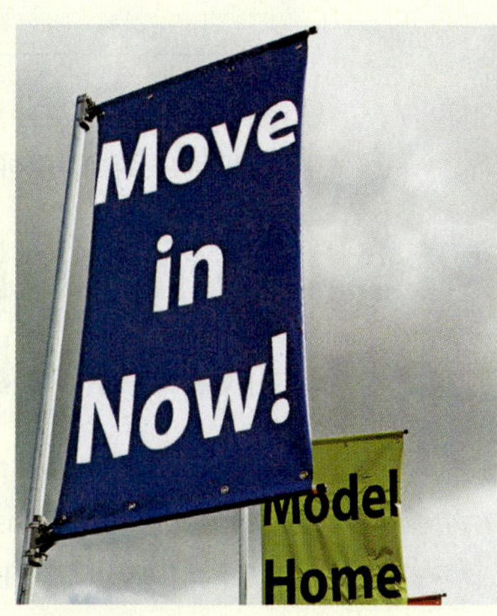

Condo sales signs

Stated main ideas express what a business or service has to offer its customers or clients.

What's the point of stated main ideas in reading and writing paragraphs?

Stated main ideas improve comprehension of lessons in academic life; help us communicate important ideas in everyday life; and improve communication on the job.

What's the Point? One Student's Response

The following paragraph is one student's response to the question "What's the point of stated main ideas in reading and writing paragraphs?"

A stated main idea helps me understand and make a point. In college life, I write the main idea of a lecture or lesson in my notes. "Think recycle!" calls us to take action in everyday life to reduce waste in landfills. In working life, a stated main idea improves communication.

Understanding the purpose and structure of a paragraph helps us to comprehend and compose main ideas. A paragraph uses different levels of information and may have several parts.

L2 Identify the Parts of a Paragraph and Levels of Information

A paragraph contains levels of information and is also made up of several parts. Including a title, a paragraph has four basic parts. Each part uses specific levels of information. The following graphic describes the function of each part of a paragraph and shows the general format of a paragraph.

Title: The title uses key words or a phrase to vividly describe the topic and tone or purpose of your paragraph.

Introduction: An introduction is usually one or more sentences that explain the importance of the topic or give necessary background information about the topic. Your topic sentence states your narrowed topic and your point about the topic.

Body: The body of a paragraph is made up of a series of sentences that offer major details in support of your topic sentence. If needed, provide minor details that support the major details. Link sentences within the paragraph with organizational words such as *first, second, last, trait, type, similarity, difference, cause,* or *effect* so your reader can easily follow your thoughts.

Conclusion: The conclusion restates or sums up your paragraph's main idea in one or more sentences.

A **paragraph** is an essential component of the reading/writing process. A paragraph is a series of closely related sentences that develop and support the writer's point about a narrowed topic. To make a point, a writer organizes levels of information into a logical unit of thought. A reader then identifies the levels of ideas in that paragraph to determine the writer's point.

A **paragraph** is a piece of writing that begins on a new line, is usually indented, and develops a main idea about a topic with appropriate major and minor supporting details.

Four Levels of Information in a Paragraph

The following outline defines the four levels of information that may be in a paragraph and shows a logical flow among the levels within a paragraph.

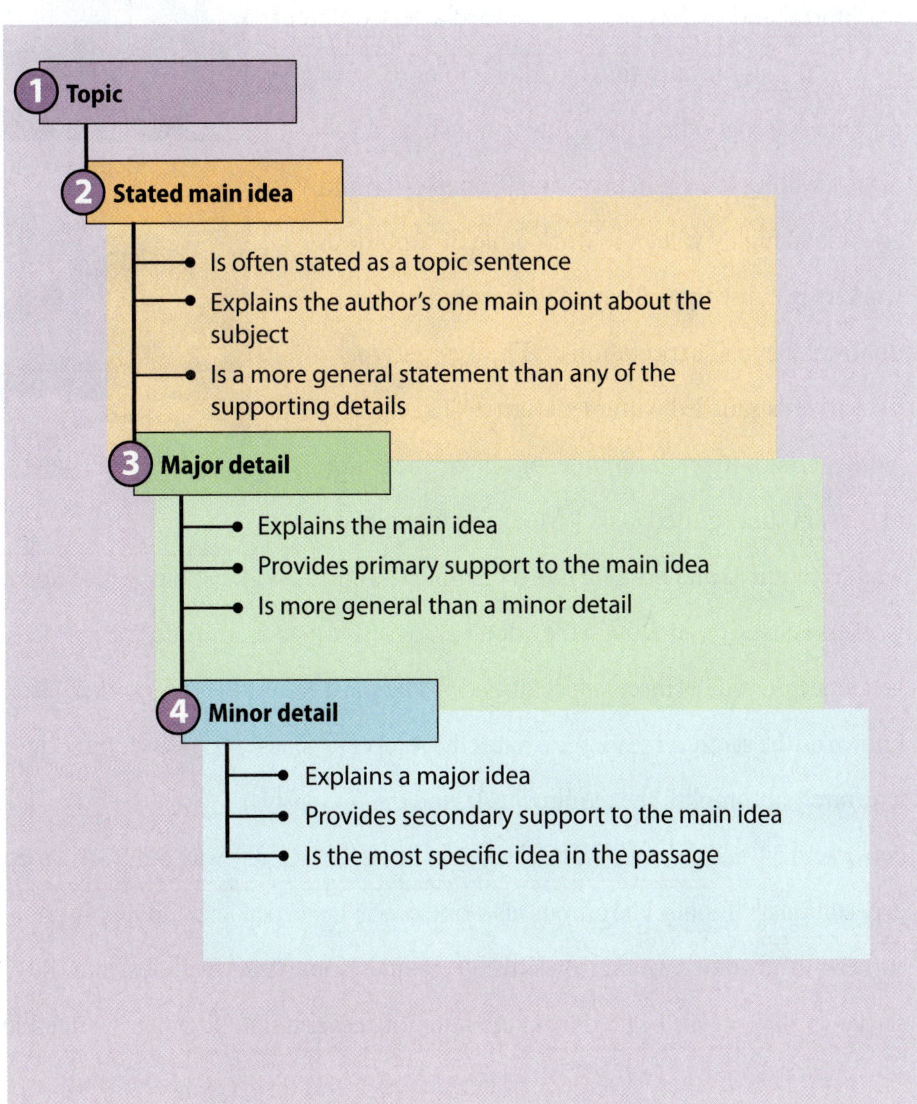

1 Topic
2 Stated main idea
Is often stated as a topic sentence
Explains the author's one main point about the subject
Is a more general statement than any of the supporting details
3 Major detail
Explains the main idea
Provides primary support to the main idea
Is more general than a minor detail
4 Minor detail
Explains a major idea
Provides secondary support to the main idea
Is the most specific idea in the passage

Example

The following student paragraph by Adam Stewart illustrates the use of a title and the three parts of a paragraph. Underline the topic sentence. Draw a box around each of the three parts of the paragraph: Introduction, Body, and Conclusion. Circle organizational words. Finally, provide a title for the paragraph.

Three Types of Workers and Their Futures

Ambitious worker

Mediocre worker

Lazy worker

[1] Although everyone has to work at one point in his or her life and a strong work ethic is looked upon very highly, unfortunately not all workers understand the importance of hard work and a good attitude. [2] Depending upon which category they represent, workers are judged by their coworkers and employers. [3] Three different types of workers make up the workforce, and each type works toward a very different future. [4] First, the ambitious worker comes to work on time, has a good attitude, stays on task, and is always willing to help in any way. [5] Supervisors and coworkers highly value the work ethic of ambitious workers because they always get the job done and do it well beyond expectations. [6] The second type of worker is satisfied with mediocrity. [7] This type of worker comes to work on time, but he or she is not always on the required task. [8] Mediocre workers do what is required and nothing more. [9] Employers and coworkers tolerate mediocre workers because even though they don't always have a good attitude, the job does get done and usually meets expectations. [10] The third type is the lazy worker, also known as the slacker. [11] Everyone hates the slacker. [12] Slackers consistently show up late, rarely accomplish the required task, and continuously try to get the rest of their coworkers off task as well. [13] The slacker, looking for the easy way out, rarely meets expectations. [14] Finally, the ambitious workers will be the leaders and high-wage earners; the mediocre workers will likely remain at some dead-end jobs; and the slackers will probably be fired from job after job, never rethinking their work ethic.

Explanation

Compare your responses to the following student's think-aloud.

For the introduction, I drew a box around sentences 1 through 3. I underlined sentence 3 as the topic sentence because it is the only sentence that includes all three types of workers and their futures. I boxed in sentences 4 through 13 as the body of the paragraph and sentence 14 as the conclusion because it began with Finally. *I circled the organizational words* **first, second type, third type, finally.** *I made up the title "Three Types of Workers and Their Futures." For the title I used the organizational word* Types *and used unbiased words "workers and their future" because I think the writer's word choice created an informative tone and purpose. This activity opened my eyes to the different parts of the paragraph. I also think that each part uses a different level of information, too. For example, the body is made up of major and minor supporting details.*

Practice 1

Identify Parts of a Paragraph

Read the following paragraph. Underline the topic sentence. Circle each of the three parts of the paragraph: Introduction, Body, and Conclusion. Provide a title for the paragraph.

Wildlife and Rocketships

[1] Kennedy Space Center is located on a barrier island on the east coast of Florida, called Merritt Island, about 34 miles long and varying in width from five to 10 miles. [2] The total land and water area covers just over 140,000 acres; however, only 6,000 acres are actually used for space shuttle operations. [3] The Space Center

CONTINUED

PRACTICE 1 *CONTINUED*

also shares a common boundary with Merritt Island's National Wildlife Refuge. [4] The Kennedy Space Center serves as a refuge for several endangered species. [5] For one, the endangered manatee flourishes in the shadows of launch platforms. [6] Just south of launch pad 39A, more than 300 manatees graze protected in a sanctuary in the northern end of Banana River. [7] Manatees are so abundant at the Center that they make up around 30 percent of Florida's total manatee population. [8] Another endangered species at the Center is the beloved sea turtle. [9] Between May and September, thousands of endangered sea turtles come ashore on this barrier island in the dark of night to lay their eggs. [10] With its protected shoreline, Kennedy has one of the most dense turtle populations in the northern hemisphere. [11] Bald eagles also find refuge at the space center. [12] At least five active bald eagle nests exist around the Center. [13] Nests can reach more than six feet in diameter and are usually inhabited from September through May. [14] The eagles usually produce one or two chicks per year. [15] No discussion of wildlife at Kennedy is complete without mentioning alligators! [16] While the interactions between man and alligator are few, the biggest problem was during shuttle landings. [17] Prior to each Kennedy shuttle landing, it was the task of a special crew to clear the runway of all debris, including any alligators that might have been sunning themselves on the runway surface.

[18] Ultimately, the Kennedy Space Center proves wildlife and rocketships can coexist.

Merritt Island's National Wildlife Refuge

Launch platforms

Adapted from *"Alligators and Rocketships."* NASA. http://www.nasa.gov/centers/kennedy/shuttleoperations/alligators/kscovrv.html

Example

Study the following outline based on an article about types of tattoos that was published in the journal *Dermatology Nursing*. In the blanks, identify each piece of information as the topic, main idea, major detail, or minor detail.

Four Types of Tattoos *Topic*

There are four major types of tattoos: traumatic, amateur, professional, and cosmetic. *Main idea*

A. *Traumatic* *Major supporting detail*

1. *Cause: accidental embedding of colored material, which leaves pigment after healing* *Minor supporting detail*
2. *Examples: motorcycle rash, "graphite tattoo" from a puncture injury with a pencil* *Minor supporting detail*

B. *Amateur* *Major supporting detail*

1. *Cause: placed by the person being tattooed or by a friend with little experience* *Minor supporting detail*
2. *Examples: boyfriend's name; gang tattoo* *Minor supporting detail*

C. *Professional* *Major supporting detail*

1. *Cultural* *Minor supporting detail*
   a. *Cause: placed by time-honored method by members of certain cultural groups* *Minor supporting detail*
   b. *Example: Samoan tattoos* *Minor supporting detail*
2. *Modern* *Minor supporting detail*
   a. *Cause: placed by "tattoo gun" by experienced, paid artists* *Minor supporting detail*
   b. *Example: Tattoo parlors* *Minor supporting detail*

D. *Cosmetic* *Major supporting detail*

1. *Cause: placed by a cosmetic specialist as permanent makeup or camouflage* *Minor supporting detail*
2. *Example: eyeliner* *Minor supporting detail*

Gang tattoos

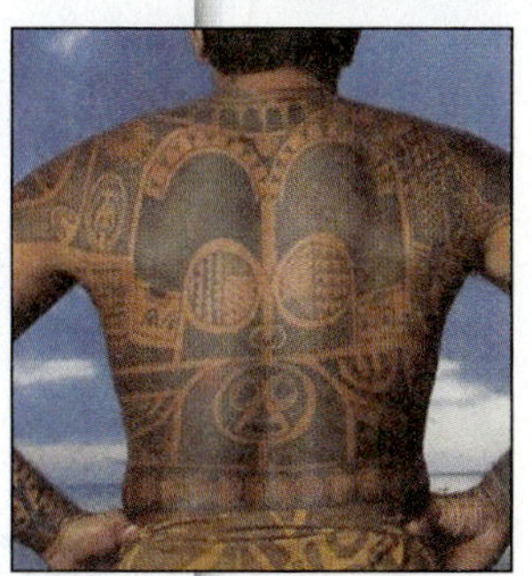

Cultural tattoos

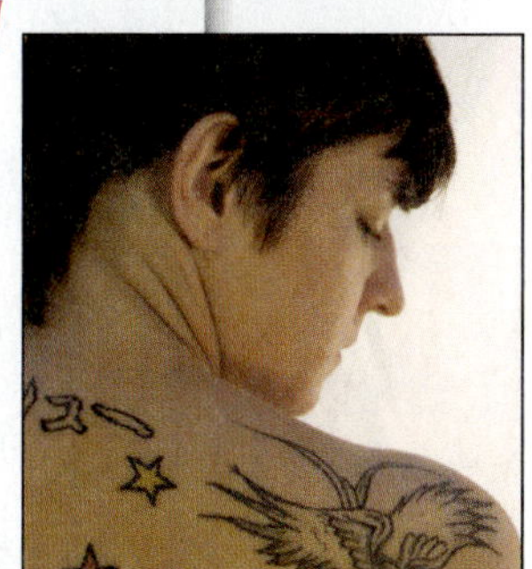

Modern tattoos

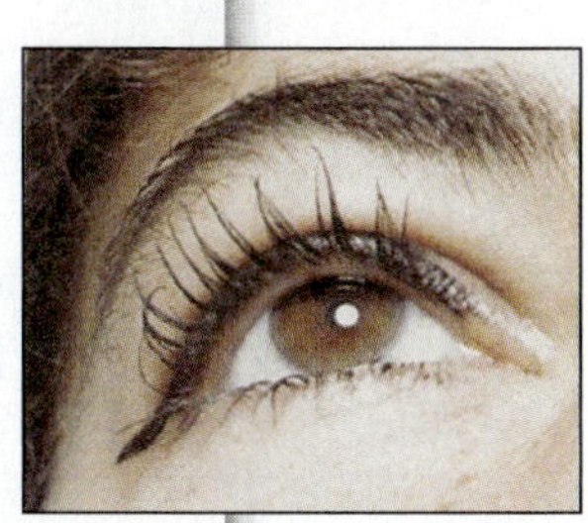

Permanent makeup

Explanation

Compare your responses to the following think-aloud.

This outline helped me see how ideas flow from a narrowed topic to a main idea to supporting details. The outline also clearly showed that a minor detail supports another detail. Based on this outline, I identified four major supporting details. These major details listed four types of tattoos. And each major supporting detail had two minor supporting details that stated causes and gave examples of each major detail. The general topic is four types of tattoos. The main idea stated the four types in one sentence. Then, the letters A, B, C, and D listed each type of tattoo as a major detail. The numbers 1 and 2 listed the minor details that explained the causes for each type of tattoo and gave examples for each. Two minor details "Cultural" and "Modern" needed more explanations, so the letters a and b indicate these additional minor details.

Practice 2

Identify Levels of Information in a Paragraph

Read the paragraph developed from the previous outline. Circle the main idea. Underline the four sentences that state the major supports.

Four Types of Tattoos

[1]There are four major types of tattoos: traumatic, amateur, professional, and cosmetic. [2]The first type, the traumatic tattoo, is caused by the imbedding of dirt or debris beneath the skin, which leaves an area of pigmentation after healing. [3]For example, this commonly occurs in "road rash" after a motorcycle accident or after a puncture injury from a lead pencil, called a "graphite tattoo." [4]The second type, the amateur tattoo, is placed by the person being tattooed or by a friend and often shows little artistry or detail. [5]A boyfriend's or girlfriend's name or a gang symbol is tattooed using a pin and India ink, pen ink, charcoal, or ashes as the pigment. [6]The third type, the professional tattoo, takes two forms: cultural and modern. [7]Cultural tattoos are placed using the time-honored methods of certain cultural ethnicities. [8]For example, the Samoans use tattoos to display the artistry of their particular heritage. [9]Modern tattoos are performed using a "tattoo gun" and are placed by experienced, paid artists. [10]The fourth type, the cosmetic tattoo, is a rapidly growing area of the tattoo industry. [11]Permanent makeup, including eyeliner, lip liner, rouge, and eyebrow

pencil, can be placed by a tattoo specialist. [12]Finally, another aspect of cosmetic tattooing is the camouflaging of an undesired tattoo or other physical flaw.

Adapted from Cronin, Terrence A., Jr. *Dermatology Nursing*. Oct. 2001 v13 i5 p. 380(4).

Identify the Elements of a Main Idea 

The main idea is a key component in a paragraph. In Module 4, you learned the importance of a writer's choice of words about a topic based on the audience, tone, and purpose of a specific reading/writing situation. Remember, tone words reveal the writer's attitude and purpose about a topic to the reader. Thus, a topic is limited or controlled by the writer's tone and purpose. A writer may also choose to limit or control a topic by using a specific **pattern of organization.**

A **pattern of organization** is the logical order of ideas within a paragraph.

Patterns of organization include time order, classification, cause and effect, and comparison and contrast, among others. Writers signal the logical flow of ideas by using words such as *first, second, next, including, finally, reasons, series, traits, groups, causes, effects, results, varieties, similarities, differences,* etc. (You will learn more about patterns of organization and their signal words in Unit 4.)

The following example illustrates the various elements of a topic sentence.

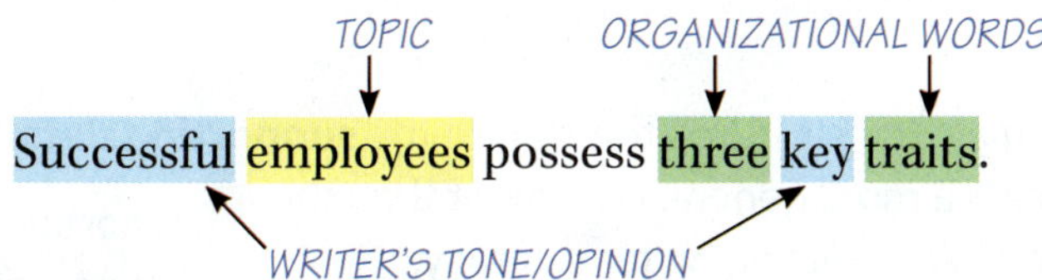

In the example, the topic is *employees*. The writer limits or controls this topic with the tone words *successful* and *key*. These two words reveal the writer's opinion and focus based on *successful* employees and *key* traits. The writer also uses the organizational words *three* and *traits* to limit the topic. These words indicate that the writer will inform the reader about three key traits of successful employees.

Example

Annotate the following topic sentences to identify their elements. Draw a box around the topic. Double underline tone words that reveal the writer's opinion. Then single underline organizational words if any are given.

1. Voting is important for a few key reasons.

2. Bullying results in several negative effects.

3. The best diet includes fresh, healthful foods from a variety of food groups.

Explanation

Compare your responses to the following student's think-aloud.

This example shows that writers choose words carefully to limit a topic. Tone words such as important, key, *or* negative *reveal the writer's opinion to the reader. Organizational words such as* a few, reasons, several, results, *or* effects *signal the logical flow of ideas. These topic sentences tell the reader what ideas to expect in the paragraphs. The following chart shows the words I annotated in each sentence.*

Topic	Tone Words	Organizational Words
1. voting	important, key	a few reasons
2. bullying	negative	results in, several, effects
3. diet	best, fresh, healthful	includes, variety, groups

Another important aspect of the main idea is its relationship to the **supporting details** in the paragraph. The topic sentence is a more general statement than the sentences that explain or support it. An effective writer carefully chooses each detail to reveal or develop his or her tone, purpose, and/or organization for a topic. An effective reader identifies each major supporting detail to find the general statement, the topic sentence, which covers all the details.

Supporting details are the specific ideas that develop, explain, or support the main idea.

A controlling point generates a set of specific supporting details. A well-written topic sentence clarifies the writer's point and enables a reader to predict what details come next.

Example

Study the outline of the following topic sentence and its major supporting details. Cross out the detail that does not support the main idea.

1. Voting is important for few key reasons.
  a. Voting is a right.
  b. Voting is a duty.
  c. Every vote counts.
  d. ~~Politicians are corrupt.~~

Generate three major details for each of the following topic sentences. Be sure that each detail supports the stated controlling point. *Answers may vary.*

2. Bullying has several negative effects.
   a. *Bullying causes anxiety.*
   b. *Bullying causes anger.*
   c. *Bullying causes low self-esteem.*

3. The best diet includes fresh, healthful foods from a variety of food groups.
   a. *lean protein*
   b. *fresh vegetables*
   c. *healthful fat*

Explanation

Compare your responses to the following think-aloud.

1. In this outline, the first three details support the topic sentence by stating important reasons for voting. However, the fourth detail, (d) "Politicians are corrupt," is not a reason to vote. In fact, it's just the opposite. Maybe the writer thinks voting is the way to get rid of corrupt politicians, but the writer hasn't made the connection between this detail and the topic sentence.

2. The supporting details for this topic sentence came easily. Bullying is something almost everyone has experienced during childhood. The negative effects of bullying I would write about are (a) bullying causes anxiety, (b) bullying causes anger, and (c) bullying causes low self-esteem. I could give examples for each of these effects.

3. I have done a lot of research about diets recently because several members of my family are overweight, and we all want to change our ways to stay healthy. The details I would write about include (a) lean protein, (b) fresh vegetables, and (c) healthful fats. I wanted to include fats because many people think a low-fat diet is best, but really our bodies need good fats, so it's an important detail.

The following paragraph from a health textbook illustrates the elements of a topic sentence and the relationship between the topic sentence and its supporting details.

The Cool-Down Period

[1]The cool-down period is an important part of an exercise workout for several reasons. [2]The cool-down involves reducing the intensity of exercise to allow the body to recover from the workout. [3]During vigorous exercise such as jogging, a lot of blood is pumped to the legs, and there may not be enough to supply the heart and brain; failure to cool down properly may result in dizziness, fainting, and, in rare instances, a heart attack. [4]By gradually reducing the level of physical activity, blood flow is directed back to the heart and brain.

—Adapted from Pruitt, B. E.., and Stein, Jane J., *Health Styles*, 2nd ed., p. 169.

To better understand the traits of a main idea, compare a paragraph to a well-planned house of ideas. In the example paragraph "The Cool-Down Period," the *topic* or general topic matter is the roof. The roof covers all the rooms of the house. The *main idea* is the frame of the house, and the supporting details are the different rooms. The following diagram shows the relationship of the ideas.

Topic: The Cool-Down Period

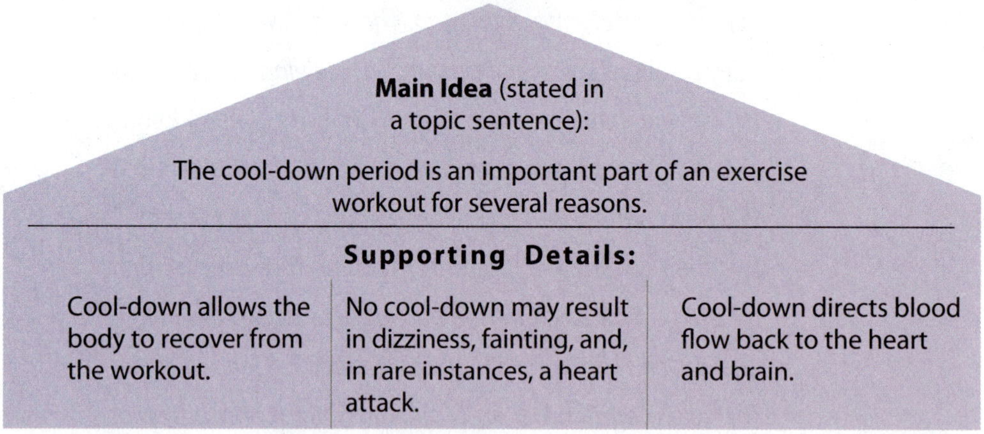

Main Idea (stated in a topic sentence):

The cool-down period is an important part of an exercise workout for several reasons.

Supporting Details:

Cool-down allows the body to recover from the workout.	No cool-down may result in dizziness, fainting, and, in rare instances, a heart attack.	Cool-down directs blood flow back to the heart and brain.

Each of the supporting details explains why the cool-down period is an important part of an exercise workout. Now that you have an overview of a paragraph and the traits of a main idea, you are better able to comprehend and compose main ideas. The following sections will guide you in using the reading/writing strategy to understand the main idea of a paragraph and to write a topic sentence that states a main idea of a paragraph you compose.

L4 Before Reading, Skim and Annotate to Identify the Topic of a Paragraph

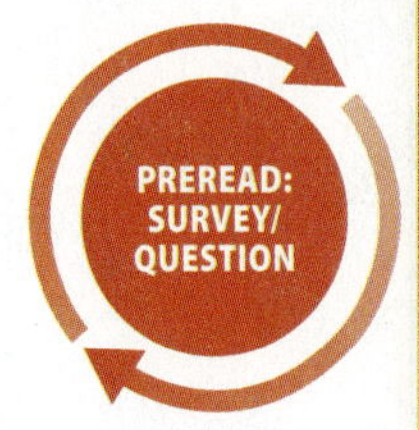

When you ask the question "Who or what is the paragraph about?" you must be sure that your answer is neither too general nor too specific. No single paragraph can discuss all the specific ideas linked to a general idea. Thus, a writer narrows the general topic so it needs only a specific set of ideas to support it. For example, the very general topic *music* can be narrowed to *hip-hop music*. And the specific details related to hip-hop music might include the different rappers, ranging from Tupac Shakur to Nicki Minaj to Jay Z. In fact, a piece of writing dealing with the very general topic *music* would include a very different set of specific ideas than the narrower topic of *hip-hop music*. Keep in mind, too, that a writer uses tone and organizational words to limit or narrow a topic.

Often a writer shows a reader the relationship between the topic and the specific details by repeating or rephrasing the narrowed topic throughout the paragraph to introduce new pieces of information about the topic. Effective readers skim a paragraph to identify the topic before reading the passage. Skimming for the topic gives a reader a preview of the writer's use of the various levels of information and parts of a paragraph.

Example

Skim the following paragraph. Circle the topic as it recurs throughout the paragraph. Answer the question that follows.

A Sincere Apology

[1]A sincere apology is a powerful human experience. [2]A sincere apology is a peace offering that honors the importance of the wronged one's feelings. [3]It defuses anger and fosters healing. [4]A genuine apology offers closure to a painful past and openness to a future built on forgiveness and empathy. [5]A genuine "I'm sorry" accepts the blame for wrongdoing and the painful results. [6]Consider the following example: as a child, Debra suffered greatly because of her abusive, alcoholic father. [7]At the age of 17, she left her father's house, and they had no contact for many years. [8]On her thirty-fifth birthday, Debra received a letter from her father, offering her a long, emotional apology. [9]Their relationship began healing that day. [10]To be brave and wise enough to apologize sincerely is to accept a lesson from life and a unique peace based on self-respect.

Which of the following best states the topic?

a. apologizing

b. a sincere apology

c. the importance of the wronged one's feelings

Explanation

Compare your responses to the following student's think-aloud.

Apologizing (a) is too general, for it could cover insincere apologies, how to apologize, or what to do if someone will not accept an apology. "The importance of the wronged one's feelings" (c) is too narrow. This idea seems more like a supporting detail. It's just one of the reasons an apology is so powerful. The topic of this paragraph is "a sincere apology" (b). I circled the following phrases: "sincere apology" (sentences 1 and 2), "genuine apology" (sentence 4), "genuine 'I'm sorry'" (sentence 5), and "apologize sincerely" (sentence 10). The writer repeated sincere three times and used the synonym genuine two times. The title of the paragraph also stated the topic. I am going to remember to repeat my topic in my details and use a title to state the topic of my own paragraphs.

Practice 3

Identify the Topic

Skim each of the following paragraphs and circle the topic as it recurs throughout the paragraph. Then identify the idea that correctly states the topic. (*Hint*: One idea is too general to be the topic; another idea is too specific.)

1.

[1]Many myths exist about the causes of acne. [2]Chocolate and greasy foods are often blamed, but foods seem to have little effect on the development and course of acne in most people. [3]Another common myth is that dirty skin causes acne; however, blackheads and other acne lesions are not caused by dirt. [4]Finally, stress does not cause acne.

Adapted from National Institute of Arthritis and Musculoskeletal and Skin Diseases, "Questions and Answers about Acne."

a. dirty skin

b. causes of acne

c. myths about what causes acne

2.

[1]Playing rigorous sports in the heat can lead to several types of heat injuries. [2]The first type of heat-related illness is dehydration, which is a lack of body fluids. [3]The second type is heat exhaustion. [4]Heat exhaustion has numerous effects, including nausea, dizziness, weakness, headache, pale and moist skin, heavy perspiration, normal or low body temperature, weak pulse, dilated pupils, disorientation, and fainting spells. [5]A third type of heat injury is heat stroke. [6]Heat stroke can lead to headaches, dizziness, confusion, and hot dry skin, possibly leading to vascular collapse, coma, and death. [7]Each of these heat injuries can be prevented.

Adapted from National Institute of Arthritis and Musculoskeletal and Skin Diseases, "Childhood Sports Injuries and Their Prevention."

a. types of heat injuries
b. injuries
c. heatstroke

MySkillsLab™

You can complete additional exercises for this section in *The Effective Reader/Writer* book-specific module in MySkillsLab.

During Reading, Question and Annotate to Identify the Topic Sentence LO5

To identify the topic sentence of a paragraph, ask the following questions:

- What is the topic of the paragraph?
- What is the writer's controlling point about the topic?
  - What tone words does the writer use about the topic?
  - What organizational words does the writer use to limit the topic?
- Which sentence includes the topic and the writer's controlling point about the topic?
- Does this sentence cover all the details in the paragraph?

As you skim a paragraph to identify its topic and topic sentence, annotate the paragraph to highlight the writer's controlling point. Circle the topic. Underline tone and organizational words that limit the topic. Look for the one sentence that states both the topic and the controlling point.

Example

The following group of ideas presents a main idea and its supporting details from an article posted on a popular website that offers health information. Circle the topic and underline words that signal the writer's controlling point. Then answer the questions.

a. Chronic Fatigue Syndrome (CFS) is marked by extreme fatigue that has lasted at least six months; is not the result of ongoing effort; is not substantially relieved by rest; and causes a substantial drop in daily activities.
b. Despite an intensive, nearly 20-year search, the cause of CFS remains unknown.
c. Much of the ongoing research into a cause has centered on the roles that the immune, endocrine, and nervous systems may play in CFS.
d. CFS is not caused by depression, although the two illnesses often coexist.

United States Department of Health and Human Services. "Risk Factors for CFS." Centers for Disease Control and Prevention. 7 June 2010. http://www.cdc.gov/cfs/cfsbasicfacts.htm#riskfactors.

1. Which of the following best states the topic?

a. symptoms of CFS
b. causes of CFS
c. definition of CFS

2. Which sentence is the stated main idea? b

Explanations

Compare your responses to the following.

1. *Item (b) "causes of CFS" is the best statement of the topic. Three of the four sentences refer to causes of CFS. The topic is stated with just a few words—a phrase, not a complete sentence.*
2. *The main idea is best stated by item (b) "Despite an intensive, nearly 20-year search, the cause of CFS remains unknown." This sentence is the only statement that is broad enough to be relevant to all the other ideas. For example, item (a) introduces the general topic CFS by stating a definition of CFS based on its major symptoms. Items (c) and (d) are supporting details that offer two views about the causes of CFS.*

Practice 4

Identify the Topic Sentence

Read the following paragraph. Circle the topic and underline the writer's controlling point. Then, answer the questions.

THE DANGERS OF DRINKING TOO MANY SODAS

[1]According to *Beverage Digest*, in 2012, the U.S. carbonated soft drink market totaled 9.17 billion cases. [2]Not surprisingly, the U.S. consumes the most sodas per person of any place in the world. [3]The American love for sodas alarms many health experts. [4]Drinking too many sodas can cause a wide range of health concerns. [5]First, drinking too many sodas is linked to obesity. [6]According to the Center for Science in the Public Interest, sodas are the single biggest source of calories in the American diet. [7]An average serving of 12 ounces of a soda contains 155 calories, 35 to 38 milligrams of caffeine, and around 40 grams of sugar. [8]Sodas provide about 7 percent of calories in most adult diets. [9]And teenagers get 15 percent of their total calories from sodas. [10]No wonder the number of obese people in America is growing. [11]Second, drinking too many sodas is harmful to bones. [12]Alarmingly, animal studies reveal that phosphorus, a common ingredient in soda, can deplete bones of calcium. [13]And two recent human studies suggest that girls who drink more soda are more prone to broken bones. [14]This finding supports the fear that drinking too many sodas may lead to osteoporosis later in life. [15]Finally, according to the Academy for General Dentistry, the acids in sodas are harmful to teeth. [16]Exposing teeth to sodas, even for a short period of time, causes dental erosion. [17]And long-term exposure can lead to significant enamel loss.

1. What is the topic of the paragraph?

   health risks of drinking too many sodas

2. Which sentence is the topic sentence that states the main idea? *4*

MySkillsLab™

You can complete additional exercises for this section in *The Effective Reader/Writer* book-specific module in MySkillsLab.

L6 Prewrite to Brainstorm and Draft a Topic Sentence

During the prewriting phase of the reading/writing strategy, a writer brainstorms ideas to discover a controlling point that will narrow the topic. Identifying your purpose, tone/opinion, or the best way to organize ideas helps you state your main idea in a complete sentence before you write your first draft.

Prewrite to Narrow the Topic

Use the following suggestions to guide your thinking as you focus a general topic into a narrowed topic.

- **Narrow the topic based on your tone or purpose.** An opinion is expressed by using tone words such as *amazing, alarming, beautiful, best, likely, should*, or any other word that states personal values, judgments, or interpretations (see Module 4). Your purpose may be *to inform, entertain, or argue* (see Module 1, p. 16). Use questions, freewriting, mapping, listing, or another brainstorming technique to discover your purpose and opinion about a topic.

Example:	General Topic	Tone/Purpose	Narrowed Topic
	Seatbelts	Negative opinion	Seatbelts can be dangerous.
		Positive opinion	Seatbelts save lives.
		Argumentative purpose	Seatbelt laws should be abolished.

- **Narrow the topic based on a *pattern of organization*.** A writer may use a pattern of organization to narrow a topic and generate details. Patterns of organization are also used to develop, organize, and express a main idea, major details, and minor details in a logical order. You will learn more about patterns of organization in Unit 4. The following list provides a few examples of patterns of organization and signal words. Use this list to narrow your topic and draft your topic sentences.

Pattern of Organization	Signal Words
Space Order	*above, below, beside, next to, underneath*
Time Order	*first, now, then, before, after, next, later*
Example	*for example, exemplify, includes, such as*
Classification	*types, kinds, levels*
Compare/Contrast	*similar, likewise, just as / however, in contrast*
Cause/Effect	*source, origin / results, impact*

Example:	General Topic	Pattern of Organization	Narrowed Topic
	Graffiti	Cause/effect	The effects of graffiti
		Classification	The types of graffiti

- **Combine the topic, opinion, and pattern of organization to generate a narrowed topic.**

Example:	General Topic	Narrowed Topic
	Seatbelts	Three reasons seatbelts can be dangerous
		Proper use of seatbelts saves lives
	Graffiti	The negative effects of graffiti
		Graffiti: A type of artistic expression

Example

Combine the topic with an opinion, purpose, and pattern of organization signal words to narrow the topic. *Answers may vary*

1. GENERAL TOPIC: *Health Issue: Weightlifting*

   OPINION: *positive* SIGNAL WORD: *effects*

   PURPOSE: *to argue*

   NARROWED TOPIC: *Benefits of Weightlifting*

2. GENERAL TOPIC: *A Public Figure: Rhianna*

   OPINION: *admirable* SIGNAL WORD: *traits*

   PURPOSE: *to entertain*

   NARROWED TOPIC: *The Admirable Traits of Rhianna*

3. GENERAL TOPIC: *Business: Saving Money*

   OPINION: *smart* SIGNAL WORD: *steps to*

   PURPOSE: *to inform*

   NARROWED TOPIC: *Smart Steps to Saving Money*

Explanation

Compare your responses to the following student's think-aloud.

Basically, I can narrow a topic in three ways. I use my opinion to narrow the topic. I can narrow a topic based on organization. Or I can use opinion and organization to narrow a topic. For example, I don't agree with the use of the word positive for the effects of weightlifting. Based on personal injuries, I would rather focus on the dangers of weightlifting. And my purpose would shift from "to inform" to "to argue." I want to convince others to focus on safety while lifting. Here are my answers and my thoughts about my answers.

1. *To argue, "Benefits of Weightlifting." The "benefits of weightlifting" uses fewer words but says the same thing as "the positive effects of weightlifting."*

CONTINUED

2. *To entertain, "The Admirable Traits of Rhianna." This topic seems like something young girls or people interested in entertainment would enjoy. I almost chose the purpose "to inform," but most people attracted to this topic are looking for entertainment.*
3. *To inform, "Smart Steps to Saving Money." I almost chose "to argue," but I think everyone wants to save money, and they don't need much convincing.*

Practice 5

Find and Narrow a Topic

Many writers respond to ideas about which they have read. They use their reading to find interesting topics about which to write. Choose two of the paragraphs you have already read in this module. Reread each paragraph. Then prewrite your response to each paragraph. Identify a topic, your own opinion about the topic, a purpose to write, and a pattern of organization you might use to develop supporting details. *Answers may vary.*

1. PARAGRAPH TITLE:

   GENERAL TOPIC:

   OPINION: SIGNAL WORD:

   PURPOSE:

   NARROWED TOPIC:

2. PARAGRAPH TITLE:

   GENERAL TOPIC:

   OPINION: SIGNAL WORD:

   PURPOSE:

   NARROWED TOPIC:

MySkillsLab™

You can complete additional exercises for this section in *The Effective Reader/Writer* book-specific module in MySkillsLab.

Draft the Topic Sentence

Once you have focused a topic into a narrowed topic with your opinion and a pattern of organization, you are ready to write a complete sentence to state the main idea. Each of the following topic sentences offers a *topic* and a controlling point: a *topic* narrowed by the writer's *tone* or *opinion* and a suggested *pattern of organization*.

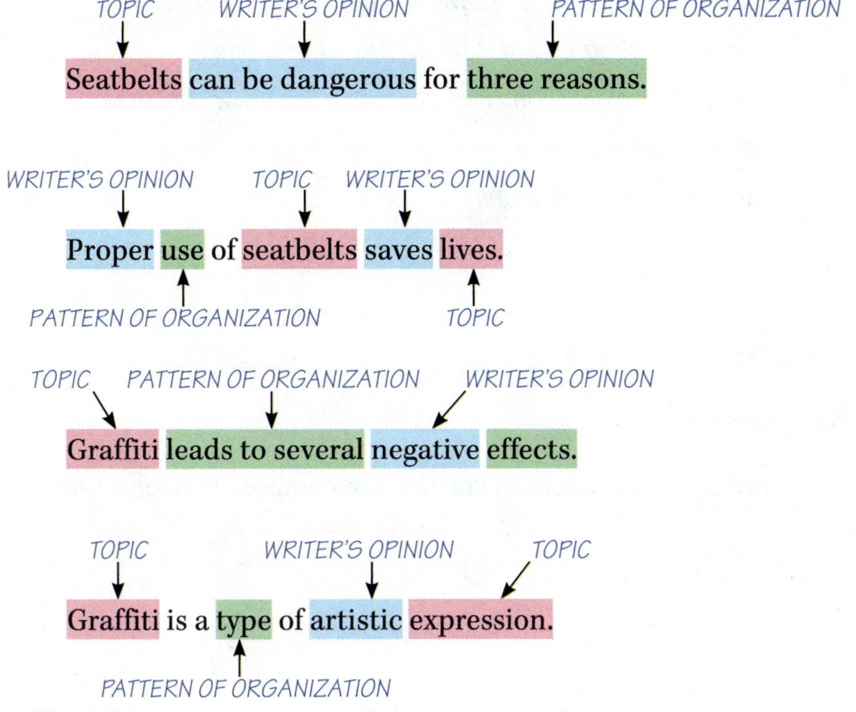

Example

Write topic sentences for each of the following narrowed topics. *Answers may vary.*

1. Narrowed Topic: Benefits of weightlifting

   TOPIC SENTENCE: *Weightlifting has several benefits.*

2. Narrowed Topic: The admirable traits of Rhianna

   TOPIC SENTENCE: *Rhianna illustrates a range of artistic abilities.*

3. Narrowed Topic: Smart steps to saving money

   TOPIC SENTENCE: *Follow three smart steps to save money.*

Explanation

Compare your responses to the following student's think-aloud.

It really helped me to have already thought about my opinion and purpose before writing these topic sentences. I was able to choose words that stated my opinion and purpose. **1.** *Weightlifting has several benefits.* **2.** *Rhianna illustrates a range of artistic abilities.* **3.** *Follow three smart steps to save money.*

Practice 6

Draft a Topic Sentence

Use the topics you identified and narrowed in Practice 5 to compose two topic sentences.

1. TOPIC SENTENCE: *Answers may vary.* ______________________________

____

2. TOPIC SENTENCE: ______________________________

____

MySkillsLab™

You can complete additional exercises for this section in *The Effective Reader/Writer* book-specific module in MySkillsLab.

L7 Identify the Central Idea and Thesis Statement of a Longer Passage

The **central idea** is the main idea of a passage made up of two or more paragraphs.

The **thesis statement** is a sentence that states the topic and the writer's controlling point about the topic for a passage of two or more paragraphs.

Just as a single paragraph has a main idea, longer passages made up of two or more paragraphs also have a main idea. You encounter these longer passages in articles, essays, and textbooks. In longer passages, the main idea is called the **central idea**. Often the writer will state the central idea in a single sentence called the **thesis statement.**

You find the central idea of longer passages the same way you locate the main idea or topic sentence of a paragraph. The thesis statement is the one sentence that is general enough to include all the ideas in the passage.

Example

Read the following passage from a college communications textbook, and identify the thesis statement, which states the central idea.

SUPPORTIVE RESPONSES

[1] Listening stops when you feel threatened. [2] No one likes to be proven wrong in front of others, criticized, or ignored. [3] Defensive individuals are usually more concerned with protecting their self-concept and saving face than promoting communication. [4] The more defensive a person becomes, the less able he is to perceive his partner's motives, values, and emotions.

[5] Your goal is to create situations that foster open communication in a supportive climate. [6] Supportive responses are based on several behaviors that encourage problem solving and build healthy relationships. [7] First, be aware of the use of "I" and "you." [8] Instead of saying, "You're never around when I need you," a supportive response says, "I felt frustrated and needed your help." [9] Second, focus on solving problems instead of placing blame. [10] Third, show empathy instead of indifference. [11] And finally, be open-minded to the views of others instead of asserting your own view as the only or correct one.

Adapted from Brownell, Judi, *Listening: Attitudes, Principles, and Skills*, p. 284.

Thesis statement: 6

Explanation

Compare your responses to the following student's think-aloud.

The first four sentences introduce the need to know about the topic "supportive responses." These sentences are designed to hook the reader's interest in the topic. Sentence 5 is a link between the need to know and the writer's central idea, which is stated in the next sentence. Sentence 6 is the central idea of the passage. It is the only sentence general enough to include most of the details in the passage. Sentence 6 includes the topic "supportive responses" and the writer's controlling point about the topic; they are "behaviors that encourage problem solving and build healthy relationships." Sentences 7 through 11 are supporting details that list the supportive responses.

Practice 7

Identify the Central Idea and Thesis Statement

Read the following passage from a college writing handbook and identify the thesis statement, which states the central idea.

CREATIVE THINKING: SHIFTING ATTENTION

[1] Sometimes in writing you come to a dead end or run out of ideas because you focus too sharply on a single aspect of your topic. [2] As you think about what you are going to write, thoughtfully shifting attention away from the chief element of your topic can lead you to additional ideas. [3] For example, in writing a paper about the effects of excessive drinking, you may be concentrating on an individual drinker. [4] Shifting your focus to the effects of alcohol on the drinker's family and friends will stimulate further thought and additional ideas. [5] So will a different kind of shift, one to a consideration of the broader social effects of alcoholism. [6] You might find yourself refocusing your paper; you may even revise your initial purpose, point, and emphasis.

[7] The following example shows how a shift of attention can lead to the solution of a problem.

[8] As a man is driving home from work, his car comes to a halt. [9] Lifting up the hood, he notices that he has a broken fan belt. [10] His solution? [11] He takes off his necktie and ties it tightly in the fan belt position. [12] He drives a quarter of a mile to the nearest service station and replaces his fan belt. [13] With the money he saved on a towing charge, he buys a new tie.

Adapted from DiYanni, Robert, and Hoy, Pat C., *The Scribner Handbook for Writers*, 3rd ed., pp. 59–60.

1. Thesis statement: 2

Reading and Writing Assignments

MySkillsLab™
Complete these assignments in MySkillsLab.

Considering Audience and Purpose

Study the sequence of photographs about the stated main idea at the beginning of this module.

Assume the student in a classroom is a peer of yours in this course. He has missed class due to an illness and has asked you what he has missed. Write a paragraph that explains one or more key skills or concepts you learned in this module.

Reading and Writing for Everyday Life

Assume you are the parent or friend of a girl who is being bullied at the local middle school. You read the following short article on the government website *stopbullying.gov*. How could this information be of help to a person who is being bullied? Write an email to the girl being bullied using the main idea from the article to encourage her. Give her advice about how to respond.

Kids Who are Bullied

Kids who are bullied can feel like they are different, powerless, unpopular, or alone. Kids who are bullied have a hard time standing up for themselves. They think the kid who bullies them is more powerful than they are. Bullying can make them feel sad, lonely, nervous, or sick. Bullying can make kids have problems at school or bully other kids.

Kids Who Bully Others

Kids bully others for many reasons. They may want to copy their friends, think bullying will help them fit in, or think they are better than the kid they are bullying.

What to Do If You're Bullied

There are things you can do if you are being bullied:

- Look at the kid bullying you and tell him or her to stop in a calm, clear voice. You can also try to laugh it off. This works best if joking is easy for you. It could catch the kid bullying you off guard.
- If speaking up seems too hard or not safe, walk away and stay away. Don't fight back. Find an adult to stop the bullying on the spot.

There are things you can do to stay safe in the future, too.

- Talk to an adult you trust. Don't keep your feelings inside. Telling someone can help you feel less alone. They can help you make a plan to stop the bullying.
- Stay away from places where bullying happens.
- Stay near adults and other kids. Most bullying happens when adults aren't around.

Source: United States Department of Human Health and Services. Stopbullying.gov. 20 Nov. 2012. <http://www.stopbullying.gov/kids/what-you-can-do/index.html>.

Reading and Writing for College Life

Assume you are taking a college sociology class. Your professor has assigned "Chapter 2—Culture" in your textbook as the basis of this week's reading and writing assignments. In your survey of the chapter, you read the following paragraph in the chapter's Summary and Review section. To call up your prior knowledge, write a paragraph that restates the key points in your own words and gives examples from everyday life, college life, or working life.

WHAT IS CULTURE?

All human groups possess culture—language, beliefs, values, norms and material objects that are passed from one generation to the next. Material culture consists of objects (art, buildings, clothing, weapons, tools). Nonmaterial (or symbolic) culture is a group's way of thinking and its patterns of behavior. Ideal culture is a group's ideal values, norms, and goals. Real culture is people's actual behavior, which often falls short of their cultural ideals.

Henslin, James M., *Essentials for Sociology: A Down-to-Earth Approach*, 9th ed., p. 56.

Reading and Writing for Working Life

Assume you are the supervisor of a department of workers employed in the local office of a regional company. You have recently received the following employee complaint about working conditions. Read the letter and write a response that explains your solution to the problem.

Dear Ms. Cain,

This letter is to request action to repair the air conditioning units in our department. It has been at least three months since the units quit working properly, and there has been no action to fix them, despite our repeated verbal complaints about the units. Employees are inconvenienced due to the poor working conditions resulting from stale, uncirculated, hot air. It should be a priority for this company to think about the effects of working without air conditioning in this sweltering heat. Certainly, the company doesn't want productivity reduced due to the lack of such a simple repair.

I anticipate that the repairs will proceed without delay, but I'm prepared to send a letter to the regional office after two weeks if suitable action has not been taken. The employees of this company enjoy their work and appreciate everything that management does to meet their needs. Thank you in advance.

Sincerely,

Dan Lyons

Local Union Representative

Workshop: Compose a Paragraph

Choose a passage to read and respond to in writing. You may select a passage in an example, practice, or writing assignment within this module. Or you may select a passage of your own choosing. Use the following guide to comprehend and respond to the passage. Apply what you have learned about stated main ideas to your reading/writing strategy.

Preread: Survey and Question

Prereading/Writing Questions based on text features (vocabulary):

____

____

____

____

____

Standard prereading/writing questions:

What is the passage about?

____

How is the material organized?

____

What do I already know about this topic? (What is my prior knowledge about the vocabulary?)

____

What is my purpose for reading/writing?

____

What is the writer's purpose and tone?

____

What main ideas or details may I want to address or include in my written response?

____

____

____

Read and Annotate

As you read, annotate key ideas, particularly those details that answer your prereading questions.

Recite, Review, and Brainstorm

Recite the information. Summarize the most important parts. Answer your prereading questions.

Rephrase ideas into your own words. Record changes in your opinions based on the new information. **Review** the information. **Brainstorm** ideas for your written response to the passage. **Freewrite** a response to what you have read. **Map** the relationship among ideas you have annotated in the text. **Outline** or list key ideas and details in blocks of thought.

Write a Draft of Your Response

Using the ideas you generated by brainstorming, compose a draft of your response. Use your own paper.

Revise Your Draft

Once you have created a draft of your paragraph, read the draft and answer the questions in the "Questions for Revising a Paragraph" box that follows. Indicate your answers by annotating your paper. If you answer "yes" to a question, underline, check, or circle examples. If you answer "no" to a question, write additional details in the margins and draw lines to indicate their placement. Revise your paragraph based on your reflection. (*Hint*: Experienced writers create several drafts as they focus on one or two questions per draft.)

Step by Step: Questions for Revising a Paragraph

- ☐ Have I stated or implied a focused main idea?
- ☐ Have I made my purpose clear?
- ☐ Is my tone appropriate for my audience and purpose?
- ☐ Is the logical order of the ideas clear? Have I used organizational words to guide my reader, such as *first, second, next*, etc.?
- ☐ Have I made my point with adequate details?
- ☐ Do all the details support my point?
- ☐ What impact will my paragraph make on my reader?

Proofread Your Draft

Once you have made any revisions to your paragraph that may be needed, proofread your paragraph to eliminate careless errors. Work with a classmate to give and receive feedback about your paragraphs.

Review Test

MySkillsLab™
Complete this Exercise on myskillslab.com

Score (number correct) ______ x 25 = ______%

Read the following passage from a college anatomy and physiology textbook. Answer the questions that follow.

1130L/10.2 GE/505 words

SKIN CANCER

[1]Numerous types of neoplasms (tumors) arise in the skin. [2]Most skin neoplasms are benign and do not spread (metastasize) to other body areas. [3](A wart caused by a virus is one such example.) [4]However, some skin neoplasms are malignant, or cancerous, and they tend to invade other body areas. [5]Indeed, skin cancer is the single most common type of cancer in humans. [6]One in five Americans now develops skin cancer at some point in his or her life. [7]The most important risk factor is overexposure to ultraviolet radiation in sunlight. [8]Frequent irritation of the skin by infections, chemicals, or physical trauma also seems to be a predisposing factor. **Basal Cell Carcinoma** [9]Basal cell carcinoma (kar'/sĭno'/mah) is the least malignant and most common skin cancer. [10]Cells of the stratum basale, altered so that they cannot form keratin, no longer honor the boundary between epidermis and dermis. [11]They proliferate, invading the dermis and subcutaneous tissue. [12]The cancer lesions occur most often on sun exposed areas of the face and appear as shiny, dome-shaped nodules that later develop a central ulcer with a "pearly" beaded edge. [13]Basal cell carcinoma is relatively slow-growing, and metastasis seldom occurs before it is noticed. [14]Full cure is the rule in 99 percent of cases in which the lesion is removed surgically.

Squamous Cell Carcinoma [15]Squamous cell carcinoma arises from the cells of the stratum spinosum. [16]The lesion appears as a scaly, reddened papule (small, rounded elevation) that gradually forms a shallow ulcer with a firm, raised border. [17]This variety of skin cancer appears most often on the scalp, ears, dorsum of the hands, and lower lip. [18]It grows rapidly and metastasizes to adjacent lymph nodes if not removed. [19]This epidermal cancer is also believed to be sun-induced. [20]If it is caught early and removed surgically or by radiation therapy, the chance of complete cure is good.

Malignant Melanoma [21]Malignant melanoma (mel"ah-no'mah) is a cancer of melanocytes. [22]It accounts for only about 5 percent of skin cancers, but its incidence is increasing rapidly and it is often deadly. [23]Melanoma can begin wherever there is pigment; most such cancers appear spontaneously, but some develop from pigmented moles. [24]It arises from accumulated DNA damage in a skin cell and usually appears as a spreading brown to black patch that metastasizes rapidly to surrounding lymph and blood vessels. [25]The chance for survival is about 50 percent, and early detection helps. [26]The American Cancer Society

CONTINUED

suggests that people who sunbathe frequently or attend tanning parlors examine their skin periodically for new moles or pigmented spots and apply the **ABCD rule** for recognizing melanoma:

A. Asymmetry. [27]The two sides of the pigmented spot or mole do not match.

B. Border irregularity. [28]The borders of the lesion are not smooth but exhibit indentations.

C. Color. [29]The pigmented spot contains areas of different colors (blacks, browns, tans, and sometimes blues and reds).

D. Diameter. [30]The spot is larger than 6 millimeters (mm) in diameter (the size of a pencil eraser).

[31]Some experts have found that adding an **E**, for elevation above the skin surface, improves diagnosis. [32]The usual therapy for malignant melanoma is wide surgical excision along with immunotherapy.

Marieb, Elaine N., *Essentials of Human Anatomy & Physiology*, 9th ed., pp. 125–126.

1. What is the topic of the passage?

a. cancer
b. causes of skin cancer
c. skin cancer
d. three types of skin cancer

2. Which sentence states the main idea of paragraph 2 (sentences 9–14)?

a. sentence 9
b. sentence 10
c. sentence 12
d. sentence 14

3. Sentence 20 states a

a. main idea.
b. supporting detail.

4. Which sentence states the central idea of the passage?

a. sentence 1
b. sentence 4
c. sentence 5
d. sentence 26

What Do You Think?

According to the passage, what is the most important risk factor that causes skin cancer? What are some of the other factors? What steps should be taken to avoid the risks of developing skin cancer? Assume you are involved in a service learning project for a college health class. Your class has agreed to speak to youth groups at local community centers and churches. Your goal is to educate youth about the risks of developing skin cancer and the steps they can take to protect themselves. Write a draft of the speech you will give. In addition, create a PowerPoint® presentation to make your points vivid and clear. Consider working with a peer or small group of classmates.

Academic Learning Log: Module Review

Summary of Key Concepts of Stated Main Ideas in Reading and Writing Paragraphs

Assess your comprehension of stated main ideas.

LO1 LO2 LO3

1. A paragraph is *a piece of writing that begins on a new line, is usually indented, and develops a main idea about a topic with appropriate major and minor supporting details*.

2. The four levels of information in a paragraph are the *topic*, *main idea*, *major details*, and *minor details*.

3. The four parts of a paragraph are the *title*, an *introduction*, the *body*, and a *conclusion*.

LO1 LO2 LO3 LO4 LO5 LO6

4. The main idea is *the writer's controlling point about a topic*.

5. A topic sentence states *the writer's main idea or controlling point in one complete sentence*.

6. Supporting details are *the specific ideas that develop, explain, or support the main idea*.

LO1 LO7

7. A central idea is the *main idea of a passage made up of two or more paragraphs*. The thesis statement is a sentence that *states the central point of a longer passage*.

L4 L5 L6

8. Before reading, *skim* and *annotate* to identify the *topic* of a paragraph.

9. During reading, *question* and *annotate* to identify the *topic sentence*.

10. Prewrite to *brainstorm* and draft a topic sentence.

11. Narrow a topic based on tone, *purpose*, and/or a pattern of organization.

Test Your Comprehension of Stated Main Ideas in Reading and Writing Paragraphs

Respond to the following questions and prompts. *Answers may vary.*

L1 L2 L3 L4 L5 L6

Use your own words to describe how you will use the reading/writing strategy to read and write paragraphs.

First, I will quickly look over the entire paragraph and underline the topic as it appears throughout the paragraph. As I read, I will underline the answers to the following questions: What is the writer's attitude about the topic? What pattern of organization does the writer use? Which sentence best states the writer's attitude and organization? Then, to write a paragraph, I will prewrite by writing down my attitude about a topic. I will also jot down ideas about causes, effects, types, or steps that should be included in my paragraph.

In your own words, what is the difference between a topic sentence and a thesis statement?

A topic sentence is the stated main idea of a paragraph. In contrast, a thesis statement is the stated main idea of the central point of two or more paragraphs.

1. **How will I use what I have learned?** In your notebook, discuss how you will apply to your own reading/writing strategy what you have learned about main ideas. When will you apply this knowledge to your reading/writing strategy?
2. **What do I still need to study about main ideas?** In your notebook, discuss your ongoing study needs. Describe what, when, and how you will continue studying main ideas.

MySkillsLab™

Complete the Post-test for Module 5 in MySkillsLab.

6

LEARNING OUTCOMES

After studying this module you should be able to:

- **LO 1** Answer the Question "What's the Point of Supporting Details in Reading and Writing Paragraphs?"
- **LO 2** Ask Questions to Locate and Generate Supporting Details
- **LO 3** Identify and Outline Major and Minor Supporting Details
- **LO 4** Analyze Supporting Details as Relevant and Adequate
- **LO 5** Write a Summary of a Paragraph

Supporting Details in Reading and Writing Paragraphs

To better understand the purpose of supporting details, compare a paragraph to a well-planned house of ideas. The *topic* or general subject matter is the roof. The roof covers all the rooms of the house, just like the topic covers all the details in a paragraph. The main idea determines the frame of the house, and the *supporting details* are the studs and beams that give shape to the different rooms. The frame is made up of *major* supports that bear the weight of the building and smaller *minor* supports that give shape and form to the different rooms in the house. Just as pieces of wood, steel, or blocks support and shape the house, specific and well-chosen details give strength and shape to a writer's ideas.

WHAT'S THE POINT of Supporting Details in Reading and Writing Paragraphs? LO1

When we tap into the power of the reading/writing cycle as an exchange of information, we build both knowledge and communication skills. Careful consideration of supporting details as both a reader and a writer enhances our ability to comprehend and communicate ideas.

Photographic Organizer: Supporting Details in Reading and Writing Paragraphs

Preview the definition of supporting details on page 198. Then consider the following images and their captions. Next to each photograph, predict how supporting details relate to academic life, everyday life, and working life. Finally, predict an answer to the question "What's the point of supporting details in reading and writing paragraphs?"

Answers may vary.

Learning in college requires a student to pay close attention to details. In a science experiment, the results are based on proper observation of details.

In our everyday life, we are wise consumers when we question the details of products or agreements before making a purchase or a decision.

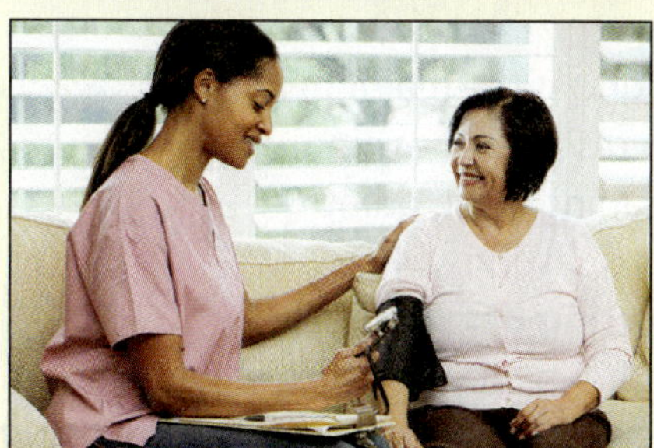

In our working life, we must gather details upon which we can make sound decisions.

What's the point of supporting details in reading and writing paragraphs?

Observation of supporting details is vital to our success in academic life, everyday life, and working life. When we understand or select key details, we can improve our learning, make sound choices, and expand our success in our career.

What's the Point? One Student's Response

The following paragraph is one student's response to the question "What's the point of supporting details in reading and writing paragraphs?"

Each of the photographs showed a person paying close attention to details. The science student has to follow the details in an experiment very closely. If she doesn't, she won't get reliable results. And then she has to observe and record the details of the result very carefully so the experiment can be done again successfully. The lady buying groceries is checking out the label, probably to see if the ingredients are healthy or unhealthy. Maybe she needs to buy low-salt or low-fat foods for her health. The nurse is observing and recording the vital signs of her patient's blood pressure. Both the health professional and the patient need this type of information to make informed decisions about well-being and possible treatments.

L2 Ask Questions to Locate and Generate Supporting Details

PREWRITE: RECITE/REVIEW/ BRAINSTORM

Asking questions is a vital step that is repeated throughout the reading/writing process. Readers and writers use questions to discover meaning. An effective reader seeks to understand a writer's meaning—the point being made. Before and during reading, a reader asks questions while searching for the writer's topic, main idea, and **supporting details** that explain, develop, or illustrate the main idea. On the other hand, an effective writer seeks to make a meaningful point to a reader. Before writing, a writer asks questions to brainstorm: to discover a topic that will impact an audience, to uncover attitudes and opinions about the controlling point, and to establish a main idea and supporting details. Readers and writers ask two types of questions: the reporter's questions and reflective questions.

Supporting details explain, develop, and illustrate the main idea.

Ask the Reporter's Questions to Locate and Generate Supporting Details						
Reporter's Questions	**Who?**	**What?**	**When?**	**Where?**	**Why?**	**How?**
Supporting Details	examples, descriptions, traits, similarities, differences	examples, descriptions, traits, similarities, differences	time order	location, descriptions	reasons or causes	explanation of a process

Reporter's questions—*who, what, when, where, why, how*—generate factual details about a topic.

The **reporter's questions** are six basic questions journalists ask to gather facts and details about a topic: *who, what, when, where, why,* or *how.* To locate and generate supporting details, effective readers and writers turn the topic or main idea into a question or set of questions based on a reporter's questions. The answer to each question will yield a specific set of supporting details.

Reflective questions use the reporter's questions to reveal the writer's attitude or opinion about a topic and the purpose for writing. Remember, the writer's attitude or opinion serves as the controlling point of a topic (see Module 5, page 171). Reflective questions vary based on the topic, but their purpose is to tap into a writer's attitude, opinion, and purpose.

- What are the writer's key attitudes or feelings about this topic?
- What is the significance of this topic?

Reflective questions are the questions used to reveal attitudes or opinions about a topic, the significance of a topic, or the purpose for knowing about a topic.

Readers ask questions and record answers as a way to learn. Usually, readers base their questions on the topic sentence and words in bold or italic print. Writers ask questions and record answers as a way to prewrite or brainstorm details. Usually writers use questions to generate details about a topic and then write a topic sentence. You may want to try out several of the reporter's questions as you read or write. Experiment to discover which question is best answered by the details in a passage you are reading, or which question best generates the details you need to make your point as a writer.

Take, for example, the topic *dog bites*. A writer might choose to write about a few of the reasons a dog might bite someone. The main idea of such a paragraph may read as follows.

Main idea: A dog's natural aggression will make it more likely to bite in certain situations.

The main idea leads us to two possible questions. Using the reporter's question *when* turns the main idea into the following question: "When is a dog likely to bite?" Or we could use the reporter's question *what* to ask "What situations are likely to make a dog bite?" In addition to these two reporter's questions, we should also ask "What is the significance of this topic?" or "What are the writer's key attitudes or feelings about the topic?" Most likely, the writer asked these questions as a step in the prewriting process to generate the details used in the final draft of the paragraph. Read the following paragraph for the answers to these questions.

A Dog's Natural Aggression and Biting

[1]A dog's natural aggression will make it more likely to bite in certain situations. [2]For example, a dog may react aggressively when its personal space is invaded. [3]Therefore, a dog that is sleeping, eating, or nurturing its puppies may very well react with violence to defend itself, its food, or its offspring. [4]Aggression may also occur when a dog has been fenced in or tethered outside. [5]In these cases, the dog may feel easily frustrated or threatened and thus feel the urge to protect itself or its territory by biting. [6]A final situation that arouses the dog's animal aggression occurs when a person runs away in fear from a dog. [7]A dog's natural desire is to pursue prey; therefore, running past or away from a dog will almost always incite the animal to give chase and perhaps bite.

The supporting details for this main idea answer the question "When?" by listing three situations that are likely to arouse a dog's aggression and lead to biting. Then the paragraph discusses why the dog behaves this way in each situation.

The question "What is the writer's opinion about the topic?" is answered with the phrase "more likely to bite in certain situations." Note the relationship between this controlling point and the supporting details—"when personal space is invaded," "when fenced in or tethered outside," and "when a person runs away in fear." The controlling point generates the details.

Notice also that these three details directly explain the main idea. However, additional supporting details are also given in the paragraph. Each of the main supporting details needed further explanation. This paragraph shows us that there are two kinds of supporting details: major details that explain the main idea and minor details that explain other details. You will learn more about major and minor details in the next section.

Example

Read the paragraph. Turn the topic sentence into a question using one of the reporter's questions (*Who? What? When? Where? Why? How?*). Write the question in the space provided. Fill in the chart with the answers to the question you have created.

The Healthful Traits of Olive Oil

[1]Olive oil has several traits that benefit our health. [2]First, olive oil is a monounsaturated fat. [3]Monounsaturated fats lower blood cholesterol levels; they keep arteries free of blockages; and they reduce the chances of heart attacks and strokes. [4]Second, olive oil contains antioxidants. [5]Just like rust on a car, oxidation damages our cells. [6]Antioxidants help prevent oxidation. [7]They also may help increase immune function; thus they

may decrease risk of infection and cancer. [8]Third, olive oil also has polyphenols. [9]Polyphenols also strengthen the immune system and protect the body from infection. [10]They have been linked to preventing cancer and heart disease.

Question based on topic sentence:

What are several traits of olive oil that benefit our health?

Topic sentence:

Olive oil has several traits that benefit our health.

First Trait/Benefit	Second Trait/Benefit	Third Trait/Benefit
(1) *Monounsaturated fats* *Lower blood cholesterol levels, Keep arteries free of blockages, Reduce the chances of heart attacks and strokes*	(2) *Antioxidants* *Prevent oxidation, Increase immune function, Decrease risk of infection and cancer*	(3) *Polyphenols* *Strengthen immune system, Prevent cancer and and heart disease*

Explanation

Compare your response to the following student's think-aloud:

Using the reporter's question What? *turns the topic sentence into the following question: "What are several traits of olive oil that benefit our health?" This question includes the topic* olive oil *and the writer's controlling point "several traits . . . that benefit . . . health." The answer to this question yields three major supporting details: (1) monounsaturated fats, (2) antioxidants, and (3) polyphenols.*

Practice 1

Ask Questions to Locate Details

Read the paragraph. Turn the topic sentence into a question using one of the reporter's questions (*Who? What? When? Where? Why? How?*). Write the question in the space provided. Fill in the chart with the answers to the question you have created.

REASONS FOR HALITOSIS

[1]Halitosis, more commonly known as bad breath, occurs due to several specific circumstances. [2]As certain foods are digested, they result in bad breath. [3]Foods such as garlic and onions are absorbed into the bloodstream, carried to the lungs and expelled as bad breath through the mouth. [4]When dry mouth occurs and the flow of saliva decreases, bad breath occurs because saliva cleanses the mouth. [5]When oral hygiene is poor, bad breath is the result. [6]Improper brushing and flossing leaves food particles in the mouth. [7]In these instances, bacteria grow and create sulfur compounds that also result in bad breath. [8]Finally, bad breath occurs when a medical disorder is present. [9]Bad breath may be a warning sign of infections of the sinuses or respiratory tract, liver or kidney problems, and diabetes.

Question based on topic sentence:

When does halitosis or bad breath occur?

Topic sentence:

Halitosis, more commonly known as bad breath, occurs due to several specific circumstances.

First Circumstance	Second Circumstance	Third Circumstance	Fourth Circumstance
(1) *as certain foods are digested*	**(2)** when dry mouth occurs	**(3)** *when oral hygiene is poor*	**(4)** when a medical disorder is present

Often, effective writers study the work of other writers to learn how to improve their own writing. To study another writer, you assume the role of the writer and look for the questions the writer most likely asked and answered. By asking and answering these questions, you learn about the thinking process that goes into limiting a topic and generating details to support a main idea.

Example

Assume the role of the writer of the paragraph "A Dog's Natural Aggression and Biting" on page 200. Answer the following questions based on the details in the paragraph. Keep in mind that some questions may not apply. For those, write **DA** for "Do not Apply."

Ask the reporter's questions to identify a topic, purpose, and audience.

- What is the topic?

A Dog's Natural Aggression and Biting

- Why write about this topic?

to inform the reader so dog bites can be avoided

- Who is the audience?

dog owners or people who are around dogs

Ask the reporter's questions to generate details about the topic.

- Who?

DA

- What?

dogs' aggression and biting

- When?

Dogs are likely to bite when personal space is invaded, when fenced in or tethered outside or when people run away in fear.

- Where?

DA

CONTINUED

EXAMPLE *CONTINUED*

- Why?

Dogs are likely to bite to defend themselves or their territory, out of frustration, or out of a natural desire to chase prey.

- How?

DA

Ask reflective questions to identify the writer's attitude and controlling point about the topic.

- What are key attitudes or feelings about this topic?

understanding of dogs' natural aggression

- Why is this topic important?

Dog bites can be avoided by knowing when they are likely to occur.

Explanation

Compare your response to the following student's think-aloud.

I learned a lot about reading and writing by studying this paragraph. I tried to figure out which questions the writer used based on the information in the paragraph. For example, the topic is "A Dog's Natural Aggression and Biting." And the supporting details answer the question <u>when</u> by describing three situations. The details also explain <u>why</u> a dog bites—like to defend itself or its territory, or out of frustration, or because of the natural urge to chase prey. I had to think longer about the questions about the purpose, audience, and attitudes. I found that some questions lead to the same answer. For example, the questions "Why write about this topic?" and "Why is this topic important?" have the same answer. The purpose is to inform the reader about when dogs bite. It's important because dog bites can be avoided if we know when they are likely to occur. When I asked questions about the purpose and attitudes, I saw how closely related purpose and attitudes are to the supporting details.

So far you have used questions as a reader to identify the supporting details to comprehend a writer's main idea. You have also studied the way a writer uses questions to generate details to make a point to a reader. You are ready to ask questions to generate details as a writer.

Practice 2

Ask Questions to Generate Details

Choose a topic of high interest in the current news, or select one from the following list of topics. Then complete the following thinking guide to generate details about your topic.

Legalizing Marijuana

Helping the Homeless

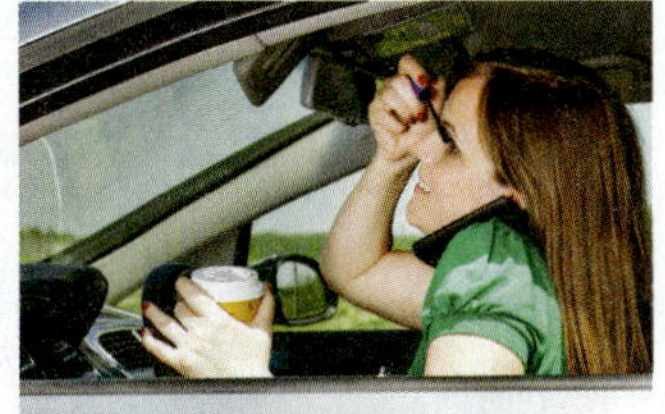

Distracted Driving

Use the reporter's questions to identify a topic, purpose, and audience.

Answers may vary.

- What is my topic? ______________________________

____

- Why am I writing? ______________________________

____

- Who is my audience? ______________________________

____

Use the reporter's questions to generate details about the topic.

- Who? ______________________________

____

- What? ______________________________

____

- When? ______________________________

CONTINUED

PRACTICE 2 *CONTINUED*

____

- Where? _______________

____

- Why? _______________

____

- How? _______________

____

Use reflective questions to identify attitudes and generate a controlling point about the topic.

- What are key attitudes or feelings about this topic? _______________

____

- Why is this topic important? _______________

____

L3 Identify and Outline Major and Minor Supporting Details

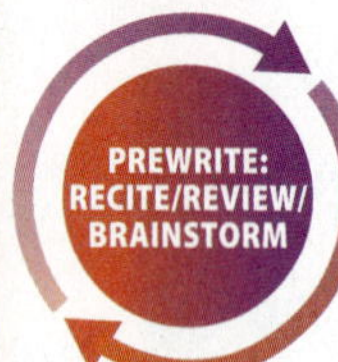

Readers and writers rely on supporting details to comprehend and make a point. During reading, effective readers often underline key supporting details. Then after reading, they outline a passage to identify the supporting details and their logical flow from general to specific: main idea to major supporting detail to minor supporting detail. Likewise, a writer uses an outline as a prewrite to generate and organize ideas into a logical flow. A supporting detail will always be one of two types.

A **major detail** is directly tied to the main idea. Without the major details, the writer's main idea would not be clear because the major details are the principal points the writer is making about the topic.

A **major detail** directly explains, develops, or illustrates the main idea.

In contrast, a **minor detail** explains a major detail. The minor details could be left out, and the main idea would still be clear. Thus minor details are not as important as major details. Minor details are used to add interest and to give further descriptions, examples, testimonies, analysis, illustrations, and reasons for the major details. To better understand the flow of ideas, study the diagram at the top of the next page.

A **minor detail** explains, develops, or illustrates a major detail.

As ideas move from general to specific details, the writer often uses signal words to introduce a new detail. These signal words—such as *first, second, next, in addition*, or *finally*—can help you identify major and minor details. Many readers and writers use an outline to identify and organize details. An **outline** lists ideas in blocks of thought, as shown in the following outline for a paragraph.

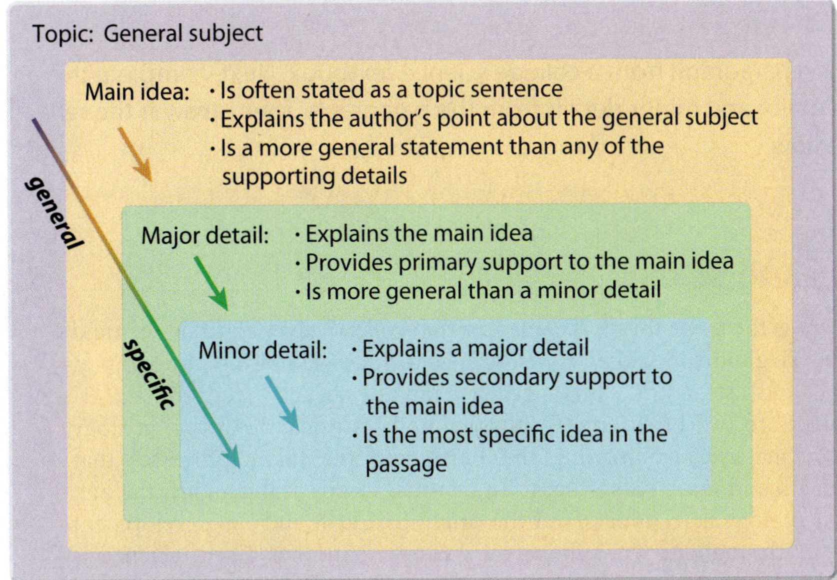

Topic: General subject
Main idea: • Is often stated as a topic sentence
• Explains the author's point about the general subject
• Is a more general statement than any of the supporting details
general
Major detail: • Explains the main idea
• Provides primary support to the main idea
• Is more general than a minor detail
specific
Minor detail: • Explains a major detail
• Provides secondary support to the main idea
• Is the most specific idea in the passage

I. Main Idea Statement: Topic Sentence

A. Major supporting detail
   1. Major detail
   2. Minor detail

B. Major supporting detail
   1. Major detail
   2. Minor detail

C. Major supporting detail
   1. Major detail
   2. Minor detail

Two types of outline are topic outlines and sentence outlines. A **topic outline** uses a word or phrase to state major and minor details. A **sentence outline** states each detail as a complete sentence.

An **outline** organizes ideas into a list of headings and subheadings that shows the flow of ideas from main idea to major supporting details to minor supporting details.

A **topic outline** uses a word or short phrase to identify each main idea, major detail, or minor detail in the outline.

A **sentence outline** states each main idea, major detail, or minor detail as a complete sentence in the outline.

Thinking Guide to Outlining

Create an outline of the main idea, major supporting details, and minor supporting details.

- ❑ List and identify each item with Roman numerals, capital letters, Arabic numerals, and lowercase letters, in that order, to show the flow of ideas.
- ❑ Place a period after each numeral or letter.
- ❑ Capitalize each item.
- ❑ For topic outlines, state each item with a word or phrase.
- ❑ For sentence outlines, state each item as a complete thought.

As you distinguish between major and minor details as a reader, consider how this skill will help you generate major and minor details as a writer.

Example

Read the following paragraph from a college science textbook. Next, complete the outline with the major and minor details from the paragraph. Then, answer the reflective questions that follow.

What Is Earth Science?

[1]**Earth science** is the name for all the sciences that collectively seek to understand Earth and its neighbors in space. [2]Earth science includes geology, oceanography, meteorology, and astronomy. [3]First, **geology** literally means "study of Earth" and is divided into two broad areas—physical and historical. [4]Physical geology examines the materials comprising the Earth and the many processes that operate beneath and upon its surfaces. [5]In contrast to physical geology, the aim of historical geology is to understand the origin of Earth and the development of the planet through its 4.5-billion-year history. [6]Another Earth science is oceanography. [7]**Oceanography** includes all the study of the composition and movement of sea water, as well as coastal processes, seafloor topography, and marine life. [8]Oceanography is actually not a separate and distinct science. [9]Rather, it involves the application of all sciences in the study of the ocean. [10]A third Earth science is meteorology. [11]**Meteorology** is the study of the atmosphere and the processes that produce weather and climate. [12]Like oceanography, meteorology involves the application of all other sciences. [13]Finally, because Earth is related to all the other objects in space, the science of **astronomy** is very useful. [14]Astronomy is the study of the universe. [15]Indeed, Earth is subject to the same physical laws that govern the many other objects populating the great expanses of space.

Adapted from Lutgens, Frederick K., Tarbuck, Edward J., and Tasa, Dennis G., *Foundations of Earth Science*, 6th ed., pp. 2–3.

Outline of "What Is Earth Science?"

Main idea stated in a topic sentence: Earth science is the name for all the sciences that collectively seek to understand Earth and its neighbors in space.

A. *Geology literally means "study of Earth" and is divided into two broad areas—physical and historical.*

1. *Physical geology* examines the materials comprising the Earth and the many processes that operate beneath and upon its surfaces.
2. *In contrast to physical geology, the aim of historical geology is to understand the origin of Earth and the development of the planet through its 4.5-billion-year history.*

B. *Another Earth science is oceanography.*

1. Oceanography includes all the study of the composition and movement of sea water, as well as coastal processes, seafloor topography, and marine life.
2. *Oceanography is actually not a separate and distinct science.*
3. Rather, it involves the application of all sciences in the study of the ocean.

C. *A third Earth science is meteorology.*

1. *Meteorology is the study of the atmosphere and the processes that produce weather and climate.*

2. Like oceanography, meteorology involves the application of all other sciences.

D. *Finally, because Earth is related to all the other objects in space, the science of astronomy is very useful.*

1. Astronomy is the study of the universe.

2. *Indeed, Earth is subject to the same physical laws that govern the many other objects populating the great expanses of space.*

Reflective Questions *Answers may vary.*

- How does outlining major and minor details help me as a reader?

Outlining major and minor details will help me generate and organize details to support my point.

- How does knowing about major and minor details help me as a writer?

Outlining details helps me to see which ideas are the most important ones to remember. It also helps me see the flow of the writer's ideas.

Explanation

Compare your response to the following think-aloud.

Every detail in the paragraph gives additional information that explains and supports the main idea or topic sentence. The topic sentence states a broad definition of Earth science. The writer expands this definition by offering major and minor details about each of the four sciences that make up Earth science. Thus, the major details are sentences 3, 6, 10, and 13. Note that each of these major details is signaled by a transition: First *(sentence 3),* Another *(sentence 6),* A third *(sentence 10), and* Finally *(sentence 13). Each of these major details is explained with minor supporting details. For example, the major detail geology is further defined by being divided into two subgroups. Thus, sentences 4 and 5 offer*

CONTINUED

EXPLANATION *CONTINUED*

minor details about these two subtopics of geology: physical geology and historical geology. The other minor details in this paragraph are sentences 7, 8, 11, 12, 14, and 15. Note that some of these minor details are also introduced with transitions: In contrast *(sentence 5),* Like *(sentence 12), and* Indeed *(sentence 15).*

Practice 3

Identify and Outline Major and Minor Details

Read the following passage from a popular online site for health information. Then, identify the major and minor details by completing the outline that follows it.

WHAT IS INSOMNIA?

[1]Insomnia (in-SOM-ne-ah) is a common condition in which you have trouble falling or staying asleep. [2]This condition can range from mild to severe, depending on how often it occurs and the type of insomnia it is.

[3]Insomnia can be chronic (ongoing) or acute (short-term). [4]Chronic insomnia means having symptoms at least 3 nights a week for more than a month. [5]Acute insomnia lasts for less time. [6]Some people who have insomnia may have trouble falling asleep. [7]Other people may fall asleep easily but wake up too soon. [8]Others may have trouble with both falling asleep and staying asleep. [9]As a result, insomnia may cause you to get too little sleep or have poor-quality sleep. [10]You may not feel refreshed when you wake up.

[11]There are two types of insomnia. [12]The most common type is called secondary or comorbid insomnia. [13]This type of insomnia is a symptom or side effect of some other problem. [14]More than 8 out of 10 people who have insomnia are believed to have secondary insomnia. [15]Certain medical conditions, medicines, sleep disorders, and substances can cause secondary insomnia. [16]In contrast, primary insomnia isn't due to a medical problem, medicines, or other substances. [17]It is its own disorder. [18]A number of life changes can trigger primary insomnia, including long-lasting stress and emotional upset.

[19]Finally, if you have insomnia, you may experience a variety of symptoms. [20]Insomnia can cause excessive daytime sleepiness and a lack of energy. [21]It also can make you feel anxious, depressed, or irritable. [22]You may have trouble focusing on tasks, paying attention, learning, and remembering. [23]This can prevent you from doing your best at work or school. [24]Insomnia also can cause other serious problems. [25]For example, you may feel drowsy while driving. [26]In this case, insomnia could lead to an accident.

Adapted from U.S. Department of Health and Human Services and National Institutes of Health. "What Is Insomnia?" *Disease and Conditions Index*. December 2011. 7 January 2014. http://www.nhlbi.nih.gov/health/dci/Diseases/inso/inso_whatis.html.

Stated main idea: This condition can range from mild to severe, depending on how often it occurs and the type of insomnia it is.

A. *Insomnia can be chronic (ongoing) or acute (short-term).*

1. Chronic insomnia means having symptoms at least 3 nights a week for more than a month.
2. *Acute insomnia lasts for less time.*
3. Some people who have insomnia may have trouble falling asleep.
4. Other people may fall asleep easily but wake up too soon.
5. Others may have trouble with both falling asleep and staying asleep.
   a. *As a result, insomnia may cause you to get too little sleep or have poor-quality sleep.*
   b. You may not feel refreshed when you wake up.

B. *There are two types of insomnia.*

1. *The most common type is called secondary or comorbid insomnia.*
   a. This type of insomnia is a symptom or side effect of some other problem.
   b. More than 8 out of 10 people who have insomnia are believed to have secondary insomnia.
   c. *Certain medical conditions, medicines, sleep disorders, and substances can cause secondary insomnia.*
2. *In contrast, primary insomnia isn't due to a medical problem, medicines, or other substances.*
   a. It is its own disorder.
   b. *A number of life changes can trigger primary insomnia, including long-lasting stress and emotional upset.*

C. *Finally, if you have insomnia, you may experience a variety of symptoms.*

1. Insomnia can cause excessive daytime sleepiness and a lack of energy.
2. It also can make you feel anxious, depressed, or irritable.
3. You may have trouble focusing on tasks, paying attention, learning, and remembering.
4. This can prevent you from doing your best at work or school.
5. Insomnia also can cause other serious problems.
   a. *For example, you may feel drowsy while driving.*
   b. In this case, insomnia could lead to an accident.

Now that you have learned to distinguish between major and minor supporting details to comprehend a writer's main idea, you are ready to generate major and minor details to support a main idea in your own writing. Just as you asked questions about a topic to generate details, you may ask questions about details to generate additional details or organize existing details to flow from major to minor details.

Example

Study one writer's response to questions she asked and answered about Distracted Driving (Practice 2). Complete the outline that follows with the major and minor details that contained the answers to the questions. Some details have been filled in to get you started. Some details may not be used. Finally, answer the reflective question that follows.

Use the reporter's questions to identify a topic, purpose, and audience.

- What is my topic? *Texting while Driving*
- Why am I writing? *to inform people of the dangers and to persuade people to stop texting while driving*
- Who is my audience? *the general public*

Use the reporter's questions to generate details about the topic.

- Who texts and drives? *Many types of people do this. Men, women, young, and old all text while driving. Teens are most likely to text while driving. The elderly are not as comfortable with technology and are less likely to text while driving.*
- What are the effects of texting? *accidents, damaged property, injuries, lost lives*
- When does texting and driving occur? *during most common driving situations such as in heavy traffic, during traffic stops, or while speeding down the highway*
- Where does texting and driving occur? *everywhere on city, neighborhood, and rural streets as well as on highways*
- Why do people text and drive? *They have a careless, shortsighted need to stay connected to family, friends, or work.*
- How does one text while driving? *The driver must take his or her eyes off the road for many seconds to read a text. The driver's eyes remain off the road and at least one hand is off the steering wheel to use the phone keyboard to type a message and push the send button.*

Use reflective questions to identify attitudes and generate a controlling point about the topic.

- What are key attitudes or feelings about this topic? *Texting while driving is a serious problem!*
- Why is this topic important? *People of all ages are being injured or killed due to texting while driving.*

Topic Sentence: Texting while driving is a serious problem.

A. Many people text while driving.

1. Men and women, young and old are involved in texting while driving.

2. *Teens are most likely to text while driving.*

B. Texting while driving occurs everywhere and during most common driving situations.

1. People text while driving in heavy traffic and while speeding down highways.

2. *People text during traffic stops.*

C. *Texting while driving causes serious accidents.*

1. Drivers who text while driving crash into and damage other people's property such as cars, buildings, and homes.

2. *Victims can be seriously injured or killed.*

D. *Texting while driving is dangerous because of how it occurs.*

1. The driver must take his or her eyes off the road for many seconds to read a text.

2. The driver's eyes remain off the road and at least one hand is off the steering wheel to use the phone keyboard to type a message and push the send button.

E. People text and drive in a careless, shortsighted need to stay connected to family, friends, or work.

Reflective questions: *Answers may vary.*

Do you agree with the order of the major details? Why or why not?

No, I do not agree with the order of the major details. I would have listed "D. Texting while driving is dangerous because of how it occurs" as the second major supporting detail. I want readers to keep in mind how texting occurs as they think about when and where texting while driving occurs and its serious effects.

Explanation

Compare your outline and reflection with the following think-aloud by the writer.

It was very helpful to use an outline to organize the details. Asking and answering the reporter's questions produced many details, but I still had to figure out the best order to discuss each one in my paragraph. The outline helped me decide the best order of the details. It actually made writing a draft of my paragraph very easy. An outline is like a blueprint or a writing plan. I plan out what to say and when to say it, and then just follow the plan. Here is an outline

CONTINUED

that shows the order of the major supporting details.

Topic Sentence: Texting while driving is a serious problem.

A. *Many people text while driving.*

B. *Texting while driving occurs everywhere and during most common driving situations.*

C. *Texting while driving causes serious accidents.*

D. *Texting while driving is dangerous because of how it occurs.*

E. *People text and drive in a careless, thoughtless need to stay connected to family, friends, and work.*

I chose to place the description of how texting occurs near the end of my paragraph because I thought it was a powerful way to lead into my final major detail. I wanted to end on a strong point. Here is a rough draft of my paragraph based on my outline.

Texting while driving is a serious problem. Many types of people text while driving. Men and women, young and old are involved in texting while driving. Teens are most likely to text while driving. Texting while driving occurs everywhere and during most common driving situations. People text while driving in heavy traffic, during traffic stops, and while speeding down highways. Texting while driving causes serious accidents. Drivers who text while driving crash into and damage other people's property such as cars, buildings, and homes. Victims can be seriously injured or killed. Texting while driving is dangerous because of how it occurs. The driver must take his or her eyes off the road for many seconds to read a text. The driver's eyes remain off the road and at least one hand is off the steering wheel to use the phone keyboard to type a message and push the send button. People text and drive in a careless, shortsighted need to stay connected to family, friends, or work.

Practice 4

Generate and Outline Major and Minor Details

Use the details you generated about the topic you chose in Practice 2. Complete the outline that follows with a main idea and major and minor details contained the answers to the questions.

Answers may vary.

Topic Sentence: ______

A. ______

1. ______

2. ______

B. ______

1. ______

2. ______

C. ______

1. ______

2. ______

Analyze Supporting Details as Relevant and Adequate

LO4

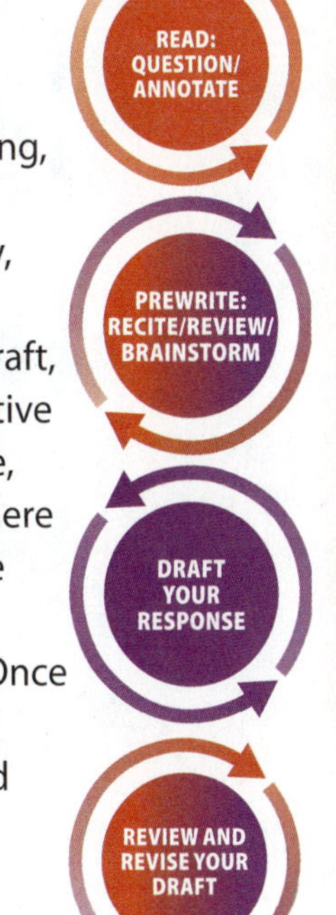

Relevant and adequate details support and develop the main idea. An effective reader doesn't just accept what he or she reads without carefully thinking about it. During reading, an effective reader asks questions to evaluate the details. Are there key details related to the main idea? Are there enough ideas to make the point clear and convincing? Similarly, an effective writer doesn't come up with supporting details without careful thought. As writers brainstorm, they usually generate many details. Before including any detail in a draft, writers evaluate the relationship between a particular detail and the main idea. An effective writer includes only the details that relate to the main idea. In addition, as writers outline, draft, and revise, they analyze the adequacy of details. They, like their readers, ask, "Are there enough details to support the main idea?" Many times, they discover the need to provide additional details to make a point clear and convincing.

Relevant details have a direct bearing or connection to the main idea.

Relevant details explain and support the writer's point. Once a writer narrows a subject into a focused main idea, he or she includes only those details that relate to his or her opinion and pattern of organization.

Thinking Guide to Check for Relevant Details

Apply the following questions to each detail to see if it is relevant to a main idea. If the answers are "no" to these questions, then the detail is most likely irrelevant and should not be included as a support.

- ❑ Does the detail reinforce the writer's opinion?
- ❑ Does the detail carry out the pattern of organization?
- ❑ Does the detail support the main idea?
- ❑ Does the detail support a major detail?

Example

The following prewrite includes a focused main idea and a set of details. Use the "Check for Relevant Details" questions given above to identify the irrelevant detail, and cross it out. Then write a relevant detail above or next to the detail you crossed out.

Main Idea: Aerobic exercise leads to several health benefits.

A. First Benefit, stronger bones	*B. Second Benefit, stronger muscles*	*C. Third Benefit, weight management*
1. builds bone mass	*1. tones muscles*	~~*1. improved looks*~~
2. reduces brittleness	*2. increases range of motion*	*2. reduces body fat*

Explanation

Compare your response to the following student's think-aloud.

The detail that is not relevant is the first minor detail "1. improved looks" under "C. Third Benefit, weight management." Improved looks may be a result of weight management, but this detail is not related to health benefits. A possible relevant detail to replace this irrelevant detail could be "burns excess calories."

Adequate details offer in-depth explanations and supports for the writer's opinion and pattern of organization. In-depth support of a main idea often requires both major and minor details. Major details directly support the main idea. Minor details support and explain the major details (review the chart on page 207 of this module).

Adequate details provide sufficient specific details to fully support a main idea.

Thinking Guide to Check for Adequate Details

Apply the following questions to see if you have adequate details to support your main idea. If the answer is "yes" to these questions, then you do not have adequate details. Additional details are most likely needed to fully support the main idea.

- ❑ Is more information needed to explain the writer's opinion?
- ❑ Is more information needed to carry out the pattern of organization?
- ❑ Does a major detail need a minor detail of support or explanation?

Example

Read the following rough draft of a paragraph. Circle the main idea. Underline the point that needs more information to adequately support the main idea.

A Winter Wonder or Winter Haven Vacation?

[1]The winter break in school calendars across the country gives families a chance to enjoy a vacation together. [2]Many families choose between two types of vacation: snow or sun. [3]A wintertime vacation actually offers distinct choices in activities, food, and clothing. [4]On the one hand, fresh snow offers plenty of opportunities for winter sports such as skiing, sledding, snowmobiling, snowboarding, or ice skating. [5]Of course, the family will need to plan on packing additional special clothing. [6]On the other hand, a family may prefer to visit a winter haven in a tropical climate. [7]Balmy beaches offer plenty of fun options such as sunbathing, snorkeling, surfing, and swimming. [8]And the family can travel light. [9]In the tropics, all they really need are their swimsuits and a few casual clothes such as shorts, t-shirts, and sandals.

Explanation

Compare your response to the following student's think-aloud:

The main idea is sentence 2 "Many families choose between two types of vacation: snow or sun." The detail that needs more support is sentence 5. What additional clothes does the family need to take? The writer could have included a sentence that says "For example, a snow vacation will require sweaters, jackets, boots, and maybe even thermal underwear." The paragraph does not contain adequate details.

Practice 5

Check for Relevant Details

Work with a peer or small group of classmates. Exchange the outlines you generated in Practice 4. Use the thinking guides for checking relevant and adequate details to evaluate the details in the outline of one of your peers. Then, give the writer of the outline your feedback based on your evaluation.

Thinking Guide to Check for Relevant Details

Apply the following questions to each detail to see if it is relevant to a main idea. If the answers are "no" to these questions, then the detail is most likely irrelevant and should not be included as a support.

- ☐ Does the detail reinforce the writer's opinion?
- ☐ Does the detail carry out the pattern of organization?
- ☐ Does the detail support the main idea?
- ☐ Does the detail support a major detail?

Thinking Guide to Check for Adequate Details

Apply the questions from the Thinking Guide to Check for Adequate Details to see if you have adequate details to support your main idea. If the answer is "yes" to these questions, then additional details are most likely needed to fully support the main idea.

- ☐ Is more information needed to explain the writer's opinion?
- ☐ Is more information needed to carry out the pattern of organization?
- ☐ Does a major detail need a minor detail of support or explanation?

Feedback to writer:

____

____

L5 Write a Summary of a Paragraph

DRAFT YOUR RESPONSE

Reading for main ideas and major supporting details is an excellent study technique that uses writing to learn. After reading, an effective strategy to deepen your understanding and provide study notes for review is to write down main ideas and major supporting details in a summary. A **summary** condenses a paragraph or passage down to only its primary points by restating the main idea and major supporting details. A summary is often the reader's first response to a passage. Accurate restatement of the writer's key ideas enables a reader to connect these ideas to the world, other ideas, and personal experience.

A **summary** is a brief, clear restatement of the most important points of a paragraph or passage.

Often you will want to paraphrase, that is, restate the ideas in your own words. Other times, you may need to use the exact language of the text to ensure accuracy. For example, scientific or medical terms have precise meanings that must be memorized; thus your summaries of these types of ideas would include the original language of the text.

A Strategy for Writing a Summary

The length of a summary will vary, depending on the length of the original text. For example, a short paragraph can be summarized in one sentence, and a longer paragraph in a few sentences. A passage of several paragraphs can be reduced to a one-paragraph summary, and a much longer selection such as a chapter in a textbook may require a summary of a page or two.

To create a summary, you can annotate, or mark, your text during reading. For example, as you read, circle the main idea and underline the major supporting details and cross out unnecessary or repetitive information. To learn more about annotating a text, see pages 43–49 in Module 2. Use the following strategy to write a summary.

A Strategy for Writing a Summary

1. Determine the Main Idea.

2. Create and Record a Question.

Create a question based on the main idea or title.

Record the question in the margin.

3. Identify and Label Details.

Locate major supporting details that answer the question based on the main idea.

Assign a number to each major supporting detail.

4. Condense Details.

Shorten a list to one word.

Describe individual parts of an action with one word.

5. Delete Details.

Delete minor details unnecessary to a shorter version of the most important points.

Delete repetitive ideas.

6. Restate Ideas.

Rewrite the topic sentence and major supports in one or two sentences.

Use your own words.

Example

Read and annotate the paragraph. Circle the topic sentence that states the main idea. Underline major supporting details. Then, apply the strategy for writing a summary. Write one or two sentences that summarize the paragraph.

ESSENTIAL SKILLS FOR JOB SEEKERS

[1]Each employer is looking for a specific set of skills from job seekers that match the demands of a particular job. [2]However, beyond job-specific skills, employers seek certain universal skills from likely employees. [3]First, employers highly value communication skills. [4]The ability to listen, speak, read, and write well is critical to success in the workforce. [5]Employers also look for workers with strong problem-solving skills. [6]Success often depends on the ability to assess a situation, gather information, identify key issues, and offer solutions. [7]In addition, almost all jobs now require basic computer literacy skills. [8]Workers need to be skilled in use of word processing, spreadsheets, email, and a wide range of other applications. [9]Such workers are better able to secure a job and earn promotions. [10]Employers also look for workers with strong interpersonal skills. Interpersonal skills include the ability to relate to co-workers, resolve conflicts, and foster teamwork. [11]Finally, there is no doubt that employers want dependable, reliable, responsible workers. [12]Dependability means workers arrive on time, every day. [13]They are ready to work, and they take full responsibility for their actions.

Summary: *Answers may vary.*

Explanation

Compare your summary to the following annotated paragraph, summary, and think-aloud.

I read the paragraph several times as I used the strategy to write a summary. First, I turned the title into the question "What Are the Essential Skills for Job Seekers?" Then I skimmed the paragraph for the answer to my question. Immediately, I saw that sentence 2 used the same words that were in the title with the addition of the word certain. When I circled sentence 2 as the topic sentence, it occurred to me that the word certain implied that the writer was going to discuss a specific number of essential skills. Thus, I continued to skim the paragraph to see if I could locate and list the certain essential skills discussed by the writer. As I skimmed, I annotated the paragraph. My annotations describe how I applied the strategy to write a summary.

WHAT ARE THE ESSENTIAL SKILLS FOR JOB SEEKERS?

~~[1]Each employer is looking for a specific set of skills from job seekers that match the demands of a particular job. [2]However, beyond job-specific skills~~, employers seek certain universal skills from likely employees. [3]First, employers highly value communication skills. ~~[4]The ability to listen, speak, read, and write well is critical to success in the workforce.~~ [5]Employers also ~~look for workers with~~ strong problem solving skills. ~~[6]Success often depends on the ability to assess a situation, gather information, identify key issues, and offer solutions.~~ [7]In addition, ~~almost all jobs now require~~ basic computer literacy skills. ~~[8]Workers need to be skilled in use of word processing, spreadsheets, email, and a wide range of other applications. [9]Such workers are better able to secure a job and earn promotions. [10]Employers~~ also look ~~for workers with~~ strong interpersonal skills. ~~[11]Interpersonal skills include the ability to relate to co-workers, resolve conflicts, and foster teamwork.~~ [12]Finally, ~~there is no doubt that employers want dependable, reliable, responsible~~ workers. [13]Dependability mean~~s workers arrive on time, every day. [14]They are ready to work, and they take full responsibility for their actions.~~

Summary:

Employers seek workers who have five universal skills, which are communication skills, problem solving skills, basic computer literacy skills, interpersonal skills, and dependability.

Steps 1 and 2: This is the main idea of the paragraph. I turned this idea into the question "What are the universal skills employers seek?"

Step 3: Words such as *First, also, in addition*, and *finally* helped me find and underline each essential skill. I underlined each of these words as labels for each skill. I then underlined the phrases "communication skills," "problem solving skills," "basic computer literacy skills," "interpersonal skills," and "dependability." Identifying these details confirmed that sentence 2 was the main idea stated as a topic sentence.

Steps 4 and 5: Each major detail lists a certain universal skill. Then, the writer offers additional details that give the traits or examples of each skill. For example, sentence 4 is a list of some specific "communication skills." This list of minor details about communication is not necessary to include in a summary of key points. I also deleted sentences 6, 8, 9 11, 13, and 14 as unnecessary minor details. So by deleting this additional information and using the writer's name for each skill, I both deleted and condensed ideas.

Step 6: I deleted sentence 1 and part of sentence 2 because these ideas are general ideas that introduce the topic. They are not necessary to include in a summary.

Step 7: Finally, I revised the topic sentence to replace "certain skills" with "five skills" and then listed the five skills.

Practice 6

Write a Summary

Read and summarize the following paragraph from a college accounting textbook. Use the strategy for writing a summary. *Answers may vary.*

LIQUID ASSETS

[1]**Liquid assets** are financial assets that can be easily sold without a loss in value. [2]They are especially useful for covering upcoming expenses. [3]Some of the more common liquid assets are cash, checking accounts, and savings accounts. [4]Cash is handy to cover small purchases, while a checking account is convenient for large purchases. [5]Savings accounts are desirable because they pay interest on the money that is deposited. [6]For example, if your savings account offers an interest rate of 4 percent, you earn annual interest of $4 for every $100 deposited in your account.

Madura, Jeff, *Personal Finance Update*, p. 40.

Summary:

Cash, checking accounts, and savings accounts are three common types of liquid assets that can be easily sold without a loss in value.

Reading and Writing Assignments

MySkillsLab™
Complete these assignments in MySkillsLab.

Considering Audience and Purpose

Study the sequence of photographs about supporting details at the beginning of this module.

Assume one of the students in the classroom is a peer of yours in this course. She has stated she is not convinced she needs to pay attention to supporting details as a reader or writer. Write a paragraph that explains the importance of paying attention to supporting details to a student, a consumer, or a worker.

Reading and Writing for Everyday Life

Assume you have received the following letter from the preschool your toddler attends while you go to school or work. Read the letter. Write a response to Elizabeth Long, Director of Bright Beginnings Preschool.

Dear Parents:

Many changes are taking place at Bright Beginnings, and we want you to be well informed about each one. First, we are excited to announce that we will be moving to a new location. While the location is 30 minutes further away, we are confident you will find the new facilities a great improvement. Second, we are thinking about extending our hours of service for an additional fee per hour of extended care. Currently, the school operates from 9:30 a.m. until 5:00 p.m., Monday through Friday. Please let us know what additional hours or days you need our services. Finally, we are raising our base rate from $500 a month to $550 a month. The new rate begins at the first of next month. Thank you for the opportunity to serve your family.

Dr. Elizabeth Long, Director of Bright Beginnings

Reading and Writing for College Life

Assume you are taking a college sociology class. Your assignment this week is to find a short article in a newspaper or online news site about a significant current event. Write a two-paragraph response to the article. In the first paragraph, write a summary of the article. In the second paragraph, write your response to the ideas in the article. In your response, answer the following questions: Why is this topic important or relevant? Who needs to know about this information and why? What are the most significant details?

Reading and Writing for Working Life

Assume you are applying for a job as youth counselor at a summer camp or you know someone who is applying. Read the following job description. Then either write a letter in which you apply for the job, or write a letter in which you recommend someone you know for the job. Be sure to include relevant and adequate details. Address your letter to Mr. Roy Lively, Director of Horseshoe Camp.

Camp Counselor Job Description

Camp Counselor Job Description: Counselors will be chaperones and advisors for boys and girls whose ages range from 8 to 13. Counselors need to be able to participate in or lead activities that range from crafts to outdoor activities such as horseback riding, hiking, and canoeing. Counselors supervise children as they complete assigned chores and learn new skills. Counselors also need to know CPR and basic first aid.

Workshop: Compose a Paragraph

Choose a passage to read and respond to in writing. You may select a passage in an example, practice, or writing assignment within this module. Or you may select a passage of your own choosing. Use the following guide to comprehend and respond to the passage. Apply what you have learned about supporting details to your reading/writing strategy.

Preread: Survey and Question

Prereading/Writing Questions based on text features (vocabulary):

____

____

____

Standard prereading/writing questions:

What is the passage about?

____

How is the material organized?

____

What do I already know about this topic? (What is my prior knowledge about the vocabulary?)

____

What is my purpose for reading/writing?

____

What is the writer's purpose and tone?

____

What main ideas or details may I want to address or include in my written response?

____

Read and Annotate

As you read, annotate key ideas, particularly those details that answer your prereading questions.

Recite, Review, and Brainstorm

Recite the information. Summarize the most important parts. Answer your prereading questions. Rephrase ideas into your own words. Record changes in your opinions based on the new information. **Review** the information. **Brainstorm** ideas for your written response to the passage. **Freewrite** a response to what you have read. **Map** the relationship among ideas you have annotated in the text. **Outline** or list key ideas and details in blocks of thought. Use your own paper.

Write a Draft of Your Response

Using the ideas you generated by brainstorming, compose a draft of your response. Use your own paper.

Revise Your Draft

Once you have drafted a paragraph, read the draft and answer the questions in the "Questions for Revising a Paragraph" box that follows. Indicate your answers by annotating your paper. If you answer "yes" to a question, underline, check, or circle examples. If you answer "no" to a question, write additional details in the margins and draw lines to indicate where the details should be placed. Revise your paragraph based on your reflection. (*Hint*: Experienced writers create several drafts as they focus on one or two questions per draft.)

Step by Step: Questions for Revising a Paragraph

- ☐ Have I stated or implied a focused main idea?
- ☐ Have I made my purpose clear?
- ☐ Is my tone appropriate for my audience and purpose?
- ☐ Is the logical order of the ideas clear? Have I used strong transitions to guide my reader, such as *first, second, next,* etc.?
- ☐ Have I made my point with adequate details?
- ☐ Do all the details support my point?
- ☐ What impact will my paragraph make on my reader?

Proofread Your Draft

Once you have made any revisions to your paragraph that may be needed, proofread your paragraph to eliminate careless errors. Work with a classmate to give and receive feedback about your paragraphs.

Review Test

MySkillsLab™
Complete this Review Test in MySkillsLab.

Score (number correct) ______x10 = ______%

Read the following passage from a college business textbook. Answer the questions that follow. Apply your reading/writing strategy to comprehend the writer's point and write your response.

1130L/10.1 GE/625 words

CAPITALISM: COMPETING IN A FREE MARKET

[1]Competition doesn't suddenly disappear from your life when you finish the marathon, quit the football team, or refuse to play another game of Rock Band. [2]You can't even go out for fast food without running into competition: McDonald's competes with Burger King, Coca-Cola competes with PepsiCo. [3]Whether you're ordering a chicken sandwich or working in the back flipping burgers, those companies' competitive relationships shape your fast food experience by affecting how much customers pay for their meals, how much the burger-flipper is paid, which items are on the menu, what the quality of the food is, and many other details. [4]If you live in a capitalistic economy—an economic system in which the means to produce goods and services are owned by private interests—you can't avoid competition.

[5]So the United States is a capitalist economy, right? [6]Well, not exactly. [7]It's more of a mixed market economy. [8]This just means that the United States borrows elements from different economic systems, like capitalism or socialism, to create an ideal system. [9]In both capitalistic and mixed market economies, competition plays a very big role.

[10]For example, let's say you decide to open a business installing swimming pools. [11]You'll get the materials you need, hire employees, and prepare advertising. [12]In return, any profits you make belong to you. [13]But can you charge as much as you want to install a new pool? [14]Of course not. [15]If your prices are too high, nobody will buy your product. [16]If your prices are too low, you won't earn a profit. [17]In a capitalistic economy, the types of goods and services produced, the prices charged, and the amount of income received are all determined through the operation of the free market.

[18]Of course, the free market doesn't mean that everything is free of cost. [19]In this case, the word free refers to people's freedom to choose what they buy and sell. [20]For example, when you buy a DVD, you voluntarily exchange your money for a copy of the latest Oscar-winning film; no one is forcing you to buy that particular movie from that particular store. [21]An employee voluntarily exchanges his or her time and labor for money. [22]In return, a company voluntarily exchanges money for employees' time and labor. [23]Both parties take part in an exchange because they have something to gain. [24]If they didn't expect to gain, they wouldn't agree to the exchange.

[25]Think about that swimming pool company you started in the last section. [26]You're competing with other swimming pool builders for customers and money in order to make your business a financial success. [27]But how, exactly, do you measure success? [28]Is a company successful if it earns a profit for six months, one year, or maybe 10 years?

[29]Often, if people see profits early on for a new company, they may call the company a success. [30]However, focusing on short-term profitability doesn't give

you the big picture. [31]Today, a better measure of success is sustainability. [32]In 1987, the World Commission on Environment and Development defined sustainable development as meeting "the needs of the present without compromising the ability of future generations to meet their own needs."

[33]What does that mean exactly? [34]**Sustainability** is the capacity for an organization to create profit for its shareholders today while making sure that its business interests are also in the best interests of the environment and other stakeholders for the future. [35]Stakeholders are all people who have an interest in an organization. [36]This may include employees, suppliers, and the community. [37]Shareholders are the people who actually own a company and directly benefit from its profits. [38]The good news about a sustainable business is that it stands an excellent chance of beating out the competition, being more successful tomorrow, and remaining successful for generations.

Adapted from Van Syckle, Barbara, and Tietje, Brian, *Anybody's Business*, pp. 56–57.

1. The central idea or thesis statement is
- **a.** sentence 1.
- **b.** sentence 2.
- **c.** sentence 6.
- **(d.)** sentence 9.

2. Sentence 10 is a
- **a.** main idea.
- **(b.)** major supporting detail.
- **c.** minor supporting detail.

3. Sentence 19 is a
- **(a.)** main idea.
- **b.** major supporting detail.
- **c.** minor supporting detail.

4. Sentence 34 is a
- **(a.)** main idea.
- **b.** major supporting detail.
- **c.** minor supporting detail.

5. Sentence 37 is a
- **a.** main idea.
- **(b.)** major supporting detail.
- **c.** minor supporting detail.

Summary Response

Restate the writer's main idea in your own words. Begin your summary response with the following: *The main idea of the passage "Capitalism: Competing in a Free Market" by Van Syckle & Tietje is. . . .*

What Do You Think?

Assume you are taking a college business class and that you are studying to become a business owner. An upcoming exam in your business class gives you an opportunity to test your understanding. Write a short-answer response of one paragraph for the following essay exam question: "What is the role of competition in capitalism?"

Academic Learning Log: Module Review

Summary of Key Concepts of Supporting Details

Assess your comprehension of supporting details.

LO1 LO2 LO3

1. To locate supporting details in a passage, an effective reader turns the topic or *stated main idea* into a *question* by asking the reporter's questions.

2. The answers to the reporter's questions, which are *who, what, when, where, why*, and *how*, yield a specific set of supporting details.

3. A reader uses an outline, which *lists ideas in blocks of thought*, to identify supporting details and see how the details flow; a writer uses an outline to *generate* and *organize* ideas into a logical flow.

LO1 LO2 LO3 LO4

4. A major supporting detail *directly explains, develops, or illustrates the main idea*.

5. A minor supporting detail *explains, develops, or illustrate the major supporting detail*.

6. *Relevant* details explain and support only the writer's controlling point; *adequate* details offer in-depth explanations and supports for the writer's opinion and pattern of organization.

L1 L2 L3 L4 L5

7. A *summary* is a *brief, clear restatement of the most important points of a paragraph or longer passage*.

L2 L4 L5

8. Often you will want to *paraphrase* or restate the ideas in your own words.

9. *Annotating* or marking your text *during* reading will help you create a *summary* after you read.

10. To create a summary for a passage with a stated main idea, *ask and answer questions based on the main idea*.

Test Your Comprehension of Supporting Details

Respond to the following questions and prompts. *Answers may vary.*

L1 L2 L3

In your own words, discuss how major and minor supporting details differ.

A major detail directly supports or explains the main idea of a passage. In contrast, a minor detail supports or explains a major detail. By giving information about a major detail, a minor detail indirectly supports the main idea. So major details are more important to the main idea than are minor details.

LO2 LO3 LO4 LO5

In the space below, outline the strategy for writing a summary for stated main ideas. See page 219.

Topic: *Writing a Summary*

Main Idea: *An effective reader can use headings, main ideas, and major supporting details to create a summary of a textbook passage.*

A *Determine the main idea.*

B *Create a question based on the main idea and record the question in the margin.*

C *Identify and number major supporting details that answer the question based on the main idea.*

D *Condense a list into a word or individual parts of an action into a word.*

E *Delete minor details and repetitive ideas unnecessary to a summary of the most important points.*

F *Restate in your own words the topic sentence and major details in one or two sentences.*

LO1 LO2 LO3 LO4 LO5

1. **How will I use what I have learned?** In your notebook, discuss how you will apply to your own reading/writing strategy what you have learned about supporting details. When will you apply this knowledge to your reading/writing strategy?
2. **What do I still need to study about supporting details?** In your notebook, discuss your ongoing study needs. Describe what, when, and how you will continue studying and using supporting details.

Complete the Post-test for Module 6 in MySkillsLab.

7

LEARNING OUTCOMES

After studying this module you should be able to:

- L1 Answer the Question "What's the Point of Implied Main Ideas in Reading and Writing Paragraphs?"
- L2 Define the Terms *Infer, Imply,* and *Implied Main Idea*
- L3 Before Reading, Skim and Annotate to Identify the Topic of an Implied Main Idea
- L4 During Reading, Question, Annotate, and Analyze Details to Infer the Implied Main Idea
- L5 After Reading, State the Implied Main Idea in a Sentence
- L6 Prewrite to Generate Supporting Details to Imply a Main Idea
- L7 Write a Paragraph That Implies a Main Idea
- L8 Determine the Implied Central Idea of a Longer Passage

Implied Main Ideas in Reading and Writing Paragraphs

One of the best ways to make writing interesting to a reader is to follow the saying "Show, don't tell." Consider the following example from a college textbook.

Skills for Behavior Change: How Many of These Healthy Behaviors Do You Practice?

- Get a good night's sleep (minimum of 7 hours)
- Maintain healthy eating habits and manage your weight
- Participate in physical recreational activities
- Practice safe sex
- Limit your intake of alcohol and avoid tobacco products
- Schedule regular self-exams and medical checkups

Donatelle, Rebecca J. *Health: The Basics*, Green Ed., 2011, p. 13.

The writer suggests or implies her point by giving a title and a list of specific details. She could have easily stated "Practice the Following Healthy Behaviors." However, her purpose is to prompt readers to think

about the choices they make and come to their own understanding of the main idea based on the details. An implied main idea is like buried treasure—one seeks to discover it, and once the discovery is made, values the find.

WHAT'S THE POINT of Implied Main Ideas in Reading and Writing Paragraphs? LO1

You already have much experience with understanding and suggesting an implied idea. You already know how to make your meaning quite clear without directly stating your point. For example, you suggest powerful ideas by using a certain tone of voice or a facial expression. Users of social media such as Facebook, Instagram, and Pinterest also tap into the power of implied main ideas by choosing and posting visual images to send meaningful messages to their friends and followers. A student often determines which ideas to remember based on the teacher's emphasis of the idea in a lecture or lesson. A job seeker dresses for an interview to make a professional first impression. In each of these situations, the details work together to suggest or imply a main idea.

Photographic Organizer: Implied Main Ideas

Assume each of the following photographs has been posted on the Internet to send a specific message to a particular audience. Read the captions that identify the audiences. Next to each photograph, write a sentence that states the point suggested by the details in the photograph. Finally, answer the question "What's the point of an implied main idea?" *Answers may vary.*

Picture posted on a college's admissions page

Come study at a college where the students are diverse and the learning is fun.

Picture posted on a father's Facebook page

I love my children and enjoy spending time with them.

Picture posted by a member of LinkedIn, a professional network on the Internet

I am a highly skilled mechanic.

What's the point of stated main ideas in reading and writing paragraphs?

Learning about stated main ideas will improve our comprehension of lessons in our academic life; help us communicate important ideas and motivate us to take action in our everyday life; and allow us to understand what a business or service has to offer us as customers or clients.

What's the Point? One Student's Response

The following paragraph is one student's response to the question "What's the point of implied main ideas in reading and writing paragraphs?"

These photographs have shown me how often we rely on implied main ideas to send and receive messages. Each photograph was chosen to send a specific message based on the details in the image. For example, the photograph posted by the college shows young men and women of various races smiling as they study together. To me, the photograph says, "Come study at a college where the students are diverse and the learning is fun." This photograph also made me think that students need to be able to figure out key ideas implied in a lecture or book. I really related to the message in the second photograph of a father reading to his children. In everyday life, our actions suggest what is important to us. Obviously, this father cares about spending quality time with his children and wants them to know how to read. His message is "I love my children and enjoy reading to them." In our working life, we can send and get powerful messages that are implied with just a few words or images. The picture of a female mechanic may be a surprising message to some people about the kind of work women are expected to do. This woman's photograph says, "I am a highly skilled mechanic." We need to be able to identify implied main ideas in all areas of our lives so we can know what ideas we are responding to.

Define the Terms *Implied Main Idea, Imply,* and *Infer*

The power of suggestion is very strong. Politicians, advertisers, and writers know this. They know an audience is more likely to accept a suggestion or **implied main idea** over a direct statement. Thus, instead of directly stating a main idea, they omit the topic sentence and provide clues through details, organizational words, and tone to suggest or **imply** the point. Think of the commercials you see and hear on television, radio, and billboards. All of them use memorable details and arouse emotions to suggest strong reasons to buy a product or accept an idea. The task of the reader is to determine or **infer** the implied main idea based on the evidence provided by the details. A writer implies and the reader infers the main idea.

Knowing the difference between *infer* and *imply* enables writers and readers to effectively send and receive implied main ideas.

An **implied main idea** is a main idea that is not stated directly, but is strongly suggested by the supporting details, organization, or tone of a passage.

Infer is to determine an idea based on the given details.

Imply is to suggest, not directly state, an idea.

Example

For sentences 1 through 5, underline the correct **bold** word. For sentences 6 through 9, fill in the blank with a form of *imply* or *infer*. Then, write your own sentence using a form of *imply* or *infer*.

1. Henry yawned, **implying/inferring** that he was bored.
2. Jenny **inferred/implied** from the smell in the kitchen that cookies were in the oven.
3. The student's test score **implied/inferred** that she had studied.
4. The surprised look on George's face **implied/inferred** he wasn't expecting Anne.
5. The police officer pulled the driver over, **implying/inferring** from the slow and weaving pace of the driver's car that the driver was drunk.
6. Tamika *inferred* from Colin's silence that he was asleep.
7. From the long line of slow moving cars on the highway, Roxanne *inferred* that a wreck had occurred.
8. Carlos *implied* that Tamar looked beautiful.
9. Kuniko smiled and eagerly shook Bob's hand, *implying* that she was glad to see him.
10. *Answers may vary.*

Explanation

Compare your responses to the following student's think-aloud.

I have often confused the words imply *and* infer. *Now I know that when I imply something I make a point, and when I infer something*

CONTINUED

EXPLANATION *CONTINUED*

I understand a point. A writer gives details to imply a point, and a reader infers a point from the details a writer gives.

1. *Implying. Henry's yawn makes the point that he is bored. He is sending a message.*
2. *Inferred. Jenny recognized the smell of cookies and, based on that smell, believed cookies were in the oven. She received a message.*
3. *Implied. The student's scores send the message that the student was prepared to take the test.*
4. *Implied. A look sends a message without saying a word.*
5. *Inferring. The police officer's belief that the driver was drunk was based on the evidence of the "slow and weaving pace."*
6. *Inferred. Colin's silence leads Tamika to believe he is asleep.*
7. *Inferred. To Roxanne, the long line of slow moving cars was evidence that an accident had occurred.*
8. *Implied. Carlos is sending a message about Tamar.*
9. *Implying. Kuniko's behaviors send the message that she is glad to see Bob.*
10. *I actually wrote two sentences to show how the same details can be used to infer or imply. Janine inferred that she had a cold based on her symptoms of a runny nose, sore throat, and cough. The symptoms of a runny nose, sore throat, and cough imply that Janine may have a cold.*

Now that you understand the terms *imply*, *infer*, and *implied main ideas*, you are ready to apply the skills of inferring and implying main ideas as a reader and a writer.

L3 Before Reading, Skim and Annotate to Identify the Topic of an Implied Main Idea

PREREAD: SURVEY/ QUESTION

In Module 5 you learned to ask the question "Who or what is the paragraph about?" to identify the topic of a paragraph with a stated main idea. You also learned that your answer must be neither too general nor too specific. This same skill will help you identify the topic of a paragraph that implies a main idea. Remember, a writer shows a reader the relationship between the topic and the specific details by repeating or rephrasing the topic throughout the paragraph to introduce new pieces of information. Effective readers skim a paragraph to identify the topic before reading the passage. Skimming for the topic gives a reader a preview of the writer's use of the details to suggest a main idea.

Example

Skim the following list of supporting details. Circle the topic as it recurs throughout the list of details. Answer the question that follows.

- Many pharaohs (ancient Egyptian rulers) built the pyramids to house themselves and their family and staff after death.
- The pyramids commemorate the greatness of the pharaohs.
- Crews of up to 100,000 men hauled and lifted stones to build pyramids.
- The first great pyramid was built about 2600 B.C.E.
- The largest pyramid, located at Giza, took 20 years to build.
- This pyramid contains 2 million blocks of stone, each stone weighing 5.5 tons.
- Egyptians were not very advanced technologically.
- They lacked pulleys or other devices to lift the huge slabs of stones.
- Masses of workers rolled stones over logs and onto barges before assembling the massive monuments on the banks of the Nile River.

Adapted from Sterns, Peter N., Adas, Michael, Schwartz, Stuart B., and Gilbert, Mark J., *World Civilization: The Global Experience*, 6th ed., pp. 37–38.

What is the topic of the list of ideas?

a. ancient monuments in Egypt
b. the Egyptian pyramids
c. technology in ancient Egypt
d. pharaohs (ancient Egyptian rulers)

Explanation

Compare your responses to the following student's think-aloud.

The topic is (b) the Egyptian pyramids. The word pyramid *is repeated six times and appears in all but the last three sentences in this list of details. However, even the last sentence uses the word* monuments *as another way to refer to pyramids. The first sentence lets us know that the details describe ancient Egyptian pyramids, not ones in other parts of the world or modern pyramids. The last three sentences did give details about the technology in ancient Egypt, but these details are related to the way the pyramids were built.*

L4 During Reading, Question, Annotate, and Analyze Details to Infer the Implied Main Idea

Remember, a stated main idea (the topic sentence) has two parts. A main idea is made up of the topic and the writer's controlling point about the topic. One trait of the controlling point is the writer's tone based on his or her opinion or bias (see Module 5). A second trait is the writer's pattern of organization, such as time order, space order, classification, comparison/contrast, cause/effect, examples, and so on. Often organizational words are used to signal a pattern of organization and to point out key details. Examples of organizational words include *first, next, next to, types, traits, similarity, difference, reason, result,* and others. Consider, for example, the topic sentence "Volunteer work results in several benefits." "Volunteer work" is the topic. "Benefits" states the opinion, and "results in several" states the pattern of organization. When you read material that implies the main idea, you should mentally create a topic sentence based on the details in the material.

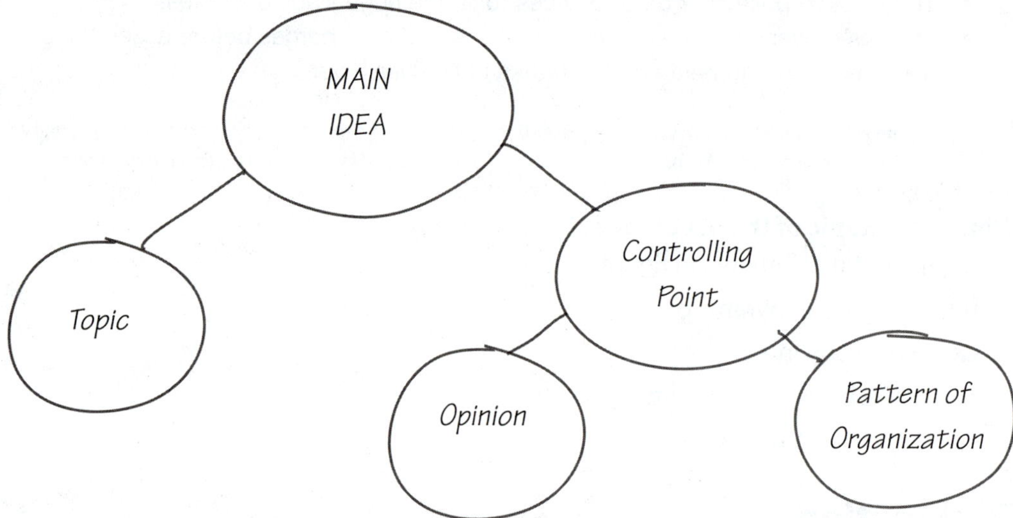

Remember that the main idea of a paragraph is like the frame of a house. Just as the frame includes all the rooms, a main idea must cover all the details in a paragraph. Therefore, the implied main idea will be general enough to cover all the details, but it will not be so broad that it becomes an overgeneralization or a sweeping statement that suggests details not given; nor can it be so narrow that some of the given details are not covered. Instead, the implied main idea must cover *all* the details given. The only difference between a main idea and an implied main idea is that the main idea is directly stated and the implied main idea is not.

To identify the implied main idea of a paragraph, ask the following questions:

- What is the topic of the paragraph?
- What is the writer's controlling point about the topic?
- What tone words does the writer use about the topic?
- What words does the writer use to limit the topic?

As you skim a paragraph, identify its topic and analyze the supporting details. Annotate the paragraph to highlight the writer's controlling point. Circle the topic. Underline tone words and words that limit the topic.

Example

Read the following details from a college criminal justice textbook. Circle the topic as it recurs throughout the details. Underline biased or opinion words and tone words. Then choose the statement that best expresses the writer's controlling point about the topic.

- The American frontier was a vast and wild place until late in the nineteenth century.
- The backwoods areas of the frontier proved a natural haven for outlaws and bandits.
- For example, Henry Berry Lowery, a famous outlaw of the Carolinas, the James Gang, and many lesser-known desperadoes felt at home in the frontier's swamps and forests.
- Only the boldest of settlers tried to police the frontier.
- In the late eighteenth century, citizen posses and vigilante groups were often the only law available to settlers on the American frontier.
- Several popular frontier figures of the nineteenth century took it upon themselves to enforce the law on the books as well as the standards of common decency.
- For example, Judge Roy Bean, "Wild Bill" Hickok, Bat Masterson, Wyatt Earp, and Pat Garrett policed the frontier, sometimes in a semiofficial role.

Adapted from Schmalleger, Frank, *Criminal Justice Today: An Introductory Text for the 21st Century*, 10th ed., p. 155.

Which statement best expresses the implied main idea?

a. The American frontier was a dangerous place.

b. Bold settlers and citizens enforced the law on the American frontier.

c. By the late nineteenth century, the vast and wild American frontier was policed by bold settlers, citizens, and popular figures who enforced the law.

d. The American frontier was home to outlaws, bandits, and desperadoes.

Explanation

Compare your responses to the following student's think-aloud.

The most frequently recurring idea is the "American frontier." At first, I thought another topic, "the law," was also the focus. But since this idea appears less often, and in several forms such as "police" and "law," I determined it was an important detail about the frontier. Several biased words describe the lack of law or the need for law on the American frontier. These words include wild, haven, outlaw, bandit, swamps, forests, desperadoes, *and* vigilantes. *A few other biased words describe the people who worked to bring law to the frontier. These words include* boldest, citizen

CONTINUED

EXPLANATION *CONTINUED*

posse, popular figures, standards of common decency, and semiofficial. Two phrases gave the time of the American frontier and its law: "until the late nineteenth century" and "in the late eighteenth century." The only statement that covers all these details is item (c). Item (a) states a general idea, and items (b) and (d) restate supporting details.

Practice 1

Infer the Main Idea

Read the following group of supporting details. Circle the topic as it recurs throughout the list of details. Underline words to help you locate the major details. Also underline biased words to determine the writer's opinion. Then, select the sentence that best expresses the implied main idea.

- Cognitive therapy helps a person deal with negative or painful thoughts and behaviors.
- This therapy, a psychological treatment, was developed by a medical doctor, Aaron T. Beck, in the 1970s.
- First, a person seeks to change thinking patterns such as assumptions and core beliefs.
- Changes in feelings and actions will follow.
- To aid change, a person learns how to replace harmful thoughts and behaviors with positive coping tactics.
- Some of these tactics may include anger management and relaxation training.

Which sentence best states the implied main idea?

a. Cognitive therapy is a psychological treatment.

b. Cognitive therapy is a psychological treatment that helps a person replace negative or painful thoughts and behaviors with positive coping skills.

c. Cognitive therapy was developed by Aaron T. Beck, M.D., in the 1970s.

d. Cognitive therapy focuses on negative or painful thoughts and behaviors.

So far as a reader, you have learned to recognize the implied main idea by studying the specific details in a group of sentences. In this next step, the sentences will form a paragraph, but the skill of recognizing and suggesting the implied main idea is exactly the same. As you work through the rest of this section and the next section as a reader, you are preparing yourself as a writer. Think about how you can use what you learn as a reader to imply a main idea as a writer.

Example

Read the following paragraph from a college business textbook. Circle the topic as it recurs throughout the paragraph. Underline words to help you locate the major details. Also underline biased words to determine the writer's opinion. Then, select the sentence that best expresses the implied main idea.

Levels of Management

[1]**Top managers** are responsible for the overall performance and effectiveness of a firm. [2]Common titles for top managers are *president, vice president, treasurer, chief executive officer* (CEO), and *chief financial officer* (CFO). [3]They set general policies, plan strategies, approve all major decisions. [4]They also represent the company in dealing with other firms and government officials. [5]Just below the ranks of top managers is another group of managers called **middle managers**. [6]Middle managers go by titles such as *plant manager, operations manager,* and *division manager*. [7]In general, middle managers carry out the strategies, policies, and decisions made by top managers. [8]**First-line managers** have titles such as *supervisor, office manager*, and *group leader*. [9]First-line managers spend most of their time working with and supervising the employees who report to them.

Adapted from Ebert, Ronald J., and Griffin, Ricky W., *Business Essentials*, 8th ed., pp. 165–166.

The best statement of the implied main idea is:

a. Top managers have the most responsibility and receive the highest pay.

b. Managers are known by a variety of titles.

(c.) Management of a firm or company can be divided into three levels of managers.

Explanation

Compare your responses to the following student's think-aloud.

The title and the supporting details of this paragraph give strong clues that helped me figure out the implied main idea. The word management appears in the title, and the word managers appears in almost all of the sentences. In addition, the writer describes three levels of managers: top, middle, and first-line. So I think the best statement of the implied main idea is item (c). Item (a) states a supporting detail, and it includes the idea of "the highest pay," which is not mentioned in any of the details. Item (b) seems too general for a main idea statement.

Practice 2

Identify the Implied Main Idea

Read the following paragraphs. In each paragraph, circle the topic as it recurs throughout the paragraph. Underline organizational words to help locate the major details. Also underline the biased words to determine the writer's opinion. Then select the sentence that best expresses the implied main idea for each.

Green Tea: The Miracle Drink

[1]Green tea has been used for thousands of years in Asia as both a beverage and an herbal medicine. [2]This herbal tea contains catechin, which is a type of tannin that acts as an astringent. [3]Research suggests that men and women in Japan who drink five to six cups of green tea each day have much lower rates of cancer than people who do not. [4]Green tea is also thought to lower cholesterol and blood sugar, control high blood pressure, stop tooth decay, and fight viruses. [5]Green tea has even been credited with the power to slow down the aging process.

1. Which sentence best states the implied main idea?

a. Green tea is an ancient herbal drink.

b. Green tea has caught the attention of medical researchers.

c. Green tea lowers cholesterol and blood sugar and controls high blood pressure.

d. Green tea, an ancient Asian herbal drink, is thought to have many health benefits.

One Handsome Young Man

[1]At 6-foot-4, Van stood taller than most young men. [2]The Florida sun tanned his skin to a deep bronze and bleached his dark brown hair to varying shades of sandy blond. [3]Endowed with the high cheekbones of his Indian ancestors, sapphire eyes, and a luminous smile, he drew attention. [4]He moved like an athlete at ease in his own skin. [5]In neighborhood orange wars, Van could throw an orange farther and more accurately than any of us. [6]In fact, he could outrun, outswim, outhunt, outfish, outdo all of us, and still we loved him. [7]Guys felt proud to be his friend; girls clamored to be his sweetheart. [8]Even now, 30 years later, at our high school reunion, Van looms larger than life to those of us he left behind: an unaging memory, a tragic loss.

2. Which sentence best states the implied main idea?

a. Van was a handsome, talented, well-liked young man who died and is still missed.

b. Van was a tall, good-looking young man.

c. Van is a tragic figure.

d. Van is still missed by his high school friends.

After Reading, State the Implied Main Idea in a Sentence

LO5

Stating an implied main idea in your own words is a way to use your writing skills to learn. Up to now, you have developed the skill of figuring out main ideas that are not directly stated. This ability to reason from specific details to main ideas will serve you well throughout college. One further step will also help your reading and studying: the ability to state the implied main idea in your own words. After reading, summarize the most important details into a one-sentence statement; in other words, you must create a topic sentence. In Module 5, you learned to write a topic sentence by narrowing a topic based on an opinion or pattern of organization. You will apply this same skill to formulate this one-sentence summary, find the topic, determine the writer's opinion by examining the biased words, and use the pattern of organization to locate the major details. Then you will combine these ideas into a single sentence. The summary sentence includes the topic and the writer's controlling point, just like a topic sentence. The statement you write must not be too narrow, for it must cover all the details given. On the other hand, it must not be too broad or go beyond the supporting details. Remember that a main idea is always written as a complete sentence.

Example

Read the list of specific ideas that follows. Circle the topic as it recurs throughout each group of details. Underline words that reveal patterns of organization and bias to discover the controlling point. Then write a sentence that best states the implied main idea.

- Ranked number one on the Forbes list as the most powerful celebrity, Oprah Winfrey made $77 million between June 2012 and June 2013. While other people may have made more money, Oprah's fame and social networking power pushed her to the top.
- Ranked number two as a power figure is Lady Gaga. In spite of a hip injury, Gaga earned $80 million dollars and is one of the most often mentioned celebrities in the press.
- Number three on the list, Steven Spielberg earned an estimated $100 million. His highly acclaimed film *Lincoln* earned two Oscars and $275 million worldwide.
- At number four, Beyoncé earned $53 million after taking a year off due to giving birth to her baby Blue Ivy. Her "Mrs. Carter World Tour" has earned her over $2 million in every city she has played. She also derives income from her classical hits, deals with Pepsi and H&M, and her own House of Dereon clothing line.
- Rounding out the top five on the 2013 Forbes list of the most powerful celebrities is Madonna. She made $125 million through her music, Material Girl clothing line, Truth or Dare fragrance, and other wise investments. Her MDNA tour grossed $305 million and earned her the Top Touring Award at the Billboard Music Awards.

Implied main idea: *Answers will vary. One possible answer: The 2013 Forbes list of most influential celebrities is dominated by women.*

CONTINUED

Explanation

Compare your responses to the following student's think-aloud.

I tried to summarize the important details into a one-sentence summary. The topic is the "Forbes list of most powerful celebrities." The organizational words include ranked number one, ranked number two, number three, at number four, rounding out the top five. *I noticed that the details were organized as a list of celebrities. Interestingly, the list was mostly made up of women, and three of the women are singers who also have clothing lines. The details of their earnings gave them their ranking on the list. I wrote the following sentence to state the implied main idea: "The 2013 Forbes list of most influential celebrities is dominated by women."*

Example

Read the following paragraph. Circle the topic as it recurs throughout the paragraph. Underline words that reveal patterns of organization and bias to discover the controlling point. Then write a sentence that best states the implied main idea. Remember: not too narrow, not too broad—find that perfect fit!

MAKE IT RIGHT IN THE LOWER NINTH WARD, NEW ORLEANS

[1]In 2005, Hurricane Katrina destroyed more than 4,000 homes in New Orleans' Lower Ninth Ward. [2]In 2007, Brad Pitt founded Make It Right to build 150 homes for families living in the Lower 9th Ward when the storm hit. [3]Importantly, Make It Right homes are storm resistant. [4]Make It Right homes include pervious concrete, escape hatches and attic windows, increased durability (able to withstand 160 mph winds), raised elevations, and hurricane window fabric. [5]Additionally, Make It Right homes are energy efficient. [6]Energy efficient features include metal roofs, hyper-insulation, solar panels, and Energy Star appliances. [7]Make It Right homes also use eco-friendly landscape designs. [8]Make It Right landscapes use native plants, rain gardens, edible gardens, roof-top gardens, xeric plantings, and street trees. [9]Finally, Make It Right homes are affordable. [10]Returning residents pay Make It Right what they're able—usually about $75,000. [11]And Make It Right lends them the rest. [12]The cost of a single Make It Right home is in the $150,000 range; a double is about $200,000. [13]The repayment policy varies. [14]For some, the loan is free, if the recipient agrees to live in the house for five to 20 years. [15]By April 2013, 90 Make It Right homes had been completed. [16]And the organization breaks ground on new homes every month—making it right for dozens of families who survived Hurricane Katrina.

Implied main idea: *Answers will vary. One possible answer: In the years after Hurricane Katrina, Brad Pitt established the Make It Right foundation to build 150 storm-resistant, energy-efficient, affordable homes in the Lower Ninth Ward of New Orleans.*

Explanation

Compare your responses to the following student's think-aloud.

I figured out the topic is Make It Right because this phrase was repeated so often in the paragraph. Then I recognized the signal words Importantly *(sentence 3),* Additionally *(sentence 5), and* Finally *(sentence 9). These words point out the most important details that explain the topic. Also, as I circled recurring words to identify the topic, the word* homes *was used repeatedly. Make It Right is all about building new homes. I wrote the following topic sentence to state the implied main idea: "In the years after Hurricane Katrina, Brad Pitt established the Make It Right foundation to build 150 storm-resistant, energy-efficient, affordable homes in the Lower Ninth Ward of New Orleans."*

Practice 3

State the Implied Main Idea

A. Read the following group of supporting details. Circle the topic as it recurs throughout the details. Underline organizational words and biased words to discover the controlling point. Then write a sentence that best states the implied main idea. After writing, check the sentence by asking if all the major details support it.

Group of Details

- Recent DNA testing has proved several people on death row innocent of the crimes for which they were sentenced to death.
- The cost to taxpayers for death penalty appeals is staggeringly high.
- Many people believe that the death penalty is morally wrong and a form of legalized homicide.
- Many also believe that the death penalty does not deter crime.
- Finally, many believe that the death penalty unfairly targets the poor and the African American population.

1. Implied main idea: *Answers will vary. One possible answer: People oppose the death penalty for several reasons.*

CONTINUED

PRACTICE 3 *CONTINUED*

B. Read the following paragraph. Circle the topic as it recurs throughout the paragraph. Underline organizational words and biased words to discover the controlling point. Then write a sentence that states the implied main idea.

Indoor Tanning: The Risks of Ultraviolet Rays

[1]The serious risk of skin cancer is not the only damage caused by tanning. [2]First, tanning causes premature aging. [3]Tanning causes the skin to lose elasticity and wrinkle prematurely. [4]This leathery look may not show up until many years after you've had a tan or sunburn. [5]Second, tanning suppresses the immune system. [6]UV-B radiation may suppress proper functioning of the body's immune system and the skin's natural defenses, leaving you more vulnerable to diseases, including skin cancer. [7]Third, tanning causes eye damage. [8]Exposure to UV radiation can cause irreversible damage to the eyes. [9]Fourth, tanning may develop an allergic reaction. [10]Some people who are especially sensitive to UV radiation may develop an itchy red rash and other adverse effects. [11]Advocates of tanning devices sometimes argue that using these devices is less dangerous than sun tanning because the intensity of UV radiation and the time spent tanning can be controlled. [12]But there is no evidence to support these claims. [13]In fact, sunlamps may be more dangerous than the sun because they can be used at the same high intensity every day of the year—unlike the sun whose intensity varies with the time of day, the season, and cloud cover.

Adapted from FDA Consumer Health Information. U.S. Food and Drug Administration. 22 Aug. 2013. http://www.fda.gov/ForConsumers/ConsumerUpdates/ucm186687.htm

2. Implied main idea: *Answers will vary. One possible answer: The ultraviolet rays of indoor tanning devices can cause several serious health problems.*

L6 Prewrite to Generate Supporting Details to Imply a Main Idea

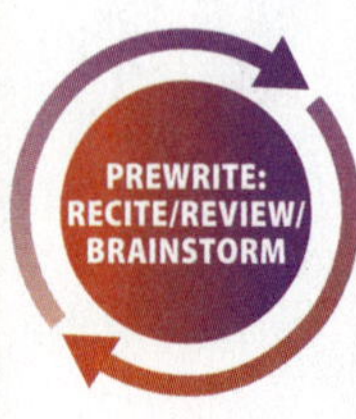

To imply a main idea about a topic, writers carefully choose details as clues that work together to lead the reader to understand the implied point. Now that you have practiced inferring a topic and main idea by analyzing supporting details as a reader, apply this skill as a writer. Before writing, a writer makes several decisions about how to best imply a main idea. First, a writer chooses the topic and identifies his or her attitude about the topic. To generate details, most writers find it helpful to also choose a pattern of organization. For example, a writer may ask, "Will the point be best made by providing details in a list or by discussing types, causes, effects, similarities, or differences?" Then the writer generates details based on these decisions.

Example

Choose a topic, opinion, and pattern of organization from the following list. Think about a specific point you would like to make about the topic. Then write a list of three major details that make your point about the topic. After creating your list of details, exchange your list with a peer. Study your peer's list of ideas. Circle the topic as it recurs throughout the list of details. Underline words to help you locate the major details. Also underline biased words to determine the writer's opinion. Then write a sentence that you think best expresses the main idea implied by your classmate. *Answers may vary.*

Topics	movie(s)	diet(s)	role model(s)
Attitudes	good	horrible	neutral
Pattern of Organization	examples	reasons	type

List of details:

1. ______________________________

2. ______________________________

3. ______________________________

Implied main idea: ______________________________

____

Explanation

Read the following student's think-aloud about providing details to imply a main idea.

I chose to write about horrible role models by giving examples. I chose this topic because of all the reality shows on television. Most of these shows make rude or odd people into famous stars who have lots of fans.

1. *Kim Kardashian is one example of a horrible role model on reality television.*
2. *Another awful role model made famous by a reality show is June "Mama" Thompson on* Here Comes Honey Boo Boo.
3. *A third example of a horrible role model from reality TV is Abby Lee Miller from* Dance Moms.

I wrote the following sentence to state my implied main idea.

CONTINUED

EXPLANATION *CONTINUED*

"Reality television offers horrible role models by turning rude or odd people into famous stars."

My classmate gave me the following list of details. After highlighting the topic, transitions, and biased words, I wrote the following sentence to state the implied main idea.

Implied Main Idea: "The grapefruit diet is a horrible diet for several reasons."

1. *The grapefruit diet is horrible because it offers very little nutrition.*
2. *Another reason is that the acidic citrus fruit in this diet may cause a stomach ulcer.*
3. *A final reason to avoid this horrible diet is that it is dangerous to mix grapefruit juice with some medications.*

Practice 4

Imply a Main Idea

Choose a topic, opinion, and pattern of organization from the following list. Think about a specific point you would like to make about the topic. Then write a list of three major details that make your point about the topic. After creating your list of details, exchange your list with a peer. Study your peer's list of ideas. Circle the topic as it recurs throughout the list of details. Underline words to help locate the major details. Also underline biased words to determine the writer's opinion. Then write a sentence that you think best expresses the main idea implied by your classmate. *Answers may vary.*

Topics	a habit	a person	a place
Opinions	admirable	fun	annoying
Pattern of Organization	examples	reasons	description

List of details:

1. ______

2. ______

3. ______

Implied main idea: ______

Write a Paragraph That Implies a Main Idea 

Now that you have practiced determining the implied main idea as a reader and stating an implied main idea, you are ready to write a paragraph that implies a main idea. Think of how a photographer captures the details of a scene to influence an audience. The photographer carefully considers which details of the scene to capture in a picture to make a specific point. Likewise, an effective writer carefully chooses specific details to suggest a main idea that will affect or inspire the reader. To develop a paragraph that implies a main idea, a writer uses the writing process to prewrite, write, revise, and proofread a paragraph. Many writers find it helpful to prewrite a topic sentence that states the point that they want to imply, but then they do not include that topic sentence in the final draft. The topic sentence simply serves as a guide as they draft, revise, and proofread.

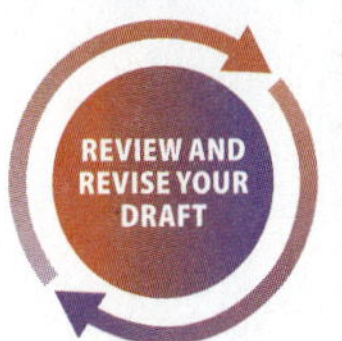

Example

Study the following photographs of Hurricane Sandy during and after the storm. What do these pictures imply about the storm? Choose details captured in these photographs, a pattern of organization, and an opinion to imply a main idea about the storm. Use the writing process to develop a paragraph that implies a main idea based on these images. Remember, you can write a main idea to help keep your thoughts organized, but then remove it before finalizing your paragraph. Your goal is to use details to "show, don't tell" the main idea. *Answers may vary.*

Hurricane Sandy

October 29, 2012, Brooklyn, NY

November 1, 2012, Brooklyn, NY

Prewrite: Think about a specific point you would like to make based on the details in the photographs. Narrow the topic "Hurricane Sandy" by identifying your opinion and a pattern of organization. You may choose from the given list. Then brainstorm a list of three major details that make your point about the topic. Write a topic sentence that states the main idea you will imply.

Topic	Hurricane Sandy		
Opinions	destructive	frightening	surprising
Pattern of Organization	examples	time order	description

CONTINUED

EXAMPLE *CONTINUED*

List of details:

1. ______________________

2. ______________________

3. ______________________

Implied main idea: ______________________

____

Draft: Write a draft of your paragraph. Do not include the topic sentence. Instead, word and organize your details to imply the main idea.
Revise: Reread your paragraph. Make sure each detail offers a strong clue that reveals your implied main idea.
Proofread: Mark any errors in punctuation and mechanics. Then create a final, polished draft.

Explanation

Read the following paragraph that implies a main idea based on the photographs. Then read the writer's think-aloud that records some of the decisions she made throughout the writing process.

On October 29, 2012, Hurricane Sandy moved into Brooklyn, New York. Torrential rains flooded the streets with a destructive force. During the night, the high winds and raging waters threatened business buildings, homes, cars, and the very lives of the people. The next morning, the dawn revealed the extent of the damage. The storm had splintered buildings into mounds of rubble. The region looked like a war zone destroyed by bombs.

Think-aloud: I really enjoyed writing this paragraph. It was really helpful to have the pictures because they showed so many specific details about the effect of Hurricane Sandy. I was really struck by how destructive the storm was. The time line of the pictures showing what happened during the night and then the results also inspired me. In my first draft, I did include words and details about how frightening the storm must have been. However, during my revision, I deleted or reworded ideas to focus just on the destruction of the storm.

Practice 5

Write a Paragraph That Implies a Main Idea

Use the writing process to develop a paragraph that implies a main idea. You may use the following images or develop a topic of your own choosing.

Prewrite: Identify your topic. Think about a specific point you would like to make based on the details in the photographs. Narrow the topic by identifying your opinion and a pattern of organization. You may choose a pattern of organization from the given list. Then brainstorm a list of three major details that make your point about the topic. Write a topic sentence that states the main idea you will imply. *Answers may vary.*

Topic: ____________________

Opinion: ____________________

Pattern of Organization effects traits time order

List of details:

1. ____________________

2. ____________________

3. ____________________

Implied main idea: ____________________

____

Draft: Write a draft of your paragraph. Do not include the topic sentence. Instead, word and organize your details to imply the main idea expressed in the topic sentence you created during the prewriting phase.

Revise: Reread your paragraph. Make sure each detail offers a strong clue that reveals your implied main idea. Make sure each detail is in its proper order to make sense. Reword, delete, add, or move details as needed to make your implied main idea clear to your reader.

Proofread: Reread your paragraph. Mark any errors in punctuation and mechanics. Then create a final, polished draft.

L8 Determine the Implied Central Idea of a Longer Passage

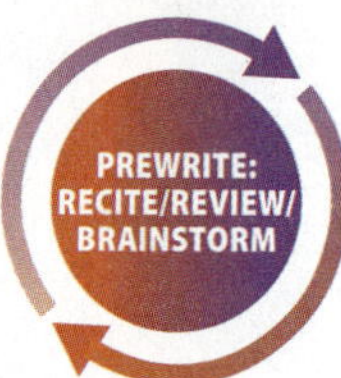

Just as a single paragraph can have an implied main idea, longer passages made up of two or more paragraphs can also have an implied main idea. You encounter these longer passages in articles, essays, and textbooks. As you learned in Module 5, the stated main idea or central idea of these longer passages is called the *thesis statement*. When the main idea of several paragraphs is implied, it is called the **implied central idea**. You use the same skills to infer or imply a central idea of a longer passage that you use to infer or imply the main idea of a single paragraph.

The **implied central idea** is the main idea suggested by the details of a passage made up of two or more paragraphs.

Before and During Reading, Skim, Question, Annotate to Identify the Topic and Analyze Details

Annotating the text is a helpful tool in determining the implied central idea. Just as you did to grasp the implied main idea for paragraphs, circle the topic as it recurs throughout the passage. Underline biased words or organizational words that reveal the controlling point. Remember, organizational words introduce supporting details. A writer often pairs these words with major supporting details. Consider the following examples: *the first reason, a second cause, the final effect, another similarity, an additional difference*, and so on. A reader may use these phrases to summarize the implied main idea in a single sentence.

Example

Read the following passage from a college psychology textbook. Annotate the text. Circle the topic as it occurs throughout the passage. Underline organizational words and biased words that reveal the controlling point. Then answer the question that follows.

CHUNKING

[1]A chunk is a meaningful unit of information. [2]A chunk can be a single letter or number, a group of letters or other items, or even a group of words or an entire sentence. [3]For example, the sequence 1-9-8-4 consists of four digits, each of which is a chunk when they are remembered separately. [4]However, if you see the digits as a year or the title of George Orwell's novel *1984*, they constitute only one chunk, leaving you much more capacity for other chunks of information.

[5]See how many chunks you can find in this sequence of 20 numbers: 19411917186518121776. [6]You can answer "20" if you see the sequence as a list of unrelated digits or "5" if you break down the sequence into the dates of major

wars in U.S. history. [7]If you do the latter, it's easy for you to recall all the digits in the proper sequence after one quick glance. [8]It would be impossible for you to remember them from a short exposure if you saw them as 20 unrelated items.

Gerrig, Richard J., and Zimbardo, Philip G., *Psychology and Life*, 19th ed., p. 225.

The sentence that best summarizes the central idea is:

a. A chunk is a small part of a larger set of information.

b. Chunking is a strategy that increases memory by organizing large pieces of information into smaller units of thought.

c. Chunking is an excellent method of memorizing important dates in history.

d. Chunking is helpful.

Explanation

Compare your responses to the following student think-aloud.

The title clearly states the topic of the passage as "Chunking." Then the word chunk is repeated four times throughout the paragraph. The writer explains what a chunk of information is and then gives examples. These examples show the reader how to chunk information. The sentence that best summarizes these details is (b), "Chunking is a strategy that increases memory by organizing large pieces of information into smaller units of thought." Sentences (a) and (c) are too narrow; sentence (d) is too broad.

Practice 6

Identify the Implied Central Idea

Read the following passage. Circle the topic as it recurs throughout the passage. Underline organizational words and biased words that reveal the controlling point. Then answer the question that follows.

THE THREE PHASES OF LYME DISEASE

[1]The first stage of Lyme disease shows up three to 30 days after a person is bitten by an infected tick. [2]During this phase, a red-rimmed circular spot or spots emerge, often described as a "bull's-eye" rash. [3]The centers of these expanding spots become pale, and the infected person experiences exhaustion, headaches, a fever, and joint and muscle pains.

[4]The second stage of Lyme disease can develop within weeks or take months to appear. [5]One symptom is Bell's palsy, which causes one side of the face to droop and the eye on that side to stay opened. [6]In addition, nerve problems can occur, the heart can become inflamed, and the rash seen in stage one can return.

[7]The third stage of Lyme disease, which can occur within weeks or take years to develop, is arthritis, the painful swelling of joints.

[8]Of course, not all cases of Lyme disease exhibit all these symptoms. [9]Some cases may have only one or two of these signs.

The sentence that best summarizes the central idea is:

a. Lyme disease can have long-term consequences.

b. Lyme disease affects different people in different ways.

c. Lyme disease can attack the nerves and heart.

d. Lyme disease, a serious illness caused by a tick bite, occurs in three stages.

After Reading, Write the Implied Central Idea of a Longer Passage

Remember, stating an implied idea in your own words is a way to use your writing skills to learn. By skimming and annotating the text before and during reading to identify the topic, the organizational words, and the biased words, you have a pretty good sense of the implied central idea. By writing a one-sentence summary of the implied central idea in the form of a thesis sentence, you clarify and deepen your understanding.

Example

Before reading the following passage from a college health textbook, skim and annotate the text. Circle the topic as it recurs throughout the passage. Underline organizational and biased words. Finally, write a sentence that states the implied central idea of the passage in a thesis statement.

TYPES OF DRUGS ABUSED OR MISUSED

[1]Some drugs stimulate the body. [2]Some depress body functions. [3]Others produce hallucinations (images, auditory or visual, that are perceived but are not real). [4]All types also include psychoactive drugs. [5]**Psychoactive drugs** change the way the brain works. [6]They have the potential to alter mood or behavior.

- [7]**Prescription drugs** can be obtained only with a prescription from a licensed health practitioner. [8]More than 10,000 types of prescription drugs are sold in the United States.

- [9]**Over-the-counter drugs (OTC)** can be purchased without a prescription. [10]More than 300,000 OTC products are available. [11]An estimated 3 out of 4 people routinely self medicate with them. [12]Prescription drugs are available at approximately 58,000 pharmacies nationwide. [13]In contrast, OTC medicines are available for consumers at over 750,000 retailers in the United States. [14]Studies show that Americans are making more use of widely available OTC medicines each year.

- [15]**Recreational drugs** belong to a somewhat vague category. [16]The boundaries depend upon how the term *recreation* is defined. [17]Generally, recreational drugs contain chemicals used to help people relax or socialize. [18]Most of them are legal even though they are psychoactive. [19]Alcohol, tobacco, and caffeine products are included in this category.

- [20]**Herbal preparations** include approximately 750 substances. [21]These include herbal teas and other products of botanical (plant) origin that are believed to have medicinal properties.

- [22]**Illicit (illegal) drugs** are the most notorious type of drug. [23]Laws governing their use, possession, cultivation, manufacture, and sale differ from state to state. [24]However, illicit drugs are generally recognized as harmful. [25]All of them are psychoactive.

- [26]**Commercial preparations** are the most universally used. [27]Yet they are the least commonly recognized chemical substances. [28]More than 1,000 of them exist. [29]Many seem to be benign items such as perfumes, cosmetics, household cleansers, paints, glues, inks, dyes, and pesticides.

[30]Those who misuse or abuse drugs may think drugs are helping them relax, improve concentration, or enhance social enjoyment. [31]However, those effects are short term. [32]They are nothing compared to the many negative effects those same drugs can have on their lives and health. [33]Are a few moments of excitement worth a lifetime of trouble?

Donatelle, Rebecca J. *Access to Health*, 12th ed., pp. 406–408.

Implied central idea: *Answers will vary. One possible response: Abuse or misuse of these six types of drugs can lead to a lifetime of trouble.*

CONTINUED

Explanation

Compare your responses to the following student's think-aloud.

Including the title, the word drug *was repeated at least 13 times. In addition, the writer used synonyms like* chemical substances, prescriptions, preparations, *and* medicines. *The words* types *and* category *and the number of drugs discussed in the list let me know the writer was talking about six types of drugs. The words* abused *or* misused *also revealed the writer's focus for the topic of drugs. The biased words* negative *and* lifetime of trouble *also helped me understand the writer's point. Based on these clues, I wrote the following thesis statement for the implied central idea. "Abuse or misuse of these six types of drugs can lead to a lifetime of trouble."*

Practice 7

Write the Implied Central Ideas as a Thesis Statement

Read the following passage from a college communications textbook. Annotate the text. Write a sentence that summarizes the details and states the implied central idea.

HANDWASHING: CLEAN HANDS SAVE LIVES

[1]What is one of the most important things you can do to prevent the spread of disease and fight food poisoning? [2]Here are a few hints.

- [3]It takes only 20 seconds (if you do it the right way).
- [4]It requires only 3 ingredients.
- [5]Anyone can do it, even very young children.

[6]The answer is *Wash Your Hands*. [7]Over and over again, research proves the importance of handwashing.

What is the right way to wash your hands?

[8]When you wash your hands the right way, it takes only 20 seconds and requires only three ingredients: running water, soap, and something to dry your hands (a clean towel or air).

[9]Here's how to do it:

1. [10]Wet your hands with clean running water (warm or cold) and apply soap.

2. [11]Rub your hands together to make a lather and scrub them well; be sure to scrub the backs of your hands, between your fingers, and under your nails.

3. [12]Continue rubbing your hands for at least 20 seconds. [13]Need a timer? [14]Hum the "Happy Birthday" song from beginning to end twice.

4. [15]Rinse your hands well under running water.

5. [16]Dry your hands using a clean towel or air dry.

[17]And here's when to do it:

- [18]Before, during, and after preparing food
- [19]Before eating food
- [20]Before and after caring for someone who is sick
- [21]Before and after treating a cut or wound
- [22]After using the toilet
- [23]After changing diapers or cleaning up a child who has used the toilet
- [24]After blowing your nose, coughing, or sneezing
- [25]After touching an animal or animal waste
- [26]After handling pet food or pet treats
- [27]After touching garbage

What if I don't have soap and clean, running water?

[28]Washing hands with soap and water is the best way to reduce the number of germs on them. [29]If soap and water are not available, use an alcohol-based hand sanitizer that contains at least 60% alcohol. [30]Alcohol-based hand sanitizers can quickly reduce the number of germs on hands in some situations, but sanitizers do not eliminate all types of germs. [31]Hand sanitizers are not as effective when hands are visibly dirty. [32]Here is how to use hand sanitizers:

1. [33]Apply the product to the palm of one hand.

2. [34]Rub your hands together.

3. [35]Rub the product over all surfaces of your hands and fingers until your hands are dry.

"Handwashing: Clean Hands Save Lives." Centers for Disease Control and Prevention. 11 Jan. 2013 http://www.cdc.gov/handwashing/.

Implied central idea: *Answers will vary. One possible response: Proper handwashing helps to prevent the spread of disease, fights food poisoning, and saves lives.*

Reading and Writing Assignments

MySkillsLab™
Complete these assignments in MySkillsLab.

Considering Audience and Purpose

Review the photographs about the implied main idea at the beginning of this module. Choose one to respond to in writing. Study the photograph. Then write a paragraph that suggests the same message intended by the picture.

Reading and Writing for Everyday Life

Assume you are the parent of a child who loves stories in which the characters are animals. Together, you have read the following short story from the collection of *Aesop's Fables*, which always have a moral or teach a lesson about life. After reading, your child asks you what the story means, and then asks you to make up your own story to share. Read the fable. Write a topic sentence that states the implied main idea. Then write an original short story that implies a lesson about life.

The Dog and the Shadow

It happened that a Dog had got a piece of meat and was carrying it home in his mouth to eat it in peace. Now on his way home he had to cross a plank lying across a running brook. As he crossed, he looked down and saw his own shadow reflected in the water beneath. Thinking it was another dog with another piece of meat, he made up his mind to have that also. So he made a snap at the shadow in the water, but as he opened his mouth the piece of meat fell out, dropped into the water, and was never seen more.

Æsop. Fables, retold by Joseph Jacobs. Vol. XVII, Part 1. *The Harvard Classics*. New York: P.F. Collier & Son, 1909–14; Bartleby.com, 2001. www.bartleby.com/17/1/. [6 Dec. 2012].

Reading and Writing for College Life

Assume you are taking a college health class. Every week, you are expected to respond in writing to a key idea in your textbook. You have chosen to respond in writing to the following paragraph. First, write a topic sentence that states the implied main idea of the paragraph. Then describe a person or situation that implies either an external or internal locus of control.

TWO TYPES OF LOCUS OF CONTROL

Locus of control is the "location" an individual sees as the source and underlying cause of events in his or her life. Individuals who feel that they have limited control over their lives often find it more difficult to initiate positive changes. If they believe that someone or something else controls a situation or that they dare not act in a particular way because of peer repercussions, they may become easily frustrated and give up. People with these characteristics have an *external* locus of control. In contrast, people who have a stronger *internal* locus of control believe they have power over their own actions. They are more driven by their own thoughts and more likely to state their opinions and be true to their own beliefs.

Adapted from Donatelle, Rebecca J. *Health: The Basics*, Green Ed., 9th ed., p. 15.

Reading and Writing for Working Life

Assume you are a human resource specialist at a major corporation. Several department managers have complained about the unprofessional way in which their employees are dressing. Your department has drafted the following guidelines. You are in charge of conducting a series of training sessions to introduce the guidelines to each department. First, write a topic sentence that states the main idea of the guidelines. This topic sentence will be included in the memo you send out to announce the training sessions. Next, describe a situation that shows the difference between professional and unprofessional attire (to use in the training session with the departments).

Dress Standards

1. Appropriate Professional Attire

Male employees are required to wear neat and clean suits or a sports jacket, dress slacks, shirt, socks, and shoes. Ties, when worn, should be tied appropriately. It is permissible to wear a suit or sports jacket, dress slacks, and a banded collared shirt. However, banded collarless shirts are not appropriate. Accessories that do not detract from the company's professional image are appropriate. Clothing must cover tattoos, if possible.

Female employees are required to wear neat and clean business dresses, and suits, dress skirts and slacks, blouses, sweaters, jackets/ blazers, and shoes. Hosiery shall be worn when wearing a dress or skirt. During summer months, the wearing of hosiery is optional. Accessories that do not detract from the company's professional image are appropriate. Clothing must cover tattoos, if possible.

2. Headgear

Hats are not appropriate in the office. With the exception of headgear for religious purposes, or to honor cultural or ethnic traditions, all staff should remove hats, caps, or other headgear while on duty indoors.

Workshop: Compose a Paragraph

Choose a passage to read and respond to in writing. You may select a passage in an example, practice, or writing assignment within this module. Or you may select a passage of your own choosing. Use the following guide to comprehend and respond to the passage. Apply what you have learned about implied main ideas to your reading/writing strategy.

Preread: Survey and Question

Prereading/Writing Questions based on text features (vocabulary):

____

____

____

Standard prereading/writing questions:

What is the passage about? ____

____

How is the material organized? ____

____

What do I already know about this topic? (What is my prior knowledge about the vocabulary?)

____

____

What is my purpose for reading/writing? ____

____

What is the writer's purpose and tone? ____

____

What main ideas or details may I want to address or include in my written response?

____

____

____

____

____

Read and Annotate

As you read, annotate key ideas, particularly those details that answer your prereading questions.

Recite, Review, and Brainstorm

Recite the information. Summarize the most important parts. Answer your prereading questions. Rephrase ideas into your own words. Record changes in your opinions based on the new information. **Review** the information. **Brainstorm** ideas for your written response to the passage. **Freewrite** a response to what you have read. **Map** the relationship among ideas you have annotated in the text. **Outline** or list key ideas and details in blocks of thought. Use your own paper.

Write a Draft of Your Response

Using the ideas you generated by brainstorming, compose a draft of your response. Use your own paper.

Revise Your Draft

Once you have created a draft of your paragraph, read the draft and answer the questions in the "Questions for Revising a Paragraph" box that follows. Indicate your answers by annotating your paper. If you answer "yes" to a question, underline, check, or circle examples. If you answer "no" to a question, write additional details in the margins and draw lines to indicate their placement. Revise your paragraph based on your reflection. (*Hint:* Experienced writers create several drafts as they focus on one or two questions per draft.)

Step by Step: Questions for Revising a Paragraph

- ☐ Have I implied a focused main idea?
- ☐ Have I made my purpose clear?
- ☐ Is my tone appropriate for my audience and purpose?
- ☐ Is the logical order of the ideas clear? Have I used words to clearly guide my reader, such as *first, second, next,* etc.?
- ☐ Have I made my point with adequate details?
- ☐ Do all the details support my point?
- ☐ What impact will my paragraph make on my reader?

Proofread Your Draft

Once you have made any revisions to your paragraph that may be needed, proofread your paragraph to eliminate careless errors. Work with a classmate to give and receive feedback about your paragraphs.

Review Test

MySkillsLab™
Complete this Review Test in MySkillsLab.

Score (number correct) ______ x 10 = ______%

Implied Main Ideas and Implied Central Ideas

Before you read, skim the following passage from a college social science textbook. Read the passage and annotate the text. Then answer the questions.

1050L/10.1 GE/345 words

LANGUAGE IS DENOTATIVE AND CONNOTATIVE

[1]*Denotation* refers to the meaning you'd find in a dictionary; it's the meaning that members of the culture assign to a word. [2]*Connotation* refers to the emotional meaning that specific speakers-listeners give to a word. [3]Words have both kinds of meaning. [4]Take as an example the word *death*. [5]To a doctor this word might mean (or denote) the time when brain activity ceases. [6]This is an **objective** description of a particular event. [7]In contrast, when a mother is informed of her child's death, the word means (or connotes) much more. [8]It recalls her child's youth, ambition, family, illness, and so on. [9]To her it's a highly emotional, **subjective**, and personal word. [10]These emotional, subjective, or personal reactions are the word's connotative meaning.

[11]The denotative meaning of a message is general or **universal**; most people would agree with the denotative meanings and would give similar definitions. [12]Connotative meanings, however, are extremely personal, and few people would agree on the precise connotative meaning of a word or nonverbal behavior.

[13]Take another example: Compare the term *migrants* (used to designate Mexicans coming into the United States to better their economic condition) with the term *settlers* (used to designate Europeans who came to the United States for the same reason). [14]Though both terms describe essentially the same activity (and are essentially the same denotatively), *migrants* is often negatively evaluated and *settlers* is often positively valued (they differ widely in their connotations).

[15]Semanticist S. I. Hayakawa coined the terms "snarl words" and "purr words" to clarify further the distinction between denotative and connotative meaning. [16]**Snarl words** are highly negative ("She's an idiot," "He's a pig," "They're a bunch of losers"). [17]Sexist, racist, and heterosexist language and hate speech provide lots of other examples. [18]**Purr words** are highly positive ("She's a real sweetheart," "He's a dream," "They're the greatest"). [19]Although they may sometimes seem to have denotative meaning and to refer to the "real world," snarl and purr words are purely connotative in meaning. [20]They don't describe people or events; rather, they reveal the speaker's feelings about these people or events.

Adapted from DeVito, Joseph A., *Human Communication: The Basic Course*, 12th ed., p. 98.

Vocabulary in Context

1. The best definition of the word **objective** in sentence 6 is

a. personal.
b. factual.
c. honest.
d. bias.

2. The best meaning of the word **universal** in sentence 11 is

a. lofty.
b. narrow.
c. common to many people.
d. exact.

3. The best meaning of the word **subjective** in sentence 9 is

a. wrong.
b. personal.
c. unbiased.
d. general.

Stated Main Ideas

4. Which sentence is the topic sentence for the last paragraph (sentences 15–20)?

a. sentence 14
b. sentence 15
c. sentence 16
d. sentence 19

Supporting Details

5. Based on the passage, **purr words**

a. describe people and events.
b. are denotative.
c. are connotative.
d. are negative.

Concept Maps and Charts

6–8. Complete the concept map with information from the passage.

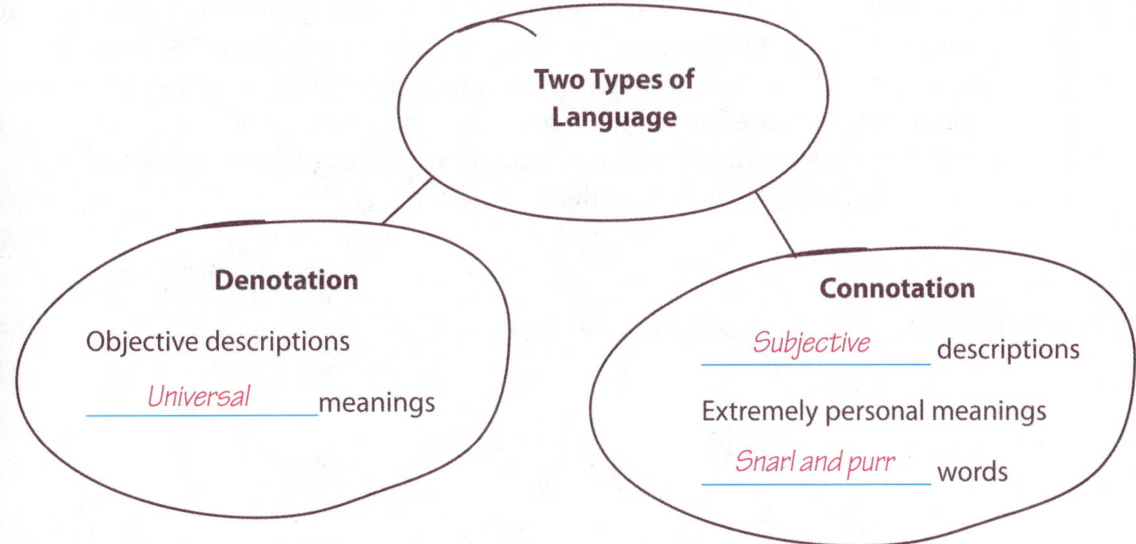

CONTINUED

Implied Main Ideas and Implied Central Ideas

9. Which sentence best states the implied main idea of the second paragraph (sentences 11–12)?

- **a.** Most people agree with denotative meanings.
- **b.** Most people disagree over connotative meanings.
- **c.** Denotative meanings are more widely agreed on than connotative meanings.
- **d.** Denotative and connotative meanings are very similar.

10. Which sentence best states the implied central idea of the passage?

- **a.** Language has the ability to communicate many meanings.
- **b.** Verbal and nonverbal language express both denotation and connotation.
- **c.** Gestures are part of nonverbal language that can express both denotation and connotation.
- **d.** Racist language is an example of connotative meaning.

Summary Response

Restate the writer's main idea in your own words. Begin your summary response with the following: *The central idea of the passage "Language Is Denotative and Connotative" by Joseph A. DeVito is. . . .*

What Do You Think?

Which type of meaning do you think is more powerful: denotative or connotative? When are we most likely to rely on the denotative meanings of words? When are we most likely to rely on connotative meanings of words? Assume you are a reporter for your college newspaper. You are writing an article about the issue of cheating in college. Write a paragraph that uses the denotative meanings of words to discuss how widespread the problem is and to explain why students might cheat. After you have written your paragraph, revise it to use connotative meanings to make your point. Share your work with a peer or small group of classmates. Discuss how the use of connotative and denotative meanings affected your writing.

Academic Learning Log: Module Review

Summary of Key Concepts of Implied Main Ideas in Reading and Writing Paragraphs

Assess your comprehension of implied main ideas.

LO1 LO2

1. Define the following terms:

- *Infer* is to *determine an idea based on the given details*.
- *Imply* is to *suggest, not directly state, an idea*.
- *Implied main idea* is *a main idea that is not stated directly but is strongly suggested by the supporting details in a passage*.

LO1 LO3 LO4 LO5

2. To determine an implied main idea, ask three questions:

- *What is the topic of the passage*?
- *What are the types of supporting details in the passage*?
- *What is the controlling point of the passage*?

LO1 LO3 LO4 LO5 LO6 LO7

3. Implied main ideas must be neither too *broad* nor too *narrow*.

LO3 LO4 LO5 LO6 LO7

4. To determine a main idea, *annotate* or mark the *topic* and the words that reveal the writer's *bias* and organization to analyze the *details* used in the passage.

5. When the idea of several paragraphs is implied, it is called the *implied central idea*.

Test Your Comprehension of Implied Main Ideas

Respond to the following questions and prompts.

In your own words, what is an implied main idea? *Answers may vary.*

An implied main idea is the main point suggested by the types of details and patterns of organization a writer uses to develop a topic.

LO3 LO4 LO5 LO6 LO7

How can the skills you use to identify the stated main idea help you determine the implied main idea?

A stated main idea is a topic sentence, and a topic sentence states the topic and the writer's controlling point about that topic. A passage that implies a main idea also has a topic and a controlling point. So I can ask questions about the topic and the supporting details to create a topic sentence that states an implied main idea.

LO6 LO7

How does a writer develop a paragraph that implies a main idea?

To develop a paragraph that implies a main idea, a writer uses the writing process to prewrite, write, revise, and proofread his or her paragraph. Many writers find it helpful to prewrite a topic sentence that states the point that they want to imply, but then they do not include that topic sentence in the final draft. The topic sentence simply serves as guide as they draft, revise, and proofread.

LO3 LO4 LO5

Study the following concept map. Then write the implied main idea suggested by the details in the map.

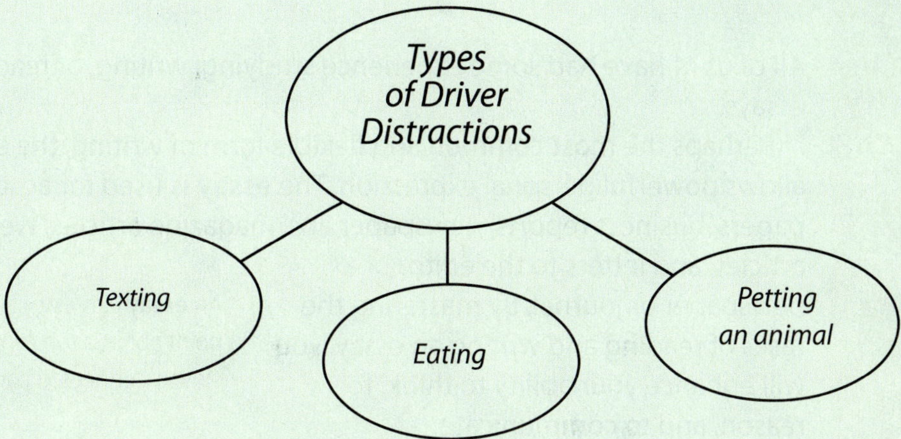

Implied main idea: *Three types of driver distractions are texting, eating, and petting an animal.*

LO1 LO2 LO3 LO4 LO5 LO6 LO7 LO8

1. **How will I use what I have learned?** In your notebook, discuss how you will apply to your own reading/writing strategy what you have learned about implied main ideas. When will you apply this knowledge to your reading/writing strategy?
2. **What do I still need to study about implied main ideas?** In your notebook, discuss your ongoing study needs. Describe what, when, and how you will continue studying implied main ideas.

MySkillsLab™

Complete the Post-test for Module 7 in MySkillsLab.

8

LEARNING OUTCOMES

After studying this module you should be able to:

- L1 Answer the Question "What's the Point of an Essay?"
- L2 Identify and Compose Effective Introductions and Conclusions
- L3 Identify and Establish a Clear Point: Central Idea or Thesis Statement
- L4 Identify and Generate Details
- L5 Recognize and Establish Logical Order
- L6 Evaluate and Use Effective Expression: Word Choice

Understanding the Essay

All of us of have had some experience studying, writing, or reading essays.

Perhaps the most common and flexible form of writing, the essay allows powerful personal expression. The **essay** is used for academic papers, business reports, newspaper and magazine articles, Web articles, and letters to the editor of a newspaper or journal. By mastering the tasks of reading and writing an essay, you will enhance your ability to think, to reason, and to communicate.

An **essay** expresses a writer's point about a topic in a series of closely connected paragraphs.

Like a paragraph, an essay is a series of closely related ideas that develop and support the writer's point about a topic. In fact, paragraphs serve as building blocks for an essay since an essay is composed of several paragraphs. Therefore, the reading/writing strategies you developed to read and write a paragraph will also help you read and write an effective essay.

WHAT'S THE POINT of an Essay?

The following set of pictures depicts several situations in which people are reading different types of essays written for specific audiences. Study each photograph. Then predict the topic or purpose for the types of essays written for each audience (write your predictions in the given spaces). Finally, answer the question "What's the point of an essay?"

Photographic Organizer: The Essay

Student writing an essay for an exam, formal report, research project, etc. as assigned by a professor

Business report or proposal written for fellow workers and supervisors

News article, letter to editor, etc., written for the general public

What's the point of an essay?

An essay gives a writer an opportunity to explain an idea or viewpoint about a topic in depth to a specific reading audience.

What's the Point? One Student's Response

The following paragraph offers one student's response to the question "What's the point of an essay?"

An essay allows a person to express an idea by using several paragraphs. So an essay lets a person get more details about a topic across to an audience. There are different types of essays. In everyday life, we read essays in newspapers, magazines, and on the Internet. For example, a newspaper has news stories, articles, editorials, and opinion columns. These are all essays. We also have the chance to respond to the essays we read by writing our own essays in online comment boxes for readers or as letters to the editor. In work life, people write and read business letters and reports. In college life, students write many essays as exams and research papers.

An essay has several basic parts: a title; a beginning, made up of an introductory paragraph that often includes a stated central idea or thesis statement; a middle, made up of body paragraphs; and an ending, often made up of a concluding paragraph. In addition to being made up of five parts, an essay offers distinct levels of information that range from general to specific. Understanding the levels and flow of ideas in essays benefits both readers and writers. Effective readers skim an essay to determine the flow of ideas before reading, annotate key general and specific details during reading, and often outline the flow of ideas after reading. The goal of the reader is to follow the flow of ideas to determine the writer's point of the essay. On the other hand, effective writers often outline or map the levels and flow of ideas before writing. Then they use the outline or map as a guide during writing and after writing to draft and revise their essays. The goal of the writer is to move from one level of information to another in such a way that the reader easily comprehends the point of the essay.

The Levels of Information in an Essay

Title

Introduction
Explains the importance of topic and the writer's point.
Offers background information about the topic.
Hooks the reader's interest.

Thesis Statement
States the central idea in a complete sentence.
Uses specific, effective wording.
Relates to all the details in the essay.

Topic Sentence
States the main idea of the paragraph.
Offers one primary support for the thesis statement.
Relates to all the details in the paragraph.
Links the details in the paragraph to the thesis statement.

Major Detail
Supports the topic sentence.
Is a secondary support for the thesis statement.
Is more general than a minor detail.

Minor Detail
Supports a major detail.
Is a secondary support for the thesis statement.
Offers the most specific details in the essay.

The Body

Conclusion
Reinforces the importance of the writer's overall point.

Compare this chart to the chart about levels of information in a paragraph on page 207.

The word *essay* means attempt, to make an effort to accomplish an end. An essay has a specific audience for a specific purpose. An effective essay supports a *central idea* or *thesis statement* with *relevant details* in *logical order***,** using *effective expression***.** An effective essay also often begins with an introduction and ends with a conclusion. Effective readers and writers use a reading/writing strategy to comprehend and make a point.

L2 Identify and Compose Effective Introductions and Conclusions

Both readers and writers use introductions and conclusions to comprehend and make a point. An effective introduction serves the following purposes:

- It introduces the essay topic.
- It explains the importance of the essay topic and/or gives necessary background information about the topic.
- It hooks the reader's interest.
- It presents the essay's main idea in a thesis statement.

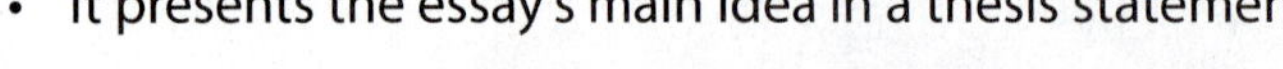

An effective conclusion fulfills the following purposes:

- It restates the essay's main idea and sums up the major points in the essay.
- It brings the essay to an end.

The following chart describes and illustrates ten of the most common types of introductions and conclusions. Many of these types may be used as either an introduction or a conclusion. Others are best used only as an introduction. The chart suggests the appropriate use of each type.

Ten Types of Introductions and Conclusions	
A question **Introduction or conclusion**	**EXAMPLE:** Don't you want to experience the well-being that results from a healthful diet and regular exercise?
A quotation **Introduction or conclusion**	**EXAMPLE:** Just as renowned coach of the Green Bay Packers Vince Lombardi said, "The difference between a successful person and others is not a lack of strength, not a lack of knowledge, but rather in a lack of will."
A definition **Introduction**	**EXAMPLE:** Hope is belief that the impossible is possible. Hope is the future counted in the present. Hope is a light, a map, and a compass. Hope gave me the will to fight and survive cancer.
A call to action **Introduction or conclusion**	**EXAMPLE:** This is not a time for indecision or hesitation. This is a time for commitment and action. Tell your federal, state, and local governments that you demand a coordinated response plan for natural disasters.
A suggestion **Introduction or conclusion**	**EXAMPLE:** Your best friend is the one who will tell you a hard truth for your own good.
A warning about consequences **Introduction or conclusion**	**EXAMPLE:** If instruments used for ear and body piercing are not properly cleaned and sterilized between clients, then you could contract HIV, hepatitis B, or hepatitis C.

Ten Types of Introductions and Conclusions	
A vivid image **Introduction or conclusion**	**EXAMPLE:** Two gas stations. A car repair shop barely visible through the rusty open hoods of dismantled racecars. A man clad in overalls selling roasted peanuts from the back of his truck. These are a few sights at the unpretentious intersection that is the small town of Barberville in Northwest Volusia. To some, the settlement along the corner of U.S. 17 and State Road 40 represents one of the area's last strongholds of unspoiled country life. Maria Herrera, "Rural Residents Wary of Road Project"
A surprising fact or statement **Introduction**	**EXAMPLE:** Nearly one in seven Americans has key clinical data missing from their medical files, according to a report in *The Journal of the American Medical Association* (JAMA). And in 44 percent of cases the absent information would have impacted a doctor's diagnosis, potentially putting patients' health at risk. You can take a few simple steps to maintain accurate and accessible personal-health records and safeguard your well-being. Adapted from "Read This Before Your Next Doctor's Appointment," *First Magazine*
A contradiction or an opposing view **Introduction**	**EXAMPLE:** Many wanna-be runners don't even try because they believe they don't have the right physique. Their legs are too short. Their stomach is too big. Their shoulders are too broad. Their body weight is too much. These people are wrong. The body is unimportant. The mind is everything. Running is not a physical sport. It's mental. "Mind Over Body," *Running Fit Prevention Guide*
Context information or a summary **Introduction or conclusion**	**EXAMPLE:** It is especially important to wash your hands before, during, and after you prepare food, before you eat, after you use the bathroom, after handling animals or animal waste, when your hands are dirty, and more frequently when someone in your home is sick. National Center for Infectious Diseases, "Wash Your Hands Often"

Often, the main idea is stated as part of the introduction and then repeated as part of the conclusion. Before reading, effective readers skim introductions and conclusions to predict the writer's main point and raise questions to ask during reading. During reading, they read to confirm the main idea and answer questions. After reading, they often review introductions and conclusions to deepen understanding and memory of what they read.

Example

Read the following introductions and conclusions. Identify the type of introduction or conclusion used in each one. Then predict the writer's main idea. Write a sentence to state the main idea of the introduction or conclusion.

a. A question
b. An interesting illustration or anecdote
c. A surprising statement or fact
d. A direct quotation
e. A definition
f. A contradiction or opposing view
g. A vivid description
h. Context information or a summary
i. A call to action
j. A warning about consequences

1. *c*

Heat kills! In fact, excessive heat is the number one weather-related killer, causing more fatalities per year than floods, lightning, tornadoes, hurricanes, winter storms, and extreme cold, according to the National Weather Service's storm data from 1994 to 2003. Therefore, when you exercise in warm, humid temperatures, protect yourself by taking a few sensible safety measures.

Main Idea: *Student answers may vary. Protect yourself by taking a few sensible safety measures.*

2. *d*

To Frederick Douglass is credited the plea that, "the Negro be not judged by the heights to which he has risen, but by the depths from which he has climbed." Judged on that basis, the Negro woman embodies one of the modern miracles of the modern World.

Mary McLeod Bethune, "A Century of Progress of Negro Women"

Main Idea: *Student answers may vary. The Negro woman embodies one of the modern miracles of the modern World.*

3. *g*

When we first saw Henry, we knew he had to be ours. He had only been recently rescued from a cruel breeder who supplied greyhounds to local racetracks. We were told that the breeder caged Henry in a metal crate with shredded newspaper for bedding for 18–22 hours each day. He fed Henry cheap 4-D meat for Greyhounds. The 'D' stands for dying, diseased, disabled, and dead livestock. Henry had barely survived the E. coli poisoning from this feed. At one time, almost every detail of Henry's skeleton could be seen beneath his thin skin. The fact is that these kinds of abuses are more common than not. Greyhound racing should be outlawed.

Main Idea: *Student answers may vary. Greyhound racing should be outlawed.*

4. *i*

Our life on earth has already reaped many benefits from past and current space exploration. The establishment of a human colony on the moon would further enhance the quality of life on this planet. Products designed for independent life on the moon will someday become part of everyday life on Earth, advancing research in robotics, communications, medicine, computer technologies, food and nutrition, clothing, environmental and architectural design, rocketry, fuel and energy, building materials, and agriculture. We should shoot for the moon!

Main Idea: *Student answers may vary. We should shoot for the moon!*

Explanation

Compare your responses to the following student's think-aloud.

These introductions and conclusions made me think more deeply about what the writer was saying. They also made me want to learn more about the topics. I recorded the main ideas stated in each introduction or conclusion.

1. *This is type (c), a surprising statement or fact. The unexpected fact that heat is the number one weather-related killer grabbed my attention and made clear the need to know about safety measures.*
Main idea: Protect yourself by taking a few sensible safety measures.
2. *This is type (d), a direct quotation. Bethune uses a quote from one of the most famous and beloved Civil Rights activists in history, former slave Fredrick Douglass. She uses this powerful quote to introduce her point about the great challenges the Negro woman has overcome.*
Main idea: The Negro woman embodies one of the modern miracles of the modern world.
3. *This type is (g), a vivid description. The writer describes a vivid personal memory to introduce his stand against Greyhound racing.*
Main idea: Greyhound racing should be outlawed.
4. *This type is (i), a call to action. At first I thought this might be a vivid description, but all the details are about what could happen if we took the action to explore the moon.*
Main idea: We should shoot for the moon!

Effective writers use introductions and conclusions to grab the reader's attention, reinforce the main idea, and make the point memorable. Writers may compose introductions before or after writing a rough draft of the body of the essay.

Example

Carefully consider the following topic sentence. Write a brief introduction and conclusion for the main idea. Identify the type of introduction and conclusion you use. *Student responses will vary.*

TOPIC SENTENCE: *To improve your study habits, follow three simple steps.*

INTRODUCTION TYPE: *A question: Are you one of the countless numbers of students with poor study habits? Do you want to learn more, gain skills, and improve your grades?*

CONCLUSION TYPE: *A call to action: Come on, start now! Follow these three easy steps into your future.*

Explanation

Compare your responses to the following student's think-aloud.

I chose to use a couple of questions to introduce this main idea. Many students will answer yes to these questions and want to read for "how to learn more, gain skills, and improve grades." Since I want my readers to apply what they learn, I used a call to action as my conclusion.

Introduction Type was "a question": Are you one of the countless numbers of students with poor study habits? Do you want to learn more, gain skills, and improve your grades?

Conclusion Type was "a call to action": Come on, start now! Follow these three easy steps into your future.

MySkillsLab™

You can complete additional exercises for this section in *The Effective Reader/Writer* book-specific module in MySkillsLab.

Identify and Establish a Clear Point: Central Idea or Thesis Statement

L3

To both the reader and the writer, the central idea is a key element in reading and writing strategies. Both a reader and a writer discover a central idea. A reader uses the reading process to identify the topic and the controlling point about the topic. Before reading, a reader skims for the repetition of key words throughout the essay; the idea most often repeated is the topic. As a reader skims for the topic, he or she also looks for words that express an opinion about the topic. Often, a reader discovers that a single sentence, the thesis statement, states the topic and the controlling point. Identifying the thesis statement early in the reading process makes it easier to comprehend the details during reading. Alternatively, a writer discovers a focused central idea during the prewriting phase of the writing process by selecting and narrowing a topic and drafting a thesis statement. A focused central idea makes the writer's point clear and powerful!

Identify the Thesis Statement: Topic and Controlling Point

A thesis statement answers the question "What's the point?" This point is the writer's opinion about the topic that is explained and supported in the essay. In fact, this point further narrows the topic. The writer's point or opinion is often referred to as the *controlling point.*

The controlling point often includes a pattern of organization (see Modules 9–13) as well as the writer's opinion. The following graphic illustrates an effective thesis statement.

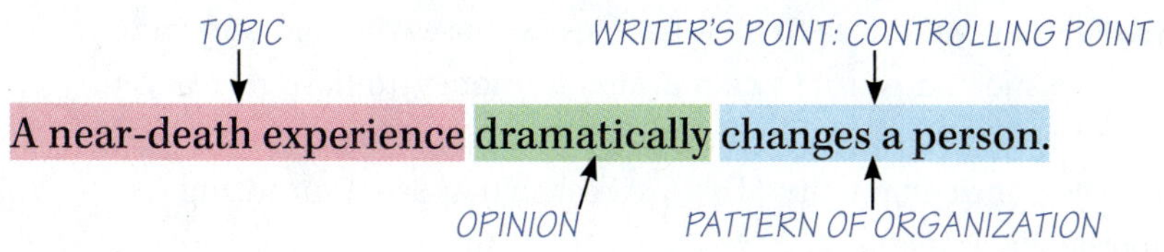

The word *dramatically* is an opinion that must be explained or supported. In addition, the word *changes* suggests a pattern of organization. This word indicates that the writer is going to compare what the person was like before the near-death experience to what the person is like after the near-death experience. The controlling point answers the question "What's the point?" of the essay.

Often, readers identify the topic and controlling point in a series of prereading steps. Effective readers keep in mind that the thesis statement can appear at or near the beginning, in the middle, or at the end of an essay. In addition, the thesis statement may be repeated or reworded as part of the conclusion, so it could appear at the beginning and the end of an essay.

Example

The following essay is from a college sociology textbook. The essay is featured in the chapter about deviance and social control. Skim the essay to identify the topic and controlling point. First, identify the topic. Skim and circle the key words (topic) recurring throughout the essay. Next, underline words that reveal the writer's opinion. Finally, double underline the thesis statement. As you read, think about the steps the writer took to select and narrow a topic.

Islands In The Street: Urban Gangs in the United States

[1]For more than ten years, sociologist Martin Sanchez-Jankowski did participant observation of thirty-seven African-American, Chicano, Dominican, Irish, Jamaican, and Puerto Rico gangs in Boston, Los Angeles, and New York City. [2]The gangs earned money through gambling, arson, mugging, armed robbery, and selling moonshine, drugs, guns, stolen car parts, and protection. [3]Sanchez-Jankowski ate, slept, and fought with the gangs, but by mutual agreement, he did not participate in drug dealings or other illegal activities. [4]He was seriously injured twice during the study.

[5]Contrary to stereotypes, Sanchez-Jankowski did not find that the motive for joining gangs was to escape from a broken home (there were as many members from intact families as from broken homes) or to seek a substitute family (the same number of boys said they were close to their families as those who said they were not). [6]Rather, the boys joined gangs to gain access to money, to have recreation (including girls and drugs), to maintain anonymity in committing crimes, to get protection, and to help the community. [7]This last reason may seem surprising, but in some neighborhoods, gangs protect residents from outsiders and spearhead political change. [8]The boys also saw the gang as an alternative to the dead-end—and deadening—jobs held by their parents.

[9]Neighborhood residents are ambivalent about gangs. [10]On the one hand, they fear the violence. [11]On the other hand, many of the adults once belonged to gangs, some gangs provide better protection than the police, and gang members are the children of people who live in the neighborhood. [12]Particular gangs will come and go, but gangs will likely always remain a part of the city. [13]Gangs fulfill the needs of poor youth who live on the margins of society.

Henslin, James M., *Essentials of Sociology: A Down-to-Earth Approach*, 9th ed., p. 145.

Explanation

Compare your responses to the following student's think-aloud.

It became pretty obvious that the topic was gangs. The writer repeated gang or gangs 14 times, including the title. Every paragraph used the word gang more than once. The writer also repeated the name of the researcher Sanchez-Jankowski three times early in the essay as a way to introduce the topic and the researcher as the source for some of the details. I underlined the following phrases that seemed to state the writer's opinion. In paragraph 1, I underlined "earned money" and "illegal activities." In paragraph 2, I underlined "Contrary to stereotypes" and "motive for joining." In paragraph 3, I underlined "Neighborhood residents are ambivalent." It seemed to me that the writer's opinion about gangs was summed in the very last sentence "Gangs fulfill the needs of poor youth who live on the margins of society." It only took me a few minutes to annotate the essay and identify the thesis statement. I will use this strategy as a study technique.

As you read the essay about gangs, did you think about the steps the writer took to select and narrow a topic? Many writers select a topic and controlling point in a series of prewriting steps. First, a writer often generates a list of topics. Many times, the writer pulls topics from reading textbooks, magazines, newspapers, or the Internet. This list serves as a bank of ideas that can be applied to a wide variety of writing situations.

Second, a writer considers the writing situation to discover the most effective controlling point for a specific audience and purpose. For example, the length of an essay often depends on your audience and purpose. A paper for an academic audience such as a history professor may have a required length, such as 1,000 words. In contrast, a local newspaper may limit the length of letters to the editor to 500 words. The scope of the topic needs to match the required length. For example, the 500-word letter to the editor cannot cover all the reasons one should volunteer at the local soup kitchen for the poor. Instead, you would need to narrow the topic to just two or three reasons. And you would choose only those details that are of interest to your specific audience.

The purpose and audience also limit the topic. A writer will choose a set of details based on the purpose and audience of the essay. For example, if a writer's purpose were to persuade city officials to take action against gangs, then the essay would have a different set of details than an essay that seeks to simply inform the public about gangs. Also, consider the audience and purpose of a college student writing in an academic course. The real audience is the professor, and the ultimate purpose is to prove learning. However, at times, college writing assignments ask students to identify and write to a specific audience for a specific purpose. For example, a sociology professor may ask students to find a news article about a significant current event and write a letter to a news editor, elected official, or local group to inform them about the issue or persuade them to take action.

For more on using prewriting techniques and selecting a topic, see pages 46–47.
For more on the writing situation, and topic, purpose, and audience, see pages 5–6.

Example

The following pictures present specific writing situations. Each picture represents an audience, and each caption states the purpose for writing to that audience. First, match the audience and purpose to its appropriate topic. Then write the letter of the topic in the appropriate space. Finally, discuss your answers with your class or in a small group.

Topics:

A. The importance of a specific lesson
B. Wisdom gained from an education
C. How to raise a child to be self-confident
D. How to best increase sales

Writing Situation 1: c
To Inform—to share, explain, or demonstrate information

Writing Situation 2: d
To Argue —to change this audience's opinion or call them to action

Writing Situation 3: b
To Express—to share personal opinions, feelings, or reactions

Writing Situation 4: a
To Reflect—to record your understandings about what you have experienced or learned

Writing situation 1: To Inform

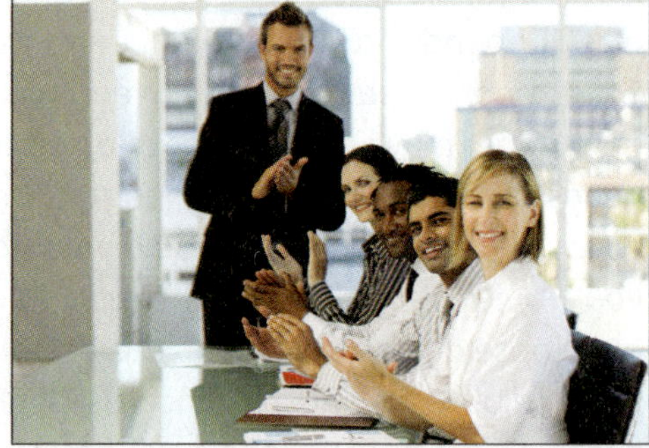
Writing situation 2: To Argue

Writing situation 3: To Express

Writing situation 4: To Reflect

Explanation

Compare your responses with the following student's think-aloud.

Topic A, "The importance of a specific lesson," matches Writing Situation 4: To Reflect. The students in the class will learn and remember if they each reflect in writing about what they are learning.

Topic B, "Wisdom gained from an education," matches Writing Situation 3: To Express. This match was tricky because the purpose could also be To Reflect. This group of graduates is most likely listening to a guest speaker at their graduation ceremony. Usually, these speakers express personal values and experiences to inspire graduates.

Topic C, "How to raise a child to be self-confident," matches Writing Situation 1: To Inform. Many parents are eager for helpful advice about how to best raise their children.

Topic D, "How to best increase sales" matches Situation 2: To Argue. These colleagues are probably listening to several arguments about this topic. They must decide which argument is the most sound for their business.

Practice 1

The Writing Situation

Reread the essay about gangs on page 278 and complete the following activities. Then share and discuss your responses with a peer or small group of classmates.

A. Based on the details in the essay, identify the writer's audience and purpose. Explain your answers.

Audience: Age *Adult* Gender *male or female*

Ethnic group *any*

Level of education *high school graduate*

Purpose: To Inform *X* To Argue ______ To Express ______ To Reflect ______

Explanation: *The audience is general adults of both genders with at least a high school education since this essay was in a college textbook. The purpose is to inform the audience about gangs. The writer isn't asking the reader to make a judgment or take a stand for or against gangs.*

B. The following writing prompts appeared in the sociology textbook at the end of the essay about gangs in a feature called "For Your Consideration." Assume your college professor is requiring a written response to the essay to demonstrate your understanding of what you have read. Identify your writing situation in terms of audience and purpose. Explain your answers. *Answers may vary.*

> **For Your Consideration:** What functions do gangs fulfill (what needs do they meet)? Suppose that you have been hired as an urban planner for the city of Los Angeles. How could you arrange to meet the needs that gangs fulfill in ways that minimize the violence and encourage youth to follow mainstream norms?

Audience: Age *Adult* Gender *male or female*

Ethnic group *any*

Level of education *college graduate with an advanced degree*

Purpose: To inform ______ To Argue *X* To Express ______ To Reflect ______

Explanation: *The actual audience is the college professor. In this situation, my essay should be suitable for males and females and any ethnic group since college professors are diverse. My main purpose for writing is to prove to my professor that I understand the essay. However, the writing prompt gives me a role and reason to write as a city planner in Los Angeles. So I may think of my audience as the city officials who hired me and who will pay for and implement any suggestions I make. I may choose to convince the city officials to take certain steps to help poor youth avoid gangs.*

Draft a Thesis Statement

Now that you have worked as a reader to identify a central idea or thesis statement, you should be aware of the importance of a well-written thesis statement to a writer. After choosing and narrowing a topic based on the writing situation, a writer composes a working draft of the thesis statement that states a controlling point about the topic. Many writers revise a thesis statement several times until it expresses a clearly focused point. The following chart offers several hints for drafting a thesis statement.

Hints for Drafting a Thesis Statement
Use specific statements. Replace vague, general words with vivid, exact words. "*Football is a dumb game*" is too vague and general. "*Football glorifies violence*" is specific and vivid.
Always state your thesis statement as a complete sentence.
Avoid asking a question. A question may introduce a topic or thesis statement, but it may never be a thesis statement. Does football glorify violence?
Avoid announcing your topic. Never say, "*I am going to write about football and violence*," or "*My essay is about football and violence*," or "*My topic is football violence.*"
Review and, if necessary, revise your thesis statement after you have written a rough draft. As you think about a topic, the point you want to make often becomes clearer.

Example

Read the following list of items. Evaluate each one for its effectiveness as a thesis statement. Mark each item **E** for Effective or **NE** for Not Effective. Explain your answers in the spaces following each item.

1. What are the major mental and physical effects of stress? *NE*

A question is not a thesis statement.

2. Stress is awful. *NE*

This statement is too vague and general.

CONTINUED

EXAMPLE *CONTINUED*

3. I am going to talk about the negative mental and physical effects of stress. *NE*

This statement makes an announcement.

4. Stress often leads to major negative physical and mental effects. *E*

This is an effective thesis statement that has a topic "stress" and a controlling point about stress—"major negative physical and mental effects."

5. My topic is the mental and physical effects of stress. *NE*

This statement makes an announcement.

Explanation

Compare your responses with the following student's think-aloud.

Item 1 is NE, not effective, because it asks a question instead of making a statement.
Item 2 is NE, not effective, because the statement is too vague and general. There is no controlling point. The reader has no idea if the writer is focused on causes or effects.
Item 3 is NE, not effective, because it makes an announcement.
Item 4 is E, effective, because it states the topic "stress" and a controlling point "major negative physical and mental effects." This statement offers a great guideline for the development of two body paragraphs.
Item 5 is NE, not effective because it also makes an announcement.

Practice 2

Draft and Revise Thesis Statements

A. Draft thesis statements for the following items. These items present a topic and a writer's point about the topic. Combine the ideas in each group to create a thesis statement. Discuss your ideas with your class or in a small group.

1. TOPIC: *workplace aggression*

WRITER'S POINT: *takes on several forms of behavior*

THESIS STATEMENT: *Workplace aggression takes on several forms of behavior.*

2. TOPIC: *cardiovascular disease*

WRITER'S POINT: *avoidable and unavoidable factors*

THESIS STATEMENT: *Although certain factors of cardiovascular disease are unavoidable, other factors are avoidable.*

3. TOPIC: *major depressive disorder*

WRITER'S POINT: *a common type of mood disorder with several long-term effects*

THESIS STATEMENT: *One common type of mood disorder with several long-term effects is major depressive disorder.*

4. TOPIC: *use of chat rooms and online discussion boards*

WRITER'S POINT: *five tips for effectiveness*

THESIS STATEMENT: *Your use of chat rooms and online discussion boards will be more effective if you follow five tips.*

5. TOPIC: *weight training machines and free weights*

WRITER'S POINT: *similarities and differences*

THESIS STATEMENT: *Although weight training with machines and with free weights are similar in several ways, important differences exist between the two methods.*

CONTINUED

PRACTICE 2 *CONTINUED*

B. Revise thesis statements. Reword the following statements into effective thesis statements.

6. What are three super foods everyone should add to their diet?

Everyone should add these three super foods to their diet.

7. I am going to write about how adoption benefits individuals and society.

Adoption benefits individuals and society.

8. Chewing tobacco is stupid.

Chewing tobacco leads to serious, even fatal results.

9. My topic is the two basic types of cellphones.

Cellphones come in two basic types.

10. How can the city meet the needs that gangs fulfill in ways that minimize the violence and encourage youth to follow mainstream norms?

The city can meet the needs that gangs fulfill in several ways.

LO4 Identify and Generate Details

Effective readers and writers pay close attention to the details in an essay. In an effective essay, the writer provides enough relevant details to adequately support the essay's central idea or thesis statement. Relevant and adequate details include **primary details** that support the thesis and **secondary details** that explain or illustrate primary details.

Often, during or after reading, a reader creates an outline or concept map of the general and specific ideas. Usually, writers use an outline or concept map as a prewriting tool to generate details. A concept map is a diagram that shows the writer's flow of ideas from topic to secondary details.

Primary details are details of key importance in support of a thesis statement.

Secondary details come after, are less important, or result from a primary detail.

Example

Read the following passage from a college textbook about self-concept. Complete the concept map with information from the passage. Discuss the value of identifying details to comprehend the writer's central idea or thesis statement.

Two Components of Self-Concept

[1]Self-concept, the image one has of oneself, is based on what people are told by others and how the sense of self is reflected in the words and actions of important people in one's life, such as parents, siblings, coworkers, friends, and teachers. [2]Two important components of the self-concept are the real self and the ideal self. [3]The real self is one's actual perception or view of characteristics, traits, and abilities that form the basis of the striving for self-actualization. [4]The ideal self is the perception of what one should or would like to be. [5]The ideal self primarily comes from important or significant others in a person's life, especially our parents when we are children. [6]Psychologist Carl Rogers believes that when the real self and the ideal self are very close or similar to each other, people feel competent and capable. [7]However, when there is a mismatch between the real self and the ideal self, anxiety and neurotic behavior can result.

[8]The two halves of the self are more likely to match if they aren't that far apart at the start. [9]When a person has a realistic view of the real self, and the ideal self is something that is actually attainable, there usually isn't a problem of a mismatch. [10]It is when a person's view of self is distorted or the ideal self is impossible to attain that problems arise. [11]Once again, how the important people (who can be either good or bad influences) in a person's life react to the person can greatly impact the degree of agreement between real and ideal selves. [12]However, as individuals develop, they look less to others for approval and disapproval, and more within themselves to decide if they are living in a way that is satisfying to them.

Adapted from Ciccarelli, Sandra K., *Psychology*, 4th ed., p. 515.

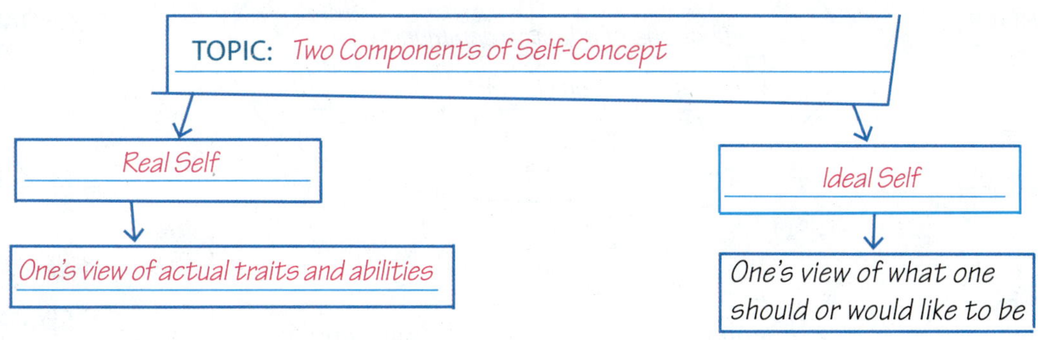

Explanation

Compare your responses with the following student's think-aloud.

Using a concept map helped me see how the writer organized the details to support the thesis statement, sentence 2. The major details are the two components of self-concept, which are the real self and the ideal self. The minor details explain the traits of each component, their sources, and why they match or mismatch.

Did you notice as you created a concept map based on the details in an essay that the concept map showed the way the writer planned out the flow of details? Most writers generate details during the prewriting stage by listing or freewriting. Then they organize the details into a writing plan. Many writers use concept mapping or outlining to help create a plan for the essay. Mapping and outlining are excellent ways to see if a writer has enough details to support the point of the essay.

Some writers begin the writing process by generating details and then drafting a thesis statement, while other writers draft a working thesis statement first and then generate details. Writers experiment to see which approach works best for them.

For concept maps of specific patterns of organization, such as time order, classification, and definition, see pages 336, 374, 419, 452, *and* 486.

Example

Study the following topic, controlling point, and list of details. Create a writing plan by filling in the concept map with groups of details from the list. Then write a one-sentence summary (a thesis statement) of the main point that they support. Discuss the value of generating details into a writing plan as a prewriting strategy.

respects others
functions of effective communication on the job
builds consensus
encourages teamwork
diffuses confrontations
states clear expectations
seeks solutions
encourages professionalism
encourages input from others

Wording may vary.

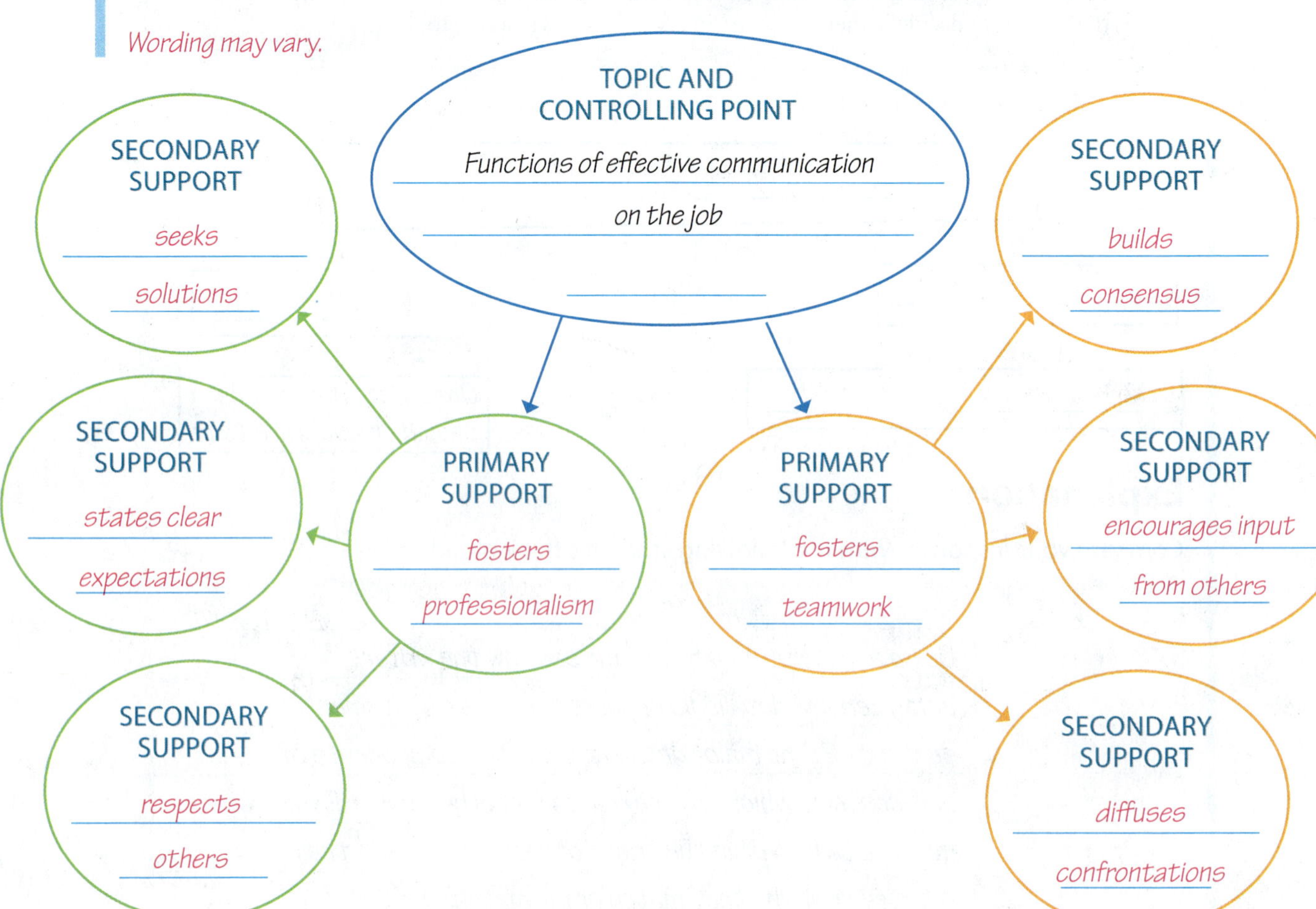

One-sentence summary of primary supports:

Effective communication on the job has several functions.

Explanation

Compare your responses with the following student's think-aloud.

I created the following writing plan using the concept map.

Topic and Controlling Point: Functions of effective communication on the job

Primary Supports:	*Fosters Teamwork*	*Fosters Professionalism*
	↓	↓
Secondary Supports:	*Builds consensus*	*Seeks solutions*
	↓	↓
	Encourages input	*States expectations*
	↓	↓
	Diffuses confrontation	*Respects others*

One-sentence summary: Effective communication fosters teamwork and communication.

Using a concept map to generate details and create a writing plan helped me think more clearly about how to support a thesis statement. As I was organizing the details into a concept map, I had to decide which details were the primary ones and which ones were secondary. First, I decided that teamwork and professionalism were the primary details. Then I had to choose which secondary details best supported each primary detail. For the first time, I realized that as a writer, I am the one who makes those decisions. After I get my writing plan set up, I know how to explain the relationship between each secondary detail and the primary detail it supports. Using a concept map to make a writing plan is very helpful because I know what I'm going to write before I have to figure out how to word it all. Also, the writing plan will help me stick to my point.

Practice 3

Identify and Generate Details

The following essay appeared in a college textbook for an introduction to technology course. Use reading/writing strategies to identify the details in this essay and generate details for your written response to the essay.

A. Complete the outline with the primary details from the essay.

Cyber Safety

[1]Making contacts and meeting friends online has never been easier. [2]Social networking services such as Facebook **(facebook.com)** are signing up users at a rapid pace. [3]Another site, YouTube **(youtube.com)**, allows you to post videos of yourself and your friends. [4]These services have you list personal information about yourself (interests, hobbies, photos, what school you attend, and so on) and encourage you to list connections to your friends. [5]When your friends log on and view your profile, they can see themselves and long chains of other acquaintances. [6]The idea is that your friends can see who else you know and get you to make appropriate introductions (or do it themselves). [7]You need to be careful when joining social networking and video sites.

[8]First, be wary of giving out too much personal information. [9]Although these two sites offer fairly tight protection of personal information, think carefully about making your personal information visible on a site and be wary of disclosing additional information to people you meet online. [10]Often children and young adults, who account for a large percentage of the users on these sites, are too trusting about revealing personal information. [11]Cybercriminals are combing these sites with the sole purpose of using the information to commit identity theft. [12]Therefore, always avoid giving out personal information such as your full name, address, Social Security number, or financial information to people you have never met. [13]Also, be careful when uploading videos of yourself or your friends. [14]Identity thieves often like to steal younger people's identities because the identity theft of minors takes longer to detect.

[15]Finally be wary of accepting computer files from people you've met online. [16]These files could contain viruses or other destructive software. [17]Just because you meet someone who is a friend of a friend of your second cousin doesn't mean that person isn't a hacker or a scam artist. [18]So, enjoy meeting new people, but exercise the appropriate amount of caution.

Adapted from Evans, Alan, Martin, Kendall, and Poatsy, Mary Anne, *Introductory Technology in Action*, 7th ed., p. 412.

1. THESIS STATEMENT: *You need to be careful when joining social networking and video sites.*

   I. *Be wary of giving out too much personal information.*

II. *Finally, be wary of accepting computer files from people you've met online.*

III. So, enjoy meeting new people, but exercise the appropriate amount of caution.

B. Assume your professor has asked you to respond in writing to the essay by answering the following question: What advice would you give a new user of one of the two social networking services listed in the essay? Draft a working thesis statement that answers the question. Then generate details by creating a concept map or outline. Use your own paper.

Evaluate Details

In an effective essay, every detail supports the thesis statement. *All* the details work together as a unit to explain and support the writer's point. Effective readers evaluate the details to make sure there are adequate, or enough, relevant details of support. When you create an outline or concept map of an essay you are reading, you are able to see how each detail relates to the other details and the thesis statement. Outlining and mapping also show if the writer included adequate relevant major and minor details. Often, a reader discovers that additional details may be needed to fully accept the writer's point.

Example

Reread the essay "Cyber Safety" in Practice 3. Underline ideas that need further support or explanation. As you read, ask yourself if the writer answered the reporter's questions *who, what, when, where, why,* and *how* in enough depth to support the thesis statement. Underline ideas that need further support. Be prepared to explain your choices.

Explanation

Compare your responses with the following student's think-aloud.

There were several ideas in the essay that I wanted to know more about. For example, the second paragraph didn't really explain how uploading videos is related to identity theft. So I underlined sentence 12. I also thought the writer should have given more details in the third paragraph about viruses and other destructive software. An example would have helped make the point stronger. So I underlined sentence 15.

During the prewriting process, a writer brainstorms many details, some of which may not be related to the focus of the main idea. Therefore, as writers create a writing plan, they think about how each detail relates to the other details and the thesis statement. Often, writers drop those details that do not support either the thesis statement or the thesis statement's primary supports. Likewise, as they evaluate details, writers discover the need for additional details. Writers usually check details for relevance once more during the revision stage of the writing process.

Example

Study the following writing plan. Cross out details that are not relevant to the thesis statement. Identify any details that need additional support. The following questions will help you test details as adequate and relevant. Share your work with your class or in a small group of peers.

- What is the topic and controlling point of the thesis statement? Circle the topic. Underline the controlling point.
- Which details are the primary or major supporting details (the ones that will be used as topic sentences for body paragraphs)? Number the three primary or major supports A, B, and C.
- What are the secondary or minor details? Number each secondary or minor detail to correspond to a primary or major detail: A1, A2, and so on; B1, B2, and so on; and C1, C2, and so on.
- Which detail(s) do not relate to the thesis statement, primary or major details, and the secondary or minor details? Cross out irrelevant details.
- Which details need additional support? Underline details that need more support.

THESIS STATEMENT:

Due to the nature of lightning, you must follow lightning safety guidelines to reduce risk of injury or death.

A	[1] *Lightning has a complex nature.*
A1	[2] *Lightning has two components: leaders and strokes.*
A2	[3] *The leader is the probing feeler sent from the cloud.*
A3	[4] *The return streaks of light are a series of strokes that produce the actual lightning bolt or flash that we see.*
B	[5] *Lightning, by nature, is unpredictable and dangerous.*

	[6]~~At any given moment, there are 1,800 thunderstorms in progress somewhere on the earth. This amounts to 16 million storms each year.~~
B1	[7]Lightning has been seen in volcanic eruptions, extremely intense forest fires, surface nuclear detonations, heavy snowstorms, and in large hurricanes.
B2	[8]No one can predict the location or time of the next stroke of lightning.
B3	[9]Lightning has been the second largest storm killer in the U.S. for the last 40 years, exceeded only by floods.
C	[10]Following proven lightning safety guidelines can reduce your risk of injury or death.
C1	[11]Count the seconds between the time you see lightning and the time you hear the thunder.
C2	[12]You should already be in a safe location if that time is less than 30 seconds.
C3	[13]The safest location during lightning activity is an enclosed building.
C4	[14]Stay inside until 30 minutes after you last hear thunder.

Explanation

Compare your responses with the following student's think-aloud.

The topic is lightning, and the writer's controlling point included "due to the nature of lightning" and "must follow safety guidelines to reduce injury or death." The writer explained the nature of lightning with two major supporting details that included "complex nature" and "unpredictable and dangerous." The details about the nature of lightning led up to the last major supporting detail "safety

CONTINUED

guidelines." The detail that was not relevant was sentence 6. This detail is about thunderstorms, which is really a different topic than lightning strikes. I would advise the writer to delete the detail from the body of the essay and perhaps use it in the introduction as a way to lead into the topic of lightning and the controlling points about the nature of lightning and the safety guidelines. Also, the writer provided adequate details to support the controlling point.

Practice 4

Evaluate Details

In Practice 3, part B, you assumed your professor had asked you to respond in writing to the essay "Cyber Safety" by answering the following question: What advice would you give a new user of one of the two social networking services listed in the essay? Review the details you generated to support your working thesis statement that answers the question.

A. Evaluate the details you generated as adequate and relevant. The following questions will help you evaluate whether your details are adequate and relevant.

- What is the topic and controlling point of the thesis statement? Circle the topic. Underline the controlling point.
- Which details are the primary or major supporting details (the ones that will be used as topic sentences for body paragraphs)? Identify the three primary or major supports A, B, and C.
- What are the secondary or minor details? Number each secondary or minor detail to correspond to a primary or major point: A1, A2, and so on; B1, B2, and so on; and C1, C2, and so on.
- Which detail(s) do not relate to the thesis statement, primary or major details, and the secondary or minor details? Cross out irrelevant details.
- Which details need additional support? Underline details that need more support.

B. After you have evaluated your details, revise your writing plan as needed to delete or add details. Your writing plan may be a concept map or an outline. Use your own paper.

Recognize and Establish Logical Order

Effective readers determine the writer's logical order to comprehend the writer's point. Effective writers arrange body paragraphs in a clear, logical order for a coherent flow of ideas. Likewise, effective writers link each paragraph to the next so that readers can follow their chain of thought. A coherent flow of ideas unfolds in several logical ways.

1. *Ideas flow in pattern(s) of organization*. At times, a writer follows a particular pattern of organization to make a point. For example, a biography of an important person is based on time order. A description of a significant place follows spatial order. Other times, a writer may need to discuss causes, effects, similarities, or differences to make a point about a topic. Many times, a writer may need to combine several patterns of organization to fully discuss a topic. For example, to logically discuss the significance of an historical event such as 9/11, a writer may need to use time order, spatial order, causes, and effects.
2. *Ideas flow in the order as presented in the thesis statement*. Often the controlling point of the thesis statement divides the topic into chunks of information. Consider the following example: "Psychological health includes mental, emotional, social, and spiritual aspects." This thesis sentence lets the reader know that the essay will be made up of four paragraphs and the order in which the listed ideas will be discussed.
3. *Ideas flow in order of importance*. Often, a writer decides upon and arranges details according to his or her opinion about the importance of the details, known as *climactic order*. Usually, climactic order moves from the least important point in the first body paragraph and builds to the essay's climax, the most important point in the final body paragraph.

Effective writers suggest the logical order of an essay in the thesis statement. Thus, readers may predict the logical order used by a writer early in the reading process and then confirm that prediction during reading.

Example

Read the following list of thesis statements. Analyze each one to predict the logical order it suggests. Some items may suggest more than one way to establish logical order. In the space before each item, write the number(s) of the logical order suggested by the thesis statement as described above. Explain your answers in the spaces following each item. (*Hint*: Annotate each statement; circle the topic and underline the controlling point.)

1, 2, 3 **1.** Stress often leads to major negative physical and mental effects.

1 **2.** Prepare for a natural disaster before it occurs.

1 **3.** The design of the iPhone is user friendly.

3 **4.** A career in health care is rewarding for several reasons.

2, 3 **5.** The poor service, awful food, and high prices of Dell's Diner make it a place to avoid.

Explanation

Compare your responses with the following reader's think-aloud.

In item 1, the writer applies all three methods. The topic is "stress," and the controlling point is "major negative physical and mental effects." First the (1) ideas flow in a pattern of organization based on "effects." Also the (2) ideas flow in the order as presented in the thesis statement, and these ideas are probably listed by (3) order of importance. I expect the writer to discuss the physical effects in the first body paragraph and the mental effects in the second body paragraph.

In item 2, the (1) ideas flow in a pattern of organization based on time order. The topic is "a natural disaster." The controlling point is "prepare . . . before it occurs." I expect the writer to explain the steps that the reader should take to prepare before the storm.

In item 3, the (2) ideas flow in space order. The topic is "iPhone." The controlling point is "design . . . user friendly." I expect the writer to describe the iPhone as user friendly based on its size, screen quality, and the layout of the Apps on the phone.

In item 4, the (3) ideas flow in order of importance. The topic is "A career in health care." The controlling point is "rewarding . . . several reasons." I expect the writer to offer a list of the rewards of a health care career. I expect the rewards to range in significance, like making money might rank lower than easing suffering.

In item 5, the (2) ideas flow in the order presented in the thesis statement. The topic is "Dell's Diner." The controlling point is "poor service, awful food, and high prices . . . avoid." I expect the writer to explain each of these complaints in the order they are listed. I also think the writer has the (3) ideas flow in order of importance. I assume the writer listed these details in the thesis statement to reflect his or her order of importance. The high price seems like the ultimate complaint.

Practice 5

Recognize and Establish Logical Order

Study the series of photographs and complete the exercises. Then share your responses with your class or in a small group.

1. **Ideas flow in pattern(s) of organization.**
   Write and arrange in space order three topic sentences (primary supports) suggested by the following thesis statement. Use the photograph to generate your primary supports. *Answers may vary.*

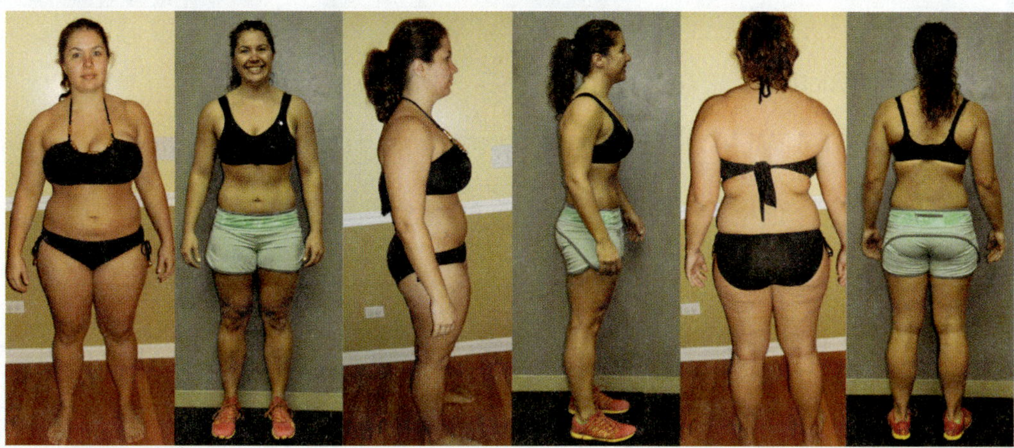

I. Introduction

THESIS STATEMENT: *After months of diet and exercise, Jennie has dramatically changed in several ways.*

II. *Jennie's physical appearance dramatically changed.*

III. *Jennie's level of physical fitness has greatly improved.*

IV. *Jennie's attitude about herself and life is completely different.*

V. Conclusion

CONTINUED

PRACTICE 5 *CONTINUED*

2. Ideas flow in order as presented in the thesis statement.
Write and arrange in time order three topic sentences (primary supports) suggested by the following thesis statement. Use the photographs to generate your primary supports. *Answers may vary.*

I. Introduction

THESIS STATEMENT: *To ensure your safety during a severe storm, you should stock up on supplies, secure your home, and be prepared to evacuate.*

II. *Stock up on several days of a variety of supplies.*

III. *Install a generator to protect against power outages.*

IV. *Educate your family about evacuation procedures and routes.*

V. Conclusion

3. Present ideas in order of importance.
Write and arrange in climactic order three topic sentences (primary supports) suggested by the following thesis statement.

I. Introduction *Answers may vary.*

THESIS STATEMENT: *Stress challenges us in almost every aspect of our lives.*

II. *Though intense, the stress we face in our academic life is short term.*

III. *Unlike academic pressures, the stress of earning a living is a long-term challenge.*

IV. *However, the most stressful pressures are those we face in our family life.*

V. Conclusion

Connect Paragraphs

In addition to ordering paragraphs coherently, writers clearly connect each paragraph to the next so that readers can follow their chain of thought. The following chart lists and illustrates several options to connect paragraphs to each other.

Connect Paragraphs	
Echo or repeat important words or phrases from the thesis statement in body paragraphs to support the thesis statement with relevant details.	
I. Thesis statement:	We can *ease* the *pain* that occurs from illness or injury in several different ways.
II. Topic sentence:	*Pain* can be *eased* by deep breathing.
III. Topic sentence:	Visualization and imagery *ease pain.*
Refer to the main idea of the previous paragraph in the topic sentence of the present paragraph.	
I. Thesis statement:	Applying the principles of computer ergonomics reduces the chances of injury and fatigue.
II. Topic sentence:	The *computer screen* should be *placed properly* to avoid painful injuries to the neck.
III. Topic sentence:	*Proper placement* of the *monitor* not only *reduces* the possibility of *neck injury* but also eases eye fatigue.
Use transitional words, phrases, or sentences to link paragraphs that follow.	
I. Thesis statement:	Sleep disorders can deprive sufferers of much needed rest and complicate their lives.
II. Topic sentence:	*One type* of sleep disorder is known as night terrors.
III. Topic sentence:	*Another type* of sleep disorder, nightmares, torments many people.
IV. Transition sentence and topic sentence:	*At least the previous two disorders occur in the privacy of one's home.* Narcolepsy, a *third kind* of sleep disorder, can occur suddenly anywhere, and at any time without warning.
Tie the last idea in one paragraph to the opening of the next paragraph.	
I. Thesis statement:	Hurricane activity is on the rise, is likely to increase, and calls for new methods of preparation.
II. Topic sentence and ending idea of paragraph:	Hurricane activity is on the rise because of higher ocean temperatures and lower vertical wind shear. Therefore, these *climate changes* are likely to continue for as many as 10 to 40 years.
III. Topic sentence:	*These shifts in climate* call for new methods of hurricane preparation.

Example

Read the following essay. Underline the connections between paragraphs. Circle the key ideas that are repeated throughout the essay. Discuss with your class or in a small group the different types of connections the writer used and evaluate their effectiveness.

Answers may vary.

A SONG OF HUMILITY

[1]The neighborhood of my youth hummed with the songs of our carefree play. [2]The beat of hammers building forts and the zings of the over-ripe ammunition of our orange wars in Winter Haven, Florida, blended beautifully with the music of the times. [3]The Beatles, and all the other really groovy groups, deafened us to any world but our very own. [4]No one was more deaf than I.

[5]At that time, I was particularly deaf to the family that lived two streets over and halfway down a dusty clay side road. [6]This out of sync family lived poorer than we did. [7]They grew their own food, raised chickens, and loved loud country music. [8]Every time I passed their house, I felt sorry for them, in a smug sort of way. [9]One afternoon the mama of that family labored up the hill to our house. [10]Her son had cut a record, and she "would be obliged if we was to listen to it" and tell her what we thought. [11]I was too busy marveling at her stained clothes and dusty feet to hear how respectfully my mother responded.

[12]Mother treated everyone with respect and tried to teach her children to do so as well. [13]She insisted that the whole family listen to the twangy tune about love and shirttails, but only I took great joy in mocking it. [14]Mother told me to return the record and say she thought it "a fine tune." [15]When I objected, she said, "Janet, consider this an unavoidable duty!" [16]I stood a long time studying the rusty door of that family's dust-covered house, wondering why I hadn't the courage to do my duty.

[17]Finally, my good friend Florence appeared at the end of the alley. [18]"Florence," I cried in great relief, "come here quick." [19]I ran to meet her, and we stood a few feet away with our backs turned from the door I so dreaded. [20]In the loud, exuberant tones of an inconsiderate child, I belted out the details of my dilemma. [21]"You ought to hear this . . . stupid . . . only hicks . . . and I have to . . . Hey, wait for me," I said to her retreating back. [22]I had hoped to push my obligation into her hands. [23]"Naw, Jan," she said without looking back, "I'm already late."

[24]So, I turned to do my hated duty. [25]Then I saw the son, the singer, dart from the door into the shadows of the house. [26]I wheeled about and cried, "Florence, come back." [27]I ran to her, begging, "He heard me.

[28]What should I do? [29]He heard everything I said." [30]Florence shrugged and turned away. [31]I pivoted and marched to the steps. [32]The son stepped out to meet me. [33]My words resonated in the silence that loomed between us, and I cursed the supper time desertion of the dusky streets. [34]"Young lady," he said gently. [35]I looked at him. [36]"Thank ya for bringing back my demo."

[37]To this day, the timbre of his voice shames me. [38]I had mocked him, yet he sought to soothe my soul. [39]And, now, when I feel the deafness of prejudice threaten me, I remember the song of humility I learned that day from a fine young singer.

Explanation

Compare your responses with the following reader's think-aloud.

The writer used a variety of connections between paragraphs. First, the writer echoed or repeated key terms. The word song *or a word related to music recurred 14 times, and in every paragraph. Other repeated words included* mock, deaf, duty, obligation, shame, *and* humility. *Some of these words were repeated in different forms such as* mocking *and* deafened. *I also think the word* prejudice *repeats the meaning of* deafness *and* deaf. *I think prejudice is a form of deafness. In addition, the first sentence of the third paragraph ties into the last sentence of the second paragraph. The writer also used transitions such as "At that time," "Finally," "So," and "To this day." These transitions kept me in the flow of the story and emphasized "power of prejudice."*

Practice 6

Connect Paragraphs

Return to the writing plan you created and revised in response to the essay "Cyber Safety" (see Practices 4 and 5). Identify the ways in which you plan to connect the paragraphs in your response essay. Write a draft of your essay using techniques to connect paragraphs. Then exchange your rough draft with a peer or small group of peers. Underline the connections in an essay written by a peer. Suggest connections as needed.

L6 Evaluate and Use Effective Expression: Word Choice

One of the most important traits of an essay is the use of effective expression or word choice. Word choice refers to the specific words carefully chosen by a writer to express an idea. Word choice usually reflects the writer's attitude or opinion about a topic. Similarly, effective readers and writers consider the connotations of words. Connotation refers to the meanings associated with or suggested by a word in addition to its literal or exact meaning. Think about the words *house* and *home*. The literal or exact meaning of *house* is a dwelling place. The word *home* means more than a building; it suggests an emotion. For many, the connotation of *home* suggests love, warmth, safety, and comfort. For a person in a troubled family, *home* may have negative connotations. An effective reader evaluates word choice to understand the meaning intended by the writer.

Evaluating word choice is a valuable reading/writing strategy that will improve your abilities as both a reader and a writer. The following thinking guide offers a few simple steps that use writing to learn to evaluate word choice.

Writing to Learn: Evaluate Word Choice

Write to reflect about the meaning of a writer's word choice.

Step 1 Identify a single word of significance (avoid a whole phrase or list of several words).

Step 2 Explain the connotation of the word based on what it makes you think of or what it suggests to you.

Step 3 Explain how the word supports the writer's point or reveals the writer's attitude about the topic.

Example

Reread the last example essay "Song of Humility." Evaluate the writer's choice of the word *deaf* in sentence 5. Complete steps 2 and 3 in the thinking guide "Writing to Learn: Evaluate Word Choice." Sentence 5 appears below for your study. Use your own paper.

> 5 At that time, I was particularly deaf to the family that lived two streets over and halfway down a dusty clay side road.

Answers may vary.

Explanation

Compare your responses with the following writer's think-aloud.

Step 2: The word deaf suggests several things to me. First, it is a handicap, a limitation. Being deaf means you don't have use of a basic sense, so your experience in the world is really different from the norm. Being deaf also makes me think of isolation, being cut off from others and the joy of sound.

Step 3: When the writer describes herself as deaf, I think she is suggesting that she didn't have a basic sense of decency. She was rude and mocking to the family because she was limited in her view of the world and other people. She looked down on them. She stereotyped and judged others harshly. She couldn't take in the idea that the singer might be talented. The word deaf suggests isolation, too. And then, her friend left her, so she had to face the singer alone. I like the way the writer admitted she was deaf. To me the point of the essay is that she learned a lesson; she changed. She wasn't deaf by the end of the essay.

Practice 7

Evaluate Effective Expression

Choose another key word from the essay "A Song of Humility." Use the thinking guide "Writing to Learn: Evaluate Word Choice" to evaluate the word you have chosen.

Answers may vary.

Evaluating word choice as a reader strengthens you as a writer. An effective writer carefully chooses words to support a point and create a specific impact on readers. Effective writers often refer to a thesaurus to find the exact words needed to make their point. A thesaurus is a collection of words, their synonyms (words of similar meaning), and their antonyms (words of opposite meaning). Thesauruses come in print and online versions. Online thesauruses, such as *merriam-webster.com*, provide a search box so you can search a specific word for its related words.

Type a word in the search box. Press enter.

In addition to the common features, many online thesauruses also provide additional information in a single search such as full entries for related words. In a writer's search for the right words, a thesaurus provides a resource of a wide range of words with varying connotations.

Example

The narrator of "Song of Humility" shows that she is careless in her treatment of the other family. Assume you have decided to write an essay about another way somebody can be careless. For example, think about the ways the following people may be careless: parent, teenager, boss, spouse, and so on. To prewrite, study the following screen shots of two entries for the word *careless* from *Merriam-Webster.com*. Circle four synonyms or related words, or antonyms, or near antonyms that you may use in your essay. Then evaluate one of your word choices by completing the thinking guide that follows the screenshots.

careless *adjective*

8+1 Like

1 not paying or showing close attention especially for the purpose of avoiding trouble <a *careless* reporter who often doesn't get his facts straight> <a *careless* mistake that caused the plane to crash>

Synonyms heedless, incautious, mindless, unguarded, unsafe, unwary

Related Words bold, impetuous, rash, reckless; inattentive, regardless; blithe, inconsiderate, thoughtless; absentminded, forgetful, unmindful; lax, neglectful, negligent, remiss, slipshod; imprudent, indiscreet, injudicious; inadvertent, unintentional, unplanned

Near Antonyms attentive, chary, observant, vigilant, watchful; foresighted, forethoughtful, provident; calculating, scheming, shrewd; considerate, thoughtful; ultracareful, ultracautious

Antonyms alert, cautious, circumspect, gingerly, guarded, heedful, safe, wary

2 failing to give proper care and attention <a *careless* effort that made an unnecessary mess>

Synonyms careless, derelict, disregardful, lax, lazy, neglectful, neglecting, remiss, slack

Related Words heedless, incautious, irresponsible, reckless, wild; unguarded, unwary; forgetful; disregardful, disregarding, inattentive, oblivious, thoughtless, unheeding, unmindful, unthinking; apathetic, disinterested, indifferent, unconcerned, uninterested; delinquent; loose

Near Antonyms meticulous, painstaking, punctilious; cautious, chary, circumspect, gingerly, guarded; alert, heedful, heeding, mindful, observant, regardful, regarding, vigilant, wary, watchful; foresighted, forethoughtful, provident, responsible; thinking, thoughtful; concerned, interested

Antonyms attentive, careful, conscientious, nonnegligent

"careless." By permission. From *Merriam-Webster's Collegiate® Dictionary*, 11th Edition ©2014 by Merriam-Webster Inc. (www.Merriam-Webster.com).

Writing to Learn: Evaluate Word Choice

Write to reflect about the meaning of a writer's word choice.

Step 1 Identify a single word of significance (avoid a whole phrase or list of several words).

Step 2 Explain the connotation of the word based on what it makes you think of or what it suggests to you.

Step 3 Explain how the word supports your point or reveals your attitude about the topic.

Explanation

Compare your responses with the following writer's think-aloud.

Step 1: I identified the four words absentminded, reckless, negligent, oblivious.
I decided to reflect about my choice of reckless.

Step 2: I chose reckless *because I am going to write about how texting while driving shows a careless disregard for the safety of others. The word* reckless *makes me think of someone who does dangerous things without thinking about the consequences.*

Step 3: The word reckless *supports my point that texting while driving is more than inconsiderate; it is dangerous. When texting, you are not aware of your surroundings, including pedestrians and other drivers. Just like driving while on drugs or booze shows a reckless disregard for human life, so does texting while driving.*

Writers may evaluate their word choices throughout the writing process, especially during prewriting and drafting. Writers fine-tune their word choices at these points to clearly support their controlling point and to make the greatest impact on the reader.

Practice 8

Evaluate and Use Effective Expression

Return to your rough draft of your essay in response to "Cyber Safety." Choose a key word in your rough draft to evaluate. Use a thesaurus to find a related word that may better support your point. On your own paper, follow the thinking guide to evaluate the word you chose from your essay and the related word you found in the thesaurus. In the space below, explain which word you will use and why. *Answers may vary.*

Reading and Writing Assignments

MySkillsLab™
Complete these assignments in MySkillsLab.

Considering Audience and Purpose

Study the sequence of photographs about the essay at the beginning of this module. Assume the woman reading the newspaper is a peer of yours in this course, and you are study partners. She has suggested that you both identify and explain the most important things you have learned in this module. Write an essay that explains three key skills or concepts that she needs to know.

Reading and Writing for Everyday Life

Assume you are the parent of a middle school student and you serve as president of the Parent–Teacher Association (PTA). The PTA publishes a monthly newsletter. A recurring feature in the newsletter is a "Letter from the President" about an issue of current concern to parents, students, and teachers. Recently, the community has reported growth in gang membership of teenagers. You plan to publish the essay "Islands in the Street: Urban Gangs in the United States" on page 278 in the next newsletter to educate your membership about the causes for gang membership. In your "Letter from the President," call for teachers, parents, and students to read the essay and offer ways to address the problem. How can the community offer other options for teenagers that make gang life less attractive?

Reading and Writing for College Life

Assume you are a reporter for your college newspaper. The editor of the paper plans to do a series of feature articles about student success that will appear throughout the semester. The first feature focuses on the traits of a successful college student and the barriers to success that students face. The editor plans to publish the essay "Two Components of Self-Concept" by Sandra K. Ciccarelli (page 287). The editor has asked you to write an essay to be published as a companion piece. The two essays will run side by side in the newspaper. Reread the essay by Ciccarelli. Then write a 400-word essay that describes the ways in which self-concept affects student success.

Reading and Writing for Working Life

Assume you work in the human resource department of a local hospital. Your department sends a newsletter each month to the staff describing upcoming training opportunities. The next session is about effective workplace communication. You are to write a brief essay that describes the session and invites employees to attend. Revisit the prewrite for "Functions of Effective Communication on the Job" on page 288. Use the ideas generated in the prewrite to compose your essay. Explain how the functions of effective communication will enhance job performance that could lead to salary increases.

Workshop: Compose an Essay

Choose an essay to read and respond to in writing. You may select an essay in an example, practice, or writing assignment within this module. Or you may select an essay of your own choosing. Use the following guide to comprehend and respond to the essay. Apply what you have learned about the essay to your reading/writing strategy.

Preread: Survey and Question

Ask questions about the text's features.

What is the passage about?

____

____

How is the material organized?

____

____

What do I already know about this topic? (What is my prior knowledge about the vocabulary?)

____

____

What is my purpose for reading/writing?

____

____

What points may I want to address or include in my written response?

____

____

Read and Annotate

As you read, annotate key ideas, particularly those details that answer your prereading questions.

Recite, Review, and Brainstorm

Recite the information. Summarize the most important parts. Answer your prereading questions. Rephrase ideas into your own words. Record changes in your opinions based on the new information. **Review** the information. **Brainstorm** ideas for your written response to the passage. **Freewrite** a response to what you have read. **Map** the relationship among ideas you have annotated in the text. **Outline** or list key ideas and details in blocks of thought. Use your own paper.

Write a Draft of Your Response

Using the ideas you generated by brainstorming, compose a draft of your response. Use your own paper.

Revise Your Draft

Once you have created a draft of an essay, read the draft and answer the questions in the "Questions for Revising an Essay" box that follows. Indicate your answers by annotating your paper. If you answer "yes" to a question, underline, check, or circle examples. If you answer "no" to a question, write additional details in the margins and draw lines to indicate their placement. Revise your essay based on your reflection. (*Hint:* Experienced writers create several drafts as they focus on one or two questions per draft.)

Step by Step: Questions for Revising an Essay

- ☐ Have I stated or implied a focused central point?
- ☐ Have I made my purpose clear?
- ☐ Is my tone appropriate for my audience and purpose?
- ☐ Is the logical order of the ideas clear? Have I used strong transitions to guide my reader, such as *first, second, next,* etc.?
- ☐ Have I made my point with adequate details?
- ☐ Do all the details support my point?
- ☐ What impact will my essay make on my reader?

Proofread Your Draft

Once you have made any revisions to your essay that may be needed, proofread your essay to eliminate careless errors. Work with a classmate to give and receive feedback about your essays.

Review Test

MySkillsLab™
Complete this Review Test in MySkillsLab.

Score (number correct) ______ x 25 = _______%

Use reading/writing strategies to comprehend and respond to the following passage. Read the following passage. Answer the questions that follow. Then respond to the essay by answering the prompts "Summary Response" and "What Do You Think?"

Vocabulary Preview

prevalence (**4**): frequency of occurrence
adolescence (**5**): teenage years
surveyed (**9**): studied, questioned
symptoms (**16**): warning signs
compulsiveness (**24**): urgent desire or driven behavior
deviant (**24**): abnormal, strange

1150L/383 words

Binge Drinking

1Despite laws that make it illegal for anyone under the age of 21 to purchase or possess alcohol, young people report that alcohol is easy to obtain and that many high school and college students drink with one goal in mind—to get drunk. 2Binge drinking is defined as consuming five or more drinks in a row for boys and four or more in a row for girls. 3The alarming aspects of binge drinking cannot be overlooked or underestimated.

4One troubling aspect of binge drinking is its **prevalence** among youth and college students. 5Often starting as young as age 13, these drinkers tend to increase bingeing during **adolescence**. 6The behavior peaks in young adulthood, which includes the ages from 18 to 20. 7After age 22, this **perilous** conduct slowly decreases. 8One study on youth risk behavior reported that 24% of high school students binge drank. 9Numerous studies consistently indicate that about 40% of college students **surveyed** engaged in binge drinking. 10More than 80% of American youth consume alcohol before their twenty-first birthday. 11About 90% of the alcohol consumed by them is in the form of binge drinking.

12Binge drinking is risky behavior that has serious **consequences**. 13The most grave effect is **alcohol poisoning**, which is an **acute** physical reaction to an overdose of the alcohol. 14During bingeing, the brain is deprived of oxygen. 15This lack of oxygen eventually causes the brain to shut down the heart and lungs. 16Alcohol poisoning has several **symptoms**. 17They include vomiting and unconsciousness. 18In addition, the skin becomes cold, clammy, pale or bluish in color. 19Breathing becomes slow or irregular.

20Binge drinking brings about other disturbing behaviors or effects as well. 21In schools with high binge drinking rates, binge drinkers are likely to insult, **humiliate**, push, or hit their peers. 22Frequent binge

CONTINUED

drinkers were eight times more likely than nonbinge drinkers to miss a class, fall behind in schoolwork, get hurt or injured, and damage property. [23]Binge drinking during college may be linked with mental health disorders. [24]These disorders include **compulsiveness**, depression or anxiety, or early **deviant** behavior. [25]Alarmingly, nearly one out of every five teenagers has experienced "blackout" spells. [26]During these spells, they could not remember what happened the previous evening because of heavy binge drinking. [27]Finally, many who are frequent binge drinkers also drink and drive.

Adapted from U.S. Department of Human and Health Services, "Binge Drinking in Adolescents and College Students."

Vocabulary in Context

1. In sentence 7 of the passage, the word **perilous** means

a. adventurous.
(b.) dangerous.
c. fun-loving.
d. disgusting.

2. In sentence 13 of the passage, the word **acute** means

a. unavoidable.
b. short-term.
c. invisible.
(d.) severe.

Central and Main Ideas

3. Which sentence states the central idea of the passage?

a. sentence 1
b. sentence 2
(c.) sentence 3
d. sentence 4

4. Which sentence is the topic sentence of the fourth paragraph?

(a.) sentence 20
b. sentence 21
c. sentence 26
d. sentence 27

Supporting Details

5–7. Complete the summary with information from the passage.

Alcohol poisoning is *an acute physical reaction to an overdose of alcohol*. Symptoms include vomiting; *unconsciousness*; cold, clammy, pale or bluish skin; slow or irregular *breathing*.

8–10. Complete the following informal outline of the fourth paragraph by filling in the blanks. *Wording of answers may vary.*

Stated main idea:

Binge drinking brings about other disturbing behaviors or effects.

A. *Binge drinkers are likely to harass their peers.*

B. *Binge drinkers are more likely to do poorly in school, get hurt, cause damage.*

C. *Binge drinking may be linked to mental health disorders.*

D. *Binge drinkers may have blackout spells.*

E. *Many binge drinkers drink and drive.*

Summary Response

Restate the writer's main idea in your own words. Begin your summary response with the following: *The central idea of the passage "Binge Drinking" is . . . .*

What Do You Think?

Why is binge drinking so prevalent among youth and college students? Why do you think binge drinking is related to mental disorders? Should colleges address the problem of binge drinking? If so, how? Write a letter to a college or school newspaper explaining the dangers of binge drinking. Include real-life examples if you know of any.

Academic Learning Log: Module Review

Summary of Key Concepts of Understanding the Essay

Assess your comprehension of the essay.

L1 L2

1. The parts of an essay are *title*, *introduction*, *thesis*, *body*, *conclusion*.

2. The four levels of information in an essay are *thesis statement*, *topic sentence*, *major details*, *minor details*.

3. An effective essay begins with an *introduction* and ends with a *conclusion*.

L1 L2 L3 L4 L5

4. Two types of details in an essay are *primary details* and *secondary details*.

5. The two levels of secondary supports are *major details* and *minor details*.

6. A *concept map* shows the writer's flow of ideas.

7. Four ways to connect paragraphs are: **A.** Echo or repeat words or phrases from the *thesis statement* in body paragraphs. **B.** Refer to the *main idea* of the previous paragraph in the topic sentence of the next paragraph. **C.** Use *transitional* words and phrases. **D.** Tie the *last* idea in one paragraph to the *opening* of the next paragraph.

L1 L2 L3 L4 L5 L6

8. The traits of an effective essay are *an introduction and conclusion*, *a clear point*, *relevant* details, *logical* order, and *effective* expression.

9. *Connotation* refers to the meanings associated with or suggested by a word in addition to its literal or exact meaning.

Test Your Comprehension of Implied Main Ideas

Respond to the following questions and prompts. *Answers may vary.*

In your own words, what is an essay?

An essay is a piece of writing that expresses the writer's point about a topic in a series of closely related paragraphs.

LO1 LO4 LO5

In your own words, explain how you can use outlines and concept maps as reading/writing strategies to comprehend an essay and write an essay.

Outlines and concept maps show the flow of ideas and the levels of information in an essay. So as a reader, I can use outlines and concept maps to see the writer's flow of ideas. As a writer I can use an outline or concept map to generate details. Seeing the flow of ideas will help me see if I have enough details to support my point.

In your own words, describe the steps to evaluate word choice as a reading/writing strategy to comprehend an essay and write an essay.

(1) Identify a single word. (2) Explain the connotation of the word. (3) Explain how the word supports your point about the topic. Readers evaluate the writer's word choice for a deeper understanding of the writer's point. Writers choose words that support a point or impact a reader.

LO1 LO2 LO3 LO4 LO5 LO6

1. **How will I use what I have learned?** In your notebook, discuss how you will apply to your own reading/writing strategy what you have learned about the essay. When will you apply this knowledge to your reading/writing strategy?
2. **What do I still need to study about the essay?** In your notebook, discuss your ongoing study needs. Describe what, when, and how you will continue studying and using the essay.

MySkillsLab™
Complete the Post-test for Module 8 in MySkillsLab.

9

LEARNING OUTCOMES

After studying this module you should be able to:

- **L1** Answer the Question "What's the Point of Time Order and Space Order?"
- **L2** Comprehend and State a Main Idea Using Time Order and Space Order
- **L3** Identify and Generate Relevant Details Using Time Order and Space Order
- **L4** Recognize and Create Logical Order Using Time Order and Space Order
- **L5** Analyze and Use Effective Language with Time Order and Space Order

Time Order and Space Order: Narration, Process, and Description

Clear communication between a writer and a reader comes from clear organization. Clear organization is based on logical connections between ideas. **Transitions** and **patterns of organization** are used to organize and express these logical connections. Time order, also known as *chronological order*, presents ideas based on the time in which they occurred. Time order enables us to tell about and understand an event, a series of actions, or a process. Space order tells where something occurs. Space order creates a clear visual image of a person, place, object, or scene. Time and space are closely linked in our thinking. Action occurs in both time and space.

Transitions are words or phrases connecting one idea to another.

A **pattern of organization** is the arrangement of ideas in a logical order to make a specific point.

WHAT'S THE POINT of Time Order and Space Order? 

Before you study this module, predict the importance of time order and space order patterns of organization. Study each photograph in the following series. Think about how a writer would use time order to make a point about this sequence of events. Would the writer tell a story or describe a series of steps? Would the writer also need to describe the place in which the actions occur? Also think about how a reader would use time order and space order to comprehend the writer's point. Write a caption for each image by answering the questions in the spaces given. Next, write a topic sentence to state the overall main idea. Finally, predict an answer to the question "What's the point of time order and space order?"

Photographic Organizer: Time Order and Space Order

FIRST EVENT

What happened? *They pitched their tent.*

Where did it happen? *in the forest by a river*

When did it happen? *early in the day*

SECOND EVENT

What happened? *They went fishing.*

Where did it happen?r *by the river*

When did it happen? *after pitching the tent, during the day*

THIRD EVENT

What happened? *They enjoyed the view.*

Where did it happen? *outside, beside their tent, by the river*

When did it happen? *early evening, during the sunset*

Topic sentence: *They had a fun and relaxing vacation camping by the river.*

What's the point of time order and space order?

Time order and space order help readers see actions or steps unfold as they read about an event or a set of directions. Time order describes when or how something occurs. Space order describes where something happens. The time and space order patterns work together to describe actions and places related to an event or to give clear directions about how to do something.

What's the Point? One Student's Response

The following paragraph offers one student's response to the images of the couple camping and her prediction about the importance of learning about time order and space order.

I thought the pictures told a story more than they showed how to do something. Each image did make me think about the steps that you have to go through to set up a campsite or fish, but really the pictures seem to capture a fun day. As a reader, knowing about time order will help me follow a writer's ideas. As a writer, time order will help me tell about an important event or give directions about how to do something. These pictures also show the importance of space order. You have to know how to fit things together to pitch a tent as well as where the best place is to put the tent. And you would need space order to describe the view.

Two types of **time order** are narration and process.

1. *Narration* conveys an event or story. For example, narration records the important events in the life of a famous person or the details of a significant event in history. Narration is also used to organize a piece of fiction.
2. *Process* gives directions to perform a task, or lists stages of a task in time order.

Space order offers descriptive details to help readers create vivid mental pictures of what the writer is describing.

The **time order** or ***chronological*** thought pattern relays a chain of actions or events in the order in which they occur.

Space order, also known as ***spatial*** order or ***description***, describes details based on their physical location in a given area.

What's the Point of Narration?

Getting a mental picture of the action of an event helps a writer to discover the point he or she wishes to make. The following sequence of photographs documents a series of events that took place in the life of Jennifer Hudson over the course of several years. Study each photograph in the timeline. Write a caption that states the topic of each picture. Then answer the question "What's the point?" with a one-sentence statement of the overall main idea.

Practice 1

Photographic Organizer: Time and Space Order in a Narration

FIRST EVENT
American Idol, 2004

What happened?

Jennifer Hudson loses American Idol.

SECOND EVENT
Oscar Ceremony, 2007

What happened?

She wins an Oscar for her role in Dreamgirls.

THIRD EVENT
Memorial for Hudson's mother, brother, and nephew, 2008

What happened?

Her mother, brother, and nephew die.

FOURTH EVENT
Weight Watchers Spokesperson, 2010

What happened?

She becomes a spokesperson for Weight Watchers.

FIFTH EVENT
United States Presidential Inaugural Ball, 2013

What happened?

She sings at the Presidential Inaugural Ball.

What's the point?

Topic Sentence: *Jennifer Hudson has overcome many losses in her life.*

One Student's Response

The following paragraph offers one student's narrative inspired by the photographs of Jennifer Hudson. Read the narrative paragraph, the explanations, and activities in **bold type** in the annotations. Complete the activities.

JENNIFER HUDSON'S FAITH AND DETERMINATION

[1]Jennifer Hudson's life reveals a strength that overcomes challenges. [2]In 2004, fans surprisingly booted Hudson off of the third season of *American Idol*. [3]Losing did not stop Hudson. [4]She hoped and watched and worked for her next big break. [5]In 2006, Hudson exploded back onto the national stage with the release of the smash-hit movie *Dreamgirls*. [6]By 2007, her show-stopping performance as Effie White in *Dreamgirls* had won her acclaim across the globe, an Academy Award, and many other awards. [7]In 2008, she snagged a Grammy as Outstanding New Artist. [8]At the height of her success, Jennifer Hudson endured a horrible tragedy. [9]On October 24, 2008, Hudson's mother, Darnell Donerson, and her brother Jason Hudson were found shot to death in Donerson's home. [10]Three days later, Hudson's nephew, 7-year-old Julian King, was also found shot and killed in a sport-utility vehicle belonging to Jason Hudson. [11]Even then, Hudson revealed her strength and determination. [12]Immediately, she and her family created *The Hudson-King Foundation for Families of Slain Victims* in honor of her mother, brother, and nephew. [13]As Jennifer Hudson faced profound loss, she also struggled with a vicious cycle of unhealthful dieting and eating. [14]In 2010, after losing 80 pounds with Weight Watchers, she became a national spokesperson for the organization. [15]She inspires millions across the world to overcome inner challenges as well as those from outside influences. [16]How fitting that she sang at the Presidential Inaugural Ball in 2013.

Main Idea: The main idea is the point of the narration. The topic is Jennifer Hudson's life. **Underline the writer's point.**

Chronological Order: Time order is established with the phrase "In 2006." **Circle two more words that indicate time order.**

Effective Language: Vivid words such as *exploded* create a mental picture and emphasize action or deepen meaning. **Double underline one more vivid word.**

Spatial Order: Space order is established with the word *across*. This phrase tells us where Jennifer Hudson was successful. **Circle two more words that establish space order.**

What's the Point of Process?

Visualizing the steps helps a reader/writer discover the point about a process. Study each photograph in the timeline. Write a caption that briefly describes each picture. Then answer the question "What's the point?"

Practice 2

Photographic Organizer: Time and Space Order in a Process

STEP ONE

What is happening?

A woman is sitting on a mat with a straight back and with her arms and legs extended.

STEP TWO

What is happening?

The woman has rounded her back and bent over at her waist into a deep stretch.

STEP THREE

What is happening?

The woman has drawn up into a ball.

STEP FOUR

What is happening?

The woman has rolled onto her back and shoulders.

What's the point?

This set of exercises increases the strength and flexibility of the body's core that supports the spine.

One Student's Response

The following paragraph offers one student's point about the set of exercises depicted in the photographs. Read the process and the explanations; then complete the activities in **bold type** in the annotations.

Spine Stretch and Roll Like a Ball

[1]"Spine stretch and roll like a ball" is an exercise sequence that builds strength and flexibility in the body's core. [2]First, sit tall and straight on your mat as if you were sitting next to a wall. [3]Open your legs slightly wider than hip-width apart, placing your heels on the outside edges of the mat. [4]Pull your navel up and in. [5]Extend your arms at shoulder height parallel to your legs and flex your feet, pressing through your heels and pointing your toes toward the ceiling. [6]Next, round your torso up and over. [7]Continually press your lower back behind you and scoop in your abdominals. [8]As you deepen the curve of your spine, press your navel further in to kiss your spine. [9]Imagine your body forming a U-shape. [10]Once you are fully extended, hang your head between your shoulders. [11]To roll like a ball, bend your knees and draw both ankles toward the core of your body and balance on your sit bones. [12]Grasp your ankles; pull your feet close to you, and place your head between your knees. [13]Imagine your body taking the shape of a small, tight C. [14]Then, inhale and roll back. [15]Throughout the roll, keep your C-shape and keep your navel pressed into your spine. [16]Finally, exhale as you roll back into your starting position.

Main Idea: The main idea is the point the writer is making about the topic. The topic is "Spine stretch and roll like a ball." **Underline the writer's point about this topic.**

Chronological Order: The transition "First" signals time order. **Circle four more time order signal words.**

Spatial Order: Space order is established with the word *outside*. To properly do this exercise, the body must assume correct positions. **Double underline two more words that establish space order.**

Relevant Details: Relevant details explain specific steps that build strength and flexibility. Extending your arms, flex your feet, pressing through your heels... builds flexibility. **Draw a box around a step in the process that builds strength.**

Effective Expression: Vivid details such as "press your navel further in to kiss your spine" creates a mental picture for the reader. **Underline three more vivid descriptive details.**

Comprehend and State a Main Idea Using Time Order and Space Order

L2

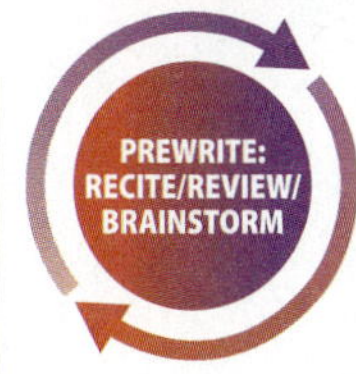

Narration records a specific event that occurs at a specific time and in a specific place. In contrast, process records a series of steps, phases, cycles, or directions that may be repeated time and again with the same results. The same transitions and signal words are used to indicate narration and process. The following chart lists a few examples of time order transitions or signal words.

Time Order Transitions and Signal Words for Narration and Process

after	currently	last	once	soon
afterward	during	later	over (time)	then
ago	eventually	meanwhile	previously	ultimately
as	finally	next	quickly	until
around	first	now	second	when
before	formerly	often	since	while

Transition or signal words of space order indicate a logical order based on two elements: (1) how the object, place, or person is arranged or occurs in space, and (2) the starting point from which the writer chooses to begin the description. The following chart lists just a few of the many transition and signal words writers use to establish space order.

Space Order Transitions or Signal Words for Description

above	back	center	in	outside
across	behind	close to	inside	over
adjacent	below	down	into	right
around	beneath	far away	left	there
at the bottom	beside	farther	middle	under
at the side	beyond	front	nearby	underneath
at the top	by	here	next to	within

Most often, we explain events and actions in terms of *where* they occur. Thus, writers often use space order along with time order to describe an event or process. Time order and space order may be combined to state a main idea. The following topic sentence effectively combines time and space order in a topic sentence.

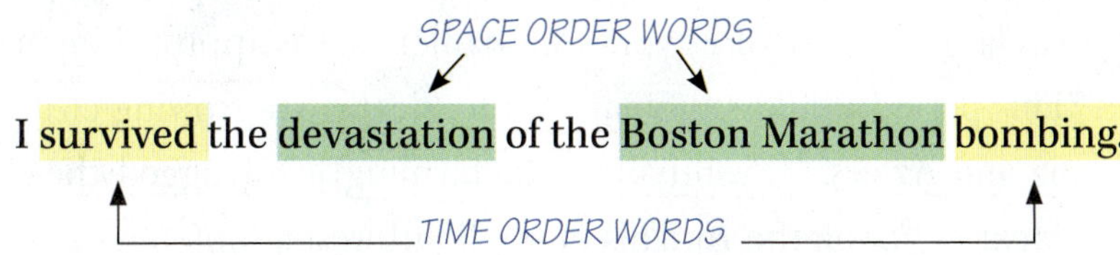

SPACE ORDER WORDS
I survived the devastation of the Boston Marathon bombing.
TIME ORDER WORDS

The words *survived* and *bombing* suggest time order. These words suggest that the writer will tell about the sequence of the bombing and how she survived. The words *devastation* and *Boston Marathon* are space order words. The words *Boston Marathon* tell where the bombing took place. They also suggest that the survivor will describe where she was when the bombs went off. The word *devastation* suggests that the writer will describe the scene after the bombs exploded. She may describe the scene on the street, but she may also describe her physical injuries.

Narration: A Chain of Events

Transitions of time signal that the writer is describing *when* an event occurred and *the sequence or order* of the actions as the event unfolded. Most often, the event occurred in a particular place. Transitions of space tell *where* the event or action occurred. Thus the details follow a logical order based on time and space. Readers take note of a writer's use of time order and space order to comprehend the point of a narrative paragraph.

Example

Survey the following paragraph from a college history textbook for the writer's use of time and space order. As you read, circle the topic as it appears throughout the paragraph. Underline the time and space order transitions, signal words, and the key details related to them. Then double underline the topic sentence, the sentence that best covers all of the details. After reading, complete the study chart with information from the paragraph.

The Maize Revolution

[1]**Maize** did not exist 7,000 years ago. [2]Then, around that time, perhaps far earlier, Indians in southern Mexico interbred various species of grasses. [3]They exploited subtle changes and perhaps significant mutations. [4]Eventually they created maize. [5]A geneticist writing in *Science* in 2003 declared this to be "arguably man's first, and perhaps his greatest, feat of genetic engineering." [6]The original ears were too small to provide much food. [7]Within several thousand years, however, farmers in Central America had developed maize that resembled modern corn. [8]The Neolithic revolution—the transition from hunting and gathering to farming—had come to Central America. [9]Soon most valleys in central Mexico bristled with cornstalks. [10]Population grew and cities emerged. [11]By AD 100 Teotihuacan, forty miles north of what is now Mexico City, had a population approaching 100,000. [12]This city featured miles of paved streets and a pyramid as large as those of Egypt. [13]Mesoamerica was approaching its classical period. [14]This period would culminate in the great corn-growing civilizations of the Mayans and Aztecs. [15]Eventually, corn farming leapfrogged the deserts of northern Mexico. [16]Soon the Indians of the Southwest adopted corn as a crop.

Carnes, Mark, and Garraty, John, *The American Nation: A History of the United States*, 14th ed., pp. 5–6.

Study Chart: The Maize Revolution				
	Who	**What**	**When**	**Where**
1.	Indians	interbred grasses created maize	around 7,000 years ago	in southern Mexico
2.	Farmers	developed maize that resembled modern corn Neolithic revolution	within several thousand years	in Central America
3.	Population of 100,000	Teotihuacan, city	by AD 100	forty miles north of what is now Mexico City
4.	Indians	adopted corn as crop	eventually	of the Southwest

Explanation

Compare your answers to the following student's think-aloud.

Before reading, I previewed the paragraph to identify the topic. The title "The Maize Revolution" told me that the paragraph is about maize. But as I previewed, I also noticed the writer used other similar words to talk about maize. For example, the word maize *appears three times in the paragraph. But the writer also uses the words* corn, cornstalks, corn crop, corn growing, *and* corn farming *to talk about the development of maize. So I circled all those words as the topic. I also circled the words* Neolithic revolution *for they seem like a synonym for the title Maize Revolution. My preview of the paragraph also gave me a good idea of the close*

CONTINUED

relationship between the time and place maize developed. Annotating the topic, transitions, signal words, and key details helped me stay focused during reading. I didn't want to underline every word, so the act of annotating slowed me down and made me think about which ideas were most important and worth underlining. After reading, it was quick work to fill in the chart with the annotated ideas. I really like the study chart. It is a great way to review information for a quiz or test. I recorded my answers below by turning each row of the chart into a sentence. I marked sentence 8 as the topic sentence. This sentence used the word revolution, which also is in the title for the paragraph. It also tied Neolithic to farming, and the whole point of the paragraph is that farming corn was a big change.

1. *Indians interbred grasses and created maize around 7,000 years ago in southern Mexico.*
2. *Farmers developed maize that resembled corn and began the Neolithic revolution within several thousand years in Central America.*
3. *A population of 100,000 in Teotihuacan, a city, emerged by AD 100, forty miles north of what is now Mexico City.*
4. *Indians of the Southwest eventually adopted corn as a crop.*

Practice 3

Comprehend a Main Idea Using Time and Space Order: Narration

Survey the following paragraph from the website of the United States Library of Congress for the writer's use of time and space order. As you read, circle the topic as it appears throughout the paragraph. Underline the time and space order transitions, signal words, and the key ideas related to them. Then double underline the topic sentence, the sentence that best covers all of the details. After reading, complete the study chart with information from the paragraph.

Colonial America (1492–1763)

[1]European nations came to the Americas to increase their wealth and broaden their influence over world affairs. [2]The Spanish were among the first Europeans to explore the New World and the first to settle in what is now the United States. [3]By 1650, however, England had established a dominant presence on the Atlantic coast. [4]The first colony was founded at Jamestown, Virginia, in 1607. [5]Many of the people who settled in the New World came to escape religious persecution. [6]The Pilgrims, founders of Plymouth, Massachusetts, arrived in 1620. [7]In both Virginia and Massachusetts, the colonists flourished with some assistance from Native Americans. [8]New World grains such as corn kept the colonists from starving while, in Virginia, tobacco provided a valuable cash crop. [9]By the early 1700s enslaved Africans made up a growing percentage of the colonial population. [10]By 1770, more than 2 million people lived and worked in Great Britain's 13 North American colonies.

"Colonial America (1492-1763)." *America's Story from America's Library*. United States Library of Congress. Web. 22 May 2013. <http://www.americaslibrary.gov/jb/colonial/jb_colonial_subj.html.>.

Study Chart: Colonial America (1492–1763)

	Who	What	When	Where
1.	Spanish, Europeans	explore and settled	first	in what is now the United States
2.	Europeans Native Americans	first colony founded	in 1607	in Jamestown, Virginia
3.	Pilgrims Native Americans	arrived and founded	in 1620	Plymouth, Massachusetts
4.	England	established presence	by 1650	on Atlantic coast
5.	More than 2 million people	lived and worked	by 1770s	Great Britain's North American colonies

To write a narration, you limit your topic to an event that occurred during a specific time and in a particular place. Most likely, a writer has an opinion or attitude about the event. This attitude or opinion shapes the controlling point of your main idea. A writer also reveals an opinion in the description of the event and the place in which the event takes place. The following topic sentence illustrates the use of time and space order to state a main idea for a narrative.

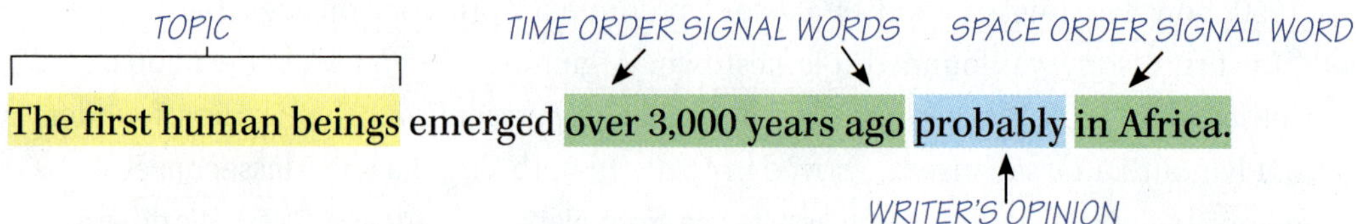

The topic is *the first human beings*. This topic is controlled or limited by the writer's use of time and space order. The time order signal words *over 3,000 years ago* tell when the first human beings emerged. The space order signal word in signals where the first humans emerged. The writer also states an opinion of uncertainty about the place with the word *probably.*

Example

Practice creating topic sentences. You are given a topic, an opinion, and time and space order signal word(s). Combine the ideas in each group to create a topic sentence for a narration. *Answers may vary.*

1. TOPIC: *Jimmie Johnson*

OPINION: *squeaked to a narrow victory, treacherous*

TIME ORDER SIGNAL WORDS: *during the last lap*

SPACE ORDER SIGNAL WORDS: *on the Daytona 500 racetrack*

TOPIC SENTENCE: *Jimmie Johnson squeaked to a narrow victory during the last lap on the treacherous Daytona 500 racetrack.*

2. TOPIC: *honesty*

OPINION: *I learned the value of*

TIME ORDER SIGNAL WORDS: *during my internship*

SPACE ORDER SIGNAL WORDS: *at City Hall*

TOPIC SENTENCE: *I learned the value of honesty during my internship at City Hall.*

Explanation

Compare your answers to the following student's think-aloud.

Working with this example showed me how the different parts of a topic sentence come together to narrow a topic and state a main idea. It was helpful to see two ways to narrow a topic. One way is to use time and space order signal words. The other way is to state an opinion about the topic. I can already think of specific details that explain when (time), where (space), and how (opinions such as "squeaked to a narrow victory, treacherous" and "I learned the value of"). I also learned that there are several ways to word a topic sentence. I had to decide where each word would appear in the sentence. For example, in the first item, I had to think about what the word treacherous described. Was it the victory or the racetrack? It made more sense to me that treacherous described the racetrack. Here are my topic sentences.

1. *Jimmie Johnson squeaked to a narrow victory on the treacherous Daytona 500 racetrack.*
2. *I learned the value of honesty during my internship at City Hall.*

Practice 4

State a Main Idea Using Time and Space Order: Narration

Practice creating topic sentences. Identify a topic, an opinion, and time and space order signal word(s) by filling in the blanks in each group of items. Combine the ideas in each group to create a topic sentence for a narrative. *Answers may vary.*

1. TOPIC: ______

OPINION: ______

TIME ORDER SIGNAL WORDS: ______

SPACE ORDER SIGNAL WORDS: ______

TOPIC SENTENCE: ______

CONTINUED

PRACTICE 4 *CONTINUED*

2. TOPIC:

OPINION:

TIME ORDER SIGNAL WORDS:

SPACE ORDER SIGNAL WORDS:

TOPIC SENTENCE:

Process: Steps, Stages, or Directions

Process is a time order thought pattern for a series of steps, stages, or directions. In a process, time order reveals the logical sequence of actions that can be repeated at any time with similar results. Space order often plays a part in the steps or stages of a process. For example, the directions for putting together a toy or assembling a piece of furniture include details about the physical or spatial aspects of the object. Effective readers pay attention to time and space order to comprehend the point of a process paragraph.

Example

Survey the following paragraph from a college ecology textbook for the writer's use of time and space order for process. As you read, circle the topic as it appears throughout the paragraph. Underline the time and space order transitions, signal words, and the key details related to them. Then double underline the topic sentence, the sentence that best covers all of the details. After reading, complete the study chart with information from the paragraph.

EARTH AS A SYSTEM: THE ROCK CYCLE

[1]Earth is a system. [2]This means that our planet consists of many interacting parts that form a complex whole. [3]Nowhere is the system of earth better illustrated than when we examine the rock cycle. [4]To begin, magma is molten material that forms inside the Earth. [5]Eventually magma cools and solidifies. [6]This process is called **crystallization**. [7]It may occur either beneath the surface or, following a volcanic eruption, at the surface. [8]The resulting rocks are called **igneous rocks**. [9]As igneous rocks are exposed at the surface, they will undergo weathering, in which the day-in and day-out influences of the atmosphere slowly disintegrate and decompose rocks. [10]Then, the materials that result are often moved downslope by gravity before being picked up and transported by any of a number of erosional agents, such as running water, glaciers, wind, or waves. [11]Eventually, these particles and dissolved substances, called **sediment**, are deposited. [12]Although most sediment ultimately comes to rest in the ocean, other sites of deposition include river floodplains, desert basins, swamps, and sand dunes. [13]Next, the sediments undergo **lithification**, a term meaning "conversion into rock." [14]Sediment is usually lithified into **sedimentary rock** when compacted

by the weight of overlying layers or when cemented as percolating groundwater fills the pores with mineral matter. [15]When the resulting sedimentary rock is buried deep within Earth and involved in the dynamics of mountain building or intruded by a mass of magma, it will be subjected to great pressures and/or intense heat. [16]This phase is called **metamorphism**. [17]The sedimentary rock will react to the changing environment and turn into the third rock type, **metamorphic rock**. [18]Finally, if metamorphic rock is subjected to still higher temperatures, it will melt, creating magma, which will eventually crystallize into igneous rock, starting the cycle all over again.

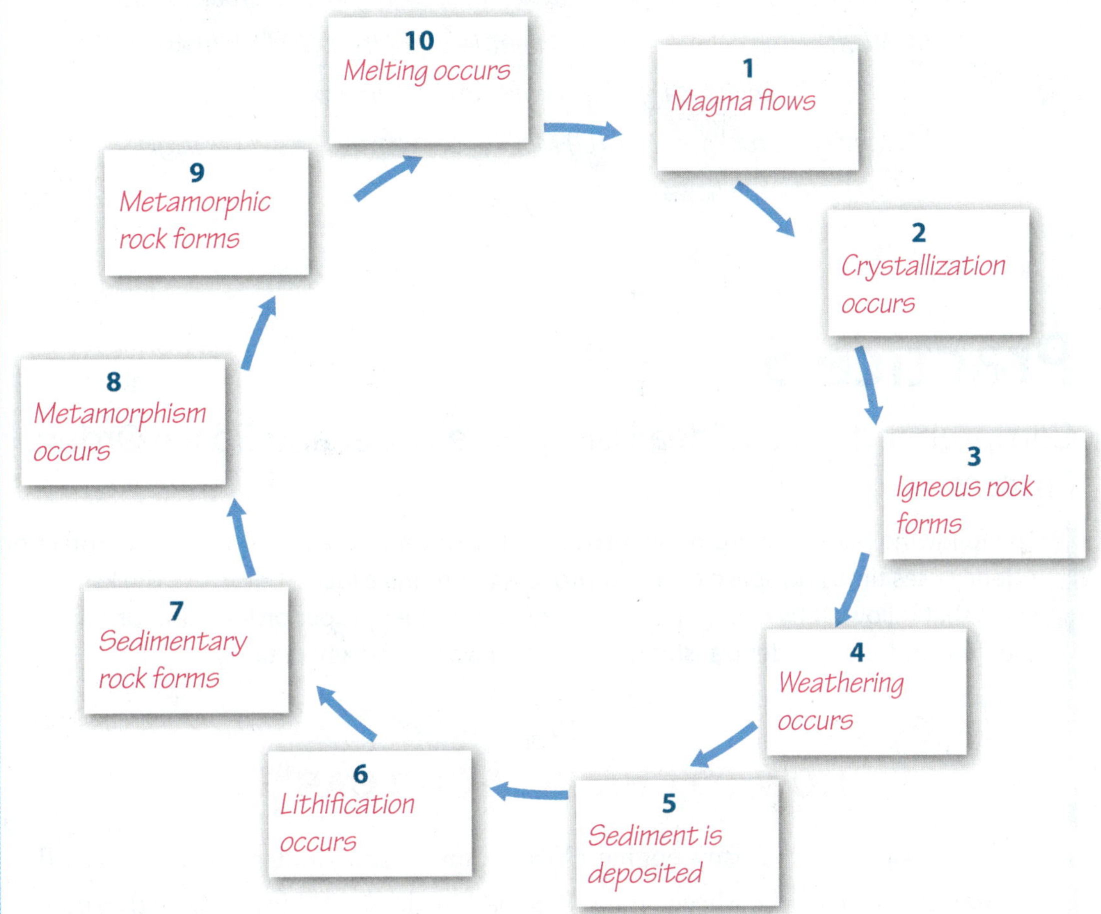

Explanation

Compare your answers to the following student's think-aloud.

The writer's use of bold print helped me in several ways. First, I think the writer highlighted these words because they are important parts of the topic. The title states that the writer is bringing two topics together: "Earth as a System" and "The Rock Cycle." It's like the rock

CONTINUED

cycle is just one example of earth as a system. So each word in bold print was a statement of one part of the topic. It helped to circle these topic words each time they were used because it helped me see how each one fit into the whole process based on the transitions and signal words. Sentence 3 is the topic sentence because it states the relationship between earth as a system and the rock cycle. I filled in the chart with the following details.

(1) Magma flows; (2) Crystallization occurs; (3) Igneous rock forms; (4) Weathering occurs; (5) Sediment is deposited; (6) Lithification occurs; (7) Sedimentary rock forms; (8) Metamorphism occurs; (9) Metamorphic rock forms; (10) Melting occurs; and the cycle begins again (1) Magma flows.

Practice 5

Comprehend a Main Idea Using Time Order and Space Order: Process

The following paragraph from the website of the United States Environmental Protection Agency uses time and space order for process to organize ideas. Complete the list of steps that follows it by giving the missing details in their proper order. (Hint: Underline the time and space order transitions and signal words and key details.)

HOW TO CHANGE YOUR CAR'S OIL

[1]First, warm up your car's engine. [2]Next, before getting under your car, turn off the engine, block the wheels, and set the parking brake. [3]Third, remove the drain plug on the bottom of the engine's oil pan, and allow the used oil to drain from your car into a drip pan. [4]Fourth, tightly replace the drain plug. [5]Fifth, carefully add the new engine oil. [6]Do not overfill. [7]Sixth, with the parking brake still set, and in a well-ventilated area, start the car, and allow the engine to run for a few minutes. [8]Seventh, turn off the engine and check the oil level. [9]Also check around the oil filter and drain plug for leaks. [10]Eighth, so you know when to change your oil next, write down the date, mileage, grade, and brand of the motor oil you installed. [11]Next, carefully pour the used oil from the drip pan into a suitable recycling container. [12]Finally, protect the environment and conserve resources

by taking your used oil to the nearest public used-oil collection center, such as a service station or lube center. [13]Also look for the "oil drop." [14]This is a petroleum industry symbol indicating that used oil is collected for recycling or reuse.

U.S. Environmental Protection Agency, "Collecting Used Oil for Recycling/Reuse."

How to Change Your Car's Oil

Step 1: *Warm up your car's engine*.

Step 2: *Turn off the engine, block the wheels, and set the parking brake*.

Step 3: *Remove the drain plug on the bottom of the engine's oil pan, and drain oil into a drip pan.*

Step 4: *Tightly replace the drain plug*.

Step 5: *Add the new engine oil.*

Step 6: *Start the car, and run the engine for a few minutes.*

Step 7: *Turn off the engine, check the oil level, and check the oil filter and drain plug for leaks.*

Step 8: *Write down the date, mileage, grade, and brand of the motor oil you installed*.

Step 9: *Pour the used oil from the drip pan into a suitable recycling container.*

Step 10: *Take your used oil to your nearest public used-oil collection center*.

To write a process, you limit your topic to a series of steps, phases, or directions. Many times, a step or phase of a process is closely tied to where it occurs. Most likely, a writer has an opinion or attitude about the process. This attitude or opinion shapes the controlling point of your main idea. A writer also reveals an opinion in the description of how the process unfolds or develops.

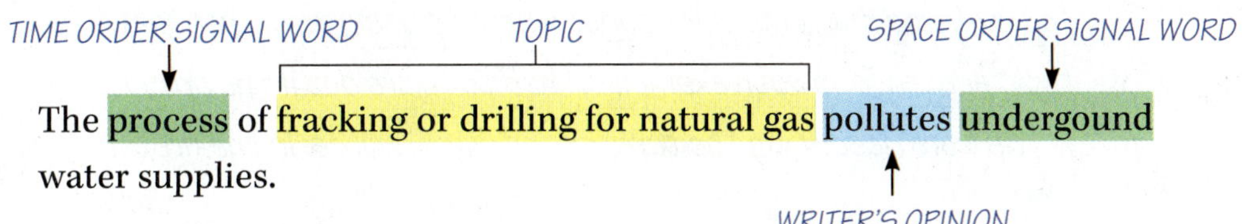

The topic is *fracking or drilling for natural gas*. This topic is controlled or limited by the writer's use of time and space order. The time order signal word *process* states that the writer will focus on the steps of fracking. The space order signal word *underground* states where water pollution occurs in the process. The writer chose the verb *pollutes* to state a negative opinion about the process of fracking. The reader should expect the writer to explain *how* and *when* fracking pollutes *underground* water supplies. While the topic sentence as worded included the time order and space order signal words, the same idea could be easily stated by implying time and space order. Consider the following topic sentence that states the same idea. *Fracking or drilling for natural gas pollutes water supplies.* The word *process* is implied in the terms *fracking* or *drilling*. Also, the location of the water supplies is a detail that will logically be explained in order to support the main idea.

Example

Practice creating topic sentences. You are given a topic, an opinion, and time and space order signal word(s). Combine the ideas in each group to create a topic sentence for a process. *Answers may vary.*

1. TOPIC: *Exercise*

OPINION: *effective, must be*

TIME ORDER SIGNAL WORDS: *program, designed for*

SPACE ORDER SIGNAL WORDS: *a specific body composition*

TOPIC SENTENCE: *An effective exercise program must be designed for a specific body composition.*

2. TOPIC: *communication*

OPINION: *especially important*

TIME ORDER SIGNAL WORDS: *during, process*

SPACE ORDER SIGNAL WORDS: *two areas of a person's body*

TOPIC SENTENCE: *Two areas of a person's body are especially important during the communication process.*

Explanation

Compare your answers to the following student's think-aloud.

This exercise made me think about where to use opinion words in a topic sentence. In both examples, I had to figure out if the opinion words were describing the topic or the signal words. In the first example, I put the topic Exercise with the signal word program and then decided the word effective described the topic. Then I put the opinion "must be" with the signal words "designed for." In the second example, I decided the opinion "especially important" describes the space order signal words "two areas of a person's body." Usually, I begin a topic sentence with the topic, but in this case I started with the space order signal words. Here are my sentences.

1. *An effective exercise program must be designed for a specific body composition.*
2. *Two areas of a person's body are especially important during the communication process.*

Practice 6

State a Main Idea Using Time and Space Order: Process

Practice creating topic sentences. Identify a topic, an opinion, and time and space order signal word(s) by filling in the blanks in each group of items. Combine the ideas in each group to create a topic sentence for a process. *Answers may vary.*

1. TOPIC: ______________________

OPINION: ______________________

TIME ORDER SIGNAL WORDS: ______________________

SPACE ORDER SIGNAL WORDS: ______________________

TOPIC SENTENCE: ______________________

____

2. TOPIC: ______________________

OPINION: ______________________

TIME ORDER SIGNAL WORDS: ______________________

SPACE ORDER SIGNAL WORDS: ______________________

TOPIC SENTENCE: ______________________

____

L3 Identify and Generate Relevant Details Using Time Order and Space Order

To identify and generate details based on time and space, readers and writers often ask the reporter's questions who, what, when, where, and how. Who is the person or people involved in a narrative? Who is carrying out the steps of a process? What are the specific actions that occur? When does each action occur? Where does the action occur? How does the event unfold or how are specific steps accomplished? What sensory details (such as sight, sound, smell, taste, or touch) are involved? Effective readers ask these questions to identify time order details. Likewise, effective writers ask and answer these questions to generate details to narrate an event or explain a process. Usually, time order and space order transitions and signal words introduce these details. Some major and minor details may also explain the writer's opinion about the event or process. Many readers and writers use a concept map to organize answers to the reporter's questions.

Example

Assume you are taking a college history course. Your professor has required you to find and respond to information about the Dust Bowl of the 1930s. You found the following article on a government website. Survey the paragraph for the writer's use of time and space order. As you read, underline the time and space order transitions, signal words, and the key details related to them. Then double underline the topic sentence, the sentence that best covers all of the details. After reading, complete the time-space graphic organizers with information from the paragraph. *Answers may vary.*

THE DUST BOWL

[1]Between 1930 and 1940, the southwestern Great Plains region of the United States suffered a severe drought. [2]Once a semi-arid grassland, the treeless plains became home to thousands of settlers when, in 1862, Congress passed the Homestead Act. [3]Most of the settlers farmed their land or grazed cattle. [4]The farmers plowed the prairie grasses and planted dry land wheat. [5]As the demand for wheat products grew, cattle grazing was reduced, and millions more acres were plowed and planted. [6]The poor farming and ranching techniques of the 1920s and 30s depleted the land and created the Dust Bowl. [7]Dry land farming on the Great Plains systematically destroyed all of the prairie grasses. [8]The dry land farming process entailed several steps. [9]In the fall, farmers deeply plowed the soil to allow rain to sink in quickly. [10]After rainfall, they practiced "dragging"

the fields to eliminate weeds and improve absorption. [11]Repeatedly, farmers raked the fields to eliminate water-devouring weeds. [12]They used tractors, combines, plows, and trucks to accomplish this intense working of the fields. [13]In the ranching regions, overgrazing also destroyed large areas of grassland. [14]Gradually, the land was laid bare, and significant environmental damage began to occur. [15]Among the natural elements, the strong winds of the region were particularly devastating. [16]With the onset of drought in 1930, the overfarmed and overgrazed land began to blow away. [17]Winds whipped across the plains, raising billowing clouds of dust. [18]The sky could darken for days. [19]People tried to seal their homes by hanging wet sheets as filters on doors and windows. [20]Even well-sealed homes could have a thick layer of dust on the furniture. [21]In some places, the dust drifted like snow, covering farm buildings and houses. [22]People spit out dust clogs as large around as a pencil. [23]They became sick with dust pneumonia. [24]Animals died. [25]Nineteen states in the heartland of the United States became a vast dust bowl. [26]On April 14, 1935, known as "Black Sunday," 20 of the worst "black blizzards" occurred across the entire sweep of the Great Plains, from Canada south to Texas. [27]With no chance of making a living, tens of thousands of farm families abandoned their homes and land, fleeing westward to become migrant laborers. [28]By 1940, 400,000 people left the Great Plains, victims of the combined action of severe drought and poor soil conservation practices.

Adapted from The Library of Congress. "The Dust Bowl." *American Memory Timeline*. Web. 29 May 2014. http://www.loc.gov/teachers/classroommaterials/presentationsandactivities/presentations/timeline/depwwii/dustbowl/

CONTINUED

EXAMPLE *CONTINUED*

Time-Space Order/Narration-Description Concept Chart

TOPIC (WHO OR WHAT): The Dust Bowl of the 1930s		
TOPIC SENTENCE: The poor farming and ranching techniques of the 1920s and 30s depleted the land and created the Dust Bowl.		
REPORTER'S QUESTIONS: WHEN, WHAT WHO, WHERE		**SENSORY DETAILS: SIGHT (SEE), SMELL, SOUND (HEAR), TASTE, TOUCH (FEEL)**
1862	Homestead act passed by Congress Thousands of settlers *Great Plains*	*semi-arid, grassland, treeless plains*
1920s–1930s	*poor farming and ranching techniques (dry farming, overgrazing)* farmers and ranchers	land was laid bare
1930	onset of drought, 19 states in the heartland of United States tried to seal homes, doors, windows	*land blew away, billowing clouds of dust, sky darkened for days, thick layer of dust on furniture, dust drifted like snow, covering buildings and houses, whipping wind, wet sheets*
During these years		*Animals died.* *People spit out dust clogs as large around as a pencil.* *They became sick with dust pneumonia.*
April 14, 1935	*20 black blizzards* tens of thousands of farm families fled the Great Plains from Canada south to Texas, migrated westward	
By 1940	400,000 people *left Great Plains*	

Time-Space Order/Narration-Description Concept Chart

TOPIC (WHO OR WHAT): Steps of Dry Land Farming		
MAJOR DETAIL: The dry land farming process entailed several steps.		
REPORTER'S QUESTIONS: WHEN, WHAT WHO, WHERE		**SENSORY DETAILS: SIGHT (SEE), SMELL, SOUND (HEAR), TASTE, TOUCH (FEEL)**
Step 1 *In the Fall*	*farmers* *deeply plowed* *soil to allow rain to sink in quickly*	semi-arid, grassland, treeless plains use of tractors, combines, plows, and trucks
Step 2 *After rainfall*	*farmers* *dragging* fields	improve water absorption
Step 3 Repeatedly	*farmers* *raked* *fields*	eliminate water-devouring weeds

Explanation

Compare your answers to the following student's think-aloud.

Completing the graphic organizers made me think deeply about the way the details worked together to tell about an important event in history. I noticed that most of the details in this paragraph were based on sight, describing how the land looked. Some sentences used more than one type of detail. For example, spitting out dust as large around as a pencil uses both taste and sight. Sometimes, the details made me think about sounds, like the use of tractors, combines, and trucks. And the word drought made me think of how hot and dry it was. It must have been very uncomfortable. It was also helpful to see how the process of dry farming was a part of the narrative. Because I had to think so much about how to fill in the chart, I am going to remember these details. They are vivid in my mind's eye. I completed the charts with the following details.

The Dust Bowl of the 1930s

1862 Where: Great Plains, Sight: Semi-arid grassland, treeless plains

1920s–30s What: Poor farming and ranching techniques (dry farming, overgrazing)

CONTINUED

EXPLANATION *CONTINUED*

1930, Sight: Land blew away, billowing clouds of dust, sky darkened for days, thick layer of dust on furniture, dust drifted like snow, covering buildings and houses
During these years, Sight: Animals died. Taste: people spit out dust clogs as large around as pencils. Touch: They became sick with dust pneumonia.
April 14, 1935, What: Black Blizzards
By 1940, What: 400,000 people left
Steps of Dry Land Farming
Step 1: In the fall, What: deeply plowed. Where: soil to allow rain to sink in quickly.
Step 2: After rainfall, What: dragging. Where: fields, Sight: improve water absorption.
Step 3: Repeatedly, What: raked. Where: fields, Sight: eliminate water-devouring weeds.

Just as a reader may use a time-order graphic organizer to comprehend a writer's point, a writer often uses the same graphic organizer to generate details. A time and space order graphic organizer helps a writer create or access vivid details to make or support a point. At this point in the reading/writing process, a writer focuses on brainstorming details. In the next step, those details can be organized into a smooth and logical flow of ideas. A time-space order chart will make the next step easier to accomplish.

Example

Assume you are continuing to work on your college history class assignment. You are ready to brainstorm a written response to the paragraph about the Dust Bowl. To guide your response, your professor has provided the following historical photograph and topic suggestions. Write a diary entry or letter from one of the following points of view: (1) a farmer who is dry farming, (2) a mother nursing a child sick with dust pneumonia, or (3) a family surviving a dust storm. Complete the time-space graphic organizer. Feel free to use details from the picture below and from the example paragraph "Dust Bowl" on pages 334–335. *Answers may vary.*

A dust storm hits a southwestern town, 1937

CONTINUED

Time-Space Order/Narration-Description Concept Chart

TOPIC (WHO OR WHAT):		
TOPIC SENTENCE:		
REPORTER'S QUESTIONS: WHEN, WHAT WHO, WHERE		**SENSORY DETAILS: SIGHT (SEE), SMELL, SOUND (HEAR), TASTE, TOUCH (FEEL)**

Explanation

Compare your answers to the following student's think-aloud.

To generate details, I first studied the photograph. The picture helped me see the size of the dust clouds. It also made the details in the paragraph become real. I chose the third topic, the point of view of a family writing a letter about surviving a storm on Black Sunday. I made up some details, like about the family members. I also tried to put myself in the situation and think about what it might have been like. For example, I believe they would have seen the storm before they heard it due to how big the clouds were. It's like you see lightning before you hear thunder.

CONTINUED

EXPLANATION *CONTINUED*

Also because the dust cloud could be seen so far away, I imagined that the sky would be clear and the sun shining before the clouds arrived. I also wanted to include details about how the family must have felt fearful and sweaty as they worked to protect their home. The paragraph also provided important details that I included in my chart.

Time-Space Order/Narration-Description Concept Chart

TOPIC (WHO OR WHAT): A family surviving a dust storm		
TOPIC SENTENCE: Dear Grandmother, we survived the dust blizzard that hit our area on Black Friday.		
REPORTER'S QUESTIONS: WHEN, WHAT WHO, WHERE		**SENSORY DETAILS: SIGHT (SEE), SMELL, SOUND (HEAR), TASTE, TOUCH (FEEL)**
April 14, 1935, Black Sunday, Before the Storm	a family of three: mother, father, preteen child outside a home in Dodge City, Kansas	blue sky, golden sunlight scorched no sound, no wind
Suddenly	the blizzard approached on the horizon behind the houses	towering, rolling, boiling black dust
Quickly	family rushed inside house covered doors and window	hung wet sheets
Within minutes	house family	pounding wind, gravel clatters against windows and on roof inky darkness complete blindness, sweating, nauseous, choking on gritty dirt fearful
Afterwards	mounds of sand	almost buried house dead cows spat clogs of dust

Practice 7

Generate Relevant Time Order and Space Order Details

Choose one of the topic sentences you created in Practices 4 or 6. Use the following time-space order concept map to generate details to support your topic sentence.
Answers may vary.

Time-Space Order/Narration-Description Concept Chart

TOPIC (WHO OR WHAT):		
TOPIC SENTENCE:		
REPORTER'S QUESTIONS: WHEN, WHAT WHO, WHERE		**SENOSRY DETAILS: SIGHT (SEE), SMELL, SOUND (HEAR), TASTE, TOUCH (FEEL)**

Practice 8

Identify and Generate Details Using Time Order and Space Order

Assume you are taking a college health course. Read the following paragraph from the unit in your textbook you are currently studying. Survey the paragraph for the writer's use of time and space order. As you read, underline the time and space order transitions, signal words, and the key details related to them. Then double underline the topic sentence, the sentence that best covers all of the details. After reading, complete the flow chart with information from the paragraph. Finally, generate details to answer the reading response question that appears after the selection. *Answers may vary.*

How Can You Make Healthier Behavior Choices?

[1]Maria needs to change several behaviors to improve her wellness. [2]Her exercise, eating, sleeping, and time management habits could all be improved. [3]Changing her current behaviors will require some effort on her part, and it will not happen overnight. [4]Unhealthy habits and patterns develop over time, so

CONTINUED

PRACTICE 8 *CONTINUED*

she cannot expect to change them without time and effort. [5]Fortunately, Maria is committed to improving her health. [6]She is going to use the Stages of Change Model to make lifestyle behavior changes. [7]The Stages of Change Model suggests that there is a series of five stages to behavior change. [8]Individuals in the first stage, **precontemplation**, of behavior change do not plan to change their unhealthy behavior. [9]They might not realize the need to change, or they just might not want to change. [10]Because people in this stage are not thinking about changing their behaviors, they might need friends and family to help move to the next stage. [11]The goal for people in this first stage is to get good information about healthy behaviors, so they can begin to look at their unhealthy behavior differently. [12]In the second phase, the **contemplation** stage, a person is aware of the need to change and intends to do so within the next 6 months. [13]People in this stage also need information about healthy behaviors and about the small steps they can make to get closer to changing. [14]During the third stage, **preparation**, the person is getting ready to make the change within the next 30 days. [15]In some cases, the person might already be making some changes (e.g., increasing lifestyle activity before starting an exercise program). [16]People also begin to take practical steps, such as keeping a detailed schedule in a cell phone or on the computer to list and prioritize daily tasks. [17]In the **action** stage, the behavior change has occurred, but for fewer than 6 months. [18]Using the behavior modification strategies discussed in the next section can help make the new behavior become a habit. [19]After sustaining the behavior change for 6 months, the person enters the last stage, **maintenance**. [20]During this stage, the behavior change is more of a habit and requires less conscious effort. [21]As this stage progresses, the temptation to resume old habits steadily decreases. [22]Continuing to use the behavior modification strategies that helped to advance through the earlier stages will help to maintain the change long term. [23]The length of time that one spends in each stage is highly individual. [24]Often, people move back and forth between the stages multiple times before they are able to make the behavior change permanent. [25]Note that a setback does not mean failure. [26]If you experience a lapse to an earlier stage, evaluate why you had the setback, and develop a new plan. [27]Learn from this experience, and do not let it discourage you. [28]The key element in any behavior change plan is the desire to change. [29]Without a genuine desire to make lifestyle changes, the best behavior change plan is doomed to fail.

Adapted from Powers, Scott K., Dodd, Stephen L., and Jackson, Erica M., *Total Fitness & Wellness*, 6th ed., pp. 11–12.

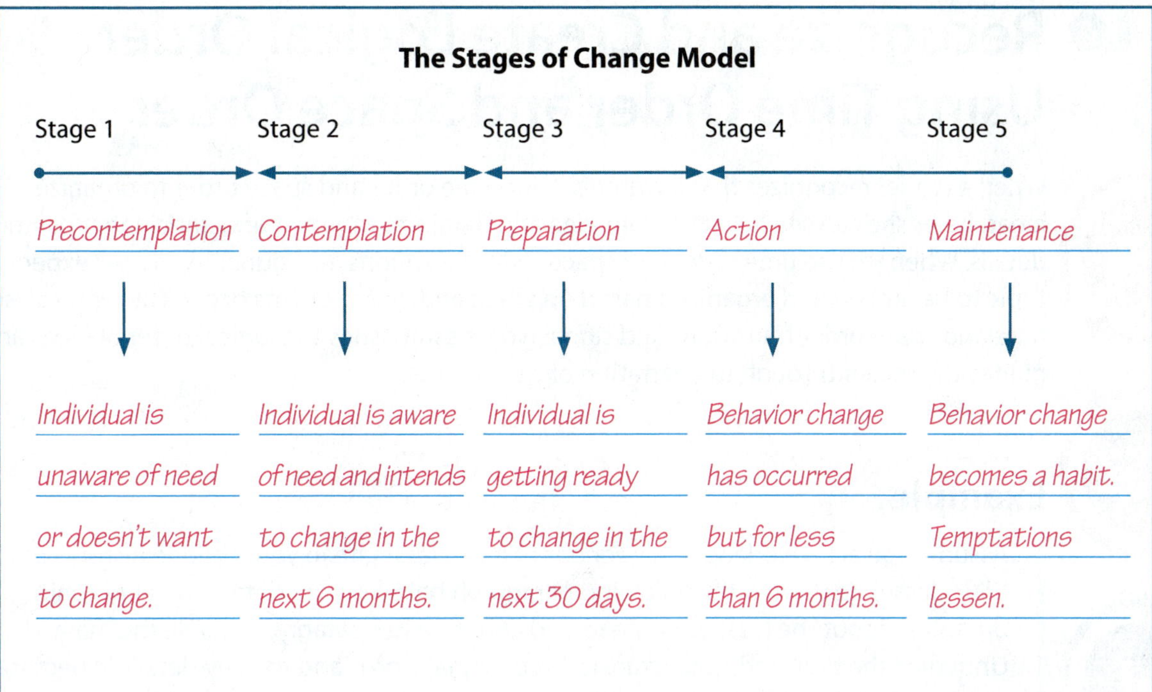
The Stages of Change Model
Stage 1
Stage 2
Stage 3
Stage 4
Stage 5
Precontemplation
Contemplation
Preparation
Action
Maintenance
Individual is unaware of need or doesn't want to change.
Individual is aware of need and intends to change in the next 6 months.
Individual is getting ready to change in the next 30 days.
Behavior change has occurred but for less than 6 months.
Behavior change becomes a habit. Temptations lessen.

Reading Response Question: Identify a person who has an unhealthy habit or pattern of behavior that needs to change. The person can be you or someone you know. In the following space, brainstorm answers to the following questions: What is the unhealthy habit? What stage in the Stages of Change Model is the person currently in? What steps should the person take to reach the maintenance stage? Use a time-space graphic organizer or a flow chart to brainstorm your response.

L4 Recognize and Create Logical Order Using Time Order and Space Order

When a reader recognizes that a writer is using time order and space order to organize ideas, he or she can see how the main idea and details fit together and anticipate upcoming details. When we use time order and space order transitions and signal words, we expect the topic to be limited and organized based on when and where events occur. The writer's use of time and space order transitions and signal words establishes the logical order of ideas and guides the reader through the narration or the process.

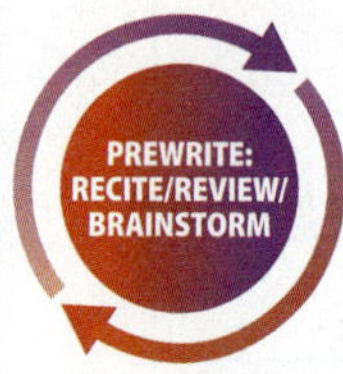

Example

Assume you are a working as a peer editor for a classmate in your college history course. Your classmate drafted the following paragraph based on the details in her graphic organizer about the Dust Bowl. Read and annotate her paragraph. Circle the main idea. Underline the time and space transitions or signal words and the key details. If necessary, cross out any details that are not relevant to the main idea. *Answers may vary.*

Dear Grandmother,

[1]We survived the dust blizzard that hit our area Sunday. [2]The day began with a beautiful blue sky and golden sunlight. [3]Mom, Dad, and I were out in the yard shoveling dirt from the last dust storm away from the house. [4]Suddenly, Dad shouted for us to look at the horizon behind the house. [5]We saw a towering cloud of dust roiling and boiling as it marched directly at us. [6]We felt no wind. [7]We heard no sound. [8]Quickly, we all dashed into the house. [9]We rushed to wet sheets and hang them over the doors and windows. [10]Within minutes, an inky darkness fell upon us. [11]We were completely blinded, not able to see our own hands in front of our faces. [12]At the same time, the wind pounded our house, and gravel clattered against the windows and on the roof. [13]We huddled together choking on the gritty dirt, sweating with fear, and sick to our stomachs. [14]When it was over, all the cows were dead, smothered by the dust. [15]Mounds of sand nearly buried the house. [16]For days, we spit globs of dirt as big around as pencils. [17]I am never going to forget Black Sunday, April 15, 1935.

Explanation

Compare your answers to the following student's think-aloud.

The first sentence states the main idea of the letter. The use of time order signal words and transitions such as "began," "Suddenly," "Quickly," "Within minutes," "When it was over," and "For days" guided me through the events of the dust blizzard. The use of space order signal words such as "out in the yard," "the horizon behind the house," "towering cloud," "into the house," "against the windows," "on the roof" showed me where each action occurred. The use of sensory details such as "blue sky," "golden sunlight," "shouted," "roiling," "boiling," "inky darkness," "wind pounded," "gravel clattered," "gritty dirt," "sick to our stomachs," "smothered," "spit globs of dirt as big around as pencils" created a vivid picture of the event in my mind. I liked the way the writer pulled details from both the photograph and paragraph about the dust storm and turned them into a story from the point of view of the daughter. I thought all the details were relevant to the main idea. I do have one suggestion. This is a letter from a granddaughter to her grandmother. I would suggest adding a sentence that gives the grandmother an idea about how the family is doing. After all, it was a pretty horrible thing to live through. I think a grandmother would want to know that they really are okay physically and emotionally.

Practice 9

Create Logical Order Using Time and Space Order

Work with the time-space order concept map you completed in Practice 7 or Practice 8. Write a rough draft of your paragraph using the details you generated. Work with a peer to review each other's rough drafts. Exchange, read, and review your drafts to make sure all details are relevant to the main ideas. Complete a time-space order concept map of the draft you are peer editing. Circle the main idea. Underline the time and space transitions or signal words and the key details. Cross out any details that are not relevant to the main idea. Suggest a change to improve the paragraph. Point out what you like about the use of time and space order in the paragraph. Return your reviewed paragraphs to each other. Revise as needed.

L5 Analyze and Use Effective Language with Time Order and Space Order

Precise word choice communicates exact meaning. Words chosen for a specific emotional or visual impact create strong images in the reader's mind and carry out the writer's purpose. Effective readers and writers understand and use the **denotative** and **connotative** meanings of words to grasp and create vivid images and impressions.

Denotation refers to the exact, literal, or neutral meaning of a word—the dictionary definition.

Consider the connotative and denotative meanings of the word *snake*. The denotative meaning of *snake* is an elongated, legless, meat-eating reptile. However, the connotative meaning of *snake* is often used to imply evil or danger and arouse emotions or feelings such as fear or dread. Connotations of words may be positive or negative. For example, based on personal or cultural experience, to some, the word *snake* may imply rebirth, a powerful life force or even healing.

Connotation refers to the associations or emotional connections suggested by a word.

Example

Complete the following chart of denotative and connotative meanings for words or phrases. Go to Thesaurus.com and type each word into the search box as needed. Discuss and compare your responses among a small group of peers. *Answers may vary.*

Denotative Meaning	Positive Connotation	Negative Connotation
1. thin	*slender*	*skinny*
2. politician	*public servant*	*crook*
3. loud speech	*cheering*	*screaming*
4. *youthful*	child-like	childish
5. determined	persistent	*stubborn*
6. intelligent	*brilliant*	*nerd*

Explanation

Compare your responses to the following student's think-aloud.

As we shared our work in our small group, we noticed that we each thought of different words. The connotations of words are often based on personal or subjective experiences. For example, in item 1, I chose slender for its positive connotation and the word skinny for its negative connotation. However, another person chose svelte for its positive connotation and scrawny for its negative connotation of the neutral or denotative word thin. Here are the rest of my responses: 2. Public servant (positive), Crook (negative). 3. Cheering (positive), Screaming (negative). 4. Youthful (denotative or neutral). 5. Stubborn (negative). 6. Brilliant (positive), Nerd (negative).

Effective writers use the connotations of words to create **figures of speech** that are fresh and vivid. Effective readers carefully analyze a writer's choice of words and figures of speech to comprehend the writer's point. The following three figures of speech are among the most commonly used.

A **figure of speech** is a word or phrase that departs from literal meaning to create a special effect or fresh meaning.

1. **Metaphor:** A direct comparison (not using *like* or *as*) between two things, using one thing to describe the other thing

   Forgiveness *is* a **well of water.**

   A **wave** of **grief** swept over him

2. **Simile:** An indirect comparison between two things, usually using *like, as,* or *than*

   Daniel, *like* a **giant oak**, stands firm and tall.

   Life blooms and fades as quickly as a **flower**.

3. **Onomatopoeia:** A word that imitates the sound it represents

   The car **zoomed** around the racetrack.

   The motor **purred** with power.

   The water **hissed** as it splashed on the hot burner.

Example

Analyze the following items based on each one's use of figures of speech. Identify the figure of speech used.

1. "Snap, crackle, pop" —Rice Krispies
   a. metaphor b. simile (c.) onomatopoeia

2. "…love should grow vaster than empires and more slow" —Andrew Marvell, "To His Coy Mistress"
   a. metaphor (b.) simile c. onomatopoeia

3. "The Sea of Faith was once, too, at the full, and round earth's shore lay" —Matthew Arnold, "Dover Beach"
   (a.) metaphor b. simile c. onomatopoeia

4. "Boom Boom Pow" —Song title by Black Eyed Peas
   a. metaphor b. simile (c.) onomatopoeia

Explanation

Compare your answers to the following student's think-aloud.

It is so much more fun to read when a writer uses figures of speech. I enjoy the way figures of speech create sights and sounds in my head. I identified the following figures of speech for each item.

1. *"Snap, crackle, pop" is (c), onomatopoeia, the sounds Rice Krispies make when you pour milk over them. I think using these sounds is a very clever and catchy advertisement for the cereal. It makes you remember and even want the cereal.*
2. *This statement uses (b), simile, to compare love to empires using the words than, vaster, and more slow. Empires are not grown overnight. They take time. And by their nature, empires are large or vast. So the idea is that immense love grows slowly over time.*
3. *The "Sea of Faith" uses (a), metaphor. Matthew Arnold makes a direct comparison between the sea and faith. So I think the statement means that faith is like the tide; sometimes it's high and sometimes it's low.*
4. *The title of the Black Eyed Peas' song "Boom Boom Pow" uses (c), onomatopoeia, to describe the beat of the music the group makes in the song.*

Practice 10

Analyze Effective Expression with Time Order and Space Order

The following paragraph is a tribute to a beloved family member of the writer. Read the paragraph. In the spaces that follow, identify the figure of speech in each sentence. Also, in your own words write the meaning of each figure of speech.

[1]My cousin's life slipped away as quickly as the setting sun in the evening sky. [2]Nedra was a warrior who fought the good fight against ignorance, apathy, and prejudice. [3]She was a trailblazer who cleared paths for others to follow. [4]She was a servant who worked to meet the needs of others before her own. [5]I can still hear her chortles, giggles, and guffaws as she saw the humor in almost every situation. [6]I can still hear the fast clip-clip of her heels as she bustled from moment to moment. [7]Like a pebble dropped in a pond, her life still radiates ever-widening circles of love.

Sentence 1. Figure of Speech: *Simile*

Meaning: *She died unexpectedly and quickly.*

Sentence 2. *Metaphor*

Meaning: *She was brave and stood up for what was right.*

Sentence 3. *Metaphor*

Meaning: *She was a leader who was the first to try new things and solve problems.*

Sentence 4. *Metaphor*

Meaning: *She was humble and kind to others. She was selfless.*

Sentence 5. *Onomatopoeia*

Meaning: *She was fun loving and had a good sense of humor.*

Sentence 6. *Onomatopoeia*

Meaning: *She was active and on the go accomplishing tasks.*

Sentence 7. *Simile*

Meaning: *She continues to affect many people.*

As you move through your own writing process, think about the impact you want to have on your reader. For the greatest impact, revise general or vague expressions into concrete and precise words and phrases. Use figures of speech to make your writing vivid and memorable.

Example

Each item below presents a general sentence using vague words. The phrase in parentheses before each sentence—(A customer to a mechanic) in item 1, for example—identifies the writer and audience of each statement. Revise each sentence to replace vague wording with figures of speech. Identify the figure of speech you used in each revised sentence. Consider the point of the writing situation. *Answers may vary.*

1. (A customer to a mechanic): My car makes a funny sound sometimes.

My car's engine screeches and whirs during acceleration. My brakes squeal.

Figure of Speech: *Onomatopoeia*

2. (A student commenting to his or her companion): The restaurant was disappointing.

The dark and dirty restaurant smelled like an old mop.

Figure of Speech: *Simile*

3. (A weather reporter on a morning broadcast): The weather is nice (or horrible).

Today's weather will be sizzling with temperatures above 100 degrees.

Figure of Speech: *Onomatopoeia*

4. (A running coach to an athlete in training): You are a fast runner who will beat all competitors.

You are a Cheetah who will overtake all you competitors.

Figure of Speech: *Metaphor*

Explanation

Compare your answers to the following student's think-aloud.

I used my senses to think of words to describe sights, sounds, smells, or touch. For example, I remembered how my car sounded when an engine belt broke. I also remembered how my brakes sounded when they were worn down. I tried to get a visual picture in my mind and then smells, sounds, and feelings came to mind. Then I chose the figure of speech that would best express my mental image. Here are my revised sentences.

1. *My car's engine screeches and whirs during acceleration. My brakes squeal.*
2. *The dark and dirty restaurant smelled like an old mop.*
3. *Today's weather will be sizzling with temperatures above 100 degrees.*
4. *You are a Cheetah who will overtake all your competitors.*

Practice 11

Use Effective Expression with Time Order and Space Order

Work with the rough draft of the paragraph you completed in Practice 9. Choose two sentences. Revise each sentence you chose to create effective expression. Use the following space to record your original and revised sentences. *Answers may vary.*

Original sentence: ______________________________

____

Revised sentence: ______________________________

____

Original sentence: ______________________________

____

Revised sentence: ______________________________

____

Reading and Writing Assignments: Narrative Using Time Order and Space Order

MySkillsLab™
Complete these assignments in MySkillsLab.

Considering Audience and Purpose

Study the sequence of photographs of Jennifer Hudson in the photographic organizer in the beginning of the module. Assume the pictures are to be used to document her achievements on a website designed to promote her career. Write a narrative that will be recorded as a voice-over and heard as the pictures flash on the screen.

Reading and Writing for Everyday Life

Assume one of your friends and you are exchanging emails about your most recent vacations. You just received the following message from her about the caves she just finished exploring. Respond to her message. In your response, comment on an aspect of the caves you find most interesting. Then describe a place you have visited that you think she would enjoy.

RE: The Amazing Caves at Ruby Falls

You would love the eerie caves at Ruby Falls. Our tour group was a small one of about ten people. We all piled onto an elevator, stuffy from all the bodies and stinking like a dirty sock, to sink 250 feet underground. We exited the elevator and gasped for air because of the lack of oxygen and the dampness of the cave. The cave was dark with barely any light. We wore helmets mounted with lights. I looked like a real spelunker. We saw stalactites hanging from the ceiling and stalagmites growing up from the ground. The columns, drapes, and flowstone created vast formations. We walked through an onyx jungle flowing with layers of limestone. The massive monuments were smooth and damp. Some were slimy like a snail. Water trickled from the ceiling in my hair and down my face. We squeezed through narrow stone pathways littered with rock shapes resembling everything from bacon, to a dragon foot, to a form that looked like New York City. We came across a huge formation that appeared lifelike. The icicle stalactites looked like they could break free and assault us. You and I need to see these amazing caves together.

Reading and Writing for College Life

Assume you are taking a college course in communication. Your professor has assigned the following paragraph from the introduction of the chapter on listening along with a writing prompt to call up your prior knowledge about listening.

Listening in Human Communication

According to the International Listening Association, **listening** is "the process of receiving, constructing meaning from, and responding to spoken and/or nonverbal messages." In this chapter, we will look at the importance of listening, the nature of the listening process, the varied styles of listening you might use in different situations, and some cultural and gender differences in listening. Throughout this chapter, we'll identify ways to avoid the major barriers to listening and guidelines for more effective listening.

DeVito, Joseph A., *Human Communication: The Basic Course*, 12th ed., p. 77.

Writing prompt: Why is listening so important? How do you make sure you listen well? How can you tell if someone is really listening to you? Recount a time in your life or the life of someone you know that reveals the importance of listening.

Reading and Writing for Working Life

Assume you work at a local retail store called Sports Gear, Inc. and you have fallen off a ladder while stocking shelves and shattered your leg; you require surgery and will be unable to work for six weeks. You are filing for workers' compensation to cover expenses and lost wages due to the injury. Read the following section from the company's Employee Handbook. Then write a paragraph to notify the company of your injury and request workers' compensation. In your paragraph, record the events of the injury as they occurred and describe the physical aspects of the injury.

Employee Handbook: Workers' Compensation

Employees who are injured on the job at Sports Gear, Inc. are covered by Workers' Compensation Insurance. It is your responsibility to immediately notify Ms. Kathleen Mann in Human Resources of any injuries you sustain while on the job at Sports Gear, Inc. In a brief letter, describe the nature of your injury: What is your injury? When, where, and how did it occur? We encourage injured employees to seek immediate medical attention at approved medical facilities. All medical expenses related to the treatment of an injury sustained on the job are paid in full directly to the medical providers. After a specified waiting period, you are also eligible for disability payments set forth by state law, where necessary.

Reading and Writing Assignments: Process Using Time Order and Space Order

MySkillsLab™
Complete these assignments in MySkillsLab.

Considering Audience and Purpose

Study the sequence of photographs about the set of Pilates exercises in Practice 2. Assume you are an instructor of an exercise class for an elderly group. Think about specific movements in each step of the exercise that might have to be adapted due to the poor balance or stiffness of joints some elderly experience. Write a paragraph for the Senior Citizens' Health Club Newsletter that describes these adapted exercises.

Reading and Writing for Everyday Life

Assume that a friend or family member has asked you for advice about how to respond to bullying. You have found the following information on a government website. Read the information; then in your own words, write a paragraph that gives advice about how to respond to a bullying at school, in a neighborhood, or at a public park.

Stop Bullying on the Spot

When adults respond quickly and consistently to bullying behavior they send the message that it is not acceptable. Research shows this can stop bullying behavior over time. There are simple steps adults can take to stop bullying on the spot and keep kids safe.

Do:

Intervene immediately. It is ok to get another adult to help.

Separate the kids involved.

Make sure everyone is safe.

Meet any immediate medical or mental health needs.

Stay calm. Reassure the kids involved, including bystanders.

Model respectful behavior when you intervene.

Avoid these common mistakes:

Don't ignore it. Don't think kids can work it out without adult help.

Don't immediately try to sort out the facts.

Don't force other kids to say publicly what they saw.

Don't question the children involved in front of other kids.

Don't talk to the kids involved together, only separately.

Don't make the kids involved apologize or patch up relations on the spot.

"Stop Bullying on the Spot." *stopbullying.gov* 19 July 2012 <http://www.stopbullying.gov/respond/on-the-spot/index.html>.

Reading and Writing for College Life

Assume you are taking a college course in communication. Your class has completed the chapter "Listening in Human Communication." As a graded assignment, you are to give a speech to the class that explains the listening process and gives real life examples of each phase of the process. Read the following excerpt from the chapter's summary section. Then write a draft of your speech. Use your own words and give examples of each stage.

The Listening Process

Listening is a five-part process that begins with receiving, and continues through understanding, remembering, evaluating, and responding. First, receiving consists of hearing the verbal signals and perceiving the nonverbal signals. Second, understanding involves learning what the speaker means, not merely what the words mean. Third, remembering involves retaining the received message, a process that involves considerable reconstruction. Fourth, evaluating consists of judging the message you receive. Finally, responding involves giving feedback while the speaker is speaking and taking your turn at speaking when the speaker has finished.

DeVito, Joseph A., *Human Communication: The Basic Course*, 12th ed., p. 77.

Reading and Writing for Working Life

Assume you have an interview for a job that pays a good salary, with benefits and opportunities for promotion. To prepare for the interview, you have researched the most common questions asked during a job interview. Review the list of possible questions you have compiled. Choose one and write a one-paragraph response.

- What major challenges and problems did you face at a previous job? How did you handle them?
- How do you handle stress and pressure?
- How do you evaluate success?
- How would you fire someone?
- How would you handle a customer complaint?

Workshop: Compose a Narrative or Process Paragraph Using Time Order and Space Order

Choose a paragraph to read and respond to in writing. You may select a paragraph in an example, practice, or writing assignment within this module. Or you may select a paragraph of your own choosing. Use the following guide to comprehend and respond to the paragraph. Apply what you have learned about time and space order (narration, process, and description) to your reading/writing strategy.

Preread: Survey and Question

Ask questions about the text's features.

____

____

What is the passage about?

____

____

How is the material organized?

____

____

What do I already know about this topic? (What is my prior knowledge about the vocabulary?)

____

____

What is my purpose for reading/writing?

____

____

What points may I want to address or include in my written response?

____

____

Read and Annotate

As you read, annotate key ideas, particularly those details that answer your prereading questions.

Recite, Review, and Brainstorm

Recite the information. Summarize the most important parts. Answer your prereading questions. Rephrase ideas into your own words. Record changes in your opinions based on the new information. **Review** the information. **Brainstorm** ideas for your written response to the passage. **Freewrite** a response to what you have read. **Map** the relationship among ideas you have annotated in the text. **Outline** or list key ideas and details in blocks of thought. Use your own paper.

Write a Draft of Your Response

Using the ideas you generated by brainstorming, compose a draft of your response. Use your own paper.

Revise Your Draft

Once you have created a draft of a process, read the draft to answer the questions in the "Questions for Revising a Process Paragraph" box that follows. Indicate your answers by annotating your paper. If you answer "yes" to a question, underline, check, or circle examples. If you answer "no" to a question, write needed information in margins and draw lines to indicate placement of additional details. Revise your paragraph based on your reflection. (*Hint*: Experienced writers create several drafts as they focus on one or two questions per draft.)

Step by Step: Questions for Revising a Paragraph Using Time and Space Order

- ☐ Have I stated or implied a focused main idea?
- ☐ Is the order of the event, steps, directions, or phases within the process clear? Have I used strong transitions of time and space?
- ☐ Have I made my point with adequate details?
- ☐ Have I included only the details that are relevant to my topic sentence?
- ☐ Have I used vivid images to make the process clear to my readers?
- ☐ Have I used concrete details to make my point?

Proofread Your Draft

Once you have made any revisions to your paragraph that may be needed, proofread your paragraph to eliminate careless errors.

Review Test

MySkillsLab™ Complete this Review Test in MySkillsLab.

Score (number correct) _____ x 10 =____%

Read the following passage from a college health textbook. Answer the questions, complete the concept map, and then respond to the writing prompts "Summary Response" and "What Do You Think?"

1280L/12 GE/940 words

The General Adaptation Syndrome

[1]When a body is in **homeostasis**, the body's systems operate smoothly and maintain equilibrium. [2]Stressors trigger a crisis-mode physiological response, after which the body attempts to return to homeostasis by means of an **adaptive response**. [3]First characterized by Hans Selye in 1936, the internal fight to restore homeostasis in the face of a stressor is known as the **general adaptation syndrome** (GAS). [4]The GAS has three distinct phases: alarm, resistance, and exhaustion.

Alarm Phase [5]When the body is exposed to a real or perceived stressor, the fight-or-flight response kicks into gear. [6]Stress hormones flow, and the body prepares to do battle. [7]The subconscious perceptions and appraisal of the stressor stimulate the areas in the brain responsible for emotions. [8]This emotional stimulation triggers the physical reactions we associate with stress. [9]The entire process takes only a few seconds.

[10]Suppose that you are walking to your residence hall after a night class on a dimly lit campus. [11]_____ you pass a particularly dark area, you hear someone cough behind you, and you sense that this person is fairly close. [12]You walk faster, only to hear the quickened footsteps of the other person. [13]Your senses become increasingly alert, your breathing quickens, your heart races, and you begin to perspire. [14]The stranger is getting closer and closer. In desperation you stop, clutching your book bag in your hands, determined to use force if necessary to protect yourself. [15]You turn around quickly and let out a blood-curdling yell. [16]To your surprise, the only person you see is your classmate, who has been trying to stay close to you out of her own anxiety about walking alone in the dark. [17]You look at her in startled embarrassment. [18]You have just experienced the alarm phase of GAS.

[19]When the mind perceives a real or imaginary stressor, the cerebral cortex, the region of the brain that interprets the nature of an event, triggers an **autonomic nervous system** (ANS) response that prepares the body for action. [20]The ANS is the portion of the central nervous system regulating body functions that we do not normally consciously control, such as heart function, breathing, and glandular function.

[21]The ANS has two branches: sympathetic and parasympathetic. [22]The **sympathetic nervous system** energizes the body for fight or flight by signaling the release of several stress hormones that speed the heart rate, increase the breathing rate, and trigger many other stress responses. [23]The **parasympathetic nervous system**

functions to slow all the systems stimulated by stress. [24]In effect, it counteracts the actions of the sympathetic branch. [25]In a healthy person, these two branches work together in a balance that controls the negative effects of stress.

[26]The responses of the sympathetic nervous system to stress involve a series of biochemical exchanges between different parts of the body. [27]The **hypothalamus**, a structure in the brain, functions as the control center of the sympathetic nervous system and determines the overall reaction to stressors. [28]When the hypothalamus perceives that extra energy is needed to fight a stressor, it stimulates the adrenal glands, located near the top of the kidneys, to release the hormone **epinephrine**, also called adrenaline. [29]Epinephrine causes more blood to be pumped with each beat of the heart, dilates the airways in the lungs to increase oxygen intake, increases the breathing rate, stimulates the liver to release more glucose (which fuels muscular exertion), and dilates the pupils to improve visual sensitivity. [30]The body is then poised to act immediately. [31]As epinephrine secretion increases, blood is diverted away from the digestive system, possibly causing nausea and cramping if the distress occurs shortly after a meal and drying of nasal and salivary tissues, which produces dry mouth.

[32]The alarm phase also provides for longer-term reaction to stress. [33]The hypothalamus uses chemical messages to trigger the pituitary gland within the brain to release a powerful hormone, adrenocorticotropic hormone (ACTH). [34]ACTH signals the adrenal glands to release cortisol, a hormone that makes stored nutrients more readily available to meet energy demands. [35]Finally, other parts of the brain and body release endorphins, the body's naturally occurring opiates, which relieve pain that a stressor may cause.

Resistance Phase [36]The resistance phase of GAS is similar to the alarm phase in that the same organs and systems are mobilized, but at a less intense level. [37]The body tries to return to homeostasis, but because some perceived stressor still exists, the body does not achieve complete rest. [38]Instead, the body stays activated or aroused at a level that causes a higher metabolic rate in some organ tissues. [39]These organs and systems of resistance are working "overtime" and after prolonged stress will become depleted to the point at which they cannot function effectively.

Exhaustion Phase [40]Stress promotes adaptation, but a prolonged response leads to **allostatic load**, or exhaustive wear and tear on the body. [41]In the exhaustion phase of GAS, the physical and emotional energy used to fight a stressor has been depleted. [42]The toll that the stress takes on the body depends on the type of stress or how long it lasts. [43]Short-term stress probably would not deplete all energy reserves in an otherwise healthy person, but chronic stress can create continuous states of alarm and resistance, resulting in total depletion of energy and susceptibility to illness.

[44]As the body adjusts to chronic unresolved stress, the adrenal glands continue to release cortisol, which remains in the bloodstream for longer periods of time as a result of slower metabolic responsiveness. [45]Over time, without relief, cortisol can reduce **immunocompetence**, or the ability of the immune system to respond to various assaults. [46]Blood pressure can remain dangerously elevated, you may catch colds more easily, or your body's ability to control blood glucose levels can be affected.

Donatelle, Rebecca J., *Health: The Basics* Green Edition, 9th ed., pp. 59–60.

1. What is the main time order pattern of organization used in this passage?

a. narration **b.** process

2. During which phase is the hormone adrenaline released into the body?

a. alarm phase **b.** resistance phase **c.** exhaustion phase

3. Which transition word best completes sentence 11?

a. before **c.** as

b. afterward **d.** since

4. The ***hypothalamus*** is located in the brain.

Complete the following concept map with information from the passage.

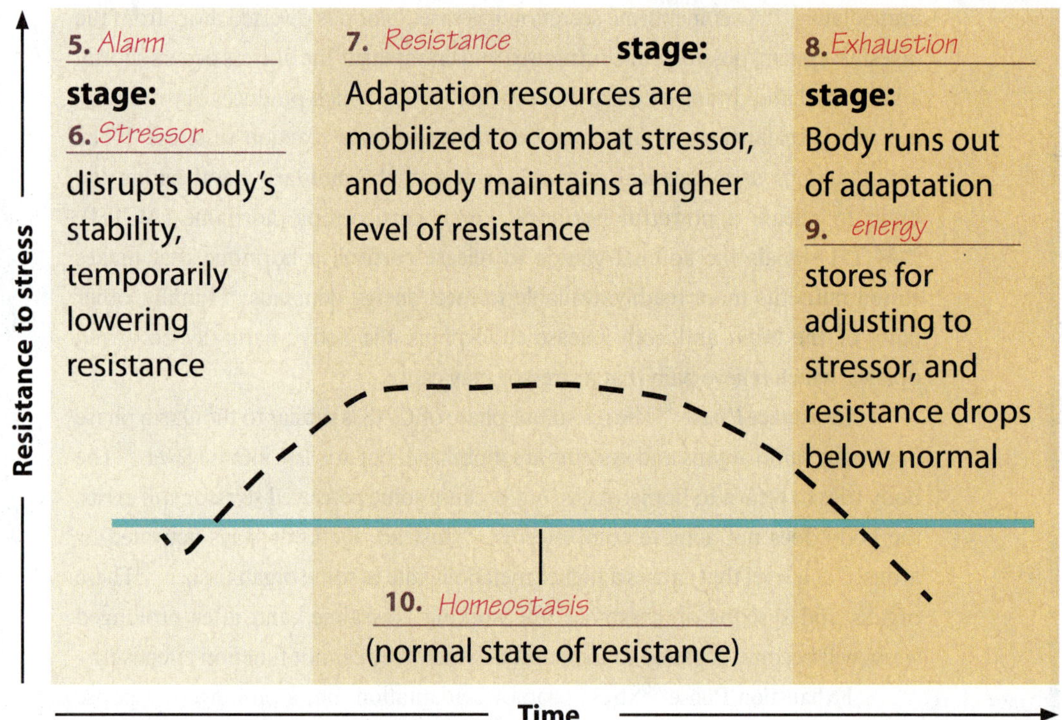
5. Alarm
stage:
6. Stressor
disrupts body's stability, temporarily lowering resistance
7. Resistance stage:
Adaptation resources are mobilized to combat stressor, and body maintains a higher level of resistance
8. Exhaustion
stage:
Body runs out of adaptation
9. energy
stores for adjusting to stressor, and resistance drops below normal
10. Homeostasis
(normal state of resistance)
Resistance to stress
Time

Summary Response

Restate the author's central idea in your own words. Begin your summary response with the following: *The central idea of the passage "The General Adaptation Syndrome" by Rebecca J. Donatelle is....*

What Do You Think?

Assume you have a friend or know a classmate who has extreme test anxiety that results in poor performance. Explain the alarm, resistance, and exhaustion phases of the general adaptation syndrome. Offer advice about how to control the body's physical response to stress.

Academic Learning Log: Module Review

Summary of Key Concepts of Time Order and Space Order

Assess your comprehension of time order and space order patterns.

LO1

1. The two time order patterns of organization are _narration_ and _process_.

2. _Narration_ is the time order pattern used to show a series of events by describing _when_ things occurred and in _what order_.

3. _Process_ is the time order pattern used to show _steps_, _stages_, or _directions_ that can be repeated at any time with similar results.

4. Space order is _the location or arrangement in space of a person, place, object, or scene._

LO1 LO2 LO3 LO4 LO5

5. Sensory details are _sights_, _sounds_, _smells_, _tastes_, and _feelings_.

LO1 LO2 LO3 LO4

6. Readers and writers ask the reporter's questions _who_, _what_, _where_, and _how_ to identify and generate relevant details using time order and space order.

LO1 LO2 LO3 LO5

7. *Denotation* refers to the exact, literal, or neutral meaning of a word—the dictionary definition. *Connotation* refers to the associations or emotional connections suggested by a word.

8. A figure of speech is *a word or phrase that departs from literal meaning to create a special effect or fresh meaning.*

9. Three of the most common figures of speech are *simile*, *metaphor*, and *onomatopoeia*.

Test Your Comprehension of Time and Space Order

Respond to the following questions and prompts. *Answers may vary.*

LO1 LO2

Identify which type of time order and space order pattern is used in each of the following topic sentences.

Narration, Description 1. Hammurabi, king of Babylon from 1800 to 1750 BCE, was one of the great rulers of early civilized history.

Process, Description 2. Perception is a continuous series of five stages that blend into one another.

Process, Description 3. Relaxation techniques to reduce stress have been practiced for centuries, and there is a wide selection from which to choose.

Narration, Description 4. Michael Dell of Dell Computer illustrates a director style of management.

LO1 LO2

Write a topic sentence for a narration paragraph.

Write a topic sentence for a process paragraph.

LO1 LO2 LO3 LO4 LO5

Complete the following blank space order concept map with details about the following topic: How to Prepare for a Local Natural Disaster.

Time-Space Order/Narration-Description Concept Chart

TOPIC (WHO OR WHAT):		
TOPIC SENTENCE:		
REPORTER'S QUESTIONS: WHEN, WHAT WHO, WHERE		**SENSORY DETAILS: SIGHT (SEE), SMELL, SOUND (HEAR), TASTE, TOUCH (FEEL)**

1. **How will I use what I have learned?** In your notebook, discuss how you will apply to your own reading/writing strategy what you have learned about the time and space order patterns. When will you apply this knowledge to your reading/writing strategy?
2. **What do I still need to study about the time and space order patterns?** In your notebook, discuss your ongoing study needs. Describe what, when, and how you will continue studying and using these patterns.

Complete the Post-test for Module 9 in MySkillsLab.

10 The Classification Pattern

LEARNING OUTCOMES

After studying this module you should be able to:

- **LO1** Answer the Question "What's the Point of Classification?"
- **LO2** Comprehend and State a Main Idea Using the Classification Pattern
- **LO3** Identify and Generate Relevant Details Using the Classification Pattern
- **LO4** Recognize and Create Logical Order Using the Classification Pattern
- **LO5** Analyze and Use Effective Language with the Classification Pattern

Identifying and labeling groups or types help both readers and writers to discover the point about a particular topic. Whether we are studying, working, shopping, or social networking, we classify information, things, and people into groups or types. In fact, we use classification as a basic thinking skill in many areas of our lives. In everyday life, we fulfill various social roles such as life partner, parent, sibling, friend, employee, or student. In working life, we promote people to higher levels of responsibility and pay based on particular types of skills and attitudes. In college life, each of us probably prefers certain kinds of courses, likes particular types of teachers, and does better on specific types of tests.

A **classification** is a division of a topic into clearly identified subgroups.

Classification divides a topic into groups and subgroups (or smaller related groups) based on shared traits or qualities. The writer lists and often labels each subgroup, describes its traits, and offers examples that best represent the group. Because groups and subgroups are listed, transitions of addition are often used to guide the reader through the flow of ideas.

WHAT'S THE POINT of Classification? 

Before you study this module, predict the point of classification. Study the following set of photographs. In the space provided, (1) identify the types of music represented by the three photographs; (2) list the traits of each subgroup; (3) describe specific examples based on the photographs; and (4) answer the question "What's the point?" with a one-sentence statement of the overall main idea.

Photographic Organizer: The Classification Pattern

TOPIC: TYPES OF MUSIC

1st Type

Garth Brooks

2nd Type

Ludacris and Queen Latifah

3rd Type

Marc Anthony

1. What type of music does each artist in the photographs represent? *Answers may vary.*

1st Type	2nd Type	3rd Type
Country music	*Hip Hop music*	*Salsa music*

2. Traits:

Traits:	Traits:	Traits:
Folk music, Southern, Western; expresses strong personal emotions; guitar, fiddle, banjo	*Urban music, African American; rap; rhymes spoken over music; beat driven; expresses political / social views; drum beats*	*Club music, Latin-American, Cuban, Afro-Caribbean; calls for dance, fast and energetic tempo; claves, cowbells, trombone, conga*

3. Examples:

Examples:	Examples:	Examples:
Garth Brooks	*Ludacris and Queen Latifah*	*Marc Anthony and Alejandro Fernandez*

What's the point of stated main ideas in reading and writing paragraphs?

Three major types of music reveal the traits of their cultures.

What's the Point? One Student's Response

The following paragraph offers one writer's point about the types of music illustrated by the photographs. Read the classification paragraph below and the explanations; complete the activities in **bold type** given in the annotations.

MUSIC'S VARIETY IS MUSIC'S POWER

[1]Music expresses our individuality; music connects us to one another; music carries our culture. [2]The power of music comes from the variety of the lives it expresses. [3]Three major types of popular music illustrate the powerful variety of music. [4]The first major type of music is country music. [5]Country music is based on the traditional folk music of the rural South and the cowboy music of the West. [6]Country songs express strong personal emotions about topics such as mother, home, love, hard work, prison, the rambling man, and religion. [7]Country musicians like Garth Brooks typically play such instruments as the guitar and fiddle. [8]The second major type of music that reveals the diversity of music is Hip Hop or rap music. [9]Rap music is a form of music that came about in African American urban communities. [10]Rap is characterized by beat-driven rhymes spoken over instruments or mixed recordings. [11]Rappers like Queen Latifah and Ludacris often express strong political and social views. [12]A third major type that illustrates the powerful variety in music is Salsa music. [13]Salsa, with its origin in Cuba, is a popular form of Latin-American dance music. [14]Salsa is characterized by Afro-Caribbean rhythms; its fast, energetic tempo stirs the urge to dance. [15]Performers like Marc Anthony use percussion instruments such as claves, congas, and cowbells.

Effective Expression: Parallelism refers to the similarity in the way ideas are worded. To achieve parallelism in this sentence, the writer repeats the subject music and uses the same form to express each verb (*expresses, connects, carries*).
Double underline three other expressions that repeat a pattern of wording.

Main Idea: The main idea is the point the author is making about the topic. The topic is *popular music.*
Underline the author's point about this topic.

Listing Order: The transitional phrase "first major type" signals that the paragraph is developed based on classification.
Circle two more phrases that signal a list of types.

Relevant Details: Relevant details use descriptive details of traits and examples. Descriptive details include sensory details based on sight, sound, smell, or touch, such as "fast, energetic tempo stirs the urge to dance."
Draw a box around two more details that appeal to the senses.

Comprehend and State a Main Idea Using the Classification Pattern

L2

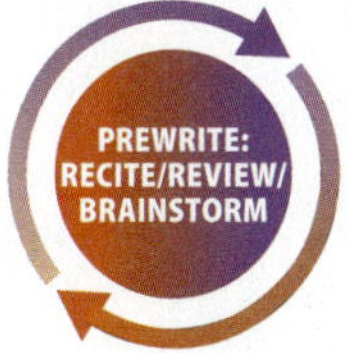

Readers rely on classification to learn about the relationships among ideas based on their traits, types, grouping, or rank. For example, think about buying a cell phone. A wise shopper researches to find out the answers to the following questions; "What type of phone do I want—an iPhone or an Android? Which phones are the highest rated? What are the traits or features I need? What types of apps do I want—maps, games, e-reader?" The answers to these questions would divide all cell phones into different categories based on their traits.

Writers use classification by sorting ideas into subgroups based on shared traits or characteristics. The writer labels, lists, and describes the traits of each subgroup.

Because groups and subgroups are listed in a piece of writing, transitions of addition (*and, also, first, last, and so on*) are also often used to order those groups and subgroups. Transitions of addition are coupled with signal words that indicate classes or groups. Examples of classification transitions and signal words (where the first word is the classification transition and the second word is the signal word) are *first type, second kind,* and *another group.*

Classification Signal Words That Are Used to Organize Groups, Types, or Traits

aspect	classify	group	quality	style
attribute	classification	ideal	rank	trait
branch	collection	kind	section	type
brand	division	level	set	typical
categories	element	order	sort	variety
characteristic	feature	part	status	
class	form	principle	stratum	

Transitions That Combine with Signal Words to List Groups, Types, or Traits

also	final	for one thing	last of all	second
and	finally	furthermore	moreover	third
another	first	in addition	next	
besides	first of all	last	one	

To comprehend the main idea, a reader skims to identify the classification transitions and signal words in the body of the paragraph. Then the reader looks for the sentence that best covers all the given groups, types, or traits of the topic. The topic sentence most often uses classification signal words to state an overview of the details. After reading, an effective reader may choose to recite the main idea and list the major details in the form of study notes. Just as a reader relies on classification signal words to identify the main idea, an effective writer uses classification signal words to discover the point about a topic. During the prewriting phase, a writer brainstorms using classification words such as *groups, types,* or *traits* to narrow the topic. Most often, the writer then includes these classification signal words in the topic sentence.

Example

Survey the following paragraph about the environment from a government website to observe the writer's use of classification. As you read, underline the classification transitions and signal words. Then double underline the topic sentence that best covers all the details. After reading, complete the study notes with the topic sentence and a list of major details based on types or traits.

TYPES OF WETLANDS

[1]Wetlands is a general term that includes several types of vital links between water and land. [2]One type of wetland is a bog, one of North America's most distinctive wetlands; it is characterized by spongy peat deposits, acidic waters, and a floor covered by a thick carpet of sphagnum moss. [3]Another type of wetland is the marsh, which is frequently or continually swamped with water; it is characterized by soft-stemmed vegetation adapted to saturated soil conditions. [4]Finally, a swamp is a type of wetland dominated by woody plants.

Adapted from U.S. Environmental Protection Agency, "America's Wetlands."

Study Notes for (Topic) *Types of Wetlands*

Topic Sentence: *Wetlands is a general term that includes several types of vital links between water and land.*

Major details (Types or Traits):

1. *Bog*
2. *Marsh*
3. *Swamp*

Explanation

Compare your answers to the following student's think-aloud.

Skimming for the classification transitions and signal words helped me quickly identify the major details and topic sentence. I underlined the following words. Title:

Types, Wetlands. Sentence 1: Wetlands, several types. Sentence 2: One type, wetland, bog, characterized. Sentence 3: Another type, wetland, marsh, characterized. Sentence 4: Finally, swamp, type, wetland. Based on these details, I underlined sentence 1 as the topic sentence because the words several types overview all the details. I recited the topic sentence and major details I had annotated in the study notes.

Study Notes for (Topic) *Types of Wetlands*

Topic Sentence: Wetlands is a general term that includes several types of vital links between water and land.

Major details: Bog
Marsh
Swamp

Practice 1

Comprehend a Main Idea Using the Classification Pattern

Assume you are interested in earth science and want to learn about volcanoes. Skim and annotate the following paragraph from a government website. Underline the classification transitions and signal words that focus the topic and introduce the major details. Then double underline the topic sentence that best states an overview of the details. Finally, complete the study notes with information from the paragraph.

TYPES OF VOLCANIC ERUPTIONS

[1]During an episode of activity, a volcano commonly displays a distinctive pattern or type of eruption. [2]One type of eruption is a Vesuvian eruption; during this type of eruption, great quantities of ash-laden gas are violently discharged. [3]These gases form a cauliflower-shaped cloud high above the volcano. [4]A second kind of eruption is the Strombolian. [5]In a Strombolian-type eruption, huge clots of molten lava burst from the summit crater to

CONTINUED

PRACTICE 1 *CONTINUED*

form luminous arcs through the sky. [6]The lava collects on the flanks of the cone, and then lava clots combine to stream down the slopes in fiery rivulets. [7]Another kind of eruption is the Vulcanian type. [8]In this eruption, a dense cloud of ash-laden gas explodes from the crater and rises high above the peak. [9]Steaming ash forms a whitish cloud near the upper level of the cone. [10]A fourth kind of eruption is a Peléan or Nuée Ardente (glowing cloud) eruption. [11]A large amount of gas, dust, ash, and incandescent lava fragments are blown out of a central crater, fall back, and form tongue-like glowing avalanches. [12]These avalanches move down slope at speeds as great as 100 miles per hour.

Adapted from U.S. Geological Survey, "Types of Volcanic Eruptions."

Study Notes for (Topic) *Types of Volcanic Eruptions*

Topic Sentence: *During an episode of activity, a volcano commonly displays a distinctive pattern or type of eruption.*

Major details (Types or Traits):

1. *Vesuvian eruption*
2. *Strombolian eruption*
3. *Vulcanian eruption*
4. *Peléan or Nuée Ardente (glowing cloud) eruption*

When you write a classification piece, you limit your topic to a set of ideas or groups based on types, shared traits, or common principles. Most likely, you also have an opinion or point of view about that set of ideas. This opinion or attitude becomes your controlling point or main idea. You also reveal your opinion by discussing the groups or traits in a particular order of importance. A topic sentence states the point or purpose of the groups, types, or traits.

For example, the following topic sentence contains (1) the topic, (2) the writer's opinion about the topic, and (3) the pattern of organization used to organize details.

The topic is *friendship*. The pattern of organization is established with the phrase "three types of." The writer's opinion is stated with the phrase "equally important interpersonal relationships."

TOPIC — PATTERN OF ORGANIZATION: CLASSIFICATION SIGNAL WORDS

Friendships offer three types of equally important interpersonal relationships.

WRITER'S OPINION

Example

Practice creating topic sentences. You are given a topic, an opinion, and classification signal word(s). Combine the ideas in each group to create a topic sentence for a classification. Then work with a peer or small group of classmates to answer the question that follows each item. *Answers may vary.*

1. TOPIC: *leisure activities*

OPINION: *strengthen family ties*

CLASSIFICATION SIGNAL WORDS: *several types*

TOPIC SENTENCE: *Several types of leisure activities strengthen family ties.*

What specific details need to be described to support this topic sentence? *The types of leisure activities that appeal to all parents and children and the traits of each activity that strengthen the family are needed.*

2. TOPIC: *diet*

OPINION: *healthful*

CLASSIFICATION SIGNAL WORDS: *several traits*

TOPIC SENTENCE: *A healthful diet has several traits.*

What specific details need to be described to support this topic sentence? *Traits of a healthful diet may include the food groups, examples from each food group, nutritional values of food, and portion sizes.*

Explanation

Compare your answers to the following student's think-aloud.

This activity helped me see how to use an opinion and classification signal words to focus a topic into a topic sentence that states a main idea. Thinking about the details needed to support the topic sentence also helped me see the connection between the topic sentence and the supporting details before writing. Here are the topic sentences I wrote and the supporting details our group thought were needed.

CONTINUED

EXPLANATION *CONTINUED*

1. *Several types of leisure activities strengthen family ties.*
   The supporting details will include a list of specific types of leisure activities such as sports like skating and bowling and media like watching television or movies. Then the details should explain the aspects or traits that strengthen family ties.
2. *A healthful diet has several traits.*
   The supporting details may include the major food groups, examples from each food group, nutritional values of foods, and portion sizes.

Practice 2

State a Main Idea Using the Classification Pattern

Practice creating topic sentences. For each topic given, provide an opinion, along with classification transitions and signal word(s). Then combine the ideas in each group to create a topic sentence for a classification paragraph. *Answers may vary.*

1. TOPIC: (people) *Roommate*

OPINION: *best, positive*

CLASSIFICATION TRANSITIONS AND SIGNAL WORDS (as needed): *three traits*

TOPIC SENTENCE: *The best roommate has three positive traits.*

2. TOPIC: (employment) *Job skills*

OPINION: *key*

CLASSIFICATION TRANSITIONS AND SIGNAL WORDS (as needed): *three types*

TOPIC SENTENCE: *Three types of job skills are key to finding and keeping a job.*

Identify and Generate Relevant Details Using the Classification Pattern

L3

To identify and generate details based on the classification pattern of organization, readers and writers primarily ask the reporter's questions *what* and *how*. *What* are the types, traits, and examples of people, places, or objects? *How* are people, places, or things grouped? Answers to these questions enable readers to identify and writers to generate details about groups, subgroups, types, traits, and examples. Usually, classification transitions and signal words introduce these details. Some major and minor details may also explain the writer's opinion about the groups, types, and traits and how they are being classified. Many readers and writers use a classification concept map to identify and generate details.

Example

Assume you are taking a college course in interpersonal communication. Your class is learning about the types of interpersonal relationships such as friendship. Read the following textbook passage. During reading, annotate the text. Underline the classification transitions, signal words, and major supporting details. Double underline the topic sentence. After reading, complete the classification concept map with information from the passage.

Friendship Types

[1]Not all friendships are the same. [2]Friendships can be classified into three major types: friendships of reciprocity, receptivity, and association.

[3]The friendship of reciprocity is the ideal type. [4]It is characterized by loyalty, self-sacrifice, mutual affection, and generosity. [5]A friendship of reciprocity is based on equality. [6]Each individual shares equally in giving and receiving the benefits and rewards of the relationship.

[7]The second type is the friendship of receptivity. [8]A main trait in this type of friendship is an imbalance in giving and receiving. [9]One person is the primary giver and one the primary receiver. [10]This is a positive imbalance, however, because each person gains something from the relationship. [11]The different needs of both the person who receives and the person who gives affection are satisfied. [12]This is the friendship that may develop between a teacher and a student or between a doctor and a patient. [13]In fact, a difference in status is essential for the friendship of receptivity to develop.

[14]The third type, friendship of association, is a transitory one. [15]It might be described as a friendly relationship rather than a true friendship. [16]Associative friendships are the kind we often have with classmates, neighbors, or coworkers. [17]There is no great loyalty, no great trust, no great giving or receiving. [18]The association is cordial but not intense.

Adapted from DeVito, Joseph A., *The Interpersonal Communication Book*, 12th ed., pp. 248–249.

CONTINUED

EXAMPLE *CONTINUED*

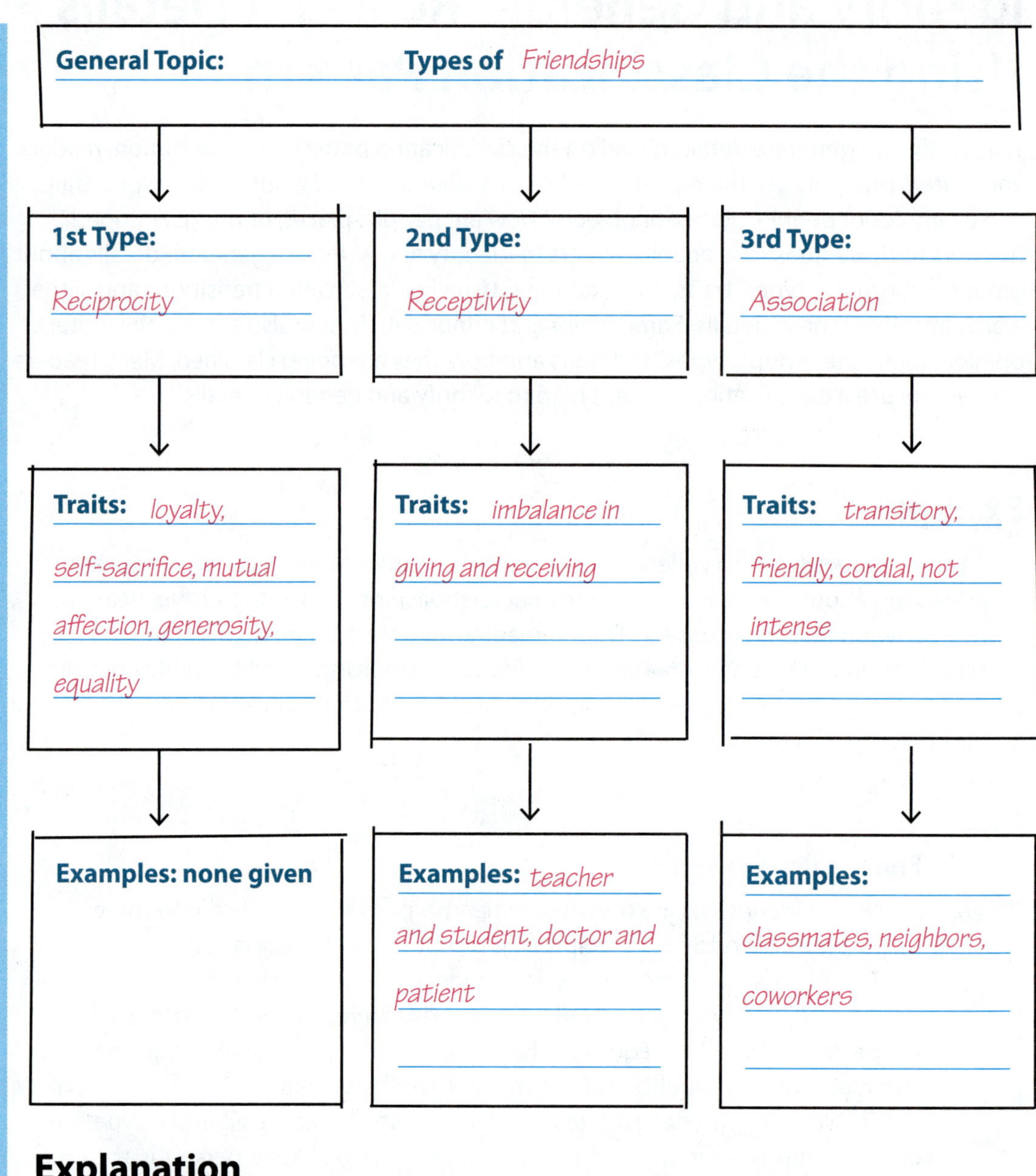

Explanation

Compare your answers to the following student's think-aloud.

Annotating the text helped me to quickly see how the writer used classification to organize ideas. The classification transitions and signal words helped me find the major details—the three types of friendship. Transitions also pointed out the minor details, the traits and examples of each group. I also like the way a classification concept map will help me study and remember new ideas. I completed the concept map with the following ideas.

Topic: *Types of Friendship*			
Subgroup:	*Reciprocity*	*Receptivity*	*Association*
Traits:	*loyalty, self-sacrifice mutual affection, generosity*	*Imbalance in giving-receiving*	*transitory, friendly, cordial, not intense*
Examples:	*none*	*teacher/ student doctor/ patient*	*classmates, neighbors, coworkers*

Practice 3

Identify Relevant Details Using the Classification Pattern

Assume you are attending a professional development seminar at your place of work. You are in a training program to become a manager. Read the following passage from the training manual. During reading, annotate the text. Underline the classification transitions, signal words, and major supporting details. Double underline the topic sentence. After reading, complete the classification concept map with information from the passage.

LEADERSHIP STYLES

[1]Effective leaders understand all the various leadership styles. [2]Leaders need to know how to select the most effective style for a given situation. [3]Although there are many leadership styles, leaders often fall into three basic categories.

[4]**Autocratic leaders** typically tell employees what to do and how to get it done, usually without seeking feedback from others. [5]They make all the decisions and watch over their employees very closely. [6]Autocratic leaders can be necessary in situations that call for such leadership. [7]For example, in an emergency room having one leader calling all the shots can be useful. [8]If all the information required

CONTINUED

PRACTICE 3 *CONTINUED*

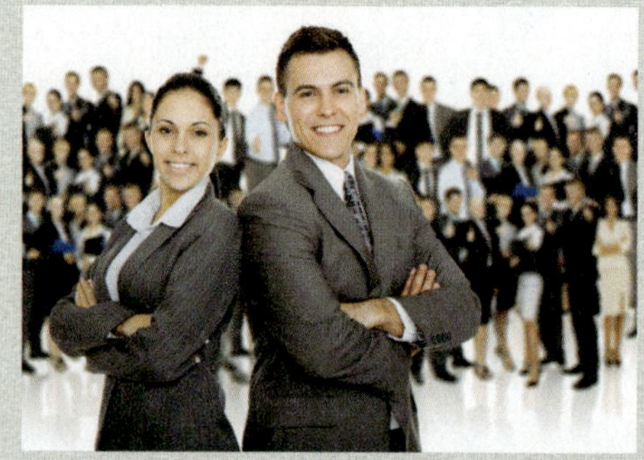

to solve a problem is on hand, time is limited, and employees are already well motivated, the autocratic leadership style can be appropriate,

[9]**Democratic leaders** work with employees to find the best way to complete the job while maintaining final authority. [10]Being a democratic leader means that you value the opinions of the others in your group. [11]That's why democratic leaders surround themselves with skillful employees. [12]This is a useful leadership style when both the leader and employees know about the task and can work together to come up with the best decision. [13]Democratic leaders get the best of both worlds. [14]They empower others, and their decisions are better informed because of the input of their fellow employees.

[15]**Free-reign leaders** (or *laissez-faire* leaders) are "hands-off" leaders. [16]They allow others to have complete freedom in their work environment. [17]Such leaders provide their followers with the materials they need to accomplish their goals. [18]But they offer little to no direction. [19]Because all authority is handed over to the employees, employees are responsible for the outcomes of the work. [20]Although the free-reign leader can get a bum rap, there is a time and place for this style. [21]For example, say you are thrust into a management position for a task you know nothing about. [22]If employees understand what's going on, who are you to tell them what to do? [23]The hands-off approach can be helpful when employees are knowledgeable, self-motivated, and trustworthy.

[24]To be effective, leaders need to be flexible and know when to apply the right leadership style in a particular situation. [25]Sir Richard Branson, chairman of the Virgin Group, is a good example of a leader who uses various leadership styles to good effect. [26]He has a strong personality. [27]Yet he has learned the importance of the free-reign style. [28]He often steps back and allows others to run the company. [29]Considering the Virgin Group comprises over 40 different companies, being able to delegate is a necessity for Branson.

[30]While Branson makes liberal use of the free-reign style, he also incorporates the democratic style into his leadership. [31]Branson writes letters to many of his employees. [32]He keeps them up-to-date on his activities and encourages them to speak up with their questions and comments. [33]To facilitate communication, Branson gives out his home address and phone number to his employees so that they can always reach him. [34]Branson's unique combination of free-reign and democratic leadership styles helps employees feel empowered and motivated, a crucial ingredient in the massive Virgin Group's continued success.

Van Syckle, Barbara, and Tietje, Brian, *Anybody's Business*, p. 136.

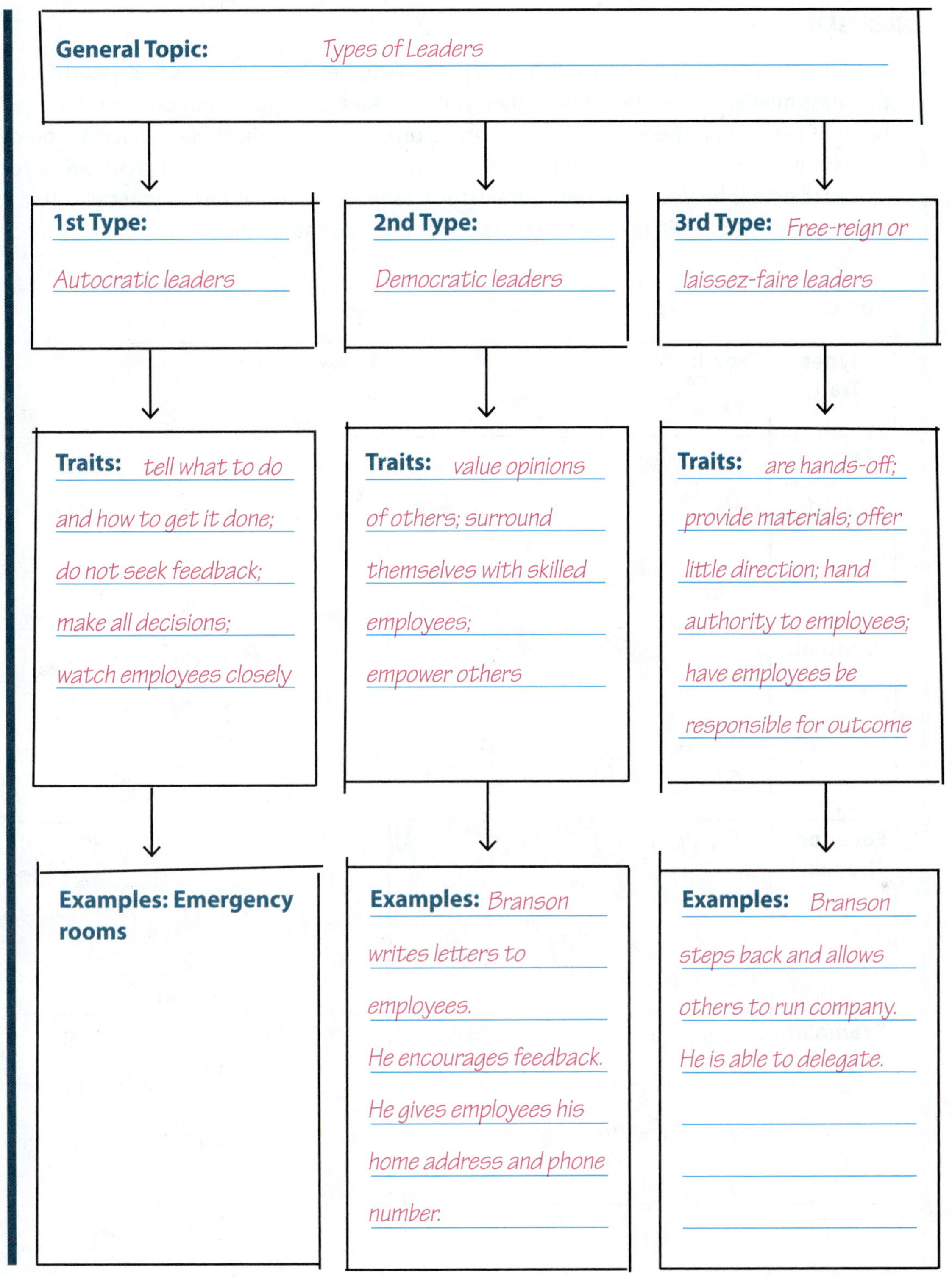

General Topic: Types of Leaders
1st Type: Autocratic leaders
2nd Type: Democratic leaders
3rd Type: Free-reign or laissez-faire leaders
Traits: tell what to do and how to get it done; do not seek feedback; make all decisions; watch employees closely
Traits: value opinions of others; surround themselves with skilled employees; empower others
Traits: are hands-off; provide materials; offer little direction; hand authority to employees; have employees be responsible for outcome
Examples: Emergency rooms
Examples: Branson writes letters to employees. He encourages feedback. He gives employees his home address and phone number.
Examples: Branson steps back and allows others to run company. He is able to delegate.

Using a classification concept map to identify details in a paragraph as a reader prepares you to generate details in an organized way as a writer. Just as a reader asks the reporter's questions to identify details, a writer asks questions to generate details. During the brainstorming phase of the writing process, use a classification concept map to generate details based on groups, types, traits, and examples. Classification concept maps may vary in their set-up. One type is a flow chart as in the last example and practice. Another type is a graphic organizer with rows and columns with headings that identify groups or types, the traits of each group or type, and examples.

Example

Assume you are taking a college course in cultural studies. Your class has been studying the mass media. Your professor has asked you to write a paragraph that classifies two types of popular programs on television based on traits of length, content (such as source of material, language, violence, type of cast), and focus or theme. Use the chart below to generate details for your paragraph. Brainstorm as many details as fast as you can. After you complete the chart, review it to cross out any details that do not relate to your topic. *Answers may vary.*

Topic:	*Two types of comedy that dominate television*	
Types Traits	**Type 1:** *Sketch comedy*	**Type 2:** *Situation comedy*
Length:	*Short scenes or sketches (1–10 minutes)*	*30-minute story line*
Content:	*Actors improvise/write scripts* *Avoids violence, uses bad language* *Has ensemble cast*	*Writers create scripts* *Avoids violence and bad language* *Has ensemble cast*
Focus or Theme:	*Politics, current events, controversial issues*	*Social relationships at home and work*
Examples:	*Mr. Show, Upright Citizens Brigade, SNL, Mad TV, Chappelle's Show, Ed Sullivan (best show of all)*	*Parks and Recreation, Brooklyn Nine-Nine, Seinfeld, How I Met Your Mother, Madea's Family Reunion*

Explanation

Compare your answers to the following student's think-aloud.

This topic was so general. There are so many different types of popular shows on TV. Using the classification concept map helped me narrow the topic. I love comedies, and television offers bunches of them. For example, there are the HBO specials that showcase stand-up comics. The hosts of late night shows always have a comedy monologue. And then there are the skits on shows like Saturday Night Live (SNL) and the weekly sitcoms. There are also tons of situation comedies. They've been popular a long time. Think of I Love Lucy or Friends. As I thought about these examples, I noticed two basic types of comedy dominate TV. They are sketches and situation comedy. Once I got the ideas flowing, they came quickly. After I finished the concept map, I reviewed it to see if all my details related to my topic. I crossed out the detail that didn't seem to fit.

Topic *Two types of comedy that dominate television*		
Types **Traits**	**Type 1** *Sketch comedy*	**Type 2** *Situation comedy*
Length:	*Short scenes or sketches (1–10 minutes.)*	*30-minute story line*
Content:	*Actors improvise/write scripts* *Avoids violence, uses bad language* *Has ensemble cast*	*Writers create scripts* *Avoids violence and bad language* *Has ensemble cast*
Focus or Theme:	*Politics, current events, controversial issues*	*Social relationships at home and work*
Examples:	*Mr. Show, Upright Citizens Brigade, SNL, Mad TV, Chappelle's Show, Ed Sullivan (best show of all)*	*Parks and Recreation, Brooklyn Nine-Nine, Seinfeld, How I Met Your Mother, Madea's Family Reunion*

Practice 4

Generate relevant details using the classification pattern

Choose one of the topic sentences you created in Practice 2. Use the following classification concept map to generate details to support your topic sentence.

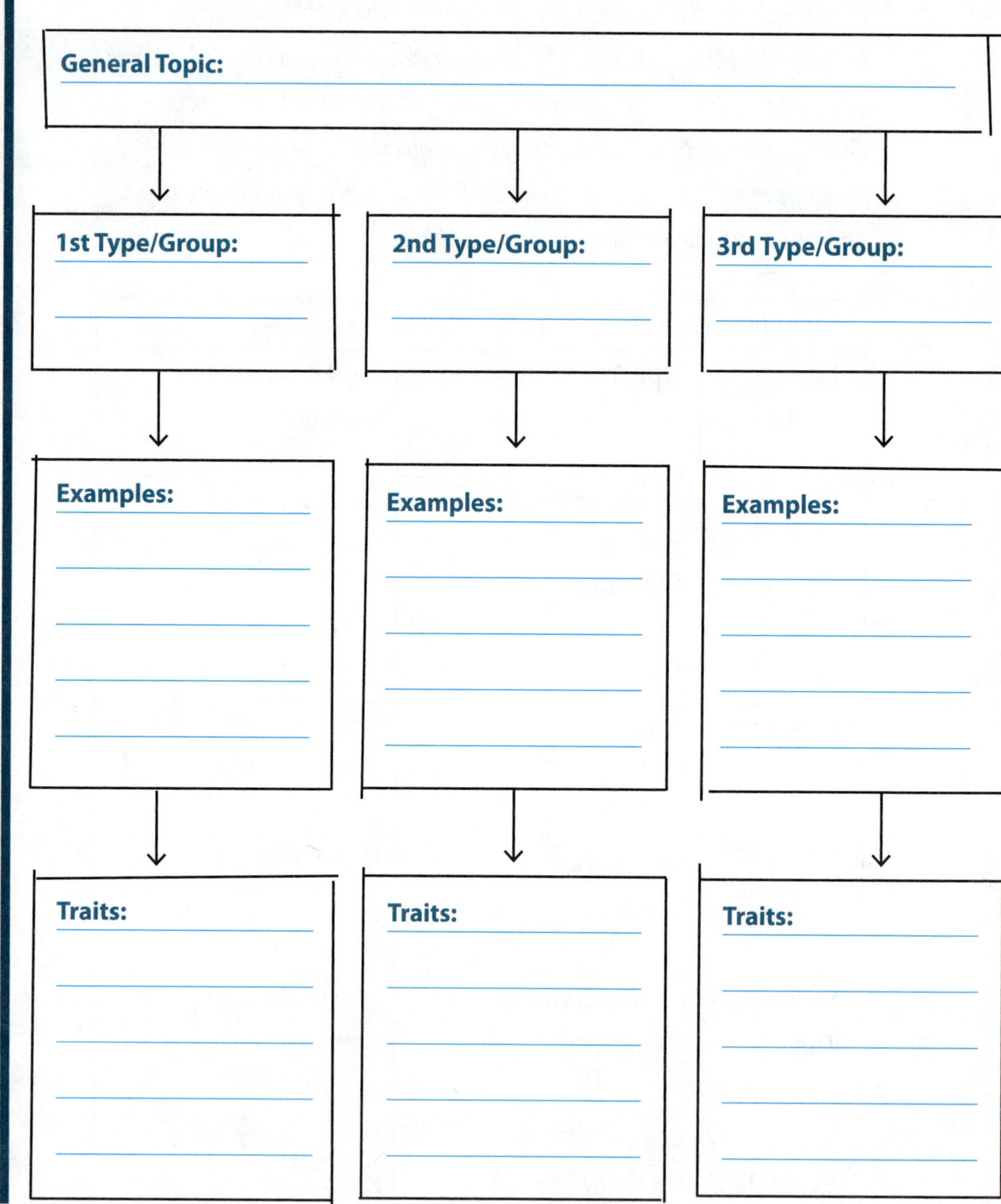

Recognize and Create Logical Order Using the Classification Pattern

L4

When a reader recognizes that a writer is using classification order to organize ideas, he or she can see how the main idea and details fit together and anticipate upcoming details. When we use classification transitions and signal words, we expect the topic to be limited and organized based on groups, types, traits, and examples. The writer's use of classification transitions or signal words establishes the logical order of ideas and guides the reader through the classification.

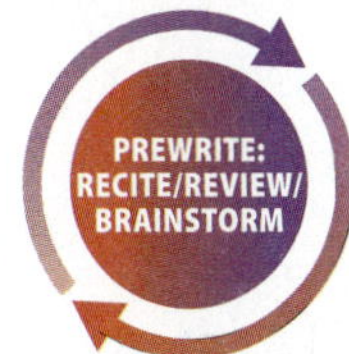

Example

Assume you are a working as a peer editor for a classmate in your college course in cultural studies. Your classmate drafted the following paragraph based on the details in his graphic organizer about types of popular television programs (see the last example). Read and annotate his paragraph. Circle the main idea. Underline the classification transitions or signal words and the types, traits, and examples. Cross out any details that are not relevant to the main idea. Share your annotations and personal reaction to the paragraph with your classmate. Suggest a change to improve the paragraph. Point out what you like about the use of classification in the paragraph. *Answers may vary.*

Television Comedy: Sketches and Sitcoms

[1]Two types of comedy have long dominated television. [2]One type is sketch comedy. [3]Sketch comedy is a series of short comedy scenes that typically range from one to ten minutes. [4]Often the actors improvise the sketch, making it up as they go; then they write the script based on their improvisation. [5]This kind of humor avoids violence, often uses offensive language, and focuses on politics, controversial issues, and current events. [6]Well-known examples of sketch comedy include *Saturday Night Live*, *Mad TV*, and *Chappelle's Show*. [7]However, *The Ed Sullivan Show* remains the all time best variety show to have appeared on television. [8]A second type of comedy dominating television is the sitcom or situation comedy, also an ensemble routine. [9]Sitcoms are usually set in a specific location such as a home or office, and they present amusing story lines about a group of characters such as a family, friends, or co-workers in an office. [10]Often episodes are self-contained stories that are resolved in less than 30 minutes; some sitcoms do use ongoing story lines based on developing relationships between characters. [11]This type of humor avoids violence, rarely uses offensive language, and focuses on social relationships. [12]Well-known examples of situation comedy include *Parks and Recreation*, *Seinfeld*, and *How I Met Your Mother*. [13]~~Overall, sitcoms are more appropriate for family viewing than sketch comedy.~~

Explanation

Compare your answers to the following student's think-aloud.

The title told me that the paragraph was about two types of comedy. The first sentence is the topic sentence. Sentence 1 uses the classification words "two types" to focus the topic comedies in the topic sentence. Sentence 1 also states the author's opinion "long dominated television." Sentence 2 uses the words "One type" to talk about "sketch comedy." Sentences 4 and 5 describe the traits of "this kind" of comedy. Sentences 6 and 7 list some examples. Sentence 8 uses the words "A second type" to talk about situation comedy. Sentences 9 through 11 give the traits of "This type of humor." Sentence 12 gives examples. I liked the way the paragraph used the classification words. It made it so easy to follow and understand. I think sentence 13 kind of goes off topic and should be taken out. Sentence 13 is a personal opinion that somebody may want to argue about. The writer could add the trait "audience" to each type of comedy and identify the audience of each one.

Practice 5

Create Logical Order Using the Classification Pattern

Work with the classification order concept map you completed in Practice 4. Write a rough draft of your paragraph to establish the classification order of details. Work with a peer to review each other's rough drafts. Exchange, read, and review your drafts to make sure all details are relevant to the main ideas. Annotate your peer's paragraph. Then complete a classification order concept map of the draft you are peer editing. Return your reviewed paragraphs to each other. Revise as needed.

Analyze and Use Effective Language with the Classification Pattern

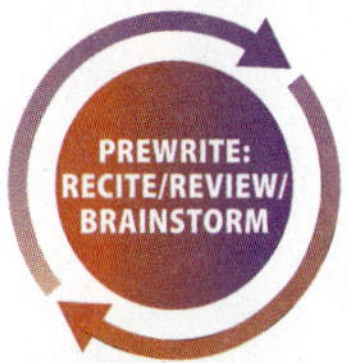

Effective writers may rely on descriptive language to clearly classify a topic into types, groups, traits, and examples. Sensory details and figures of speech such as metaphors and similes create vivid images of a group, type, trait, or example in the reader's mind. Therefore, to comprehend the writer's classification of a topic, effective readers analyze the writer's use of descriptive language.

Metaphor: A direct comparison (not using *like* or *as*) between two things, using one thing to describe the other

> Three common *types* of **leaders** *are* the **dictator**, the **coach**, and the **investor**.

Simile: An indirect comparison between two things, usually using *like*, *as*, or *than*.

> Basic **leadership** *styles* may be described *as* **closed-fists**, **helping-hands**, and **hands-off.**

Sensory Details: Details that appeal to our senses of sight, sound, smell, taste, and touch to create a vivid mental image, including onomatopoeia, a word that imitates a sound.

> The dictator-leader may **shoot** out orders in **rapid fire** to lower-level employees.

> The coach-leader **builds** a team and **cheers** members on to **heights** of success.

Example

Analyze the following classification topic sentences and supporting details based on figures of speech. Underline the figure of speech in each sentence. Then choose the answer that identifies the figure of speech used.

1. One common type of human personality is the "Firecracker" Type A, first identified most likely to have heart disease by cardiologists Friedman and Rosenman in the 1950s.

a. metaphor **b.** simile **c.** sensory detail

2. Just like a firecracker, this personality type is volatile.

a. metaphor **b.** simile **c.** sensory detail

3. People with this type of personality sizzle with hostility, time urgency, and impatience.

a. metaphor **b.** simile **c.** sensory detail

4. Their tempers are often short fuses set off by minor events.

a. metaphor **b.** simile **c.** sensory detail

Explanation

Compare your responses to the following student's think-aloud.

As I analyzed each sentence, I noticed that metaphors and similes could also use sensory details. Here are my answers and explanations.

1. *Firecracker is a metaphor (a) for "Type A" personality. I often hear this label used to describe people who are workaholics or controlling. In this sentence, Type A is a metaphor for "heart attack" inducing behaviors.*
2. *"Just like a firecracker" is a simile (b) that indirectly compares Type A to a firecracker. I was tempted to say this was a sensory detail because a firecracker brings to mind the fire, smoke, pop, and lights made when the firecracker explodes. But the phrase "just like" set up a strong indirect comparison between Type A and the sensory details of a firecracker.*
3. *The word sizzle is a sensory detail (c). This is an example of onomatopoeia, the sound the word represents.*
4. *The idea temper is directly compared to "short fuses set off." The answer is metaphor (a). The word short could be a sensory detail. However, the detail is part of the metaphor.*

Practice 6

Analyze Effective Expression with the Classification Pattern

Read the following paragraph that describes Daytona Beach, Florida. Underline three figures of speech and sensory details. Identify and explain the meaning of the three details you underlined. *Answers may vary.*

[1]The balmy breezes, hard-packed white sand, and motor events of Daytona Beach, Florida, the "World's Most Famous Beach," attract roughly 8 million visitors each year. [2]Basically, there are three Daytona Beaches. [3]First, there is the Daytona Beach of the tourists who swarm in like bees and buzz with the activity of special events. [4]Tourists come in hordes of heavily tattooed bikers revving their engines on Main Street during Bike Week or Biketoberfest. [5]They are

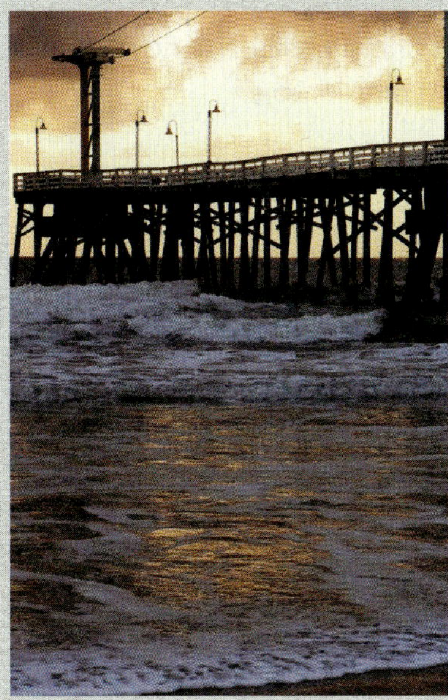

packs of avid race fans deafened by the roaring hum of stock cars at the Daytona 500. [6]They are crowds of Spring Breakers thronging the beach for a drive, a stroll, or a party. [7]Second is the Daytona Beach of the transplants who wilt soon enough. [8]Many have fled the northern cold for sunny warmth. [9]Often, transplants quickly droop with the stress of summer's heat, hungry mosquitoes, and violent weather. [10]Many are not hardy enough to endure. [11]The third Daytona Beach is of the townspeople who are the true vines that flourish. [12]These are those—whether native born or transplanted—who sink deep roots into the exotic beauty of the natural environment and the coastal culture. [13]From surfer, to shopkeeper, to developer, townspeople respect the roaming bears, gators, and sharks. [14]They graciously defer to the mighty thunderstorms and calmly prepare for the hurricane.

Figure of Speech	Sensory Detail	Explanation
bees in hives	*swarm, hum*	*Bees are a simile for tourists who come for special events. The tone is negative.*
transplant	*wilts soon, droops*	*Transplant is a metaphor for those who relocate and can't endure the environment. They are plants repotted in the wrong soil. The tone is negative.*
true vines	*flourish, sink deep roots, exotic beauty*	*True vines are a metaphor for the townspeople who enjoy living in the area. The tone is positive.*

As you move through your own writing process, think about the impact you want to have on your reader. For the greatest impact, revise general or vague expressions of types, groups, traits, or examples into concrete and precise words and phrases. Use figures of speech and sensory details to make your classification vivid and memorable.

Example

The following items include the first draft of a classification topic, topic sentence, and three statements of detail. Revise each item to use the descriptive language of a metaphor, simile, or sensory detail.

First Draft	Revision
1. Types of shoppers	*Shoppers Are Animals*
2. There are three types of shoppers.	*Three typical shoppers are the chameleons, the predators, and the scavengers.*
3. One type of shopper is the kind who is always changing shopping styles based on a mood or situation.	*The first type, the chameleon shopper, changes shopping style based on a mood or situation.*
4. Another type of shopper is the kind who is aggressive, focused, and fast.	*The second type, the predator, is an aggressive, focused, and fast shopper.*
5. The final type of shopper is the kind who loves to shop for fun.	*The final type of shopper, the scavenger, loves to shop for the thrill of pouncing on a good buy.*

Explanation

Compare your answers to the following student's think-aloud.

Revising these items required some time spent in thought. I have always loved animals. My favorite television shows are animal and nature shows like Discovery Channel's Animal Planet. I often find myself thinking of people in terms of animals and their traits, such as "stubborn as a mule" or "she has her claws out." So I decided to use animals as metaphors to classify shoppers. Here are my revisions.

1. *Shoppers Are Animals*
2. *Three typical shoppers are the chameleons, the predators, and the scavengers.*
3. *The first type, the chameleon shopper, changes shopping style based on a mood or situation.*
4. *The second type, the predator, is an aggressive, focused, and fast shopper.*
5. *The final type of shopper, the scavenger, loves to shop for the thrill of pouncing on a good buy.*

Practice 7

Use Effective Expression with the Classification Pattern

Work with the rough draft of the paragraph you completed in Practice 5. Choose two sentences and revise them to use descriptive language. Use the following space to record your original and revised sentences.

Original sentence: ______________________________

____

____

Revised sentence: ______________________________

____

____

Original sentence: ______________________________

____

____

Revised sentence: ______________________________

____

____

Reading and Writing Assignments

Considering Audience and Purpose

Study the set of photographs about the types of music at the beginning of the module. Assume you are a mentor to a young person who is just becoming interested in music. You have decided to start a collection of music for him or her. First, identify the type(s) of music you want to include in this gift collection, spanning at least three different categories. Create a list of specific artists and songs for the type or types of music you have chosen. Then write a note to go with the gift that includes a paragraph explaining the type(s) of music in the collection.

Reading and Writing for Everyday Life

Assume your doctor has recommended that you begin an exercise program. To help you understand and set up your exercise program, she has given you the following flyer about muscle contractions. Read the flyer. Then write a paragraph that describes an exercise program that includes these types of exercises.

Three Primary Types of Muscle Contractions

There are three primary types of contractions: isotonic, isometric, and isokinetic. **Isotonic** contractions are characterized by a consistent muscle tension as the contraction proceeds and a resulting movement of body parts. An arm curl with a 10-pound hand weight involves isotonic contractions throughout your arm. **Isometric** contractions are characterized by a consistent muscle length throughout the contraction with no visible movement of body parts. An example of an isometric contraction is when you hold a hand weight at arm's length in front of you; your arm is not moving, but you feel tension in your arm muscles. **Isokinetic** contractions are characterized by a consistent muscle contraction speed within a moving body part. In order to perform isokinetic contractions, you need specialized equipment that holds the speed of movement constant as your arm, leg, or other muscles contract with varying forces. Stationary bikes and treadmills engage isokinetic contractions. Isotonic contractions are the most common in exercise programs. Lifting free weights, working on machines, and doing push-ups are all examples of isotonic contractions. Isotonic contractions can be either concentric or eccentric. **Concentric** contractions occur when force is developed in the muscle as the muscle is shortening--for example, when you curl a free weight up toward your shoulder. In **eccentric** muscle contractions, force remains in the muscle while the muscle is lengthening. This occurs as you lower a free weight back to its original position.

Hopson, Janet L., Donatelle, Rebecca J., and Littrell, Tanya R., *Get Fit, Stay Well!*, pp. 111–112.

Reading and Writing for College Life

Assume you are taking a college course in sociology. The next unit you will be studying is about human love. In preparation, your professor has given the following assignment from your textbook. Read the paragraph and compose a paragraph in response to the questions.

Three Aspects of Love

Researcher Robert Sternberg describes love as a combination of three traits—intimacy, passion, and commitment. **Intimacy**, the emotional aspect of love, includes sharing, communicating, and mutual support. **Passion**, the motivational aspect, consists of physical attraction and romantic passion. **Commitment**, the mental aspect, consists of the decisions you make concerning your lover. When you have all three aspects to about equal degrees, you have complete or consummate love. Do you agree with Sternberg's description of love? Do you think many people experience consummate love? How would you rate your love (or the love of someone you know) on a scale of 1 to 5, with 1 = Incomplete and 5 = Consummate?

Adapted from DeVito, Joseph A., *The Interpersonal Communication Book,* 12th ed., p. 225.

Reading and Writing for Working Life

Assume you work for a local marketing firm that helps businesses increase their sales in your area. The family-owned Cuban-Mexican restaurant Los Amigos has been highly successful in a nearby town. Management wants to open a second location in your town. You have received the following memo from your supervisor. Read the memo and compose a response.

From: Carla Weeks, Director of Marketing
RE: Identify Local Market Segments for Los Amigos

The current Los Amigos is a highly successful, award-winning family-owned Cuban-Mexican restaurant serving uniquely delicious and authentic Cuban-Mexican dishes made from the highest quality ingredients at a reasonable price in a relaxed atmosphere from 11 a.m. until 11 p.m. every day with a 4–7 p.m. Happy Hour. You are to write a report that identifies the market segment in your town for Los Amigos. Your findings may be used to create an advertisement campaign. Use the following criteria:

Geographic traits: Which part of town would draw the most business for Los Amigos? Identify at least two specific locations.

Demographic traits: Identify the ages, gender, and income levels of people likely to go to Los Amigos based on the time of day. What type of customer is most likely to lunch at Los Amigos? What type is most likely to enjoy Happy Hour? What type is most likely to eat dinner? Do the locations you suggest support each type of customer?

Psychographic traits: Identify the lifestyle, personality traits, values, and opinions of potential customers. What kind of experience do customers want when they come to Los Amigos?

Workshop: Compose a Classification Paragraph

Choose a paragraph to read and respond to in writing. You may select a paragraph in an example, practice, or writing assignment within this module. Or you may select a paragraph of your own choosing. Use the following guide to comprehend and respond to the paragraph. Apply what you have learned about classification to your reading/writing strategy.

Preread: Survey and Question

Ask questions about the text's features.

____

____

What is the passage about?

____

____

How is the material organized?

____

____

What do I already know about this topic? (What is my prior knowledge about the vocabulary?)

____

____

What is my purpose for reading/writing?

____

____

What points may I want to address or include in my written response?

____

____

Read and Annotate

As you read, annotate key ideas, particularly those details that answer your prereading questions.

Recite, Review, and Brainstorm

Recite the information. Summarize the most important parts. Answer your prereading questions. Rephrase ideas into your own words. Record changes in your opinions based on the new information. Review the information. Brainstorm ideas for your written response to the passage. Freewrite a response to what you have read. Map the relationship among ideas you have annotated in the text. Outline or list key ideas and details in blocks of thought. Use your own paper.

Write a Draft of Your Response

Using the ideas you generated by brainstorming, compose a draft of your response. Use your own paper.

Revise Your Draft

Once you have created a draft of an essay, read the draft and answer the questions in the "Questions for Revising a Classification Paragraph" box that follows. Indicate your answers by annotating your paper. If you answer "yes" to a question, underline, check, or circle examples. If you answer "no" to a question, write additional details in the margins and draw lines to indicate their placement. Revise your essay based on your reflection. (Hint: Experienced writers create several drafts as they focus on one or two questions per draft.)

Step by Step: Questions for Revising a Classification Paragraph:

- ☐ Have I stated or implied a focused central point?
- ☐ Have I made my purpose clear?
- ☐ Is my tone appropriate for my audience and purpose?
- ☐ Is the logical order of the ideas clear? Have I used strong classification transitions and signal words to guide my reader?
- ☐ Have I made my point with adequate details?
- ☐ Do all the details support my point?
- ☐ What impact will my paragraph make on my reader?

Proofread Your Draft

Once you have made any revisions to your paragraph that may be needed, proofread your essay to eliminate careless errors. Work with a classmate to give and receive feedback about your essays.

Review Test

MySkillsLab™ Complete this Review Test in MySkillsLab.

Score (number correct) ______ x 10 = _______%

Use reading/writing strategies to comprehend and respond to the following passage from a college psychology textbook. Read the passage. Complete the classification concept map with the relevant information from the passage. Finally, respond to the two writing prompts, "Summary Response" and "What Do You Think?"

1180L/9.8 GE/1135 words

TYPES OF COMPUTER VIRUSES

[1]Although thousands of computer viruses and variants exist, they can be grouped into six broad categories based on their behavior and method of transmission.

Boot-Sector Viruses

[2]What are boot-sector viruses? A **boot-sector virus** replicates itself into a hard drive's master boot record. [3]The master boot record is a program that executes whenever a computer boots up, ensuring that the virus will be loaded into memory immediately, even before some virus protection programs can load. [4]Boot-sector viruses are often transmitted by a flash drive left in a USB port. [5]When the computer boots up with the flash drive connected, the computer tries to launch a master boot record from the flash drive, which is usually the trigger for the virus to infect the hard drive. [6]Boot-sector viruses can be extremely destructive.

Logic Bombs and Time Bombs

[7]What is a logic bomb? [8]A **logic bomb** is a virus that is triggered when certain logical conditions are met—such as opening a file, or starting a program a certain number of times. [9]A **time bomb** is a virus that is triggered by the passage of time or on a certain date. [10]For example, the Michelangelo virus, first launched in 1992, was a famous time bomb that was set to trigger every year on March 6, Michelangelo's birthday. [11]The BlackWorm virus (otherwise known as Kama Sutra, Mywife, or CME-24), another time bomb, spreads through e-mail attachments. [12]Opening the attachment infects the computer, and on the third day of every month, the virus seeks out and deletes certain file types (such as executable or EXE files) on Windows computers. [13]The effects of logic bombs and time bombs range from display of annoying messages on the screen to reformatting of the hard drive, which causes complete data loss.

Worms

[14]What is a worm? [15]A **worm** is slightly different from a virus in that a worm attempts to travel between systems through network connections to spread an infection. [16]A virus infects a host file and waits until that file is executed on another computer to replicate. [17]A worm, however, works independently of host file execution and is much more active in spreading itself. [18]The Conficker worm broke out in November 2008 and quickly infected an estimated 9 to 15 million individual computers. [19]This worm spread through vulnerabilities in the Windows code and compromised computers by disabling certain software services and utility programs (such as Windows Update). [20]Fortunately, it is easy to protect yourself from most worms. [21]Installing antivirus software and a firewall is a good start. [22]You also should apply software patches (code issued by the manufacturers of software such as Windows that repairs known security problems) to your computer whenever they are issued.

Script and Macro Viruses

[23]What are script and macro viruses? [24]Some viruses are hidden on Web sites in the form of scripts. [25]A **script** is a series of commands—actually, a miniprogram—that is executed without your knowledge. [26]Scripts are often used to perform useful, legitimate functions on Web sites such as collecting name and address information from customers. [27]However, some scripts are malicious. [28]For example, say you receive an e-mail encouraging you to visit a Web site full of useful programs and information. [29]When you click a link to display a video on the Web site you were directed to, a script runs that infects your computer with a virus without your knowledge.

[30]A **macro virus** is a virus that attaches itself to a document (such as a Word or Excel file) that uses macros. [31]A macro is a short series of commands that usually automates repetitive tasks. [32]However, macro languages are now so sophisticated that viruses can be written with them. [33]In March 1999, the Melissa virus became the first major macro virus to cause problems worldwide. [34]It attached itself to a Word document.

[35]The Melissa virus was also the first practical example of an **e-mail virus**. [36]E-mail viruses use the address book in the victim's e-mail system to distribute the virus. [37]Anyone opening an infected document triggered the virus, which infected other Word documents on the victim's computer. [38]Once triggered, the Melissa virus sent itself to the first 40 people in the address book on the infected computer. [39]This helped ensure that Melissa became one of the most widely distributed viruses ever released.

Encryption Viruses

[40]What are encryption viruses? [41]**Encryption viruses** are the newest form of virus. [42]When these viruses infect your computer, they run a program that searches for common types of data files (such as Microsoft Word and Excel files) and compresses them using a complex encryption key that renders your files unusable. [43]You then receive a message that asks you to send money to an account if you want to receive the program to decrypt your files. [44]The flaw with this type of virus, which keeps it from being widespread, is that law enforcement officials can trace the payments to an account and may possibly be able to catch the perpetrators. [45]Still, we see these types of viruses from time to time.

Virus Classifications

[46]How else are viruses classified? [47]Viruses can also be classified by the methods they take to avoid detection by antivirus software:

- [48]A polymorphic virus changes its own code (or periodically rewrites itself) to avoid detection. [49]Most polymorphic viruses infect one type of file (.exe files, for example).
- [50]A multipartite virus is designed to infect multiple file types in an effort to fool the antivirus software that is looking for it.
- [51]Stealth viruses temporarily erase their code from the files where

CONTINUED

REVIEW TEST *CONTINUED*

they reside and then hide in the active memory of the computer. [52]This helps them avoid detection if only the hard drive is being searched for viruses. [53]Fortunately, antivirus software developers are aware of, and have designed software to watch for, these tricks. [54]Given the creativity of virus programmers, you can be sure we'll see other types of viruses emerge in the future.

Virus Symptoms

[55]If your computer displays any of the following symptoms, it may be infected with a virus:

1. [56]Existing program icons or files suddenly disappear. [57](Viruses often delete specific file types or programs.)
2. [58]Changes appear in your browser. [59]If you fire up your browser and it takes you to an unusual home page (one you didn't set) or it has new toolbars, then you may have a virus.
3. [60]Odd messages or images are displayed on the screen or strange music or sounds play.
4. [61]Data files become corrupt. [62]Although files become corrupt for many reasons, a virus is one cause.
5. [63]Programs don't work properly. [64]This could be caused by either a corrupted file or a virus.

[65]If you think you have a virus, boot up your computer with an antivirus software DVD (or CD) in your DVD/CD drive. [66]This allows you to run the antivirus software before potential viruses load on the computer. [67]Are you looking for free antivirus software? [68]Consider downloading AVG Antivirus Free Edition (free.avg.com).

Evans, Alan, Martin, Kendall, and Poatsy, Mary Anne, *Technology in Action, Introductory Version*, 7th ed., pp. 406–407.

Types of Computer Viruses		
Type	**Traits**	**Examples**
Boot-Sector Virus	replicates itself into *a hard drive's master boot record* often transmitted by flash drive loads when computer starts up	
Logic Bomb *Time Bomb*	triggered when certain preset conditions are met such as opening a file or starting a program a number of times triggered by *passage of time or certain date*	In 1992, Michelangelo was set to trigger on March 6 every year; BlackWorm (Karma Sutra, Mywife, CME-24) was triggered by opening e-mail attachments.

continues

Type	Traits	Examples
Worm	travels between computer systems through network connections to spread infection	In November 2008, the Conficker worm infected 9 to 15 million computers
Script **Macro Virus**	a series of commands—a miniprogram—infects computer without user's knowledge attaches itself to a document such as Word or Excel that uses macros	A link to a video on a website runs a script to infect a computer. Melissa was the first e-mail virus using the address book in the victim's e-mail system to distribute the virus.
Encryption Virus	renders files unusable and charges money to decrypt files	
Virus Classifications based on methods they use to avoid detection by antivirus software	A polymorphic virus changes its own code (or periodically rewrites itself) to avoid detection. A multipartite virus is designed to infect multiple file types in an effort to fool the antivirus software that is looking for it. A stealth virus temporarily erases its code from the files where it resides and then hides in the active memory of the computer.	

Summary Response

Restate the main idea of the passage. Begin your summary response with the following: *The main idea of the passage "Types of Computer Viruses" by Evans, Martin, and Poatsy is. . . .*

What Do You Think?

Assume you work at the Snap-Tite company, a small manufacturer of specialty fasteners. Recently, the company computers have been behaving strangely and running slowly. Employees complain that since last Tuesday important Word documents are unreadable (looking like strings of code instead of words) or cannot be opened at all. In addition, key data has been completely lost. You suspect one or more computer viruses might be the problem. Your boss has asked you to write a report that identifies which virus may be a problem and recommends a solution.

Academic Learning Log: Module Review

Summary of Key Concepts of the Classification Pattern

Assess your comprehension of the classification pattern.

L1 L2

1. Classification *divides* a topic into *subgroups*, based on shared *traits* or *qualities*.

2. In a classification the writer lists *and labels each subgroup, describes its traits, and offers examples that best represent the group*.

3. Readers rely on classification to learn about the relationship of ideas based on *traits, types, grouping, or rank*.

4. Writers use classification to create meaning by *sorting ideas into smaller groups and describing the traits of each group*.

L1 L2 L3

5. Because groups and subgroups are listed, transitions of *addition*, such as *and*, *also*, and *first* are used.

6. Readers and writers primarily ask the reporter's questions *what* and *how* to identify and generate relevant details using classification.

L1 L2 L3 L4

7. The *writer's* use of classification *transitions* or *signal words* establishes the logical order of ideas and guides the *reader* through the classification.

L1 L2 L3 L4 L5

8. Many readers and writers use a classification concept map to *identify* and *generate* details.

9. Writes use sensory details and figures of speech such as metaphors and similes to create vivid images of a group, type, trait, or example in the reader's mind.

10. To comprehend a writer's classification of a topic, effective readers analyze the writer's use of descriptive language .

Test Your Comprehension of the Classification Pattern

Respond to the following prompts. Answers may vary

Complete a chart of signal words used to establish classification order.

Words That Are Used to Signal Groups, Types, or Traits				
aspect	classify	group	quality	style
attribute	classification	ideal	rank	trait
branch	collection	kind	section	type
brand	division	level	set	typical
categories	element	order	sort	variety
characteristic	feature	part	status	
class	form	principle	stratum	

On your own paper create a blank classification concept map.

1. **How will I use what I have learned?** In your notebook, discuss how you will apply to your own reading/writing strategy what you have learned about the classification pattern. When will you apply this knowledge to your reading/writing strategy?
2. **What do I still need to study about the classification pattern?** In your notebook, discuss your ongoing study needs. Describe what, when, and how you will continue studying and using the classification pattern.

Complete the Post-test for Module 10 in MySkillsLab.

11

LEARNING OUTCOMES

After studying this module you should be able to:

- L1 Answer the Question "What's the Point of Example Patterns?"
- L2 Comprehend and State a Main Idea Using Example Patterns
- L3 Identify and Generate Relevant Details Using Example Patterns
- L4 Recognize and Create Example Patterns
- L5 Analyze and Use Effective Expression with Example Patterns

The Example Patterns

When we communicate—with family members, employers, teachers, or friends—we often use **examples** to clarify a general idea or define a new word or concept. Think of a situation you were in recently where you used examples to make a point. What makes an example effective?

An **example**, also called an ***exemplification***, is a specific illustration or representation of a more general idea.

In everyday life, we illustrate our decorating ideas with paint chips and swatches of fabric, or we define our values using illustrations. In working life, we define our goals and offer examples of our hard work and successes when we apply for jobs and promotions. In college life, professors and textbook writers use examples to teach new words and concepts in every discipline.

To write an example paragraph, a writer moves from a general idea to specific examples that support and clarify the main point. Sometimes, as in a science lab report, a writer may present the specific examples first and then come to a general conclusion based on the examples.

WHAT'S THE POINT of Example Patterns?

Identifying and analyzing examples help a reader to understand the point of a paragraph. Generating and organizing examples help a writer to discover his or her point about a particular topic. The following photographs offer three examples of a thrifty lifestyle. Study each photograph. Write a caption that briefly describes each example of thrifty living. Then answer the question "What's the point?" with a one-sentence statement of the overall main idea.

Photographic Organizer: Examples of a Thrifty Lifestyle

What is this?

adjusting the thermostat

What is this?

saving loose change

What is this?

packing a lunch

What's the point?

A thrifty lifestyle saves money.

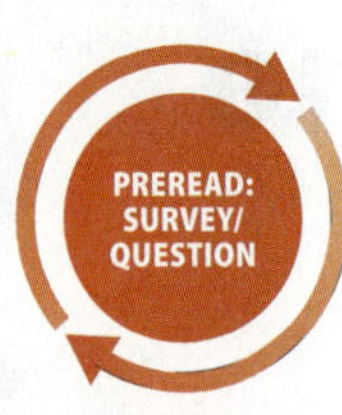

What's the Point? One Student's Response

The following paragraph offers one student's point about what the people in the photographs exemplify. Read the exemplification and the explanations; complete the activities in **bold type** in the annotations. *Answers may vary.*

Main Idea: The main idea is the point the writer is making about the topic. The topic is "A thrifty lifestyle." **Underline the writer's point about this topic.**

Listing Order: The transitional phrase "for example" signals that the paragraph is developed by examples. **Circle two more transitional phrases that indicate a list of examples.**

Effective Expression: Parallelism refers to the way ideas of equal importance are worded. To achieve parallelism, a writer uses the same form of wording for a set, series, or list of ideas or details. Repeating a form of wording or type of phrase makes your ideas easier to follow. **Double underline two more ideas with *–ing* phrasing.**

Relevant Details: Concrete details list specific minor details for each major example of "a thrifty lifestyle." **Draw boxes around two more concrete minor details that support a major example.**

EXAMPLES OF A THRIFTY LIFESTYLE

[1] Thrift is wise use of money, goods, and resources. [2] That old saying "a penny saved is a penny earned" exemplifies the ideal of thrift. [3] A thrifty lifestyle saves money. [4] For example, adjusting our thermostats can lower our energy bill up to 10% a month. [5] In the winter, we should set the thermostat to 68°F while we're awake and even lower while we're asleep or away from home. [6] In the summer, we should set the thermostat to 78°F. [7] If we usually pay $300.00 a month for energy, we could save $30.00 a month. [8] A second example of thrifty living is saving loose change. [9] Most of us have tons of change in our wallets, at the bottom of our purses and backpacks, in our cars, and even in our sofas and chairs. [10] We can put that money to good use by rolling loose change and depositing the rolls into a savings account. [11] Saving 50 cents a day in loose change adds up to $15 a month. [12] Another example of thriftiness is packing a lunch. [13] Typically, each of us spends $6 to $12 every time we eat out during a work or school day. [14] If one person packed a lunch every day, he or she would save $60 to $120 a week! [15] That means we could save as much as $480 a month, and that's just for one person. [16] Think of what a family could save by packing lunches. [17] As these three examples prove, living a thrifty lifestyle can save each of us thousands of dollars in just one year.

Comprehend and State a Main Idea Using Example Patterns

LO2

PREWRITE: RECITE/REVIEW/BRAINSTORM

Readers and writers rely on examples to support generalizations, such as a main idea, or to define new or difficult words. Effective readers often skim for key examples as a way to locate, confirm, or infer a main idea or comprehend the definition of a new or difficult word or concept. Effective writers often include key words in the topic sentence and paragraph body to signal the use of either the generalization-example pattern or the definition-example pattern.

In the **generalization-example pattern**, the writer makes a general statement and then offers an example or a series of examples to clarify the generalization.

The Generalization-Example Pattern

Statement of a general idea

Example

Example

Key words may introduce the example pattern in the topic sentence (general statement), and key words along with transition words may signal specific examples (supporting details) as they occur throughout the paragraph. The following chart lists a few of the key words and transition words used to signal examples.

The **generalization-example pattern** first states an overall idea and then gives examples to illustrate or explain that idea.

Key Words Used to Signal Examples			
an illustration	for instance	once	to illustrate
for example	include/including	such as	typical, typically

Transition Words Used to List Examples				
also	final	for one thing	last of all	second
and	finally	furthermore	moreover	specifically
another	first	in addition	next	third
besides	first of all	last	one	
certain				

Example

Read each of the following items and fill in the blanks with an appropriate example word or phrase. Circle the general statement (topic sentence) in each item.

1. Food labels *include* important information. *For example*, the label on Dark Whole Grain bread states that one slice has 120 calories.
2. Fatigue *typically* interferes with performance. *For example*, Carla was so tired after working straight through two shifts at the restaurant that she made careless mistakes on her math exam.
3. Tyler's intelligence and energy allow him to excel in a variety of areas *such as* sports, academics, and community service.

Explanation

Compare your answers to the following student's think-aloud.

1. *I used the signal word* include *in the first sentence. The word* include *suggests to me that other important information is also on the label. Calories is just one example of important information. So I expect other examples, such as the serving size or the amount of sugar. I circled this first sentence as the general statement. Some key words and transitions that signal examples are so close in meaning, they seem more like synonyms. For example, in the second sentence, either the phrase "for example" or "for instance" makes sense. I used "for example."*

2. *I used the word* typically *in the first sentence. I looked up the meaning of* typically*, which is "in the usual way, as a rule." The word* typically *signals something recurring in time. I circled the first sentence as the general statement. Again, either "For example" or "For instance" makes sense in the second blank. I took time to look up the meaning of "for instance." It means "an*

example of a particular type of action or situation: an occasion of something happening."[1] *So I thought "for instance" better signaled events of poor performance commonly occurring due to fatigue.*

3. *I think this whole sentence is a topic sentence. I circled the first part of the sentence "Tyler's intelligence and energy allow him to excel in a variety of areas" as a general statement. I used "such as" to signal that a list of examples is included in the sentence. I liked that the rest of the sentence lists the specific examples of areas in which Tyler excels. I expect the paragraph to explain how each area is an example of Tyler's intelligence and energy.*

The definition-example pattern is similar to the generalization-example pattern. Both offer general statements followed by specific examples. However, the definition-example pattern serves a very specific purpose. A **definition-example pattern** clarifies the meaning of a word or concept. Writers may use either a simple definition example or an extended definition example.

The **definition-example pattern** introduces a new word or specialized term, gives its definition, and provides examples to illustrate or explain the word or term.

In the **simple definition-example pattern**, the writer makes a general statement that introduces and gives the meaning of a new, specialized, or difficult term. Definition statements often include words such as *is*, *are*, and *means*. The writer then offers one or more examples to show how the word and its meaning are used or applied in a specific context or situation. Simple definitions are often short—no more than just a few sentences.

The **simple definition-example pattern** defines and exemplifies a word or term in one sentence or a few sentences.

The Simple Definition-Example Pattern

Term and definition

Example

Example

[1]*Merriam-Webster Learner's Dictionary*. 14 March 2013. Web. <http://www.learnersdictionary.com/search/instance>.

In the **extended definition-example pattern**, the writer makes a general statement introducing a term or word that represents a more difficult concept. To define the concept, the writer identifies and explains its traits, describes what the concept is like or similar to, and offers examples. Often, to clarify meaning, a writer may also include an explanation and example of what the term is *not*. The extended definition can be a paragraph or longer in length.

The **extended definition-example pattern** develops a deeper meaning of a word or term by using classification, comparison, contrast, and examples or illustration in one or more paragraphs.

The Extended Definition-Example Pattern

Concept and definition

Traits	Example
What it is similar to	Example
What it is *not*	Example

Both the simple and extended definition-example patterns use many of the same key words and transition words used in the generalization-example pattern. However, effective writers use additional words to signal the use of definitions. The following chart includes just a few of the key words that signal definition.

Key Words That Signal Definition

as	consists of	i.e. (that is to say)	means
are	constitutes	in particular	suggests
category	defined as	indicates	trait
characteristics	denotes	is, is called, is known as	unlike
characterized by	differs	is not	
connotes	distinguished from	like	

Examples

Read the following paragraphs and answer the questions that follow.

A. The Simple Definition-Example Pattern

Read the following paragraph from a college communications textbook. Annotate the paragraph. Double underline the topic sentence. Single underline two key supporting details. Then answer the questions that follow. *Answers may vary.*

DOWNSHIFTING

[1]Downshifting is a deliberate effort to reduce stress by choosing to live more simply. [2]For example, a person may give up a high-paying job in the city to take a lower-paying job in a small town. [3]Some people who choose to downshift may also avoid the use of televisions, computers, and cell phones.

1. What word or concept is being defined and what is its definition?

Downshifting is the choice to live more simply to reduce stress.

2. What are the two examples that illustrate the term being defined?

Give up a high-paying job in the city for a lower-paying job in a small town

and *avoid the use of television, computers, and cell phones*.

3. Which words signal each example? *For example* and *also*.

B. The Extended Definition-Example Pattern

Read the following paragraph from a college health textbook. Annotate the paragraph. Double underline the topic sentence. Single underline the key supporting details. Then answer the questions that follow the paragraph. *Answers may vary.*

PHYSICAL ACTIVITY

[1]The terms *physical activity* and *exercise* are often used as synonyms. [2]However, they do not mean the same thing. [3]Physical activity includes all physical movement, regardless of the level of energy used or the reason for it. [4]Physical activity can be occupational, lifestyle, or leisure time. [5]Occupational activity is the activity that you carry out in the course of your job. [6]Two examples are a restaurant server and a construction worker. [7]Lifestyle activity includes housework, walking to class, or climbing the stairs to your apartment or dorm room. [8]Leisure-time physical activity is any activity you choose to do in your free time. [9]Exercise is a type of leisure-time physical activity. [10]Basically, all conditioning activities and sports are considered exercise. [11]Exercise is planned and helps maintain or improve physical fitness. [12]Unlike other types of physical activity, exercise is done specifically for health and fitness. [13]The term *physical activity* includes exercise. [14]But *exercise* does not include all types of physical activity. [15]For example, riding your bike to work for transportation is lifestyle physical activity. [16]Lifting heavy boxes at work is occupational physical activity. [17]Both of these activities will improve health. [18]Both are examples of how an active lifestyle or job can affect health even when a person does not participate in a regular structured exercise program. [19]Typically, exercise produces the greatest health benefits. [20]Still, you can receive a lot of health benefits with regular physical activity.

Adapted from Powers, Scott K., Dodd, Stephen L., and Jackson, Erica M., *Total Fitness and Wellness*, 6th ed., p. 6.

CONTINUED

EXAMPLES *CONTINUED*

1. Which sentence is the topic sentence of the paragraph?
   - a. 1
   - (b.) 3
   - c. 5
   - d. 20

2. What is the relationship of ideas between sentences 5 and 6?
   - a. generalization-example
   - (b.) definition-example

3. What is the relationship of ideas between sentences 15 and 16?
   - (a.) generalization-example
   - b. definition-example

4. Exercise is an example of which type of physical activity?
   - a. occupational
   - b. lifestyle
   - (c.) leisure

5. Exercise is unlike other physical activities because it
   - a. improves health.
   - b. is planned.
   - c. is a leisure activity.
   - (d.) is done specifically to improve health and fitness.

Explanations

Compare your responses to the following student's think-aloud.

Thinking about how writers use the definition-example pattern helps me better understand the writer's main idea. Before reading, I skimmed the paragraphs to find the signal words for the examples. Then I was really able to see the general statements that introduced the terms and the definitions. Part A was really simple because it was so short. Part B was more challenging. At first, I wanted to say the last sentence was the topic sentence of the paragraph "Physical Activity." But none of the examples really explained or supported the health benefits. All the examples supported sentence 3. Here are my answers.

A.
1. *Downshifting is the choice to live more simply to reduce stress.*
2. *Two examples are "giving up a high-paying job in the city for a lower-paying job in a small town" and "avoid the use of television, computers, and cell phones."*
3. *Signal words are "For example" and "also."*

B. 1. (b) sentence 3 is the topic sentence. All the examples explain and illustrate this main idea.

2. The relationship of ideas between sentences 5 and 6 is (b) definition-example. Sentence 5 defines the term "occupational activity." And sentence 6 gives two examples. The signal words "is" and "Two examples" state the relationship.

3. The relationship between sentences 15 and 16 is (a) generalization-example. The word exercise is already defined in sentence 11. So sentence 15 is a general statement that explains physical activity is not just exercise. Then sentence 16 gives an example to clarify the point.

4. Exercise is an example of (c) leisure physical activity.

5. Exercise is unlike other physical activities because it (d) is done specifically to improve health and fitness.

Practice 1

Identify Example Patterns, Transitions, Signal Words, and Topic Sentences

Read the following two paragraphs from the college textbook *The Essentials of Public Speaking*. Answer the questions that follow each paragraph.

Message

[1] **Messages** conveyed in public speaking include both verbal and nonverbal signals. [2] In both conversation and public speaking, your message has a purpose. [3] For example, in conversation, you might want to tell a friend about what happened at a recent basketball game. [4] In this case, your purpose would be to inform. [5] Or you might want to convince a coworker to switch vacation schedules with you. [6] Here your purpose would be to persuade. [7] And in public speaking, too, you communicate with a purpose.

1. The relationship of ideas within sentence 1 is
a. generalization-example. (**b.**) definition-example.

2. The relationship of ideas between sentences 2 and 3 is
(**a.**) generalization-example. **b.** definition-example.

CONTINUED

PRACTICE 1 *CONTINUED*

3. The main pattern of organization for the paragraph is
(a.) generalization-example. **b.** definition-example.

4. The topic sentence of the paragraph is sentence
a. 1. **c.** 3.
(b.) 2. **d.** 7.

Noise

[1]**Noise** is anything that distorts the message and prevents the listeners from receiving your message as you intended it to be received. [2]It's revealing to distinguish noise from "signal." [3]In this context, the term *signal* refers to information that is useful to you, information that you want. [4]So for example, an e-mail list or electronic newsgroup that contained lots of useful information would be high on signal and low on noise. [5]If it contained lots of useless information, it would be high on noise and low on signal. [6]Spam is high on noise and low on signal, as is static on the radio, television, or telephone. [7]Noise may be physical (others talking loudly, cars honking, illegible handwriting, "garbage" on your computer screen), psychological (preconceived ideas, wandering thoughts), or semantic (misunderstood meanings). [8]Public speaking involves visual as well as spoken messages. [9]Sunglasses that conceal nonverbal messages from your eyes is an example of noise. [10]Another example would be dark print on a dark background on your slides. [11]All public speaking situations involve noise.

DeVito, Joseph A., *The Essentials of Public Speaking*, 4th ed., pp. 5–8.

5. The relationship of ideas within sentence 1 is
(a.) generalization-example. **b.** definition-example.

6. The relationship between sentences 3 and 4 is
a. generalization-example. **(b.)** definition-example.

7. The relationship of ideas between sentences 8 and 9 is
a. generalization-example. **(b.)** definition-example.

8. The main pattern of organization for the paragraph is
a. generalization-example. **(b.)** definition-example.

9. An electronic newsgroup with lots of useful information is an example of
a. noise. **c.** spam.
(b.) signal. **d.** garbage.

10. Illegible handwriting is an example of which type of noise?
(a.) physical **c.** psychological
b. semantic **d.** nonverbal

11. The topic sentence of the paragraph is sentence
a. 1. **c.** 7.
b. 2. **(d.)** 11.

When you write using the generalization-example pattern, you limit your topic to a set of specific examples, instances, or cases. Most likely, you also have an opinion or point of view about the examples, and this opinion or attitude is your point or main idea. You may reveal your opinion by listing the examples in a particular order of importance. A topic sentence states the point or purpose of the examples.

For example, the following topic sentence contains (1) the topic; (2) the writer's opinion about the topic; and (3) the pattern of organization used to organize details.

The topic is "body art." The pattern of organization is established with the phrase "such as tattooing and piercing" and the verb "exemplifies." The writer's opinion is stated with the phrase "self-expression."

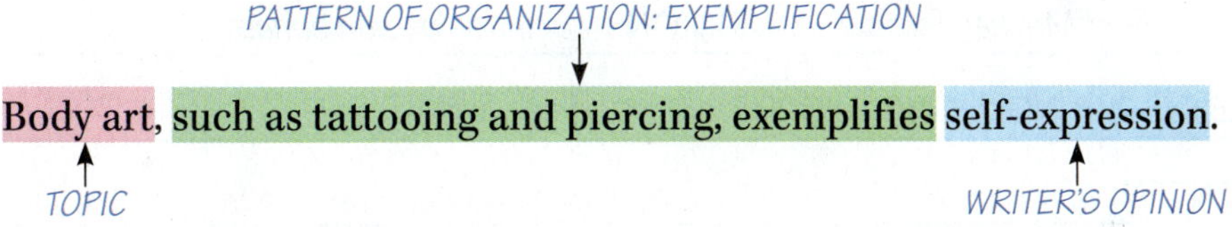

PATTERN OF ORGANIZATION: EXEMPLIFICATION
Body art offers opportunities for self-expression.
Body art, such as tattooing and piercing, exemplifies self-expression.
Body art offers opportunities for self-expression.
TOPIC
WRITER'S OPINION

Sometimes in an example paragraph, a topic sentence only implies the pattern of organization as in the following version.

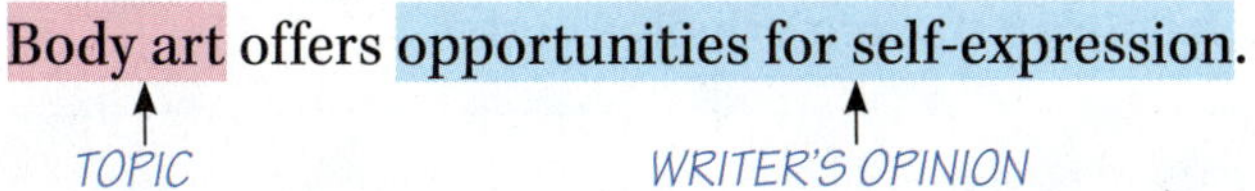

When the example pattern of organization is only implied by the topic sentence, transitions that signal and list examples establish the pattern of organization within the body of the paragraph. Notice in the following example that the two major detail sentences state the topic, pattern of organization, and writer's opinion.

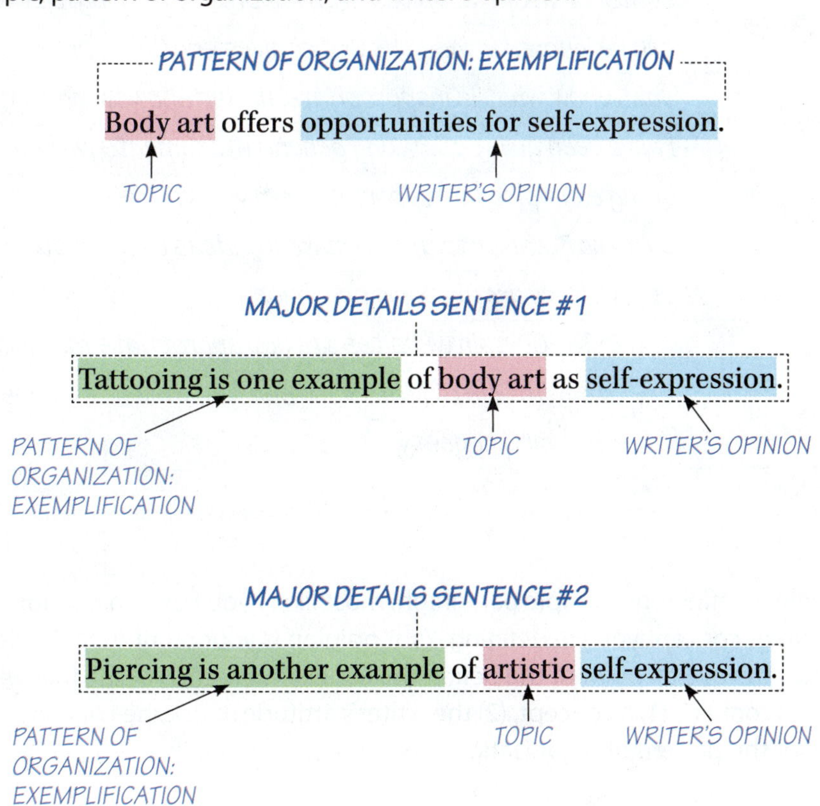

Example

The items below present a topic, an opinion, and example signal word(s). Combine the ideas in each group to create a topic sentence for a generalization-example paragraph.

Answers may vary.

1. TOPIC: *Websites* OPINION: *are not appropriate for minors*

   EXAMPLE (OR LISTING) SIGNAL WORDS: *certain*

   TOPIC SENTENCE: *Certain websites are not appropriate for minors.*

2. TOPIC: *The life of Mother Teresa* OPINION: *compassion and honesty*

   EXAMPLE (OR LISTING) SIGNAL WORDS: *illustrates*

   TOPIC SENTENCE: *The life of Mother Teresa illustrates compassion and honesty.*

Explanation

Compare your responses to the following student's think-aloud.

Creating these topic sentences showed me that general statements are really somebody's opinion that needs to be backed up with examples. For example, the topic sentence about websites is an important warning. But it can be ignored unless the writer gives specific examples that show what is inappropriate. It also showed me that I have been guilty of making general statements without giving examples to support my own views. This skill is going to make it easier for me to make my ideas clear to other people. Here are my topic sentences.

1. *Certain websites are not appropriate for minors.*
2. *The life of Mother Teresa illustrates compassion and honesty.*

When you write a definition-example paragraph, most likely you have an opinion or belief about the word or concept you are defining. Your opinion is your point or main idea. A topic sentence states the overall point of the definition. For example, each of the following two topic sentences contains (1) a concept, (2) the writer's attitude about the concept, and (3) the signal words for the pattern of organization used to organize details.

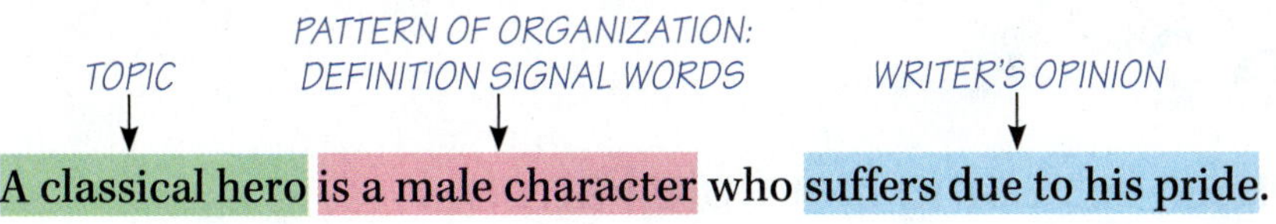

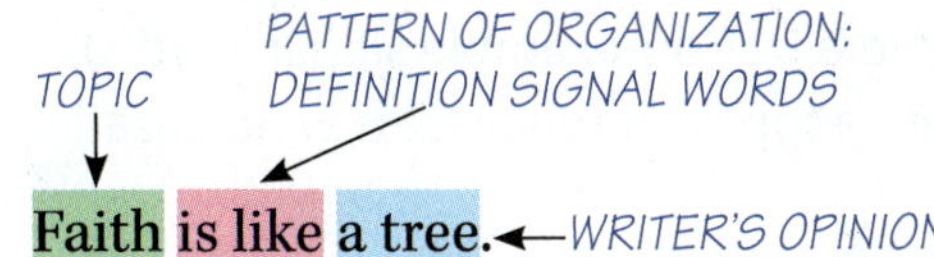

Example

The items below present a topic, an opinion, and example signal word(s). Combine the ideas in each group to create a topic sentence for a definition-example paragraph. *Answers may vary.*

1. TOPIC: *Bosses* OPINION: *good, respectful, honest, inspiring*

   EXAMPLE (OR LISTING) SIGNAL WORDS: *are*

   TOPIC SENTENCE: *Good bosses are respectful, honest, and inspiring.*

2. TOPIC: *Bullying* OPINION: *cruel power*

   EXAMPLE (OR LISTING) SIGNAL WORDS: *is*

   TOPIC SENTENCE: *Bullying is the cruel use of power.*

Explanation

Compare your responses to the following student's think-aloud.

Creating these topic sentences led to an "Aha" moment in my understanding. A generalization-example topic sentence states an overview or overall opinion about a topic. It is a broad statement that needs examples to support it. A definition-example topic sentence is a specific type of generalization that also needs examples as support. However, a definition-example topic sentence states a specific meaning of a particular word or concept. Then examples show the meaning of the word. Here are the topic sentences I wrote.

1. *Good bosses are respectful, honest, and inspiring.*
2. *Bullying is the cruel use of power.*

Practice 2

Write Topic Sentences Using Example Patterns

A. Practice creating topic sentences. The two items present a general topic. You are to narrow the topic. State an opinion. Choose generalization-example signal word(s). Then combine the ideas in each group to create a topic sentence for a generalization-example paragraph. *Answers may vary.*

TOPIC: (alternative energy source) *Solar energy* OPINION: *is versatile and cheap*

EXAMPLE (OR LISTING) SIGNAL WORDS: *not included; only implied*

TOPIC SENTENCE: *Solar energy is versatile and cheap.*

TOPIC: (vehicle) *Sport Utility Vehicles (SUVs)* OPINION: *rugged, aggressive*

EXAMPLE (OR LISTING) SIGNAL WORDS: *exemplify*

TOPIC SENTENCE: *SUVs exemplify the rugged, aggressive lifestyle.*

B. The two items present a general topic. You are to narrow the topic. State an opinion. Choose definition-example signal word(s). Then combine the ideas in each group to create a topic sentence for a definition-example paragraph. *Answers may vary.*

TOPIC: (mental condition or state of being) *Depression*

OPINION: *treatable illness that affects the body and mind*

DEFINITION SIGNAL WORDS: *is a*

TOPIC SENTENCE: *Depression is a treatable illness that affects the body and mind.*

TOPIC: (dishonest person) *A hypocrite*

OPINION: *a spy or traitor*

DEFINITION SIGNAL WORDS: *is*

TOPIC SENTENCE: *A hypocrite is a spy and a traitor.*

Identify and Generate Relevant Details Using Example Patterns

LO3

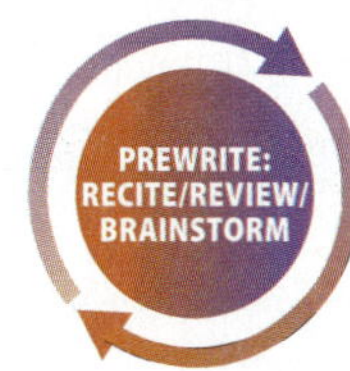

To identify and generate details based on the example patterns of organization, readers and writers may use some of the reporter's questions such as *who, what, when,* and *how*. To identify key details, effective readers ask questions. The following chart lists some questions you may ask to identify key details.

Ask Questions to Identify Key Details
What is the general idea being illustrated?
What is the term or concept being defined?
Who or what serves as an example of this idea?
What examples are given?
How do the examples illustrate the general idea or specific word or concept?

Effective writers use these same questions to generate relevant details during the prewriting phase of the writing process. Then they usually include the signal words and transitions of the example pattern to introduce these details and guide readers. Thus, readers look for example signal words and transitions to locate the key details that answer the questions they have asked. Many readers and writers use example concept maps to identify and generate details.

Example

Read the following two paragraphs from college textbooks. These paragraphs are typical of the kind of information you will read in introductory courses for earth science and economics. During reading, annotate the paragraphs. Use the example signal words and transitions to locate major supporting details. Underline the topic sentence and key examples. After reading, complete the example concept maps with information from the paragraphs. Then discuss the value of using example concept maps as study tools.

Answers may vary.

Why Study Rocks?

[1]Every rock contains clues about the environment in which it formed. [2]For example, some rocks are composed entirely of small shell fragments. [3]This tells Earth scientists that the rock originated in a shallow marine environment. [4]Other rocks contain clues that indicate they were formed from a volcanic eruption or deep in the Earth during mountain building. [5]Thus, rocks contain a wealth of information about events that have occurred over Earth's long history.

Lutgens, Frederick K., Tarbuck, Edward J., and Tasa, Dennis G., *Foundations of Earth Science,* 6th ed., p. 44.

CONTINUED

EXAMPLE *CONTINUED*

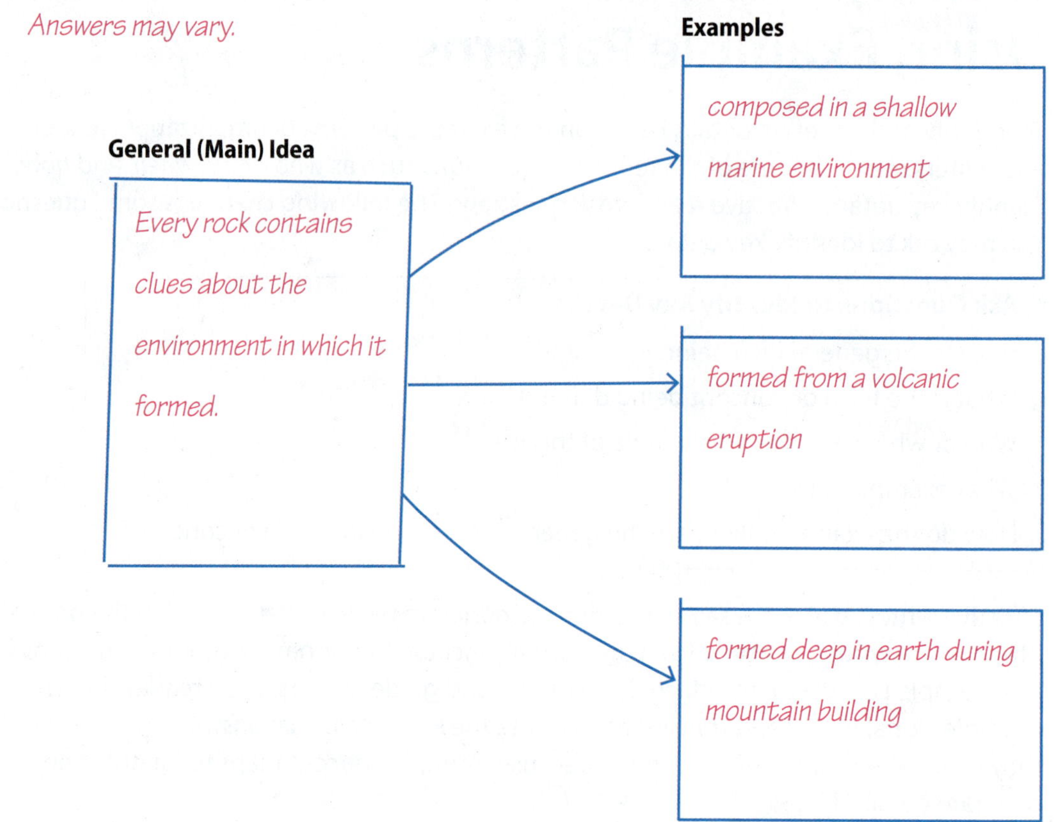

Answers may vary.
Examples
General (Main) Idea
Every rock contains clues about the environment in which it formed.
composed in a shallow marine environment
formed from a volcanic eruption
formed deep in earth during mountain building

SCARCITY

[1] Our inability to satisfy all our wants is called **scarcity**. [2] The ability of each of us to satisfy our wants is limited by the time we have, the incomes we earn, and the prices we pay for the things we buy. [3] These limits mean that everyone has unsatisfied wants. [4] The ability of all of us as a society to satisfy our want is limited by the productive resources we have. [5] These resources include the gifts of nature, our labor and ingenuity, and the tools and equipment we have made. [6] Everyone, poor and rich alike, faces scarcity. [7] A student wants Beyoncé's latest album and a paperback but has only $10.00 in his pocket. [8] He faces scarcity. [9] Brad Pitt wants to spend a week in New Orleans discussing plans for his new eco-friendly housing, and he wants to spend that week promoting his new movie. [10] He faces scarcity. [11] The U.S. government wants to increase defense spending and cut taxes. [12] It faces scarcity. [13] An entire society wants improved health care, an Internet connection in every classroom, an ambitious space program, clean lakes and rivers, and so on. [14] Society faces scarcity.

Bade, Robin, and Parkin, Michael, *Foundations of Economics*, 6th ed., p. 2.

Term	Definition	Traits	What It Is Not	Examples
Scarcity	our inability to satisfy all our wants	Ability to satisfy wants is limited by the time we have, the incomes we earn, and the prices we pay for the things we buy. Also limited by availability of productive resources such as gifts of nature, labor, ingenuity, tools, and equipment.	Poverty: Rich and poor alike face scarcity.	A student (lacks money); Brad Pitt (lacks time); U.S. government (lacks money); society (lacks money and productive resources)

Explanation

Compare your answers to the following student's think-aloud.

Example concept maps are great study tools. First, filling out the concept maps forced me to really think about how the general idea or the key term related to the examples given as supporting details. For example, in the first paragraph, my original question was based on the title "Why Study Rocks?" Before reading, I expected the answer to include specific names of rocks and descriptions of what they were made of. But when I went to fill in the chart, I changed my question to "Where in the environment are rocks formed?" So this chart made me think and helped me see that where a rock is formed is a key idea in earth

CONTINUED

EXPLANATION *CONTINUED*

science. The concept map for the second paragraph about scarcity also deepened my understanding. As I filled in the examples, I thought about what type of scarcity each example represented. Example concept maps make the information easy to review and remember. I can cover up certain pieces of information to test my ability to recall related information. For example, I can cover up the definition of a word and try to say it from memory. I filled the concept maps in with the following information.

Why Study Rocks?

- *Every rock contains clues about the environment in which it formed.*
  - *composed in a shallow marine environment*
  - *formed from a volcanic eruption*
  - *formed deep in earth during mountain building*

Scarcity

- *Definition: Our inability to satisfy our wants*
  - *ability to satisfy wants is limited by time, income, and prices*
  - *ability to satisfy wants is limited by productive resources such as gifts of nature, labor, ingenuity, tools, and equipment*
- *Examples: student, Brad Pitt, U.S. government, society*

Practice 3

Identify Relevant Details Using Example Patterns

Assume you are taking a college course in sociology. Your class is learning about issues in aging. Read the following two paragraphs from a college textbook. During reading, annotate the paragraphs. Use the example signal words and transitions to locate major supporting details. Underline the topic sentence and key examples. After reading, complete the example concept maps with information from the paragraphs. Answer the questions that follow each.

Ageism

[1]Some years ago Robert Butler coined the term *ageism* to describe negative attitudes toward the aging. [2]The International Longevity Center defines **ageism** as "Ideas, attitudes, beliefs, and practices on the part of individuals that are biased against persons or groups based on their older age." [3]According to Butler, ageism "reflects a deep seated uneasiness on the part of the young and middle-aged—a personal revulsion to and distaste for growing old, disease, disability, fear of powerlessness, uselessness, and death." [4]However, studies show ageism is not limited to young or middle aged people. [5]Older adults showed just as strong an age bias as did younger adults. [6]The media provide current examples of ageism. [7]The cartoon show *The Simpsons* depicts Grandpa Simpson as ignorant, forgetful, and timid. [8]In one episode he and his nursing-home friends break out of the home to freedom. [9]They make it to the sidewalk, look around, get scared, and shuffle back inside.

Term	Definition	Traits	Example
Ageism	*ideas, attitudes, beliefs, and practices on the part of individuals that are biased against persons or groups based on their older age*	a deep-seated uneasiness on the part of the young and middle aged—a personal revulsion to and distaste for growing old, disease, disability, fear of powerlessness, uselessness, and death; not limited to young or middle aged people; older adults showed just as strong an age bias as did younger adults.	*Media depiction of older people as in Grandpa Simpson on The Simpsons*

CONTINUED

PRACTICE 3 *CONTINUED*

1. The relationship of ideas within sentence 2 is
a. generalization-example. **(b.)** definition-example.

2. The relationship between sentences 6 and 7 is
(a.) generalization-example. **b.** definition-example.

3. The topic sentence of the paragraph is sentence
a. 1. **c.** 3.
(b.) 2. **d.** 9.

VICTIMIZATION BY FRAUD

[1]Older people seem more susceptible to certain types of crime than others. [2]Con artists and swindlers, for example, tend to target this population. [3]Older people have savings that make them attractive targets. [4]They also may have fewer social supports to help them steer clear of bogus deals such as home repair and medical and insurance scams. [5]Cons and swindles take many forms. [6]For instance, con artists often use the "bank examiner" swindle on older people. [7]In that case, a con artist calls an older person, often a woman who lives alone, and says that someone is embezzling money from her bank. [8]The caller asks if she will help catch the thief. [9]The caller tells her to withdraw money from her account and give the money to a bank messenger who will arrive at her door. [10] The caller explains that the messenger will take the money back to the bank. [11] The bank will then check the serial numbers and catch the crooked teller. [12] The messenger, of course, works for the con artist and gets away with the money. [13] In another instance, home repair con artists also target older people. [14] They look for homes that need repairs—loose shingles or a broken eaves trough. [15] The swindler then knocks on the older person's door and offers to estimate the cost of repairs. [16] He or she gives a low estimate and says that the older person will have to pay for the work right away to get this deal. [17] The con artist usually asks for cash payment before any work gets done.

Adapted from Novak, Mark., *Issues in Aging*, pp. 3, 5, 11.

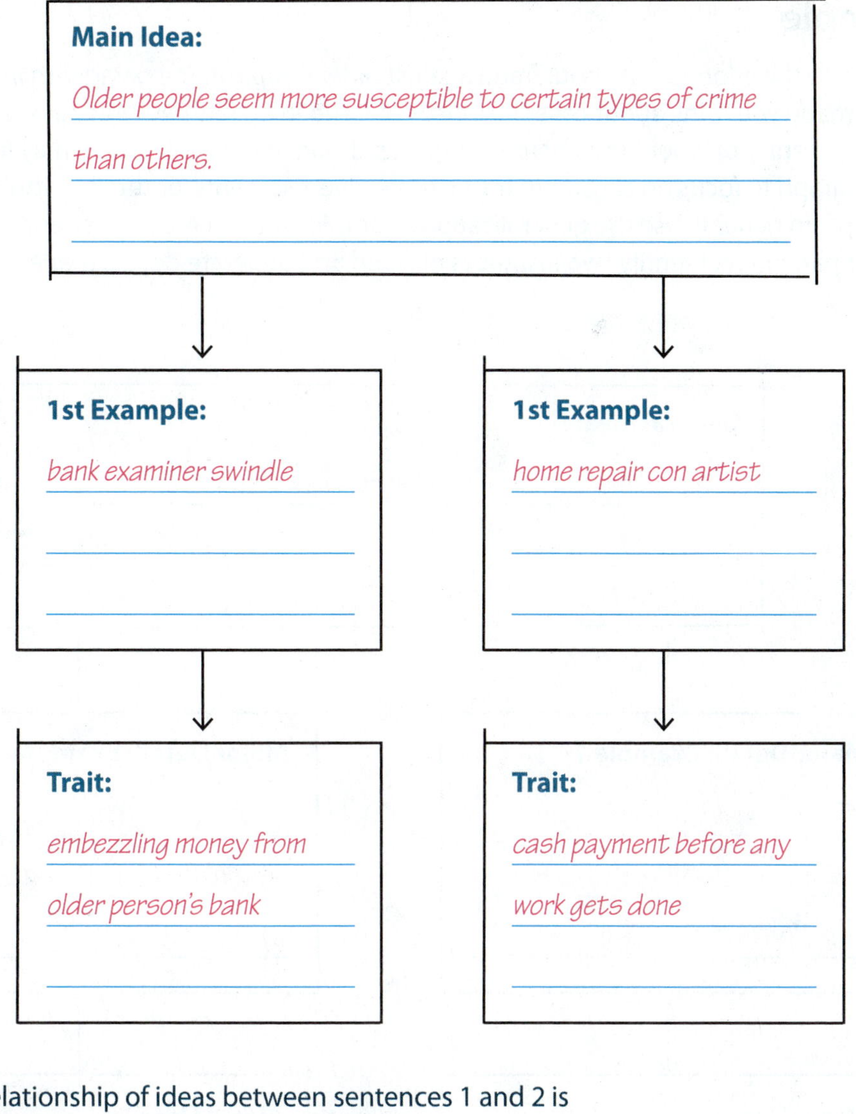

1. The relationship of ideas between sentences 1 and 2 is
(a.) generalization-example. **b.** definition-example.

2. The relationship between sentences 6 and 7 is
(a.) generalization-example. **b.** definition-example.

3. The topic sentence of the paragraph is sentence
(a.) 1. **c.** 5.
b. 2. **d.** 17.

Using concept maps based on example patterns as a reader prepares you to generate details as a writer. During the prewriting phase of the writing process, use an example concept map to generate details to clarify a generalization or define a key word or concept. The generalization-example concept map usually flows from the main or general idea to key examples that are the major supporting details. Often, you will also provide minor details that describe or further explain an example.

Example

Assume the information about fraud against older people in the paragraph in Practice 3 has made you think about other instances of fraud in our culture. You have decided to post an entry on your blog about examples of fraud in our society. You may limit your paragraph to focus on consumer fraud, false advertisements, or the deceitful behaviors of people in general. Use the generalization-example concept map to generate details for your paragraph. Identify two instances of fraud and generate details that explain them.

Answers may vary.

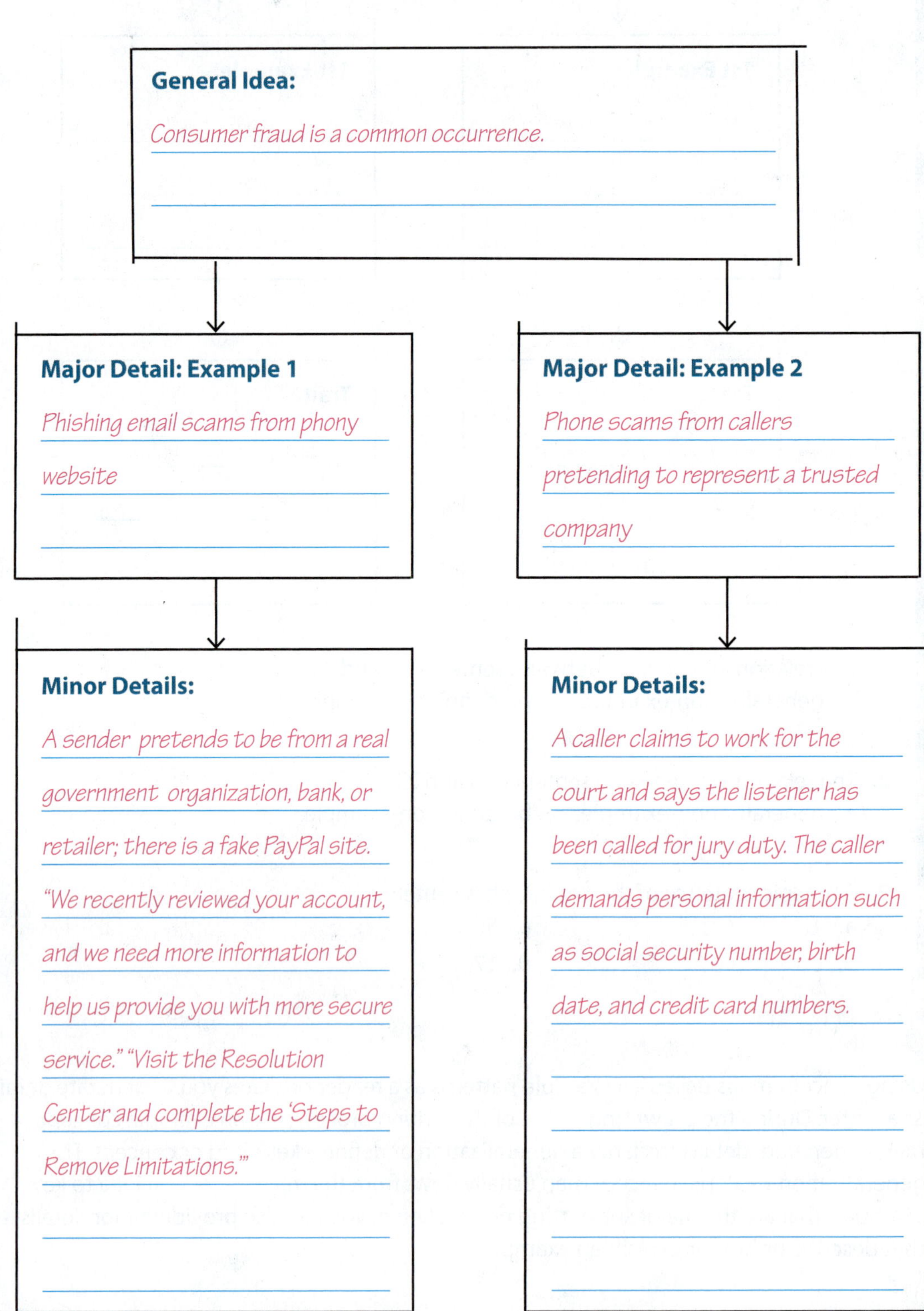
General Idea:
Consumer fraud is a common occurrence.
Major Detail: Example 1
Phishing email scams from phony website
Major Detail: Example 2
Phone scams from callers pretending to represent a trusted company
Minor Details:
A sender pretends to be from a real government organization, bank, or retailer; there is a fake PayPal site. "We recently reviewed your account, and we need more information to help us provide you with more secure service." "Visit the Resolution Center and complete the 'Steps to Remove Limitations.'"
Minor Details:
A caller claims to work for the court and says the listener has been called for jury duty. The caller demands personal information such as social security number, birth date, and credit card numbers.

Explanation

Compare your answers to the following student's think-aloud.

I have been hassled by emails and phone calls trying to rip me off. It drives me crazy especially because I am on the Do Not Call list and use a junk mail service to filter my email. So here are the details I generated based on personal experience.

General Idea: Consumer fraud is a common occurrence.

- *Major Detail: Example 1*
  Phishing email scams from a phony website
  - *Minor Details: A sender pretends to be from a real government organization, bank, or retailer. There is a fake PayPal site. "We recently reviewed your account, and we need more information to help us provide you with more secure service." "Visit the Resolution Center and complete the 'Steps to Remove Limitations.'"*
- *Major Detail: Example 2*
  Phone scams from callers pretending to represent a trusted company
  - *Minor Details: A caller claims to work for the court and says the listener has been called for jury duty. The caller demands personal information such as social security number, birth date, and credit card numbers.*

The definition-example concept map also usually flows from the main idea to key examples that are the major supporting details. However, the extended definition-example concept map also prompts you to generate additional details. To define a word or concept, you may generate details that explain the traits of the concept, what the concept is like, and what the concept is not.

Example

Assume you are taking a literature class that is beginning a unit on the classical hero in literature. To prepare you for the lesson (by calling up your prior knowledge), your professor has asked you to define your concept of what a hero is. Use the following extended definition-example concept map to generate details for your paragraph.

Answers may vary.

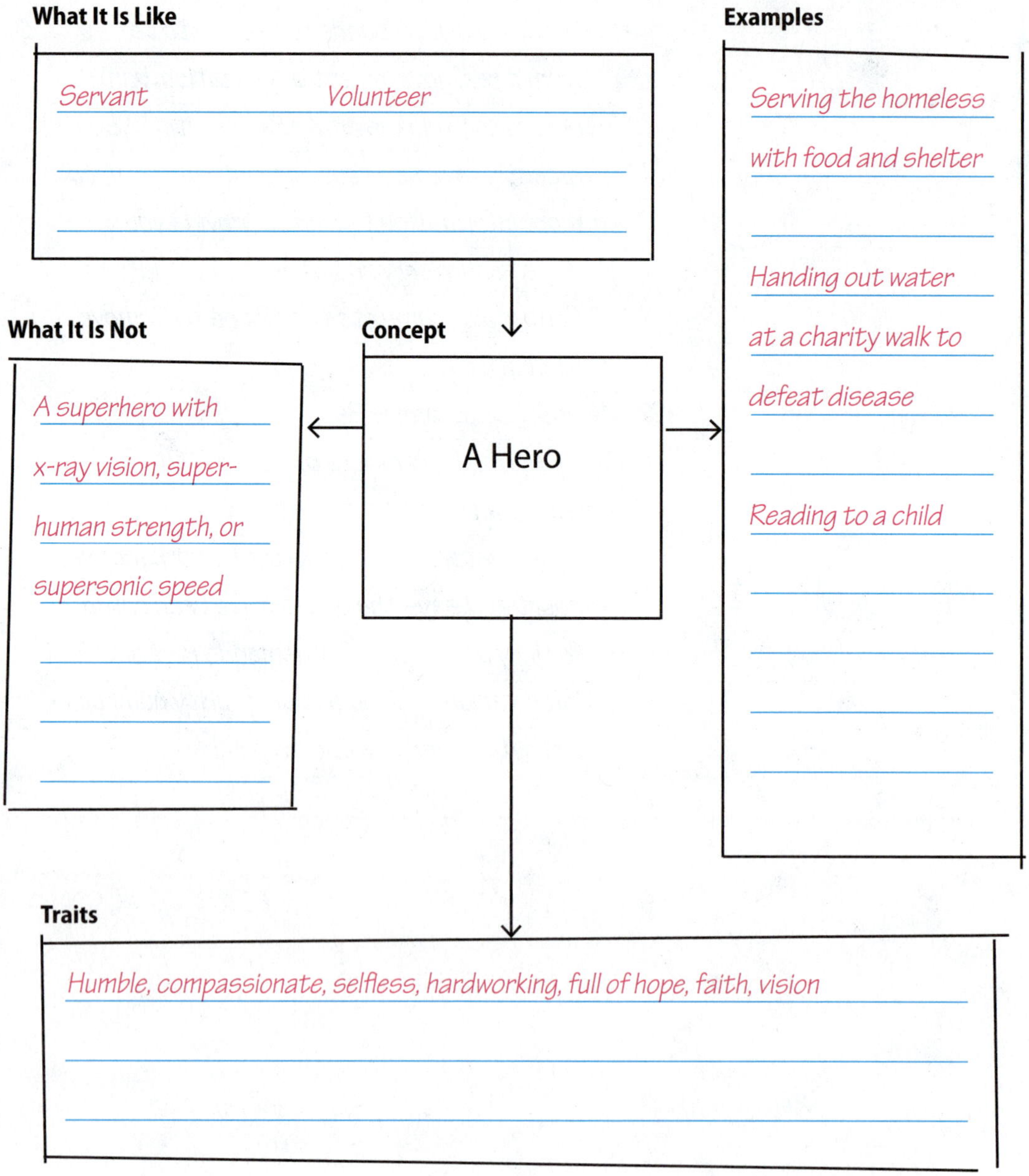

What It Is Like

Servant *Volunteer*

Examples

Serving the homeless with food and shelter

Handing out water at a charity walk to defeat disease

Reading to a child

What It Is Not

A superhero with x-ray vision, super-human strength, or supersonic speed

Concept

A Hero

Traits

Humble, compassionate, selfless, hardworking, full of hope, faith, vision

Explanation

Compare your answers to the following student's think-aloud.

This topic was a lot of fun. It will be interesting to see how my definition of a hero compares to literature's definition of a classical hero. The first thing the term "classical hero" made me think of was superheroes like Superman, Iron Man, and Batman. But even those heroes are really based on the best qualities of an everyday real hero. So I defined my hero as the Real Hero. Here are the details I generated.

Concept: A Real Hero

What it is like: A servant, volunteer

What it is not: A superhero with x-ray vision, superhuman strength, or supersonic speed

Traits: humble, compassionate, selfless, hardworking, full of hope, faith, vision

Examples: Serving the homeless with food and shelter, handing out water at a charity walk to defeat disease, reading to a child

Practice 4

Generate Relevant Details Using Example Patterns

Choose one of the topic sentences you created in Practice 2. Use one of the following example pattern concept maps to generate details to support your topic sentence.

Generalization-Example Map

General Idea:

Major Detail: Example 1

Major Detail: Example 2

Minor Details:

Minor Details:

Definition-Example Map

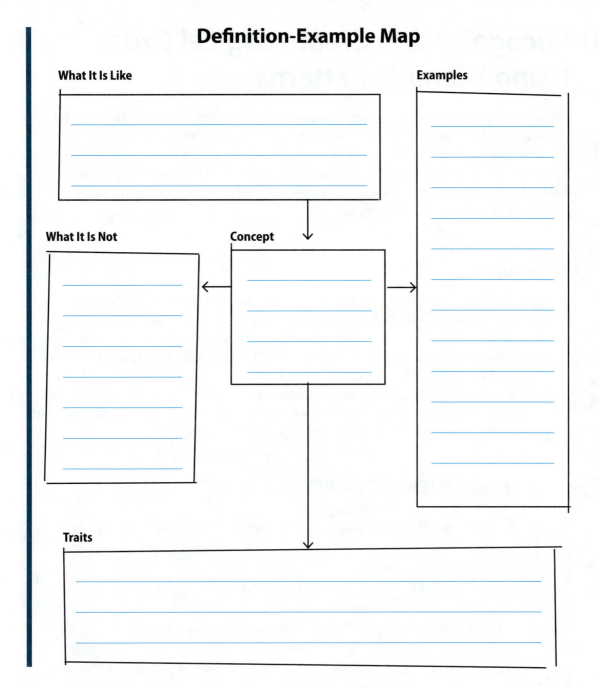

What It Is Like

Examples

What It Is Not

Concept

Traits

L4 Recognize and Create Logical Order Using Example Patterns

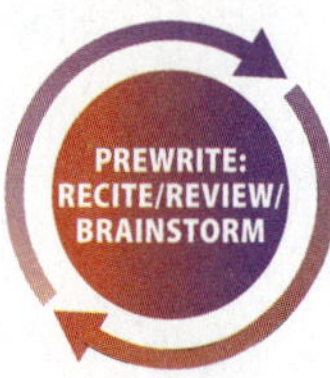

When a reader recognizes that a writer is using an example pattern to organize ideas, he or she can see how the main idea and details fit together and anticipate upcoming details. When we use example transitions and signal words, we expect the logical order to flow from a general idea to specific examples. The writer's use of example transitions or signal words establishes the logical order of ideas and guides the reader through the generalization-example or definition-example pattern.

Example

Assume you are a friend or family member of a person who has a blog with a large following. The blogger drafted the following paragraph about consumer fraud (see the example on p. 420). Before posting the paragraph, she has asked you to read it and give her feedback. Read and annotate her paragraph. Circle the main idea. Use example signal words and transitions to locate and underline key details. Cross out any details that are not relevant to the main idea. Share your annotations and your personal reaction to the paragraph with a classmate. Suggest a change to improve the paragraph. Point out what you like about the use of examples in the paragraph. *Answers may vary.*

CONSUMERS BEWARE!

[1]Have you recently received an email telling you that you are eligible to receive thousands of dollars if you just reply with key personal information? [2]Well, if you have, beware!

[3]It is probably a scam designed to steal your money or your identity. [4]Consumer fraud is a common occurrence. [5]One example is the phishing email from a phony website. [6]A sender pretends to be from a real government organization, bank, or retailer. [7]In one case, the phishing email came from a fake PayPal site. [8]The email stated, "We recently reviewed your account, and we need more information to help us provide you with more secure service." [9]The message may also direct the consumer "to visit the Resolution Center and complete the 'Steps to Remove Limitations.'" [10]Another example is the phone scam from callers also pretending to represent a trusted company. [11]The caller also tries to gather key personal information. [12]In one instance, a caller claimed to work for the court and said the listener had been called for jury duty. [13]Then the caller demanded personal information such as a social security number, birth date, bank account information, and credit card numbers. [14]~~Of course, not all request for information are scams.~~

Explanation

Compare your answers to the following student's think-aloud.

This paragraph showed me how to use example signal words and transitions. The use of "One example" in sentence 5 and "Another example" in sentence 10 let me quickly find these two main examples. Then the words "In one case" in sentence 7 and "In one instance" in sentence 12 introduced the minor details for each major example. The ideas were really easy to follow. I did cross out the last sentence. It didn't seem to relate to the topic at all. I suggest writing a concluding sentence that restates the main idea.

Example

Assume you are working as a peer editor for a classmate in your college literature course. Your classmate drafted the following paragraph as her definition of a hero (see the example on p. 422). Read and annotate her paragraph. Circle the main idea. Use example signal words and transitions to locate key details. Cross out any details that are not relevant to the main idea. Share your annotations and your personal reaction to the paragraph with your classmate. Suggest a change to improve the paragraph. Point out what you like about the definition and examples in the paragraph.

What Is a Hero?

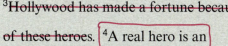

[1]When I think of the word hero, images of all the superheroes such as Superman, Batman, and Wonder Woman come to mind. [2]These are not real heroes. ~~[3]Hollywood has made a fortune because of these heroes.~~ [4]A real hero is an ordinary person who makes a significant difference in the lives of others. [5]For example, real heroes are compassionate people who care about others as much as they care about themselves. [6]They are humble people who want to serve others without looking for a reward. [7]They are hard-working people who don't quit no matter what. [8]Exemplifying

CONTINUED

EXAMPLE *CONTINUED*

selflessness, a real hero serves the hungry and homeless by giving them hot meals and safe, warm shelter. [9]A real hero fights diseases such as AIDS or cancer by handing out water at a charity walk. [10]A real hero volunteers to read to a child to combat illiteracy. [11]A real hero doesn't have x-ray eyesight, superhuman strength, or supersonic speed. [12]A real hero has better gifts—a vision of hope, the strength of faith, and the speed of good will.

Explanation

Compare your answers to the following student's think-aloud.

Right away I noticed that the third sentence didn't really add anything to the definition of a hero. Hollywood making money isn't related to the writer's main point, so I crossed it out. I thought the use of superheroes was a good way to say what a "real hero" is not. I like the way the writer began and ended the paragraph with the contrast between superheroes and real heroes. I didn't think enough was said about how real heroes "don't quit no matter what." I think an example of not quitting would be powerful.

Now that you have recognized the logical order of a paragraph and the ways in which readers can use example signal words and transitions to comprehend a generalization or the definition of a new term, you are ready to create logical order using examples in your own piece of writing.

Practice 5

Create Logical Order Using Example Patterns

Work with the example pattern concept map you completed in Practice 4. Write a rough draft of your paragraph to establish either the generalization-example or definition-example order of details. Work with a peer to review each other's rough drafts. Exchange, read, and review your drafts to make sure all details are relevant to the main ideas. Annotate your peer's paragraph. Then complete an example pattern concept map of the draft you are peer editing. Return your reviewed paragraphs to each other. Revise your paragraph as needed. Use your own paper.

Analyze and Use Effective Expression with Example Patterns

LO5

Readers and writers give thoughtful attention to the effective use of language in example patterns. Effective writers may rely on descriptive language to clearly exemplify a general idea or define a key word. Sensory details and figures of speech such as metaphors and similes create vivid images in the reader's mind that can clarify the main idea. Often, a writer uses figurative language to state a generalization as the main idea and then provide examples and illustrations as supporting details that clarify the point. Likewise, writers may use figurative language to define a key term based on its similarities to concepts more familiar to the reader. Therefore, to comprehend the writer's general idea or definition, effective readers analyze the writer's use of descriptive or figurative language.

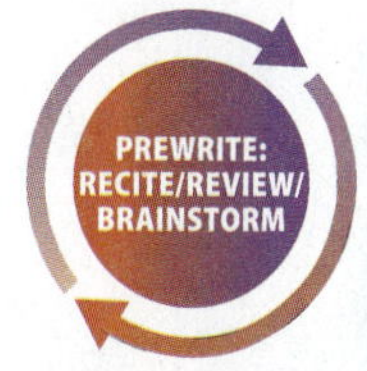

My **mother** *is* my **rock.**

METAPHOR: A DIRECT COMPARISON (NOT USING LIKE OR AS) BETWEEN TWO THINGS, USING ONE THING TO DESCRIBE THE OTHER THING (see Module 10, p. 383)

A **tornado** *is like* a **whirlpool.**

SIMILE: AN INDIRECT COMPARISON BETWEEN TWO THINGS, USUALLY USING LIKE, AS, OR THAN (see Module 10, p. 383)

Jealousy **devours** love.

SENSORY DETAILS: DETAILS THAT APPEAL TO OUR SENSES OF SIGHT, SOUND, SMELL, TASTE, AND TOUCH TO CREATE A VIVID MENTAL IMAGE, INCLUDING ONOMATOPOEIA, A WORD THAT IMITATES A SOUND (see Module 10, p. 383)

Example

The following items are topic sentences using the generalization-example or definition-example patterns. Analyze each topic sentence based on its use of figures of speech. Underline the figure of speech in each sentence. Then choose the answer that identifies the figure of speech used.

1. The Internet is like a worldwide library at your fingertips.
a. metaphor **(b.)** simile **c.** sensory detail

2. Alzheimer's disease is a thief of memory, relationships, and physical health.
(a.) metaphor **b.** simile **c.** sensory detail

3. A collapsed star is like a black drain hole in space.
a. metaphor **(b.)** simile **c.** sensory detail

4. The earth boils in pollution.
a. metaphor **b.** simile **(c.)** sensory detail

Explanation

Compare your responses to the following student's think-aloud.

I thought that some of these sentences used sensory details to create a metaphor or simile. For example, sentence 1 created a visual image in my mind with the words "at your fingertips." Sentence 3 also created a visual image with the words "black drain hole." However, both of these sentences used "is like" to link the key word or idea to these images, so I identified them as similes. Here are my answers.

1. *(b) A simile that uses "is like" to indirectly compare the Internet to a library.*
2. *(a) A metaphor that uses "is" to directly compare Alzheimer's to a thief.*
3. *(b) A simile that uses "is like" to indirectly compare a collapsed star to a drain hole.*
4. *(c) Sensory details that create the image of pollution heating up the earth until it boils.*

Practice 6

Analyze Effective Expression

Assume you are taking a college psychology class. Your professor posted the following information to help you study for an upcoming exam. Read the paragraph. Underline key terms, the figures of speech, and sensory details. Then complete the chart with information from the paragraph. *Answers may vary.*

Freud's Iceberg Metaphor for the Mind

[1]Sigmund Freud, an Austrian neurologist who lived from 1856 to 1939, is the father of psychoanalysis. [2]Psychoanalysis is a method of understanding mental life based on the function of the mind. [3]This method assumes that powerful mental forces shape personality and motivate behavior. [4]According to Freud, the mind is like an iceberg, mostly submerged. [5]The visible tip of the iceberg is our conscious or awareness, such as feelings of hunger and thirst or knowledge of our

surroundings. [6] Just under the water lies our preconscious or dream state that includes recallable thoughts and feelings such as phone numbers or recent experiences. [7] The largest part of the iceberg lays deep below hidden from view, just as we remain unaware of our unconscious. [8] Our unconscious stores instincts, passions, fears, and shameful or long-forgotten experiences. [9] Often pieces of the submerged parts of an iceberg break off and float to the surface. [10] Likewise, Freud believed bits of our unconscious may break off and float to the surface of our awareness as mental problems.

Key Term	Figure of Speech	Sensory Detail	Examples	Explanation
The mind	*iceberg*	mostly submerged		Many forces shape personality and motivate behavior.
Conscious		*tip of iceberg*	feelings of hunger and thirst, knowledge of our surroundings	*Our conscious mind is aware of just a small part of what our mind is and does.*
Preconscious		*just under water*	dream state, recallable thoughts and feelings such as phone numbers or recent experiences	*This information is easily remembered.*
Unconscious		*largest part deep below hidden from view*	instincts, passions, fear, shameful or long-forgotten experiences	*We remain unaware of most of the forces that shape personality and motivate behavior.*

As you move through your own writing process, think about the impact you want to have on your reader. For the greatest impact, revise vague statements of general ideas, definitions, and examples into concrete and precise words and phrases. Use figures of speech and sensory details to make your general ideas, definitions, and examples vivid and memorable.

Practice 7

Use Effective Expression

Work with the rough draft of the paragraph you completed in Practice 5. Choose two sentences and revise them to use descriptive language. Use the following space to record your original and revised sentences.

Original sentence:

Revised sentence:

Original sentence:

Revised sentence:

Reading and Writing Assignments

MySkillsLab™
Complete these assignments in MySkillsLab.

Considering Audience and Purpose

Study the set of photographs about the examples of a thrifty lifestyle at the beginning of the module. Assume you want to start a blog called "Living Wisely, Living Well" that you will post to once a week. Write a paragraph that exemplifies or defines "Living Wisely, Living Well." Or assume you have already begun your blog and have a following and want to write an entry about "A Thrifty Lifestyle." Define the term "Thrifty Lifestyle" and give and explain a few examples.

Reading and Writing for Everyday Life

Assume you are greatly concerned about the "right to bear arms" and gun control in the United States. You want to form a definite opinion so you can vote wisely about the issue. You have found a copy of the Second Amendment to the Constitution in the Bill of Rights in the government's online archives. Read the amendment. Then write a letter to an elected official of your choice that answers the question "Does the government have the right to control guns?" Define or exemplify "the right of the people to keep and bear arms." You may need to use a dictionary to define terms such as "well regulated," "Militia," and "infringe" in your discussion.

> Amendment II
>
> A well-regulated Militia, being necessary to the security of a free State, the right of the people to keep and bear Arms, shall not be infringed.

"Charters of Freedom." National Archives and Records Administration. <http://www.archives.gov/exhibits/charters/bill_of_rights_transcript.html>.

Reading and Writing for College Life

Assume you are taking a college art appreciation course. Throughout the course, your class has been discussing the definition of art. Your professor has asked you to respond to the following prompt: "Is It or Isn't It Art?" You are to write a paragraph that defines a current art form or explains why something is not a form of art. The professor handed out the following paragraph as an example of a well-written response to the topic. Read the paragraph and then compose your own response to the prompt. For example, you may define graffiti as art. Or you may choose to define another means of expression such as rap or break-dancing.

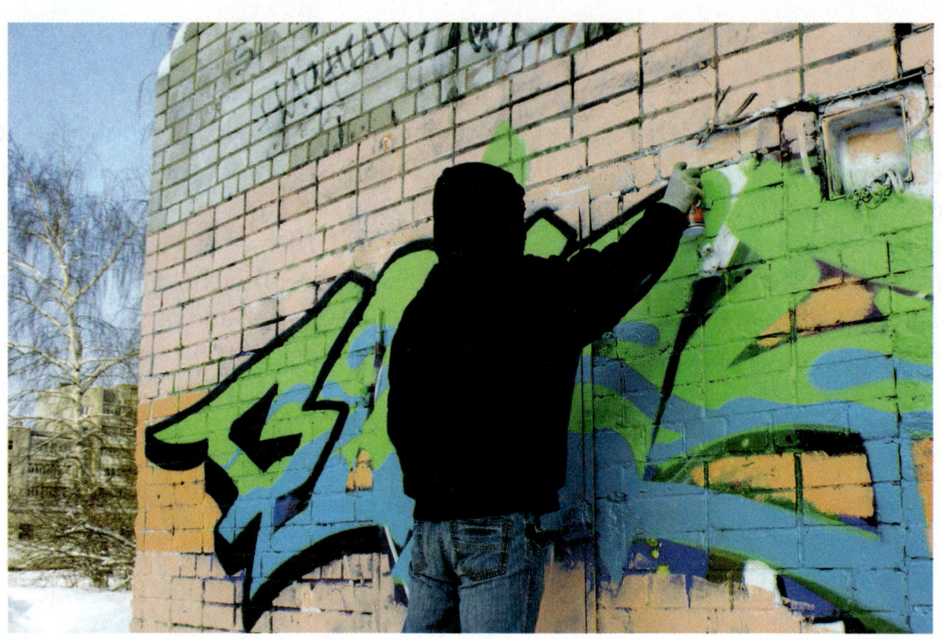

Graffiti: Vandalism, Not Art

Although graffiti is a common sight, many do not understand its true nature. Graffiti is vandalism, not art. Graffiti, a form of personal expression, is the unlawful markings of an individual or group on private and public surfaces. Unlike more widely accepted forms of art, graffiti is not generally regarded as aesthetically pleasing, nor is it thought of as a means to explore or enhance the appreciation of beauty. Graffiti is actually vandalism and defacement, and seen as evidence of a gang or a neighborhood in decline. One type of graffiti is known as a tag, a stylized signature of a tagger or writer. A tag is quickly created with one color that starkly contrasts with the background upon which it is written. Tags can be written with spray paint, fat-tipped markers, etching tools, or pre-tagged stickers. Another kind of graffiti is the throw-up, a two-dimensional image made with large bubble letters that are outlined in black or white and filled in with another color. A writer often uses throw-ups to bomb an area in a short amount of time. A third type of graffiti, similar to a mural, is the "piece," short for masterpiece. Time-consuming to create, a piece is a large, colorful, and complex image that usually reflects a political or social issue. Piecing demonstrates a high level of aerosol paint control. Instances of graffiti are evident in both urban and suburban public areas such as parks, restrooms, buildings, and trains.

Reading and Writing for Working Life

Assume you are a supervisor of a sales team at a local store of a retail chain. You have attended a training session about sexual harassment. You are expected to share this information with your employees. Read the following definition from the workshop. Then compose a memo that defines sexual harassment and gives examples you may have noticed on the job. Use your own words.

Sexual Harassment

Sexual harassment is a form of sex discrimination. Specifically, unwelcome sexual advances, requests for sexual favors, and other verbal or physical conduct of a sexual nature are sexual harassment when submission to or rejection of this conduct affects an individual's employment, interferes with an individual's work performance, or creates a hostile or offensive work environment. Sexual harassment can occur in a variety of situations, such as the following. First, the victim as well as the harasser may be a woman or a man. The victim does not have to be of the opposite sex. Second, the harasser can be the victim's supervisor, an agent of the employer, a supervisor in another area, a co-worker, or a non-employee. Third, the victim does not have to be the person harassed but could be anyone affected by the offensive conduct. Fourth, unlawful sexual harassment may occur without economic injury to or discharge of the victim. Finally, the harasser's conduct must be unwelcome. An example is a co-worker who regularly tells sexually explicit jokes and makes demeaning comments about male coworkers and clients.

Adapted from United States Equal Employment Opportunity Commission.

Workshop: Compose a Paragraph Using Example Patterns

Choose a paragraph to read and respond to in writing. You may select a paragraph in an example, practice, or writing assignment within this module. Or you may select a paragraph of your own choosing. Use the following guide to comprehend and respond to the paragraph. Apply what you have learned about example patterns to your reading/writing strategy.

Preread: Survey and Question

Ask questions about the text's features.

____

____

What is the passage about?

____

____

How is the material organized?

____

____

What do I already know about this topic? (What is my prior knowledge about the vocabulary?)

____

____

What is my purpose for reading/writing?

____

____

What points may I want to address or include in my written response?

____

____

Read and Annotate

As you read, annotate key ideas, particularly those details that answer your prereading questions.

Recite, Review, and Brainstorm

Recite the information. Summarize the most important parts. Answer your prereading questions. Rephrase ideas into your own words. Record changes in your opinions based on the new information. **Review** the information. **Brainstorm** ideas for your written response to the passage. **Freewrite** a response to what you have read. **Map** the relationship among ideas you have annotated in the text. **Outline** or list key ideas and details in blocks of thought. Use your own paper.

Write a Draft of Your Response

Using the ideas you generated by brainstorming, compose a draft of your response. Use your own paper.

Revise Your Draft

Once you have created a draft of your essay, read the draft and answer the questions in the "Questions for Revising a Paragraph" box that follows. Indicate your answers by annotating your paper. If you answer "yes" to a question, underline, check, or circle examples. If you answer "no" to a question, write additional details in the margins and draw lines to indicate their placement. Revise your essay based on your reflection. (*Hint:* Experienced writers create several drafts as they focus on one or two questions per draft.)

Step by Step: Questions for Revising a Paragraph

- ☐ Have I stated or implied a focused central point?
- ☐ Have I made my purpose clear?
- ☐ Is my tone appropriate for my audience and purpose?
- ☐ Is the logical order of the ideas clear? Have I used strong example transitions and signal words to guide my reader?
- ☐ Have I made my point with adequate details?
- ☐ Do all the details support my point?
- ☐ What impact will my paragraph make on my reader?

Proofread Your Draft

Once you have made any revisions to your paragraph that may be needed, proofread your essay to eliminate careless errors. Work with a classmate to give and receive feedback about your essays.

Review Test

MySkillsLab™
Complete this Review Test in MySkillsLab.

Score (number correct) ______ x 10 = _______%

Use reading/writing strategies to comprehend and respond to the following passage from a college history textbook. Read the passage. Complete the study notes based on an example concept map with three general ideas and examples for each from the passage. (One general idea and one example have been provided.) Write a paragraph in response to "What Do You Think?"

1140L/11.1 GE/392 words

DISEASE AND POPULATION LOSSES OF AMERICAN INDIANS IN THE NEW WORLD

[1]Almost as soon as Europeans set foot on American soil, Indians began to die. [2]Of all the weapons the Europeans brought to the Americas, the most powerful was one they could not see and of which they were mostly unaware: microorganisms. [3]Europeans carried diseases such as smallpox, measles, bubonic plague, diphtheria, influenza, malaria, yellow fever, and typhoid. [4]For centuries, these diseases had ravaged Asia, Europe, and Africa. [5]By the 1500s, Eurasian and African populations had acquired some resistance to such diseases. [6]An outbreak of smallpox or diphtheria might take a severe toll on infants and the elderly. [7]But these diseases no longer would destroy entire populations.

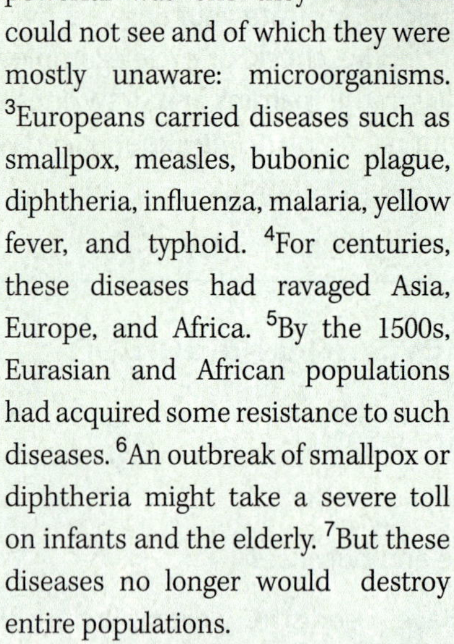

[8]American Indians had evolved over hundreds of generations without contact with these diseases. [9]They lacked the necessary biological defenses. [10]When these diseases first struck, many Indian villages were nearly wiped out. [11]In 1585, for example, Sir Francis Drake, preparing for a raid against the Spanish, stopped at the Cape Verde Islands. [12]While there some of his men contracted a fever—probably typhus—but sailed for Florida undaunted by their discomfort. [13]When they landed at St. Augustine, the disease spread to the Indians who, according to Drake, "died verie fast and said amongst themselves, it was the Englisshe God that made them die so faste."

[14]After the initial infestation by Europeans, the diseases then spread among Indians, rippling outward, far beyond the areas initially visited by the explorers. [15]De Soto's journey spread diseases throughout what is now the Southeast, virtually destroying the mound communities of Mississippian culture.

[16]Indian losses from diseases were incalculable. [17]However, the lowest estimates begin in the millions. [18]Scholars agree on only one fact concerning the population history of the North American Indians following the arrival of Columbus. [19]The number of Indians declined quickly.

[20]Another reason why so many Indians succumbed to disease was that they suffered from malnutrition. [21]European plants and animals had disrupted the Indian ecosystem. [22]For example, pigs and cattle, brought in the first Spanish ships, were set

loose in the Americas. [23]Without the predators and diseases that thinned their numbers in Europe and Asia, the pigs reproduced rapidly. [24]And they ate their way through fields of maize, beans, and squash. [25]Rats, stowaways on most European ships, also reproduced in the Americas and infested Indian crops. [26]Europeans also brought plants such as dandelions and other weeds that choked the Indian crops.

Carnes, Mark, and Garraty, John, *The American Nation: A History of the United States*, 14th ed., p. 25.

General Idea	Example
Of all the weapons the Europeans brought to the Americas, the most powerful was one they could not see and of which they were mostly unaware: microorganisms.	*Europeans carried diseases such as smallpox, measles, bubonic plague, diphtheria, influenza, malaria, yellow fever, and typhoid.*
When these diseases first struck, many Indian villages were nearly wiped out.	*Sir Francis Drake's men contracted a fever, maybe typhus, in the Cape Verde Islands and then landed in St. Augustine and infected Indians, who died fast.*
After initial infestation by Europeans, the diseases spread among Indians, rippling outward beyond areas initially visited by explorers.	*De Soto's journey spread diseases throughout the Southeast, destroying the mound communities of Mississippian culture.*
European plants and animals had disrupted the Indian ecosystem.	*Pigs, cattle, and rats from European ships were set loose, reproduced, and ruined Indian crops.*

What Do You Think?

Assume you are taking a college course in history. The following prompt for a short written response appears on the chapter exam. On your own paper, respond to the prompt based on the information in the passage "Disease and Population Losses of American Indians in the New World." Use your own words.

Test Prompt: Explain and illustrate the Indian defenselessness against European diseases.

Academic Learning Log: Module Review

Summary of Key Concepts of Example Patterns

Assess your comprehension of the example patterns.

LO1 LO2

1. In the generalization-example pattern, the writer makes a *general* statement and then offers an *example* or series of *examples* to clarify the *generalization.*.

2. In a simple definition-example pattern, the writer makes a general statement that *introduces and gives the meaning of a new, specialized, or difficult term.*.

3. Two types of definition-example patterns are the *simple definition* and the *extended definition*.

4. In an extended definition-example pattern, a writer makes a general statement that introduces a difficult concept. To define the concept, the writer identifies and explains its *traits, describes what the concept is like or similar to, and offers examples*.

5. To clarify meaning, a writer may also include an explanation and example of *what the term is not*.

Test Your Comprehension of Example Patterns

Respond to the following prompts. *Answers may vary.*

LO1 LO2 LO3 LO4 LO5

Complete a chart of transitions and signal words used to establish example patterns.

Key Words and Transitions Used to Signal Examples				
an illustration	*for instance*	*once*	*to illustrate*	
for example	*include/ including*	*such as*	*typical, typically*	
also	*final*	*for one thing*	*last of all*	*second*
and	*finally*	*furthermore*	*moreover*	*specifically*
another	*first*	*in addition*	*next*	*third*
besides	*first of all*	*last*	*one*	
certain				
Words Used to Signal Definitions				
as	*category*	*differs*	*is, is called, is known as*	*trait*
are	*consists of*	*distinguished from*	*is not*	*unlike*
characteristics	*constitutes*	*i.e (that is to say)*	*like*	
characterized by	*defined as*	*in particular*	*means*	
connotes	*denotes*	*indicates*	*suggests*	

On your own paper, create a generalization-example concept map and a definition-example concept map.

LO1 LO2 LO3 LO4 LO5

1. **How will I use what I have learned?** In your notebook, discuss how you will apply to your own reading/writing strategy what you have learned about examples. When will you apply this knowledge to your reading/writing strategy?
2. **What do I still need to study about examples?** In your notebook, discuss your ongoing study needs. Describe what, when, and how you will continue studying and using examples.

Complete the Post-test for Module 11 in MySkillsLab.

12

The Comparison/ Contrast Pattern

LEARNING OUTCOMES

After studying this module you should be able to:

- **LO 1** Answer the Question "What's the Point of the Comparison/ Contrast Pattern?"
- **LO 2** Comprehend and State a Main Idea Using the Comparison/Contrast Pattern
- **LO 3** Identify and Generate Relevant Details Using the Comparison/ Contrast Pattern
- **LO 4** Recognize and Create the Comparison/ Contrast Pattern
- **LO 5** Analyze and Use Effective Expression with the Comparison/ Contrast Pattern

Comparing and contrasting ideas is an essential part of critical thinking. A comparison examines how two or more things are similar. A contrast looks at how two or more things are different. When we choose between Subway and McDonald's or an iPhone and an Android we are weighing the similarities or differences of products and services and making a choice by comparison shopping. In everyday life, we compare or contrast the neighborhoods we want to live in and the prices of homes we want to buy, or the honesty and policies of political candidates as we decide for whom we will vote. In working life, we compare or contrast the salaries, benefits, and working conditions among several career opportunities. In college life, we compare and contrast leaders, governments, cultures, literature, technology, writers, or philosophies in a wide range of courses.

To read or write a comparison/contrast paragraph, you identify or establish the comparable points between two (or more) topics. As a reader, you identify the writer's list of similarities and differences between the topics and evaluate the explanations given for them. Your goal is to understand the point the writer is making by comparing/contrasting the topics. As a writer, you choose two topics to discuss based on their similarities and differences. You state the points of comparison or contrast between the topics and explain each point of similarity or difference. The writer's goal is to make a specific point by choosing, developing, and guiding the reader through comparable points between the topics.

WHAT'S THE POINT of the Comparison/ Contrast Pattern? 

Often ideas become clearer when they are analyzed based on how they relate to one another. The comparison/contrast pattern of organization allows a writer to explore the ways in which ideas are related. The following set of photographs documents some similarities and differences between electric and gas vehicles. Study the sets of images. Answer the following questions about each comparable point. Then answer the question "What's the point?" with a one-sentence statement of the overall main idea.

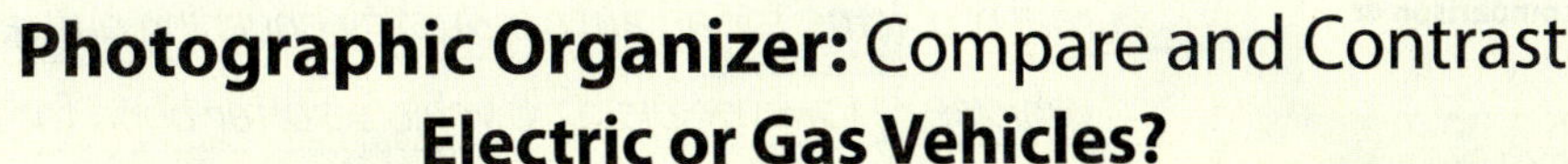

Photographic Organizer: Compare and Contrast

Electric or Gas Vehicles?

Electric Vehicles (Nissan Leaf)

SIMILAR TO OR DIFFERENT FROM

Gas Vehicles (Hyundai Accent)

What is the **1st** comparable point?

looks sporty and has standard features

looks sporty and has standard features

SIMILAR TO OR DIFFERENT FROM

What is the **2nd** comparable point?

powered by lithium ion battery

powered by V-8 engine

SIMILAR TO OR DIFFERENT FROM

What is the **3rd** comparable point?

uses electricity

uses gas

What's the point?

A comparison between electric vehicles and gas vehicles shows pleasing similarities but some major differences.

What's the Point? One Student's Response

The following paragraph offers one student's point about the similarities and differences between electric and gas vehicles as illustrated by the photographs. Read the comparison/contrast paragraph below and the explanations; then, complete the activities in **bold** type in the annotations. *Answers may vary.*

Logical Order: Words of comparison or contrast (such as *likewise, however*) signal similarities or differences. **Circle two more signal words or phrases for comparison or contrast.**

Main Idea: The main idea is the point the author is making about the topic. **Underline the two topics being compared and contrasted, and underline the author's point about the two topics.**

Relevant Details: Relevant details include descriptive details about similarities or differences between comparable points. **Draw a box around two more details of similarities or differences.**

Effective Expression: This sentence uses a semicolon to join ideas and give equal weight to both types of vehicles. **Double underline another sentence that expresses equal ideas with the use of semicolon.**

Electric or Gas Vehicles?

[1] Pollution, global warming, and the price of fuel pose real problems for an auto industry churning out gas vehicles. [2] However, electric vehicles offer hope for the future. [3] A comparison between electric vehicles and gas vehicles shows pleasing similarities and differences. [4] Most electric vehicles look just like a gas vehicle. [5] For example, the electric-powered Nissan Leaf resembles the gas-powered Hyundai Accent. [6] Both sport the sleek look of a family hatchback, and both have all the standard features, such as seating for five and plenty of storage space. [7] They even perform similarly; both go from 0 to 60 mph in 6 seconds. [8] Although these similarities promise to please, many drivers will really like the differences between electric and gas vehicles. [9] For example, the lithium-ion battery of the Nissan Leaf uses far less energy than the gas-guzzling engine of the Hyundai Accent. [10] The Nissan Leaf can go 102 to 129 miles between charges and costs about $6 to $12 a week in electricity; in contrast, the Hyundai Accent averages 28 miles per gallon in the city and 37 on the highway. [11] Plus, based on the price of oil, gasoline can cost as much as $5 a gallon, and those dollars add up with the miles. [12] The final difference is price. [13] A new Hyundai Accent sells for $18,235. [14] In contrast, a new Nissan Leaf retails for $31,820. [15] However, to promote electric cars, the government offers a $7,500 discount for the Nissan Leaf, bringing the cost down to $25,635. [16] Basically, one must decide if the higher cost of the electric car is worth it.

Comprehend and State a Main Idea Using the Comparison/Contrast Pattern

L2

A **comparison** states or explains the similarities between two or more topics.

A **contrast** states or explains the differences between two or more topics.

A **comparison/contrast** states or explains both the similarities and the differences between two or more topics.

A **comparison** makes a point by discussing the *similarities* between two or more topics. A **contrast** makes a point by discussing the *differences* between two or more topics. Sometimes, combining the two into a single comparison/contrast paragraph best supports a specific point or main idea. Effective readers take note of a writer's use of key words that signal the use of comparison/contrast patterns. **Comparison/contrast** signal words help readers grasp the main idea and flow of information. Thus, effective writers often include signal words in the topic sentence and paragraph body to indicate the use of the comparison/contrast pattern.

Words That Signal Comparison				
alike	equally	in the same way	likewise	similarity
as	in a similar fashion	just as	resemble	similarly
as well as	in a similar way	just like	same	
equal	in like manner	like	similar	

Words That Signal Contrast				
although	conversely	differently	more	on the other hand
as opposed to	despite	even though	most	still
at the same time	difference	in contrast	nevertheless	to the contrary
but	different	in spite of	on the contrary	unlike
by contrast	different from	instead	on the one hand	yet

The comparison/contrast pattern can be limited in three ways. Sometimes, the main idea focuses on just the similarities of the topics. Other times, the focus is only on the differences. The third focus includes both the similarities and the differences. Effective writers often include signal words in the topic sentence and paragraph body to indicate the focus on a comparison, a contrast, or a combination comparison/contrast. Thus, effective readers skim for comparison/contrast words to locate and comprehend a writer's focus and main idea.

Example

Survey the following paragraphs for the writers' uses of the comparison/contrast pattern. As you skim each paragraph, circle the topic as it appears throughout the paragraph. Underline the comparison/contrast signal words and the key details related to them. Then double underline the topic sentence, the sentence that best covers all of the details. After reading, identify the focus of the main idea as a comparison, a contrast, or a comparison/contrast.

HUMANS AND MICE: GENETIC SIMILARITIES

[1]The genetic similarities between humans and mice support the use of mice in scientific research. [2]Humans and mice both have about 30,000 genes. [3]In addition, 99 percent of the 30,000 genes in humans and mice are the same. [4]Another important similarity is that 90 percent of genes linked to diseases are identical in the human and the mouse.

1. This pattern of organization for this paragraph is
a. comparison. **b.** contrast. **c.** comparison/contrast.

Alec's Changed Behavior: Before versus After Counseling

[1]Alec behaved very differently after attending a series of counseling sessions aimed at improving his communication skills. [2]Quiet and withdrawn before counseling, Alec rarely spoke, smiled, or made eye contact with his coworkers as he passed them in the hallways or at their desks. [3]However, after counseling, he became more friendly and outgoing, taking time to make eye contact and speak with colleagues. [4]Even though Alec had rarely spoken to others in the hallways, he had often interrupted coworkers who were speaking during meetings. [5]In contrast, after counseling, he listened politely to others as they spoke during meetings.

2. This pattern of organization for this paragraph is
a. comparison. **b.** contrast. **c.** comparison/contrast.

Yoga and Pilates: The Similarities and Differences

[1]Although yoga and Pilates share similar characteristics, an important difference exists. [2]Both yoga and Pilates are low-impact forms of exercise that improve posture, flexibility, and concentration. [3]In addition, both emphasize that a balance between body and mind is important. [4]However, the primary goal of Pilates is to strengthen the midsection and buttocks. [5]Pilates calls this area of the body the "powerhouse." [6]On the other hand, yoga does not focus on any one part of the body. [7]Rather, yoga works the opposing muscles of the entire body.

3. This pattern of organization for this paragraph is
a. comparison. **b.** contrast. **c.** comparison/contrast.

Explanation

Compare your answers to the following student's think-aloud.

In the first paragraph the two topics being compared are humans and mice. I underlined the following signal words in the title and body of the paragraph: similarities, both, and, similarity, same, identical. *Key details introduced by the signal words are "both have about 30,000 genes," "99 percent of the 30,000 genes are the same," "90 percent of genes linked to diseases are identical." The topic sentence is the first sentence.*

In the second paragraph, the two topics being contrasted are Alec's behaviors before counseling and Alec's behaviors after counseling. This topic made me stop and think because it seemed at first that there was only one topic, which was Alec. But really, the topic is his "changed behavior." So I circled all the words that referred to or described Alec's behavior before and after counseling throughout the paragraph. I underlined the following signal words: Before, after, differently, however, even

CONTINUED

EXPLANATION *CONTINUED*

though, in contrast. *The topic sentence is sentence 1. In paragraph 3, the two topics being compared and contrasted are yoga and Pilates. I circled these topics as they appeared throughout the paragraph. The title states that the paragraph is going to focus on similarities and differences between the two exercises. I underlined the following signal words:* similarities, differences, although, and, similar, difference, both, however, on the other hand, rather. *The topic sentence of the paragraph is sentence 1. It is the only sentence that contains comparison/contrast signal words.*

1. (a) comparison. 2. (b) contrast. 3. (c) comparison/contrast

Practice 1

Comprehend a Main Idea Using Comparison/Contrast Order

Survey the following paragraph to identify the main idea. As you skim, annotate to identify the comparable topics, comparison/contrast signal words, and key details. Then answer the questions, state the main idea, and complete the chart that follows. Finally, in the blank below, provide a title for the paragraph that includes the topic and an appropriate comparison or contrast signal word. *Answers may vary.*

1. *The Similarities between Christianity and Islam*

[1]Two of the most influential religions, Christianity and Islam, actually share many similarities. [2]Both religions are monotheistic, worshipping one God, and the God of both religions is an all-powerful and all-knowing being. [2]Both Islam and Christianity believe God has a special relationship with humans. [3]Muslims and Christians have a similar view of God as the creator to whom they submit in obedience. [4]Islam and Christianity share a moral code based on a Covenant, or agreement, established by God. [5]Both religions view Satan in the same way, as an enemy of God and humanity.

[6]Likewise, Muslims and Christians agree that humans have free will and are going to face a final judgment based on their actions in light of God's moral code. [7]In a similar fashion, both revere Jesus Christ as a prophet of God who lived a holy life.

2. The pattern of organization for this paragraph is

a. comparison. **b.** contrast. **c.** comparison/contrast.

3. The sentence that best states the main idea is sentence 1.

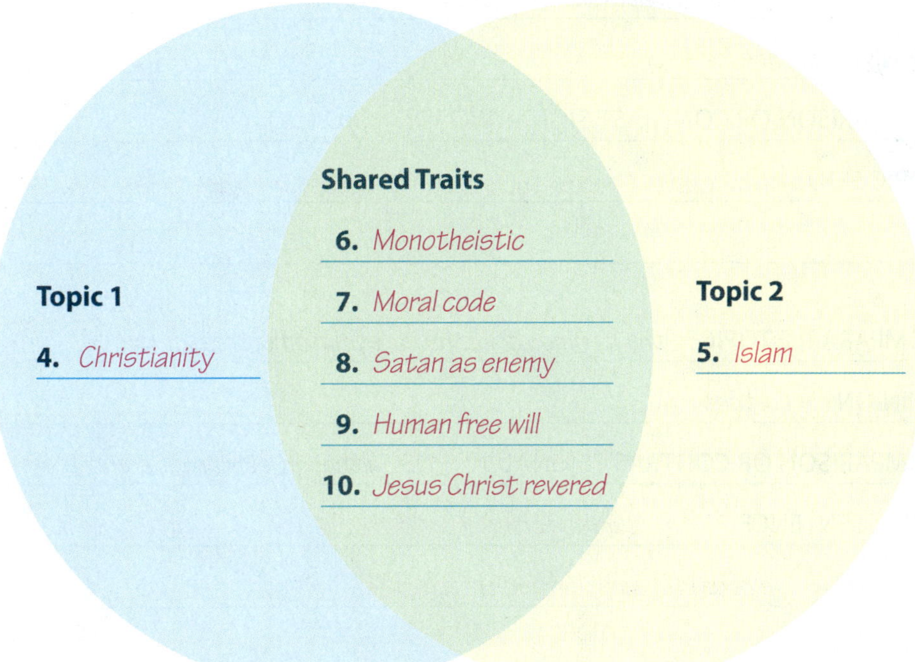

To write a comparison or a contrast piece, you limit your thoughts to a set of topics based on their relationship to each other. While several topics can be compared/contrasted, often writers limit their comparison/contrast to two. Most likely you have an opinion or belief about the two topics and their comparable points. Your opinion is your point or main idea. In a comparison or contrast paragraph, you also reveal your opinion by describing the points of similarity or difference between the topics in the order of your own choosing. A topic sentence states the overall point of the comparison, the contrast, or the comparison/contrast between the two topics.

For example, the following topic sentence contains (1) the comparable topics, (2) the writer's opinion about the topic, and (3) a signal word for pattern of organization used to organize details.

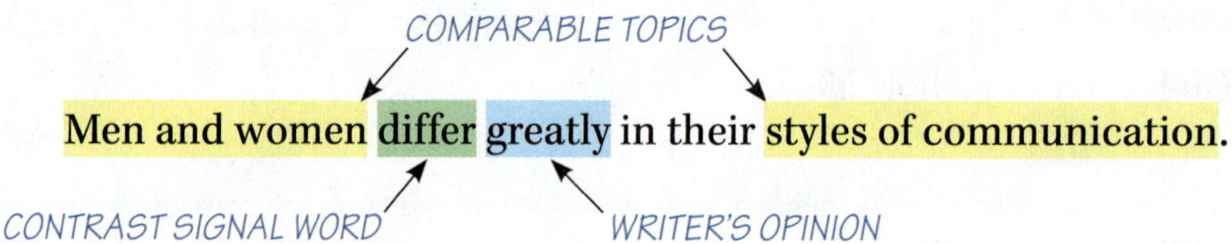

Example

Each of the items below presents a topic, an opinion, and comparison/contrast signal word(s). Combine the ideas in each group to create a topic sentence for a comparison, contrast, or comparison/contrast paragraph. *Answers may vary.*

1. COMPARABLE TOPICS: *capitalism, socialism*

OPINION: *visions for a society*

COMPARISON OR CONTRAST SIGNAL WORDS: *opposite*

TOPIC SENTENCE: *Capitalism and socialism offer opposite visions for a society.*

2. COMPARABLE TOPICS: *the common cold, the flu, symptoms, treatments*

OPINION: *important*

COMPARISON OR CONTRAST SIGNAL WORDS: *although, similar, differences*

TOPIC SENTENCE: *Although the common cold and flu seem similar, they do have important differences in symptoms and treatments.*

3. COMPARABLE TOPICS: *parental authority, peer pressure*

OPINION: *powers*

COMPARISON OR CONTRAST SIGNAL WORDS: *opposing*

TOPIC SENTENCE: *Parental authority and peer pressure are opposing powers.*

Explanation

Compare your responses to the following student's think-aloud.

I worked with these topic sentences for quite a while to reword each one different ways until I came up with sentences that seemed to flow smoothly and make sense. These ideas can be said in several different ways. This activity showed me how to use the comparison/contrast signal words to focus a topic on a comparison, a contrast, or a comparison/contrast. I can also see how each of these statements needs specific details to explain and support it. For example, I want to know the difference in symptoms and treatments between the cold and the flu. And I want to talk about the opposing powers of parents and peers. My final drafts for each topic sentence are the following.

1. *Capitalism and socialism offer opposite visions for a society.*
2. *Although the common cold and the flu seem similar, they do have important differences in symptoms and treatments.*
3. *Parental authority and peer pressure are opposing powers.*

Practice 2

State a Main Idea Using the Comparison/Contrast Pattern

Practice creating topic sentences. The three items present general comparable topics. You may choose your own topics. You are to narrow the comparable topics into a topic sentence. State an opinion. Choose comparison/contrast signal word(s). Then combine the ideas in each group to create a topic sentence for a comparison/contrast paragraph. *Answers may vary.*

1. COMPARABLE TOPIC: *an effective boss, an ineffective boss*

OPINION: ______

CONTINUED

PRACTICE 2 *CONTINUED*

COMPARISON/CONTRAST SIGNAL WORDS: ______

TOPIC SENTENCE: ______

______

2. COMPARABLE TOPICS: *walking, jogging*

OPINION: ______

COMPARISON/CONTRAST SIGNAL WORDS: ______

TOPIC SENTENCE: ______

______

3. COMPARABLE TOPICS: *infatuation, real love*

OPINION: ______

COMPARISON/CONTRAST SIGNAL WORDS: ______

TOPIC SENTENCE: ______

______

L3 Identify and Generate Relevant Details Using the Comparison/Contrast Pattern

To identify and generate details based on comparison or contrast, readers and writers may ask the reporter's questions *who*, *what*, *when*, *where*, *why*, and *how*. *Who* is being compared or contrasted? *What* places, objects, or ideas are being compared or contrasted? *What* are the specific similarities between the two ideas? *What* are the differences? *When* do the similarities or differences occur? *Where* do they occur? *Why* is this comparison or contrast significant? *How* do the people, places, things, or ideas differ? *How* do they agree? Answers to these questions enable readers to identify and writers to generate details to compare or contrast people, places, objects, and ideas. Usually, comparison/contrast transitions and signal words introduce these details. Some major and minor details may also explain the writer's opinion about the comparison or contrast. Many readers and writers use a concept map to identify and generate details.

Example

Assume you are taking a course in communication. Your professor has required you to read and respond to the following paragraph. Survey the paragraph for the writer's use of the comparison/contrast pattern. As you read, underline the compare/contrast signal words and the key details related to them. Then double underline the topic sentence. After reading, complete the comparison/contrast graphic organizer with information from the paragraph. *Answers may vary.*

CONFIRMATION AND DISCONFIRMATION

[1]The terms confirmation and disconfirmation refer to the extent to which you acknowledge another person. [2]*Disconfirmation* is a communication pattern in which you ignore someone's presence as well as that person's communications. [3]You say, in effect, that this person and what this person has to say are not worth serious attention or effort, that this person and this person's contributions are so unimportant or insignificant that there is no reason to concern yourself with them. [4]Note that disconfirmation is not the same as rejection. [5]In rejection you acknowledge but disagree with the person; you indicate your unwillingness to accept something the other person says or does. [6]In disconfirming someone, however, you deny that person's significance; you claim that what this person says or does simply does not count. [7]*Confirmation* is the opposite communication pattern. [8]In confirmation you not only acknowledge the presence of the other person but also indicate your acceptance of this person, of this person's self-definition, and of your relationship as defined or viewed by this other person. [9]Consider this situation. [10]You've been living with someone for the past six months, and you arrive home late one night. [11]Your partner, let's say Pat, is angry and complains about your being so late. [12]Which of the following is most likely to be your response?

- [13]Stop screaming. [14]I'm not interested in what you're babbling about. [15]I'll do what I want, when I want. [16]I'm going to bed.
- [17]What are you so angry about? [18]Didn't you get in three hours late last Thursday when you went to that office party? [19]So knock it off.
- [20]You have a right to be angry. [21]I should have called to tell you I was going to be late, but I got involved in an argument at work, and I couldn't leave until it was resolved.

[22]In the first response, you dismiss Pat's anger and even indicate dismissal of Pat as a person. [23]In the second response, you reject the validity of Pat's reasons for being angry but do not dismiss either Pat's feelings of anger or Pat as a person. [24]In the third response, you acknowledge Pat's anger and the reasons for it. [25]In addition, you provide some kind of explanation and, in doing so, show that both Pat's feelings and Pat as a person are important and that Pat has the right to know what happened. [26]The first response is an example of disconfirmation, the second of rejection, and the third of confirmation.

DeVito, Joseph A., *Interpersonal Messages: Communication and Relationship Skills*, 2nd ed., pp. 114–115.

Comparison/Contrast Concept Chart						
1	**Comparable Topics**	**Topic A:** *Disconfirmation*	**Like or Unlike**	**Topic B:** *Rejection*	**Like or Unlike**	**Topic C:** *Confirmation*
2	**1st Point of Comparison /Contrast**	communication pattern	*Like*	communication pattern	*Like*	communication pattern
3	**2nd Point of Comparison /Contrast**	*You ignore someone's presence as well as that person's communications.*	*Unlike*	You acknowledge the person.	*Unlike*	You acknowledge the presence of the other person.
4	**3rd Point of Comparison /Contrast**	*You deny that person's significance; you claim that what this person says or does simply does not count.*	*Unlike*	You disagree with the person. You indicate your unwillingness to accept something the other person says or does.	*Unlike*	*You indicate your acceptance of this person, of this person's self-definition, and of your relationship as defined or viewed by this other person.*
5	**4th Point of Comparison /Contrast (Examples)**	*I'm not interested in what you're babbling about.*	*Unlike*	*What are you so angry about?*	*Unlike*	*You have a right to be angry.*

Explanation

Compare your answers to the following student's think-aloud.

The writer discusses each comparable topic in a block of information. For example, the main comparable points of disconfirmation are discussed in sentences 3 and 4. Then sentences 4 through 6 discuss the topic of rejection. And sentences 7 and 8 discuss confirmation. A single sentence often states several comparable points. Completing the chart helped me pull out each comparable point for the three topics and see how each point relates to the others. Underlining the compare/contrast signal words made it clear that this is a contrast paragraph. The only similarity is that each of the three topics is "a communication pattern." I completed the chart with the following details. The fourth comparable point was the examples. The author gave each example and then later identified which communication pattern each one stood for. I only underlined and put in the chart the key part of each example.

1. Disconfirmation. Rejection. Confirmation.
2. Like. Like.
3. Unlike. You ignore someone's presence as well as that person's communications. Unlike.
4. You indicate your acceptance of this person, of this person's self-definition, and of your relationship as defined or viewed by this other person. Unlike. You deny that person's significance; you claim that what this person says or does simply does not count. Unlike.
5. You have a right to be angry. Unlike. I'm not interested in what you're babbling about. Unlike. What are you so angry about?

Just as a reader may use a compare/contrast concept map to comprehend a writer's point, a writer often uses a similar graphic organizer to generate details. A compare/contrast graphic organizer helps a writer create or access the major and minor similarities, differences, or both to make or support a point. At this point in the reading/writing process, a writer focuses on brainstorming details. In the next step, those details can be organized into a smooth and logical flow of ideas. A compare/contrast chart will make the next step easier to accomplish.

Example

Assume you are continuing to work on the assignment you received in your college communication class. You are ready to brainstorm a written response to the paragraph about the three patterns of communication: confirmation, disconfirmation, and rejection. Your professor has provided the following writing prompt to guide your response.

Assume you are the president of the Parent–Teacher Association (PTA) at your teenager's high school. You have decided to write an article for the PTA's online newsletter to discourage disconfirmation. Use the following scenario to make your point. The scenario asks you to write a confirming, a rejecting, and a disconfirming response. Explain the significance of each type of response and why a confirming response is the best.

CONTINUED

EXAMPLE *CONTINUED*

Enrique receives his semester grades. They are much better than last semester's grades, but they are still not great. After seeing his grade report, he says, "I really tried hard to get my grades up this semester." Enrique's parents respond (a) with disconfirmation, (b) with rejection, (c) with confirmation.

Use the compare/contrast concept chart to generate details for your response.

Compare/Contrast Concept Chart					
Comparable Topics	**Topic A:**	**Like or Unlike**	**Topic B:**	**Like or Unlike**	**Topic C:**
1st Point of Comparison/ Contrast					
2nd Point of Comparison/ Contrast					
3rd Point of Comparison/ Contrast					

Explanation

Compare your answers to the following student's think-aloud.

To contrast these three responses to Enrique, I organized the ideas in the following way. I first contrasted the parents' disconfirming, rejection, and confirming statements. The disconfirming statement says, "You are worthless." The confirming statement says, "I understand."

Next, I contrasted the significance of the responses. The disconfirming words ignore Enrique's value as a person. The confirming response offers support.

Finally, I contrasted the effects on Enrique. The disconfirming and rejection harm his self-worth. The confirming statement offers support.

Practice 3

Generate Relevant Comparison/Contrast Details

Choose one of the topic sentences you created in Practice 2. Use the following compare/contrast concept map to generate details to support your topic sentence. *Answers may vary.*

Compare/Contrast Concept Chart			
Comparable Topics	**Topic A:**	**Like or Unlike**	**Topic B:**
1st Point of Comparison/ Contrast			
2nd Point of Comparison/ Contrast			
3rd Point of Comparison/ Contrast			

Practice 4

Identify and Generate Details Using Comparison/Contrast Order

Assume you are taking a college sociology course. Your professor has asked you to select a current issue of importance, find and read an article about the issue, and respond to what you have read in writing. You found the following summary of a research project about distracted driving. Survey the paragraph for the writer's use of the comparison/contrast pattern. As you read, underline the comparison/contrast signal words and the key details related to them. Then double underline the topic sentence, the sentence that best covers all of the details. After reading, complete the compare/contrast chart with information from the paragraph. Finally, generate details to answer the reading response question that appears after the selection.

CONTINUED

COMPARISON OF THE CELL PHONE DRIVER AND THE DRUNK DRIVER

Objective: [1]The objective of this research was to determine the relative impairment associated with talking on a cellular telephone while driving. **Background:** [2]Research suggests that the relative risk of being in a traffic accident while using a cell phone is similar to the hazard associated with driving with a blood alcohol level at the legal limit. [3]The purpose of this research was to provide a direct comparison of the driving performance of a cell phone driver and a drunk driver in a controlled laboratory setting. **Method:** [4]We used a high-fidelity driving simulator. [5]We compared the performance of cell phone drivers with drivers who were intoxicated from ethanol. [6]Intoxicated drivers had a blood alcohol concentration at 0.08% weight/volume. **Results:** [7]When drivers were talking on either a handheld or hands-free cell phone, their braking reactions were delayed. [8]They took longer to recover speed lost after braking. [9]They were involved in more traffic accidents than when they were not conversing on a cell phone. [10]Finally, the driving distraction caused by talking on a cell phone was temporary, and attention quickly returned. [11]By contrast, when drivers were intoxicated from ethanol they exhibited a more aggressive driving style. [12]Unlike drivers distracted by cell phones, drunk drivers followed closer to the vehicle immediately in front of them. [13]They applied more force while braking than did drivers talking on cell phones. [14]And they had less time to collision after braking. [15]A final difference, driving distraction due to alcohol persists for prolonged periods of time, is systemic, and leads to chronic impairment. **Conclusion:** [17]When driving conditions and time on task were controlled, the impairments associated with using a cell phone while driving can be as profound as those associated with driving while drunk. **Application:** [18]This research may help to provide guidance for regulation addressing driver distraction caused by cell phone conversations.

Compare/Contrast Concept Chart		
Comparable Topics	**Topic A:** Driving while talking on a cell phone	**Topic B:** Driving while intoxicated
1st Point of Comparison /Contrast	Had delayed reactions Delayed braking reactions and took longer to recover speed lost after braking	Had more aggressive driving style Applied more force when braking
2nd Point of Comparison /Contrast	Longer following distances	Followed closer to the vehicle immediately in front of them
3rd Point of Comparison /Contrast	More accidents than when not using cell phone	Less time to collision after braking
4th Point of Comparison /Contrast	Driving distraction is temporary while on phone and attention quickly returns.	Driving distraction caused by alcohol persists for long periods of time, is systemic, and leads to chronic impairment.
Conclusion (Main Idea)	The impairments associated with using a cell phone while driving can be as profound as those associated with driving while drunk.	

CONTINUED

PRACTICE 4 *CONTINUED*

Reading Response Question: Write a letter to your local legislators asking them to support strong legislation about using a cell phone while driving. In your letter, compare cell phone drivers to drunk drivers in order to convince legislators to ban cell phone use while driving. Use a time-space graphic organizer or a flow chart to brainstorm your response. *Answers may vary.*

L4 Recognize and Create the Comparison/ Contrast Pattern

PREWRITE:
RECITE/REVIEW/
BRAINSTORM

DRAFT
YOUR
RESPONSE

When a reader recognizes that a writer is using the comparison/contrast pattern to organize ideas, he or she can see how the main idea and details fit together and anticipate upcoming details. When we use comparison/contrast transitions and signal words, we expect the topic to be limited and organized based on the similarities or differences between people, places, objects, or ideas. The writer's use of comparison/contrast transitions and signal words establishes the logical order of ideas and guides the reader through the comparison/ contrast argument.

Example

Assume you are working as a peer editor for a classmate in your college communication course. Your classmate drafted the following paragraph based on the details in her concept chart about disconfirming, rejecting, and confirming parents. Read and annotate her paragraph. Circle the main idea. Underline the comparison/contrast signal words and the key details. Cross out any details that are not relevant to the main idea. Suggest a change to improve the paragraph. Point out what you like about the use of comparison/ contrast in the paragraph. *Answers may vary.*

PTA NEWSLETTER: ARE YOU DISCONFIRMING, REJECTING, OR CONFIRMING YOUR STUDENT?

[1]For many students and parents, one of the most stressful times in the semester is when grades are reported. [2]Although parents may share their teenager's feelings of stress in the pressure to achieve high grades and get into college, parents need to understand the different and powerful role they play. [3]As parents, we can make the situation better or worse depending on our response when our teenagers do not perform as well as expected. [4]Consider the following scenario. [5]Enrique receives his semester grades. [6]They are much better than last semester's grades, but they are still not great. [7]After seeing his grade report, he says, "I really tried hard to get my grades up this semester." [8]Enrique's parents can respond three ways. [9]They can disconfirm, reject, or confirm Enrique and his efforts. [10]A disconfirming response says, "You are worthless. [11]When I was your age, I got straight A's." [12]This response ignores Enrique's statement that he tried. [13]It also ignores Enrique's value as a person by comparing his accomplishments to those of his parents. [14]Disconfirming responses harm a student's self-worth by ignoring him as a person and his efforts. [15]I heard too many disconfirming statements as a student. [16]A second slightly different way his parents may respond is by rejecting Enrique. [17]A rejecting response says, "You just didn't try hard enough. I know you can do better." [18]While this response does acknowledge Enrique as a person who is able to do better, it disagrees with his statement that he tried. [19]Rejecting statements harm the student's self-worth by ignoring his efforts; in contrast, the final and best response is the confirming response. [21]A confirming response says, "I understand you are discouraged, but you did improve. [22]Let's see what additional steps you can take to reach your goal." [23]Unlike the other two responses, this response recognizes Enrique's feelings and efforts and offers support. [24]Confirming responses build the student's self-worth by acknowledging his efforts and his beliefs.

Explanation

Compare your answers to the following student's think-aloud.

The third sentence states the main idea of the paragraph. This sentence lets the reader know that the purpose is to look at three different ways parents may respond to students. The writer's use of comparison/contrast words like both, better or worse, or, different, in contrast, *and* unlike *made the ideas easy to follow and understand. I crossed out sentence 15. This sentence stated the personal experience of the writer. In this paragraph, the writer's personal experience is not relevant to the main idea. It seemed out of place. I liked that the writer ended with the best response, confirming. While the third sentence did state the main idea of the paragraph, it didn't really focus on the contrast among the three responses. I suggest ending the paragraph with a more focused main idea statement that answers the question posed in the title, like this, "Rather than disconfirming or rejecting, confirming a student is the best response."*

Practice 5

Create Logical Order Using the Comparison/Contrast Pattern

Work with the compare/contrast concept chart you completed in Practice 3 or Practice 4. Write a rough draft of your paragraph using the details you generated. Work with a peer to review each other's rough drafts. Exchange, read, and review your drafts to make sure all details are relevant to the main ideas. Complete a compare/contrast concept chart of the draft you are peer editing. Circle the main idea. Underline the comparison/contrast signal words and the key details. Cross out any details that are not relevant to the main idea. Suggest a change to improve the paragraph. Point out what you like about the use of the comparison/contrast pattern in the paragraph. Return your reviewed paragraphs to each other. Revise as needed.

Analyze and Use Effective Expression with the Comparison/Contrast Pattern

L5

Effective expression reflects a writer's thoughtful match of ideas to words and structure. Two types of sentence structures enable effective expression of comparison or contrast: coordination and subordination.

Coordination expresses an **equal** relationship between topics. Coordination expresses similarities with words such as *and, likewise, similarly, also*. Coordination expresses an equal relationship between **differences** with words such as *but, yet, or, however, in contrast*.

A **compound** sentence is an example of **coordination**.

Examples

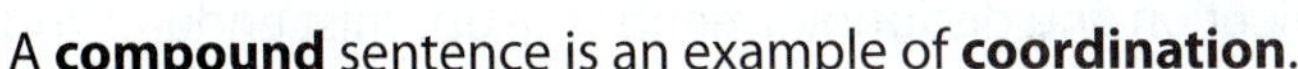

An athlete trains the body for competitions; *likewise*, a student trains the mind for final exams.

Althea enjoys watching sports, *but* she doesn't like participating in them.

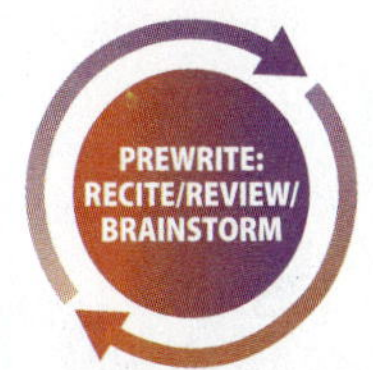

Subordination expresses an **unequal** relationship between topics. Subordination expresses **similarities** with words such as *as, just as, just like, like*. **Subordination** expresses an **unequal** relationship between **differences** with words such as *although, even though, while*.

A **complex sentence** is an example of **subordination**.

Examples

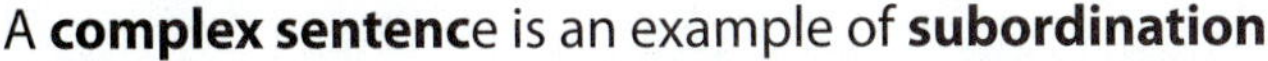

Just as an athlete trains the body for competitions, a student trains the mind for final exams.

Althea enjoys watching sports *even though* she doesn't like participating in them.

For more information about coordination and subordination see pages 635–646.

Example

Label each of the following sentences as a compound or a complex sentence. Identify the pattern of organization expressed by each sentence as comparison, contrast, or comparison/contrast.

1. Although the pessimist and the optimist face many of the same challenges in life, they differ greatly in their actions, words, and thoughts.

   SENTENCE TYPE: *complex*

   PATTERN OF ORGANIZATION: *comparison/contrast*

2. Just as the pessimist faces rejection and disappointments, the optimist endures those same hardships common to all humans.

   SENTENCE TYPE: *complex*

   PATTERN OF ORGANIZATION: *comparison*

3. The pessimist focuses on problems and remains passive; in contrast, the optimist focuses on solutions and takes action.

   SENTENCE TYPE: *compound*

   PATTERN OF ORGANIZATION: *contrast*

Explanation

Compare your answers to the following student's think-aloud.

1. *To help me figure out the sentence type and the pattern of organization, I underlined the comparison/contrast signal words. In the first sentence I underlined* although, same, differ. *These three words signal that the writer is going to compare and contrast the pessimist and the optimist. The word* although *signals a contrast and makes the first idea subordinate to the second idea. The word* same *states that the pessimist and optimist share challenges. The word* differ *signals a focus on the contrast of the reactions between the pessimist and the optimist. Sentence type: complex. Pattern of organization: comparison/contrast.*

2. *I underlined the signal words* just as, same, common. *These words signal that the writer is going to compare the hardships faced by both the pessimist and the optimist.* Just as *also makes the first idea subordinate to the second. Sentence type: complex. Pattern of organization: comparison.*

3. *I underlined the signal words* in contrast. *These words signal that the writer is going to contrast the focus of the pessimist to the focus of the optimist. The words* in contrast *signal that both ideas are equal, and the sentence uses coordination. Sentence type: compound. Pattern of organization: contrast.*

Practice 6

Analyze Effective Expression

Review the paragraph "PTA Newsletter: Are You Disconfirming, Rejecting, or Confirming Your Student?" given in the example on page 461. Analyze the writer's use of coordination and subordination. Identify two sentences that use coordination or subordination to make a comparison, contrast, or comparison/contrast. In the given spaces, record the sentences and the pattern of organization each one uses.

1. *Although parents may share their teenager's feelings of stress in the pressure to achieve high grades and get into college, parents need to understand the different and powerful role they play.*

   SENTENCE TYPE: *complex*

   PATTERN OF ORGANIZATION: *comparison/contrast*

2. *They are better than last semester's grades, but they are still not great.*

   SENTENCE TYPE: *compound*

   PATTERN OF ORGANIZATION: *contrast*

Practice 7

Use Effective Expression

Work with the rough draft of the paragraph you completed in an earlier practice. Choose two sentences and revise them to create effective expression through coordination and subordination. Use the following space to record your original and revised sentences.

Original sentence: ______________________________

____

____

Revised sentence: ______________________________

____

____

Original sentence: ______________________________

____

____

Revised sentence: ______________________________

____

____

Reading and Writing Assignments

MySkillsLab™
Complete these assignments in MySkillsLab.

Considering Audience and Purpose

Study the set of photographs at the beginning of the module that show the similarities and differences between electric and gas vehicles (page 443). Write a letter to your U.S. Senator or to the editor of your local newspaper. In your letter, call for support for either the electric or the gas vehicle. Explain the points of comparison that prove one better than the other.

Reading and Writing for Everyday Life

Assume that as the parent of a preteen, you are concerned about the trend to legalize marijuana. You have found the following information published by the Office of National Drug Control Policy. The article contrasts the myths with the facts about using marijuana. You want to share this information on a blog you write that is followed by several hundred families. Write a paragraph to the teenagers. Contrast the *two most important myths* about marijuana use with the *reality* of marijuana use.

WHAT AMERICANS NEED TO KNOW ABOUT MARIJUANA

Many of the things Americans "know" about marijuana are myths or misperceptions. People need to know the difference between the myths and the truth about this harmful drug. The first myth is the belief that marijuana is harmless. To the contrary, marijuana is far from harmless; in fact, recent scientific findings about the drug are startling. Most of the drug treatment for young people in the United States is for marijuana alone. Marijuana emergency-room mentions have skyrocketed over the past decade, and the drug is associated with an increased risk of developing schizophrenia, even when personality traits and pre-existing conditions are taken into account. Using marijuana may promote cancer of the respiratory tract and disrupt the immune system. The second myth asserts that marijuana is not addictive. However, marijuana has been proven to be a psychologically addictive drug. Scientists at the National Institute on Drug Abuse have demonstrated that laboratory animals will self-administer THC in doses equivalent to those used by humans who smoke marijuana. The third myth is youth experimentation with marijuana is inevitable. Just the opposite is true. Drug use can be prevented. The majority of young people do not use drugs, and there are proven ways to keep kids from starting. Contrary to popular belief, marijuana use is not a rite of passage. It is a risky behavior with serious consequences. Every American has a role to play in the effort to reduce marijuana use—at home and on the job, in schools, in places of worship, and in civic or social organizations. Working together, we can reaffirm healthy attitudes about marijuana use. Finally, a fourth myth is that marijuana is not associated with violence, as are drugs like cocaine and heroin. The criminalization of marijuana is what leads to crime, not the drug itself. It's not simply the trafficking of drugs that causes crime at home and abroad. Crime also results from the behavior of people who have drug dependencies.

Adapted from "What Americans Need to Know about Marijuana: Important Facts about Our Nation's Most Misunderstood Illegal Drug." Office of National Drug Policy. National Criminal Justice Reference Service. < https://www.ncjrs.gov/ondcppubs/publications/pdf/mj_rev.pdf>

Reading and Writing for College Life

Assume you are taking a college sociology class. Your professor has assigned the following passage as an introduction to the chapter "Socialization." You are to read the passage and write a response to the following prompt: How does childhood currently differ from childhood as described in the passage? Be prepared to share and discuss your response in class.

Childhood (From Birth to About Age 12) Differs Based on Geography and History

Consider how different your childhood would have been if you had grown up in another historical era. Historian Philippe Aries (1965) noticed that in European paintings from about A.D. 1000 to 1800 children were always dressed in adult clothing. If they were not depicted stiffly posed, as in a family portrait, they were shown doing adult activities.

The Artist's Family by Sofonisba Anguissola

From this, Aries drew a conclusion that sparked a debate among historians. He said that Europeans of this era did not regard childhood as a special time of life. They viewed children as miniature adults and put them to work at an early age. At the age of 7, for example, a boy might leave home for good to learn to be a jeweler or a stonecutter. A girl, in contrast, stayed home until she married, but by the age of 7 she assumed her share of the household tasks. Historians do not deny that these were the customs of that time, but some say that Aries' conclusion is ridiculous, that other evidence of that period indicates that these people viewed childhood as a special time of life (Orme 2002).

Having children work like adults did not disappear with the Middle Ages. This practice was still common around the world in the 1800s. Even today, children in the Least Industrialized Nations work in many occupations—from blacksmiths to waiters. As tourists are shocked to discover, children in these nations work as street peddlers, hawking everything from shoelaces to chewing gum.

In contemporary Western societies such as the United States, children are viewed as innocent and in need of protection from adult responsibilities such as work and self-support. Ideas of childhood vary historically and cross-culturally. From paintings, such as this 1559 Italian painting by Sofonisba Anguissola (1532–1625), "The Artist's Family," some historians conclude that Europeans once viewed children as miniature adults who assumed adult roles early in life.

Henslin, James M., *Essentials of Sociology: A Down-to-Earth Approach*, 9th ed., pp. 89–90.

Reading and Writing for Working Life

Assume you are a top manager at a 300-room upscale hotel. Your upper-level management team is meeting to consider two candidates for the assistant front-office manager position. Read the following memo from the hotel's human resource manager. Write a memo in response that offers your recommendation in support of one of the candidates. In your report answer the following questions: What are the qualifications for the job that should be considered for both candidates? Who would be the better person for the job? Why?

MEMO: HUMAN RESOURCE SUMMARY: CHARLES Y. AND NANCY X.

Charles Y. and Nancy X. both applied for the assistant front-office manager position at a 300-room upscale hotel. Charles has worked for a total of eight years in three different hotels and has been with this hotel for three months as a front-office associate. Initially, he had a lot of enthusiasm. Lately, however, he has been dressing a bit sloppily, and his figures, cash, and reports have been inaccurate. In addition, he is occasionally rattled by demanding guests.

Nancy recently graduated from college with honors, with a degree in hospitality management. While attending college, she worked part-time as a front desk associate at a budget motel. Nancy does not have a lot of experience working in a hotel or in customer service in general, but she is quite knowledgeable as a result of her studies and is eager to begin her career.

It appears that Charles would be considered a prime candidate for the office manager position because of his extensive experience in other hotels and his knowledge of the hotel's culture. In view of his recent performance, however, the division manager of rooms will need to sit down with Charles to review his future career development track.

Adapted from Walker, John R., *Introduction to Hospitality*, 6th ed., p. 548.

Workshop: Compose a Comparison/Contrast Paragraph

Choose a paragraph to read and respond to in writing. You may select a paragraph in an example, practice, or writing assignment within this module. Or you may select a paragraph of your own choosing. Use the following guide to comprehend and respond to the paragraph. Apply what you have learned about the comparison/contrast pattern to your reading/writing strategy.

Preread: Survey and Question

Ask questions about the text's features.

____

____

What is the passage about?

____

____

How is the material organized?

____

____

What do I already know about this topic? (What is my prior knowledge about the vocabulary?)

____

____

What is my purpose for reading/writing?

____

____

What points may I want to address or include in my written response?

____

____

Read and Annotate

As you read, annotate key ideas, particularly those details that answer your prereading questions.

Recite, Review, and Brainstorm

Recite the information. Summarize the most important parts. Answer your prereading questions. Rephrase ideas into your own words. Record changes in your opinions based on the new information. **Review** the information. **Brainstorm** ideas for your written response to the passage. **Freewrite** a response to what you have read. **Map** the relationship among ideas you have annotated in the text. **Outline** or list key ideas and details in blocks of thought. Use your own paper.

Write a Draft of Your Response

Using the ideas you generated by brainstorming, compose a draft of your response. Use your own paper.

Revise Your Draft

Once you have created a draft of a comparison/contrast response, read the draft to answer the questions in the "Questions for Revising a Comparison/Contrast Paragraph" box that follows. Indicate your answers by annotating your paper. If you answer "yes" to a question, underline, check, or circle examples. If you answer "no" to a question, write needed information in margins and draw lines to indicate placement of additional details. Revise your paragraph based on your reflection. (*Hint*: Experienced writers create several drafts as they focus on one or two questions per draft.)

Step by Step: Questions for Revising a Comparison/ Contrast Paragraph:

- ❑ Have I stated or implied a focused main idea?
- ❑ Have I stated or implied the specific points of comparison or contrast?
- ❑ Is the order of the comparison or contrast of specific points clear? Have I used strong transitions of comparison or contrast?
- ❑ Have I used concrete details to make my point?
- ❑ Have I made my point with adequate details?
- ❑ Have I included only the details that are relevant to my topic sentence?
- ❑ Have I used coordination and subordination to make the contrast or comparison clear to my readers?

Proofread Your Draft

Once you have made any revisions to your paragraph that may be needed, proofread your paragraph to eliminate careless errors.

Review Test

MySkillsLab™ Complete this Review Test in MySkillsLab.

Score (number correct) _____ x 10 =_____%

Read and annotate the following paragraph from a college business textbook. Underline the main idea, comparison/contrast signal words, and key details. Then, complete the study chart. Finally, respond to the writing prompts "Summary Response" and "What Do You Think?"

1350L/11.5 GE/225 words

WHICH IS BETTER—A STRONG DOLLAR OR A WEAK DOLLAR?

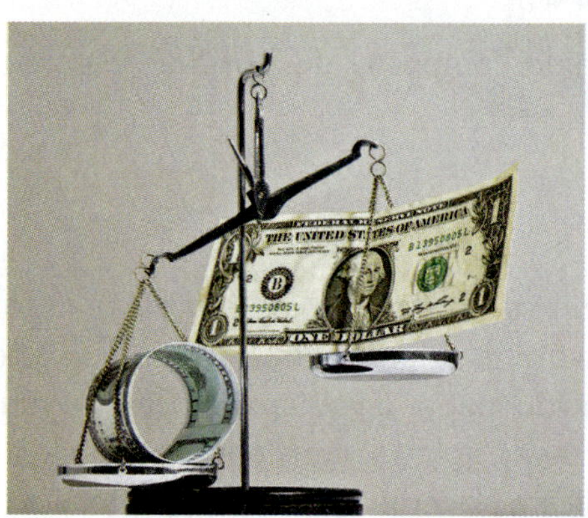

[1]The answer to this question depends on the type of business a firm undertakes. [2]Companies that do a lot of exporting—such as vehicle manufacturers, chemical manufacturers, and farmers—prefer a weak dollar because their product's price is lower in the global marketplace, so their sales and profits will be higher. [3]However companies that import components or finished goods for resale in the domestic market prefer a strong dollar because the relative price of their imports is lower. [4]From a consumer's perspective, a strong dollar is typically preferred because import prices are lower, which has a tendency to keep domestic competitors' prices low as well. [5]As an employee, if you work for a company that exports much of its product, you would prefer a weak dollar to stimulate sales and ensure your job security. [6]The benefits of a strong dollar for a nation as a whole are lower-priced imports, such as oil, lower prices, and a lower inflation rate in general. [7]A weak dollar, on the other hand, is good for domestic international business because it stimulates employment and raises standards of living. [8]The drawback of a weak dollar is the higher costs of energy and other imports that create higher rates of inflation. [9]So, which is better—a strong dollar or a weak dollar? [10]Like most real-world issues, the answer depends on your perspective.

Solomon, Michael R., *Better Business*, 3rd ed., p. 108.

Comparison/Contrast Study Chart:		
Points of Comparison	Topic 1: **(1)** *Strong Dollar*	Topic 2: **(2)** *Weak Dollar*
Companies that **(3)** *export* and their employees		preferred because products' price is lower and profits are higher, stimulates sales, ensures job security
Companies that **(4)** *import*	preferred because price of imports is **(5)** *lower*	
(6) *Consumers*	preferred because prices are lower	
National **(7)** *benefits*	causes **(8)** *lower prices and lower inflation*	stimulates **(9)** *employment, raises standard of living*
National drawbacks		causes **(10)** *higher costs of energy and higher rates of inflation*

Summary Response

Restate the writer's main ideas in your own words. Begin your summary response with the following: *The main idea of the paragraph "Which Is Better—A Strong Dollar or a Weak Dollar?" by Michael R. Solomon is . . .*

What Do You Think?

Assume you are taking a college class in business. Your professor has indicated that the differences between the strong dollar and the weak dollar will be a test question requiring a short-answer written response. In a paragraph, compare and contrast the strong dollar with the weak dollar. Use evidence from the text and provide real-world examples to illustrate the differences.

Academic Learning Log: Module Review

Summary of Key Concepts of the Comparison/Contrast Pattern

Assess your comprehension of the comparison/contrast pattern of organization.

LO1 LO2 LO3 LO4

1. To read or write a comparison/contrast paragraph, you identify or establish the *comparable points* between two (or more) topics.
2. The comparison/contrast pattern can be limited in *three* ways.
3. A comparison focuses on the *similarities* between topics.
4. A contrast focuses on the *differences* between topics.
5. A *comparison/contrast piece* focuses on the both the similarities and the differences between topics.
6. Signal words for comparison include *alike*, *as*, *equally*, *similarly*, *likewise*.
7. Signal words for contrast include *although*, *but*, *conversely*, *differently*, *unlike*.
8. To identify and generate details based on comparison or contrast, readers and writers may ask the reporter's questions *who*, *what*, *when*, *where*, *why* and *how*.

LO5

9. Coordination expresses an *equal* relationship between topics. A *compound* sentence is an example of coordination.
10. Subordination expresses an *unequal* relationship between topics. A *complex* sentence is an example of subordination.

Test Your Comprehension of the Comparison/Contrast Pattern

Respond in your own words to the following questions and prompts. *Answers may vary.*

Identify the focus of the comparison/contrast pattern used in each of the following topic sentences. Is the focus of the sentence a comparison, a contrast, or a comparison/contrast?

Contrast 1. Significant differences exist among children based on their birth order as first, middle, or last born.

Comparison/contrast 2. While iPhones and Android phones offer similar features, the differences between the two are worth noting.

Comparison 3. The writing style of Dean Koontz is similar to the style of Edgar Allen Poe.

L1 L2 L3 L4

On your own paper, create a blank compare/contrast concept chart.

L1 L2 L3 L4 L5

1. **How will I use what I have learned?** In your notebook, discuss how you will apply to your own reading/writing strategy what you have learned about comparison/contrast patterns. When will you apply this knowledge to your reading/writing strategy?
2. **What do I still need to study about the comparison/contrast patterns?** In your notebook, discuss your ongoing study needs. Describe what, when, and how you will continue studying and using the comparison/contrast patterns.

Complete the Post-test for Module 12 in MySkillsLab.

13 The Cause and Effect Pattern

LEARNING OUTCOMES

After studying this module you should be able to:

- **LO 1** Answer the Question "What's the Point of the Cause and Effect Pattern?"
- **LO 2** Comprehend and State a Main Idea Using the Cause and Effect Pattern
- **LO 3** Identify and Generate Relevant Details Using the Cause and Effect Pattern
- **LO 4** Recognize and Create the Cause and Effect Pattern
- **LO 5** Analyze and Use Effective Expression with the Cause and Effect Pattern

A *cause* is the reason an event takes place. An *effect* is the result of an event. Cause leads to effect. Understanding the relationship between cause and effect is a vital critical thinking skill used in all aspects of life. For example, when an illness strikes us, our physician must correctly identify the cause of our symptoms in order to treat us. In addition, the side effects of any medication prescribed to treat the illness must be taken into account. Thinking about cause and effect points out the relationship between events based on reasons and results. For example, in your personal life, you may have identified that stress causes you to overeat. In working life, you may have identified the need to master certain software programs to be competitive in the job market. In college life, you may have identified how logical causes and effects play a role in the study of history, science, or economics.

When you read or write a cause and effect paragraph, you analyze the reasons for and the results of an action, event, condition, decision, or belief. The focus of the paragraph may be only on the causes, only on the effects, or include both. As a reader, you identify the writer's focus, list the given causes or effects, and comprehend the main idea supported by the writer's explanation of causes or effects. As a writer, you must choose the causes or effects on which to focus. Often, there are too many causes or effects to explain in one paragraph or essay. So the writer decides which are the key causes or effects, and then establishes and explains the flow between cause and effect. An effective writer presents details in a logical order that explains why each cause leads to a specific effect. Both readers and writers test the truth of each cause.

WHAT'S THE POINT of the Cause and Effect Pattern?

Often ideas become clearer when they are analyzed based on how they relate to one another. The cause and effect pattern of organization allows readers and writers to explore the ways in which ideas are related based on reasons and results. The following photographs document a set of causes and effects. Study the images and write captions that identify the appropriate causes and effects illustrated. Answer the following questions: What is this? Why did it happen? What is this further effect? Then answer the question "What's the point?" with a one-sentence statement of the overall main idea. *Answers may vary.*

Photographic Organizer: Cause and Effect

One Cause—Multiple Effects

CAUSE

Effect 1

What is this effect?

healthy weight

Effect 2

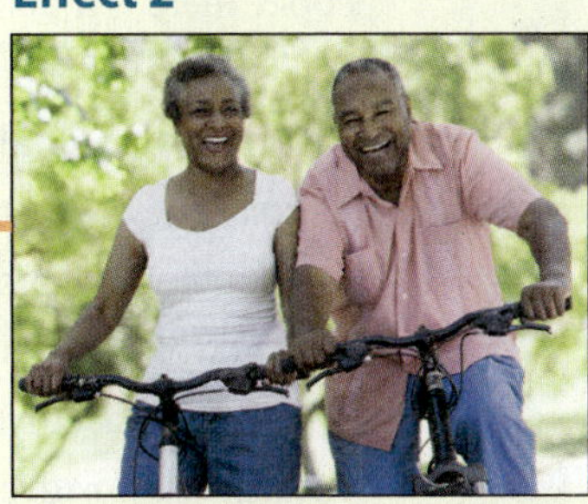

What is this effect?

well-being, long life

Effect 3

What is this effect?

restful sleep

What's the point?

Daily exercise leads to several benefits.

What's the Point? One Student's Response

The following paragraph offers one student's point about the causes and effects of daily exercise as illustrated by the photographs. Read the cause and effect paragraph below and the explanations; then complete the activities in **bold** type in the annotations.

Strong Transitions: The transitional word *because* signals that health and fitness are the result of daily exercise. **Circle two more transitional words or phrases that signal cause and effect.**

Relevant Details: Relevant details include examples or descriptions of causes and effects. **Draw boxes around two more relevant details that give examples or describe a cause or effect.**

Effective Expression: Precise word choice makes a point credible. Writers often confuse the word *affect*, a verb that means "to influence," with *effect*, a noun that means "result." **Double underline a verb that can be replaced with *affect(s)*. Double underline a noun that can be replaced with *effect*.**

THE BENEFITS OF EXERCISE

MARTIN AMEZCUA

[1] What can a person do to improve his or her life and live a long and healthy life? [2] It's not something that's a big secret or is in certain people's genes; it's regular exercise. [3] Studies have shown that people live long, healthy, and fit lives because of daily exercise. [4] It doesn't have to be some killer workout routine; it can be as simple as walking, playing sports, dancing, jogging, swimming, or walking the dog on a regular basis. [5] The most important benefit of exercise is that people who live active lives are less likely to get ill and generally live longer. [6] For example, lifting weights builds strong bones and muscles. [7] Walking, jogging, and swimming strengthen the heart and lungs. [8] Since illness occurs less frequently in active people, there is a possibility of avoiding some huge medical bills. [9] Aside from keeping one physically fit, another benefit is exercise helps improve mental health and general sense of well-being. [10] For example, one of the most commonly known benefits of exercise is the reduction of stress. [11] With less stress, a person is better able to focus on what's at hand. [12] On the other hand, exercise can cause a boost in self-esteem and confidence—one of the most overlooked benefits. [13] A positive mindset affects the way a person feels about self, others, and life. [14] One of the least obvious benefits of exercise is that it can help a person get good sleep. [15] Many suffer from sleeping disorders or don't get a good night's rest because they still have a lot on their mind. [16] Exercising exhausts a person's body and mind, helping to reduce anxious thoughts, and in return helps with sleep. [17] Regular exercise promotes health and well-being.

Main Idea: The main idea is the point Martin is making about the topic *exercise*. **Underline his point about this topic**.

Comprehend and State a Main Idea Using the Cause and Effect Pattern

LO2

Readers and writers rely on cause and effect to understand or communicate a variety of factors that connect ideas. These factors or connections focus on specific aspects of the cause and effect pattern. A **cause** states why something happens. An **effect** states a result or outcome. At times, a single cause leads to several effects. For example, "Stress leads to short- and long-term effects." Other times, several causes contribute to a single effect. For example, "Several factors contribute to success on the job." Still other times, a chain of causes and effects occurs in a series of events known as a causal chain. A **causal chain** is a sequence of events in which any one event in the chain causes the next one, leading up to a final effect. For example, "A series of events led to the fall of ancient Rome." Effective readers skim a paragraph for use of cause and effect signal words to identify the writer's focus and main idea. To ensure that readers grasp their focus and point, effective writers often use cause and effect transitions and signal words in the topic sentence.

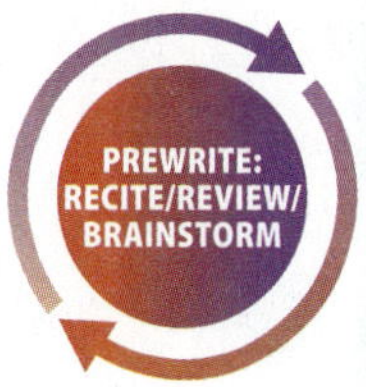

A **cause** is something or someone that creates an effect, brings about a result, has a consequence, or is the reason for a condition.

An **effect** is a result, condition, or consequence that is brought about by a cause or agent of change.

A **causal chain** is a linked sequence of events in which any one event in the chain causes the next one, leading up to a final effect.

Transitions That Signal Cause and Effect

accordingly	consequently	hence	on account of	so
as a result	due to	if…then	results in	therefore
because of	for that reason	leads to	since	thus

Verbs That Signal Cause and Effect (sample list)

affect	constitute	create	force	initiate	restrain
benefit	construct	damage	harm	institute	stop
cause	contribute	determine	induce	preclude	
compose	control	facilitate	influence	prevent	

Nouns That Signal Cause and Effect (sample list)

actor	consequence	end	impact	product
agent	creation	event	influence	result
author	creator	factor	issue	source
benefit	damage	grounds	outcome	
condition	effect	harm	outgrowth	

The cause and effect pattern can be limited in several ways. A writer may choose to limit the focus to include only causes or only effects or expand the discussion to both causes and effects. Effective writers often include signal words in the topic sentence and paragraph body to indicate the focus on causes, effects, or causes and effects. Thus, effective readers skim for cause and effect transitions and signal words to locate and comprehend a writer's focus and main idea.

Example

Survey the following paragraphs for the writers' uses of the cause and effect pattern. As you skim each paragraph, circle the topic as it appears throughout the paragraph. Underline the cause and effect transitions and signal words and the key details related to them. Then double underline the topic sentence, the sentence that best covers all of the details. After reading, identify the focus of the main idea: cause, effect, or cause and effect.

THE REASONS WE SELF-DISCLOSE

[1]Self-disclosure refers to communicating information about yourself to another person. [2]Usually, this is information that you normally keep hidden. [3]It may involve information about your values, beliefs, and desires. [4]You probably self-disclose for a variety of reasons. [5]Perhaps you feel the need for catharsis—a need to get rid of guilty feelings to confess wrongdoing. [6]You might also disclose to help the listener—to show the listener, for example, how you dealt with an addiction or succeeded in getting a promotion. [7]And you may self-disclose to encourage relationship growth, to maintain or repair a relationship, or even as a strategy for ending a relationship.

DeVito, Joseph A., *Interpersonal Messages: Communication and Relationship Skills,* 2nd ed., p. 189.

1. The focus of the cause and effect pattern for this paragraph is

(a.) multiple causes with one effect.

b. one cause with multiple effects.

c. causal chain—a cause leads to an effect, which becomes the cause of the next effect, and so on.

THE ORIGIN AND INFLUENCE OF MASS MEDIA

[1]Far beyond serving simply as sources of information, mass media influence many of our attitudes. [2]Mass media affect our views toward social issues, the ways that we view other people, and even our self-concept. [3]Because media significantly shape public opinion, all governments attempt to influence them. [4]Totalitarian governments try to control them. [5]The mass media are relatively new in human history. [6]They owe their origins to the invention of the printing press in the 1400s. [7]This invention had profound consequences on all social institutions. [8]The printing of the Bible altered religion, for instance. [9]The publication of political broadsides and newspapers altered politics. [10]From these beginnings, a series of inventions—from radio and movies to television and the microchip—has made the media an increasingly powerful force. [11]One of the most significant questions we can ask about this social institution is, Who controls mass media?

[12]That control, which in totalitarian countries is obvious, is much less visible in democratic nations. [13]Some might conclude that the media in a democratic nation represent the varied interests of many groups that make up that nation. [14]Others see the matter quite differently: the mass media—at least the country's most influential newspapers and television stations—represent the interest of the political elite. [15]They give coverage to mildly dissenting opinions, but they stand solidly behind the government. [16]The most obvious example is the positive treatment that media give to the inauguration of a president. [17]Since the mass media are so influential in our lives, it is vital to understand who controls the media.

Adapted from Henslin, James M., *Sociology: A Down-to-Earth Approach,* 10th ed., pp. 102–103.

2. The focus of the cause and effect pattern for this paragraph is

- **a.** multiple causes with one effect.
- **b.** one cause with multiple effects.
- **c.** causal chain—a cause leads to an effect, which becomes the cause of the next effect, and so on.

The Cause and Result of the Mass Extinction Event

[1]Scientists believe that around 65 million years ago—at the end of the Cretaceous period, in the region of the Yucatan Peninsula—a large meteorite struck Earth's surface. [2]The impact left a crater 180 km in diameter under the waters of the Caribbean. [3]Evidence from deep-sea sediment cores reveals a remarkable record of the meteorite's impact and the resulting debris. [4]The debris blasted high into the atmosphere. [5]This cloud of debris may have triggered a major decline in Earth's temperature. [6]Scientists now believe the assault by this massive asteroid or comet was largely responsible for the extinction of 70 percent of all species inhabiting Earth at that time, including the dinosaurs. [7]In the period that followed, the various species that eventually dominated the oceans and land surface changed dramatically from the previous inhabitants. [8]Scientists refer to the loss of species at the end of the Cretaceous as a mass extinction event.

Adapted from Smith, Thomas M., and Smith Robert Leo, *Elements of Ecology,* 8th ed., p. 566.

3. The focus of the cause and effect pattern for this paragraph is

- **a.** multiple causes with one effect.
- **b.** one cause with multiple effects.
- **c.** causal chain—a cause leads to an effect, which becomes the cause of the next effect, and so on.

Explanation

Compare your answers to the following student's think-aloud.

In the first paragraph, I circled the terms self-disclosure, disclose, and self-disclose. *I also circled the word* confess *in sentence 5 as a synonym for disclose. I underlined the cause and effect signal word* reasons, *once in the title and in sentence 4. I double underlined sentence 4 as the topic sentence because the topic "self-disclose" was limited by the cause and effect signal words "for a variety of reasons." This sentence best covers all the details in the paragraph. The writer used the verbs "to help," "to show," "to encourage" as the "variety of reasons" for self-disclosure. This paragraph mainly focuses on the causes for self-disclosure.*

In the second paragraph, I circled the words Mass Media *in the title and every time they appeared in the paragraph. I also circled* printing press *and* printing *because they are examples of mass media. I underlined the following words that signaled cause or effect:* origin, Influence, sources, affect, consequences, altered, force, control. *Identifying the focus of the paragraph required careful analysis of the writer's use of these words. For example, the wording of sentence 10 suggests a causal chain that begins with the printing press and then leads systematically to the microchip. But this idea isn't the focus of the whole paragraph, only this one sentence. The focus is really on various effects of mass media from their origin to the present. Sentence 17 is the topic sentence that best covers all the details.*

In the third paragraph, I circled the words Mass Extinction Event, meteorite, debris, assault, asteroid, comet. *I underlined the cause and effect signals "Cause and Result," "impact," "resulting," "may have triggered," "responsible." I also underlined the following key details: "left crater 180km in diameter," "decline in temperature," "extinction of 70 percent of species," "including dinosaurs." Sentence 8 is the topic sentence.*

1. (a) multiple causes with one effect. 2. (b) one cause with multiple effects. 3. (c) causal chain—a cause leads to effect, which becomes a cause of the next effect, and so on.

Practice 1

Comprehend a Main Idea Using the Cause and Effect Pattern

Survey the following paragraph from a college communication textbook to identify the main idea. As you skim, annotate the topic, cause and effect transitions or signal words, and key details. Then answer the questions. Complete the chart that follows the paragraph. Finally, in the blank below, provide a title for the paragraph. In your title, include the topic and appropriate cause and effect signal words. *Answers may vary.*

1. *Communication Effects*

[1]Communication always has some effect on those involved in the communication act. [2]For every communication act, there is some consequence. [3]For example, you may gain knowledge or learn how to analyze, synthesize, or evaluate something. [4]These are intellectual or cognitive effects. [5]You may acquire affective effects such as new feelings, attitudes, or beliefs, or change existing ones. [6]You may also gain psychomotor effects by learning new bodily movements such as how to throw a curve ball, paint a picture, give a compliment, or express surprise.

DeVito, Joseph A., *Essentials of Human Communication*, 4th ed., p. 9.

2. The focus of the cause and effect pattern for this paragraph is

a. multiple causes with one effect.

(b.) one cause with multiple effects.

c. causal chain—a cause leads to an effect, which becomes a cause of the next effect, and so on.

3. The sentence that best states the main idea is sentence *1 or 2*.

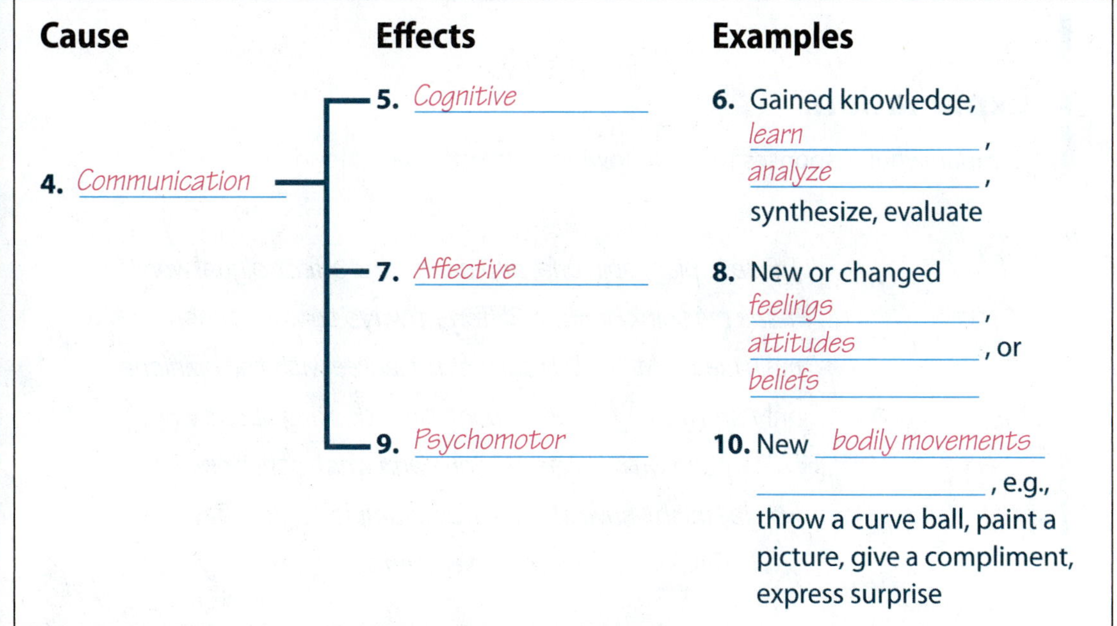

To write a cause and effect paragraph you limit your thoughts to the reasons and/or results of an action, event, condition, decision, or belief. Most likely you have an opinion or belief about the causes or effects of the action, event, condition, decision, or belief. Your opinion is your point or main idea. In a cause and effect paragraph, you also reveal your opinion by the value or importance you assign to each cause or effect you discuss. A topic sentence states the overall point of the cause and effect paragraph. For example, the following topic sentence contains (1) a topic, (2) the writer's opinion about the topic, and (3) signal words for the cause and effect pattern of organization.

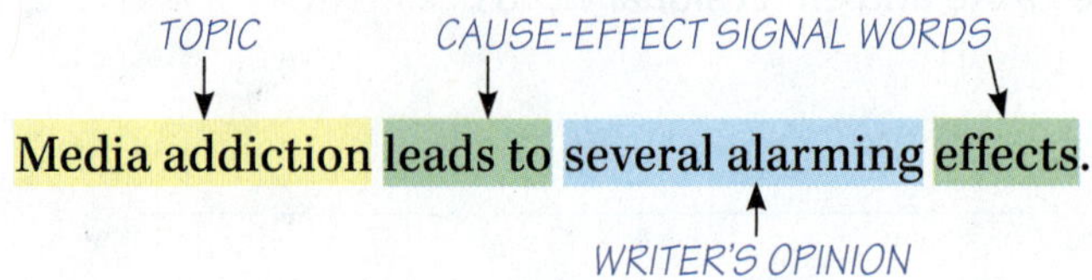

Example

Each of the items below presents a topic, an opinion, and cause and effect signal word(s). Combine the ideas in each group to create a topic sentence for a paragraph based on cause, effect, or cause and effect. *Answers may vary.*

1. TOPIC: *smoking cigarettes* OPINION: *only adverse*

CAUSE OR EFFECT SIGNAL WORDS: *leads to physical effects*

TOPIC SENTENCE: *Smoking cigarettes only leads to adverse physical effects.*

2. TOPIC: *bullying* OPINION: *mainly low self-esteem and anger*

CAUSE OR EFFECT SIGNAL WORDS: *stems from*

TOPIC SENTENCE: *Bullying mainly stems from low self-esteem and anger.*

Explanation

Compare your responses to the following student's think-aloud.

These topics, opinions, and cause and effect signal words made me think of many different ways to word these main ideas. At first, I really didn't agree with the opinions only and mainly. Thus, I spent time thinking about why I disagreed with these opinions and what other opinion words I might have chosen. For example, I might have said, "Smoking cigarettes may lead to adverse physical effects." I wanted to avoid taking such a harsh stand, thinking it more fair to take a softer tone. However, after thinking it through, I feel more comfortable with the harsher approach due to the real physical harm smoking causes. I did move the word only *to describe "leads to" instead of "adverse physical effects." I'm still not sure I agree that the main causes of bullying are "low self-esteem and anger." But that's the point. These words state an opinion about the cause of bullying that must be explained. I wrote the following sentences.*

1. *Smoking cigarettes only leads to adverse physical effects.*
2. *Bullying mainly stems from low self-esteem and anger.*

Practice 2

State a Main Idea Using the Cause and Effect Pattern

Each of the items presents a topic. Limit the topic by filling in the blanks with an opinion and cause or effect signal word(s). Then combine the ideas in each group to create a topic sentence for a cause and effect paragraph. *Answers may vary.*

1. TOPIC: *academic cheating* OPINION: ______

CAUSE OR EFFECT SIGNAL WORDS: ______

TOPIC SENTENCE: ______

______

2. TOPIC: *stress* OPINION: ______

CAUSE OR EFFECT SIGNAL WORDS: ______

TOPIC SENTENCE: ______

______

L3 Identify and Generate Relevant Details Using the Cause and Effect Pattern

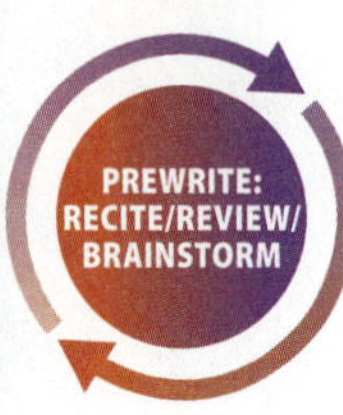

To identify and generate details based on cause and effect, readers and writers may ask the reporter's questions *why* and *what*. *Why* has this occurred? *What* are the causes? *What* are the effects? These questions may also focus on one or more of the following traits of causes and effects: major or minor, long term or short term, obvious or subtle. *What* are the major causes? *What* are the major effects? *What* are the minor causes or effects? *What* are the long-term causes or effects? *What* are the short-term or immediate causes or effects? *What* are the obvious or clear causes or effects? *What* are the subtle, unseen, or indirect causes or effects? Answers to these questions enable readers to identify and writers to generate details to explain the causes or effects of an action, event, condition, decision, or belief. Usually, cause and effect transitions and signal words introduce these details. Since causes and effects are often listed or occur in time, transitions such as *first*, *next*, and *ultimately* are also used to identify or introduce a cause or effect. Some details may also explain the writer's opinion about the cause or effect. Many readers and writers use a cause and effect flow chart or concept map to identify and generate details.

Example

Assume you are taking a college health course. Your professor has asked you to read and respond to the following two paragraphs in the textbook *Access to Health*. Survey the paragraphs for the writer's use of cause and effect. As you read, underline the cause and effect signal words and key details. Then double underline the topic sentence of each paragraph. After reading, answer the questions that follow. Complete the cause and effect concept map with information from both paragraphs. *Answers may vary.*

CHOOSE HEALTH NOW FOR IMMEDIATE BENEFITS

[1]Almost everyone knows that overeating leads to weight gain, or that drinking and driving increases the risk of motor vehicle accidents. [2]But other, subtler choices you make every day may be influencing your well-being in ways you're not aware of. [3]For instance, did you know that the amount of sleep you get each night could affect your body weight, your ability to ward off colds, your mood, and your driving? [4]What's more, inadequate sleep is one of the most commonly reported barriers to academic success. [5]Another example is smoking. [6]Smoking has many immediate health effects. [7]Some include fatigue, throat irritation, and breathing problems. [8]Smoking also increases your vulnerability to colds and other infections. [9]A second example is drinking alcohol. [10]Drinking alcohol reduces your immediate health and your academic performance. [11]It also sharply increases your risk of unintentional injuries—not only motor vehicle accidents, but also falls, drownings, and other harm or damage. [12]This is especially significant

because for people between the ages of 15 and 44, unintentional injury—whether related to alcohol use or any other factor—is the leading cause of death. [13]Clearly, healthy choices have immediate benefits. [14]When you're well nourished, fit, rested, and free from the influence of nicotine, alcohol, and other drugs, you're more likely to avoid illness, succeed in school, maintain supportive relationships, participate in meaningful work and community activities, and enjoy your leisure time.

CHOOSE HEALTH NOW FOR LONG-TERM REWARDS

[1]The choices you make today are like seeds: Planting good seeds means you're more likely to enjoy the fruits of good health. [2]Good health includes not only a longer life, but also a higher quality of life. [3]In contrast, poor choices increase the likelihood of a shorter life, as well as persistent illness, addiction, and other limitations on quality of life. [4]In other words, successful aging starts now. [5]Personal choices influence your life expectancy. [6]According to current statistics, the average life expectancy at birth in the United States is projected to be 78.5 years for a child born in 2012. [7]In other words, we can expect that American infants born today will live to an average age of over 78 years. [8]This is much longer than the 47-year life expectancy for people born in the early 1900s. [9]That's because life expectancy 100 years ago was largely determined by our susceptibility to infectious disease. [10]In 1900, over 30 percent of all deaths occurred among children under 5 years old. [11]And the leading cause of death was infection. [12]Even among adults, infectious diseases such as tuberculosis and pneumonia were the leading causes of death. [13]And widespread epidemics of infectious diseases such as cholera and influenza crossed national boundaries to kill millions. [14]With the development of vaccines and antibiotics, life expectancy increased dramatically. [15]At the same time, premature deaths from infectious diseases decreased. [16]As a result, the leading cause of death shifted to chronic diseases. [17]These included heart disease, cerebrovascular disease (which leads to strokes), cancer, and chronic lower respiratory diseases. [18]At the same time, advances in diagnostic technologies, heart and brain surgery, radiation and other cancer treatments, as well as new medications continued the trend of increasing life expectancy into the twenty-first century. [19]Another significant benefit of good choices is the increase of your healthy life expectancy. [20]Your

CONTINUED

EXAMPLE *CONTINUED*

healthy life expectancy is the number of years of full health you enjoy without disability, chronic pain, or significant illnesses. [21]Another aspect of healthy life expectancy is **healthy related quality of life (HRQoL).** [22]HRQoL includes physical, mental, emotional, and social function. [23]HRQoL focuses on the impact the health status has on overall quality of life.

Adapted from Donatelle, Rebecca J., *Access to Health*, 13th ed., pp. 4–5.

1. Which sentence is the topic sentence for paragraph 1?

a. sentence 1
b. sentence 2
c. sentence 3
(d.) sentence 13

2. Which sentence is the topic sentence for paragraph 2?

(a.) sentence 1
b. sentence 2
c. sentence 3
d. sentence 5

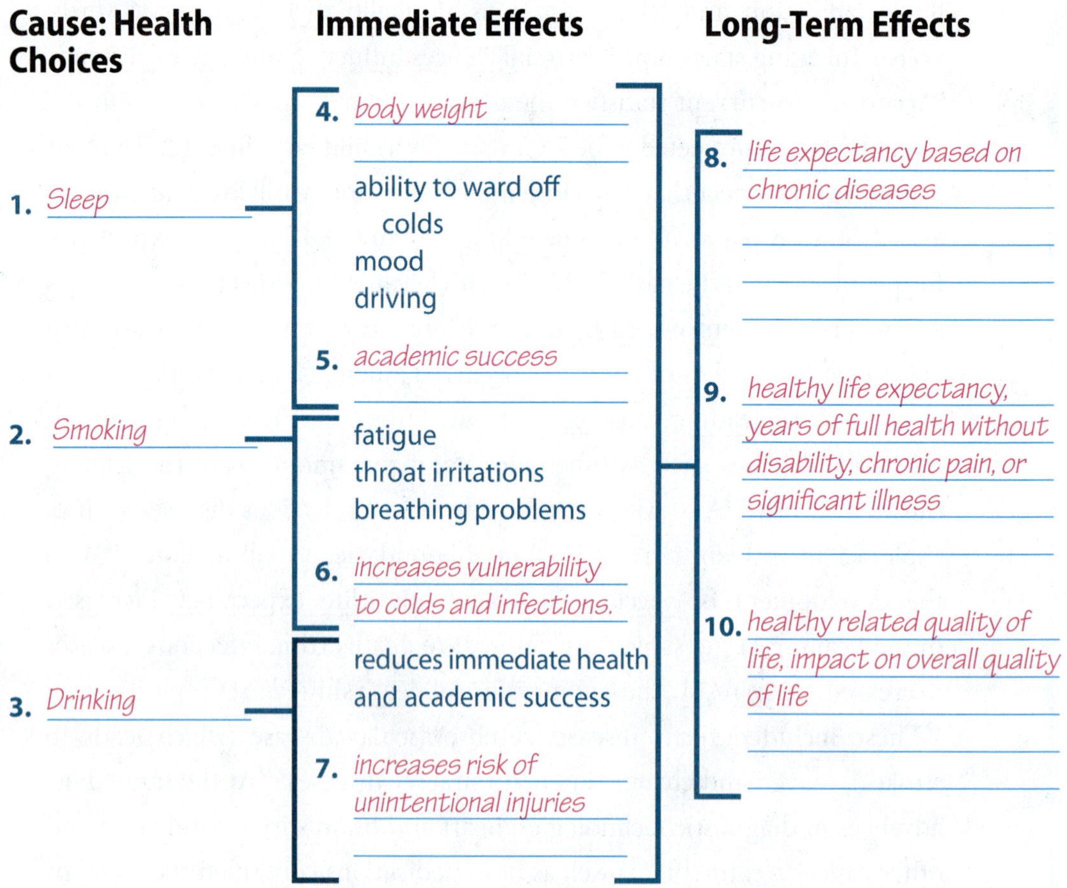

Cause: Health Choices	Immediate Effects	Long-Term Effects
1. *Sleep*	**4.** *body weight* ability to ward off colds mood driving **5.** *academic success*	**8.** *life expectancy based on chronic diseases*
2. *Smoking*	fatigue throat irritations breathing problems **6.** *increases vulnerability to colds and infections.*	**9.** *healthy life expectancy, years of full health without disability, chronic pain, or significant illness*
3. *Drinking*	reduces immediate health and academic success **7.** *increases risk of unintentional injuries*	**10.** *healthy related quality of life, impact on overall quality of life*

Explanation

Compare your answers to the following student's think-aloud.

Annotating the paragraphs helped me in two ways. For one thing, annotating helped identify the topic sentences in both paragraphs. First, I skimmed for the cause and effect signal words and underlined the key details in both paragraphs. Then I looked for the sentences that best covered the details and stated the main ideas. In the first paragraph, I underlined cause and effect words like immediate, benefits, leads to, increases, influencing, affect, effects, reduces, leading cause, influence. *These words stated the effects of health choices such as* sleep, smoking, *and* drinking alcohol. *In the second paragraph, I underlined the cause and effect signal words* long-term rewards, increase, determined, leading cause, increased, as a result, benefit, impact. *These words stated the effects of personal choices on life expectancy, healthy life expectancy, and healthy related quality of life. Annotating also helped me complete the cause and effect concept map with the details I underlined.*

1. *The topic sentence is (d) 13. The title of the paragraph states the focus is "immediate benefits," and this sentence summarizes that focus. Sentence 1 (a) states facts, not a main idea that needs to be explained. Sentence 2 (b) focuses on "subtler choices." I think the writer used these details to emphasize the importance of making healthy choices. Sentence 3 (c) is an example of sentence 2.*

2. *The topic sentence is (a) sentence 2. This sentence states both of the long-term benefits to healthy choices that are discussed throughout the paragraph. Sentence 1 (a) is a general statement that introduces the topic. Sentence 3 (c) states a detail that contrasts the effects of poor health choices with the rewards of good health choices. Sentence 5 (d) states a major detail, a major reward of good health choices.*

Just as a reader may use a cause and effect concept map to comprehend a writer's point, a writer often uses a similar graphic organizer to generate details. A cause and effect graphic organizer helps a writer create or access the major and minor, long-term and short-term, obvious and subtle causes and effects. At this point in the reading/writing process, a writer focuses on brainstorming details. In the next step, those details can be organized into a smooth and logical flow of ideas. A cause and effect map will make the next step easier to accomplish.

Example

Assume you are continuing to work on the assignment you received in your college health class. You are ready to brainstorm a written response to the paragraphs about the immediate and long-term benefits or rewards of good health choices. Your professor has provided the following writing prompt to guide your response:

> Identify two healthy choices an individual can make that lead to immediate and long-term effects. Explain the immediate effects of these two choices and how they affect life expectancy and healthy life expectancy.

Use the cause and effect concept map to generate details for your written response.
Answers may vary.

Cause and Effect Concept Map		
Causes: Health Choices	**Immediate Effects**	**Long-Term Effects**
Healthful diet	*weight management* *better body functions* *increased energy* *ability to ward off colds and other infections*	*reduces chances of chronic illnesses such as heart disease* *extends life expectancy* *increases number of healthy years lived* *HRQoL*
Daily exercise	*weight management* *strengthens heart, lungs, bones* *better mental function* *self-discipline*	*reduces chances of chronic illnesses* *increases number of healthy years lived* *HRQoL*

Explanation

Compare your answers to the following student's think-aloud.

The two healthy choices I decided to discuss are a healthy diet and daily exercise. As I generated details for the cause and effect concept map, it became clear that both choices led to the same immediate and long-term effects. It's like healthful diet and daily exercise work together to make the body stronger and last longer. The cause and effect concept map let me see how to set up the flow of details when I start my first draft.

Cause and Effect Concept Map		
Causes: Health Choices	**Immediate Effects**	**Long-Term Effects**
Healthful diet	*weight management* *better body functions* *increased energy* *ability to ward off colds and other infections*	*reduces chances of chronic illnesses such as heart disease* *extends life expectancy* *increases number of healthy years lived* *HRQoL*
Daily exercise	*weight management* *strengthens heart, lungs, bones* *better mental function* *self-discipline*	*reduces chances of chronic illnesses* *extends life expectancy* *increases number of healthy years lived* *HRQoL*

Practice 3

Generate Relevant Cause and Effect Details

Choose one of the topic sentences you created in Practice 2. Use or adapt the following cause and effect concept map to generate details to support your topic sentence.

Answers may vary.

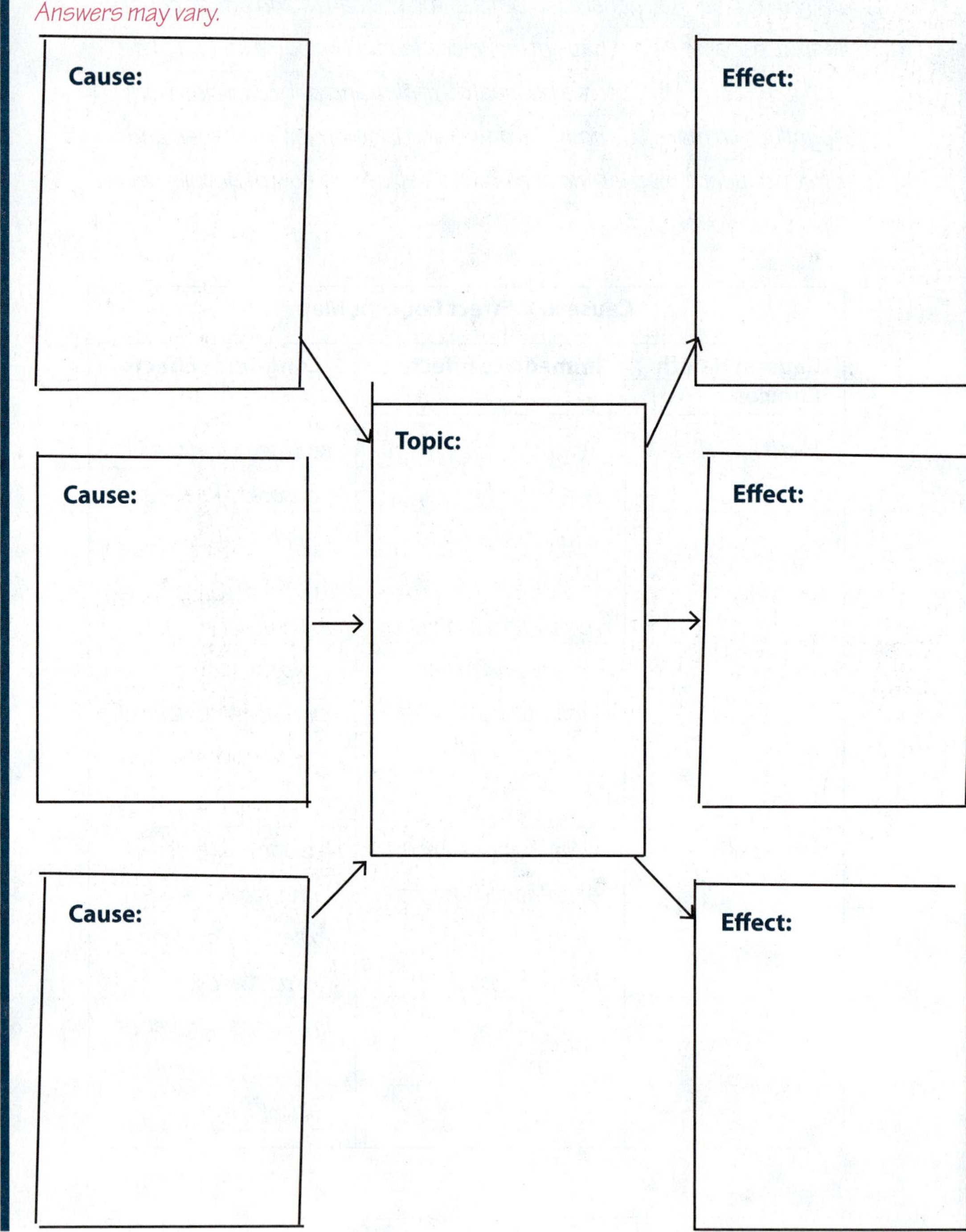

Practice 4

Identify and Generate Details Using Cause and Effect

Assume that you are taking a college health course. Your professor requires that you read and respond to the following paragraph from your textbook. Survey the paragraph for the writer's use of the cause and effect pattern. As you read, underline the cause and effect signal words and the key details related to them. Then double underline the topic sentence, the sentence that best covers all of the details. After reading, complete the cause and effect graphic organizer with information from the paragraph. Finally, generate details to answer the reading response question that appears after the selection.

Answers may vary.

Fight the Anger Urge

[1]Anger usually results when we feel we have lost control of a situation or are frustrated by a situation that we can do little about. [2]Major sources of anger include (1) perceived threats to self or others we care about; (2) reactions to injustice such as unfair actions, policies, or behaviors; (3) fear, which leads to negative responses; (4) faulty emotional reasoning or misinterpretation of normal events; (5) low frustration tolerance, often fueled by stress, drugs, lack of sleep, and other factors; (6) unreasonable expectations about ourselves and others; and (7) people rating, or applying derogatory ratings to others. [4]Each of us learned by this point in our lives that there are three main approaches to dealing with anger: expressing it, suppressing it, or calming it. [5]You may be surprised to find out that expressing your anger is probably the healthiest thing to do in the long run, if you express anger in an assertive rather than an aggressive way. [6]However, it's a natural reaction to want to respond aggressively, and that is what we must learn to keep at bay. [7]You can use several strategies to control your anger.

- [8]Identify your anger style. [9]Do you express anger passively or actively? [10]Do you hold anger in, or do you explode? [11]Do you throw the phone, smash things, or scream at others?
- [12]Learn to recognize patterns in your anger responses and how to de-escalate them. [13]For 1 week, keep track of everything that angers you or keeps you stewing. [14]What thoughts or feelings lead up to your boiling point? [15]Keep a journal and listen to your anger. [16]Try to change your self-talk. [17]Explore how you can interrupt patterns of anger, such as counting to 10, getting a drink of water, or taking some deep breaths.
- [18]Find the right words to de-escalate conflict. [19]Recent research has shown that when couples are angry and fight, using words that suggest thoughtfulness can reduce conflict. [20]Words such as think, because, reason, why demonstrate more consideration for your partner and the issues under fire, as well as a more rational approach.
- [21]Plan ahead. [22]Explore options to minimize your exposure to anger-provoking situations such as traffic jams.
- [23]Vent to your friends. [24]Find a few close friends in whom you can confide or

CONTINUED

PRACTICE 4 *CONTINUED*

to whom you can vent your frustration. [25]Allow them to listen and perhaps provide insight or another perspective that your anger has blinded you to. [26]Don't wear down your supporter with continual rants.

- [27]Develop realistic expectations of yourself and others. [28]Anger is often the result of unmet expectations, frustrations, resentments, and impatience. [29]Are your expectations of yourself and others realistic? [30]Try talking with those involved about your feelings at a time when you are calm.
- [31]Turn complaints into requests. [32]When frustrated or angry with someone, try reworking the problem into a request. [33]Instead of screaming and pounding on the wall because your neighbors' blaring music woke you up at 2 A.M., talk with them. [34]Try to reach an agreement that works for everyone.
- [35]Leave past anger in the past. [36]Learn to resolve issues that have caused pain, frustration, or stress. If necessary, seek the counsel of a professional to make that happen.

Donatelle, Rebecca J., *Access to Health*, 13th ed., pp. 85–87.

Cause	Effect	Cause	Effect
1. perceived threats 2. reactions to injustice 3. fear, negative responses 4. faulty emotional reasoning, misinterpretation of normal events 5. low frustration tolerance, fueled by stress, drugs, lack of sleep, and other factors 6. unreasonable expectations 7. people rating	8. Anger	Identify your anger style. Recognize patterns in your anger. Find the right words to de-escalate anger. 9. Plan ahead Vent to friends. 10. Have realistic expectations. Turn complaints into requests. Leave past anger in past.	Controlled Anger

Reading Response Question: One of the most common displays of anger is seen in road rage, the aggressive or angry behavior of the driver of a vehicle. Assume you are going to write a letter to the editor of your local newspaper identifying the causes and effects of road rage to raise awareness and offer solutions to this dangerous problem. Identify the causes and effects of road rage. Offer advice to drivers about how to control their road rage. Use or adapt the following cause and effect graphic organizer to generate details to use in your letter.

Answers may vary.

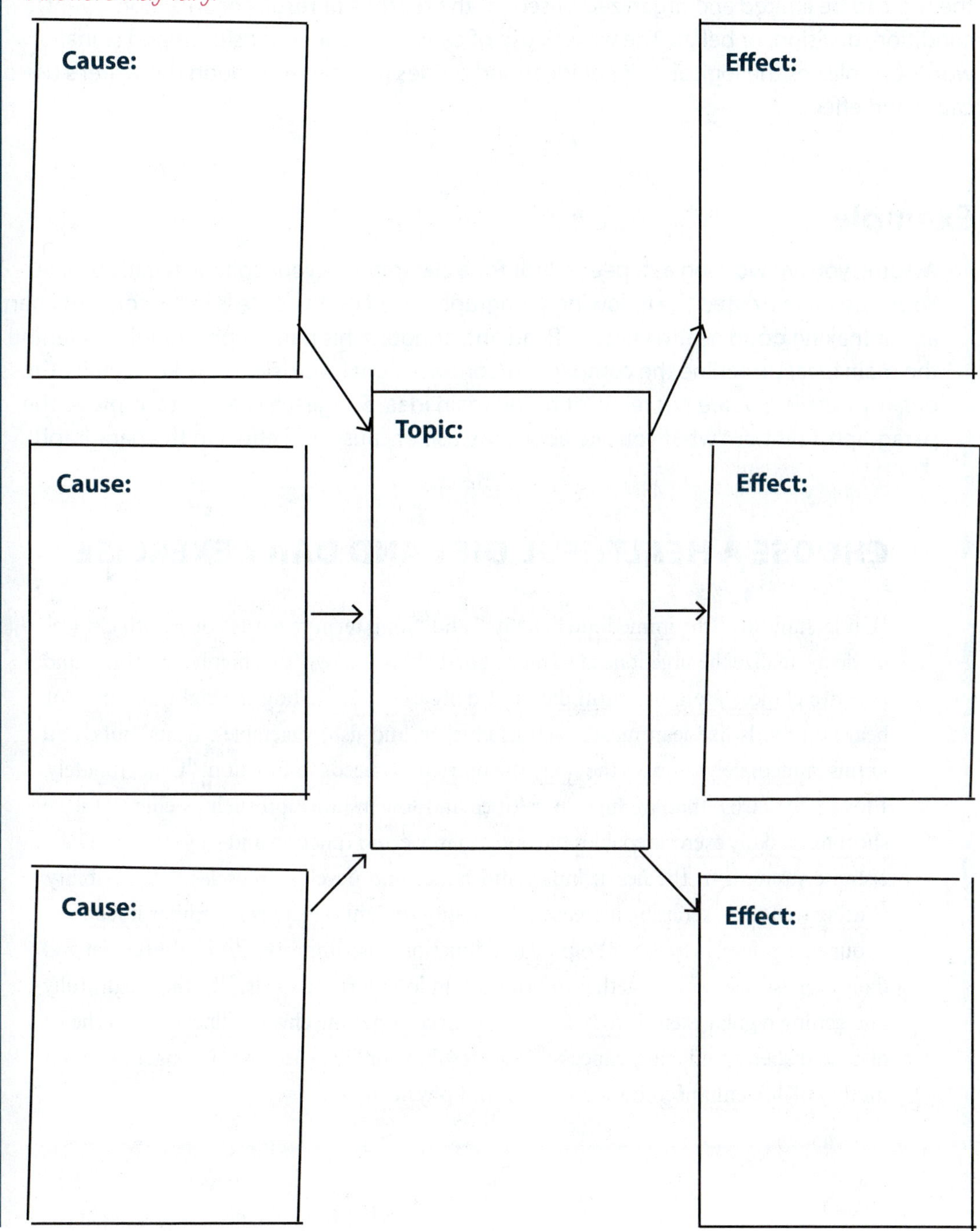

L4 Recognize and Create the Cause and Effect Pattern

When a reader recognizes that a writer is using the cause and effect pattern to organize ideas, the reader can see how the main idea and details fit together and anticipate upcoming details. When we use cause and effect transitions and signal words, we expect the topic to be limited and organized based on the reasons or results of an action, event, condition, decision, or belief. The writer's use of cause and effect transitions and signal words establishes the logical order of ideas and guides the reader through the writer's use of cause and effect.

Example

Assume you are working as a peer editor for a classmate in your college health course. Your classmate drafted the following paragraph based on the details in his concept chart about making good health choices. Read and annotate his paragraph. Double underline the main idea. Underline the comparison/contrast signal words and the key details. Cross out any details that are not relevant to the main idea. Suggest a change to improve the paragraph. Point out what you like about the use of cause and effect in the paragraph.

Answers may vary.

CHOOSE A HEALTHFUL DIET AND DAILY EXERCISE

[1]Understanding "the immediate benefits" and "long term rewards" of health choices made me realize the urgent need to make good choices now. [2]Two highly important and effective choices are a healthful diet and daily exercise. [3]Eating the right amounts of healthful foods like lean meats such as chicken and fish, vegetables, fruits, nuts, and grains immediately supplies the body the nutrients it needs to function. [4]~~Unfortunately, I love salty carbs that are high in calories and low in nutrition such as chips.~~ [5]In the short term, daily exercise enables the body to move and function and stay strong. [6]Daily exercise strengthens the heart, lungs, and bones and develops muscles and flexibility. [7]Eating well and exercising increase your ability to fight off colds and other infections. [8]Your energy level increases. [9]Your mental functions also improve. [10]A healthful diet and daily exercise also work together to bring about long-term rewards. [11]Eating healthfully and getting regular exercise reduces your chances of getting chronic illness such as heart disease, diabetes, and many cancers. [12]As a result, your life expectancy is longer and your quality of life enhanced both mentally and physically.

Explanation

Compare your answers to the following student's think-aloud.

The first sentence introduces the topic health choices *and explains its importance. The second sentence states the main idea of the paragraph. This sentence states the writer's focus and attitude with the phrases "two highly important and effective," "healthful diet," "daily exercise." I liked the way the writer set up the flow of details from the immediate and short-term effects to the long-term rewards. I crossed out sentence 4 because it was off topic as it talked about an unhealthy choice and the focus is choosing a "healthful diet." I also would like to know more details about how eating a healthful diet and getting daily exercise lead to a better quality of life. What are the specific effects of a better quality of life?*

Practice 5

Create Logical Order Using the Cause and Effect Pattern

Work with the cause and effect concept chart you completed in Practice 3 or Practice 4. Write a rough draft of your paragraph using the details you generated. Work with a peer to review each other's rough drafts. Exchange, read, and review your drafts to make sure all details are relevant to the main ideas. Complete a cause and effect concept chart of the draft you are peer editing. Double underline the main idea. Underline the cause and effect signal words and the key details. Cross out any details that are not relevant to the main idea. Suggest a change to improve the paragraph. Point out what you like about the use of the cause and effect pattern in the paragraph. Return your reviewed paragraphs to each other. Revise as needed.

LO5 Analyze and Use Effective Expression with the Cause and Effect Pattern

Effective expression reflects a writer's thoughtful choice of words for impact on the reader. Some words, such as *affect* and *effect,* seem closely related because they are similar in their sounds and spellings. These similarities often cause confusion and lead to the misuse of the words. However, their meanings are clearly distinct, so thoughtful writers use the correct word for effective expression.

Affect is a verb that means **to influence** or **to cause.**

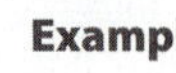

Example

Video games affect learning by improving concentration and visual skills.

PREWRITE: RECITE/REVIEW/ BRAINSTORM

Effect is a noun that means **result.**

Example

Video games have a positive effect on learning by improving concentration and visual skills.

Effect is a verb that means to **bring about** or **cause.**

Example

The new law will effect a change in the sentencing of sex offenders.

Example

Identify and analyze the writer's use of *affect* and *effect* in the following paragraph. First, underline the words *affect* and *effect* and the key details they signal. Then complete the cause and effect concept map with details from the paragraph. (*Hint:* Substitute the words *influence* or *result* as a test for exact meaning in the context of the sentence.)

SAD: Seasonal Affective Disorder

[1]The lack of bright light during winter months produces an effect known as Seasonal Affective Disorder (SAD), a form of depression. [2]The long, dark hours of winter affect as much as 6 percent of the population. [3]The effects of SAD include loss of energy, social withdrawal, overeating, weight gain, and difficulty concentrating. [4]Researchers believe that reduced sunlight affects the biological rhythms that control the body's internal clock and disrupts sleep patterns. [5]Researchers also believe that heredity, age, and the body's chemical balance effects the onset of SAD. [6]However, there is a source for relief from SAD's negative effects. [7]Exposure to sun and sun lamps for one to three hours a day effects a positive change in the mood of one who suffers from SAD.

Create a Cause and Effect Concept Map

Answers may vary.

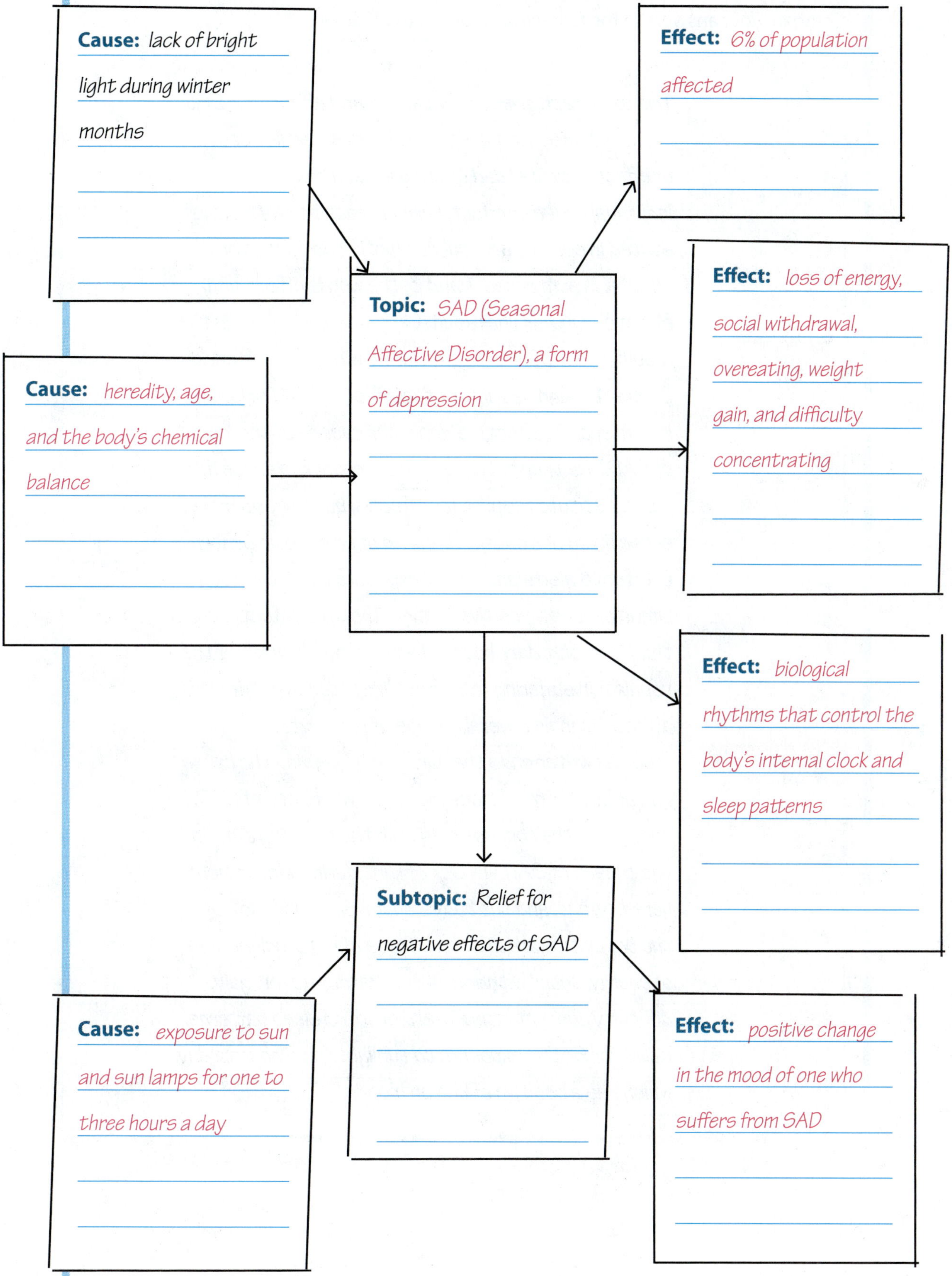

Cause: lack of bright light during winter months

Effect: 6% of population affected

Topic: SAD (Seasonal Affective Disorder), a form of depression

Cause: heredity, age, and the body's chemical balance

Effect: loss of energy, social withdrawal, overeating, weight gain, and difficulty concentrating

Effect: biological rhythms that control the body's internal clock and sleep patterns

Subtopic: Relief for negative effects of SAD

Cause: exposure to sun and sun lamps for one to three hours a day

Effect: positive change in the mood of one who suffers from SAD

EXPLANATION

Compare your answers to the following student's think-aloud.

This paragraph gives many causes and effects for SAD in a very few sentences. Several sentences list causes or effects. So instead of filling in each box with an individual cause or effect, I filled in each box with ideas stated in specific sentences that listed causes or effects. In sentences 1 and 3, the words effect and effects signaled the results. In sentence 1, SAD is the result of lack of bright light during winter. In sentence 3, effects signals a list of five effects of SAD. However, in sentence 5, effects signals the causes of the "onset of SAD." Neither of these sentences makes sense if you substitute results for effects, but they do make sense if you use causes instead of effects. In sentence 6, effects also signals that exposure to sun and sun lamps causes a positive change. The word affect signals that "the long, dark hours of winter" result in 6% of the population suffering from SAD. In sentence 4, the word affects signals several results of reduced sunlight. Also the writer ends the paragraph by giving the cause and effect for relief from the negative effects of SAD. I completed the concept map with the following details. The causes of SAD are lack of light during winter months, heredity, age, and the body's chemical balance. 6% of the population are affected. These effects include loss of energy, social withdrawal, overeating, weight gain, difficulty concentrating, and disrupted sleep patterns. Relief for SAD is exposure to sunlight for 3 hours a day, which has a positive effect on moods.

Practice 6

Use Effective Expression

Work with the rough draft of the paragraph you completed in an earlier practice. Choose two sentences and revise each one to create effective expression through the thoughtful and proper use of *affect* and *effect*. Use the following space to record your original and revised sentences.

Original sentence:

Revised sentence:

Original sentence:

Revised sentence:

Reading and Writing Assignments

MySkillsLab™
Complete these assignments in MySkillsLab.

Considering Audience and Purpose

Study the set of photographs at the beginning of the module. Assume Martin Amezcua is a personal trainer with whom you have been working. Write him a letter thanking him as your coach. Explain the effects that exercise has had on you physically, mentally, and emotionally.

Reading and Writing for Everyday Life

Assume you are a concerned citizen who wants to make a difference in your community after reading about the effects of climate change. Read the following article from a government website. Write a letter to the editor of your local newspaper that calls the public to take steps to reduce the harmful effects of climate change. Explain the need for action and what people can do at home, work, or school to effect change.

Climate Change

Our Earth is warming. Earth's average temperature has risen by 1.4°F over the past century, and is projected to rise another 2 to 11.5°F over the next hundred years. Small changes in the average temperature of the planet can translate to large and potentially dangerous shifts in climate and weather. The evidence of the effects is clear. Rising global temperatures have been accompanied by changes in weather and climate. Many places have seen changes in rainfall, resulting in more floods, droughts, or intense rain, as well as more frequent and severe heat waves. The planet's oceans and glaciers have also experienced some big changes—

oceans are warming and becoming more acidic, ice caps are melting, and sea levels are rising. As these and other changes become more pronounced in the coming decades, they will likely present challenges to our society and our environment. Humans are largely responsible for recent climate change. Over the past century, human activities have released large amounts of carbon dioxide and other greenhouse gases into the atmosphere. The majority of greenhouse gases come from burning fossil fuels to produce energy, although deforestation, industrial processes, and some agricultural practices also emit gases into the atmosphere. Greenhouse gases act like a blanket around Earth, trapping energy in the atmosphere and causing it to warm. This phenomenon is called the greenhouse effect and is natural and necessary to support life on Earth. However, the buildup of greenhouse gases can change Earth's climate and result in dangerous effects to human health and welfare and to ecosystems. The choices we make today will affect the amount of greenhouse gases we put in the atmosphere in the near future and for years to come. You can take action. You can take steps at home, on the road, and in your office to reduce greenhouse gas emissions and the risks associated with climate change. Many of these steps can save you money; some, such as walking or biking to work can even improve your health! Buy light fixtures, bulbs, appliances, and vehicles that are energy efficient. Reducing, reusing, and recycling in your home and at work helps conserve energy and reduces pollution and greenhouse gas emissions from resource extraction, manufacturing, and disposal. If there is a recycling program in your community, recycle your newspapers, beverage containers, paper, and other goods. Also, composting your food and yard waste reduces the amount of garbage that you send to landfills and reduces greenhouse gas emissions. Use water efficiently. It takes lots of energy to pump, treat, and heat water, so saving water reduces greenhouse gas emissions. You can also get involved on a local or state level to support energy efficiency, clean energy programs, or other climate programs.

"Climate Change Is Happening." *Climate Change*. United States Environmental Protection Agency. <http://www.epa.gov/climatechange/basics/>

Reading and Writing for College Life

Assume you are taking a college course in literature. Your professor has given you the following information in a handout about the effects of conflict on a character in a piece of fiction, along with a study question for an upcoming exam. Read the paragraph and answer the study question.

CONFLICTS CAUSE A DYNAMIC CHARACTER

In a piece of fiction, a character may go through an important inner change in attitude, values, or personality. A character who changes is known as a dynamic character. A change in a dynamic character is usually the result of one or more conflicts that arise throughout the story. Five major conflicts may result in the dynamic growth of the character. First, person versus self is an inner conflict, such as the conflict between ambition and honor. Second, a character may change because of an external conflict with another person, such as a struggle between a father and a son. Third, a character may change due to another external conflict—person versus society. Conflicts with society include a citizen and the government or a human against technology. A fourth conflict, person against nature, is also an external conflict. This struggle to survive a wildfire, a hurricane, a tornado, or any power of nature may bring about a deep personal change in the character's values and priorities. A final conflict, person versus God or the supernatural, may be experienced as either an external conflict with a powerful external force or as an inner battle based on a moral code.

Exam Study Question: Choose a dynamic character from a movie you have watched recently. What conflicts caused the character to change? Why or how did the character change?

Reading and Writing for Working Life

Assume you are preparing for a job interview as an assistant manager at a local movie theatre. The counselor at the Employment Office gave you the following information to help you prepare for your interview. Read the information. Then choose a question and write a response as practice for the interview.

Job Interview Questions

Job interviews can cause great stress to the prospective employee. However, the first impression you make can cause you to either get the job or lose the opportunity for employment. The best way to reduce stress and make a great first impression is to prepare before the interview. Take time to review the following common interview questions that you are likely to be asked. Write out responses to these questions and rehearse your answers until you feel comfortable.

Why do you want this job?

What contributions will you make to our company?

Why should we hire you?

What causes you stress and how do you handle stress?

Workshop: Compose a Cause and Effect Paragraph

Choose a paragraph to read and respond to in writing. You may select a paragraph in an example, practice, or writing assignment within this module. Or you may select a paragraph of your own choosing. Use the following guide to comprehend and respond to the paragraph. Apply what you have learned about the cause and effect pattern to your reading/writing strategy.

Preread: Survey and Question

Ask questions about the text's features.

____

____

What is the passage about?

____

____

How is the material organized?

____

____

What do I already know about this topic? (What is my prior knowledge about the vocabulary?)

____

____

What is my purpose for reading/writing?

____

____

What points may I want to address or include in my written response?

____

____

Read and Annotate

As you read, annotate key ideas, particularly those details that answer your prereading questions.

Recite, Review, and Brainstorm

Recite the information. Summarize the most important parts. Answer your prereading questions. Rephrase ideas into your own words. Record changes in your opinions based on the new information. **Review** the information. **Brainstorm** ideas for your written response to the passage. **Freewrite** a response to what you have read. **Map** the relationships among ideas you have annotated in the text. **Outline** or list key ideas and details in blocks of thought.

Write a Draft of Your Response

Using the ideas you generated by brainstorming, compose a draft of your response. Use your own paper.

Revise Your Draft

Once you have created a draft of a cause and effect paragraph, read the draft to answer the questions in the "Questions for Revising a Cause and Effect Paragraph" box that follows. Indicate your answers by annotating your paper. If you answer "yes" to a question, underline, check, or circle examples. If you answer "no" to a question, write needed information in margins and draw lines to indicate placement of additional details. Revise your paragraph based on your reflection. (**Hint:** Experienced writers create several drafts as they focus on one or two questions per draft.)

Step by Step: Questions for Revising a Cause and Effect Paragraph

- ☐ Have I stated or implied a focused main idea?
- ☐ Have I stated or implied the specific causes and effects?
- ☐ Is the order of the causes and effects clear? Have I used strong transitions and signal words for cause and effect?
- ☐ Have I used concrete details to make my point?
- ☐ Have I made my point with adequate details?
- ☐ Have I included only the details that are relevant to my topic sentence?
- ☐ Have I used *affect* and *effect* precisely?

Proofread Your Draft

Once you have made any revisions to your paragraph that may be needed, proofread your paragraph to eliminate careless errors.

Review Test

MySkillsLab™
Complete this Review Test in MySkillsLab.

Score (number correct) ______ x 10 = ______ %

Use reading/writing strategies to comprehend and respond to the following passage. Read the passage from the college textbook *Encyclopedia of Stress*. Answer the questions that follow. Finally, respond to the writing prompts "Summary Response" and "What Do You Think?"

Vocabulary Preview

provokes (**4**): causes, stirs up
phobia (**5**): deep, irrational fear
interacting with (**13**): relating to working with
inflammation (**21**): swelling

1140L/10.6 GE/369 words

TECHNOSTRESS

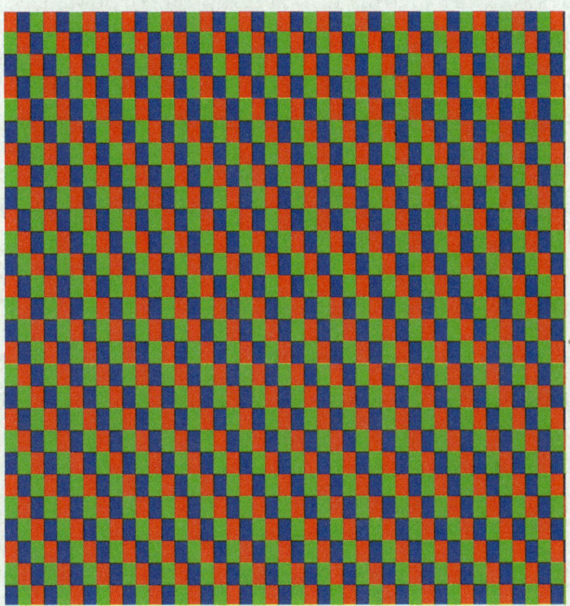

[1]The computer revolution has created a new form of stress that is threatening the physical and mental health of many workers. [2]"Technostress" is a modern disorder caused by an inability to cope in a healthy manner with the new computer technology.

[3]Technostress reveals itself in several distinct ways. [4]It can surface as a person struggles to learn how to use computers in the workplace, which often **provokes** anxiety. [5]Some people develop a **phobia** about modern technology and need professional help to deal with their fears.

[6]Technostress can also surface as overidentification with computers. [7]Some people develop a machinelike **mind-set** that reflects the traits of the computer itself. [8]Some who were once warm and sensitive people become cold, lose their friends, and have no patience for the easy give-and-take of conversation. [9]In addition, they watch television as their major or only leisure activity.

CONTINUED

[10]Further, **technostress** is the term used for such physical stress reactions as computer-related eyestrain, headaches, neck and shoulder tension, and backache. [11]Also, many people who use computer keyboards often develop carpal tunnel syndrome.

[12]These various reactions to technostress arise from long-term use of computers. [13]If someone spends most of their working hours **interacting with** only a computer screen and a keyboard, then that person may develop a number of the following symptoms.

[14]Eyestrain is caused by focusing continuously on a screen at close range. [15]The person who focuses for a long time on one specific colored screen may see the **complementary** color when looking up at a blank wall or ceiling. [16]This color reversal is normal and quickly lessens. [17]Headaches, though sometimes caused by eyestrain, are most often due to tension involving muscles of the brow, temples, jaw, upper neck, and base of the skull. [18]These headaches can be affected by improper height of the chair and screen. [19]Even the lack of an armrest can contribute. [20]Lack of an armrest causes the arms to pull down on the shoulders, creating, in turn, tension at the shoulder tip and base of the skull and spasms radiating up into the head. [21]Carpal tunnel syndrome, a numbness, tingling, or burning sensation in the fingers or wrists, may be induced by **inflammation** of the ligaments and tendons in fingers and wrists.

Adapted from McGuigan, F. J., *Encyclopedia of Stress*, pp. 237–238.

Vocabulary in Context

1. The term **mind-set** in sentence 7 means

a. stubbornness. **(c.)** attitude.

b. decision. **d.** opinion.

2. The best synonym for **complementary** in sentence 15 is

a. beautiful. **c.** praise.

(b.) opposite. **d.** similar.

Concept Map

3–4. Finish the concept map by filling in the missing idea with information from the passage.

Long-Term Effects

Technostress
- *Eyestrain*
- *Headaches*
- *Carpal tunnel syndrome*

Central Idea and Main Idea

5. Which sentence states the central idea of the passage?

a. sentence 1
(b.) sentence 2
c. sentence 12
d. sentence 13

Supporting Details

6. Sentence 19 is a

a. major supporting detail.
(b.) minor supporting detail.

Transitions

7. The word **further** in sentence 10 is a signal word that shows

a. comparison.
b. cause.
(c.) addition.

8. The word **though** in sentence 17 signals

a. cause and effect.
(b.) contrast.
c. addition.

Thought Patterns

9. The primary thought pattern for the entire passage is

(a.) cause and effect.
b. generalization and example.
c. comparison and contrast.

10. The thought pattern for the fourth paragraph (sentences 10–11) is

a. cause and effect.
b. generalization and example.
(c.) listing.

Summary Response

Restate the writer's main idea in your own words. Begin your summary response with the following: *The main idea of the passage "Technostress" from the* Encyclopedia of Stress *is. . . .*

What Do You Think?

Assume you are an office manager, and you are giving a presentation about technostress at a training session for new employees. Write a draft of your presentation. Warn new employees about the dangers of technostress and offer ways in which they can avoid or reduce technostress.

Academic Learning Log: Module Review

Summary of Key Concepts of the Cause and Effect Pattern

Assess your comprehension of the cause and effect pattern of organization.

L1 L2 L3 L4

1. To read or write a cause and effect paragraph, you analyze the *reasons* for and the *results* of an *action*, *event*, condition, *decision*, or belief.

2. The *focus* of the paragraph may be only on the causes, only on the effects, or include both.

3. A *cause* states why something happens.

4. An *effect* states a result or outcome.

5. A *causal chain* is a *sequence* of events in which any one event in the chain causes the next one, leading up to a final *effect*.

6. Signal words for cause and effect may be transitions, *verbs*, or *nouns*.

7. Transition words for cause and effect include *accordingly*, *as a result*, *consequently*, *if . . . then*, and *therefore*.

8. Verbs that signal cause and effect include *affect*, *benefit*, *contribute*, and *influence*.

9. Nouns that signal cause and effect include *agent*, *benefit*, *condition*, *event*, *factor*, and *impact*.

L5

10. *Affect* is a verb that means to *influence* or to *cause*. *Effect* is a noun that means *results*. *Effect* may also be a *verb* that means to bring about or *cause*.

Test Your Comprehension of the Cause and Effect Pattern

Respond to the following questions and prompts. *Answers may vary.*

LO1 LO2

Read the following topic sentences. In the given spaces identify the cause and effect stated in each sentence.

1. Alcohol damages the brain in several ways.

   Cause: *alcohol* Effect: *damages the brain in several ways*

2. The volunteer and the community benefit from volunteer work.

   Cause: *volunteer work* Effect: *the volunteer and community benefit*

3. An effective team is the result of a series of decisions made by leadership.

   Cause: *a series of decisions made by leadership* Effect: *an effective team*

LO1 LO2 LO5

Write cause and effect topic sentences for the following topics. *Answers may vary.*

1. Topic: Academic cheating

   Topic sentence: *A variety of factors affect academic cheating* _____.

2. Topic: Distracted driving

   Topic sentence: *Distracted driving often leads to devastating effects* _____.

LO1 LO2 LO3 LO4

On your own paper, create a blank cause and effect concept chart.

LO1 LO2 LO3 LO4 LO5

1. **How will I use what I have learned?** In your notebook, discuss how you will apply to your own reading/writing strategy what you have learned about cause and effect. When will you apply this knowledge to your reading/writing strategy?
2. **What do I still need to study about cause and effect?** In your notebook, discuss your ongoing study needs. Describe what, when, and how you will continue studying and using cause and effect in your writing.

Complete the Post-test for Module 13 in MySkillsLab.

14

LEARNING OUTCOMES

After studying this module you should be able to:

- **L1** Answer the Question "What's the Point of Fact and Opinion?"
- **L2** Distinguish Between Fact and Opinion
- **L3** Comprehend and State a Main Idea Using Fact and Opinion
- **L4** Evaluate and Generate Relevant Details Using Fact and Opinion
- **L5** Recognize and Create Logical Order Using Fact and Opinion
- **L6** Analyze and Use Effective Expression with Fact and Opinion

Fact and Opinion

Janine and Robert were involved in a car accident. Robert said Janine was texting and caused the accident. Janine said Robert had road rage and ran into her on purpose. The fact is that a car accident occurred. The drivers involved gave two different opinions about the cause of the accident. The traffic officer who responds to the accident will gather evidence to separate fact from opinion and determine the true cause of the accident. The evidence may come from eyewitnesses who observed the accident as it occurred. Or the evidence may be physical evidence such as skid marks on the road or the specific damage to the cars. Facts can be proven; opinions are so personal that they cannot be proven. The ability to distinguish between fact and opinion affects how you react to what you see or read and how you pass the information on as a writer. Effective readers and writers are able to accurately recognize and clearly communicate facts and opinions.

WHAT'S THE POINT of Fact and Opinion? 

You probably are familiar with the terms *fact* and *opinion*, and you may already have an idea about what each one means. Test what you know about the difference between fact and opinion. Study the following photographs that illustrate the nature of facts and opinions. In the blanks below each photograph, state the purpose of the opinion or fact as illustrated. Then predict how fact and opinion differ by answering the question "What's the point of fact and opinion?"

Photographic Organizer: Fact and Opinion

The following set of photographs illustrates some of the ways in which facts and opinions are used.

FACTS

Purpose: *to give information about nutrition so consumers can make wise choices*

Purpose: *to gather information about an accident*

OPINIONS

Purpose: *to find out what customers think or feel about a product or service*

Purpose: *to see if others agree or disagree with an idea*

What's the point of facts and opinions?

Facts state what happened or what is. Opinions state what people think or believe.

What's the Point? One Student's Response

The following paragraph offers one student's point about the difference between fact and opinion.

The nutritional information about the tomato gives details that can be proven by science. This information helps us make healthful choices about what we eat. The form that asks for information such as "employment," "diagnosis," and "date of accident" creates a record of what happened (such as the date of an accident and diagnosis of injuries) or what is (such as employment). These things can be checked out to see if they are accurate. The answers to these will not change. The other two illustrations are forms or checklists that ask what people think or believe. Different people would answer differently. Facts state something that actually is or has occurred. In contrast, opinions just state what someone thinks or believes and can't be proven as the truth.

L2 Distinguish Between Fact and Opinion

Both readers and writers must distinguish between fact and opinion to effectively comprehend and make a point. Consider the following two statements.

Fact: Jennifer Lopez is a dancer, singer, actress, and reality television performer.

Opinion: Jennifer Lopez is a positive role model for young women.

The first sentence states a set of details about Jennifer Lopez that can be proven as true or false. The second sentence relays a personal view with which others may agree or disagree.

Separating fact from opinion requires you to think critically because opinion is often presented as fact. For example, advertisements combine fact and opinion to sell you a product. Likewise, politicians rely on facts and opinions to gain your vote. The following clues will help you separate fact from opinion.

A **fact** is a specific detail that is true based on objective proof. A fact is discovered.

An **opinion** is an interpretation, value judgment, or belief that cannot be proved or disproved. An opinion is created.

Objective proof can be physical evidence, an eyewitness account, or the result of an accepted scientific method.

Fact	Opinion
Is objective Is discovered States reality Can be verified Is presented with unbiased words	Is subjective Is created Interprets reality Cannot be verified Is presented with biased words
Example of a fact	**Example of an opinion**
Spinach is a source of iron.	Spinach tastes awful.

A fact is a specific, objective, and verifiable detail; in contrast, an opinion is a biased, personal view created from feelings and beliefs.

Example

Read the following statements, and mark each one **F** if it states a fact or **O** if it expresses an opinion.

O **1.** Michelangelo is the greatest painter of all time.

F **2.** The Sistine Chapel is the private chapel of the popes in Rome.

F **3.** Between 1508 and 1512, Michelangelo produced frescos for the chapel's ceiling; the murals depict scenes from the Book of Genesis, from the Creation to the Flood.

O **4.** Many of the images Michelangelo created are terrifying.

Explanation

Compare your answers to the following student's think-aloud.

Sentences 2 and 3 state facts that can be verified through research. Sentences 1 and 4 express opinions, personal reactions to Michelangelo's work as an artist. Sentence 1 expresses a positive personal opinion; sentence 4 expresses a negative personal opinion.

Most people's points of view and beliefs are based on a blend of fact and opinion, and a person's purpose for communicating influences his or her use of facts and opinion. If the main purpose is to inform, a writer relies mainly on facts. For example, textbooks, news articles, and medical research rely on facts. In contrast, if the purpose is to entertain or persuade, writers may rely more heavily on opinion. For example, editorials, advertisements, and fiction often mix fact and opinion. An effective reader, then, distinguishes between facts and opinions. Three questions help effective readers and writers distinguish between facts and opinions.

Questions to Distinguish Between Fact and Opinion

- Can the statement be proved or demonstrated to be true?
- Can the statement be observed in practice or operation?
- Can the statement be verified by witnesses, manuscripts, or documents?

If the answer to any of these questions is "no," the statement is an opinion—not a fact. Often, you will find the answer is both "yes" and "no" as many statements include both fact and opinion.

Example

A. Read the following statements, and mark each one **F** if it states a fact or **O** if it expresses an opinion.

F **1.** Jay Z, also known as Shawn Corey Carter, is married to Beyoncé.

O **2.** Jay Z's music promotes bad values.

F **3.** Carter's net worth is nearly $500 million; he has sold nearly 50 million albums worldwide and received 17 Grammy Awards.

O **4.** Jay Z's lyrical skills are unmatched, and we will never see another one as talented as he.

B. Choose a public figure, such as a singer, actor, reality show personality, or elected official. Write two sentences—one that states only a fact and another that states an opinion about that public figure. Exchange your sentences with a classmate. Use "Questions to Distinguish Between Fact and Opinion" to determine which one of your classmate's sentences states a fact and which one states an opinion. *Answers may vary.*

5. ______________________________

____

6. ______________________________

____

Explanation

Compare your answers to the following student's think-aloud.

Sentences 1 and 3 state facts because they can be verified by official written records or documents. Sentences 2 and 4 express opinions that cannot be proved or demonstrated as true or verified by objective proof. For example, in sentence 2, what do the words bad values *mean? And what proof is there that connects his music to bad values? This sentence states a negative opinion. In sentence 4 the word unmatched and phrase "will never see another as talented as he" are broad generalizations that cannot be proven to be true. This sentence states a positive opinion. I chose to write about Taylor Swift.*

***5.** Taylor Swift's songs are awesome. This sentence states a personal opinion that others can disagree with. What is "awesome" to one person may be annoying to another. This statement cannot be proven.*

***6.** Taylor Swift has earned numerous awards and millions of dollars. This sentence states facts that can be proved by research and documentation.*

Biased words are often loaded with emotion. The box below contains a small sample of these kinds of words.

Biased words express opinions, value judgments, and interpretations.

Biased Words					
amazing	best	favorite	great	miserable	stupid
awful	better	frightful	greatest	more	ugly
bad	disgusting	fun	handsome	most	unbelievable
beautiful	exciting	good	horrible	smart	very

A **qualifier** may express an absolute, unwavering opinion using words such as *always* or *never*. Qualifiers may also express an opinion in the form of a command as in *must*, or the desirability of an action with a word such as *should*. Qualifiers may indicate different degrees of doubt with words such as *seems* or *might*. The box below contains a few examples of these kinds of words.

Qualifiers are words that describe or modify the meaning of another word.

Words That Qualify Ideas					
all	could	likely	never	possibly, possible	sometimes
always	every	may	often	probably, probable	think
appear	has/have to	might	only	seem	though/although/ even though
believe	it is believed	must	ought to	should	usually

At times, a sentence can include both facts and opinions. The part of the sentence that includes a biased word may be an opinion about another part of the sentence that is a fact. At other times, a paragraph blends facts and opinions. One sentence may state a fact; surrounding sentences then offer opinions about the stated fact.

Example

A. Read the following sentences. Underline the biased words and circle the qualifiers.

1. Even though actor George Clooney is over 50 years old, he is still very handsome.
2. The grasslands of the American West were tragically plowed under for crops.
3. Every good citizen who wants to be informed about current events should subscribe to at least two newspapers and never miss the nightly news.
4. Amber, fossilized tree resin, was one of the first substances used for decoration. It was believed to exert a healthful influence on the endocrine system, spleen, and heart.

B. Choose a movie or television show that you would or would not recommend to others. Write a sentence or two that states a fact and your opinion about the movie or TV show. Use biased words and qualifiers as needed. Exchange sentences with a classmate and underline each other's use of biased words and qualifiers.

5. *Answers may vary.*

Explanation

Compare your answers to the following student's think-aloud.

1. *The phrase "George Clooney is over 50 years old" is a fact that can be proved by research. However, the qualifier "even though" ties the fact of his age to the opinion "he is still very handsome" in the second part of the sentence.*
2. *In the second sentence, "the grasslands of the American West were plowed under for crops" is a fact, but whether that fact is tragic is a matter of opinion.*

3. *The qualifiers in this sentence are every, should, and never. The fact is that newspapers and the nightly news do cover current events, but these qualifiers express a personal opinion about this fact.*

4. *The first sentence in this item states a fact that can be verified. The second sentence begins with the qualifier "it was believed." This second sentence states a "belief" about the fact.*

5. *I wrote one sentence that had both fact and opinion about the movie* The Hunger Games. *The biased words and qualifiers are underlined. "*The Hunger Games *is an amazing movie that everyone must see featuring favorite stars Jennifer Lawrence, Liam Hemsworth, Woody Harrelson, and Donald Sutherland."*

Practice 1

Distinguish Between Fact and Opinion

A. Read the following statements. Mark each one **F** if it states a fact, **O** if it expresses an opinion, or **F/O** if it combines fact and opinion. Underline biased words and qualifiers as needed.

F/O **1.** Unhealthy diets and lack of exercise are serious national problems that must be addressed; 300,000 deaths each year are linked to these two problems.

F **2.** Tobacco use kills more Americans than motor vehicle crashes, AIDS, cocaine use, heroin use, homicide, and suicide combined.

F/O **3.** Tobacco products cause cancer and should be outlawed.

F **4.** Diets high in fruits, vegetables, and fiber lower the risk for some types of cancer.

O **5.** Public schools ought to serve fruits and vegetables instead of pizza and hamburgers.

F/O **6.** Sandra Bullock stars in the thrilling space adventure *Gravity*; the award-winning actress gives the best performance of her career.

F/O **7.** The Nine Steakhouse, which serves prime aged steaks and imported spirits, is Chicago's most popular night spot.

CONTINUED

PRACTICE 1 *CONTINUED*

B. Study the following editorial cartoon. Then based on the issue as expressed in the cartoon, write three sentences: one stating a fact, one stating an opinion, and one combining a fact and an opinion. Use biased word and qualifiers as needed. *Answers will vary.*

8. Fact: *Texting while driving distracts drivers and causes accidents.*

9. Opinion: *Texting while driving should be illegal.*

10. Fact/Opinion: *Distracted driving is a stupid behavior that results in the death of thousands each year.*

Now that you have learned some strategies to identify and use facts and opinions, you are ready to apply the use of fact and opinion to your reading/writing process.

Comprehend and State a Main Idea Using Fact and Opinion

LO 3

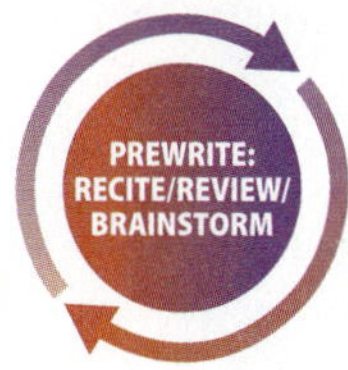

As you learned in Module 5, effective readers and writers use facts and opinions to comprehend and state a main idea. Remember, a topic sentence states the writer's opinion or controlling point about a topic in a complete sentence. At times, the topic sentence may also include facts about the topic. At other times, the topic sentence states only the writer's opinion about the topic. In the following example, the topic sentence includes both fact and opinion.

In the above example, the writer's opinion is revealed by the words "better" and "than." These words suggest a specific pattern of organization—the words combine to imply a comparison and contrast between the iPhone and an Android.

Distinguishing between fact and opinion is an important reading/writing strategy. For example, before reading, an effective reader looks for the writer's use of fact and opinion to comprehend the main idea.

Before reading:

- Skim to locate the topic sentence.
- Annotate the topic sentence to make clear the writer's topic and use of facts and opinion.
- Predict the details you expect the writer to give.

Example

Analyze facts and opinions to comprehend the writer's main idea. Read the following topic sentences. Circle the topic. Single underline facts about the topic. Double underline the writer's opinion about the topic. Discuss with a peer or small group of classmates the types of details you expect.

1. Jennifer Lawrence, who plays Katniss Everdeen in the *Hunger Games* films, is a gifted actor.

2. A common industrial chemical used in plastic containers, BPA causes serious adverse health effects and should be banned from use in food storage items.

3. Employers seek workers highly skilled in communication, problem solving, and decision making.

4. If you are one of the 70% of all American students who procrastinate, you may overcome this problem by following three simple steps.

Explanation

Compare your answers to the following student's think-aloud.

Most of these topic sentences combined fact and opinion. The facts offered helpful or attention-grabbing background information about the topics.

1. *The topic is Jennifer Lawrence. The fact "who plays Katniss Everdeen in the* Hunger Games*" gives the reader an example of the fact that she is an "actor." The writer's opinion is "gifted." I expect the writer to explain how Lawrence is gifted as an actor.*
2. *The topic is BPA. The fact "a common industrial chemical used in plastic containers" tells the reader what BPA is. This fact emphasizes the importance of the topic since everyone frequently uses plastic containers. The phrase "adverse health effects" is also a fact that can be verified. The writer qualifies the adverse health effects as "serious" and offers the opinion that BPA "should be banned from use in food storage items." I predict that the writer will list and explain the harmful effects of BPA to support the call to ban use of BPA in food storage containers.*
3. *The topic is "Employers seek workers." At first it seems like there are two topics—employers and workers. But I infer that the real topic is getting hired. I did not detect any facts in this topic sentence. This sentence only lists three skills; however, there are other skills than these that employers seek. So I infer that the listed skills reflect the writer's opinion. The writer's opinion is "highly skilled in communication, problem solving, and decision making." I predict the writer will define these skills and explain why they are important.*
4. *The topic is stated twice in this sentence with the words* procrastinate *and* problem. *The statement "70% of all American students who procrastinate" is a fact because the percentage of students who procrastinate can be verified. The word* problem *is part of the writer's opinion "may overcome this problem by following three simple steps." The phrase "If you are one of the" also states an opinion in the form of an uncertain condition. The writer doesn't know if the reader is one who procrastinates or not.*

Effective writers know that a topic sentence is never a statement of fact alone. A statement of fact may be proved or disproved, but it is not an idea that lends itself to further development or support. A fact is a detail, never a main idea. Thus, to make a point, a writer may or may not combine fact and opinion in a topic sentence. Sometimes, the topic sentence states only an opinion about a topic. Other times, a topic sentence may state an opinion in response to a fact or set of facts. In these cases, a writer may state the fact(s) first in a sentence that introduces the topic sentence.

Example

The following items present a topic, an opinion, a fact, and signal word(s) of various patterns of organization. Combine the ideas in each group to create a topic sentence based on combined patterns. *Answers may vary.*

1. TOPIC: *Sleep deprivation*

OPINION: *suffer, alarming*

FACT: *40 million Americans*

PATTERN OF ORGANIZATION SIGNAL WORDS: *effects*

TOPIC SENTENCE: *Sleep deprivation has alarming effects on millions of Americans.*

INTRODUCTORY SENTENCE OF FACT AND TOPIC SENTENCE: *Forty million Americans suffer from lack of sleep. The effects of sleep deprivation are alarming.*

2. TOPIC: *Technology, learning*

OPINION: *greatly*

FACT: *college students spend average of 12 hours each day using some type of media*

PATTERN OF ORGANIZATION SIGNAL WORDS: *as, impacts*

TOPIC SENTENCE: *As college students spend an average of 12 hours each day using some type of media, technology greatly impacts learning.*

INTRODUCTORY SENTENCE OF FACT AND TOPIC SENTENCE: *College students spend an average of 12 hours each day using some type of media. Clearly, technology greatly impacts learning.*

Explanation

Compare your answers to the following student's think-aloud.

I decided to write each topic sentence two ways. First, I composed topic sentences that combined fact and opinion. Next I wrote topic sentences that only stated the opinion about the topic, and then I also wrote two sentences using the facts to introduce those topic sentences. To use facts to introduce a topic sentence, it was necessary to change or add words so ideas flowed smoothly.

1. *Topic sentence combining fact and opinion: Sleep deprivation has alarming effects on millions of Americans.*

   A sentence stating a fact introducing a topic sentence: Forty million Americans suffer from severe lack of sleep. The effects of sleep deprivation are alarming.

2. *Topic sentence combining fact and opinion: As college students spend an average of 12 hours each day using some type of media, technology greatly impacts learning.*

   A sentence stating a fact introducing a topic sentence: College students spend an average of 12 hours each day using some type of media. Clearly, technology greatly impacts learning.

Practice 2

Comprehend and State a Main Idea Using Facts and Opinions

Read the following paragraph from the college sociology textbook *The Family*. Complete the reading/writing activities that follow.

WHAT IS THE FAMILY?

[1]Traditionally, and legally, *the family* refers to two or more persons related by birth, marriage, or adoption who reside together in a household. [2]This definition is how the U.S. Census defines families. [3]Families in the United States are perhaps as diverse as anywhere in the world. [4]Yet, most of us have an image of what a family is and should be. [5]This image is perhaps best illustrated by popular television shows of the 1950s such as *Father Knows Best, Leave it to Beaver*, and *Ozzie and Harriet*. [6]In these shows, the family is one of a loving, two-parent family with children. [7]The father is the breadwinner and "head." [8]The stay-at-home mother cares for the house and children and is the loving and supportive wife. [9]And the children, while exhibiting occasions of sibling rivalry and mischief, are basically conforming and obedient. [10]Does this image comply with what we know about the family of the 1950s? [11]Or is it the product of nostalgia for a better time? [12]Family historians have shown that this image is one that may have fit a minority of mostly middle-class families but is far from an accurate portrayal of family during that time for most Americans.

Eshleman, J. Ross, and Bulcroft, Richard, *The Family*, 12th ed., pp. 4, 44–45.

A. Comprehend a Main Idea Using Fact and Opinion.
The following list contains the topic sentence and key supporting details from the paragraph. First, identify each of the sentences as **F** for fact, **O** for opinion, or **F/O** if it combines fact and opinion. Then underline the sentence that states the main idea of the paragraph, the topic sentence.

F **1.** Traditionally, and legally, *the family* refers to two or more persons related by birth, marriage, or adoption who reside together in a household.

F **2.** This definition is how the U.S. Census defines families.

O **3.** Families in the United States are perhaps as diverse as anywhere in the world.

O **4.** Yet, most of us have an image of what a family is and should be.

F/O **5.** This image is perhaps best illustrated by popular television shows of the 1950s such as *Father Knows Best, Leave it to Beaver*, and *Ozzie and Harriet.*

CONTINUED

PRACTICE 2 *CONTINUED*

B. State a Main Idea Using Fact and Opinion.

Assume you are taking a college course in sociology. Your teacher requires you to respond in writing to the paragraph defining the family. To assist you, your teacher has provided the following reader's response prompt:

Write a one-paragraph response to the ideas in "What is *The Family*?" Use the following questions to focus your response.

- Do you agree with the definition of *family* given in the passage? Why or why not?
- How would you define *the family*?
- Which television shows or movies best depict your view of *the family*? How so?

Write a topic sentence that states the main idea of your response. Answers may vary.

Topic sentence: *The family is far more than the definition given by the U.S. Census or the popular television shows of the 1950s.*

LO4 Evaluate and Generate Relevant Details Using Facts and Opinions

Distinguishing between fact and opinion is a key strategy in identifying and generating details throughout the reading/writing process. While a statement of fact can never be a topic sentence, it is a convincing supporting detail. And, while an opinion is a basic part of a topic sentence, it may also serve as a strong supporting detail. Therefore, during reading, effective readers analyze the writer's use of facts and opinions as details to determine if the writer has provided relevant or adequate support. They evaluate the following to infer the effectiveness of the writer's details: the context of the passage, the context of the writer, and the context of the source.

Evaluate the Context of the Passage

One way to distinguish between fact and opinion is to evaluate the context. A reader analyzes a writer's language to decide whether a statement can be backed up with evidence and proven in some way. Language also indicates whether the statement is someone's point of view, judgment, or belief. You have already studied biased words and qualifiers that signal an opinion. Also consider the following examples of language that expresses facts and opinions.

Examples of Language Expressing Facts	Examples of Language Expressing Opinions
According to the results of the latest poll	The prosecution **argues** that
The latest studies **confirm**	The defense **claims** that
The research has **demonstrated**	In the President's **view**
Researchers have recently **discovered**	Most experts in this field **suspect** that

In addition to the wording of an idea, relationships between ideas and thought patterns may also signal a fact or an opinion.

Patterns of Organizations That May Imply Facts and Opinions

Patterns That May Imply Facts	**Patterns That May Imply Opinions**
Definition	Comparisons
Causes and Effects	Reasons (explanations and interpretations)
Examples	Quality, Traits, Attributes

Of course, some comparisons and traits are factual. And writers can present possible or probable causes and effects that haven't been proven. So an effective reader must analyze the context of each statement.

The mixture of fact and opinion occurs when a writer interprets or evaluates a fact. Look at the following three statements in which the facts are highlighted in yellow and the opinions are highlighted in green.

Fact: One in three adults owns a tablet computer.

Opinion: Tablets are too expensive, easy to break, and lead to eyestrain.

Fact and **Opinion:** Tablets enrich education by giving access to the Internet and storing hundreds of books and files on one device.

The first statement is a fact that can be verified. The second statement offers a negative opinion about tablets. The third statement offers factual details about tablets; it is common knowledge that the key features of a tablet are access to the Internet and the memory to hold hundreds of books and files. However, the writer has also offered an opinion with the biased phrase "enrich education." Not everyone agrees with this view.

Example

Read the following passage. Next, identify each sentence as follows: **F** if it states a fact, **O** if it expresses an opinion, **F/O** if it combines fact and opinion. Underline the topic sentence. Then discuss with a peer or small group of classmates the answer to the following question: How effective was the writer's use of facts and opinions as supporting details? Write your response in a few sentences.

ALEXANDER THE GREAT

[1]Alexander III, more commonly known as Alexander the Great, was one of the greatest leaders in world history. [2]History confirms that he was born in Pella, Macedonia, in 356 B.C. to King Phillip of Macedon and his wife Olympias. [3]He seemed capable beyond his years. [4]For example, after his father's assassination, Alexander, at the age of 20, took the throne and brutally murdered all his rivals

CONTINUED

EXAMPLE *CONTINUED*

to power. [5]Through the course of 13 years of war, he established a civilization that included the Mediterranean, most of Europe, and reached to the borders of India. [6]He also established Greek as the common language of the land. [7]Some historians argue that Alexander's use of Greek as a common language was his wisest decision. [8]Greek as a common language expanded Greek culture, developed commerce, and created unity among diverse groups of people. [9]Shortly before his 33rd birthday, Alexander the Great died. [10]The cause of his death remains unknown.

1. *F/O* **2.** *F* **3.** *O* **4.** *F/O* **5.** *F*
6. *F* **7.** *O* **8.** *F/O* **9.** *F* **10.** *F*

Written Response: How effective was the writer's use of facts and opinions as supporting details?

Answers may vary. See the explanation.

Explanation

Compare your answers to the following student's think-aloud.

1. *F/O: His name and title are factual, but the value word greatest is an opinion with which some people may disagree.*
2. *F: The phrase "history confirms" indicates that this statement can be verified through research.*
3. *O: This sentence describes a quality of Alexander: the ability to lead early in life.*
4. *F/O: The phrase "for example" signals the facts that Alexander became king as a young man of 20 years of age and that he killed rivals. These details can be confirmed by research. However, the phrase "brutally murdered" is a biased description of the event.*

5. F: This statement can be checked and verified as true.
6. F: This statement can be checked and verified as true.
7. O: The phrase "historians argue" signals this statement is an opinion. Also, the word wisest states the writer's value judgment of Alexander's decision to use Greek as the common language.
8. F/O: Proving a direct connection between the effect of using the Greek language on culture and commerce and unifying the people may be difficult. This is a complicated assertion that needs research to be verified.
9. F: This statement can be checked and verified as true.
10. F: This is a factual statement that something isn't known.

Written Response: How effective was the writer's use of facts and opinions as supporting details?

My peers and I think the writer effectively used a mixture of facts and opinions to support the main idea. The first sentence is the topic sentence, and it states that Alexander was "one of the greatest leaders in world history." The facts in sentences 2, 4, 5, and 6 support this main idea. We also thought that the last two sentences state facts about his death that do not relate to his leadership.

Evaluate the Context of the Writer

Even though opinions can't be proved true like facts can, many opinions are still sound and valuable. To infer the reliability or value of an opinion, you may consider the source, the author of the opinion. Writers offer two types of valid opinions: **informed opinions** and **expert opinions.**

A writer develops an **informed opinion** by gathering and analyzing evidence.

A writer develops an **expert opinion** through much training and extensive knowledge in a given field.

Example

Read the topic and study the list of writers who have written their opinions about the topic. Identify each person as **IO** if he or she is more likely to offer an informed opinion and **EO** if he or she is more likely to offer an expert opinion. Discuss with a peer or small group of classmates the answer to the following question: *Which source(s) are best suited for an academic research essay?* Write your response.

How to Parent a Teen

EO **1.** Dr. Lisa Boesky, a leading child psychologist, television guest expert, national speaker, and author of several books such as *When to Worry: How to Tell if Your Teen Needs Help—and What to Do About It*

IO **2.** An advice columnist such as Ann Landers or Dear Abby responding to a reader's question

EO **3.** A pediatrician giving advice to the parents of one of his patients

IO **4.** A high school science teacher who writes a lesson plan about disciplining children for a unit on human development in a health class

Written response: Which source(s) are best suited for an academic research essay?

Answers may vary. See the explanation.

Explanation

Compare your responses to the following student's think-aloud.

1. *Dr. Boesky is considered to be an expert in the field of childrearing as she holds an advanced degree and has published books about the topic.*
2. *Advice columnists offer informed opinions on a wide range of topics. They often cite experts in their advice.*
3. *A pediatrician is a medical doctor for children. A pediatrician has had extensive training in child development.*
4. *A health teacher offers an informed opinion based on research to prepare the lesson. The teacher's main field is not child development, but science.*

Written response:

My peers and I agree that the expert opinion of Dr. Lisa Boesky would be the best source to use in an academic research essay. Her education, professional experience, and publications establish her as a reliable source. Ann Landers may be able to give an informed decision based on her years of experience as an advice columnist. However, she is not an expert in child psychology. We did consider using the advice of a pediatrician. However, professional advice to one patient may not apply to all parenting situations. The high school science teacher is also offering an informed opinion about one of many topics covered by a degree in science education. We did think that we could use the informed opinions of Ann Landers, the pediatrician, or the science teacher as an introduction or conclusion.

Evaluate the Context of the Source

Often people turn to factual sources to find the factual details. Factual details serve as convincing evidence in support of a point. They also may serve as the basis for informed opinions and expert opinions. The following chart lists just a few types and examples of sources for facts.

Types of Sources for Facts	
Type	**Example(s)**
Atlas: a collection of information given in a graphic format to include maps, photographs, timelines, etc.	**General atlas:** *Atlas of World History* **Subject atlas:** *Human Anatomy Atlas* **Road atlas:** *Rand McNally Road Atlas*
Dictionary: an alphabetical list of words with their meanings, pronunciation, and etymology	**Language dictionary:** *Merriam-Webster's Collegiate Dictionary* **Subject dictionary:** *The Dictionary of Baseball*
Encyclopedia: a reference volume(s) summarizing information from all fields of study or from one particular subject area	**General encyclopedia:** *The World Book Encyclopedia* **Subject encyclopedia:** *Encyclopedia of Human Nutrition*
Handbook: a reference book that gives quick access to facts, terms, concepts, directions, and so on about a specific subject	*Handbook for Writers* *Job Searcher's Handbook*

Example

Read the passage. Answer the questions that follow it. Then with a peer or small group of your classmates, discuss the answer to the following question: *Was the writer's use of facts and opinions effective? Why or why not?* Write your response.

The Growing Need for EMTs and Paramedics

[1]According to the U.S. Department of Labor's *Occupational Outlook Handbook*, employment of emergency medical technicians (EMTs) and paramedics is growing. [2]The number of jobs in this field will rise by 33 percent from 2010 to 2020. [3]This growth is much faster than the average for all careers. [4]*The Emergency Medical Training Handbook* states, "The primary focus of the EMT is to provide basic medical care and transportation for patients who access the emergency medical system." [5]*The Encyclopedia of Emergency Medicine* states the difference between EMTs and paramedics. [6]For example, paramedics provide advanced emergency care. [7]Also, paramedics are trained to give medication orally and intravenously. [8]In addition, they are also trained to use complex monitors or equipment. [9]*The Emergency Preparedness Atlas* stresses the role of EMTs and paramedics in responding to acts of terror or outbreaks of infectious diseases. [10]First responders must detect such threats. [11]They also must quickly relay such threats to proper authorities. [12]Leroy McCraney is a veteran paramedic who has bravely responded to emergencies caused by war, crime, and natural disasters over the course of his 30-year career. [13]He says, "EMTs and paramedics are dedicated to saving lives. [14]There is no more noble profession."

1. Sentence 2 is
(a.) a fact. **b.** an opinion. **c.** fact and opinion.

2. Sentence 8 is
(a.) a fact. **b.** an opinion. **c.** fact and opinion.

3. Sentence 12 states
a. a fact. **b.** an opinion. **(c.)** fact and opinion.

4. Sentence 13 states
a. a fact. **b.** an informed opinion. **(c.)** an expert opinion.

5. How many types of sources did the writer give in the passage?
a. 3 **(c.)** 5
b. 4 **d.** 6

Written response: Was the writer's use of facts and opinions effective? Why or why not?

Answers may vary. See the explanation.

Explanation

Compare your responses to the following student's think-aloud.

1. *Sentence 2 is (a) a fact. This detail can be verified in the* Occupational Outlook Handbook.
2. *Sentence 8 is (a) a fact. I assume this detail can be verified in* The Encyclopedia of Emergency Medicine, *a source for the special traits of a paramedic.*
3. *Sentence 12 states (c) fact and opinion. The facts about Leroy McCraney's career can be verified through research. However, the word* bravely *is biased and states the writer's opinion about the facts.*
4. *Sentence 13 states (c) an expert opinion. As a veteran, 30-year paramedic, McCraney has acquired extensive hands-on experience and training.*
5. *The writer used 5 types of sources.*
   - *in sentences 1 and 4, two handbooks—the* Occupational Outlook Handbook *and* The Emergency Medical Training Handbook
   - *in sentence 5, an encyclopedia—*The Encyclopedia of Emergency Medicine
   - *in sentence 9, an atlas—*The Emergency Preparedness Atlas
   - *in sentence 12, an expert opinion—Leroy McCraney, paramedic*

Written response:

My group of peers and I think the writer effectively used facts and opinions. We concluded that the writer's purpose was to persuade readers to become an EMT or paramedic based on the facts that this is a growing field with plenty of jobs in the future. The writer's use of factual sources makes this a trustworthy point. The call to action at the end of the paragraph was inspiring.

Effective writers begin thinking about their use of fact and opinion early in their reading/writing strategy. During the prewriting phase, writers may use facts and opinions to brainstorm details to support a main idea. A writer may choose to respond to a fact with opinions, or to use facts to support or disagree with an opinion. Many writers benefit from the following prewriting steps:

- Choose a topic.
- Brainstorm a list of facts, or record facts learned from reading.
- Brainstorm a list of opinions (biased words) about the topic:
  - Opinions of others that you have heard or read.
  - Your opinion(s) in response to a fact or facts.

Example

Review the paragraph and writing assignment about "The Family" in Practice 2, Part B (see page 526). Use the following chart to brainstorm details to support the topic sentence you wrote in Part B. Use relevant facts and opinions from the original paragraph, along with your own observations and opinions, to answer the following questions. *Answers may vary.*

- Do you agree with the definition of family given in the passage? Why or why not?
- How would you define *the family?*
- Which television shows or movies best depict your view of the family? How so?

Brainstorming Details: Facts and Opinions

Topic Sentence: *The family is far more than the definition given by the U.S. Census or the popular television shows of the 1950s.*

Type of Information	Information	My Opinion(s) in Response
Fact(s) and Source(s)	*Definition of the family: "The family refers to two or more persons related by birth, marriage, or adoption who reside together in a household," U.S. Census*	*This is a very limited definition of the family.*
Informed Opinion(s) and Source(s)	*"The family is a unit of people bound by a vow to the spiritual, emotional, and physical well-being of all members," Lottie Lane, foster parent to over 50 children*	*I agree with this definition. However, Lane does not make it clear who the "members" of a family are.*
Expert Opinion(s) and Source(s)	*"Most of us have an image of what a family is and should be. This image is perhaps best illustrated by popular television shows of the 1950s such as Father Knows Best,*	*Television shows that depict the family: The Fosters, ABC. One Day at a Time, The Cosby Show, NBC*

Explanation

Compare your responses to the following student's think-aloud.

I used the definition of the family from the U.S. Census: "The family refers to two or more persons related by birth, marriage, or adoption who reside together in a household." I consider this a fact as the government uses this definition to officially count families. For an informed opinion, I spoke to Lottie Lane, a long-time foster parent: "The family is a unit of people bound by a vow to the spiritual, emotional, and physical well-being of all members." I used the expert opinion of the textbook writers: "Most of us have an image of what the family is and should be. This image is perhaps best illustrated by popular television shows of the 1990s such as Father Knows Best, Leave it to Beaver, *and* Ozzie and Harriet.*" Then, I stated my reaction to each piece of information. I believe the U.S. Census definition of the family is too limited. I agree with Lane, but she does not explain who family "members" are. I listed TV shows that I believe more accurately depict the family, such as* One Day at a Time, The Cosby Show, *and* The Fosters.

Practice 3

Generate Relevant Details Using Fact and Opinion

Practice generating details to support a main idea. Study the following topic sentence and set of information from four sources. Choose information from the sources that you would use to support the topic sentence. Fill in the chart with the information you chose and your reactions. *Answers may vary.*

Topic sentence: The billion-dollar video game industry may lead to violent behavior by some users.

Source 1: "Active participation increases effective learning. Video games are an ideal environment in which to learn violence. They place the player in the role of the aggressor and reward him or her for successful violent behavior." —American Academy of Pediatrics

Source 2: "Video games profits were $6.7 billion, and 21% of bestselling video games in 2012 were shooter games. "—Essential Facts about the Computer and Video Game Industry, 2013. Entertainment Software Association

Source 3: "The images and themes in some video games are shocking and troublesome. There are popular games where players advance through acts of 'virtual' murder, assault and rape." —Congressman Jim Matheson, introducing the Video Game Ratings Enforcement Act to limit youth access to violent video games

CONTINUED

Brainstorming Details: Facts and Opinions		
TOPIC SENTENCE: The billion-dollar video game industry may lead to violent behavior by some users.		
Type of Information	**Information**	**My Opinion(s) in Response**
Fact(s) and Source(s)		
Informed Opinion(s) and Source(s)		
Expert Opinion(s) and Source(s)		

Recognize and Create Logical Order Using Facts and Opinions

L5

Effective readers note the logical relationship between facts and opinions in a passage. The order of the details reveals if the writer uses facts to support or explain an opinion. In that case, the opinion is stated first and the facts follow as supporting details. However, the order also reveals the writer's use of opinions to respond to a fact or set of facts. In this case, a fact or set of facts is stated and opinions follow that evaluate or explain their significance.

Example

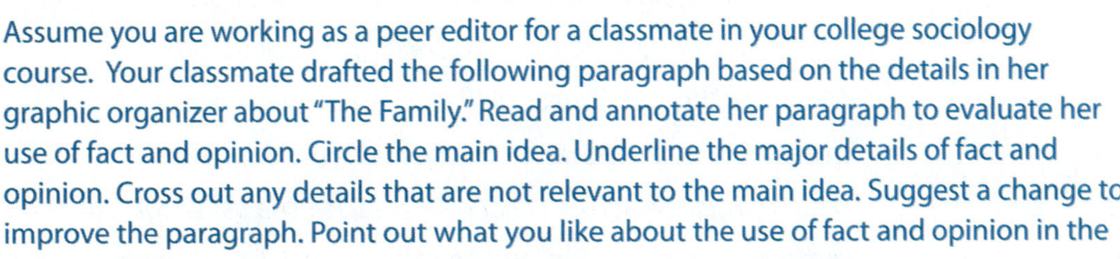
Assume you are working as a peer editor for a classmate in your college sociology course. Your classmate drafted the following paragraph based on the details in her graphic organizer about "The Family." Read and annotate her paragraph to evaluate her use of fact and opinion. Circle the main idea. Underline the major details of fact and opinion. Cross out any details that are not relevant to the main idea. Suggest a change to improve the paragraph. Point out what you like about the use of fact and opinion in the paragraph. *Answers may vary.*

What is *The Family*?

[1]What do we mean when we refer to "the family"? [2]According to the U.S. Census, "The family refers to two or more persons related by birth, marriage, or adoption who reside together in a household." [3]However, this official definition is designed to count people and does not state the true meaning of the family. [4]In the textbook *The Family*, authors Eshleman and Bulcroft claim, "Most of us have an image of what a family is and should be. [5]This image is perhaps best illustrated by popular television shows of the 1950s such as *Father Knows Best*, *Leave it to Beaver*, and *Ozzie and Harriet*." [6]~~I really like to watch the reruns of these shows.~~ [7]However, this view of the family is also very limited. [8]Many would say that other popular television shows better depict the family. [9]For example, *One Day at a Time* (1975–1984) depicted a single mother raising two children. [10]*The Cosby Show* (1984–1992) portrayed a traditional two-parent, upper-middle class African American family. [11]*The Fosters* (premiering in 2013) represents a non-traditional, multi-ethnic family made up of foster and biological children raised by two moms. [12]Perhaps the foster mother of 50 children, Lottie Lane, offers the best definition of the family, "The family is a unit of people bound by a vow to the spiritual, emotional, and physical well-being of all members." [13]Lane's definition may not clearly explain who the "members" of a family are, but she describes the heart of the family. [14]Ultimately, the family is far more than the definition given by the U.S. Census or the popular television shows of the 1950s.

Explanation

Compare your answers to the following student's think-aloud.

This paragraph effectively uses fact and opinion to lead up to the main idea stated in the last sentence. The main idea effectively disagrees with the definitions given by the U.S. Census and the textbook authors. The details also effectively combine fact and opinion to explain the main idea. The writer gives a fact, expert opinion, and informed opinion from various sources. Then the writer offers a sentence or two in reaction to them. For example, sentence 2 states the U.S. Census definition. Then sentence 3 states the writer's opinion, which disagrees with the definition. Likewise, sentences 4–5 state the textbook authors' expert opinion, and sentences 6–11 state the writer's opposing opinion. Sentence 8 states an opinion, and sentences 9–11 give factual descriptions of the television shows that "better depict the family." Finally, the writer states the informed opinion of Lottie Lane in sentence 12. Then, sentence 13 states the writer's opinion. Sentence 14 is the topic sentence. Sentence 6 is really not related to the main idea. It is not relevant that the writer "enjoys" watching the reruns of these shows. This sentence should be taken out. I also think the writer should give another example of a popular television show to illustrate the family for each decade between the 1990s and 2014.

Practice 4

Create Logical Order Using Facts and Opinions

Work with the brainstorming chart you completed in Practice 3. First, create an outline to organize your flow of facts and opinions. Next, write a rough draft of your paragraph using the details you generated. Work with a peer to review each other's rough drafts. Exchange, read, and review your drafts to make sure all details are relevant to the main ideas. Complete the following concept chart for the draft you are peer editing. Circle the main idea. Underline the key facts and opinions. Cross out any details that are not relevant to the main idea. Suggest a change to improve the paragraph. Point out what you like about the use of facts and opinions in the paragraph. Return your reviewed paragraphs to each other. Revise as needed.

Peer Review Concept Map: Facts and Opinions	
Topic Sentence:	
Supporting Details	**Type of Information and Source**
1.	
2.	
3.	

L6 Analyze and Use Effective Expression with Fact and Opinion

To effectively use fact and opinion to comprehend and state a main idea, readers and writers rely on attribution. **Attribution** is an effective way to distinguish between fact and opinion. It is also an effective tool to evaluate the reliability of a source. Two types of attribution are **quotes** and **reported speech**.

Attribution is the act of giving credit to the source of a piece of information.

A **quote**, or direct speech, is the use of the exact words of a person or passage.

Effective use of attribution is based on several rules of language. Consider the following statements. What is similar and different between the two?

Quote: Dr. McCullough states, "My studies reveal a strong connection between violence in the media and bullying."

Reported speech: Dr. McCullough stated that her studies revealed a clear link between media violence and bullying.

The quote identified the speaker and placed quotation marks before and after the exact words of the speaker. The reported speech also identified the speaker, but did not use quotation marks. Instead the word *that* linked the speaker to the speaker's ideas. In addition, the wording of reported speech changed in the use of verb tense and pronouns. A quote captures a statement made in the time it was spoken, and a speaker often uses present tense. Thus, this quote used the present tense verbs *states* and *reveal*. However, reported speech retells what was said in the past, so the verb tense changes accordingly. In this case, *states* was revised to *stated* and *reveal* to *revealed*. Likewise, the pronoun often differs between quoted and reported speech. In this example, the quote used the first person pronoun *I* while the reported speech revised *I* to *her*. Both readers and writers need to know the rules for using quotes and reported speech.

Reported speech, or indirect speech, is used to communicate what a person or passage said, but without using the exact words.

Basic Language Rules for Quotes

- Quotation marks appear before and after the exact words of the speaker.
- The attribution phrase that gives credit to the speaker or source is set off with a comma.
- A comma or period at the end of the quote is placed inside the closing quotation mark.
- The quoted material begins with a capital letter.
- When a quote is interrupted by an attribution phrase, the quoted material after the attribution is not capitalized.
- Examples:
    - Lisa states, "Using a tablet increases my learning."
    - "Using a tablet," Lisa states, "increases my learning."
    - "Using a tablet increases my learning," states Lisa.

Basic Language Rules for Reported Speech

- Reword the original idea of the speaker or the passage.
- Use *that* to link the speaker to the reported speech, the reworded original idea.
- Change the pronouns and tense of verbs as appropriate for sense.
- Example:
  - Lisa stated that her use of a tablet increased her learning.

Readers analyze sources and take notes to record ideas that they may use in their own writing. During the note-taking process, effective readers follow the rules of attribution.

Example

Assume you are writing a research paper about workplace stress for a college psychology class. Read the following information about the topic from various sources. Choose two ideas to use in your paper. Record one idea as a quote and the other idea as reported speech. Then share your response with a peer or small group of classmates. Discuss how you used attribution to evaluate and choose the ideas you recorded. *Answers may vary.*

Source 1:
Joe Tripp, Regional Manager of BigSale Retail: "Since the company reorganized, nobody feels safe. It used to be that as long as you did your work, you had a job. That's not for sure anymore. Morale is terrible."

Source 2:
U.S. Centers for Disease Control and Prevention: "Job stress can be defined as the harmful physical and emotional responses that occur when the requirements of the job do not match the capabilities, resources, or needs of the worker."

Source 3:
Princeton Survey Research Associates: "Three-fourths of employees believe the worker has more on-the-job stress than a generation ago."

Source 4:
Psychology professor, Dr. Karla Elias: "Chronic workplace stress reduces the ability of workers to do their jobs effectively."

Quote: *The CDC states, "Job stress can be defined as the harmful physical and emotional responses that occur when the requirements of the job do not match the capabilities, resources, or needs of the worker."*

Reported Speech: *Joe Tripp, Regional Manager for BigSale Retail, stated that morale is terrible at his workplace since the company reorganized.*

Explanation

Compare your answers to the following student's think-aloud.

I choose to use sources 1 and 2. Source 2 offers a definition of workplace stress from a reliable government source, the CDC. Source 1 offers a personal example of workplace stress. As a writer I would explain the relationship between these two pieces of information. I might also use the facts given by source 3, too. Each of the members of our small group made different choices based on how we wanted to limit the topic. For example, one peer decided to use sources 2 and 3. He wants to explain how workforce stress is getting worse. In contrast, I want to explain how the CDC definition applies to the real world.

Quote: The CDC states, "Job stress can be defined as the harmful physical and emotional responses that occur when the requirements of the job do not match the capabilities, resources, or needs of the worker."

Reported Speech: Joe Tripp, Regional Manager for BigSale Retail, stated that morale is terrible at his workplace since the company reorganized.

Effective readers/writers use the revision and proofreading phases of the writing process to ensure proper use of language for attribution of facts and opinions.

Practice 5

Analyze and Use Effective Expression Using Fact and Opinion

Work with the rough draft of a paragraph you completed in an earlier practice. Exchange drafts with a peer. Proofread each other's paragraphs for effective use of language for attribution of facts and opinions. Make suggestions for improvements as needed. Return your drafts to each other and revise into a new draft.

Reading and Writing Assignments

MySkillsLab™ Complete these assignments in MySkillsLab.

Considering Audience and Purpose

Study the set of photographs at the beginning of the module. Assume you work in an advertising firm and your client produces a line of tomato products called *The Mighty Tomato*. The product line includes tomato sauces, chopped tomatoes, and pureed tomatoes. The company wants to increase sales. Write a paragraph that describes the benefits of eating tomatoes. In your sales pitch for tomatoes use both facts and opinions that will convince consumers to buy them.

Reading and Writing for Everyday Life

Assume you are in the market to buy a used car. You begin your search on the Internet, and you come across a site with the following information. Skim the page. Then rate it on the following scale for trustworthiness. Highlight facts useful to you as a consumer looking to buy a used car. Complete the company's customer service survey that follows the information. *Responses may vary.*

Evaluation of Source:	**Untrustworthy**			**Trustworthy**	
BargainCarsEveryday.com	1	2	3	4	5

To improve our service, please tell us what about our page convinced you to shop with us. What can we do to improve our page? What additional information do you need?

Reading and Writing for College Life

Assume you are taking a college course in health. You are currently studying the unit on preventing violence and injury. The passage that follows is part of your required textbook reading. In addition, you have chosen to research and write about gun control. You have found the following four sources on the Internet. In the spaces given, identify each source as **P** = Pro (for) gun control, **C** = Con (against) gun control, or **O** = Objective about gun control.

P ________ Brady Campaign to Prevent Gun Violence. "4 Victories for Strong Gun Laws." Jan 2012. Web.

P ________ Children's Defense Fund. ***Protect Children Not Guns 2009***, September 2009. Web.

C ________ National Rifle Association. "Firearms Fact Card 2012." NRA Institute for Legislative Action: Gun Laws. 9 Jan. 2012. Web.

O ________ U.S. Department of Justice. *Federal Firearms Regulations Reference Guide*. 2005 Web. Jan. 2012.

Skim the passage. Predict the author's stand as pro, con, or neutral in the gun debate. Underline the key facts. Enclose statements of opinion in (parentheses). Next, write a response to the passage. In your response, agree or disagree with the author's ideas. Explain your reasons for agreeing or disagreeing.

HEALTH HEADLINES: THE GUN DEBATE

According to the most recent statistics, more than 100,000 people in the United States were shot in murders, assaults, suicides, accidents, or by police intervention in 2007. Nearly 31,000 died from gun violence. Many who survived experienced major physical and emotional effects.

- In 2007, firearm homicide was the second leading cause of injury or death for men and women aged 10 to 24, second only to motor vehicle crashes.
- Today, 35 percent of American homes have a gun on the premises. More than 283 million privately owned guns are registered. 40 percent of those registered are handguns.
- The presence of a gun in the home triples the risk of a homicide there. The presence of a gun in the home increases suicide risk by more than five times.

What factors contribute to excessive gun deaths in the United States? (Of course, by sheer numbers, if you have more guns, the likelihood of people using them in inappropriate ways increases. Critics of gun control argue that guns don't murder people. It's the person pulling the trigger on the gun who is ultimately the problem. In addition the argument about the "right to bear arms" as a constitutional right is a difficult area of debate.)

Adapted from Donatelle, Rebecca J., *Health: the Basics*, Green Edition, 9th ed., p. 105.

Reading and Writing for Working Life

Assume you are a supervisor of the receiving department in an electronics retail store. One of your employees has reported an incident to which you must respond.

- **Before Reading**: Use the reporter's questions *who, what, when, where, why,* and *how* to get an idea of what took place in the incident.
- **During Reading**: Highlight the relevant facts.
- **After Reading**: In the space following the passage, make a recommendation for action to respond to the incident.

Employee Incident Report

Name: Jamal Odum	**Date of Accident**: December 12
Age: 28	**Time**: 6 a.m.
Position: Forklift Operator	**Location**: Loading dock 3
Employee ID #: 33358	**Witnesses**: Amy Presser, John Hall

Description of Event: Jamal Odum drove the forklift at Dock 3 at the store on Beeville Road. The routine job involved unloading and storing cardboard containers delivered by truck from another store in the chain. Each bale of cardboard weighed 700 pounds, and the bales were stacked double. As Odum lifted a stack off a truck, the top bale slid off and into Carl Jones, the truck driver. The accident caused severe injury to Jones. Odum stated that he had not stabilized the load before beginning to move it. He claimed there was not room at the top of the truck. He admitted that he had previously dropped loads off his forklift and blamed the accidents on the driving surface. He said that the handling of the forklift truck was very unstable. He used his hands to describe the motion of the truck—it floated.

Comments from Witnesses: Amy Presser stated that Odum is an ideal worker who had to put up with unsafe job conditions. The surface of the floor/road at the loading dock was uneven and soft, often causing heavy loads to shift and the forklift to sink into the surface. John Hall stated that the top bale was too high, making it unsafe to lift with a fork lift. John Hall stated that Odum was careless as a forklift driver.

Workshop: Compose a Paragraph Using Fact and Opinion

Choose a paragraph to read and respond to in writing. You may select a paragraph in an example, practice, or writing assignment within this module. Or you may select a paragraph of your own choosing. Use the following guide to comprehend and respond to the paragraph. Apply what you have learned about fact and opinion to your reading/writing strategy.

Preread: Survey and Question

Ask questions about the text's features.

____

____

What is the passage about?

____

____

How is the material organized?

____

____

What do I already know about this topic? (What is my prior knowledge about the vocabulary?)

____

____

What is my purpose for reading/writing?

____

____

What points may I want to address or include in my written response?

____

____

Read and Annotate

As you read, annotate key ideas, particularly those details that answer your prereading questions.

Recite, Review, and Brainstorm

Recite the information. Summarize the most important parts. Answer your prereading questions. Rephrase ideas into your own words. Record changes in your opinions based on the new information. **Review** the information. **Brainstorm** ideas for your written response to the passage. **Freewrite** a response to what you have read. **Map** the relationship among ideas you have annotated in the text. **Outline** or list key ideas and details in blocks of thought.

Write a Draft of Your Response

Using the ideas you generated by brainstorming, compose a draft of your response.

Revise Your Draft

Once you have created a draft using facts and opinions, read the draft to answer the questions in the "Questions for Revising a Paragraph Using Fact and Opinion" box that follows. Indicate your answers by annotating your paper. If you answer "yes" to a question, underline, check, or circle examples. If you answer "no" to a question, write needed information in margins and draw lines to indicate placement of additional details. Revise your paragraph based on your reflection. (*Hint:* Experienced writers create several drafts as they focus on one or two questions per draft.)

Step by Step: Questions for Revising a Paragraph Using Fact and Opinion

- ❑ Have I stated or implied a focused main idea?
- ❑ Have I stated or implied the specific details?
- ❑ Is the order of details clear? Have I used clear transitions and signal words?
- ❑ Have I used appropriate details of fact and opinion to make my point?
- ❑ Have I made my point with adequate details?
- ❑ Have I included only the facts and opinions that are relevant to my topic sentence?
- ❑ Have I used effective language for attribution of facts and opinions?

Proofread Your Draft

Once you have made any revisions to your paragraph that may be needed, proofread your paragraph to eliminate careless errors.

Review Test

MySkillsLab™ Complete this Review Test in MySkillsLab.

Score (number correct) _____ x 10 = _____ %

Fact and Opinion

Read the following passage from a college psychology textbook. Complete the items that follow.

1150L/10.0 GE/551 words

Culture

[1]In his book *Amusing Ourselves to Death* professor and social commentator Neil Postman sounds a sociological alarm, warning readers that a culture based purely on technology and TV is not necessarily a culture worth enjoying.

[2]We are rapidly becoming a society that focuses on trivia. [3]We all know who's dating who in Hollywood and which TV star recently got arrested, but can we name the vice president? [4]If we become caught up in a culture of mindless entertainment, he argues, we spend our time thinking about insignificant trivia and ignoring important issues. [5]We are at risk of killing our culture because people are too busy focusing on the insignificant.

[6]Is Postman's warning nothing more than hyperbole? [7]Not necessarily. [8]Recently, I watched a family sitting at a table eating frozen custard. [9]The mother listened to her iPod as a Nintendo DS game hypnotized her son. [10]The father talked on his cell phone, and the five year old daughter seemed totally bored because she had no electronic toy or anyone to talk to. [11]This technophilic family was clearly caught up in our country's culture of instant, constant entertainment. [12]Entertainment is not all bad, as Postman points out, but pursuing entertainment at all costs affects our relationships and

CONTINUED

our nation. [13]Of course, there's more to culture than movies, slot machines, and electronic gizmos. [14]In fact, culture forms the foundation of society and frames our perception of life.

[15]One category of culture is material culture: items within a society that you can taste, touch, or feel. [16]The jewelry, art, music, clothing, architecture, and crafts a society creates are all examples of material culture. [17]Of course, the natural resources available to a culture can influence that culture's creations. [18]For example, while seven countries (the United States, Japan, Russia, Canada, Germany, France, and the United Kingdom) use more than 46 percent of the world's electricity and oil, these countries combined hold only about 12 percent of the world's population. [19]What do these statistics tell you about material culture? [20]On a tour of these countries, you'd be likely to stumble across plenty of cars, air conditioners, heaters, blow dryers, and a host of other modern conveniences. [21]If you took a trip to Nigeria, though, you'd notice that a lack of access to energy also influences material culture. [22]Nigeria is the ninth largest country in the world, yet it ranks 71st in the world's electricity use and 42nd in the world's use of oil. [23]Few people own a car, and many live without regular access to electricity.

[24]Not all elements of culture are items you can touch, see, or buy at your local mall. [25]Nonmaterial culture consists of the nonphysical products of society, including our symbols, values, rules, and sanctions. [26]Symbols represent, suggest, or stand for something else. [27]They can be words, gestures, or even objects, and they often represent abstract or complex concepts.

[28]How can people uphold and enforce their values in everyday life? [29]They develop rules for appropriate behavior based on those values. [30]We call these rules norms. [31]Norms provide the justification for sanctions. [32]A sanction is a prize or punishment you receive when you either abide by a norm or violate it. [33]If you do what you are supposed to do, you get a positive sanction; if you break the rules, you earn a negative sanction.

Adapted from Carl, John, *Think Sociology*, pp. 48–49.

A. Complete the following items.

1. Sentence 1 is
   (a.) a fact. b. an opinion. c. a mixture of fact and opinion.
2. Sentence 2 is
   a. a fact. (b.) an opinion. c. a mixture of fact and opinion.
3. Sentence 17 is
   a. a fact. (b.) an opinion. c. a mixture of fact and opinion.
4. In this passage, Neil Postman's ideas are
   a. factual details. b. informed opinions. (c.) expert opinions.

B. Complete the concept map with information from the passage.

5. *Material Culture*	6. *Nonmaterial Culture*
items within a society that you can taste, touch, feel, see, or hear	**Nonphysical products of society** **7.** *Symbols*: represent, suggest or stand for something (words, gestures) **8.** *Values*: standards to determine what is good, bad, right, or wrong **9.** Norms: *rules for appropriate behavior* **10.** *Sanctions*: prizes for abiding by norms; punishment for violating them

Summary Response

Restate the author's central idea in your own words. In your summary, follow the thought pattern used by the author. Begin your summary response with the following: *The central idea of "Culture" from the textbook* Think Sociology *is. . . .*

What Do You Think?

Do you agree with Neil Postman that people focus too much on entertainment technology and insignificant things in our society today? The author cites a personal experience as an example that appears to support Postman's claim. Assume you are writing a paper for a sociology class. State your position—whether you agree or disagree with Postman—and then cite personal experience to support your view. Try to add at least one detail from a factual source and one expert opinion. (You might even want to post your response to a blog!)

Academic Learning Log: Module Review

Summary of Key Concepts of Fact and Opinion

Assess your comprehension of facts and opinions.

LO1 LO2

1. A fact is *a specific detail that is true based on objective proof*.

LO1 LO2 LO3 LO4

2. An opinion is *an interpretation, value judgment, or belief that cannot be proved or disproved*.
3. Objective proof can be *physical evidence, an eyewitness account, or the result of an accepted scientific method*.
4. An informed opinion is developed *by gathering and analyzing evidence*.
5. An expert opinion is developed *through much training and extensive knowledge in the field*.
6. A fact *states* reality and uses *unbiased* words.
7. An opinion *interprets* reality and uses *biased* words.
8. Biased words express *opinions, value judgments, and interpretations*.
9. A qualifier may express an *absolute, unwavering opinion using words such as always or never*.
10. *Attribution* is the act of giving credit to the source of a piece of information. A *quote*, or direct speech, is the use of the exact words of a person or passage. *Reported speech*, or indirect speech, is used to communicate what a person or passage said, but without using the exact words.

Test Your Comprehension of Fact and Opinion

Respond to the following questions and prompts. *Answers may vary.*

LO1 LO2 LO3 LO4

In your own words, what is the difference between an informed opinion and an expert opinion?

The main difference between an informed and an expert opinion is based on a person's education and experience in relationship to a particular topic. For example, a student can form an informed opinion by writing a research paper on a topic. In contrast, a professor has formed an expert opinion by earning an advanced degree, teaching, and writing on the subject.

LO1 LO2 LO3 LO5

In your own words, describe how to distinguish between a fact and an opinion.

To distinguish between a fact and an opinion, a reader can ask the following questions: Can the statement be proved or disproved? Can the statement be observed in practice? Can the statement be verified by witnesses, manuscripts, or documents? Does the author use biased words or qualifiers?

Why is it important to distinguish between fact and opinion?

It is important to distinguish between a fact and an opinion to evaluate information as reliable and useful. Since opinions are biased viewpoints, they may not be valid, reliable, or useful. However, an opinion may be supported with facts and logical reasons. Expert opinions are built on research, education, and professional experience. Our ability to distinguish between fact and opinion helps us make wise decisions or purchases.

L1 L2 L3 L4 L5 L6

1. **How will I use what I have learned?** In your notebook, discuss how you will apply to your own reading/writing strategy what you have learned about facts and opinions. When will you apply this knowledge to your reading/writing strategy?
2. **What do I still need to study about facts and opinions?** In your notebook, discuss your ongoing study needs. Describe what, when, and how you will continue studying and using facts and opinions.

Complete the Post-test for Module 14 in MySkillsLab.

15 Argument

LEARNING OUTCOMES

After studying this module you should be able to:

- **LO 1** Answer the Question "What's the Point of Argument?"
- **LO 2** Comprehend and State a Main Idea Using Argument
- **LO 3** Identify and Generate Relevant Details for an Argument
- **LO 4** Recognize and Create Logical Order in an Argument
- **LO 5** Analyze and Use Effective Expression with Argument

In almost every area of our lives, we engage in some form of argument or persuasion. Whether convincing a friend to see a particular movie or proving we are the right candidate for a particular job, we are most effective when we use reason and logic to get others to agree with our views.

To make an argument, effective writers assert or imply a strong stand on one side of a debatable issue. Then they offer supports for that stand by providing convincing evidence such as reasons, facts, examples, and expert opinions. In addition to asserting a claim and supporting it with evidence, effective writers acknowledge and rebut (disprove or challenge) the opposition's counterclaims. An effective reader evaluates the claim and supporting details to determine or infer whether the claim is valid and the supports are relevant and adequate. In everyday life, our court system is based on proving claims of guilt or innocence. In working life, we use reasons to resolve workplace disputes or offer solutions to problems. In college life, we encounter debatable claims in every discipline.

WHAT'S THE POINT of Argument?

Argument is often a call to action or a challenge to a change of mind. The following photos represent several reasons against building a Target store in the location of a popular neighborhood park. Study the photographs. In the space provided, identify the claim, reasons, and an opposing point of view about removing the park to build a Target store. Answer the question "What's the point?" with a one-sentence statement of the overall main idea. *Answers may vary.*

Photographic Organizer: Argument

What is the issue?

Opposition to building a Target store in a city park.

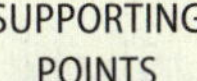

SUPPORTING POINTS

COUNTERCLAIM (Opposing Point)

What is this reason?

Target will cause more traffic.

What is this point?

Target will stimulate the local economy.

What is this reason?

Target will destroy a shady oasis.

SUPPORT THAT REFUTES COUNTERCLAIM

What is this reason?

Mega-stores bring more crime.

What is this reason?

The park gives children a safe place to play.

What's the claim?

A Target store should not be built in the park.

What's the Point? One Student's Response

The following paragraph offers one student's claim that argues against building a new Target store in her neighborhood, as illustrated by the photographs. Read the argument and the explanations; complete the activities in **bold** type in the annotations.

Let the Children Play: No Target

Dear Mayor and Commissioners:

[1]I strongly oppose relocating the recreational center at the corner of Nova Road and Main Trail to make space for a Target store. [2]I am outraged and shocked that you even think moving our playground so it sits on top of a landfill behind a new Target is an option. [3]Most likely, you think a Target will stimulate the economy, but a Target in this location is not worth the money it would generate. [4]First of all, the intersection will not be able to sustain the kind of traffic that a Target will draw. [5]This type of traffic will create added dangers for the children commuting to their "relocated" park. [6]Secondly, the development will destroy one of the few remaining ecological parks; Nova Park is not only a natural habitat, but also a shady oasis for the many families that live nearby. [7]Why pave over this natural refuge when there is so much bare land out Williamson and US 1? [8]Those roads can better bear the added traffic. [9]Thirdly, a park at the edge of the neighborhood adds more value to the neighborhood than a Target. [10]I am an expectant mother and have planned on walking my child to this park just as my parents did with me. [11]I grew up playing on those monkey bars and swinging under the beautiful canopy of oaks that you now threaten to destroy with a lame, hot parking lot and an unattractive, square building. [12]I do not wish to take my child to the back of a Target store to play. [13]Finally, this type of mega-retail store often increases crime in the surrounding area. [14]This nearsightedness is not the kind of leadership I will vote for.

Respectfully, A Concerned Citizen

Main Idea: The main idea is the point the author is claiming about the topic. **Underline the topic and circle the writer's claim about this topic.**

Effective Expression: To argue with a reader, an author uses subjective words that express opinions, attitudes, and values.

Double underline at least three more subjective words or phrases.

Strong Transition: The transition phrase "First of all" signals that the author is offering a reason in support of her claim.

Circle three more transitional words or phrases that signal a reason of support.

Relevant Details: In argument, relevant details not only include facts and consequences, but also refute opposing points. Here, the writer offers another location better suited to a retail store.

Draw a box around one other opposing point and the writer's counterpoint.

Comprehend and State a Main Idea Using Argument

LO2

Have you noticed how many of us enjoy debating issues and winning arguments? You can see this on television, where many shows thrive on conflict and debate. For example, the *Jerry Springer* show uses the conflicts between guests to amuse the audience. Programs such as *Meet the Press*, hosted by David Gregory, or *The O'Reilly Factor* with Bill O'Reilly debate political and social issues. Likewise, talk radio fills hours of airtime with debate about issues related to culture and politics. Two examples are *The Rush Limbaugh Show* and *The Diane Rehm Show*.

A **claim** is a statement, assertion, or conclusion about a specific position on a debatable issue.

Some people are so committed to their ideas that they become emotional, even angry. However, an effective **argument** is a reasonable **claim** based on logical supports. An argument also acknowledges and refutes **counterclaims**.

Argument is a process of reasoning that demonstrates a claim as valid based on the logical details given in support of that claim.

A **counterclaim** is a statement, assertion, or conclusion that opposes a specific position on a debatable issue.

You have acquired several skills that will help you master argument as a reader/writer, including stating or implying main ideas, identifying and generating supporting details, distinguishing between fact and opinion, recognizing tone and purpose, and making inferences. Think about these skills as you read the following claim.

Psycho is a movie worth seeing.

The claim certainly states the speaker's point clearly. But it probably wouldn't inspire most of us to see the movie. Instead, our first response to the claim is likely to be "Why?" We need supporting details or reasons before we can decide if we think a claim is valid. Notice that a claim, like any main idea, is made up of a topic and a controlling point. Here, *Psycho* is the topic, and the controlling point is "worth seeing."

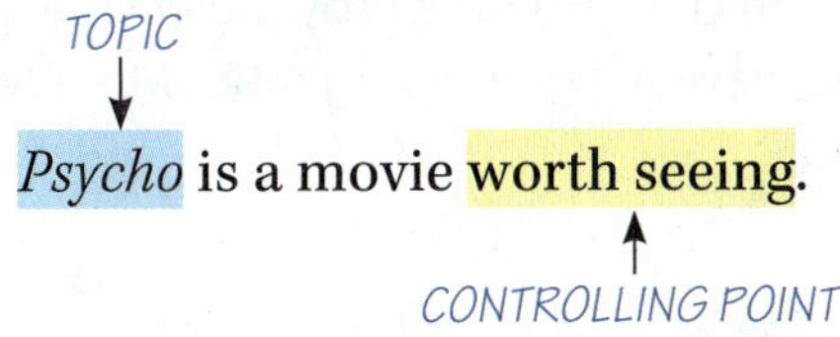

Notice that the details that follow answer a question about the controlling point: "Why is *Psycho* a movie worth seeing?"

1. It is a classic—the first "slasher" movie that inspired hundreds of slasher movies, none of which come close to it in style or substance.
2. It is suspenseful and shocking, with a haunting score by Bernard Hermann.
3. It contains the notorious "shower scene"—one of the most famous scenes in movie history.

These three sentences offer the supports for the writer's claim. We are now able to understand the basis of the argument, and we now have details about which we can agree or disagree.

Writers frequently make claims that they want us to accept as valid. In fact, a reader's main task is to infer whether a claim is reasonable based on the details. To assess whether the claim is valid, an effective reader first identifies the claim and the supports.

Example

A. Read the following groups of ideas. Identify the claim and supports in each group. Write **C** if the sentence states the writer's claim or **S** if the sentence offers support for the claim.

Group 1

[1]Dog bites pose a serious national problem. [2]Dogs bite an estimated 4.7 million people each year, with 800,000 individuals needing medical treatment.

C **1.** Sentence 1

S **2.** Sentence 2

Group 2

[1]They never wave or say hello. [2]Our neighbors are unfriendly people.

S **3.** Sentence 1

C **4.** Sentence 2

Group 3

[1]Popcorn contains only 15 calories per cup when it is air-popped. [2]Popcorn is a good snack. [3]Popcorn is a good source of fiber.

S **5.** Sentence 1

C **6.** Sentence 2

S **7.** Sentence 3

Group 4

[1]Mrs. Overby takes time to explain difficult ideas in class. [2]Mrs. Overby is always available for student conferences. [3]Mrs. Overby's students have a high passing rate. [4]Mrs. Overby is a good teacher.

S **8.** Sentence 1

S **9.** Sentence 2

S **10.** Sentence 3

C **11.** Sentence 4

B. Editorial cartoons offer arguments through the use of humor. The cartoonist has a claim to make and uses the situation, actions, and words in the cartoon as supporting details. Study the cartoon reprinted here. Then write a claim based on the supports in the cartoon.

Answers will vary. See the explanation.

The Detroit News, Larry Wright © 2002

Explanation

Compare your answers to the following student's think-aloud.

A.

Group 1

1. *Sentence 1 states the writer's claim (C). The topic is "dog bites," and the writer's opinion is "a serious national problem."* **2.** *Sentence 2 offers facts about dog bites as support for the claim (S).*

Group 2

3. *Sentence 1 describes the neighbor's behavior as evidence to support the claim (S).* **4.** *Sentence 2 states the writer's claim*

CONTINUED

EXPLANATION *CONTINUED*

(C). The topic is "our neighbors." The writer's claim is "unfriendly people."

Group 3

5. Sentence 1 offers a fact about popcorn as support for the claim (S). **6.** Sentence 2 states the writer's claim (C). The topic is popcorn. The writer's claim is "a good snack." **7.** Sentence 3 offers another fact in support of the claim (S).

Group 4

8–10. Sentences 1, 2, and 3 offer observations and facts that can be verified as support for the claim (S). **11.** Sentence 4 states the writer's claim (C). The topic is "Mrs. Overby." The writer's opinion is "a good teacher."

B. The note from school came from the school's administration. The horrible spelling is a sign that the people running the school do not have basic writing or thinking skills. Several claims may be suggested by the details in the cartoon. The following are a few possibilities.

Students must not be receiving a good education.

School administrators should not allow teachers to teach outside their fields.

School administrators are the main problem in education.

School administrators are not smart.

School administrators must not care about education.

Practice 1

Comprehend a Main Idea Using Argument

Identify the claim and supports in the following paragraph. Write **C** if the sentence states the writer's claim or **S** if the sentence offers support for the claim.

[1]School vouchers are government cash grants or tax credits for parents, equal to all or part of the cost of educating their child at an elementary or secondary school of their choice. [2]School vouchers are not the best ways to improve education. [3]The greatest gains in student achievement have occurred in places where vouchers do not exist. [4]Private schools that receive money from school vouchers are not required to adopt the academic standards, hire highly qualified teachers, or administer the assessments required of public schools. [5]School vouchers require taxpayers to fund both public and private schools.

S **1.** Sentence 1
C **2.** Sentence 2
S **3.** Sentence 3
S **4.** Sentence 4
S **5.** Sentence 5

To compose a paragraph using argument, a writer asserts his or her claim in a topic sentence. A topic sentence states the debatable topic, the writer's claim, and, possibly, a pattern of organization. Because argument is a purpose, the writer may choose a particular pattern or combined patterns of organization to support a claim. In addition, the writer's claim is often implied by the following types of signal words or phrases: *against, all, always, must, must not, never, only, oppose, should, should not,* or *support.*

For example, the following topic sentence contains (1) the debatable topic, (2) the writer's claim, and (3) a pattern of organization to signal the flow of ideas.

DEBATABLE TOPIC — WRITER'S CLAIM

Substance-free student housing on college campuses should be available for several reasons.

PATTERN OF ORGANIZATION: ARGUMENT SIGNAL WORDS

Example

The following items present a debatable topic, the writer's claim, and a pattern of organization. Combine the ideas in each group to create a topic sentence for an argumentative paragraph. *Answers may vary.*

1. TOPIC: *Merit pay for teachers*

   CLAIM: *oppose, support*

   PATTERN OF ORGANIZATION: *list, reasons*

   TOPIC SENTENCE: *The public should support merit pay for teachers for several reasons.*

2. TOPIC: *Corporal punishment (spanking) to discipline children*

   CLAIM: *negative, positive*

   PATTERN OF ORGANIZATION: *effects*

   TOPIC SENTENCE: *Parents and educators should never use corporal punishment due to its negative effects.*

Explanation

Compare your responses to the following student's think-aloud.

I had to revise these ideas several times to discover the most effective way to state my position on the issues. For both topics, I had to think about who should or would support or oppose the ideas. I didn't want to use the first person pronoun I because I wanted my argument to reflect a larger view than just my own. It seems that the "public" would be the group that needs to take a stand about merit pay. And parents and educators need to take a stand about corporal punishment. Also, it didn't seem necessary to include the pattern of organization signal words in the first topic sentence. Including them made the sentence long and awkward. It was helpful to consider the pattern of organization signal words as I thought about the stand

I wanted to state. I did include the pattern words in the second topic sentence.

1. *The public should support merit pay for teachers.*
2. *Parents and educators should never use corporal punishment due to its negative effects.*

Practice 2

State a Main Idea Using Argument

The following items present a topic. Limit the topic by filling in the blanks with a claim or position and appropriate signal word(s). Then combine the ideas in each group to create a topic sentence for an argument. *Answers may vary.*

1. TOPIC: *Raise minimum wage*

CLAIM: *for, against*

PATTERN OF ORGANIZATION: *listing, reasons*

TOPIC SENTENCE: *Compelling reasons exist for raising the minimum wage.*

2. TOPIC: *Studying*

CLAIM: *most effective*

PATTERN OF ORGANIZATION: *process, series, steps*

TOPIC SENTENCE: *The most effective studying process occurs in a series of steps.*

L3 Identify and Generate Relevant Details for an Argument

Common supports of an argumentative claim include reasons, facts, examples, effects, and expert opinions, as well as details that refute the opposing view. Both readers and writers evaluate these types of details to infer or determine if a claim is a **valid conclusion**. For a claim to be valid, supporting details must be both **relevant** and **adequate**.

A **valid conclusion** is a claim reasonably supported with details soundly based in logic or fact.

Adequate details satisfy in quality and quantity the requirements of a claim.

Relevant details have a significant and clear relationship to the claim.

To decide whether the details, or supports, are relevant to the claim, apply what you already know about main ideas and details. A claim, like any main idea, is made up of a topic and a controlling point. Relevant details carry out the controlling point. Irrelevant supports change the topic or ignore the controlling point. Relevant supports answer the reporter's questions (*who, what, when, where, why, how*). Ask and answer these questions to infer whether the supports for a claim are relevant.

For example, read the following argument a teenager makes about her curfew. Identify the support that is irrelevant to her claim.

> [1]"I am mature enough to make my own decisions about my curfew. [2]When I work the closing shift at McDonald's, I am out until 2 a.m., and no matter where I am, I always make sure to stick with a group of people. [3]And I am not just out roaming the streets; I only want to stay out late for specific events like a concert or a late movie. [4]None of my friends even have curfews. [5]Just like always, I will tell you ahead of time where I will be and when I will be home, and I do have my cell phone in case you get worried and want to call me. [6]Or I can call you if I need help."

By turning this teenager's claim into a question, she and her parents can test her ability to offer valid reasons: "How have I shown I am mature enough to make my own decisions about my curfew?" Sentences 2, 3, 5, and 6 offer relevant factual examples of her maturity. However, sentence 4 states an irrelevant support that changes the topic. The argument is about *her* curfew based on *her* maturity, not her friends' curfews.

Effective readers and writers also evaluate details to determine if they are adequate. A valid argument is based not only on a claim and relevant support but also on the amount and quality of the support given. That is, supports must give enough evidence for the writer's claim to be convincing. Just as you use the reporter's questions to decide whether supports are relevant, you also can use them to test whether supports are adequate. Asking and answering questions to test details keeps you from jumping to an **invalid conclusion** or false inference.

An **invalid conclusion** is a claim not adequately supported with enough relevant details, a false inference.

For example, you may argue, "A vegetarian diet is a more healthful diet. I feel much better since I became a vegetarian." However, the reporter's question "Why?" reveals that the support is inadequate. The answer to "Why is a vegetarian diet a more healthful diet?" should include expert opinions and facts, not just personal opinion. Often in the quest to support a claim, people oversimplify their reasons. Thus, they do not offer enough information to prove the claim. Instead of facts and logical details, they may offer emotional false causes, false comparisons, or forced choices, or leave out facts that hurt the claim. When evaluating an argument, it is important to test each piece of supporting evidence to determine that details are relevant and adequate.

Example

Test each of the following sets of supporting details to determine if they are relevant and adequate in relationship to the stated claims.

A. Relevant Details: Read the following lists of claims and supports. After reading, mark each support **R** if it is relevant to the claim or **N** if it is not relevant to the claim.

Claim:

Online shopping offers a lot of benefits.

Supports

R **a.** You can shop at any time of the day or night.

R **b.** You don't have to leave your house.

N **c.** You can't try on clothes to see if they fit.

N **d.** You may have to pay postage to return items.

R **e.** You can save money because comparison shopping takes less time.

B. Relevant Details: Argument is also used in advertisements. It is important for you to be able to understand the claims and supports of ads. Many times advertisers appeal to emotions, make false claims, or give supports that are not relevant because their main aim is to persuade you to buy their product. Study the advertisement for milk put out by America's Dairy Farmers and Milk Processors. Mark each support **R** if it is relevant to the claim or **N** if it is not relevant to the claim.

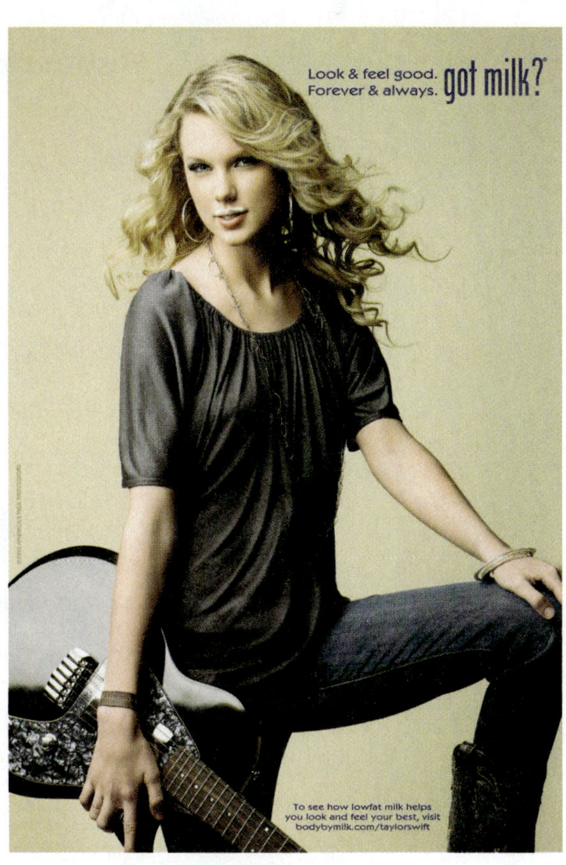

Claim:

Drinking milk is good for your health.

Supports

N **a.** Taylor Swift drinks milk.

N **b.** Exercise leads to physical fitness.

N **c.** Taylor Swift pours herself into her music.

N **d.** Taylor Swift is a popular entertainer.

R **e.** The protein and nutrients in low-fat milk build muscles.

CONTINUED

EXAMPLE *CONTINUED*

C. Adequate Details: Read the following paragraph. After reading, choose the topic sentence that best states the claim best supported by the details. Write **V** for valid by the claim that is adequately supported by the evidence in the list.

[1]When a couple fights, name-calling creates distrust, anger, and a sense of helplessness. [2]In addition, assigning blame makes others defensive during a fight. [3]When two people fight, words like *never* or *always* are usually not true and create more anger. [4]Exaggerating or making up a complaint can keep the couple's real issues hidden during a fight. [5]A couple bringing up gripes and hurt feelings stockpiled over time can lead to explosive anger in a fight.

_____ **a.** Fighting leads to violence.
__V__ **b.** Using unfair methods during a fight makes the situation worse.
_____ **c.** Everyone uses unfair fighting methods.
_____ **d.** Fighting cannot be avoided.

Explanation

Compare your answers to the following think-aloud:

A. Items (a), (b), and (e) are relevant to the claim. Items (c) and (d) are not relevant because they point out drawbacks to online shopping instead of supporting the claim that online shopping offers a lot of benefits.

B. Only item (e) is relevant to the claim that drinking milk is good for your health. Personal remarks or information about Taylor Swift are not relevant to the healthfulness of milk. Item (b) states a fact, but has nothing to do with the claim about milk.

C. Choice (a) is irrelevant. "Violence" is not mentioned in any of the details. Choices (c) and (d) use the evidence to jump to false conclusions about fighting. Choice (c) assumes that "everyone" fights with no evidence to back up that claim. Likewise choice (d) jumps to the false conclusion that fighting cannot be avoided. Choice (b) states a valid claim adequately supported by the details. Each detail is an example of "unfair fighting." And the writer explains how each example harms the couple's relationship.

Effective readers learn to use the VALID thinking process to infer if a claim is sound. The VALID approach avoids drawing false inferences and coming to false conclusions.
The **VALID** approach includes the following:

V — **V**erify and value the facts.	Writers may mix fact with opinion or use false information for their own purposes. Likewise, readers may draw false inferences by mixing the writer's facts with their own opinions. So it is important to find, verify, and stick to the factual details. Then you can begin to interpret the facts by making inferences and coming to conclusions about a claim's validity.
A — **A**ssess prior knowledge.	Once you are sure of the facts, draw on your prior knowledge. What you already have learned and experienced can help you make accurate inferences about an argument.
L — **L**earn from the text.	When you value and verify facts, you are learning from the text. A valid inference or conclusion is always based on what is stated or implied in the text. An invalid conclusion goes beyond the evidence. Many of the skills you have gained from previous modules work together to enable you to learn from the text. Context clues unlock the writer's use of vocabulary. Patterns of organization reveal the relationships among ideas.
I — **I**nvestigate for bias.	To infer if an argument is valid, bias must be identified and confronted. Each of us possesses strong personal views that affect the way we process information. Our bias may shape our reading of the writer's meaning. Likewise, it is important to recognize the writer's use of bias to make and support a claim.
D — **D**etect contradictions.	In determining the validity of an argument, contradictions occur in two ways. The first is jumping to a wrong conclusion that contradicts the evidence. For example, have you ever assumed a person was rude, only to find out later that he or she was acutely shy? Many times there may be a better explanation for a set of facts than the first one that comes to mind. Thus, consider all the possible explanations and choose the one that most reasonably explains all the details. The second contradiction occurs when a writer presents and refutes counterclaims. In both instances, effective readers search for contradictions and test them for logic.

Example

Read the following paragraph. Apply the VALID approach to evaluate the list of claims or conclusions that follow the paragraph. Underline the details of the facts. Strike through biased words. Mark each item **V** if the claim is valid or **I** if the claim is invalid. Share your responses with a peer or small group of classmates. Discuss how you used prior knowledge and how you learned from the text to arrive at your conclusions.

THE FIVE PILLARS OF ISLAM

[1]The guiding principles of the Islamic faith are known as the Five Pillars of Islam. [2]Muslims, the believers of Islam, devote their lives to these principles. [3]The first principle is called *shahadah* (shah-HAH-dah). [4]*Shahadah* is the prayer of faith that says, "There is no God but Allah, and Muhammad is his messenger." [5]The second rule is known as *salat* (sah-LAHT); *salat* is the act of praying five times a day to Allah. [6]Prayer occurs at dawn, noon, afternoon, dusk, and night. [7]The third principle is *saum* (sah-OHM); *saum* is a fast from food or drink that lasts 30 days during the holy month of Ramadan. [8]The fourth pillar is called *zakat* (zeh-KAHT); this is the act of giving money to the poor and needy. [9]The final principle of Islam is *haj* (HAHDJ); this is the journey of pilgrimage that Muslims all over the world must make to the holy city of Mecca in Saudi Arabia at least once in their lifetime.

V **1.** The word *shahadah* is a word for a very specific prayer that is always worded the same way.

V **2.** Islam teaches one to seek God and to help others.

V **3.** Islam takes discipline to practice.

I **4.** Islam is a radical belief that teaches people to think selfishly of themselves first.

Explanation

Compare your responses to the following student's think-aloud.

*Items 1, 2 and 3 are (**V**) valid inferences based on the details in the paragraph. Item 1 includes the qualifier always, which usually indicates a bias. However, based on the fact that the paragraph gives the name and exact wording of the prayer, it is reasonable to infer that the exact* *wording is the unique trait of the prayer and always used. Item 4 is an (I) invalid inference. This sentence includes two biased words:* radical *and* selfishly. *This biased statement is not grounded in the details. My own prior knowledge about the religions Christianity and Islam informed me as I read the paragraph and evaluated the claims. While I was raised to believe in Christianity and to reject all other religions as invalid, items 2 and 3 reveal similarities between these two religions and help me overcome any bias I had against Islam. The details in this paragraph support these two claims. My personal experience reinforces them as well.*

An effective writer also evaluates details to see if they are relevant to his or her claim and adequate to convince a reader that the claim is valid. As a writer narrows a topic into a focused main idea, he or she generates supporting details that answer questions such as *who*, *what*, *when*, *where*, *why*, and *how*. During the brainstorming phase, a writer naturally generates many details. Some of these details may be irrelevant to the specific claim. A writer evaluates the relevance of each detail and uses only those that imply, clarify, or support the main idea. Often, a writer uses a concept map before writing to generate ideas and after writing to determine if details are relevant and adequate.

Example

Assume you are taking a college course in sociology. The class requires students to write a report on a current issue or problem in society. You are working with a classmate to proofread each other's reports. Read the following report. Test details as relevant and adequate by completing the Argumentation Concept Map with the appropriate details from the paragraph. Underline the claim. Cross out the irrelevant detail.

Pay the Price: Stop the Shootings

[1]Public school officials should use metal detectors to screen students for possession of firearms in order to reduce the numbers of injuries and deaths. [2]The use of metal detectors signals students that safety measures

CONTINUED

EXAMPLE *CONTINUED*

are in place and that violence will not be tolerated. [3]Some oppose the use of metal detectors as a step that fosters a jail house atmosphere and condemns students as guilty without cause. [4]These opponents to metal detectors also decry the economic cost of screening students for possession of firearms. [5]Unfortunately, evidence indicates that the need to provide a safe school and the right to a safe school far outweigh these concerns. [6]According to the Centers for Disease Control and Prevention, from 1992 to 1999, 56% of homicides and suicides occurring at school involved firearms. [7]In addition, the National Education Association estimates that "on a daily basis, 100,000 students carry guns to school; 160,000 miss classes due to fear of physical harm, and 40 are injured or killed by firearms." [8]Tragic school shootings have already occurred and signal that the danger is clear and present. [9]For example, in 1999 at Columbine High School, in Colorado, two students massacred 12 fellow students and a teacher, injured 24 other people, and then committed suicide. [10]In 2005, at Red Lake High School in Minnesota, a student killed five students and injured seven others after he had killed his grandfather and his grandfather's girlfriend at home. [11]He also shot himself. [12]As recently as 2012, Adam Lanza shot and killed 20 students and 6 adults at Sandy Hook Elementary School in Newtown, Connecticut. [13]He also killed himself by gunshot. [14]All of these shooters obviously suffered mental health problems. [15]~~These incidents are extreme and few~~. [16]These incidents show that public schools must screen students for weapons. [17]The cost of not doing so is too high!

Works Cited

Centers for Disease Control and Prevention. "Source of Firearms Used by Students in School-Associated Violent Deaths—United States, 1992–1999." *Morbidity and Mortality Weekly Report* 52(09): 169–72. 7 March 2003. Web. 14 Aug. 2009.

"School Violence." National Education Association. Washington, D.C.: 1993.

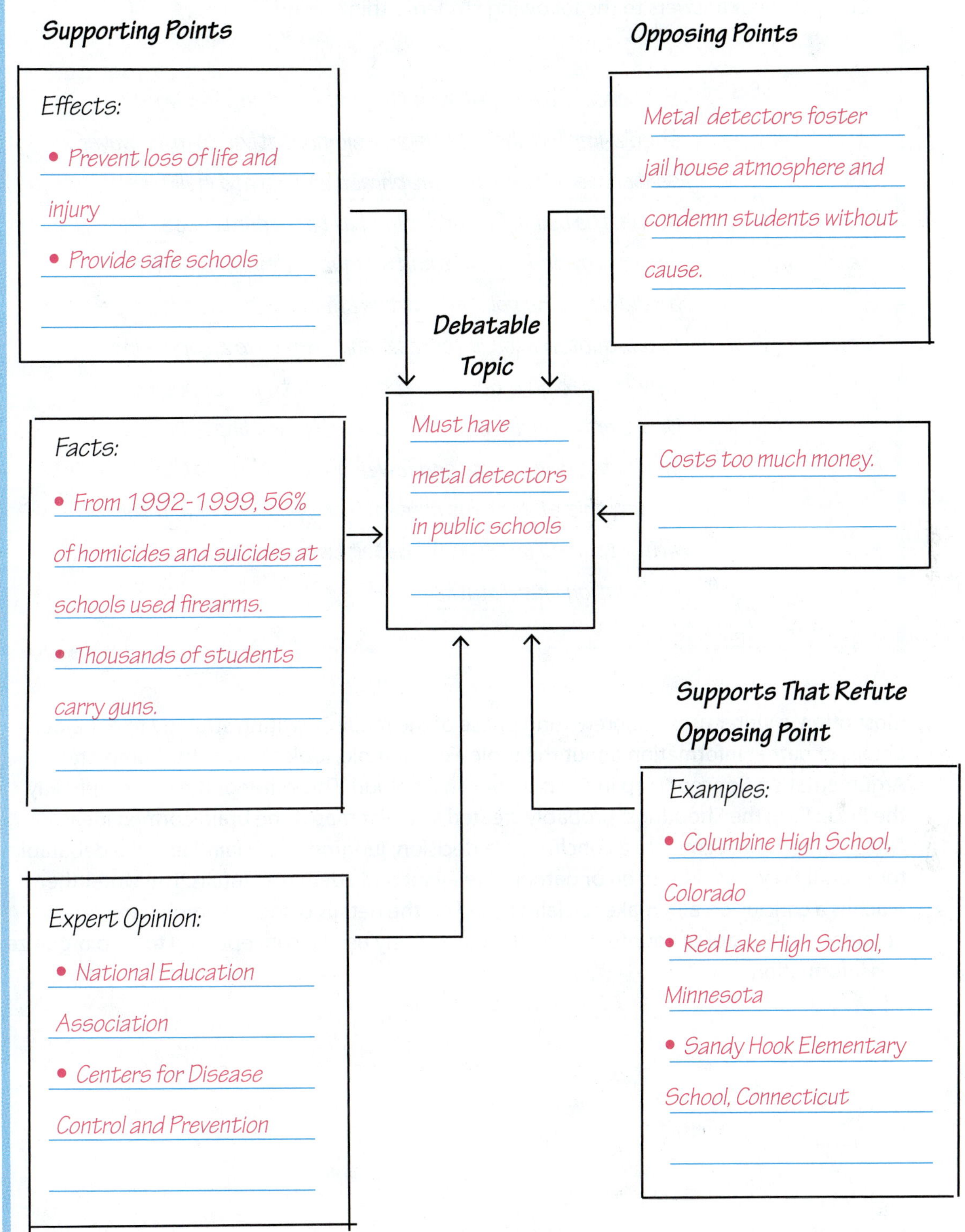
Argumentation Concept Map
Supporting Points
Effects:
• Prevent loss of life and injury
• Provide safe schools
Opposing Points
Metal detectors foster jail house atmosphere and condemn students without cause.
Debatable Topic
Must have metal detectors in public schools
Facts:
• From 1992-1999, 56% of homicides and suicides at schools used firearms.
• Thousands of students carry guns.
Costs too much money.
Supports That Refute Opposing Point
Examples:
• Columbine High School, Colorado
• Red Lake High School, Minnesota
• Sandy Hook Elementary School, Connecticut
Expert Opinion:
• National Education Association
• Centers for Disease Control and Prevention

Explanation

Compare your answers to the following student's think-aloud.

Sentence 1 clearly states the writer's claim. The word should implies that this is an argumentative claim. However, sentences 16 and 17 paraphrase, or restate in different words, the claim. So I underlined all three sentences. The writer provided relevant and adequate details to make a valid claim. He pointed out the effects, gave convincing facts, quoted expert sources, and even gave an opposing view. He also gave good reasons to refute the opposing view. Sentence 15 was irrelevant. The fact that these incidents are extreme and few does not support the claim. In fact, this statement presents an opposing view. If the writer wanted to keep this detail, I would suggest adding an explanation that refutes it.

Most often, a writer uses the prewriting phase of the reading/writing strategy to generate details or gather information about the topic. For example, look again at the completed Argumentation Concept Map in the previous think-aloud. The writer of the paragraph "Pay the Price: Stop the Shootings" probably created a similar map as he brainstormed ideas. Often, writers don't come to a conclusion (a decision, judgment, or claim) about a debatable topic until they have identified or gathered relevant and adequate details. The writer then reaches a conclusion and makes a claim based on the details of fact, examples, expert opinions, or disproof of counterclaims. The writer likely used a concept map to help organize this information.

Practice 3

Generate Relevant and Adequate Details for an Argument

Choose one of the topic sentences you created in Practice 2. Use or adapt the following concept map to generate details to support your topic sentence. *Answers may vary.*

Argumentation Concept Map

The Debatable Topic: What is the issue?

Supporting Points

Reason 1:

Reason 2:

Reason 3:

Counterclaim

Support That Refutes Counterclaim

Topic sentence that states the claim:

Practice 4

Identify and Generate Details Using Argument

Assume you are taking a college psychology course and the following passage from your textbook is part of your weekly reading assignment. During the week, you also came across an article in the newspaper that stated the following: "The American public has divided views about gender roles in the workplace. Most Americans believe jobs should be based on gender. Men are better suited to certain jobs such as firefighting or soldering while women are better suited to jobs such as teaching or hairdressing." You have decided to write a letter to the editor of the newspaper that agrees or disagrees with this claim. As you read the passage, underline details that you can use to support your claim and address any counter claim. Then, complete the graphic organizer to prewrite your letter to the editor. *Answers may vary.*

HOW DO MEN AND WOMEN DIFFER IN THINKING, SOCIAL BEHAVIOR, AND PERSONALITY?

[1]Although there are clear biological differences in males and females, even to the point of affecting the size of certain structures in the brain, what sort of differences exist in the behaviors of males and females? [2]Are those differences due to biology, socialization, or a combination of the two influences?

Cognitive Differences [3]Researchers have long held that females score higher on tests of verbal abilities than do males, but that males score higher on tests of mathematical and spatial skills. [4]Early explanations of these differences in cognitive functioning involve physical differences in the way each sex uses the two hemispheres of the brain as well as hormonal differences. [5]Other research strongly suggests that psychological and social issues may be more responsible for these differences, as these differences have become less and less obvious. [6]In particular, the supposed difference in math abilities between boys and girls have now been shown to be the effect of girls' lack of confidence rather than any biological difference in the working of the brain. [7]That the disparities (which are actually quite small) seem to be disappearing as society has begun to view the two genders as more equal in ability is taken as a sign that more equal treatment in society has reduced the gender difference.

Social and Personality Differences [8]The differences normally cited between men and women in the ways they interact with others and in their personality traits are often the result of stereotyped thinking about the sexes. [9]It is difficult to demonstrate differences that are not caused by the way boys and girls are socialized as they grow up. [10]Boys are taught to hold in their emotions, not to cry, to be "strong" and "manly." [11]Girls are encouraged to form emotional attachments, be emotional, and be open about their feelings with others.

[12]In communication, research suggests that when men talk to each other, they tend to talk about current events, sports, and other events. [13]This has been called a "report" style of communication and seems to involve switching topics frequently, with attempts to dominate the conversation by certain members of the group. [14]In contrast, women tend to use a "relate" style of communication with each other, revealing a lot about their private lives and showing concern and sympathy. [15]They tend to interrupt each other less and let everyone participate in the conversation. [16]Another study, using fMRI technology, found that men listen with the left hemisphere only, whereas women listen with both hemispheres, suggesting that women pay attention to the tone and emotion of statements as well as the content.

Ciccarelli, Saundra K., *Psychology*, 4th ed., pp. 397–398.

Argumentation Concept Map

The Debatable Topic: What is the issue?

Jobs based on gender

Supporting Points

Reason 1: Cognitive Differences

Females score higher on tests of verbal abilities, but males score higher on mathematical and spatial skills due to cognitive functioning, use of the brain, and hormonal differences.

Reason 2: Social and Personality Differences

Boys are taught to hold in their emotions, not to cry, to be "strong" and "manly." Girls are encouraged to form emotional attachments, be emotional, and be open about their feelings with others.

Reason 3: Communication

Men use a "report" style of communication. In contrast, women use a "relate" style of communication.

Counterclaim(s)

1. *These differences have become less and less obvious.*
2. *Disparities are quite small and seem to be disappearing as more equal treatment in society has reduced the gender difference.*

Support That Refutes Counterclaim(s)

Research strongly suggests that psychological and social issues may be more responsible for cognitive differences.

Conclusion/Recommendation:

Jobs should not be based on gender.

Recognize and Create Logical Order in an Argument

LO4

When a reader recognizes that a writer is using argument to organize ideas, he or she can see how the main idea and details fit together and anticipate upcoming details. To make an argument, an effective writer moves from a general idea (the claim) to a major support (a reason, fact, example, expert opinion, or argument against the opposing view) to a minor support (also a reason, fact, example, expert opinion, or argument against the opposing view). Effective readers use transitions and signal words to recognize the importance and movement among details.

Transitions That Signal Argument				
accordingly	even so	in conclusion	obviously	thus
admittedly	finally	indeed	of course	to be sure
although	first (second, third, etc.)	in fact, in truth	on the one hand	truly
because	for	in summary	on the other hand	undoubtedly
but	furthermore	last	since	
certainly	granted	meanwhile	some believe	
consequently	hence	nevertheless	some may say	
despite	however	nonetheless	therefore	

Signal Words That Qualify an Idea as an Argument (sample list)					
all	every	may	often	probably, probable	think
always	has/have to	might	only	seem	too
believe	it is believed	must	ought to	should	usually
could	likely	never	possibly, possible	sometimes	

Example

Assume you are a member of the Product Evaluation Committee at your workplace, a local grocery store. The committee is given the task of looking into switching from paper to plastic bags. The chair of the committee, the store's assistant manager, has given you a rough draft of a memo about the issue. Read and annotate his draft. Circle the main claim. Underline the supporting details. Describe the writer's use of words that signal or qualify argument in the memo. Suggest a change, if needed, to improve the memo.

Answers may vary.

TO: Department Supervisors
FROM: Assistant Manager
RE: Paper or Plastic

[1]The Product Evaluation Committee recommends that our store should continue its use of paper bags due to the harmful effects of plastic bags on the environment and related health hazards. [2]First, because plastic bags are cheaper to produce and transport, they are everywhere on the planet. [3]Unfortunately, the saturation of the earth with plastic bags raises the risk to marine life. [4]This threat to marine life posed by plastic bags is the second reason to avoid their use. [5]Sea animals, like sea turtles and whales, mistake plastic bags for food. [6]The bags clog their stomachs, and then they starve to death. [7]Third, stray plastic bags also cause another harmful chain of events. [8]Plastic bags clog sewer pipes. [9]Clogged pipes cause the collection of standing, stagnant, and polluted water. [10]Human health hazards then develop due to the water polluted by plastic bags. [11]Some argue that we should use plastic bags because they take up less space than paper bags in landfills. [12]That's true, nothing biodegrades in a landfill, not plastic, not paper. [13]However, the threat to wildlife and human health posed by plastic bags outweighs the space needed for paper bags in landfills. [14]Many may argue to switch to plastic because of the bottom line—money. [15]Plastic is indeed cheaper to produce and transport. [16]Nonetheless, our store should make the humane choice to protect wildlife and human health—even if the cost is a little more.

Explanation

Compare your answers to the following student's think-aloud.

Sentences 1 and 16 state the claim of the argument. Sentence 1 takes a stand for the use of paper bags and against the use of plastic bags. This sentence also implies the pattern of organization with the signal words for several reasons. Sentence 16 restates this claim as a logical conclusion based on the evidence provided by the details.

The signal and qualifying words for argument helped me identify the major claims and supports. The word should *in sentence 1 states a claim about what action should be taken. The words* first, *in sentence 2,* the second reason *in sentence 4, and* third *in sentence 7 indicate details or reasons that support the claim. The words* unfortunately *in sentence 3,* some argue *in sentence 11, and* many argue *in sentence 14 indicate opposing opinions. The words* however *in sentence 13 and* nonetheless *in sentence 16 indicate details that refute the opposing opinions. The word* nonetheless *also indicates a conclusion that is based on the preceding details.*

All the details seem relevant. However, the details do not seem adequate to make the claim valid. For example, the following details are lacking: No expert opinion is given. Nor are there any sources for factual details. Additionally, the argument claims paper bags are worth the extra cost. However, to make a sound decision, more information about the cost is needed. I recommend adding these missing details.

Practice 5

Create Logical Order Using Argument

Work with the argumentation concept chart you completed in Practice 3 or Practice 4. Write a rough draft of your paragraph using the details you generated. Include words that signal or qualify argumentative claims and supports. Work with a peer to review each other's rough drafts. Exchange, read, and review your drafts to make sure all details are relevant to the main ideas. Complete a concept chart of the draft you are peer editing. Circle the main idea. Underline the signal words for the various patterns of organization and the key details. Cross out any details that are not relevant to the main idea. Suggest a change to improve the paragraph. Point out what you like about the use of argument in the paragraph. Return your reviewed paragraphs to each other. Revise as needed.

L5 Analyze and Use Effective Expression with Argument

Readers and writers may encounter both objective and subjective language as they comprehend or make an argument. Effective argument is the result of the writer's careful choice of words for the greatest impact on the reader. Objective words often express facts and expert opinions based on experience and research. An objective tone often implies that the information is factual and therefore valid and reliable. Subjective words express personal opinions, emotions, judgments, and interpretations. Many writers are tempted to rely on emotionally slanted language to present either a favorable or a negative, or biased, view of the topic under debate. In addition, writers may include only the details that favor the stances they have taken. A valid argument relies on objective, factual details. To evaluate an argument for bias, ask the following questions.

- Does the writer provide mostly positive or negative supports?
- Does the writer provide mostly factual details or rely on biased language?
- Does the writer include or omit opposing views?

Example

Read the following information. Annotate the text. Circle the writer's main claim. Single underline factual details. Double underline biased language. Answer the questions that follow.

Underage Drinking

[1]Alcohol use by persons under age 21 years is a major public health problem. [2]Alcohol is the most commonly used and abused drug among youth in the United States, more than tobacco and illicit drugs. [3]And alcohol use is responsible for more than 4,700 annual deaths among underage youth. [4]Although drinking by persons under the age of 21 is illegal, people aged 12 to 20 years drink 11% of all alcohol consumed in the United States. [5]More than 90% of this alcohol is consumed in the form of binge drinks. [6]In 2010, persons under age 21 made approximately 189,000 emergency room visits for injuries and other conditions linked to alcohol. [7]The 2011 Youth Risk Behavior Survey tracked the drinking levels of high school students during the past 30 days. [8]According to the survey, 39% drank some amount of alcohol; 22% binge drank; 8% drove after drinking alcohol; and 24% rode with a driver who had been drinking alcohol.

[9]Underage drinkers face alarming social problems, such as fighting, and school problems, such as higher absence and poor or failing grades. [10]Underage drinkers are more often arrested for driving or physically

hurting someone while drunk. [11]They are more vulnerable to physical and sexual assault. [12]They are at a higher risk for suicide and homicide. [13]They are apt to engage in unwanted, unplanned, and unprotected sexual activity. [14]At the same time, alcohol use disrupts normal growth and sexual development and causes changes in brain development that may have life-long effects. [15]Underage drinkers also endure more illnesses, loss of memory, alcohol-related car crashes and other unintentional injuries, such as burns, falls, and drowning, and death from alcohol poisoning. [16]They also abuse other drugs. [17]Underage drinking has disastrous consequences.

"Fact Sheets—Underage Drinking." Centers for Disease Control and Prevention.

1. Overall, the passage mostly relies on
   - (a.) factual details.
   - b. emotionally slanted language.

2. Which of the following statements is true?
   - a. Sentence 1 offers an opposing view.
   - b. Sentence 8 offers an opposing view.
   - c. Sentence 11 offers an opposing view.
   - (d.) No opposing view is offered.

3. In this passage, the writer expresses a biased attitude
   - a. in favor of lowering the drinking age.
   - b. in favor of raising the drinking age.
   - (c.) against underage drinking.
   - d. against all alcohol consumption.

Explanation

Compare your answers to the following student's think-aloud.

1. Although the passage contains some emotionally slanted language such as alarming and disastrous, overall, the writer relies on (a) factual details that can be verified through research. 2. The writer offers no opposing view. 3. In the passage, the writer expresses a biased attitude (c) against underage drinking. In fact, this biased attitude is the writer's claim.

Effective readers also analyze the writer's use of objective and subjective words to determine the point of view of the argument. Point of view is established with the use of personal pronouns. Personal pronouns imply an objective or subjective tone. The three points of view are first person, second person, and third person.

Personal Pronouns and Points of View	
First Person (subjective tone) *I, me, mine, my, myself* *we, us, ours, our, ourselves*	First person refers to speaker/writer. First person testimonies offer powerful evidence. First person is informal. First person can be intimate, more engaging. First person may not offer reliable details. First person offers a limited point of view.
Second Person (subjective tone) *you, your, yours,* *yourself, yourselves*	Second person refers to listener/reader. Second person speaks directly to the reader. Second person is more familiar and engaging. Second person may be directive, instructional. Second person is informal. Second person may become overbearing.
Third Person (objective tone) *he, him, his, himself* *she, her, hers, herself* *it, its, itself* *they, them, their,* *theirs, themselves*	Third person refers to the person, thing, or idea being discussed. Third person creates space between writer/reader. Third person is formal. Third person may seem more credible. Third person offers a universal point of view.

Common sense tells us that we cannot shift between several individuals' points of view. However, at times, writers carelessly shift point of view, as in the following sentence.

> Television addiction contributes to our obesity. When you choose to sit in front of a television from the minute you get home until you go to bed, you leave no time for exercise.

Consistent use of point of view strengthens coherence or the clear flow of ideas. Therefore, writers carefully edit their writings to ensure appropriate and consistent use of point of view. For example, read the following edited version of the sentence above.

> Television addiction contributes to our obesity. When we choose to sit in front of a television from the minute we get home until we go to bed, we leave no time for exercise.

Example

Read the following claims and supporting statements. Identify and analyze the use of viewpoint. Underline the personal pronouns. Label each one as first person, second person, or third person. For any third person pronouns, also underline the noun to which the pronoun refers. Discuss the effectiveness of the use of viewpoint in each set of ideas.

Third Person *Second Person*

1. Parents must monitor their children's access to the Internet. You are vulnerable to predators in chat rooms and social networks.

How effective is the use of viewpoint?

Answers may vary. The viewpoint shifts from third person their *to second person* You. *This is also a shift in tone from formal to informal. The shift is jarring and doesn't make sense.*

Second Person *Third Person*

2. Getting enough sleep is crucial to your long-term health. When a person is sleep deprived, your body is unable to repair itself through rest.

Second Person

How effective is the use of viewpoint?

Answers may vary. The claim and support state two different viewpoints. The viewpoint makes an illogical shift from second person your *to third person with the noun* a person. *Then the viewpoint shifts back to second person* your. *This is also a shift in tone from informal to formal to informal. These shifts weaken the claim and support by being distracting and confusing.*

Explanation

Compare your answers to the following student's think-aloud.

Shifting viewpoint for no logical reason confuses the reader and weakens an argument.

1. *The viewpoint shifts from third person* their *to second person* you. *This is also a shift in tone from formal to informal. The shift is jarring and doesn't make sense.*

CONTINUED

EXPLANATION *CONTINUED*

2. *The claim and support state two different viewpoints. The viewpoint makes an illogical shift from second person your to third person with the noun a person. Then the viewpoint shifts back to second person your. This is also a shift in tone from informal to formal to informal. These shifts weaken the claim and support by being distracting and confusing.*

Practice 6

Identify, Analyze, and Use Effective Expression with Argument

Work with the rough draft of the paragraph you completed in an earlier practice. Choose two sentences and revise each one to create effective expression through the thoughtful choice of objective and biased language. Use the following space to record your original and revised sentences.

Original sentence:

____

____

Revised sentence:

____

____

Original sentence:

____

____

Revised sentence:

____

____

Reading and Writing Assignments

MySkillsLab™
Complete these assignments in MySkillsLab.

Considering Audience and Purpose

Study the set of photographs at the beginning of the module. Assume you are the mayor or commissioner who has received this letter from "A Concerned Citizen." Write a one-paragraph response that states your official stand on the issue. Or assume you are a representative for Target. Write a one-paragraph response to support the building of a Target at the Nova Park location.

Reading and Writing for Everyday Life

Assume your doctor has strongly suggested that you change your diet to address health issues such as high cholesterol and inflamed arteries. You are reading labels and analyzing claims about foods before you consume them. Before reading, skim the advertisement for Sunshine Sweet Potato Sticks. Write at least one question you need answered to determine if this is a food you should add to your diet. During reading, highlight the claim and the facts that support the claim. After reading, rate the product from 1 for unhealthy food to 5 for healthful food. Explain your rating. Finally, write a review to post to the product's website. In your review, state your conclusion and the reasons for your recommendation.

NATURE MADE IT SWEET,
NATURE MADE IT A SUPERFOOD
WE MAKE IT FRESH AND EASY!
Loaded with Vitamin A, Vitamin B6, Vitamin C, Calcium, and Potassium. Great source of fiber. Super anti-inflammatory.
SUNSHINE SWEET POTATO STICKS-
Superfood for the super busy!
Low in sodium, saturated fat, and cholesterol, SUNSHINE SWEET POTATO STICKS, made from sweet potatoes picked fresh from the farm, a healthy addition to any meal!

Reading and Writing for College Life

Assume you are taking a college course in sociology. The following passage is part of your weekly reading assignment from your textbook. Your professor has given you the following question based on your reading: "Although Freud was one of the most influential theorists of the twentieth century, most of his ideas have been discarded. What may have caused the rejection of Freud's ideas?" Skim the passage. Underline the major claims made by Freud in his theory of personality. Double underline the opposing views of other sociologists in the passage. Then write a response to the question posed by the professor.

Freud and the Development of Personality

As the mind and the self develop, so does the personality. Sigmund Freud (1856–1939) developed a theory of the origin of personality that has had a major impact on Western thought. Freud, a physician in Vienna in the early 1900s, founded psychoanalysis, a technique for treating emotional problems through long-term exploration of the subconscious mind. Let's look at his theory. Freud believed that personality consists of three elements. Each child is born with the first element, an **id**, Freud's term for inborn drives that cause us to seek self-gratification. The id of the newborn is evident in its cries of hunger or pain. The pleasure-seeking id operates throughout life. It demands the immediate fulfillment of basic needs: food, safety, attention, sex, and so on.

The id's drive for immediate gratification, however, runs into a roadblock: primarily the needs of other people, especially those of the parents. To adapt to these constraints, a second component of the personality emerges, which Freud called the ego. The **ego** is the balancing force between the id and the demands of society that suppress it. The ego also serves to balance the id and the superego, the third component of the personality, more commonly called the conscience. The **superego** represents culture within us, the norms and values we have internalized from our social groups. As the moral component of the personality, the superego provokes feelings of guilt or shame when we break social rules, or pride and self-satisfaction when we follow them. According to Freud, when the id gets out of hand, we follow our desires for pleasure and break society's norms.

When the superego gets out of hand, we become overly rigid in following those norms and end up wearing a straitjacket of rules that inhibit our lives. The ego, the balancing force, tries to prevent either the superego or the id from dominating. In the emotionally healthy individual, the ego succeeds in balancing these conflicting demands of the id and the superego. In the maladjusted individual, the ego fails to control the conflict between the id and the superego. Either the id or the superego dominates this person, leading to internal confusion and problem behaviors.

Sociological Evaluation Sociologists appreciate Freud's emphasis on socialization—his assertion that the social group into which we are born transmits norms and values that restrain our biological drives. Sociologists, however, object to the view that inborn and subconscious motivations are the primary reasons for human behavior. This denies the central principle of sociology: that factors such as social class (income, education, and occupation) and people's roles in groups underlie their behavior (Epstein 1988; Bush and Simmons 1990).

Feminist sociologists have been especially critical of Freud. Although what I just summarized applies to both females and males, Freud assumed that "male" is "normal." He even referred to females as inferior, castrated males (Chodorow 1990; Gerhard 2000). It is obvious that sociologists need to continue to research how we develop personality.

Adapted from Henslin, James M., *Sociology: A Down-to-Earth Approach*, 10th ed., p. 67.

Professor's Question: What may have caused the rejection of Freud's ideas?
Answers may vary.

Reading and Writing for Working Life

Assume you are a supervisor of a department in a local business. One of your employees has made a claim that she is being sexually harassed. To evaluate the claim, you have checked the employee handbook as a resource and located the following information. Before reading, skim both the handbook excerpt and the incident report. As you read the handbook excerpt, underline details you will use to evaluate the incident report. As you read the incident report, underline details that support the claim of sexual harassment. Put question marks by the details in the report that raise questions. Double underline details in the report that refute sexual harassment. After reading, draft your conclusion and recommendation based on the handbook and the incident report.

Employee Handbook: Workplace Harassment

Unlawful harassment is a form of discrimination. Harassment violates Title VII of the Civil Rights Act of 1964 and other federal authority.

Harassment is the unwelcome verbal or physical conduct based on race, color, religion, sex (whether or not of a sexual nature and including same-gender harassment and gender identity harassment), national origin, age (40 and over), disability (mental or physical), sexual orientation, or retaliation. Harassment may occur in one of two ways or both. ?

1. The conduct is severe or pervasive enough to create a hostile work environment.

2. A supervisor's harassing conduct results in a tangible change in an employee's employment status or benefits (for example, demotion, termination, failure to promote, etc.).

Hostile work environment harassment has several traits. This harassment is the unwelcome comments or conduct based on sex, race, or other legally protected ? characteristics. The harassment interferes with an employee's work performance. Or the harassment

CONTINUED

creates an intimidating, hostile, or offensive work environment. Anyone in the workplace might commit this type of harassment. A harasser could be a manager, co-worker, or non-employee. Examples of non-employees are a contractor, vendor, or guest. The victim can be anyone affected by the conduct, not just the individual at whom the offensive conduct is directed. The following are examples of actions that may create sexual hostile environment harassment.

- Leering—staring in a sexually suggestive manner.
- Making offensive remarks about looks, clothing, or body parts.
- Touching in a way that may make an employee feel uncomfortable. Patting, pinching, or intentional brushing against another's body are examples.
- Telling sexual or lewd jokes, hanging sexual posters, making sexual gestures, etc.
- Sending, forwarding or asking for sexually suggestive letters, notes, emails, or images.

What Is Not Harassment? Federal law does not prohibit simple teasing, ? offhand comments, or minor isolated incidents. Rather, the conduct must be so offensive as to alter the conditions of one's employment. Immediately report any case of harassment to your supervisor, any member of management, or the Human Resource Department.

Adapted from Federal Communications Commission. "Understanding Workplace Harassment." *FCC Encyclopedia*. FCC.gov.

Harassment Incident Report Form

Background Information

Date of Incident: September 24 **Victim Name:** Rosa Smythe

Alleged Harasser: Clint Edwards **Incident Location:** in office, email

Type of Harassment __Age __Disability __Gender __Marital Status ___National Origin __Physical Attributes __Race __ Religion ✓ Sexual

Brief Description of Incident: Ms. Smythe alleges that Mr. Edwards has continually sexually harassed her over the past several months both in the office and by email. On September 24, Mr. Edwards sent Ms. Smythe an email congratulating her on her sales figures. The content of the message complimented Ms. Smythe on her "sexy good looks and flirty ways" to which he credited her success. Shortly before receiving the email, Mr. Edwards and Ms. Smythe were in the employee break room. As Ms. Smythe was pouring her coffee, Mr. Edwards approached from behind and leaned up against her as he reached for a cup on the shelf beside the coffee pot. When Ms. Smythe objected, Mr. Edwards patted her lower back, winked, and said, "Oh, I'm sorry. You know you like it." Ms. Smythe states that this incident is only one of many similar in nature. Email sent from Edwards to Smythe on September 24 is in attachment.

List of Names of Witness(es): People in the break room during the incident: Doug Webb, Kim Majors, and Juan Rejos.

Recommendation of Supervisor: *Answers may vary.*

Workshop: Compose a Paragraph Using Argument

Choose a paragraph to read and respond to in writing. You may select a paragraph in an example, practice, or writing assignment within this module. Or you may select a paragraph of your own choosing. Use the following guide to comprehend and respond to the paragraph. Apply what you have learned about argument to your reading/writing strategy.

Preread: Survey and Question

Ask questions about the text's features.

____

____

What is the passage about?

____

____

How is the material organized?

____

____

What do I already know about this topic? (What is my prior knowledge about the vocabulary?)

____

____

What is my purpose for reading/writing?

____

____

What points may I want to address or include in my written response?

____

____

Read and Annotate

As you read, annotate key ideas, particularly those details that answer your prereading questions.

Recite, Review, and Brainstorm

Recite the information. Summarize the most important parts. Answer your prereading questions. Rephrase ideas into your own words. Record changes in your opinions based on the new information. **Review** the information. **Brainstorm** ideas for your written response to the passage. **Freewrite** a response to what you have read. **Map** the relationship among ideas you have annotated in the text. **Outline** or list key ideas and details in blocks of thought.

Write a Draft of Your Response

Using the ideas you generated by brainstorming, compose a draft of your response. Use your own paper.

Revise Your Draft

Once you have created a draft of your argument, read the draft to answer the questions in the "Questions for Revising a Paragraph Using Argument" box that follows. Indicate your answers by annotating your paper. If you answer "yes" to a question, underline, check, or circle examples. If you answer "no" to a question, write needed information in margins and draw lines to indicate placement of additional details. Revise your paragraph based on your reflection. (*Hint:* Experienced writers create several drafts as they focus on one or two questions per draft.)

Step by Step: Questions for Revising a Paragraph Using Argument

- ☐ Have I chosen an important debatable topic?
- ☐ Have I made my point? Can I state my point in one sentence?
- ☐ Have I effectively used reasons, facts, effects, examples? Have I used strong signal words of argument?
- ☐ Have I used adequate details to make my point?
- ☐ Have I included only the details that are relevant to my topic sentence? Have I used effective and relevant expert opinions? Have I addressed important opposing points effectively? Have I documented my sources properly?
- ☐ Have I used the following to make my ideas clear and interesting to my readers: vivid verbs and images, parallel language, controlled sentence structure, coordination, subordination, precise use of words such as *affect* and *effect*, and thoughtful use of biased words?
- ☐ Have I used objective words to persuade my reader?

Proofread Your Draft

Once you have made any revisions to your paragraph that may be needed, proofread your paragraph to eliminate careless errors.

Review Test

MySkillsLab™
Complete this Review Test in MySkillsLab.

Score (number correct ______ x 10 = ______ %

Use reading/writing strategies to comprehend and respond to the following passage from the college textbook *Marriage and Families: Diversity and Change*. Answer the questions that follow. Finally, respond to the writing prompts "Summary Response" and "What Do You Think?"

Vocabulary Preview

attributed (**4**): assigned to, held responsible for

intervened (**19**): came between two people or things in order to exert influence

1240L/10.8 GE/409 words

HELICOPTER PARENTS

[1]Every summer across the United States children gather on playgrounds to board buses that will carry them away to summer camp. [2]And, every summer one or more of these children cry, having trouble saying good-bye to Mom and Dad. [3]However, according to camp counselors, the camp crybabies are now the parents who are having trouble letting go. [4]Some experts call it "kid-sickness," a condition **attributed** in large part to today's involved style of parenting aided by the ever-present cell phones, email, and text message (Irvine, 2008). [5]Others, who deal with young people, including college administrators, refer to many of today's parents as hovering or helicopter parents (Fortin, 2008). [6]Even employers are finding that "helicopter parenting" extends into the workplace. [7]Parents accompany their children to job fairs and then contact employers to discuss their child's salary, benefits, and working conditions (Armour, 2007).

[8]The process is much the same regardless of the child's age. [9]These parents, though well meaning, are ever-present, making sure that the children are OK, but often preventing their children from learning to solve problems on their own. [10]Many camp counselors, college administrators, and employers see this as too much parental involvement and are taking steps to limit it. [11]Many summer camps now spend as much time preparing parents for camp as they do the campers themselves. [12]They restrict the timing and number of faxes, emails, or calls between parents and campers. [13]Camp owners have even hired full-time parent **liaisons** to address parental concerns (Kelley, 2008). [14]They also insist that the camp staff, not parents, handle routine issues like homesickness and disputes between campers. [15]Similarly, college administrators are telling parents to step back and allow their children to become independent. [16]Employers, too, say that too much parental involvement can backfire. [17]An adult child may lose a job opportunity because the employer doesn't want to deal with their parents.

CONTINUED

[18]However, the news is not all bad. [19]Data gathered for the National Survey of Student Engagement found that students whose parents were in frequent contact with them and often **intervened** on their behalf reported higher levels of engagement. [20]They also more frequently used deep learning activities such as after-class discussion with professors, intensive writing exercises, and independent research than students with less-involved parents. [21]According to the survey, children of helicopter parents were more satisfied with their college experience than were other students. [22]However, students with very involved parents had lower grades than those whose parents were not as involved (Mathews, 2007).

Adapted from Schwartz, Mary Ann A., and Scott, Barbara Marliene, *Marriage and Families: Diversity and Change*, 6th ed., pp. 249–250.

Vocabulary in Context

1. The word **liaisons** in sentence 13 refers to people who

a. counsel.
b. train.
c. lead.
d. communicate.

Tone and Purpose

2. The overall tone of the passage is

a. objective.
b. biased.

3. The primary purpose of the passage is to

a. inform.
b. entertain.
c. argue.

Central Idea and Main Idea

4. Which sentence states the central idea of the passage?

a. sentence 1
b. sentence 3
c. sentence 8
d. sentence 9

Supporting Details

5. Sentence 6 is a

a. major supporting detail for the central idea.
b. minor supporting detail for the central idea.

Transitions

6. The word **however** in sentence 18 is a signal word that shows

a. comparison.
b. cause.
c. contrast.
d. classification.

Thought Patterns

7. The overall thought pattern of the passage is

a. contrast.
b. time order.
c. cause and effect.
d. definition and example.

Fact and Opinion

8. Sentence 18 is a statement of

a. fact.

(b.) opinion.

c. fact and opinion.

Inferences

9. Based on the details in the passage, we can infer that

a. children resent helicopter parents.

b. children of helicopter parents never solve problems on their own.

(c.) separation from parents is a necessary step toward adulthood.

d. helicopter parents have only their children's interests in mind.

Argument

10. Which statement is not relevant to the following claim?

Claim: There are some positive effects of heavy parental involvement.

a. Students with heavily involved parents reported higher levels of engagement in school.

b. Students with heavily involved parents were more frequently involved in deep learning activities.

c. Students with heavily involved parents were more satisfied with their college experience.

(d.) Students with heavily involved parents tended to have lower grades.

Summary Response

Restate the writers' central idea in your own words. In your summary, state the writers' claim. Begin your summary response with the following: *The central idea of "Helicopter Parents" by Schwartz and Scott is. . . .*

What Do You Think?

Have you experienced or witnessed helicopter parenting? Do you agree with the writers that parents may hinder their children's success by over-parenting? Assume you are a summer camp counselor and you are writing a welcome letter to prepare participating families to transition their children from home to camp. In your letter discuss the following points:

- Explain how campers will develop independence and problem-solving skills.
- List some of the benefits of separating parents from their children.
- Explain when and why parents will be contacted if needed.

Academic Learning Log: Module Review

Summary of Key Concepts of Argument

Assess your comprehension of argument.

LO1 LO2 LO3 LO4

1. A claim is *a statement, assertion, or conclusion about a specific position on a controversial issue*.

2. An argument is *a process of reasoning that demonstrates a claim is valid based on the logical details given*.

3. A valid conclusion is *a claim reasonably supported with details soundly based on logic or fact*.

4. An invalid conclusion is *a false inference, a claim not adequately supported with relevant details*.

5. Relevant details *have a significant and clear relationship to the claim* while adequate details *satisfy the requirements of a claim*.

LO1 LO2 LO3 LO4 LO5

6. Transition words that signal argument include *accordingly*, *even so*, *nonetheless*, *some may argue*, *therefore*.

7. Signal words that qualify an idea as an argument include *all*, *always*, *must*, and *should*.

8. To evaluate an argument for bias, ask the following questions:
   - *Does the writer provide mostly positive or negative supports?*
   - *Does the writer provide mostly factual details or rely on biased language?*
   - *Does the writer include or omit opposing views?*

9. Points of view and examples of personal pronouns are *I* and *our* for first person, *you* for second person, and *she* or *her* for third person.

Test Your Comprehension of the Argument

Respond to the following questions and prompts. *Answers may vary*

L1 L2 L3 L4 L5

In your own words, explain the relationship between making an inference and analyzing an argument.

A valid inference is based on evidence stated in the passage. It is supported by adequate and relevant details. An invalid inference cannot be supported by the details in the passage. The same skills are needed to make a valid inference and analyze an argument for its effectiveness.

L2 L3 L4 L5

Create a valid argument. Study the photograph. Then, based on the details in the photo, write a claim and two supports that clearly support the claim.

The Impact of Marine Debris

Claim: *Marine debris is a hazard to the environment.*

Support 1: *Habitats, such as coastal beaches, are polluted with human waste.*

Support 2: *Much of marine debris is made of plastics that do not decay over time.*

1. **How will I use what I have learned?** In your notebook, discuss how you will apply to your own reading/writing strategy what you have learned about argument. When will you apply this knowledge to your reading/writing strategy?
2. **What do I still need to study about argument?** In your notebook, discuss your ongoing study needs. Describe what, when, and how you will continue studying and using argument.

MySkillsLab™

Complete the Post-test for Module 15 in MySkillsLab.

16

LEARNING OUTCOMES

After studying this module you should be able to:

L1 Answer the Question "What's the Point of Research?"

L2 Develop Your Reading/Writing Strategies for Research

L3 Choose a Topic to Research

L4 Find and Evaluate Sources of Research Information

L5 Avoid Plagiarism throughout the Research Process

A Reading/Writing Strategy for Research

Research is an act of investigation. **Research** is a thoughtful, focused study that entails a search for facts, the interpretation of these facts, the revision of ideas in the light of new facts, and the practical application of information. Through research, we learn a new concept, clarify an idea, support a viewpoint, or make a sound decision. Research gives power to your decisions, studies, and viewpoints. Knowing the best research strategies and resources will help you find and use the information you need in your college life, work life, and everyday life.

Research is the process of gathering, reading, evaluating, synthesizing, writing, documenting, and publishing information for a specific purpose.

WHAT'S THE POINT of Research? 

The following photographs illustrate several research situations in college life, work life, and everyday life. Study each photograph and its caption. In the spaces provided, state the need for research in each situation. Then state the overall point of research.

College Life:

Student selecting library books as resources for a term paper

Students gather and document information from reliable sources in research essays to learn more about specific topics in their classes.

Work Life:

A detective with evidence from a crime scene

Many careers such as law enforcement, marketing, and health care rely on the gathering and sharing of facts and expert opinions.

Everyday Life:

Woman checking food labelling

Wise consumers research the products they buy to protect their health and to get the best bargain.

What's the point?

The need for research exists in all areas of our lives. Research enables us to make the best decision about the products we buy. Research is vital in many careers, such as criminal justice, health care, education, and business. Many academic courses require student research as a main way to learn and test information.

What's the Point? One Student's Response

The following paragraph offers one student's response to the question "What's the point of research?"

When needed, you can learn more about any topic through research. Most of the time, I use the Internet to get information. Like, when shopping for a car, I went online and googled Kelley Blue Book so I would know the trade-in value of my car. Many teachers assign research to show us how to learn on our own.

L2 Develop Your Reading/Writing Strategy for Research

Effective research is based on all that you have learned about the reading/writing strategy. You have learned how to survey information to question and annotate text. You have learned to comprehend the writer's point by reciting and reviewing main ideas and supporting details. You have learned to brainstorm and organize details in response to what you have read. You have thought carefully about the use of effective expression to make your point clear to your own readers. All of these steps are also vital steps that you may apply to the research process. Developing your own reading/writing strategy for research enables you to find and use the information you need in your college life, work life, and everyday life.

A reading/writing strategy integrates the steps of reading and writing in order for a researcher to investigate a topic, comprehend information, and compose a written report of the findings of the research. The reading/writing strategy for research is recursive; steps are repeated as needed.

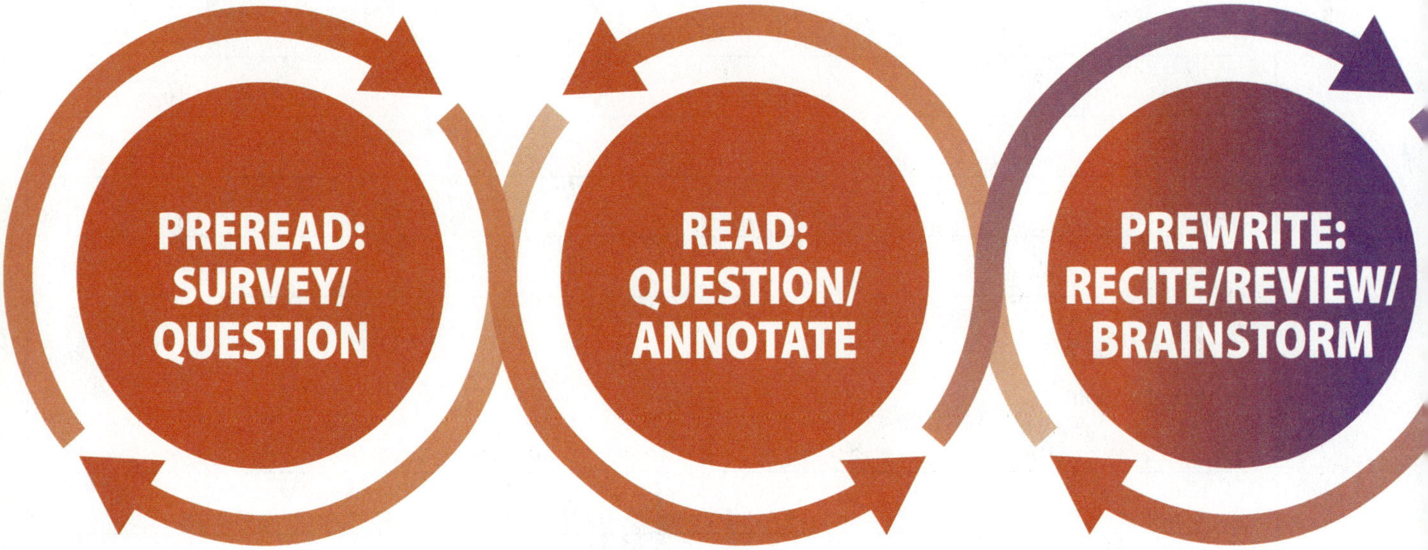

PREREAD: SURVEY/ QUESTION

READ: QUESTION/ ANNOTATE

PREWRITE: RECITE/REVIEW/ BRAINSTORM

Preread:

- Choose a topic to research.
- Create questions based on titles, headings, bold/italic terms, and visuals.
- What is my prior knowledge?
- What is my purpose for researching?
- Who is the intended audience for my research?
- Is this information relevant to my research?
- What kind of information is needed? Where can I find information? Is the information reliable?
- Find and evaluate sources.

Read:

- Ask/record questions.
- Annotate text.
- Underline main ideas.
- Circle new/key words.
- Highlight key details.
- Restate ideas out loud.
- Take notes. Record attribution of sources.

Prewrite:

- Organize notes taken.
- List, cluster, outline topics based on survey; leave room to fill in details during reading.
- Take notes. Restate ideas.
- Record quotes.
- Narrow writing topic based on reading/notes.
- Generate details based on narrowed topic, audience, and purpose for research.
- Freewrite a first response.
- Outline or map out details.

DRAFT YOUR RESPONSE

REVIEW AND REVISE YOUR DRAFT

PROOFREAD

Draft:

- Refer to notes.
- Write a thesis statement.
- Write the body, introduction, and conclusion of your research.
- Include quotes, paraphrases of expert opinions.
- Include facts from reliable sources.
- Avoid plagiarism.

Review/Revise:

- Refine ideas.
- Review draft for clear use of wording, details, and organization.
- Annotate draft with needed revisions.
- Rewrite draft based on review and annotations.
- Apply proper documentation style: MLA or APA.
- Avoid plagiarism.

Proofread:

- Polish ideas.
- Reread draft to identify/correct errors in grammar, spelling, usage, style of documentation.

Practice 1

Develop Your Reading/Writing Strategy for Research

Reflect on your research and writing process. On your own paper, in your journal or portfolio, record your prior experiences with research and writing. First, describe the steps you usually take when you research information to include in your writing. Then describe the steps you usually take when you compose a piece of writing. Finally, discuss how you plan to use the information you learn in this module about research and writing. Predict how your research and writing processes might change.

L3 Choose a Topic to Research

Most research occurs in response to a specific situation that prompts the need to learn more about a topic. For example, in everyday life, we often research a product before we buy it. We compare and contrast brands, price, and reliability. We evaluate the product's advertisement for fact and opinion in their claim. In our working life, we encounter a number of needs for research. For example, employers research the background of job seekers to determine which candidate is best suited to the job. Retailers conduct market research to determine which products to sell to whom and where. In our academic life, we use research to learn independently about a particular topic. At times, professors provide a list of suggested topics to direct your learning. At other times, students are encouraged to select a research topic of interest to them that is relevant to the course. The box "Step by Step: Discover a Research Topic" describes five steps to take to discover and limit a research topic. Effective researchers may repeat this strategy several times as they gather more information until they discover a workable topic. The thinking strategy is designed to yield an adequate depth of information for appropriate research. However, the length of the final research report plays a significant role in choosing and narrowing a topic. The shorter the report is, the narrower the focus will be; in addition, fewer subtopics will be developed. The longer the report is, the greater is your ability to develop more subtopics.

Step by Step: Discover a Research Topic

1. Describe the research situation:
   - ❑ What is the general topic or subject area of the research?
   - ❑ What is the purpose of the research?
   - ❑ What is the length of the final research report?
   - ❑ Who is the audience of the research?
2. Identify possible sources for topics and subjects:
   - ❑ What are key problems, concepts, or issues suggested by a professor, lecture notes, or textbook?
   - ❑ What are some relevant current events or issues covered in newspapers, magazines, or online news sources?

CONTINUED

3. Explore background information about a key problem, issue, or concept. Skim relevant information in sources (such as general and subject encyclopedias, research guides, or yearbook reviews) to answer the following questions:
   - ❑ What are the keywords and terms used to discuss this topic?
   - ❑ How has the issue developed or changed over time?
   - ❑ What is debatable or controversial about the topic?
   - ❑ Who are the accepted or well-known experts about the topic?
   - ❑ What are the publications that cover this topic?
4. Focus your topic. A topic that is too narrow makes it difficult to find adequate information to conduct reasonable research. A topic that is too broad becomes overwhelming and difficult to manage. Narrow your topic by applying one or more of the following focuses:
   - ❑ Content focus: biological, economic, ethical, legal, psychological, political, social, etc.
   - ❑ The timeframe for the research: historical? recent past? current? and so on.
   - ❑ Traits of the population being researched: age, culture, education, gender, nationality, occupation, social/economic class, etc.
   - ❑ Place or region being researched: neighborhood, city, county, state, nation, international region, etc.
5. State your topic as a research question. Use signal words for patterns of organization along with the focus of your topic to form a question that you can answer through research. The questions "Why?" and "How?" form the best basis of research questions, as in the following examples (subject areas listed in parentheses):
   - ❑ How does corporal punishment affect children's emotional development? (psychology, sociology, health)
   - ❑ How does plastic trash impact the environment? (biology, ecology, health, physical sciences)
   - ❑ How do violent video games affect regular players? (psychology, sociology, health)
   - ❑ How should the NFL respond to the problem of concussions suffered by players? (economics, physical fitness, health, team sports medicine)
   - ❑ Why do so many NFL players suffer from concussions? (physical fitness, health, team sports medicine)
   - ❑ Why should the national minimum wage be raised? (economics, political science, sociology)
   - ❑ Why does the cost of gas go up during certain times of the year? (economics, business)

Effective researchers often start with some exploratory searches to find the information called for throughout the thinking strategy to discover a topic. Researchers may begin by surveying a library's online catalogue or online databases (see page 607). At other times, they may do a survey of information on the Internet (see pages 610–611). To search the Internet, a researcher opens a search engine such as Google. In the search box, he or she types in a general subject and a key term from a step in the strategy. For example, a researcher may type "NFL concussions current events" or "NFL concussions controversy" for information called for in steps 2 or 3. For step 4, one might search by combining "NFL concussions" with "biological," "psychological," "ethical," "history of," or "current developments." Each of these searches builds prior knowledge about the topic and the sources of information for the topic. The researcher may then access and build upon this knowledge throughout the research process.

The thinking strategy is designed to yield an adequate depth of information for appropriate research. However, the length of the final research report plays a significant role in choosing and narrowing a topic.

Example

Assume you have chosen to research the general topic "the impact of plastic trash." Your preliminary search on the Internet using the terms "impact of plastic trash" located the information asked for in steps 1–3. Based on the given information, complete steps 4 and 5. Discuss your responses with a peer or small group of classmates.

1. Describe the research situation:

- What is the general topic or subject area of the research? *Marine Biology*
- What is the purpose of the research? *to investigate the impact of plastic trash on the environment*
- What is the length of the final report? *1–2 pages*
- Who is the audience of the research? *professor, classmates, general public*

2. Identify possible sources for topics and subjects:

- What are key problems, concepts, or issues suggested by a professor, lecture notes, or textbook? Dr. Elias, Professor of Marine Biology: *"Fatal to sea creatures. Costs millions of dollars to clean up plastic debris. Illegal dumping."*
- What are some relevant current events or issues covered in newspapers, magazines, or online news sources? *garbage patches growing in oceans, harm to habitats, sea life, human health*

3. Explore the background information about a key problem, issue, or concept.
   - What are the keywords and terms used to discuss this topic? *debris, types, causes, effects, human action, environment, habitat, biodegrade*
   - How has the issue developed or changed over time? *growing problem*
   - What is debatable or controversial about the topic? *human dependence on plastic*
   - Who are the accepted or well-known experts about the topic? *U.S. National Oceanic and Atmospheric Administration, Greenpeace*
   - What are the publications that cover this topic? National Geographic Magazine; Garbology: Our Dirty Love Affair with Trash, *book by Edward Humes; newspapers such as* LA Times *and* New York Times

4. Narrow your topic by applying one or more of the following focuses. Circle the ones that may apply:
   - Content focus: biological, economic, ethical, legal, psychological, political, social.
   - The time frame for the research: Historical. Recent past. Current.
   - Traits of population being researched: age, culture, education, gender, nationality, occupation, social/economic class.
   - Place or region being researched: neighborhood, city, county, state, national, international, regional, global.

5. State your topic as a research question.

How does plastic debris generated by humans harm sea life?

Explanation

Compare your answers to the following think-aloud.

The Step by Step: Discovering a Research Topic offered enough information to effectively limit the topic into a research question. Due to the general subject area, the source of a professor, and the audience, I infer that one of the purposes of this research is to fulfill a science course requirement. However, understanding the impact of plastic trash on the environment is the main purpose

CONTINUED

EXPLANATION *CONTINUED*

for this research. By studying the information given in steps 1–3, I circled the following focuses in step 4. I circled biological, ethical, and legal. Biological covers the physical impact on wildlife and human life. Ethical and legal address human dependence on plastic and illegal dumping. Since garbage patches in oceans are a current and growing problem, I also circled recent past and current as ways to focus the topic. The focus of culture and occupation also seem related to illegal dumping and human dependence on plastic. Finally, due to the garbage in the oceans, the focus may also range from specific regions, international territories, or global effects.

Since the final research paper is only 1–2 pages, I didn't think I could include research about all these terms. So I narrowed my focus to the following research question: "How does plastic debris generated by humans harm sea life?" As I explore the issues, expert opinions, and facts, I may need to refine my question.

Many researchers keep a journal or notebook where they record the information gained in each step of the research process. Keeping accurate research records in a journal or notebook has several benefits. First, a research journal captures information for current and future use. A journal organizes your notes and sources. A research journal offers you the opportunity to reflect about your findings, set and assess research goals, and record your efforts and research results. Recording information generated in a particular research step makes the next step easier to accomplish.

Practice 2

Choose a Research Topic: Start a Research Journal

Begin a research journal to record the steps you take throughout the research process in this module. Consider using the following supplies: a 3-hole punch folder with front and back pockets, loose leaf paper for hand-written notes, a 3-hole puncher for handouts and other printed material, a stack of 3" x 5" index cards. In your journal complete the five steps of the Step by Step: Discover a Research Topic guideline. Use one of the following general topics, or identify a general topic of your own choosing. *Responses may vary.*

Suggested General Topics:

Identity theft	Nelson Mandela	e-cigarettes
Stress	Sleep disorders	How to start a small business

Step by Step: Discover a Research Topic

1. Describe the research situation.
2. Identify possible sources for topics and subjects.
3. Explore the background information.
4. Narrow your topic by applying one or more of the following focuses: content, timeframe, population, region.
5. State your topic as a research question.

Find and Evaluate Sources of Research Information

One of the most basic and early steps in the research process is finding useful and trustworthy information. A good way to begin your research is to ask the following three questions:

- What kind of information do I need?
- Where can I find the information I need?
- How do I know the information I find is reliable or trustworthy?

The rest of this section offers you strategies and resources to answer these basic research questions.

What Kind of Information Do I Need?

Basically, two types of information guide our thinking and writing: facts and opinions. The skills you developed in Module 14 to distinguish between fact and opinion are essential to you as a researcher. Remember:

- A fact is something that can be shown to be true, to exist, or to have happened based on evidence. The following statistic is an example of a fact: "About one-third of U.S. adults (33.8%) are obese." The source of this fact is the government agency the Centers for Disease Control and Prevention (CDC).
- An opinion is a personal view somebody takes about an issue. The following statement is an example of an expert opinion given by Dr. Oz, a heart surgeon and author—a medical expert. "You can control your health destiny." This quote is his expert opinion as stated on page 2 of his best-selling book about health, *You: The Owner's Manual.*

An undeniable fact or an expert opinion is a convincing research detail. Effective researchers identify sources for facts and opinions.

Example

Assume you are continuing to research the impact of plastic trash on marine life. You are evaluating a few general sources to locate key facts and expert opinions. Identify each of the following sources as **F** for a source of facts or **EO** as a source for an expert opinion.

F 1. *Encyclopedia of Environmental Issues*
F/EO 2. *National Geographic* magazine
F/EO 3. U.S. National Oceanic and Atmospheric Administration
F/EO 4. *Credo Reference*, 100 online subject encyclopedias, dictionaries, handbooks, and more
EO 5. A marine biologist at Marine Land, FL
EO 6. A published professor with a Ph.D. in the field

Explanation

Compare your answers to the following student's think-aloud.

Item 1, the Encyclopedia of Environmental Issues, *is a published source for facts—accurate, objective, and reliable information. Item 2,* National Geographic *magazine, is a highly respected source that publishes expert opinions and facts about the physical world. The U.S. National Oceanic and Atmospheric Administration is a research branch of the federal government. It serves as a source of data and the interpretation of data by respected experts in the field. According to its website* Credo Reference *offers online access to full text reference books and library resources. So I think item 4 definitely is a source for facts, but it could also offer access to well-published expert opinions. Items 5 and 6 offer expert opinions. Both a marine biologist and a published professor with a Ph.D. in their field are educated and experienced in their subject area.*

Where Can I Find the Information I Need?

Identifying the type of information you need helps you know where to look for it. The two main storehouses of information are the library and the Internet. Both offer a variety of resources for help in locating information as well as sources of information.

Library Resources and Sources

- Seek out your library's **reference librarian**. These professionals are trained to teach you how to use the library and its resources. They can answer queries about specific information and also can recommend good sources for specific topics. Reference librarians have to stay up to date with technology and customer needs; thus they are able to assist your use of all types of research resources.

A **reference librarian** is trained in library work and is responsible for a collection of specialized or technical information or materials.

- Search the **library's online catalogue**. Easily reached from the Internet, the catalogue is used mainly to locate books and other material physically located at a library. You can search for a source by author, title, subject, or keywords. As you find a source you think you may use, write down the title, author, and call number (or other reference information) so you can locate the item on its library shelf.

The **library's online catalogue** is an index of materials held by the library.

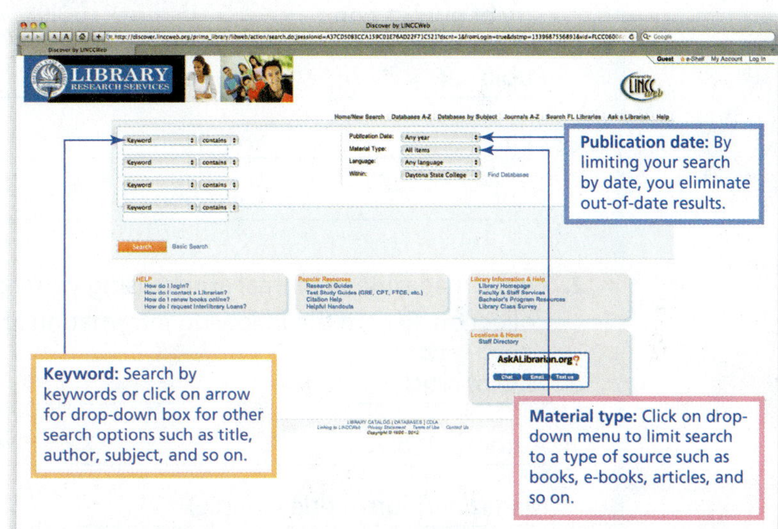

- Search the library's **electronic database collection**. This information is organized by searchable fields, such as author, title, subject, or keywords. A library's electronic database collection gives you access to thousands of sources such as magazine, journal, and newspaper articles, as well as essays, and e-books.

The library's **electronic database collection** is a computer-based collection of records or listings of a wide variety of information.

Example

Practice using your college's library as a resource for research into the impact of plastic debris on marine life. Search for sources by completing the following activities. Ask a reference librarian for assistance as needed. *Answers may vary.*

1. Find a book using your college's online catalogue. Record the following information about the book:

   Title ____________________

   Author(s) or Editor(s) ____________________

   City of publication ____________________

   Publisher __________ Year published __________

   Call # __________ Available __________ or checked out __________

   Print __________ or e-book __________

2. Find a magazine or journal article using your college library's electronic database collection. Record the following information about the article:

   Title of article ____________________

   Author(s) if given ____________________

   Magazine/journal title (Source) ____________________

   Date published __________ Page # __________

   Name of database ____________________

3. Find a newspaper article using your college library's electronic database collection. Record the following information about the article:

   Title of article ____________________

   Author(s) if given ____________________

   Newspaper title (Source) ____________________

   Date published __________ Page # __________

   Name of database ____________________

Explanation

Compare your answers to the following student's think-aloud.

As I looked for sources of information in my college's online catalogue and database, I saw many ways in which writers limit the topic "impact of plastic debris on marine life." Some focus on how the plastic debris gets into the oceans. Others focus on the types of plastic debris. Some focus on the effects of plastic debris on the different types of marine life. Surveying both online resources actually helped me figure out my focus on this topic. I am interested in learning about the large garbage patches growing in the oceans. So I used the search terms "garbage patch" and "oceans" to locate the following sources.

Book

Title: Plastic Ocean: How a Sea Captain's Chance Discovery Launched a Quest to Save the Oceans

Author(s) or Editor(s): Charles Moore

City of publication: New York

Publisher: Avery Year published: 2011

Call #: GC1085.M67 2011 Available in print.

Magazine/Journal

Title of article: "Plastic, the Great Pacific Garbage Patch, and International Misfires at a Cure"

Author(s): Grant A. Harse

Magazine/journal title (Source): UCLA Journal of Environmental Law & Policy

Date published: Fall, 2011 Vol/Page #: Vol. 29, p. 331. Name of database: LINCCWeb

Newspaper

Title of article: "The Widening Gyre"

Author(s) if given: Editorial Desk

Newspaper title (Source): New York Times

Date published: Nov. 2, 2011 Page #: A30(L)

Name of database: LINCCWeb

Internet Resources and Sources

A **search engine** looks for and retrieves information from millions of sites on the Internet. The search engine records each word within a document on the Internet. When you conduct a search, it matches your keywords to the records it has in its databases and retrieves a list of links that match your request. Examples of search engines are Yahoo, Google, Ask.com, and Bing.

> A **search engine** is a computer software program that uses keywords to search for and locate text, data, or any specific information on the Internet.

- Search by **keywords**. A keyword is a term used to indicate a word (or series of words) a researcher types in a search engine to locate specific information on the Internet.

  If a keyword is too broad, then too many results are returned. If a keyword is too narrow, then too few results are returned.

> A **keyword** is a word used as a query or point of reference for seeking more information about a topic.

  - Use quotation marks or Boolean (NOT, OR) operators to group words together. Enclosing words in quotation marks tells the search engine to search for the complete phrase, not the individual words. Searches that use the Boolean operator "NOT" tell the search engine to search for sites that mention the first item, but not the second. Finally, searches that use the Boolean operator "OR" tell the search engine to search for one term or the other. For example, a search for *"green energy" NOT nuclear* will find sites on green energy that do not mention nuclear power. Searches for *"green energy" OR nuclear* will find sources that discuss either green energy or nuclear power. Spell your keywords carefully, and consider alternate spellings.
  - Investigate your search engine's Advanced Search options. Most sites allow you to limit results by date, type of site, or many other options.

- Search by website domains. To search by domains, you need to understand a website's **URL**.

> A **URL** is a site's universal resource locator, also referred to as the website's address.

Basically, a URL has three main parts:

Notice the three letters at the end of the host name; these letters identify the type of organization that hosts the information. To search a topic by a domain, think about which domain is most likely to host the type of information you need. Then include the domain in your query by leaving a space after the last word and typing a period and the three letters of the domain.

Types of Domains That Host Websites with Examples		
.com	companies and commercial sites	msnbc.com
.edu	educational institutions	http://owl.english.purdue.edu/owl
.gov	government organizations	http://www.usa.gov
.org	nonprofit organizations	http://redcross.org

- Use an Internet bookmark. An **Internet bookmark** acts as a marker for a website. Once you find a website as a source of information, you can save it for easy and quick access. Look in the toolbar of your web browser for the Favorites or Bookmark option.

An **Internet bookmark** is a link or URL stored in a Web browser for future access.

Example

Practice using the Internet as a resource for research. Continue working with the topic of "impact of plastic debris on marine life." Find a website that offers information about your topic using a search engine such as ask.com, bing.com, firefox.com, google.com, or yahoo.com. *Answers may vary.*

Website name: ______________________________

Website address (URL): ______________________________

Title of article: ______________________________

Article's author(s) if given: ______________________________

Website sponsor: ______________________________

Date of last update: ______________ Date of access: ______________

Explanation

Compare your answers to the following student's think-aloud.

I used the keywords "garbage patch" and "oceans" to search the Internet. These keywords brought up a number of sources such as National Geographic, *the* New York Times, *and the U.S. National Oceanic and Atmospheric Administration (NOAA). Each source offered a different view on marine debris. For example, the* National Geographic *article focused on defining terms such as "Great Pacific Garbage Patch," "ocean gyre," "marine debris." The article also discussed harmful effects on specific types of marine life and how to clean up the oceans. The article from the* New York Times *focused on "expanding islands of trash afloat in the oceans." The article from NOAA focused on "science vs. myth" about the sizes or mass of the garbage patches in the oceans. I decided to use the information from*

CONTINUED

EXPLANATION *CONTINUED*

> *National Geographic about the effect of marine debris on particular species of marine life, such as sea turtles, jellyfish, and albatrosses. This source also provides links to additional sources, such as NOAA.*
>
> *Website name: National Geographic Education*
> *Website address (URL): http://education.nationalgeographic .com/education/encyclopedia/great-pacific-garbage-patch/?ara=1*
> *Title: "Great Pacific Garbage Patch: Pacific Trash Vortex"*
> *Article's author(s) if given: Kim Rutledge*
> *Website sponsor: National Geographic Society*
> *Date of last update: None given*
> *Date of access: December 20, 2013*

Track Your Sources

As you find a source you think you may use, take the following steps to track and document it.

- Write in a log or cut and paste into a Word file the information about the source's publication.
- Send to your e-mail account the record of or the link to the source.
- Download the document, or create a copy of the document by cutting and pasting it into a Word file.

Find and record the following information (consider using 3" x 5" index cards, one card per source):

- Author's full name
- Title of article
- Title of book, periodical, or site
- Publisher of book, periodical, or site
- Date of publication, or for websites, the date of latest update
- For books and articles, page numbers from which you need information
- For websites, date you accessed the information
- For websites, the URL, also called the website's address

In some websites, you may not find all the usual publication information. For example, some organizations do not identify a specific person as an author. In addition, you may need to click around in the site to find all the information.

Practice 3

Find Sources: Keeping a Research Journal

Update your research journal to record the steps you take to find sources for a topic. Continue researching the topic you chose in Practice 2. In your research journal find sources and record the information needed to track and document each source. Find a book, a magazine, and an Internet source. *Responses may vary.*

1. Book

Title

Author(s) or Editor(s)

City of publication Publisher

Year published

Call # Available or checked out

Print e-book

2. Magazine or journal article

Title of article

Author(s) if given

Magazine/journal title (Source)

Date published Page #

Name of database

3. Internet

Website name

Website address (URL)

Title of article

Article's author(s) if given

Website sponsor

Date of last update Date of your access

How Can I Know the Information I Find Is Reliable or Trustworthy?

Before publishing material in books, newspapers, magazines, and scholarly journals, editors and peers carefully evaluate sources and review information to ensure they are reliable and accurate. But even then, print materials may reveal a bias or share incomplete or misleading information. The Internet, on the other hand, allows anyone to publish information without any screening of the information for reliability or accuracy. Thus, more than ever before, we must carefully evaluate information to determine how reliable and accurate it is. The following chart offers a guide for evaluating sources from the library and the Internet. If a source qualifies as usable based on this guide, then use that source as PAART of your research.

PAART: A Guide to Evaluating Sources		
P	**P**urpose Why did the author write?	Identify the purpose of the information: to inform, to argue, to entertain. Identify the type of information: fact, opinion, expert opinion. Identify any specific bias: cultural, personal, political, religious viewpoints.
A	**A**uthority Who is the author or host?	Identify the author, publisher, source, or sponsor. Identify contact information: e-mail or street address. Identify the qualifications of the author: education, experience. For a website: Identify the type of domain that hosts the site.
A	**A**ccuracy How correct is the information?	Note errors: grammar, spelling, typographical (typos). Verify the information in another source. Identify the source of the information. Look for reviewers or editors of the publication.
R	**R**elevance How does the information relate to the topic of research?	Identify the intended audience for the publication. Evaluate how the information relates to your topic of research. Review a variety of sources before making a final choice to use a particular source.
T	**T**imeliness When was the information written?	Evaluate the need for current or historical information. Note the date of the publication. Note if the information has been updated or revised. For a website: Test the hyperlinks to make sure they still work.

The PAART guide can be used to quickly evaluate a source for research in college, work, and everyday life. We need to test information before we accept it as useful to our thinking or decision-making process.

Example

Practice using PAART to evaluate a source. Work with one of the sources identified for the topic "impact of plastic on marine life" in previous examples and explanations (see pages 602 and 608). Answer each question with a score from 5 to 1. A score of 5 means excellent, and a score of 1 means unacceptable. Then add up the total score. Discuss your experience with a peer or a small group of classmates. What makes a source excellent?

PAART: A Guide to Evaluating Sources						
Title of Source:						
Criteria	**Questions to Evaluate Source**	**Rating of Source**				
Purpose What?	Is the purpose of the publication made clear?	5	4	3	2	1
	Is the type of information appropriate for the research topic?	5	4	3	2	1
	Does a specific bias influence the information?	5	4	3	2	1
Authority Who?	Is the author, publisher, source, or sponsor of the publication stated?	5	4	3	2	1
	Is contact information available?	5	4	3	2	1
	Is the author qualified to address the topic?	5	4	3	2	1
	For a website: Is the domain that hosts the site appropriate for the topic?	5	4	3	2	1
Accuracy How?	Are there errors: grammar, spelling, typographical (typos)?	5	4	3	2	1
	Can the information be verified in another source?	5	4	3	2	1
	Is the source of information reliable?	5	4	3	2	1
	Has the information been reviewed by peers or editors in the field?	5	4	3	2	1
Relevance How?	Is the intended audience for the publication made clear?	5	4	3	2	1
	Does the information relate to the topic of research?	5	4	3	2	1
	Is the information at the appropriate level?	5	4	3	2	1
	Have a variety of sources been reviewed before making a final choice to use a particular source?	5	4	3	2	1
Timeliness When?	Does the topic of research call for current or historical information?	5	4	3	2	1
	Is the date of publication given?	5	4	3	2	1
	Is the date of publication appropriate for the need of current historical information?	5	4	3	2	1
	Has the information been updated or revised?	5	4	3	2	1
	For a website: Do the hyperlinks still work?	5	4	3	2	1
	Total score					

Score Range	**Excellent** 100–81	80–61	60–41	40–21	**Unacceptable** 20–0

Explanation

Compare your answers to the following student's think-aloud.

I chose to evaluate the article "Great Pacific Garbage Patch" on the National Geographic Education website.

EXPLANATION *CONTINUED*

Purpose: 5

For the clear purpose of disseminating information to the public, the article uses appropriate information. The article used biased language to convey a sense of urgency about the topic, but it also used facts to justify the bias.

Authority: 5

Both the source and the author of the article were given. National Geographic is a respected source about our physical world as it relies on facts and expert opinions on the topic.

Accuracy: 5

The article is error free. It offers links to additional sources that verify and expand the ideas given in the article. In addition, the credits list a team of 13 that includes the writer, editors, and reviewers.

Relevance: 5

The general public is clearly the audience. The article uses easy to understand language that clearly explains scientific terms and processes. I reviewed three sources before choosing this one.

Timeliness: 4

It offers current information. However, the date of publication is not given, nor is there any information about a recent update. However, all the links work.

As my classmates compared sources, we noticed that some sources received low ratings because the author or date wasn't given. We had to search or click through several pages to find information to evaluate. We decided that an excellent source discloses (and makes it easy to find) all the information needed for use in our research.

Practice 4

Find and Evaluate Sources: Keeping a Research Journal

Update your research journal to record the steps you took to find sources for a topic. Continue working with the sources you are gathering from Practices 2 and 3. In your research journal, use PAART to evaluate the three sources you recorded in Practice 3.

Avoid Plagiarism Throughout the Research Process

L5

Plagiarism is a form of stealing that leads to serious consequences in both the classroom and the workplace. The penalties for plagiarism in the classroom may range from failing the assignment to expulsion. Likewise, plagiarism in the workplace may result in demotion, lack of opportunity for promotion, or job loss. Plagiarism is not only unethical, it is also illegal. Original work is protected by copyright law. Thus, plagiarism can result in legal action. Many times, plagiarism is not a deliberate act. Instead, plagiarism may occur from a lack of knowledge about how to use the work of others or how to give them proper credit for their work. You can avoid plagiarism by properly **paraphrasing**, summarizing, quoting, and citing the words and ideas of other people.

The following chart outlines five steps for paraphrasing.

> **Plagiarism** is the act of presenting the words or ideas of another author as one's own or using information without giving credit to its original source.
>
> **Paraphrasing** a text is accurately restating an idea using your own words.

The Five R's of Paraphrasing: Read, Restate, Revise, Revisit, Repeat	
Read	Read the text to understand the author's meaning. Highlight key ideas. Look up words you don't know.
Restate	Put the original text out of sight. Recall in writing the author's ideas using your own words.
Revise	Wait for a space of time (from a few minutes to a few days) to create an opportunity to see your paraphrase with fresh eyes. Then revise your paraphrase for clear wording and smooth flow of ideas.
Revisit	After drafting your paraphrase, revisit the original text. Compare your paraphrase to the author's wording. Change any wording that is too close to the author's words. Double check to make sure your paraphrase correctly restates the author's message.
Repeat	Complete the preceding steps as many times as needed to draft a sound paraphrase.

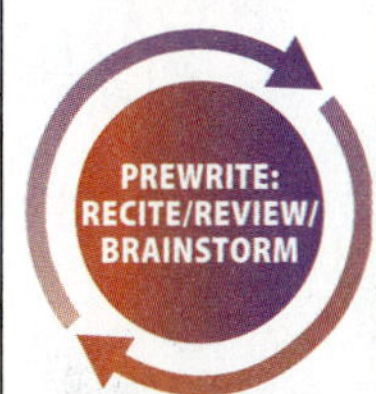

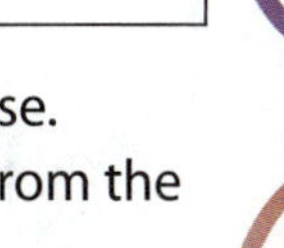

With a peer or small group of classmates, study the following example of a paraphrase. Read the original text and the paraphrase. Then discuss how the paraphrase differs from the original text. Finally, discuss how the paraphrase is similar to the original text.

Original Text:

"Health and safety procedures for body artists may be regulated by city, county, or state agencies. Reputable shops and tattoo parlors govern themselves and follow strict safety procedures to protect their clients—and their body artists."

Source of Text:

"Body Art: Tattoos and Piercings." Centers for Disease Control and Prevention (CDC), 29 Aug. 2011. Web.

Paraphrase:

Trustworthy tattooists and body piercers are rigorous in hygiene. They are also faithful to the laws set in place by different levels of government. Responsible "body artists" take steps to ensure the physical well-being of their customer and themselves ("Body Art: Tattoos and Piercings").

Notice that the paraphrase is about the same length as the original text. Also notice that in the paraphrase, any exact words taken from the original text are placed in quotation marks. Finally, the source of the paraphrase is cited in the text to avoid plagiarism. Since the source does not have an author, the title is used in the citation. Also, since this information is from the Internet, no page number is given. However, the page numbers where information appears in a print source should be included in the citation. The complete publication information will also be provided in the Works Cited page.

Example

Assume you are continuing your research about marine debris, garbage patches, and oceans. You have decided to paraphrase the following information from the article "Great Pacific Garbage Patch" on the National Geographic Education website. Read the paragraph. In the given space, write a paraphrase of the information. Use the "Five R's of Paraphrasing." Then exchange your paraphrase with a peer or small group of classmates. Evaluate each other's paraphrases and recommend specific revisions if needed.

Answers may vary.

Original Text:

"The Great Pacific Garbage Patch, also known as the Eastern Pacific Garbage Patch and the Pacific Trash Vortex, lies in a high-pressure area between the U.S. states of Hawaii and California. This area is in the middle of the North Pacific Subtropical Gyre. An ocean gyre is a circular ocean current formed by the Earth's wind patterns and the forces created by the rotation of the planet. The area in the center of a gyre tends to be very calm and stable. The circular motion of the gyre draws in debris. Debris eventually makes its way into the center of the gyre, where it becomes trapped and builds up. A similar garbage patch exists in the Atlantic Ocean, in the North Atlantic Gyre."

NOAA

Source of Text:

Rutledge, Kim. "The Great Garbage Patch." *National Geographic Education*. n.d. Web. 20 Dec. 2013.

Paraphrase:

The Great Pacific Garbage Patch is sometimes called the Eastern Pacific Garbage Patch or the Pacific Trash Vortex. It is centered in the North Pacific Subtropical Gyre, off the high-pressure coasts of Hawaii and California. An ocean gyre or vortex occurs due to the formation of a whirlpool as the ocean's current spirals in response to the force of earth's rotation and wind patterns. The powerful whirlpool then catches up and funnels floating debris into its center where it becomes a growing, whirling mass. In the North Atlantic Gyre, the Atlantic Ocean also has a garbage patch (Rutledge).

Explanation

Compare your answers to the following student's think-aloud.

Before I could start my paraphrase, I had to look up several terms in the paragraph, such as vortex, gyre, high-pressure area *just to be sure I understood the writer's use of the scientific words. Looking up the definitions of these terms helped me create a mental picture of the ocean's rotating current and how it gathers and traps debris. Certain facts could not be reworded, such as the names of the garbage patches and where they are located. Also based on the example, I gave the author's name in parentheses. Since this information came from the Internet, there wasn't a page number to include.*

Paraphrase:

The Great Pacific Garbage Patch is sometimes called the Eastern Pacific Garbage Patch or the Pacific Trash Vortex. It is centered in the North Pacific Subtropical Gyre, off the high-pressure coasts of Hawaii and California. An ocean gyre or vortex occurs due to the formation of a whirlpool as the ocean's current spirals in response to the force of earth's rotation and wind patterns. The powerful whirlpool then catches up and funnels floating debris into its center where it becomes a growing, whirling mass. In the North Atlantic Gyre, the Atlantic Ocean also has a garbage patch (Rutledge).

Summarizing and quoting are two additional ways to avoid plagiarism. You developed these skills in your studies of Module 6 (see pages 218–219) and Module 14 (see pages 540–541).

As you learned, summarizing a text entails reducing a section of text to its main points and key details. Since you paraphrase ideas in a summary, any exact words taken from the original text are placed in quotation marks. Just as with a paraphrase, the source of the summary is cited in the text and Works Cited page to avoid plagiarism. Many experts suggest that you begin a summary with the title of the original text and the author's name.

With a peer or small group of classmates, review your understanding of writing a summary. Study the following example of a summary. The original text has been annotated to illustrate the three-step process for writing a summary. Read the original text, the annotations, and the summary. Then discuss how the summary differs from the original text. Finally, discuss how the summary is similar to the original text.

Bullying Is a Big Problem

by Teenshealth.org

Every day thousands of teens wake up afraid to go to school. Bullying is a problem that affects millions of students. And it has everyone worried, not just the kids on its receiving end. Yet because parents, teachers, and other adults don't always see it, they may not understand how extreme bullying can get. Bullying is when a person is picked on over and over again by an individual or group with more power, either in terms of physical strength or social standing. Two of the main reasons people are bullied are because of appearance and social status. Bullies pick on the people they think don't fit in, maybe because of how they look, how they act (for example, kids who are shy and withdrawn), their race or religion, or because the bullies think their target may be gay or lesbian.

Some bullies attack their targets physically, which can mean anything from shoving or tripping to punching or hitting, or even sexual assault. Others use psychological control or verbal insults to put themselves in charge. For example, people in popular groups or cliques often bully people they categorize as different by excluding them or gossiping about them (psychological bullying). They may also taunt or tease their targets (verbal bullying).

Step 1. Delete unnecessary material.

Step 3. Underline, rephrase main idea.

Step 1. Delete repetitive material.

Step 2. Condense this section to list "physical, psychological, and verbal bullying."

Summary: According to "Bullying Is a Big Problem" by Teenshealth.org, bullying occurs when one or more persons of power repeatedly harass an individual of lesser "physical strength or social standing." Bullies use physical, psychological, and verbal abuse to torment others who differ from them.

Quoting a text entails repeating the exact words of the author. When you use the exact words of another person, you enclose that exact wording within a pair of quotation marks. You should use quotes rarely and purposefully in your writing. A well-placed quote adds interest, emphasis, and authority to an important point. Too many quotes make it look like you didn't take time to understand the text well enough to offer a fresh view of the topic.

With a peer or a small group of classmates, review your understanding of quoting information. Study the following use of a quote in a piece of writing. Annotate the following: Underline the information that gives the context of the quote. Double underline the attribution of the quote. Circle the publication information. Underline the quote with a squiggly line.

Example of Quoting:

> On a cold, snowy day, January 21, 1961, John F. Kennedy at the age of 43 took the oath of office as the youngest man elected to be President of the United States of America. Kennedy exclaimed, "And so, my fellow Americans, ask not what your country can do for you; ask what you can do for your country" (American Rhetoric: Top 100 Speeches). Kennedy effectively beckoned an entire generation into public service with this moving call to action.

Notice several aspects of this example of proper quoting that apply as general rules for quoting text. First, a comma follows the attribution verb *exclaimed* to introduce the quote. Second, a pair of quotation marks enclose the exact words of President Kennedy. Third, the source or publication information is placed inside a pair of parentheses and immediately follows the quote. Finally, the end sentence punctuation is placed outside the closing parenthesis.

To avoid plagiarism, effective readers/writers record information in the form of notes. Each note is recorded as a paraphrase, a summary, or a quote. And each note is clearly linked to its source.

Practice 5

Avoid Plagiarism Throughout the Research Process

Continue working with the topic you chose in Practice 4. Go to one of the sources you evaluated and select information to use in your research. Compose three types of notes from the original text: a paraphrase, a summary, and a quote. *Answers will vary.*

Reading and Writing Assignments

MySkillsLab™
Complete these assignments on MySkillsLab.

Considering Audience and Purpose

Review the photographs in the Photo Organizer about the purpose of research. Assume you volunteer at the local library and you have been asked to give a speech about the value of research in everyday life, college life, and work life. Write a draft of your speech to post on the library's website after you give your presentation. Use information you have learned from this module. Also, interview your professor for tips and advice. Track your sources and use summary, paraphrasing, and quoting to avoid plagiarism.

Reading and Writing for Everyday Life

Assume you are a member of a local consumer group. The purpose of your group is to share information that will help members wisely manage or save money. Your group publishes a newsletter online once a month. This month, you have been asked to write a column about ways to save money at the grocery store. Find two to three sources of information for your column. Track your sources and use summary, paraphrasing, and quoting to avoid plagiarism.

Reading and Writing for College Life

Assume that you are taking a college course in health, and you are interested in the health benefits of organic food. Find two or three sources about organic food. In addition to the benefits of organic food, you may want to include in your essay information about the traits, the expense, and the use of organic food. Track your sources and use summary, paraphrasing, and quoting to avoid plagiarism.

Reading and Writing for Working Life

Assume that you are preparing to enter the workforce in a profession of your choice (such as a nurse, a manager at a local retail store, a real estate salesperson, etc.). You have decided to draft a general cover letter that you can adapt to fit possible job applications. In your cover letter, you plan to discuss how well suited you are for the responsibilities of the job. Find two or three sources that describe the tasks, responsibilities, and qualifications of the type of job you are seeking. Include information from these sources in your cover letter. Track your sources and use summary, paraphrasing, and quoting to avoid plagiarism.

Workshop: Compose a Paragraph Using Research

Choose a paragraph to read and respond to in writing. You may select a paragraph in an example, practice, or writing assignment within this module. Or you may select a paragraph of your own choosing. Use the following guide to comprehend and respond to the paragraph. Apply what you have learned about research to your reading/writing strategy.

Preread: Survey and Question

Ask questions about the text's features.

____

____

What is the passage about?

____

____

How is the material organized?

____

____

What do I already know about this topic? (What is my prior knowledge about the vocabulary?)

____

____

What is my purpose for reading/writing?

____

____

What points may I want to address or include in my written response?

____

____

Read and Annotate

As you read, annotate key ideas, particularly those details that answer your prereading questions.

Recite, Review, and Brainstorm

Recite the information. Summarize the most important parts. Answer your prereading questions. Rephrase ideas into your own words. Record changes in your opinions based on the new information. **Review** the information. **Brainstorm** ideas for your written response to the passage. **Freewrite** a response to what you have read. **Map** the relationship among ideas you have annotated in the text. **Outline** or list key ideas and details in blocks of thought.

Write a Draft of Your Response

Using the ideas you generated by brainstorming, compose a draft of your response. Use your own paper.

Revise Your Draft

Once you have created a draft of a comparison/contrast, read the draft to answer the questions in the "Step by Step: Questions for Revising a Paragraph Using Research" box that follows. Indicate your answers by annotating your paper. If you answer "yes" to a question, underline, check, or circle examples. If you answer "no" to a question, write needed information in margins and draw lines to indicate placement of additional details. Revise your paragraph based on your reflection. (*Hint:* Experienced writers create several drafts as they focus on one or two questions per draft.)

Step by Step: Questions for Revising a Paragraph Using Research

- ☐ Have I stated or implied a focused main idea?
- ☐ Have I used strong transitions and signal words? Is the order of details clear?
- ☐ Have I used concrete details to make my point?
- ☐ Have I made my point with adequate details?
- ☐ Have I included only the details that are relevant to my point?
- ☐ Have I properly paraphrased, quoted, or summarized ideas?
- ☐ Have I properly documented my sources?
- ☐ Have I used effective language?

Proofread Your Draft

Once you have made any revisions to your paragraph that may be needed, proofread your paragraph to eliminate careless errors.

Review Test

MySkillsLab™
Complete this Review Test on MySkillsLab.

Score (number correct) ______ x 10 = ______ %

Use reading/writing strategies to comprehend and respond to the following passage from the college textbook *Social Psychology.* Answer the questions that follow. Finally, respond to the writing prompts "Summary Response" and "What Do You Think?"

Vocabulary Preview

intrinsic motivation (**19**): the desire to engage in an activity because we enjoy it or find it interesting, not because of external rewards or pressures

extrinsic motivation (**23**): the desire to engage in an activity because of external rewards or pressures, not because we enjoy the task or find it interesting

overjustification effect (**27**): the tendency for people to view their behavior as caused by compelling extrinsic reasons, making them underestimate the extent to which it was caused by intrinsic reasons

1170L/10.9 GE/1231 words

INTRINSIC VERSUS EXTRINSIC MOTIVATION

[1]Imagine that you are an elementary school teacher who wants your students to develop a love of reading. [2]Not only do you want your students to read more, but you also want them to develop a love of books. [3]How might you go about accomplishing this? [4]It is not going to be easy, because so many other things compete for your students' attention, such as television, video games, and text messaging.

[5]If you are like many educators, you might decide that a good approach would be to reward the children for reading. [6]Maybe that will get them to put down those cell phones and pick up a book—and develop a love of reading in the process. [7]Teachers have always rewarded kids with a smile or a gold star on an assignment, of course, but recently they have turned to more powerful incentives. [8]A chain of pizza restaurants offers elementary school students in some school districts a certificate for a free pizza when they have read a certain number of books (see "Book It!" at www.bookitprogram.com). [9]In others, teachers offer candy, brownies, and toys for academic achievement (Perlstein, 1999). [10]One school district has taken this a step further by rewarding high school students with cash prizes if they do well on advanced placement exams (Hibbard, 2011).

[11]There is no doubt that rewards are powerful motivators and that pizzas and money will get kids to read more. [12]One of the oldest and most fundamental psychological principles says that giving a reward each time a behavior occurs will increase the frequency of that behavior. [13]Whether it be a food pellet delivered to a rat pressing a bar or a free pizza given to a child for reading, rewards can change behavior.

CONTINUED

[14]But people are not rats, and we have to consider the effects of rewards on what's inside—people's thoughts about themselves, their self-concept, and their motivation to read in the future. [15]Does being paid to read, for example, change people's ideas about *why* they are reading? [16]The danger of reward programs such as Book It! is that kids begin to think they are reading to earn something, not because they find reading to be an enjoyable activity in its own right. [17]When the reward programs end and pizzas are no longer forthcoming, children may actually read less than they did before.

[18]This is especially likely to happen to children who already liked to read. [19]Such children have high **intrinsic motivation**: the desire to engage in an activity because they enjoy it or find it interesting, not because of external rewards or pressures (Harackiewicz & Elliot, 1993, 1998; Harackiewicz & Hulleman, 2010; Hirt et al., 1996; Hulleman et a1., 2010; Lepper, Corpus, & Iyengar, 2005; Ryan & Deci, 2000; Vansteenkiste et a1., 2010). [20]Their reasons for engaging in the activity have to do with themselves—the enjoyment and pleasure they feel when reading a book. [21]In other words, reading is play, not work.

[22]What happens when the children start getting rewards for reading? [23]Their reading, originally stemming from intrinsic motivation, is now also spurred by **extrinsic motivation**, which is people's desire to engage in an activity because of external rewards or pressures, not because they enjoy the task or find it interesting. [24]According to self-perception theory, rewards can hurt intrinsic motivation. [25]Whereas before many children read because they enjoyed it, now they are reading so that they will get the reward. [26]The unfortunate outcome is that replacing intrinsic motivation with extrinsic motivation makes people lose interest in the activity they initially enjoyed. [27]This result is called the **overjustification effect**, which results when people view their behavior as caused by compelling extrinsic reasons (e.g., a reward), making them underestimate the extent to which their behavior was caused by intrinsic reasons (Deci, Koestner, & Ryan, 1999a, 1999b; Harackiewicz, 1979; Lepper, 1995; Lepper, Henderlong, & Gingras, 1999; Warneken & Tomasello, 2008).

[28]In one study, for example, fourth- and fifth-grade teachers introduced four new math games to their students, and during a 13-day baseline period they noted how long each child played each math game. [29]As seen in the leftmost line in Figure 1, the children initially had some intrinsic interest in the math games, in that they played them for several minutes during this baseline period. [30]For the next several days, a reward program was introduced. [31]Now the children could earn credits toward certificates and trophies by playing the math games. [32]The more time they spent playing the games, the more credits they earned. [33]As the middle line in Figure 1 shows, the reward program was effective in increasing the amount of time the children spent on the math games, showing that the rewards were an effective motivator.

[34]The key question is what happened after the program ended and the kids could no longer earn rewards for playing the games. [35]As predicted by the overjustification hypothesis, the children spent significantly less time on the math games than they had initially, before the rewards were introduced (see the rightmost line in Figure 1). [36]The researchers determined, by comparing these results to those of a control condition, that it was the rewards that made people like the games less and not the fact that everyone became bored with the games as time went by. [37]In short, the rewards destroyed the children's intrinsic interest in the games; by the end of

the study, they were hardly playing the games at all (Greene, Sternberg, & Lepper, 1976).

[38]What can we do to protect intrinsic motivation from the dangers of society's reward system? [39]Fortunately, there are conditions under which overjustification effects can be avoided. [40]Rewards will undermine interest only if interest was initially high (Calder & Staw, 1975; Tang & Hall, 1995). [41]If a child has no interest in reading, then getting him or her to read by offering rewards is not a bad idea, because there is no initial interest to undermine.

[42]Also, the type of reward makes a difference. [43]So far, we have discussed **task contingent rewards,** meaning that people get them simply for doing a task, regardless of how well they do it. [44]Sometimes **performance-contingent rewards** are used, whereby the reward depends on how well people perform the task. [45]For example, grades are performance-contingent because you get a high reward (an A) only if you do well. [46]This type of reward is less likely to decrease interest in a task—and may even increase interest—as it conveys the message that you are good at the task (Deci & Ryan, 1985; Sansone & Harackiewicz, 1997). [47]Thus, rather than giving kids a reward for playing math games regardless of how well they do (i.e., a task-contingent reward), it is better to reward them for doing well in math. [48]Even performance-contingent rewards must be used with care; they too can backfire. [49]Although people like the positive feedback these rewards convey, they do not like the apprehension caused by being evaluated (Harackiewicz, 1989; Harackiewicz, Manderlink, & Sansone, 1984). [50]The trick is to convey positive feedback without making people feel nervous and apprehensive about being evaluated.

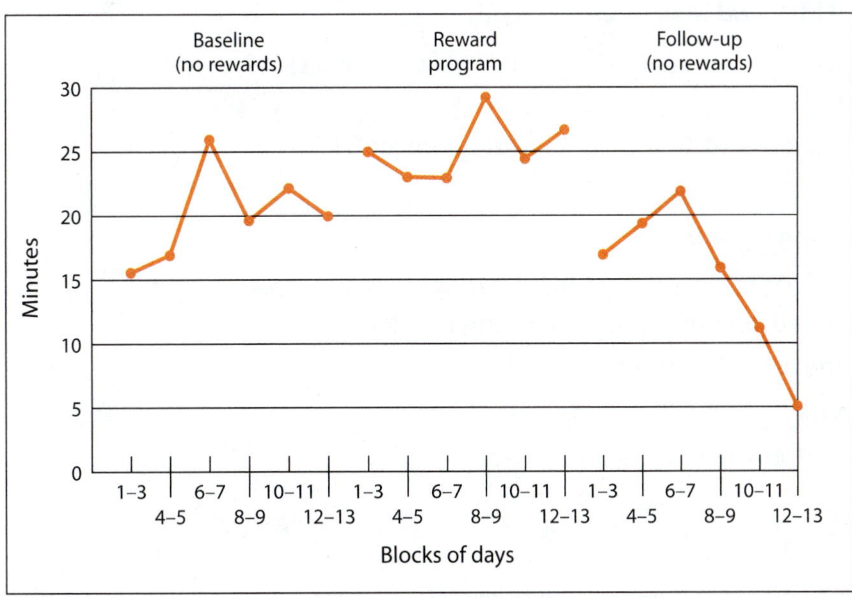

FIGURE 1

The Overjustification Effect During the initial baseline phase, researchers measured how much time elementary school students played math games. During the reward program, they rewarded the children with prizes for playing with the games. When the rewards were no longer offered (during the follow-up phase), the children played with the games even less than they had during the baseline phase, indicating that the rewards had lowered their intrinsic interest in the games. (Data from Greene, Sternberg, & Lepper, 1976)

Aronson, Elliot, Wilson, Timothy D., and Akert, Robin M., *Social Psychology,* 8th ed., pp. 115–117.

CONTINUED

REVIEW TEST *CONTINUED*

Vocabulary in Context

1. The term **intrinsic** in the title and sentence 19 means
   a. selfish.
   b. selfless.
   (c.) essential.
   d. learned.

2. The best synonym for **contingent** in sentence 43 is
   a. uncertain.
   b. planned.
   c. certain.
   (d.) dependent.

Tone and Purpose

3. The tone of sentence 13 is
   a. scholarly.
   (b.) sarcastic.
   c. encouraging.
   d. humorous.

4. The writer's primary purpose for writing the passage is to
   (a.) inform the reader about the differences between intrinsic and extrinsic motivation.
   b. entertain the reader with interesting facts about intrinsic and extrinsic motivation.
   c. convince the reader that intrinsic motivation is stronger than extrinsic motivation.

Central Idea and Main Idea

5. Which sentence states the central idea of the passage?
   a. sentence 1
   (b.) sentence 14
   c. sentence 27
   d. sentence 51

Supporting Details

6. According to the passage, high grades are an example of
   a. the success of the reading program "BookIt!"
   b. the overjustification effect.
   c. task-contingent rewards.
   (d.) performance-contingent rewards.

Transitions

7. The relationship between sentences 27 and 28 is
   a. comparison.
   b. cause.
   c. addition.
   (d.) definition-example.

Pattern of Organization

8. The main pattern of organization suggested by the title is
   a. cause and effect.
   b. generalization-example.
   (c.) comparison/contrast.
   d. classification.

Fact and Opinion

9. Sentence 8 states

a. a fact.

b. an opinion.

c. fact and opinion.

Argument

10. Sentence 16 states

a. a claim.

b. a counterclaim.

c. a relevant support.

d. an irrelevant support.

Summary Response

Restate the writer's main idea in your own words. Begin your summary response with the following: *The main idea of the passage "Intrinsic Versus Extrinsic Motivation" from the textbook* Social Psychology *is. . . .*

What Do You Think?

Assume you are taking a college sociology course. Your professor assigned this passage from the textbook as required reading. The assignment also requires you to compose a written response to the passage. Based on your reading of the passage, you created the following research questions to help you draft your response:

- How do intrinsic motivation and extrinsic motivation influence behavior?
- How do they differ from one another?
- How do rewards apply to everyday life or working life?

Use ideas and details from the passage to draft your answer to these questions. Track your sources and use summary, paraphrasing, and quoting to avoid plagiarism.

Academic Learning Log: Module Review

Summary of Key Concepts of Research

Assess your comprehension of research.

LO1 LO2 LO3 LO4

1. What are two kinds of information that inform our thinking and writing? *facts and opinions*

2. What are two main storehouses of information? *the library and the Internet*

3. What is PAART? *PAART is a guide for evaluating sources based on the source's or author's Purpose, Authority, Accuracy, Relevance, and Timeliness.*

LO1 LO2 LO3 LO4 LO5

4. What is plagiarism? *Plagiarism is the act of presenting the words or ideas of another author as one's own or using information without giving credit to its original source.*

5. What are four ways to avoid plagiarism? *Plagiarism is avoided by paraphrasing, summarizing, quoting, and citing the words and ideas of other people.*

6. What are the Five R's of paraphrasing? *read, restate, revise, revisit, and repeat*

Test Your Comprehension of Research

Respond to the following prompts and questions. *Answers may vary.*

LO1 LO2 LO3 LO4 LO5

In your own words, explain the differences among paraphrasing, summarizing, and quoting.

Paraphrasing is restating the writer's point in your own words. A main idea or details may be paraphrased. Usually, the paraphrase is about the same length as the original text. In contrast, summarizing is reducing an idea to its most important points. A summary also paraphrases the ideas. Unlike paraphrasing or summarizing, quoting is using the exact words of the writer's original text. A quote is placed in quotation marks to indicate that the writer's exact words have been used.

In your own words, explain how a researcher avoids plagiarism throughout the research process.

To avoid plagiarism throughout the research process, a researcher records the publication information for every source used in the research. During the research process, a researcher takes careful notes in the form of paraphrases, summaries, or quotes and records the source information for each note. During the writing process, a researcher uses in-text citations to give credit to the sources of researched details where they appear in the body of the essay. The researcher also provides a Works Cited or References page to list all the sources used in the research.

LO1 LO2 LO3 LO4 LO5

1. **How will I use what I have learned?** In your notebook, discuss how you will apply to your own reading/writing strategy what you have learned about research. When will you apply this knowledge to your reading/writing strategy?
2. **What do I still need to study about research?** In your notebook, discuss your ongoing study needs. Describe what, when, and how you will continue studying and using research.

Complete the Post-test for Module 16 in MySkillsLab.

17

LEARNING OUTCOMES

After studying this module you should be able to:

LO 1 Identify Types of Subjects

LO 2 Identify Types of Verbs

LO 3 Compose the Simple Sentence

Subjects, Verbs, and Simple Sentences

A simple sentence, also called an *independent clause,* includes a subject and verb and expresses a complete thought.

LO 1 Identify Types of Subjects

A **subject** is the person, place, object, or topic about which a writer expresses a focused thought or makes an assertion. To identify a subject, ask: Who or what did this? Alternatively, ask: Who or what is this?

Simple Subjects

- **Simple Subject, Type 1:** A single person, place, object, or topic is the focus of thought.

SUBJECT

Wilma Mankiller served as the first female chief of the Cherokee Nation from 1985–1995.

Make a difference by voting.

"YOU" IS UNDERSTOOD, BUT NOT STATED, AS THE SUBJECT OF THE SENTENCE, WHICH IS A COMMAND.

Compound Subject

Two or more people, places, objects, or topics are the subjects of a focused thought.

COMPOUND SUBJECTS

Florida, Texas, and California lead the national growth of online banking.

COMPOUND SUBJECTS ARE OFTEN JOINED BY THE COORDINATING CONJUNCTION "AND."

Identify Types of Verbs

A **verb** makes an assertion about a subject. Three basic types of verbs include **linking verbs, action verbs,** and **helping verbs**. (See Modules 26–27 for more information about verbs.)

Linking Verbs

A **linking verb** connects the subject to a word that renames, describes, or defines the subject. Linking verbs often describe a state of being.

Some Common Linking Verbs Are

am, is, are, was, were, am being, has been…

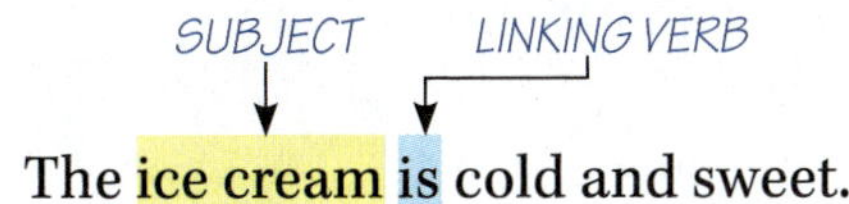

SUBJECT
LINKING VERB
The ice cream is cold and sweet.

Action Verbs

An **action verb** shows the behavior of the subject.

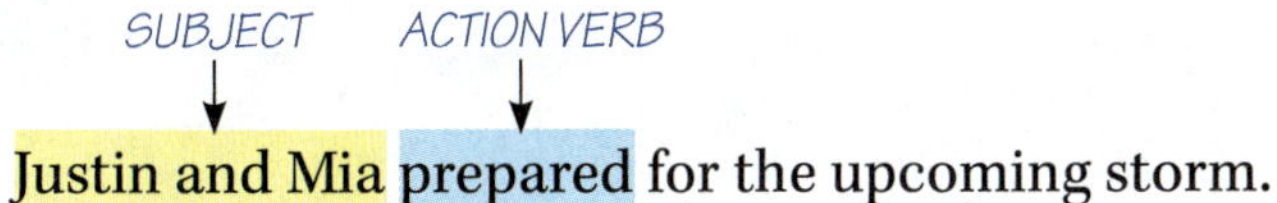

SUBJECT
ACTION VERB
Justin and Mia prepared for the upcoming storm.

Helping Verbs

A **helping verb** is used with a main verb to create a verb phrase. Helping verbs are also used to form questions. The verbs *be, do,* and *have* can be used alone or as helping verbs.

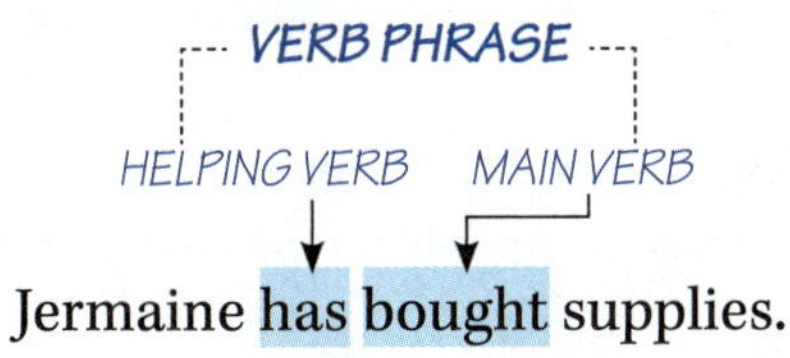

Jermaine has bought supplies.

L3 Compose the Simple Sentence

A **simple sentence** is a group of related words that includes a subject and verb and expresses a complete thought. A simple sentence is also known as an **independent clause**. An idea that is missing a subject or verb is a fragment or incomplete thought.

Distinguishing between a Fragment and the Simple Sentence

For more information on correcting fragments, see Module 23.

Fragment with Missing Subject:

VERB

Uses her status as a superstar to bring media attention to refugees around the world.

Fragment with Missing Verb:

SUBJECT

Angelina Jolie using her status as a superstar to bring media attention to refugees around the world.

Simple Sentence:

SUBJECT VERB

Angelina Jolie uses her status as a superstar to bring media attention to refugees around the world.

MySkillsLab™

Complete the Post-test for Module 17 in MySkillsLab.

Compound and Complex Sentences

A compound sentence joins together two or more independent clauses. A complex sentence combines one independent or main clause and one or more dependent clauses.

18

LEARNING OUTCOMES

After studying this module you should be able to:

- **L1** Compose a Compound Sentence
- **L2** Compose a Complex Sentence
- **L3** Compose a Compound-Complex Sentence

Compose a Compound Sentence L1

A compound sentence is made up of two or more independent clauses. A **compound sentence** links two or more independent clauses together as **equally important** ideas.

Two Ways to Combine Independent Clauses into a Compound Sentence

1. **A comma and a coordinating conjunction:** The coordinating conjunction serves as a transition that shows the relationship of ideas within the sentence. Use the acronym FANBOYS to help you remember the seven coordinating conjunctions—*for, and, nor, but, or, yet,* or *so.*

Coordinating Conjunctions (FANBOYS) and Meanings							
Coordinating Conjunction	For	And	Nor	But	Or	Yet	So
Meaning	Result	Addition	Negation	Contrast	Choice	Contrast	Result

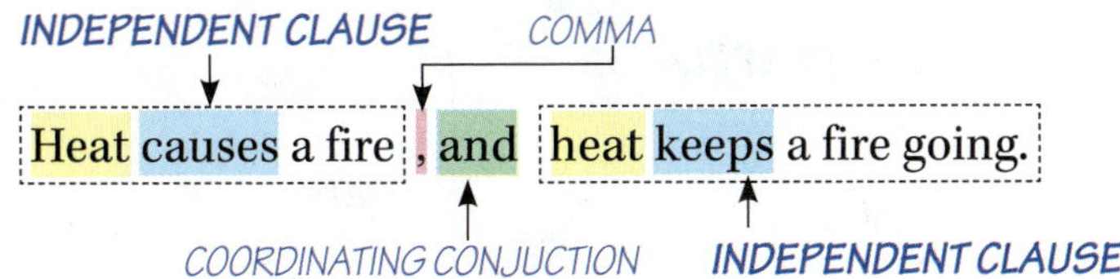

2. **A semicolon, conjunctive adverb, and a comma:** The conjunction shows the relationship of ideas within the sentence. In addition, the conjunctive adverb introduces the next clause. A comma follows the conjunctive adverb since it is an introductory element of the next clause:

[Independent clause;] conjunctive adverb, [independent clause.]

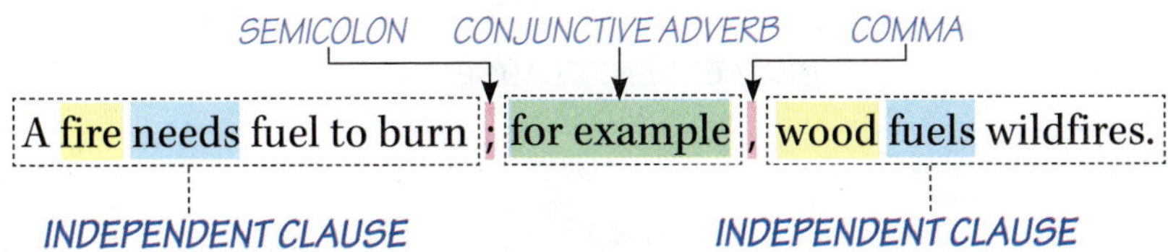

L2 Compose a Complex Sentence

A **complex sentence** contains one independent or main clause and one or more dependent clauses. A **dependent clause** expresses a **subordinate** or minor detail about an idea in the independent clause. A complex sentence joins independent and dependent clauses by placing a subordinating conjunction at the beginning of the dependent clause. **Subordinating conjunctions** state the relationship between the main clause and the subordinate clause.

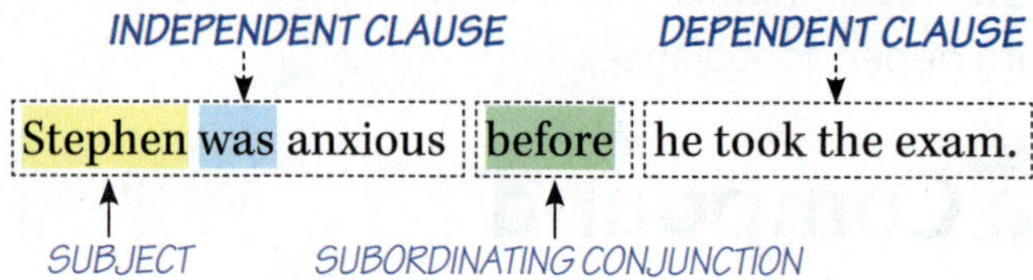

A special kind of subordinating conjunction is the relative pronoun. A **relative pronoun** connects the dependent clause to a noun in the main clause.

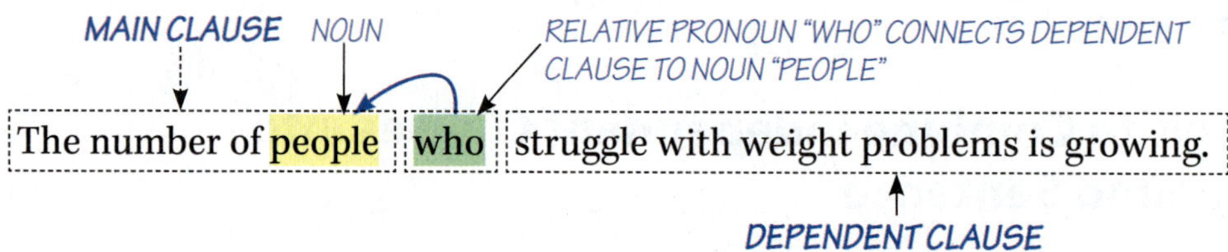

L3 Compose a Compound-Complex Sentence

A **compound-complex sentence** is two or more independent clauses and one or more dependent clauses. A compound-complex sentence joins coordinate and subordinate ideas into a single sentence. All the punctuation rules for both compound and complex sentences apply to the compound-complex sentence.

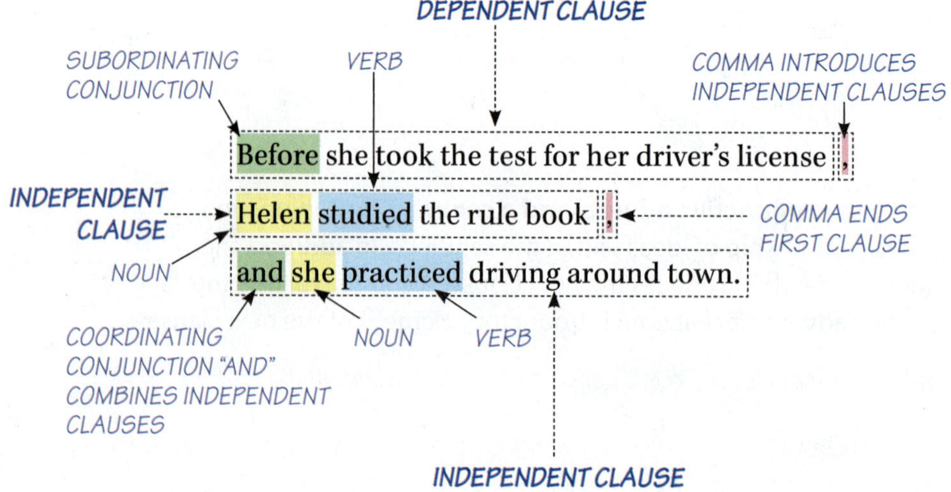

MySkillsLab™

Complete the Post-test for Module 18 in MySkillsLab.

Sentence Variety

Sentence variety adds interest and power to your writing. You can achieve sentence variety by varying the purposes, types, lengths, and openings of your sentences.

19

LEARNING OUTCOMES

After studying this module you should be able to:

LO 1 Vary Sentence Purpose

LO 2 Vary Sentence Types

LO 3 Vary Sentence Openings

LO 4 Vary Sentence Length

Vary Sentence Purpose LO 1

1. **Declarative sentences** make a statement to share information and are punctuated with a period. Declarative sentences are often used to state a main idea and supporting details.

    Carjacking is a common crime.

2. **Interrogative sentences** ask a question and are punctuated with a question mark. Usually, the writer also provides an answer to the question. An interrogative sentence may be used to introduce a topic and lead into a topic sentence.

    How can you prevent a carjacking?

3. **Imperative sentences** give a command that demands an action and are punctuated with a period. Imperative sentences are often used to give directions to complete a process or persuade a reader to take action.

    Follow three steps to prevent a carjacking.

4. **Exclamatory sentences** express a strong emotion and are punctuated with an exclamation point. Exclamatory sentences emphasize a significant point.

    Your life is more important than your car!

Vary Sentence Types LO 2

You learned in Modules 17 and 18 about the four types of sentences: simple, compound, complex, and compound-complex. When we rely on one type of sentence more than the others, our writing becomes dull and flat, like a speaker delivering a speech in a monotone. Vary your use of sentence types to show that ideas are equal in importance, or that one idea is more important than another.

Coordinating ideas makes each idea equal in importance. To combine coordinate ideas, use a comma and a coordinating conjunction (FANBOYS: *for, and, nor, but, or, yet,* or *so*).

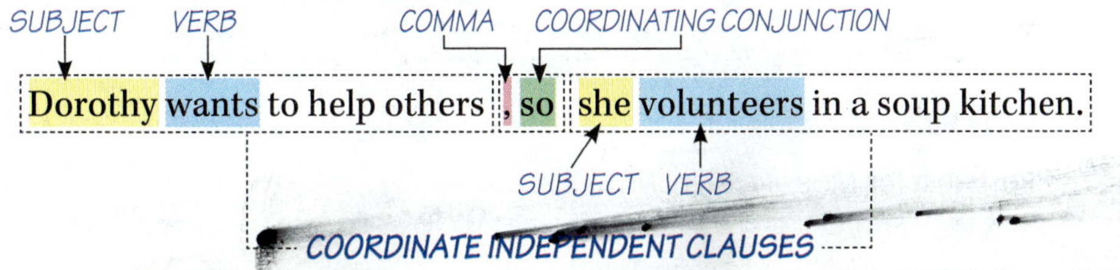

Subordinating ideas makes one idea dependent on (and less important than) another idea. To make an idea subordinate, use a subordinating conjunction (*although, after, as, because, before, since, unless,* etc.). If the new subordinate clause begins the sentence as an introductory element, include a comma at the end of the subordinate clause to set it off from the main independent clause.

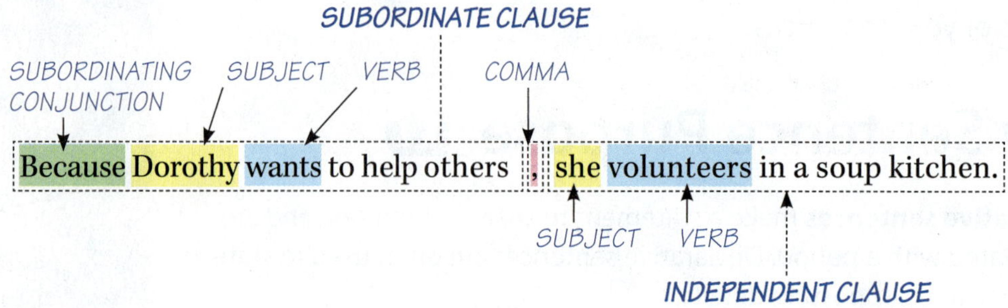

L3 Vary Sentence Openings

To add interest and to shift the emphasis of an idea, you can vary the ways in which you begin a sentence. You have already worked with several types of sentence openings: participle phrases, appositives, and dependent clauses. Two additional ways to begin a sentence include using adverbs and prepositional phrases. As introductory elements in a sentence, both an adverb and a prepositional phrase are set off with a comma.

An adverb describes or modifies another adverb, a verb, or an adjective, and usually ends in *-ly*: *angrily, beautifully, frequently*.

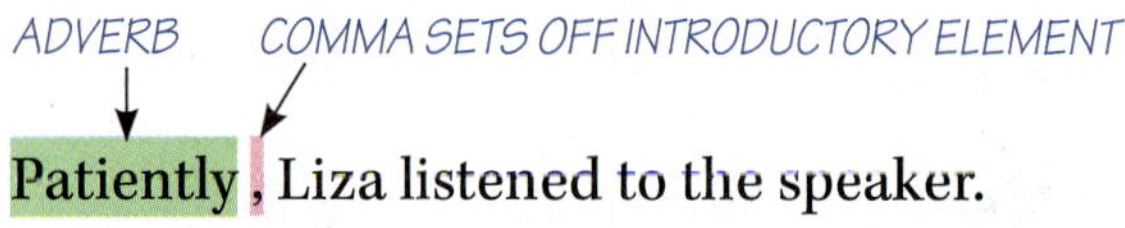

A prepositional phrase begins with a preposition and ends with a noun or pronoun, the object of the preposition.

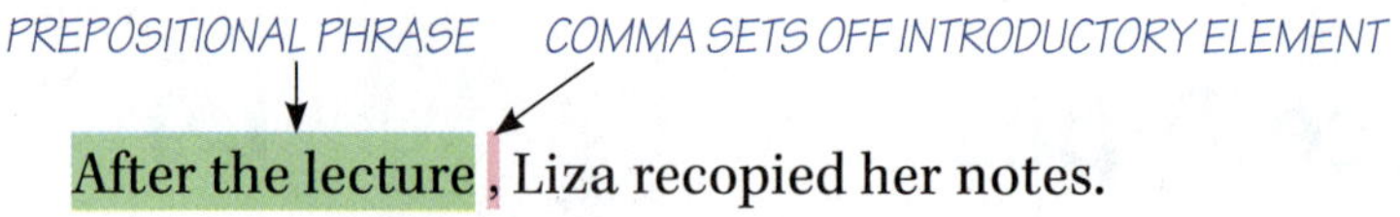

L4 Vary Sentence Length

To add interest to your writing, vary the length of your sentences. When a writer relies too heavily on one length of sentence, the writing seems dull, flat, or uninteresting. Too many long sentences make a piece boring or confusing. Too many short sentences can seem choppy and immature. The sentence-combining techniques you have learned throughout this module will also help you create sentences of varying lengths.

Complete the Post-test for Module 19 in MySkillsLab.

Sentence Clarity: Point of View, Number, and Tense

Sentence clarity creates a logical flow of ideas through consistency in person, point of view, number, and tense.

20

LEARNING OUTCOMES

After studying this module you should be able to:

- LO1 Use Consistent Person and Point of View
- LO2 Use Consistent Number
- LO3 Use Consistent Tense

Use Consistent Person and Point of View LO1

The term **person** refers to the use of pronouns to identify the difference between the writer or speaker, the one being written or spoken to, and the one being written about or spoken of. **Point of view** is the position from which something is considered, evaluated, or discussed; point of view is identified as first person, second person, or third person. Person and point of view also communicate tone.

Three Points of View

Person	Traits	Pronouns
First Person	The writer or speaker; informal, conversational tone	singular: *I, me* plural: *we, our*
Second Person	The one being written or spoken to; can remain unstated; informal, conversational tone	singular: *you* plural: *you*
Third Person	The one being written about or spoken of; formal, academic tone	singular: *he, she, it, one* plural: *they*

Illogical Shift in Person

An abrupt or **unnecessary shift in person or point of view** causes a break in the logical flow of ideas. When you revise for consistency, remember that the number of the verb may need to change as well.

Illogical Shift in Person:

THIRD PERSON ↓

Nobody should text while you drive.

↑ SECOND PERSON

Revision:

THIRD PERSON

Nobody should text while he drives.

PRONOUN AND VERB AGREE IN PERSON

L2 Use Consistent Number

The term *number* refers to the difference between a singular noun or pronoun and plural nouns and pronouns. Once you choose a point of view, carefully edit your writing to ensure **consistent use of number.**

Illogical Shift in Number

When pronouns act as the subject of a verb, they, too, must agree in number. An abrupt or **unnecessary shift in number** causes a break in the logical flow of ideas.

Illogical Shift in Number:

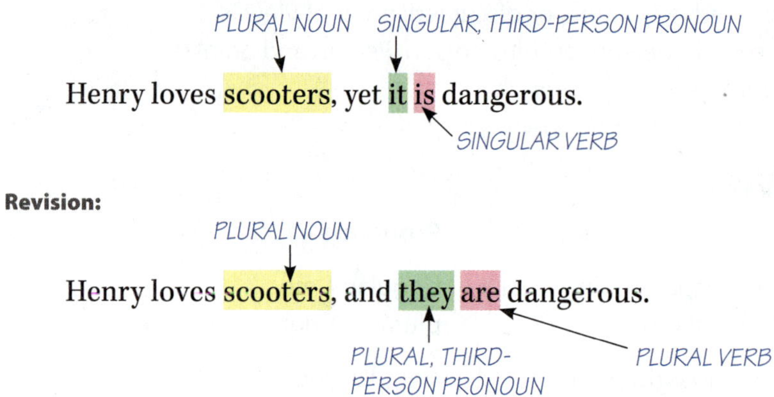

L3 Use Consistent Tense

Consistent tense expresses the logical sequence of events or existence. Verb *tense* expresses the time or duration of an action or state of being. Primary tenses include three time frames: The **past** *was*; the **present** *is*; the **future** *will be.*

Illogical Shift in Tense

Abruptly changing from one verb tense to another without a logical reason, also called an **illogical shift in tense**, breaks the logical flow of ideas and causes confusion.

Illogical Shift in Tense:

PRESENT TENSE

Monica eats dinner and went to bed.

PAST TENSE

Revision:

PRESENT TENSE

Monica eats dinner and goes to bed.

MySkillsLab™

Complete the Post-test for Module 20 in MySkillsLab.

21 Parallelism

LEARNING OUTCOMES

After studying this module you should be able to:

- LO1 Use Parallel Words
- LO2 Use Parallel Phrases
- LO3 Use Parallel Clauses
- LO4 Punctuate for Parallelism

Parallelism is the expression of equal ideas—similar words, phrases, or clauses—in a sentence in the same, matching grammatical form. Parallel expressions bring clarity, interest, and power to a piece of writing.

LO1 Use Parallel Words

Parallel structure uses a pair or series of closely related compound words to emphasize a point. Parallel words often, but not always, use similar **suffixes** (word endings).

- **Parallel Words**

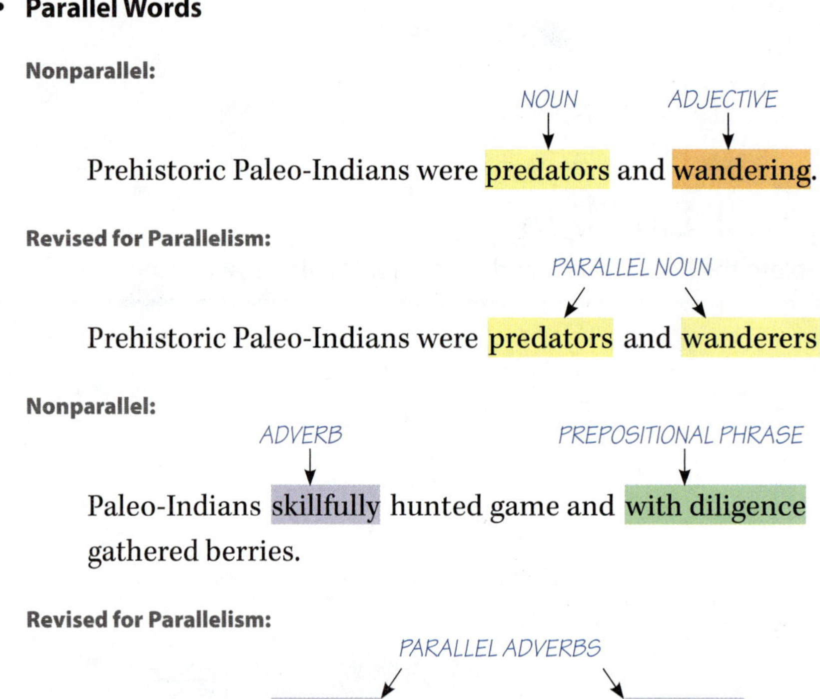

Nonparallel:

NONPARALLEL VERBS

They flaked and crafting flint into spears.

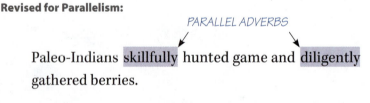

Revised for Parallelism:

PARALLEL VERBS

They flaked and crafted flint into spears.

Use Parallel Phrases

Parallel structure uses a pair or series of closely related compound phrases to emphasize a point. Parallel phrases repeat similar word patterns or groups.

- **Parallel Phrases**

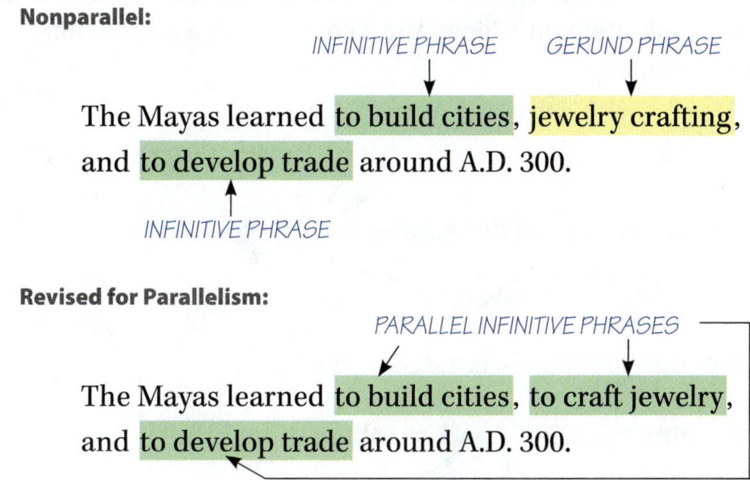

Nonparallel:
INFINITIVE PHRASE
GERUND PHRASE
The Mayas learned to build cities, jewelry crafting, and to develop trade around A.D. 300.
INFINITIVE PHRASE
Revised for Parallelism:
PARALLEL INFINITIVE PHRASES
The Mayas learned to build cities, to craft jewelry, and to develop trade around A.D. 300.

Use Parallel Clauses

Parallel structure uses a set of closely related clauses to emphasize a point. Parallel structure begins with a clause and continues with clauses to create a balanced, logical statement. Use parallel words and phrases within clauses.

- **Parallel Clauses**

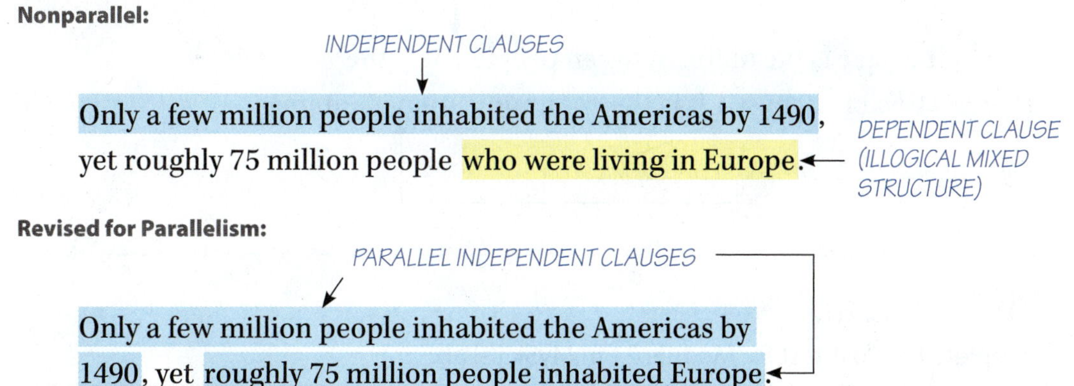

Nonparallel:
INDEPENDENT CLAUSES
Only a few million people inhabited the Americas by 1490, yet roughly 75 million people who were living in Europe.
DEPENDENT CLAUSE (ILLOGICAL MIXED STRUCTURE)
Revised for Parallelism:
PARALLEL INDEPENDENT CLAUSES
Only a few million people inhabited the Americas by 1490, yet roughly 75 million people inhabited Europe.

L4 Punctuate for Parallelism

The comma and the semicolon (sometimes along with coordinating conjunctions), and numbered, lettered, or bulleted items in a list signal ideas of equal importance. Ideas marked by these pieces of punctuation are best expressed with parallelism.

Coordinating conjunctions always signal an equal relationship among words, phrases, and clauses. Use commas between parallel items in a series. Use a comma with a coordinating conjunction to join independent clauses.

Examples:

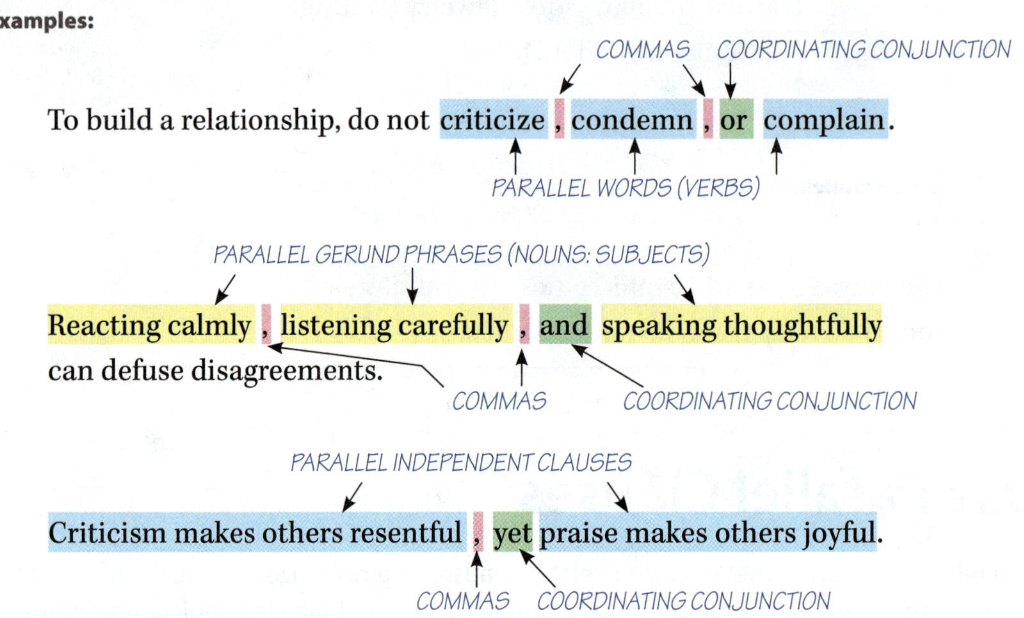

Semicolons signal two or more closely related independent clauses.

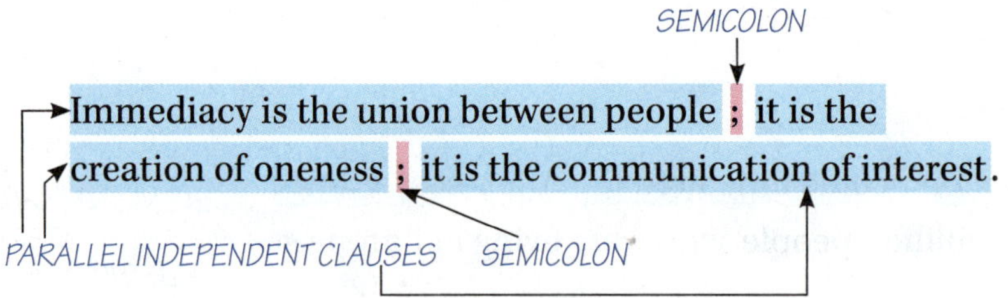

MySkillsLab™
Complete the Post-test for Module 21 in MySkillsLab.

Comma Splices and Fused Sentences

A comma splice is an error that occurs when a comma is used by itself to join two sentences. A fused sentence is an error that occurs when two sentences are joined without any punctuation.

22

LEARNING OUTCOMES

After studying this module you should be able to:

- LO 1 Identify Comma Splices
- LO 2 Identify Fused Sentences
- LO 3 Correct Comma Splices and Fused Sentences Using Four Strategies

Identify Comma Splices LO 1

A **comma splice** occurs when a comma is used by itself (without a coordinating conjunction) to join two independent clauses.

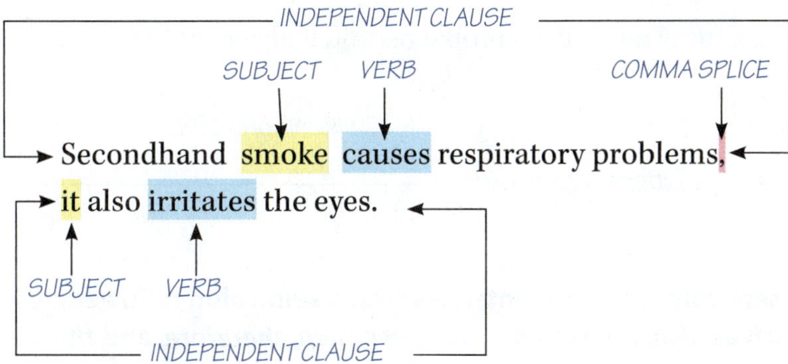

Identify Fused Sentences LO 2

A **fused sentence** sentence occurs when two independent clauses are joined without any punctuation.

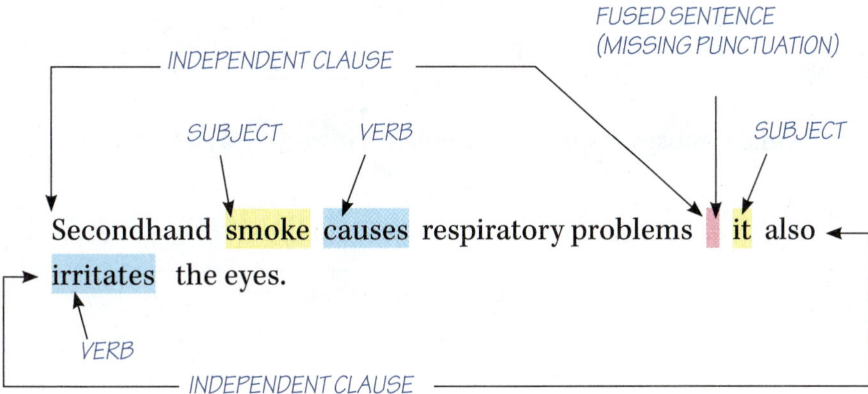

L3 Correct Comma Splices and Fused Sentences Using Four Strategies

1. Separate sentences using a period and capital letter.

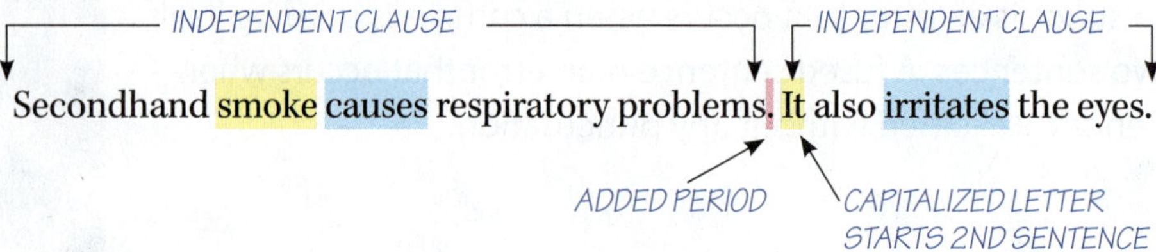
INDEPENDENT CLAUSE
INDEPENDENT CLAUSE
Secondhand smoke causes respiratory problems. It also irritates the eyes.
ADDED PERIOD
CAPITALIZED LETTER STARTS 2ND SENTENCE

2. Join sentences with a comma followed by a coordinating conjunction.

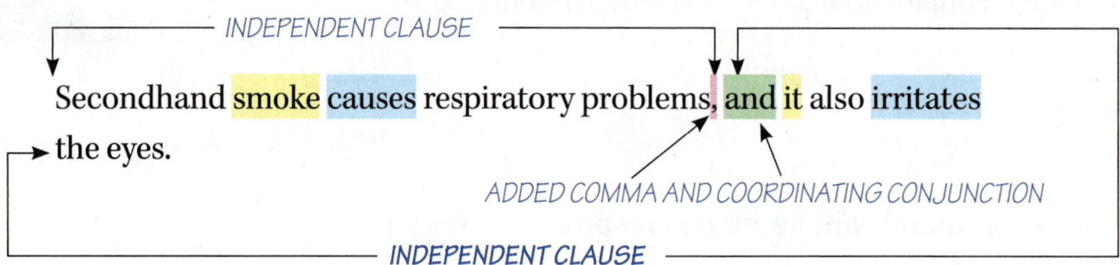
INDEPENDENT CLAUSE
Secondhand smoke causes respiratory problems, and it also irritates the eyes.
ADDED COMMA AND COORDINATING CONJUNCTION
INDEPENDENT CLAUSE

3. Join sentences with a semicolon, or join sentences with a semicolon followed by a conjunctive adverb such as *also, for example, however, then, therefore,* and *thus.*

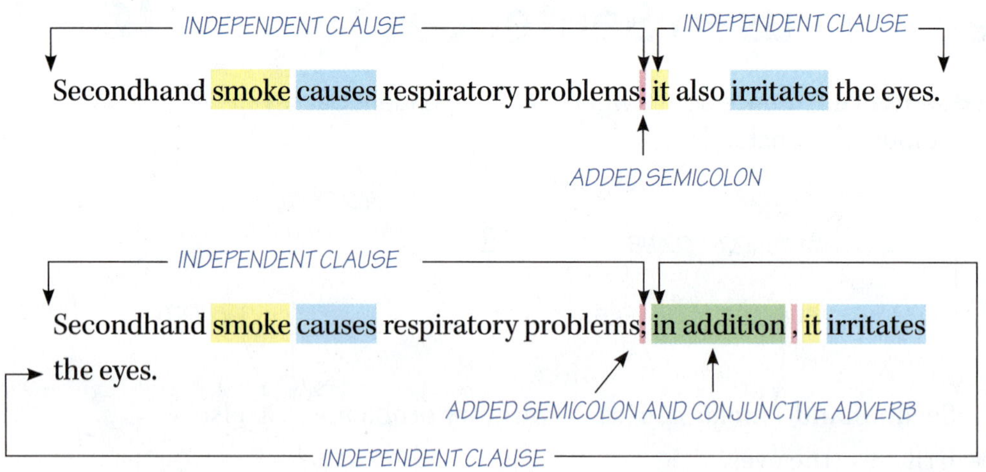
INDEPENDENT CLAUSE
INDEPENDENT CLAUSE
Secondhand smoke causes respiratory problems; it also irritates the eyes.
ADDED SEMICOLON
INDEPENDENT CLAUSE
Secondhand smoke causes respiratory problems; in addition, it irritates the eyes.
ADDED SEMICOLON AND CONJUNCTIVE ADVERB
INDEPENDENT CLAUSE

4. Join sentences using subordinate ideas.

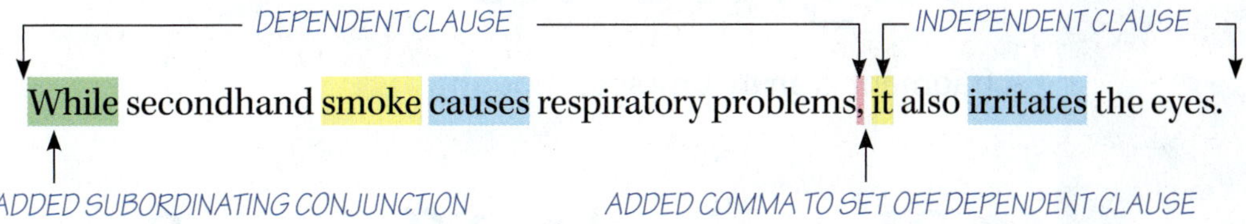

For more information on complex sentences, see Module 18, "Compound and Complex Sentences."

MySkillsLab™

Complete the Post-test for Module 22 in MySkillsLab.

23

LEARNING OUTCOMES

After studying this module you should be able to:

LO 1 Recognize the Difference Between Sentences and Fragments

LO 2 Edit to Correct Types of Fragments

Fragments

A fragment is an incomplete thought.

LO 1 Recognize the Difference Between Sentences and Fragments

A **sentence** contains a subject, a verb, and all the information needed to clearly express a complete thought.

SENTENCE: **Complete Thought-Complete Information**

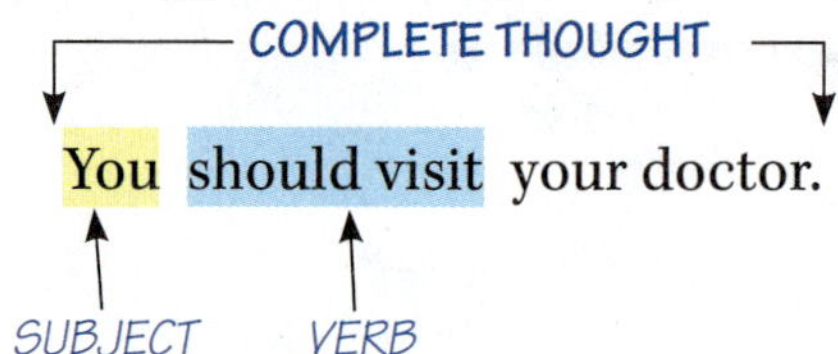

FRAGMENT: **Incomplete Thought-Missing Information**

A **fragment** is missing one of the following: a subject, a verb, or both subject and verb.

Fragment (Missing an Independent Clause):

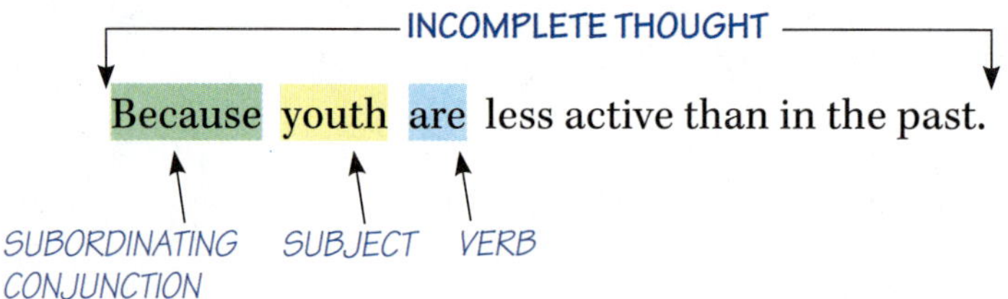

LO 2 Edit to Correct Types of Fragments

This section discusses two common types of fragments: the phrase fragment and the clause fragment. A writer may use two techniques to revise fragments into sentences:

- Combine existing ideas.
- Add missing ideas.

Phrase Fragments

A **phrase** is a group of words that acts as a single unit. A phrase is a fragment because it does not contain both a subject and a verb.

PHRASE

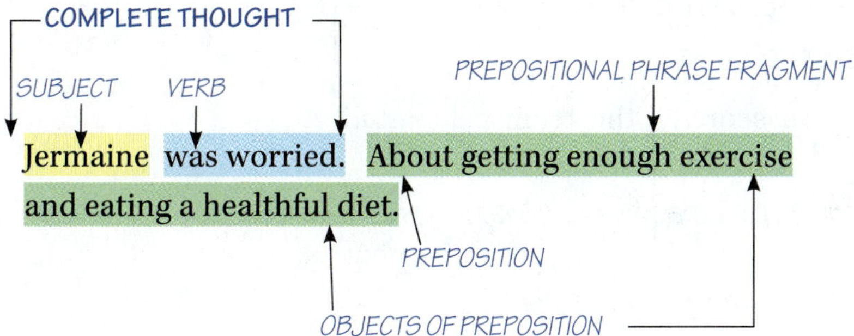

Revised to Combine Ideas:

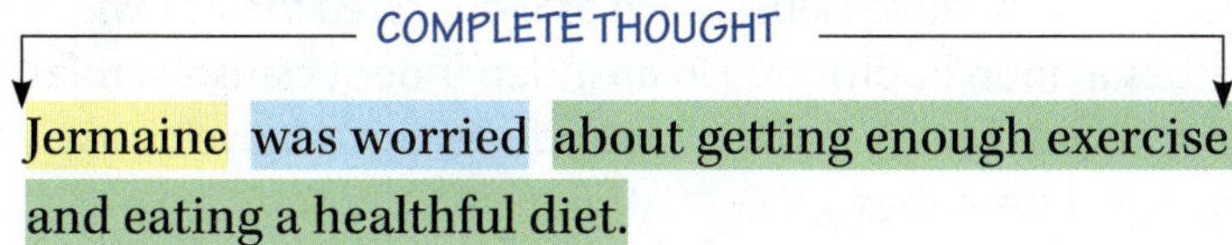

Revised to Add Ideas:

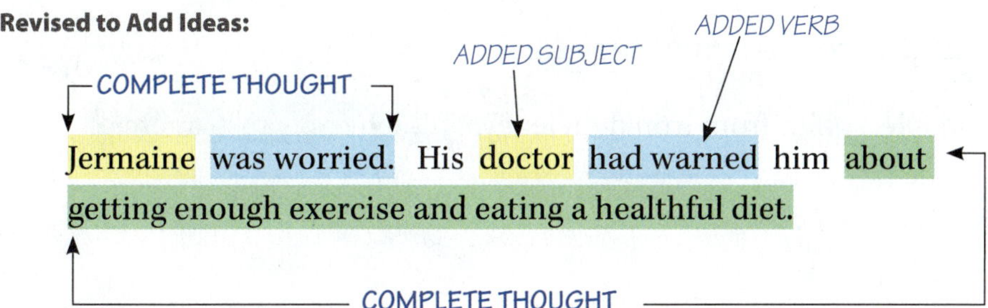

Clause Fragments

A **clause** is a set of words that contains a subject and a verb. A **dependent clause** expresses an incomplete thought or fragment.

For more on dependent and subordinate clauses, see Module 18.

Dependent Clause

A **dependent clause**, also known as a **subordinate clause**, does not make sense on its own.

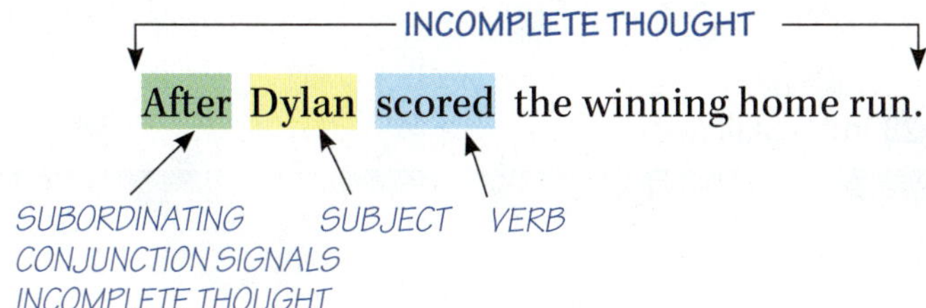

A **subordinating conjunction** states the relationship between two clauses.

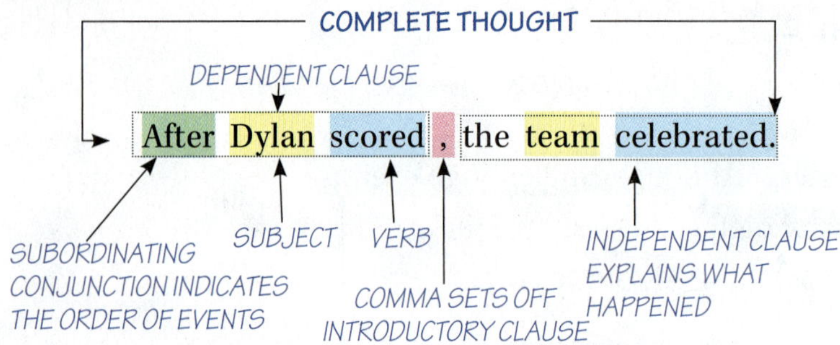
COMPLETE THOUGHT
DEPENDENT CLAUSE
After Dylan scored, the team celebrated.
SUBORDINATING CONJUNCTION INDICATES THE ORDER OF EVENTS
SUBJECT
VERB
COMMA SETS OFF INTRODUCTORY CLAUSE
INDEPENDENT CLAUSE EXPLAINS WHAT HAPPENED

Relative Clause

One type of dependent clause is the relative clause, such as *who scored the winning home run*. A **relative clause** describes a noun or pronoun in an independent clause. A **relative pronoun** (such as *who, whom, whose, which*, and *that*) introduces the relative clause and relates it to the noun or pronoun it describes.

Join the relative clause to the independent clause that contains the word it describes.

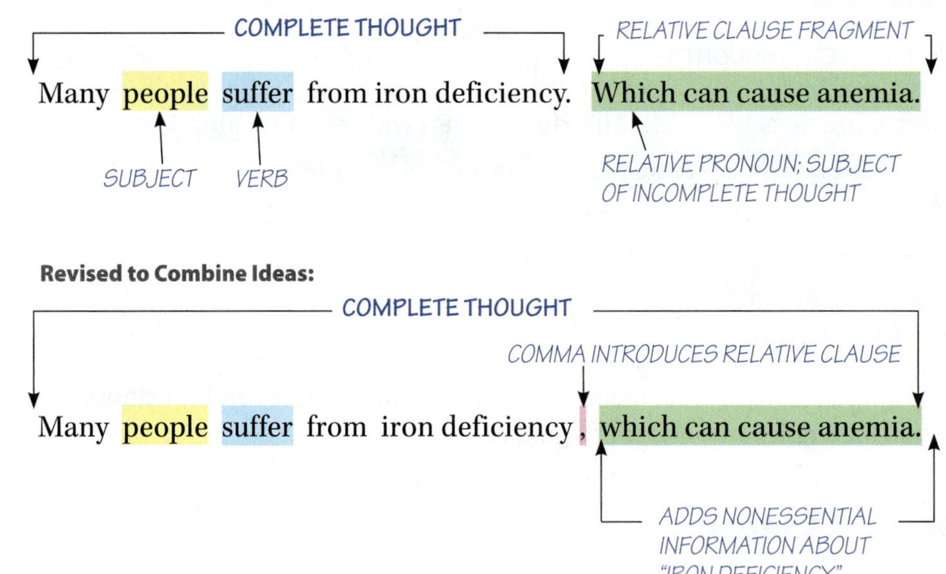
COMPLETE THOUGHT
RELATIVE CLAUSE FRAGMENT
Many people suffer from iron deficiency. Which can cause anemia.
SUBJECT
VERB
RELATIVE PRONOUN; SUBJECT OF INCOMPLETE THOUGHT
Revised to Combine Ideas:
COMPLETE THOUGHT
COMMA INTRODUCES RELATIVE CLAUSE
Many people suffer from iron deficiency, which can cause anemia.
ADDS NONESSENTIAL INFORMATION ABOUT "IRON DEFICIENCY"

MySkillsLab™

Complete the Post-test for Module 23 in MySkillsLab.

Misplaced and Dangling Modifiers

24

LEARNING OUTCOMES

After studying this module you should be able to:

- LO 1 Edit Misplaced Modifiers
- LO 2 Edit Dangling Modifiers

A modifier is a word or phrase that describes, clarifies, or gives more information about another word in a sentence.

Edit Misplaced Modifiers LO 1

A **misplaced modifier** is a word or phrase illogically separated from the word it describes. The following examples and revisions illustrate the most common types of misplaced modifiers.

Types of Misplaced Modifiers

MISPLACED WORDS A misplaced word is separated from the word it limits or restricts.

Example

WORD "ONLY" DESCRIBES ?

Belle Glade, Florida only has been flooded twice by hurricanes.

Revision #1

WORD "ONLY" DESCRIBES "TWICE"

Belle Glade, Florida has been flooded only **twice** by hurricanes.

Revision #2

Only Belle Glade, Florida has been flooded twice by hurricanes.

WORD "ONLY" DESCRIBES "BELLE GLADE"

MISPLACED PHRASE A phrase that describes a noun is placed next to the wrong noun and separated from the noun it describes.

Example

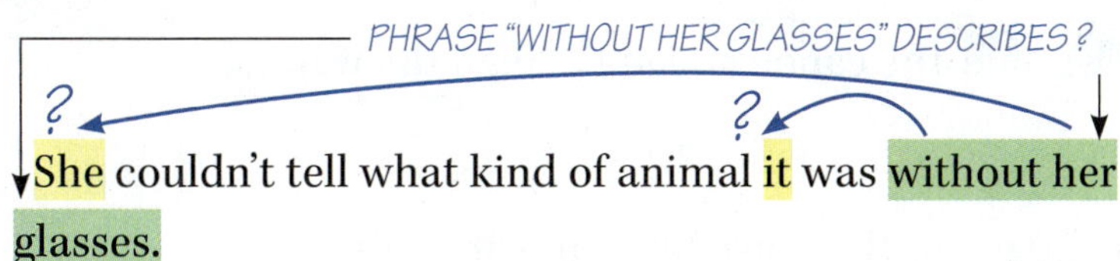

PHRASE "WITHOUT HER GLASSES" DESCRIBES ?
?
?
She couldn't tell what kind of animal it was without her glasses.

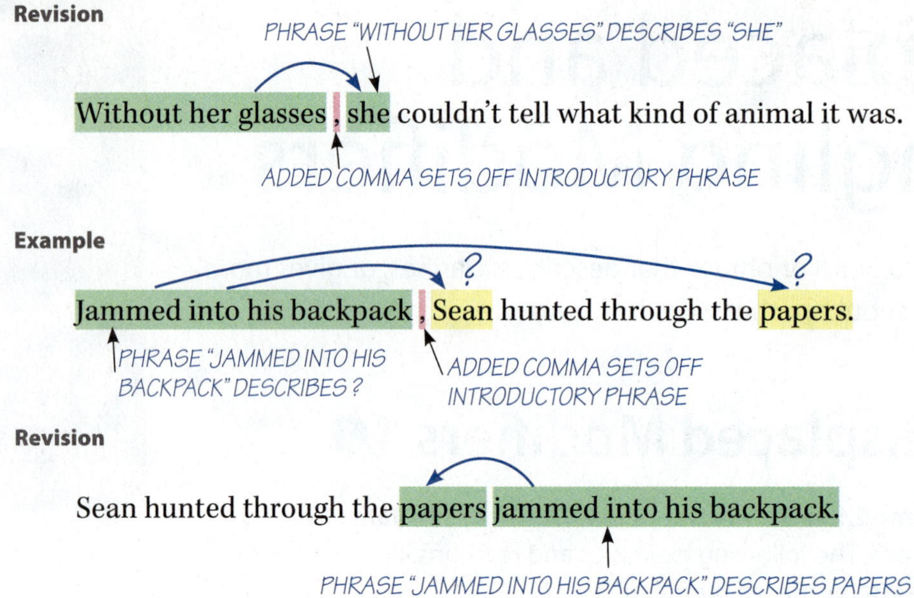

MISPLACED CLAUSE A dependent clause that describes a particular word is placed next to the wrong word and is separated from the word the clause describes.

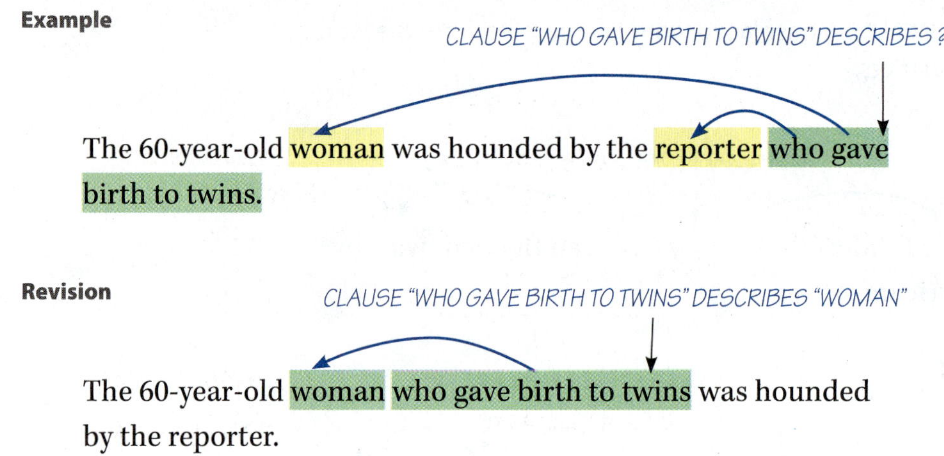

Example
Jammed into his backpack, Sean hunted through the papers.
PHRASE "JAMMED INTO HIS BACKPACK" DESCRIBES ?
CLAUSE "WHO GAVE BIRTH TO TWINS" DESCRIBES ?
The 60-year-old woman was hounded by the reporter who gave birth to twins.
Revision
Sean hunted through the papers jammed into his backpack.
PHRASE "JAMMED INTO HIS BACKPACK" DESCRIBES PAPERS
CLAUSE "WHO GAVE BIRTH TO TWINS" DESCRIBES "WOMAN"
The 60-year-old woman who gave birth to twins was hounded by the reporter.

L2 Edit Dangling Modifiers

A **dangling modifier** is a phrase that describes a word not stated in the sentence.

EXAMPLES **What or whom do these phrases describe in each sentence below?**

Sentence #1

While cleaning the house, a fifty dollar bill turned up.

Sentence #2

Observing the wildlife, the canoe glided through the waters.

Sentence #3

Running in second place, the finish line came into view.

Dangling Modifiers: Two Revision Tips

REVISION TIP #1 Change the dangling modifier into a logical clause with a subject and a verb.

Revised Sentence #1

ADDED SUBJECT AND VERB TO CREATE DEPENDENT CLAUSE

While I was cleaning the house, a fifty dollar bill turned up.

Revised Sentence #2

ADDED SUBORDINATING CONJUNCTION, SUBJECT, AND VERB TO CREATE DEPENDENT CLAUSE

As we were observing the wildlife, the canoe glided through the waters.

Revised Sentence #3

ADDED SUBJECT AND VERB TO CREATE INDEPENDENT CLAUSE

I was running in second place; the finish line came into view.

ADDED SEMICOLON JOINS TWO INDEPENDENT CLAUSES

REVISION TIP #2 Revise the main clause to include the word being modified.

Revised Sentence #1

PHRASE "WHILE CLEANING THE HOUSE" DESCRIBES ADDED SUBJECT

While cleaning the house, I found a fifty dollar bill.

ADDED SUBJECT AND VERB

Revised Sentence #2

PHRASE "OBSERVING THE WILDLIFE" DESCRIBES ADDED SUBJECT

Observing the wildlife, we glided the canoe through the waters.

ADDED SUBJECT

Revised Sentence #3

PHRASE "RUNNING IN SECOND PLACE" DESCRIBES ADDED SUBJECT

Running in second place, I saw the finish line come into view.

ADDED SUBJECT AND VERB

MySkillsLab™

Complete the Post-test for Module 24 in MySkillsLab.

25

LEARNING OUTCOMES

After studying this module you should be able to:

1. Recognize Subject-Verb Agreement
2. Create Agreement Using Key Verbs in the Present Tense: *To Have, To Do, To Be*
3. Create Subject-Verb Agreement

Subject-Verb Agreement: Present Tense

In the present tense, subjects and verbs must agree in number. Singular subjects must take singular verbs; plural subjects must take plural verbs.

LO1 Recognize Subject-Verb Agreement

The following chart uses the sample verb *think* to illustrate present tense agreement in number.

Present Tense Agreement				
	Singular **Subject** and **Verb**		Plural **Subject** and **Verb**	
First Person	I	think	We	think
Second Person	You	think	You	think
Third Person	He She It	thinks	They	think

For standard verbs, only the third person singular verb is formed by adding *-s* or *-es*.

Third person singular subject	→	present tense verb ends with *-s* or *-es*
He	→	apologizes
She	→	accepts
It	→	catches

LO2 Create Agreement Using Key Verbs in the Present Tense: *To Have, To Do, To Be*

Three key verbs are used both as main verbs and as helping verbs to express a wide variety of meanings: *to have, to do,* and *to be*. Memorize their present tense singular and plural forms to ensure subject-verb agreement.

To Have: Present Tense		
	Singular **Subject** and **Verb**	Plural **Subject** and **Verb**
First Person	I have	We have
Second Person	You have	You have
Third Person	He She — has It	They have

To Do: Present Tense		
	Singular **Subject** and **Verb**	Plural **Subject** and **Verb**
First Person	I do	We do
Second Person	You do	You do
Third Person	He She — does It	They do

The verb ***to do*** is often used with the adverb *not* to express a negative thought. Frequently this negative is stated in the form of the contractions *doesn't* and *don't* that combine the verb and the adverb into shorter words. The verb part of the contraction must still agree with its subject.

To Do and *Not:* Contraction Form		
	Singular **Subject** and **Verb**	Plural **Subject** and **Verb**
First Person	I don't agree	We don't agree
Second Person	You don't seem well	You don't seem well
Third Person	He She — doesn't care It	They don't care

The ***to be*** verb is unusual because it uses three forms in the present tense: *am*, *is*, and *are*.

To Be: Present Tense		
	Singular **Subject** and **Verb**	Plural **Subject** and **Verb**
First Person	I am	We are
Second Person	You are	You are
Third Person	He She — is It	They are

L3 Create Subject-Verb Agreement

Subjects Separated from Verbs

The standard order of ideas in a sentence places the subject first, immediately followed by the verb. However, subjects are often separated from their verbs by **prepositional phrases**. The object of the preposition can never be the subject of a sentence. The verb of a sentence agrees with the subject, not the object of the preposition.

Example

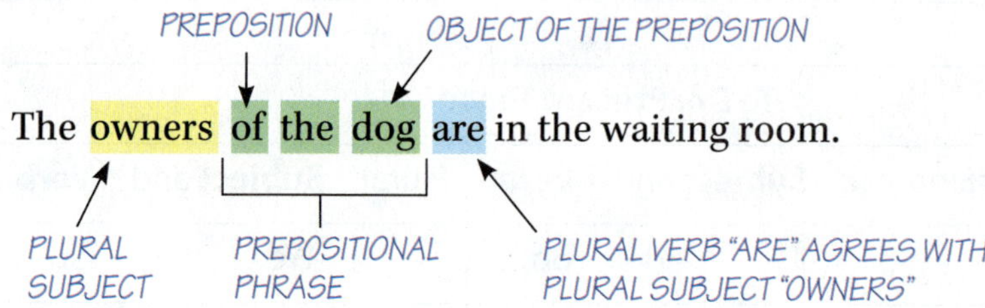

The owners of the dog are in the waiting room.

Subjects after Verbs

In some instances, a writer may choose to place the subject after the verb.

There and ***Here*** are never the subject of a sentence. Both of these words signal that the subject comes after the verb.

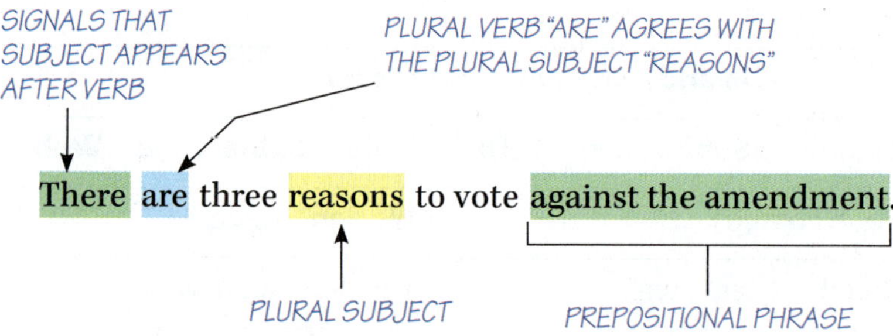

SIGNALS THAT SUBJECT APPEARS AFTER VERB

There are three reasons to vote against the amendment.

Agreement in Questions relies on understanding that the subject comes after the verb or between parts of the verb.

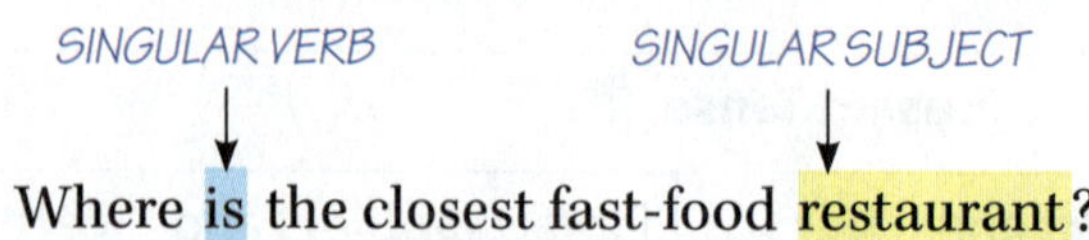

SINGULAR VERB
SINGULAR SUBJECT
Where is the closest fast-food restaurant?

MySkillsLab™

Complete the Post-test for Module 25 in MySkillsLab.

The Past Tense of Verbs

The past tense of verbs describes actions or events that have already occurred.

Identify Regular Verbs in the Past Tense LO1

The following chart states the general rule for forming the past tense of regular verbs, the spelling rules for exceptions, and examples of each rule.

Rules for Forming Past Tense of Regular Verbs			
	Base Form		**Past Tense**
General Rule: Regular verbs form the past tense by adding ***-ed*** to the base form of the verb.	walk	→	walk***ed***
Spelling Exceptions: There are several exceptions to the way in which regular verbs form the past tense:			
1. When the base form of the verb ends in ***-e***, only add ***-d***.	live save	→	live***d*** save***d***
2. When the base form of the verb ends with a consonant and ***-y***, delete the ***-y*** and add ***-ied*** in its place.	cry try	→	cr***ied*** tr***ied***
3. When the base form of the verb ends with ***-p*** or ***-it***, double the last letter before adding the ***-ed***.	stop permit	→	sto***pped*** permi***tted***

Identify Irregular Verbs in the Past Tense LO2

The past tense of irregular verbs does not use ***-ed*** or conform to uniform spelling rules with clear exceptions. The chart below lists the base form and past tense form of five of the most commonly used irregular verbs.

Five of the Most Common Irregular Verbs in the Past Tense			
Base Form	**Past Tense**	**Base Form**	**Past Tense**
get	got	see	saw
go	went	take	took
say	said		

26

LEARNING OUTCOMES

After studying this module you should be able to:

LO1 Identify Regular Verbs in the Past Tense

LO2 Identify Irregular Verbs in the Past Tense

Key Verbs in the Past Tense: *To Have, To Do, To Be*

Three key irregular verbs are used both as main verbs and as helping verbs to express a wide variety of meanings: *to have, to do,* and *to be.*

To Have	To Do	To Be
had	did	was (singular)
		were (plural)

Three Often Confused Helping Verbs: *Can, Could, Would*

- ***Can* expresses an ability in the present tense.**

"CAN" EXPRESSES A MENTAL ABILITY

I can solve mathematical equations.

- ***Could* expresses an ability, opportunity, possibility, or permission in the past tense.**

"COULD" EXPRESSES A PHYSICAL ABILITY

She could run a marathon.

"COULD" EXPRESSES A LOST OPPORTUNITY

You could have tried harder than you did.

"COULD" EXPRESSES POSSIBILITY

He could have been the culprit.

"COULD" EXPRESSES PERMISSION

He said that we could begin the driving test.

- ***Would* expresses past routine or intention in the past tense.**

"WOULD" EXPRESSES PAST ROUTINE

He would win every race.

"WOULD" EXPRESSES PAST INTENTION

She said she would do the dishes.

MySkillsLab™
Complete the Post-test for Module 26 in MySkillsLab.

The Past Participle

27

LEARNING OUTCOMES

After studying this module you should be able to:

- LO1 Identify Past Participles of Regular Verbs
- LO2 Identify Past Participles of Irregular Verbs
- LO3 Use the Present Perfect Tense
- LO4 Use the Past Perfect Tense
- LO5 Use the Passive Voice (*To Be* and the Past Participle)
- LO6 Use the Past Participle as an Adjective

A participle is a verb form that can be used to establish tenses or voices, or it can be used as a modifier, which describes, restricts, or limits other words in a sentence.

Identify Past Participles of Regular Verbs LO1

In general, regular verbs form the past participle by adding *-ed* to the base form of the verb. Just as with the simple past tense, there are several spelling exceptions for the past participle of regular verbs.

Base Form	Past Tense	Past Participle
live cry permit	liv***ed*** cr***ied*** permi***tted***	liv***ed*** cr***ied*** permi***tted***

Identify Past Participles of Irregular Verbs LO2

As with the simple past tense, irregular verbs do not use *-ed* to form the past participle. Nor does the past participle of irregular verbs conform to uniform spelling rules with clear exceptions. In addition, the past participle forms of many irregular verbs vary from their past tense forms. The following chart lists the base form, past tense form, and past participle of eight of the most commonly used irregular verbs.

For more about the simple past tense, see Module 26.

Eight of the Most Common Irregular Past Participles

Base Form	Past Tense	Past Participle
be	was, were	been
get	got	gotten
give	gave	given
go	went	gone
have	had	had
say	said	said
see	saw	seen
take	took	taken

Use the Present Perfect Tense LO3

The **present perfect tense** connects the past to the present. The present perfect tense states the relationship of a past action or situation to a current, ongoing action or situation. The present perfect tense is formed by joining the helping verbs ***has*** or ***have*** with the past participle.

The purposes of the present perfect tense are:

- **to express change from the past to the present.**

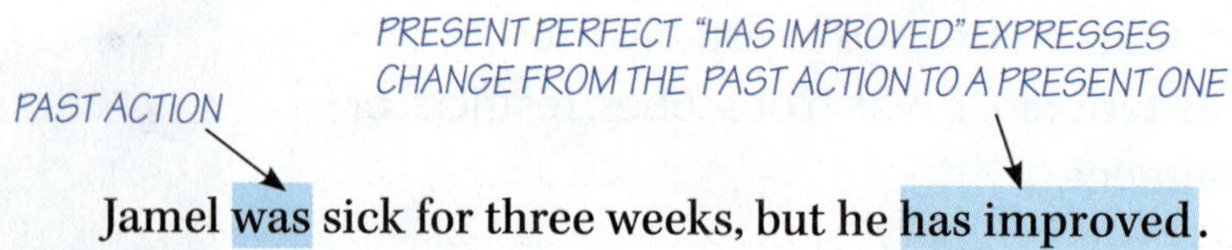

Jamel was sick for three weeks, but he has improved.

- **to express a situation or action that started in the past and continues to the present.**

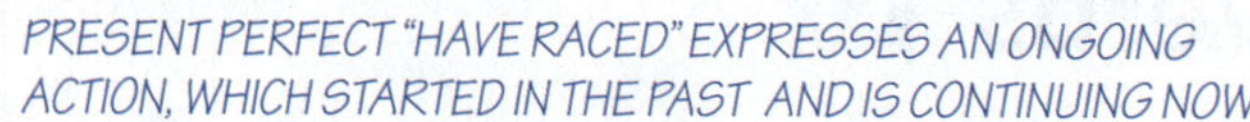

Carmen and Michelle have raced stock cars for several years.

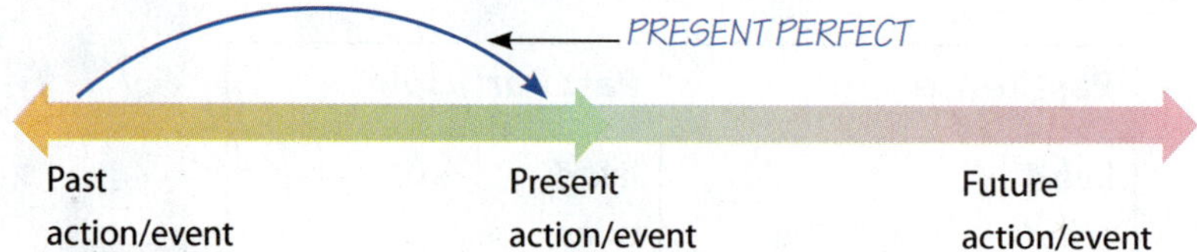

L4 Use the Past Perfect Tense

The **past perfect** connects two past actions or situations. The past perfect is formed by joining the helping verb ***had*** with a past participle.

The purposes of the past perfect tense are:

- **to connect a previous action or event with a later action or event.**

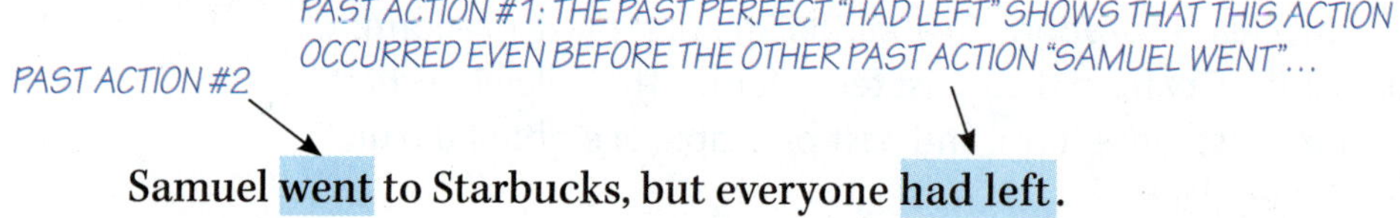

PAST ACTION #1: THE PAST PERFECT "HAD LEFT" SHOWS THAT THIS ACTION OCCURRED EVEN BEFORE THE OTHER PAST ACTION "SAMUEL WENT"...
PAST ACTION #2
Samuel went to Starbucks, but everyone had left.

- **to express an action or event that happened before a certain past time.**

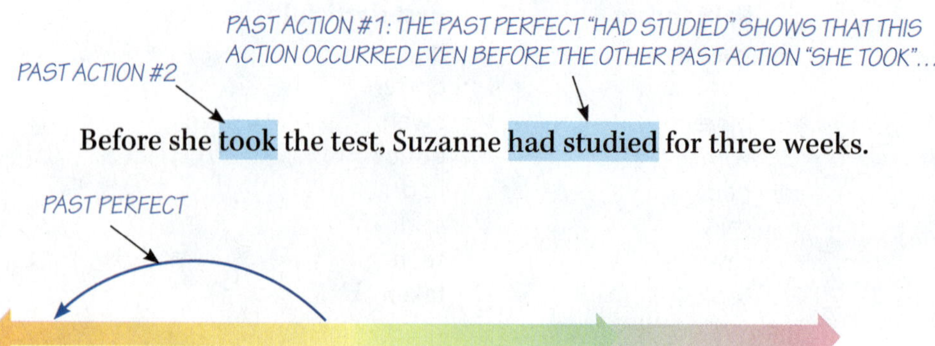

PAST ACTION #1: THE PAST PERFECT "HAD STUDIED" SHOWS THAT THIS ACTION OCCURRED EVEN BEFORE THE OTHER PAST ACTION "SHE TOOK"...
PAST ACTION #2
Before she took the test, Suzanne had studied for three weeks.
PAST PERFECT
Past action/event #1
Past action/event #2
Present
Future

Use the Passive Voice (*To Be* and the Past Participle)

LO 5

Action verbs establish the **active voice** by expressing what the subject of a sentence does. When the subject of a sentence receives the action (or is acted upon), the sentence is in the **passive voice.** The combination of *to be* with a past participle establishes the passive voice. In addition, the passive voice can be expressed in every tense.

The purpose of the passive voice is to tell the reader what is done to a subject.

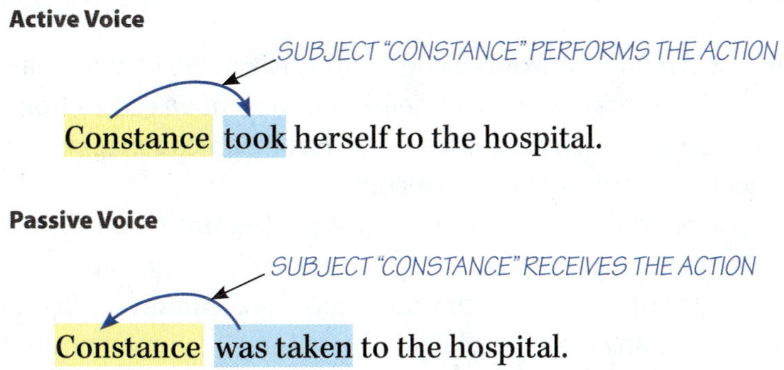

Active Voice
SUBJECT "CONSTANCE" PERFORMS THE ACTION
Constance took herself to the hospital.
Passive Voice
SUBJECT "CONSTANCE" RECEIVES THE ACTION
Constance was taken to the hospital.

Use the Past Participle as an Adjective

The past participle is often used as an adjective that modifies a noun or pronoun. Both regular and irregular forms of the past participle are used as adjectives.

The purposes of the past participle as an adjective are:

- **to describe a noun or pronoun with a word or phrase.**

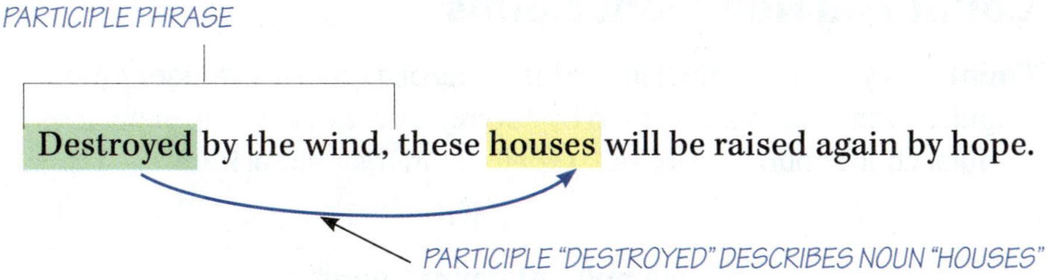

PARTICIPLE PHRASE
Destroyed by the wind, these houses will be raised again by hope.
PARTICIPLE "DESTROYED" DESCRIBES NOUN "HOUSES"

- **to describe the subject by completing a linking verb in the sentence.**

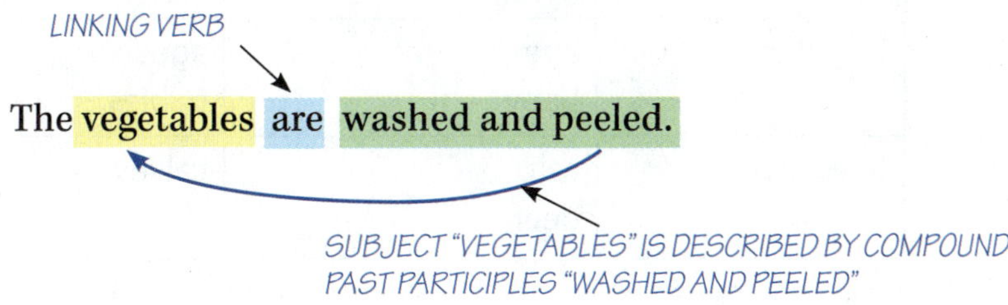

The vegetables are washed and peeled.
SUBJECT "VEGETABLES" IS DESCRIBED BY COMPOUND PAST PARTICIPLES "WASHED AND PEELED"

Complete the Post-test for Module 27 in MySkillsLab.

28

LEARNING OUTCOMES

After studying this module you should be able to:

LO 1 Recognize Types and Uses of Nouns

LO 2 Recognize Types and Uses of Pronouns

Nouns and Pronouns

A noun names a person, animal, place, or thing. A pronoun stands in the place of a noun that has been clearly identified earlier in the text.

LO 1 Recognize Types and Uses of Nouns

Often, nouns are the first words we learn to speak as we hear the names of people and things that we want or need. The word *noun* comes from the Latin word *nomen*, which means "name." A **noun** names a person, animal, place, object, element, action, or concept.

One type of noun is the proper noun. A **proper noun** names an individual person, place, or thing. A proper noun is always capitalized. The second type of noun is the common noun. A **common noun** is a general name for any member of a group or class. A common noun is not capitalized.

Two Types of Nouns	
Proper Noun	**Common Noun**
Kohl's	department store
Outback Steakhouse	restaurant

Count and Noncount Nouns

Count nouns name distinct individual units of a group or category. Most singular count nouns are formed by adding *-s* or *-es*. However, many singular count nouns use irregular spellings in their plural form.

Examples of Count Nouns		
	Singular	**Plural**
Regular	age baby	ages babies
Irregular	calf deer	calves deer

Noncount nouns name a nonspecific member of a group or category. Noncount nouns, which are typically common nouns, do not have plural forms. Noncount nouns name things that cannot be divided into smaller parts. Often, noncount nouns represent a group of count nouns.

Examples of Noncount Nouns and Corresponding Count Nouns	
Noncount Noun	**Count Noun**
air, oxygen, steam	gases
anger, happiness, grief	emotions

Articles and Nouns

An **article** is a type of adjective that describes a noun as being general or specific.

> **Indefinite articles**: ***A*** and ***an*** are used before a singular noun that refers to any member of a larger group: ***a** cat,* ***an*** *umbrella*. These articles are often used to introduce a noun for the first time in the discussion. Use *a* before a noun that begins with a consonant: ***a*** *cat*. Use *an* before a noun that begins with a vowel: ***an*** *umbrella.*

> **Definite article**: ***The*** is used before a singular or plural noun that refers to a specific member of the larger group: ***the*** *cat,* ***the*** *hat*. The article *the* is often used to indicate a noun that has already been introduced into the discussion. "A cat is at the front door; the cat looks hungry."

> **Zero article**: No article is used before the noun. An example: *Time is money*. Use zero article to refer to general ideas.

Recognize Types and Uses of Pronouns L2

Pronouns and **antecedents** work closely together to communicate an idea. A **pronoun** refers to or stands in the place of a noun that has been clearly identified earlier in the discussion. An **antecedent** is the noun to which a pronoun refers. Every pronoun should refer clearly and specifically to one particular antecedent.

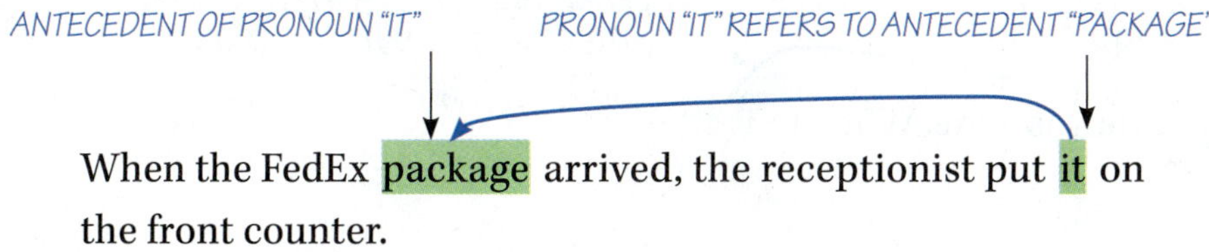

ANTECEDENT OF PRONOUN "IT"
PRONOUN "IT" REFERS TO ANTECEDENT "PACKAGE"
When the FedEx package arrived, the receptionist put it on the front counter.

In the preceding example, the pronoun "it" clearly refers to the antecedent "package." To make sure your writing is clear, avoid faulty pronoun references.

Avoid Pronoun Reference to More Than One Antecedent

PROBLEM:

The pronoun does not clearly and unmistakably refer to one specific antecedent.

PRONOUN "IT" REFERS TO ?

Jared threw the remote control at the television because it was broken.

ANTECEDENT OF "IT"?

CORRECTION:

Correct by replacing the pronoun with a noun.

> Jared threw the remote control at the television because the remote control was broken.

ADDED NOUN REPLACES PRONOUN WITH NO CLEAR ANTECEDENT
SUBJECT AND VERB IMPLY THAT "IT" IN THE ABOVE SENTENCE REFERS TO A DONUT

Avoid Pronoun Reference to Implied or Missing Antecedent

PROBLEM:

The antecedent is not stated or is missing.

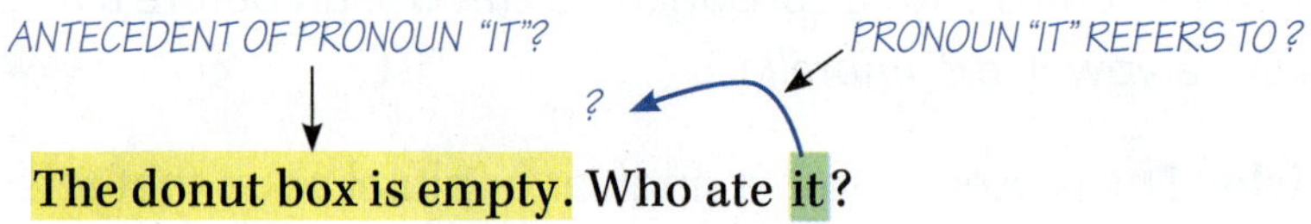

ANTECEDENT OF PRONOUN "IT"?
The last donut is gone. Who ate it?
PRONOUN "IT" REFERS TO ?
?
The donut box is empty. Who ate it?

CORRECTION #1:

Correct by replacing the pronoun with a noun.

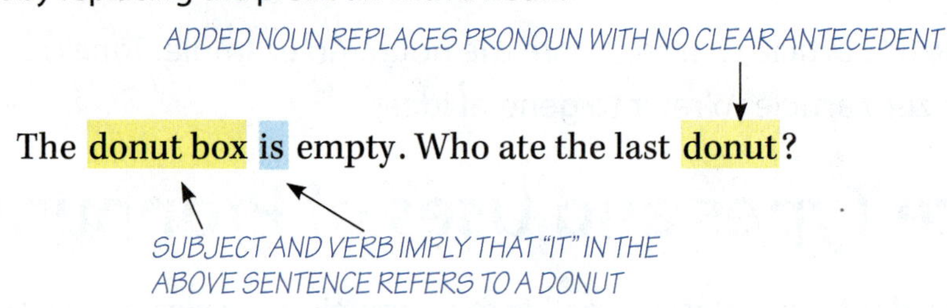

CORRECTION #2:

Correct by rewording to include a clear antecedent for the pronoun.

> **MySkillsLab™**
>
> Complete the Post-test for Module 28 in MySkillsLab.

Adjectives and Adverbs

An adjective describes a noun or a pronoun. An adverb describes a verb, an adjective, or another adverb.

29

LEARNING OUTCOMES

After studying this module you should be able to:

- **LO1** Recognize Types and Uses of Adjectives
- **LO2** Recognize Types and Uses of Adverbs

Recognize Types and Uses of Adjectives LO1

An **adjective** modifies—in other words, it describes—a noun or a pronoun. It answers one or more of the following questions:

- What kind?
- Which one?
- How many?

ADJECTIVE "LOUD" DESCRIBES NOUN "VOICE"

Maya has a loud voice.

An **adverb** modifies, or describes, a verb, an adjective, or another adverb. It answers one or more of the following questions:

- How?
- Why?
- When?
- Where?
- To what extent?

VERB "TALKS" DESCRIBED BY ADVERB "LOUDLY"

Maya talks loudly.

Participles as Adjectives

Many adjectives are formed by adding *-ed* or *-ing* to verbs. These **participle adjectives** serve two purposes: The *-ed* form describes a person's reaction or feeling; the *-ing* form describes the person or thing that causes the reaction.

The amazed crowd watched the fireworks display.

The amazing fireworks display lit up the entire sky.

Nouns and Verbs Formed as Adjectives

In addition to the *-ed* and *-ing* word endings, many adjectives are formed by other types of word endings.

Common Adjectives								
Word Endings	***-able* *-ible***	***-ful***	***-ic***	***-ish***	***-ive***	***-less***	***-ly* *-y***	***-ous***
Examples	acceptable	bashful	alcoholic	boorish	abusive	cheerless	actually	ambiguous

Placement of Adjectives

A careful writer not only chooses the precise word for impact, but also arranges words in the most effective order for the greatest impact on the reader.

Adjectives can appear before a noun.

The nervous suspect offered an alibi.

Adjectives can appear after **linking verbs** such as *is*, *are*, *were*, *seems*, and *appears*.

The alibi seemed plausible.

Adjectives can appear after **sensory verbs**—those that describe physical senses—such as *look, smell, feel, taste,* and *sound*.

The suspect looked frightened.

L2 Recognize Types and Uses of Adverbs

The most common use of adverbs is to describe verbs. In addition, adverbs modify other types of words such as adjectives and other adverbs. In purpose, adverbs answer the reporter's questions *When? Where?* and *How?*

Many adverbs are derived from adjectives, many adverbs end in *-ly*, and many adverbs are gradable based on degree or quantity. The following chart lists some of the most frequently used adverbs based on the type of information they provide.

Common Adverbs				
Time, Frequency, or Sequence **When?**	**Place** **Where?**	**Manner** **How?**	**Certainty or Negation** **How?**	**Degree or Quantity** **How much?**
already finally regularly usually	everywhere here somewhere there	badly fast quickly well	certainly clearly not never	almost completely entirely not very

How to Use the Comparative and Superlative

Adjectives and adverbs take the form of three degrees: **absolute, comparative,** and **superlative.** The degrees of adverbs are formed by adding the suffixes *-er* or *-est* or by using *more* or *most*. For example, *more* or *most* establishes a degree of comparison with adverbs that end in *-ly*.

Absolute

The absolute degree makes no comparison, or makes a one-to-one comparison (in which the adjective or adverb describes both things equally).

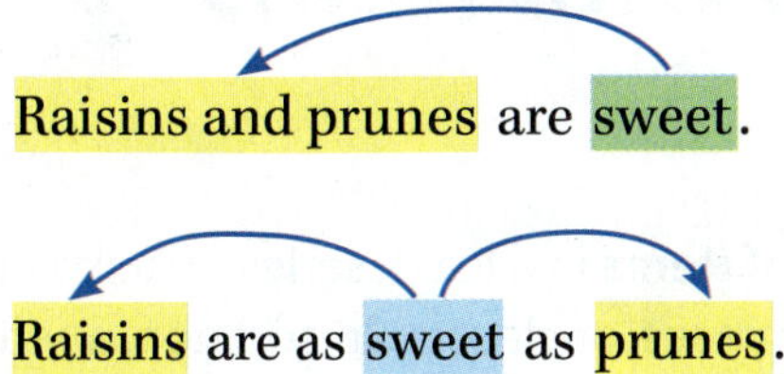

Comparative

The comparative degree compares and makes distinctions between two people or things, usually by using the adverb *more* or *less* or adding the suffix *-er*.

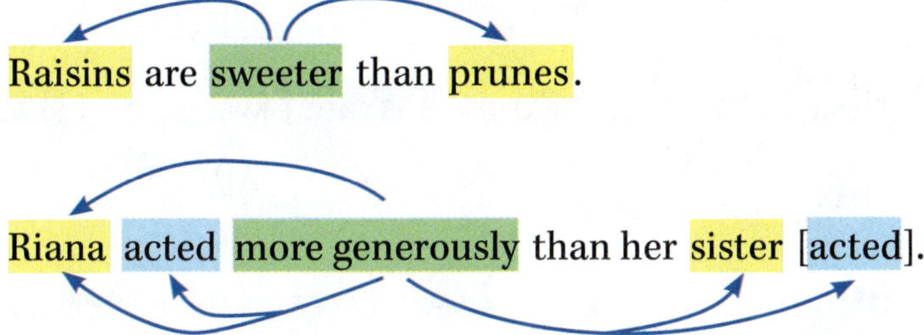

Superlative

The superlative degree makes distinctions among three or more people or things, usually by using the adverb *most* or *least* or adding the suffix *-est*.

MySkillsLab™

Complete the Post-test for Module 29 in MySkillsLab.

30

LEARNING OUTCOMES

After studying this module you should be able to:

- LO1 Use Commas with Items in a Series
- LO2 Use Commas with Introductory Elements
- LO3 Use Commas to Join Independent Clauses
- LO4 Use Commas with Parenthetical Ideas
- LO5 Use Commas with Quotations

The Comma

A comma is a valuable, useful punctuation device because it separates the structural elements of a sentence into manageable segments.

The primary purpose of the **comma** is to make a sentence easy to read by indicating a brief pause between parts of the sentence that need to be separated.

LO1 Use Commas with Items in a Series

Use commas to separate a **series of items** in a list. A series of items in a list can be **three** or more words, phrases, or clauses. In addition, a series of items can be made up of subjects, verbs, adjectives, participles, and so on. Items in a series are parallel and equal in importance.

Series of Words

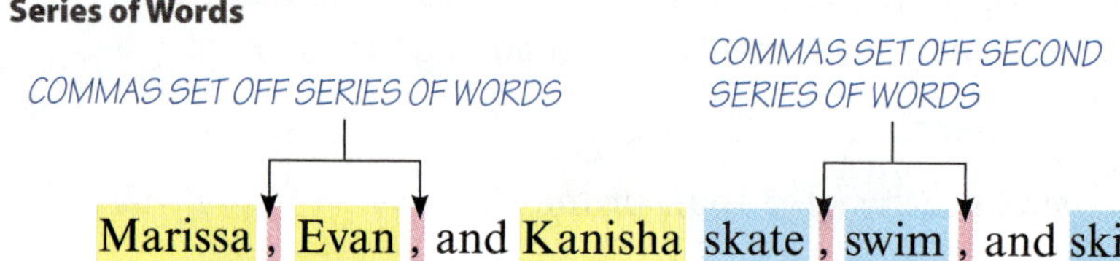

Marissa, Evan, and Kanisha skate, swim, and ski.

Series of Phrases

COMMAS SET OFF SERIES OF PHRASES
Marissa enjoys skating on ice, swimming in the ocean, and skiing down a snowy slope.

Series of Clauses

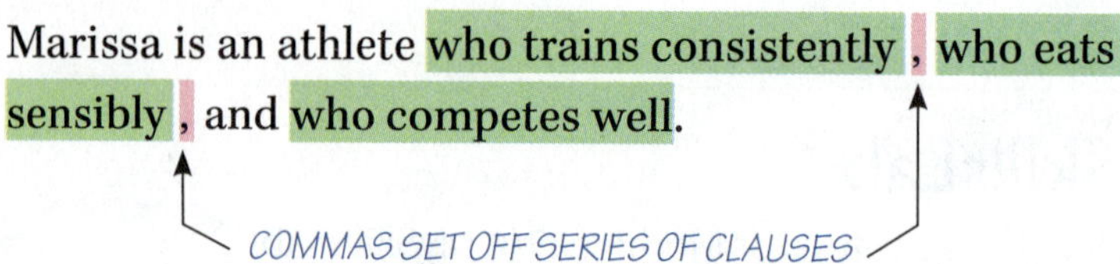

Marissa is an athlete who trains consistently, who eats sensibly, and who competes well.
COMMAS SET OFF SERIES OF CLAUSES

Use Commas with Introductory Elements

Use commas to set off the introductory element of a sentence. **Introductory elements** are ideas that appear at the beginning of a sentence. Introductory elements come before a main clause and can be a word, phrase, or clause.

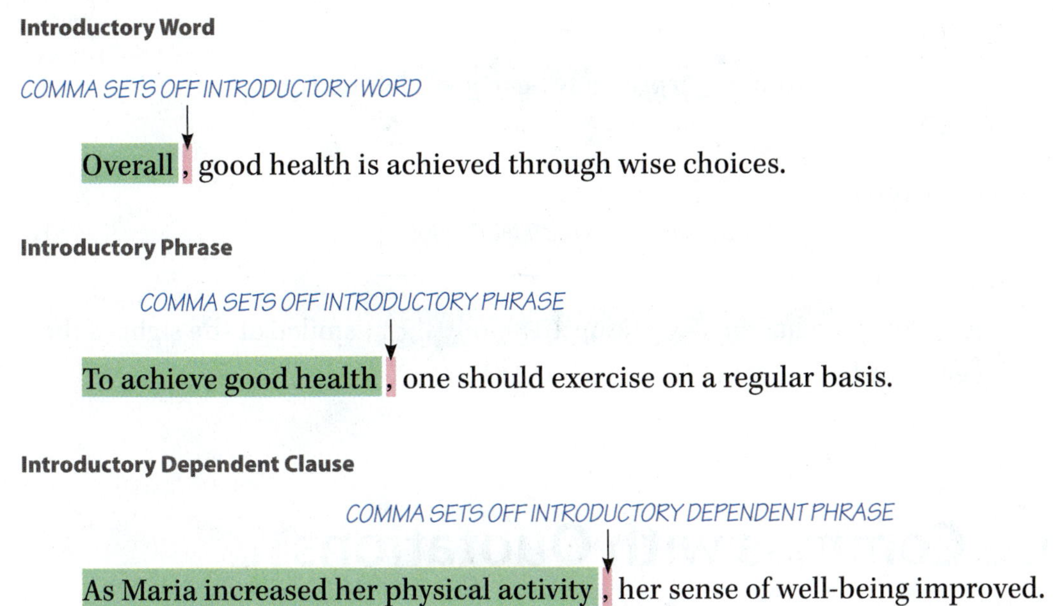

Introductory Word
COMMA SETS OFF INTRODUCTORY WORD
Overall, good health is achieved through wise choices.
Introductory Phrase
COMMA SETS OFF INTRODUCTORY PHRASE
To achieve good health, one should exercise on a regular basis.
Introductory Dependent Clause
COMMA SETS OFF INTRODUCTORY DEPENDENT PHRASE
As Maria increased her physical activity, her sense of well-being improved.

Use Commas to Join Independent Clauses

Use a comma with a coordinating conjunction to join two or more equally important and logically related independent clauses. To join sentences with a coordinating conjunction, place the comma before the conjunction. The acronym **FANBOYS** identifies the seven coordinating conjunctions: *for, and, nor, but, or, yet,* and *so.*

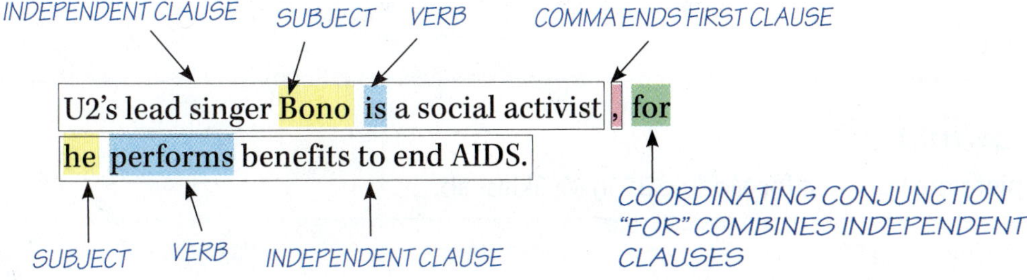

COMMA ENDS FIRST CLAUSE
U2's lead singer Bono is a social activist, for
he performs benefits to end AIDS.

Use Commas with Parenthetical Ideas

Use commas to set off a parenthetical idea. A **parenthetical idea** is an idea that interrupts a sentence with information that is **nonessential** to the meaning of the sentence. Such an idea could be enclosed in parentheses. However, more often, a comma comes before and after such an idea. These interruptions can be words, phrases, or clauses.

Parenthetical Word

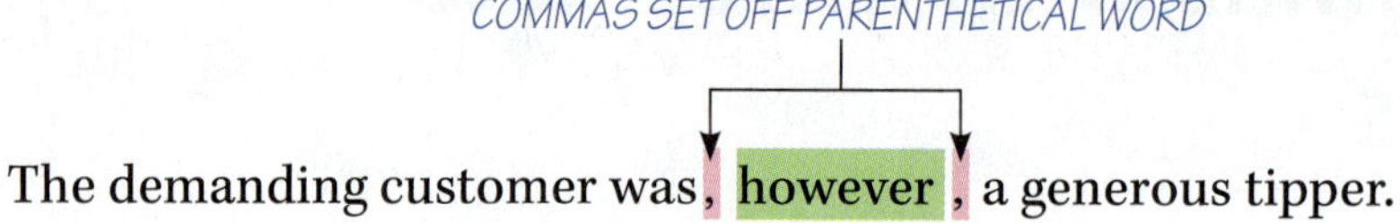

COMMAS SET OFF PARENTHETICAL WORD
The demanding customer was, however, a generous tipper.

Parenthetical Phrase

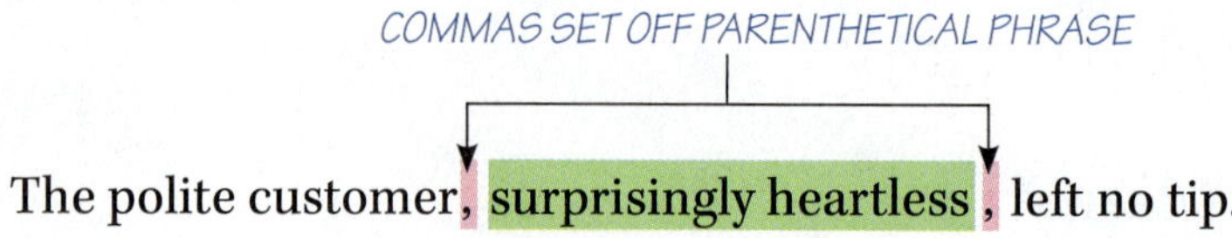

COMMAS SET OFF PARENTHETICAL PHRASE
The polite customer, surprisingly heartless, left no tip.

Parenthetical Clause

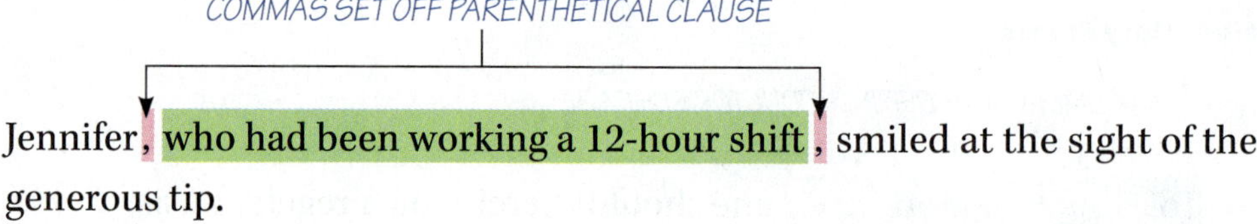

COMMAS SET OFF PARENTHETICAL CLAUSE
Jennifer, who had been working a 12-hour shift, smiled at the sight of the generous tip.

L5 Use Commas with Quotations

Use commas after a verb that introduces a quotation. The comma is used to set off the "said" clause, called the **speech tag**, and the comma is placed before the quoted information.

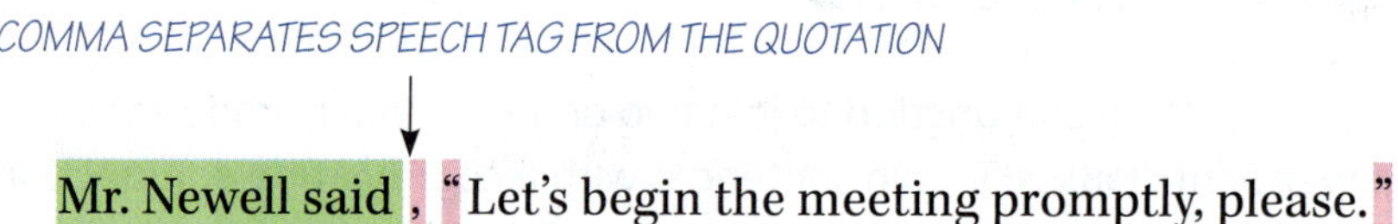

COMMA SEPARATES SPEECH TAG FROM THE QUOTATION
Mr. Newell said, "Let's begin the meeting promptly, please."

> **MySkillsLab™**
> Complete the Post-test for Module 30 in MySkillsLab.

The Apostrophe

The apostrophe is used to show ownership and to form contractions by replacing omitted letters or numbers.

31

LEARNING OUTCOMES

After studying this module you should be able to:

- LO 1 Use the Apostrophe to Show Ownership
- LO 2 Use the Apostrophe for Contractions
- LO 3 Avoid Common Misuses of the Apostrophe

Use the Apostrophe to Show Ownership LO 1

The **possessive form** of a noun and some pronouns is created by using an apostrophe followed, at times, by an *-s*. The possessive tells the reader that someone or something owns or possesses the next stated thing.

The following chart lists and illustrates the rules for using an apostrophe to show possession.

Using the Apostrophe for Ownership		
To Show Possession for	**Correct Use of Apostrophe**	**Example**
A singular noun	add '	my husband's job
A singular noun ending with *-s*	add ' or add 's	the boss' memo or James's home
A regular plural noun ending with *-s*	add '	the writers' colony
An irregular plural noun	add 's	women's clothing

Using the Apostrophe for Ownership (*continued*)		
To Show Possession for	**Correct Use of Apostrophe**	**Example**
Compound words	add 's	vice president's speech sister-in-law's business (Note: Do not confuse the possessive form with the plural form, as in *sisters-in-law*)
Joint ownership of an item	add 's to the last noun	Abbott and Costello's comedy
Individual ownership	add 's to the end of both nouns	Leigh's and Rob's cars (Each person owns a car.)
Indefinite pronouns ending with *one* or *body*	add 's	someone's computer

LO2 Use the Apostrophe for Contractions

An apostrophe is used to indicate the omission of letters to form a *contraction*. Most often, a **contraction** is formed to join two words to make one shorter word such as *don't* for *do not*. An apostrophe (') takes the place of the letter or letters that are dropped to form the contraction.

The following chart illustrates how contracted verbs are formed.

Apostrophe Use in Common Contractions The apostrophe replaces omitted letters.	
'm APOSTROPHE REPLACES "A" IN "I AM" I am = I'm	's APOSTROPHE REPLACES "I" IN "IT IS" it is = it's
're APOSTROPHE REPLACES "A" IN "YOU ARE" you are = you're	've APOSTROPHE REPLACES "HA" IN "I HAVE" I have = I've
n't APOSTROPHE REPLACES "O" IN "IS NOT" is not = isn't	'll APOSTROPHE REPLACES "WI" IN "I WILL" I will = I'll

Avoid Common Misuses of the Apostrophe

Quite often, the apostrophe is misused in several specific ways. The following chart lists and illustrates these common misuses of the apostrophe. Always base your use of an apostrophe on a specific rule. Proofread your writing for these common mistakes.

- **Do not use an apostrophe to form a plural noun.**

Correct Plural	Incorrect Plural
homes books	home's book's

- **Do not use an apostrophe to form a possessive pronoun.**

Correct	Incorrect
ours hers theirs	our's her's their's

- **Do not omit the apostrophe to form the possessive indefinite pronoun.**

Correct	Incorrect
one's everybody's	ones everybodys

- **Do not confuse contractions with similar sounding words.**

Contraction	Possessive Pronoun
it's (it is) who's (who is) they're (they are)	its whose their

MySkillsLab™

Complete the Post-test for Module 31 in MySkillsLab.

MODULE 32 QUOTATION MARKS

32

LEARNING OUTCOMES

After studying this module you should be able to:

LO1 Format and Punctuate Direct Quotations

LO2 Use Speech Tags with Direct Quotations

LO3 Use Quotation Marks Correctly with Titles

Quotation Marks

Quotation marks are used to set off exact words either written or spoken by other people or to set off titles of short works.

LO1 Format and Punctuate Direct Quotations

1. Place commas (,) and periods (.) inside the quotation marks (" ").

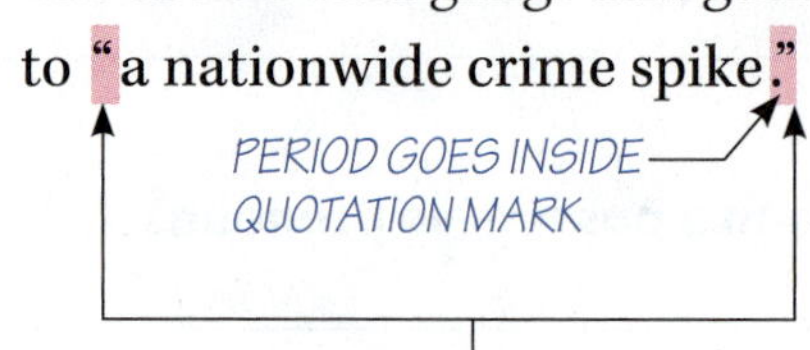

The article said gangs and guns contributed
to "a nationwide crime spike."

2. Place semicolons (;) and colons (:) outside the quotation marks.

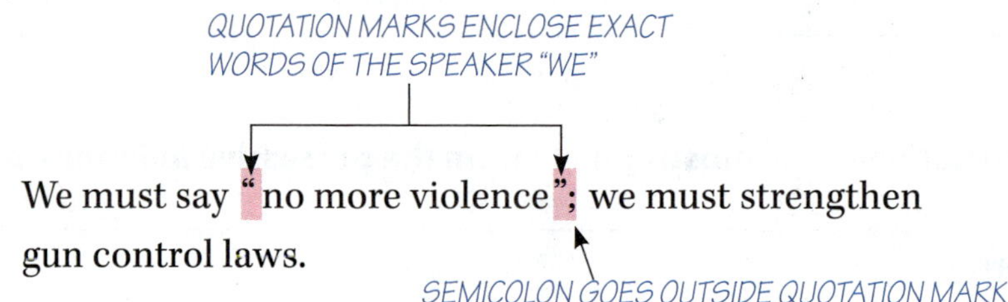

3. Place a question mark (?) inside quotation marks when it is part of the quotation. Place a question mark outside quotation marks when the larger sentence is a question, but the quotation included in it is not.

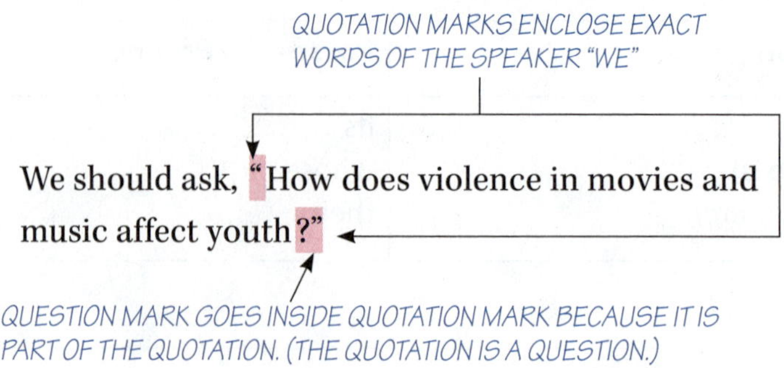

QUOTATION MARKS ENCLOSE EXACT WORDS OF THE SPEAKER "WE"
gun control laws.
We should ask, "How does violence in movies and
music affect youth?"
QUESTION MARK GOES INSIDE QUOTATION MARK BECAUSE IT IS PART OF THE QUOTATION. (THE QUOTATION IS A QUESTION.)

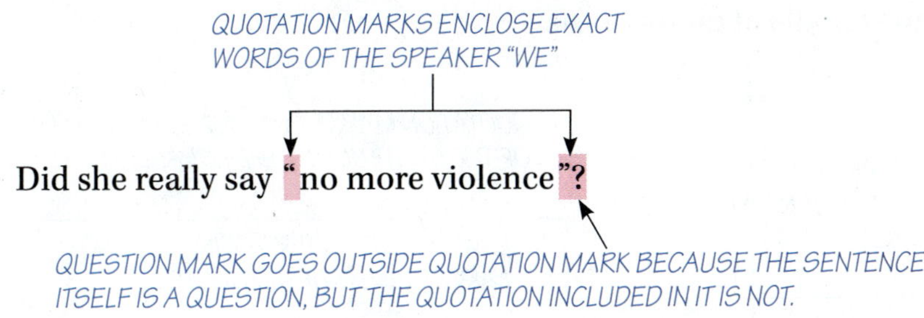

QUOTATION MARKS ENCLOSE EXACT WORDS OF THE SPEAKER "WE"
Did she really say "no more violence"?
QUESTION MARK GOES OUTSIDE QUOTATION MARK BECAUSE THE SENTENCE ITSELF IS A QUESTION, BUT THE QUOTATION INCLUDED IN IT IS NOT.

4. Use single quotation marks for quoted information—or titles of short works—that appear within direct quotation.

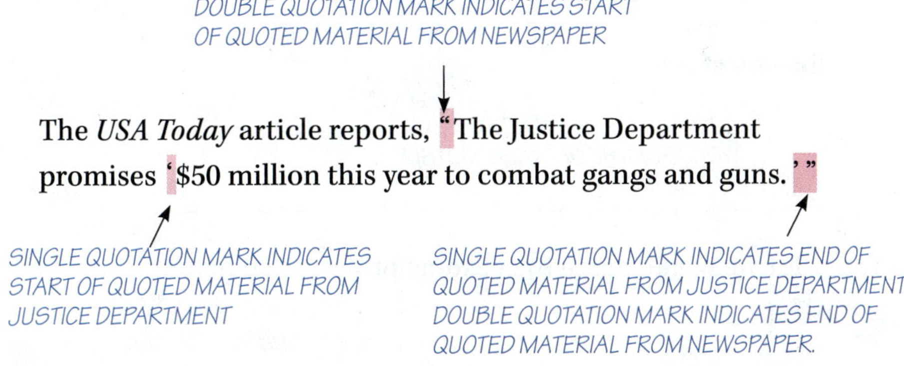

Use Speech Tags with Direct Quotations

One part of a direct quotation is the **speech tag** or the credit given to the source, the person who spoke or wrote an idea. A speech tag is formed by a subject (the speaker) and a verb that indicates the subject is speaking. The following examples highlight the correct use of commas, periods, capitalization, and quotation marks based on the placement of the speech tag.

- **Speech tag at the beginning of quote**

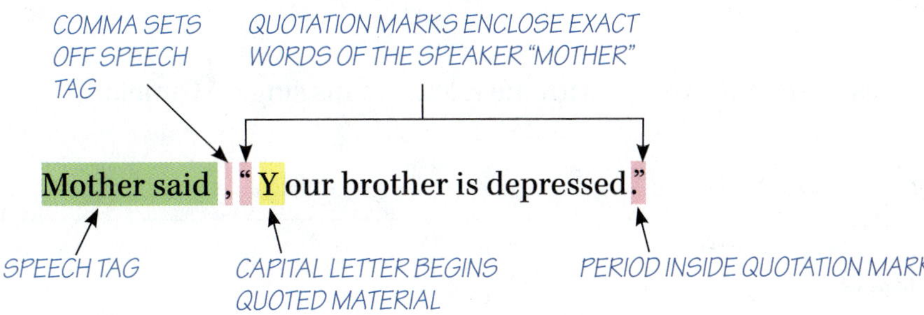

- **Speech tag in the middle of quote**

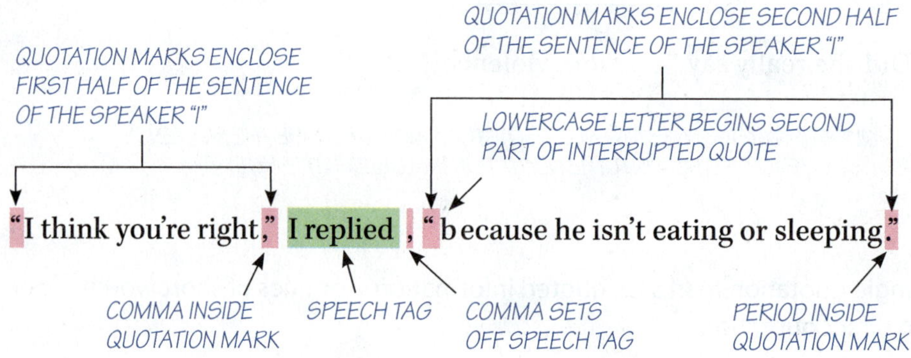

LOWERCASE LETTER BEGINS SECOND PART OF INTERRUPTED QUOTE
"I think you're right," I replied, "because he isn't eating or sleeping."

COMMA SETS OFF SPEECH TAG

- **Speech tag at the end of quote**

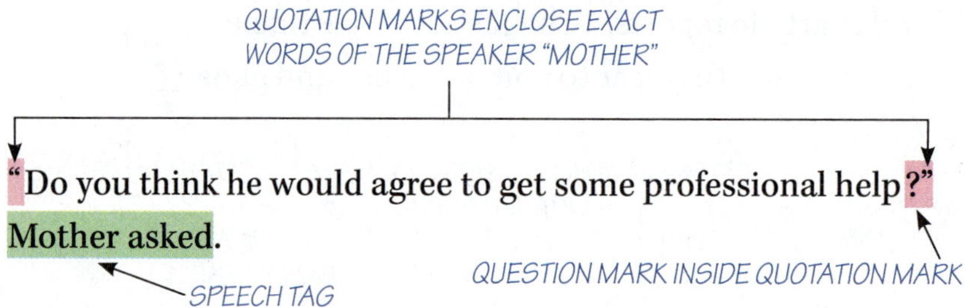

"Do you think he would agree to get some professional help?" Mother asked.

L3 Use Quotation Marks Correctly with Titles

Quotation marks are also used to set off the titles of short works such as essays, short stories, short poems, songs, articles in magazines, TV episodes, and chapter titles in books.

- Follow the general rules for using quotation marks.
- Do not use quotation marks to set off titles of larger publications such as magazines, newspapers, and books. These larger publications are set off with italics.

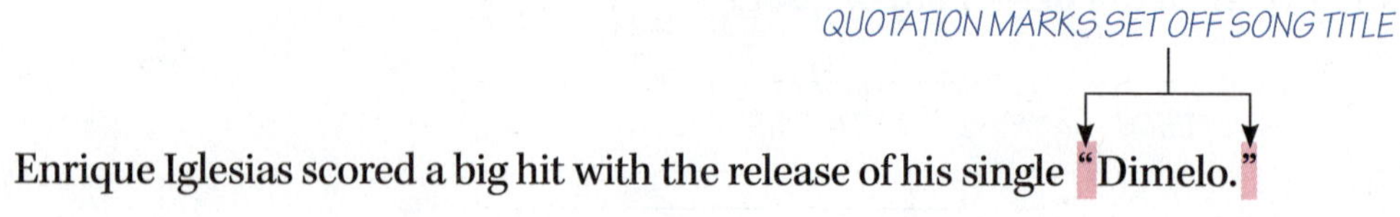

QUOTATION MARKS SET OFF SONG TITLE
Enrique Iglesias scored a big hit with the release of his single "Dimelo."

MySkillsLab™

Complete the Post-test for Module 32 in MySkillsLab.

End Punctuation

End punctuation marks the end of a complete thought. The **punctuation marks** that indicate the end of a sentence (called **end punctuation**) are **the period**, **the question mark**, and **the exclamation point**. Each of these end punctuation marks indicates the purpose or type of a sentence.

33

LEARNING OUTCOMES

After studying this module you should be able to:

LO 1 Use Periods Correctly

LO 2 Use Question Marks Correctly

LO 3 Use Exclamation Points Correctly

Use Periods Correctly LO 1

End Punctuation	Type of Sentence	Purpose of Sentence
The Period (.)	Ends a declarative statement Ends an imperative statement	To inform To command without urgency

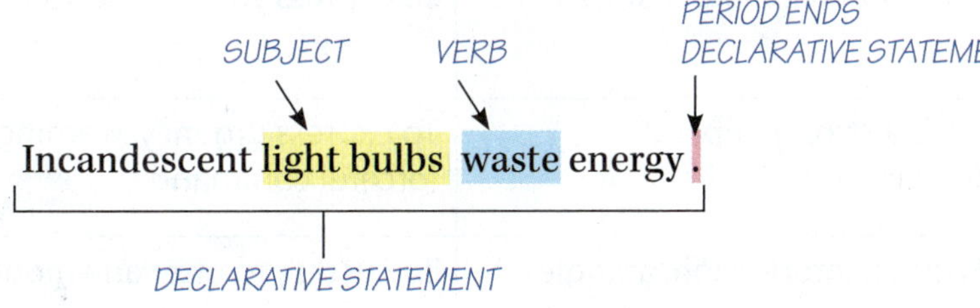

SUBJECT
VERB
PERIOD ENDS DECLARATIVE STATEMENT
Incandescent light bulbs waste energy.
DECLARATIVE STATEMENT

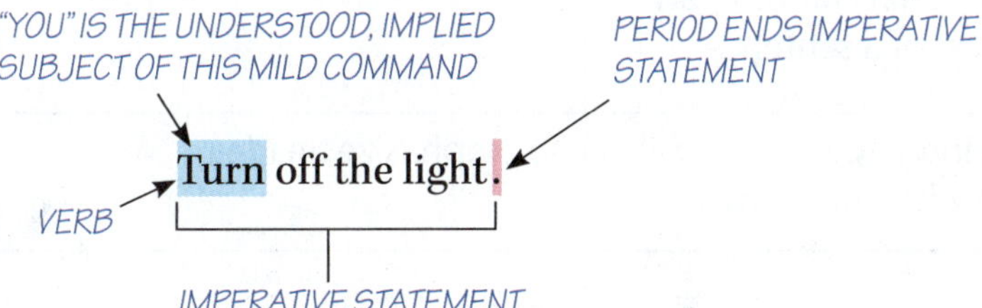

"YOU" IS THE UNDERSTOOD, IMPLIED SUBJECT OF THIS MILD COMMAND
PERIOD ENDS IMPERATIVE STATEMENT
Turn off the light.
VERB
IMPERATIVE STATEMENT

Use Question Marks Correctly 

End Punctuation	Type of Sentence	Purpose of Sentence
The Question Mark (?)	Ends an interrogative statement	To question
	May invert order of subject and helping verb	To question
	May begin with *what*, *who*, or *how*	To ask a direct question
	Often uses a helping verb such as *do*, *can*, *will*, or *would*	To make a request

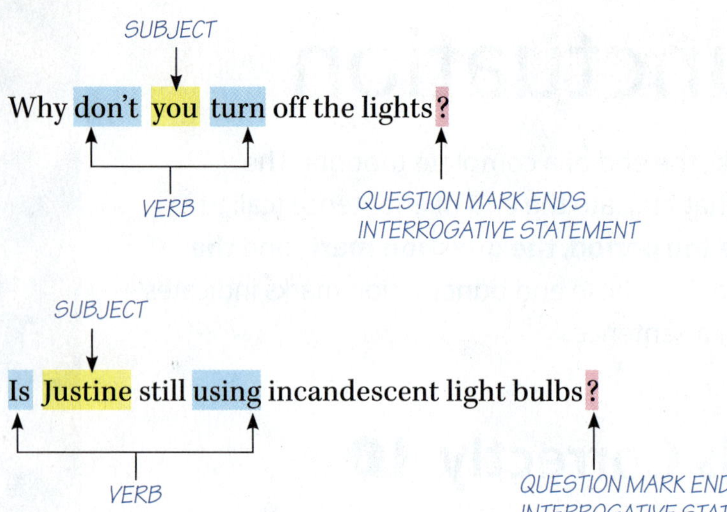
SUBJECT
Why don't you turn off the lights?
VERB
QUESTION MARK ENDS INTERROGATIVE STATEMENT
SUBJECT
Is Justine still using incandescent light bulbs?
VERB
QUESTION MARK ENDS INTERROGATIVE STATEMENT

L3 Use Exclamation Points Correctly

End Punctuation	Type of Sentence	Purpose of Sentence
The Exclamation Point(!)	Ends an exclamatory statement	To express strong emotion
	Ends a strong imperative (command)	To express urgency, warning, or a forceful command
	Ends an interjection, a single word or phrase used as an exclamation that stands apart from the rest of a sentence	To cry out, to utter an emotion
	Used with interjections beginning with *how* or *what*	To emphasize an idea

Example

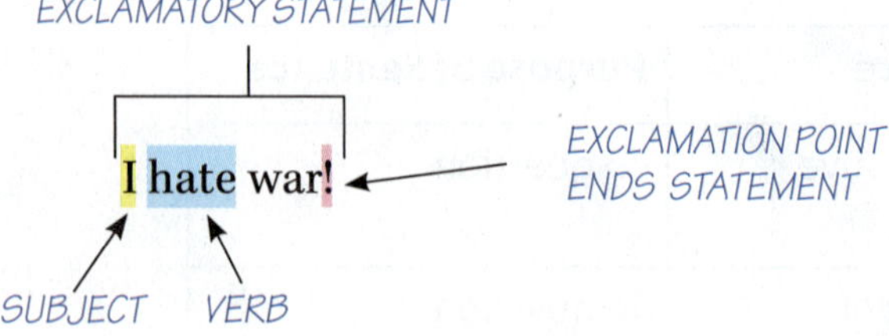
EXCLAMATORY STATEMENT
I hate war!
EXCLAMATION POINT ENDS STATEMENT
SUBJECT
VERB

MySkillsLab™
Complete the Post-test for Module 33 in MySkillsLab.

Capitalization

Capitalization clearly identifies the beginning of a new idea or the names of specific people, places, and things.

Apply the Seven Rules of Capitalization LO1

Capitalization refers to writing letters (and sometimes words) in uppercase letters. The most frequent usage of capitalization, however, is writing a word with its first letter in uppercase (and the rest of its letters in lowercase) to indicate the beginning of a sentence.

Following seven basic rules will ensure proper use of capitalization in your writing.

RULE 1: Capitalize the first word of every sentence.

INITIAL CAPITAL LETTERS IN THE FIRST WORD OF EVERY SENTENCE INDICATE THE START OF A NEW SENTENCE AND A NEW THOUGHT

Extreme horror films provide thrill rides for loyal fans.

RULE 2: Capitalize the pronoun *I*.

ALWAYS CAPITALIZE THE FIRST-PERSON SINGULAR PRONOUN "I"

Because I keep my eyes closed through most of a horror movie, I think they are a waste of my money.

RULE 3: Capitalize the first letter of the first words in written greetings and salutations (for example, *Dear friends*, or *Best regards*).

ALWAYS CAPITALIZE THE FIRST LETTER OF THE FIRST WORDS IN WRITTEN GREETINGS OR CLOSINGS (IN LETTERS, MEMOS, EMAILS, ETC.)

Dear Mr. Sanchez:

I am writing to protest your support of horror films. As a sponsor of this type of film, you foster fear and violence in our culture. Until you stop sponsoring horror films, I will no longer buy items from your company.

Sincerely,

Dorothea Simmons

34

LEARNING OUTCOMES

After studying this module you should be able to:

LO1 Apply the Seven Rules of Capitalization.

Rule 1: Capitalize the first word of every sentence.

Rule 2: Capitalize the pronoun *I*.

Rule 3: Capitalize the first letter of the first words in written greetings and salutations.

Rule 4: In titles of publications, capitalize the first letter of the first and last words, the principal words, and the first word that comes after a semicolon or a colon.

Rule 5: Capitalize the first letters in all essential words in proper nouns.

Rule 6: Capitalize the first letter of the title of a person when the title precedes the person's name.

Rule 7: Capitalize proper adjectives.

RULE 4: In titles of publications, such as books, magazines, newspapers, songs, poems, plays, and articles, capitalize the first letter of the first and last words, the principal words, and the first word that comes after a semicolon or a colon.

Do not capitalize the first letters of the following in titles, unless they are the first or last word or come after a semicolon or colon: articles (*a, an, the*), prepositions (such as *in, of,* and *with*), and conjunctions (such as *and, but,* and *for*).

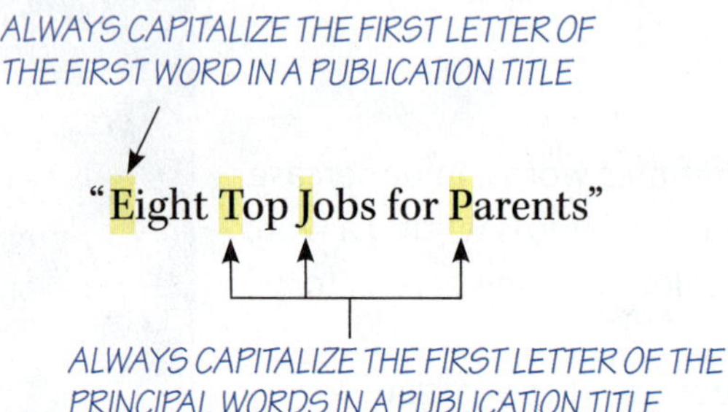
ALWAYS CAPITALIZE THE FIRST LETTER OF THE FIRST WORD IN A PUBLICATION TITLE
"Eight Top Jobs for Parents"
ALWAYS CAPITALIZE THE FIRST LETTER OF THE PRINCIPAL WORDS IN A PUBLICATION TITLE

RULE 5: Capitalize the first letters in all essential words in proper nouns.

Proper nouns name specific people, places, things, and events. Proper nouns include people's names; certain titles of people (see Rule 6 for details), places, and regions; organizations and associations; and publications. Each of the examples in the chart below illustrates various rules for capitalizing proper nouns.

Note the capitalization of abbreviations. Do not capitalize common nouns.

	Common Nouns	Proper Nouns
People	a professor an officer	Professor Walker Captain Rivera or Capt. Rivera
Places and Regions	a country a street	Mexico Main Street
Things	a language a company	English Apple, Inc.
Events, Time Periods	a day an era	Friday the Middle Ages

RULE 6: Capitalize the first letter of the title of a person when the title precedes the person's name.

Some writers capitalize the first letter of a title of very high rank even when it follows a proper name. Capitalization of the first letter of a title is also common if it appears at the end of a letter, email, or other correspondence, following the person's name. Do not capitalize those titles when they appear on their own as common nouns (without modifying a particular person's name).

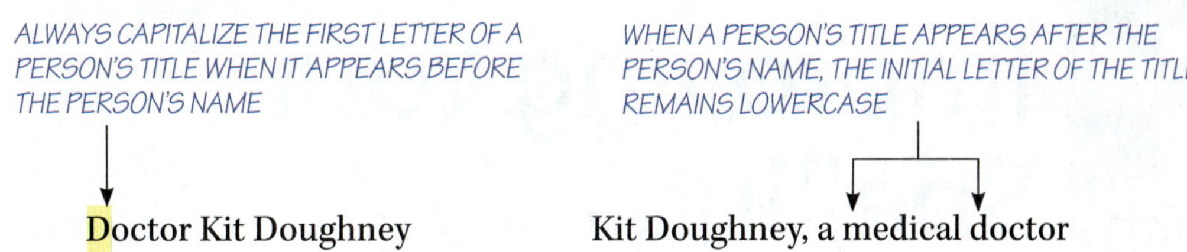
ALWAYS CAPITALIZE THE FIRST LETTER OF A PERSON'S TITLE WHEN IT APPEARS BEFORE THE PERSON'S NAME
WHEN A PERSON'S TITLE APPEARS AFTER THE PERSON'S NAME, THE INITIAL LETTER OF THE TITLE REMAINS LOWERCASE

Doctor Kit Doughney   Kit Doughney, a medical doctor

RULE 7: Capitalize proper adjectives. Proper adjectives are formed from proper nouns.

Proper Noun	Proper Adjective
Africa	African
Shakespeare	Shakespearean

Use and capitalize brand-name trademarks as proper adjectives such as Kleenex tissue or Scotch tape.

MySkillsLab™
Complete the Post-test for Module 34 in MySkillsLab.

35

LEARNING OUTCOMES

After studying this module you should be able to:

LO1 Apply the Rules for Improving Your Spelling

Rule 1: Understand How Suffixes Are Used

Rule 2: Add *-s* or *-es* to Nouns and Verbs to Form the Plural

Rule 3: Double the Final Consonant in Words with One Syllable

Rule 4: Double the Final Consonant in Words with More Than One Syllable

Rule 5: Drop or Keep the Final *E*

Rule 6: Change or Keep the Final *Y*

Rule 7: Choose *ie* or *ei*

Improving Your Spelling

To spell correctly is to understand the rules for properly arranging letters in a word.

LO1 Rules for Improving Your Spelling

Improving your spelling involves understanding rules about the use of suffixes and prefixes.

RULE 1: Understand How Suffixes Are Used

A **suffix** is added to the end of a **base word** (a word's original meaning) to change the use or meaning of the word. Suffixes begin with either a vowel or a consonant, which affects the spelling rules for adding them to base words. The following chart lists a few common vowel and consonant suffixes, along with their meanings and examples.

Vowel Suffix	Meaning	Example
-able -ible	able to	touchable, visible
-ed	past tense of a verb	talked, walked
-en	present or past participle	bitten, written
-er	one who is or does	player, adopter
-er	comparison	bigger, smaller
-es	plural of a noun	dresses, boxes
-es	singular present tense of a verb	washes, finishes
-ous	full of	dangerous, luxurious

Consonant Suffix	Meaning	Example
-ful	full of	wonderful, careful
-ly or -y	like	gently, grimy
-ness	state of being	happiness, faithfulness
-ment	state of	government, statement
-s	plural of a noun	doctors, workers
-s	singular present tense of a verb	runs, quits

The rules of spelling words with suffixes vary. The next several sections explain and illustrate the various spelling rules for adding suffixes.

RULE 2: Add *-s* or *-es* to Nouns and Verbs to Form the Plural

- **Add -s to form the plural of most regular nouns, including those that end with *o*.**

  video + s ⟶ videos

- **Add -*es* to nouns that end with a consonant immediately before a final *o*.**

  hero + es ⟶ heroes

- **Add -*s* to most regular verbs to form the singular present tense in the third person.**

  ask + s ⟶ asks

- **Add -*es* to form the plural of nouns and to third person present tense verbs that end in *ch*, *sh*, *s*, *x*, or *z*.**

Nouns		Verbs	
watch + es	watches	buzz + es	buzzes

RULE 3: Double the Final Consonant in Words with One Syllable

Many **one syllable** words end in a **consonant** with a **vowel** immediately **before** it. (*Hint*: Remember CVC.) For a word with one syllable, one consonant, and one vowel, double the final consonant when adding a vowel suffix. The final consonant is *not* doubled when adding a consonant suffix.

sit + sits OR sitter

Exception: Do not double the final consonant of words that end in *w*, *x*, or *y* as in the following examples: **snowing, boxer, obeys.**

RULE 4: Double the Final Consonant in Words with More Than One Syllable

Words with more than one syllable often end with a vowel immediately before a **consonant**. (*Hint*: Remember VC.) If the final syllable is stressed or emphasized in its pronunciation, **double the final consonant**.

control controlled controlling

RULE 5: Drop or Keep the Final *E*

- **Drop the e when the base *word ends* with a *silent e* and the *suffix begins* with a *vowel.***

advance + -ing ⟶ advancing

- **Drop the e when a *vowel comes immediately before* the silent e.**

true + -ly ⟶ truly

- **Keep the e when the base *word ends* with a silent e and the *suffix begins* with a *consonant*.**

advance + -ment ⟶ advancement

RULE 6: Change or Keep the Final *Y*

- **When a *consonant* appears before the final *y*, change the *y* to *i*.**

supply + -ies ⟶ supplies

- **When a *vowel* appears before the final *y*, keep the *y*.**

obey + -ed ⟶ obeyed

- **Keep the *y* when adding the suffix *-ing*.**

cry + -ing ⟶ crying

RULE 7: Choose *ie* or *ei*

A helpful way to remember how to use *ie* and *ei* in spelling is to think of the following rhyme:

"***i*** before ***e*** except after ***c*** or when sounds like *ay* as in *neighbor* or *weigh*"

There are, however, some exceptions to the *ie*, *ei* rule that should be memorized:

ie: species, science, conscience

ei: height, either, neither, leisure, seize, counterfeit, foreign

MySkillsLab™

Complete the Post-test for Module 35 in MySkillsLab.

Reading Selections

A Reading Strategy for a Writer

Nine Reading Selections

Reading Selections

Reading and writing are mirror reflections of the thinking process.

A Reading Strategy for a Writer

As you read the nine selections included in this section, use the following reading strategy to make the connection between reading and writing. Read each selection three times. Read it once just to enjoy the writing. Then reread the piece to annotate it for understanding. Finally, read a third time to study the piece more closely to prepare for a written response. The following steps are a guide to how to get the most out of your reading.

Reading Like a Writer

Before Reading

Write a journal entry about the topic, title, and vocabulary. What do you already know, believe, or feel about the topic? Skim the text to identify new or difficult words and look them up.

During Reading

Annotate the text. Underline or highlight key terms, definitions, and main ideas. Generate questions to guide your thinking as you read; these questions will help you recall information after you read. Look for the answers to these questions and annotate the text when you come across the answers. Many college textbooks provide comprehension questions after a section of information. Feel free to use these after reading questions to focus your attention as you read.

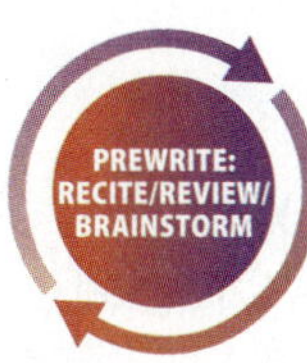

After Reading

Think, discuss, and write about what you read. Each of the reading selections has four discussion questions about the writer's main idea, relevant details, logical order, and effective expression. These directed thinking activities are called "After Reading Discussion Questions: Meaning, Structure, and Expression." Your writing will improve as you learn how other writers handle these elements.

Discuss It

Use your annotations to compare your views about a text with those of your classmates. Be open to ideas you had not considered. Add information to your notes. Discuss possible written responses.

Write About It

Respond in writing to the text. Each of the reading selections has two writing prompts under the heading "What Do You Think?" These writing prompts ask you to respond to the reading selection by composing your own piece of writing. Take the opportunity to model your writing on some of the techniques used by the writer of the reading selection. In addition, use the full writing process to draft, review, revise, and proofread your essay.

Nine Reading Selections

READING 1
Description

Snow
970L/6.0 GE/798 words

JOHN HAINES

John Haines (1924–2011), born in Norfolk, Virginia, spent more than twenty years homesteading in Alaska. He was also an award-winning author of more than ten collections of poetry and published a book of essays entitled *Fables and Distances: New and Selected Essays* (1996). The following essay is an excerpt from *The Stars, the Snow, the Fire: Twenty-five Years in the Northern Wilderness.*

Before Reading

Write a journal entry about your experience with the outdoors. Do you enjoy being outdoors? Why or why not? What is your favorite season?

Vocabulary

Before, during, and after reading the selection, annotate the text and write in your journal. Create a list of vocabulary words, along with their definitions. Give examples of their use from the selection you just read.

[1]To one who lives in the snow and watches it day by day, it is a book to be read. The pages turn as the wind blows; the characters shift and the images formed by their combinations change in meaning, but the language remains the same. It is a shadow language, spoken by things that have gone by and will come again. The same text has been written there for thousands of years, though I was not here, and will not be here in winters to come, to read it. These seemingly random ways, these paths, these beds, these footprints, these hard, round pellets in the snow: they all have meaning. Dark things may be written there, news of other lives, their sorties and excursions, their terrors and deaths. The tiny feet of a shrew or a vole make a brief, erratic pattern across the snow, and here is a hole down which the animal goes. And now the track of an ermine comes this way, swift and searching, and he too goes down that white-shadow of a hole.

[2]A wolverine, and the loping, toed-in track I followed uphill for two miles one spring morning, until it finally dropped away into another **watershed** and I gave up

following it. I wanted to see where he would go and what he would do. But he just went on, certain of where he was going, and nothing came of it for me to see but that sure and steady track in the snowcrust, and the sunlight strong in my eyes.

3Snow blows across the highway before me as I walk—little, wavering trails of it swept along like a people **dispersed**. The snow people—where are they going? Some great danger must pursue them. They hurry and fall, the wind gives them a push, they get up and go on again.

4I was walking home from Redmond Creek one morning late in January. On a divide between two watersheds I came upon the scene of a battle between a moose and three wolves. The story was written plainly in the snow at my feet. The wolves had come in from the west, following an old trail from the Salcha River, and had found the moose feeding in an open stretch of the overgrown road I was walking.

5The sign was fresh, it must have happened the night before. The snow was torn up, with chunks of frozen moss and broken sticks scattered about; here and there, swatches of moose hair. A confusion of tracks in the trampled snow—the splayed, stabbing feet of the moose, the big, furred pads and spread toenails of the wolves.

6I walked on, watching the snow. The moose was large and alone, almost certainly a bull. In one place he backed himself into a low, brush-hung bank to protect his rear. The wolves moved away from him—those moose feet are dangerous. The moose turned, ran on for fifty yards, and the fight began again. It became a running, broken flight that went on for nearly half a mile in the changing, rutted terrain, the red morning light coming across the hills from the sun low in the south. A pattern shifting and uncertain; the wolves relenting, running out into the brush in a wide circle, and closing again: another patch of moose hair in the trodden snow.

7I felt that I knew those wolves. I had seen their tracks several times before during that winter, and once they had taken a marten from one of my traps. I believed them to be a female and two nearly grown pups. If I was right, she may have been teaching them how to hunt, and all that turmoil in the snow may have been the serious play of things that must kill to live. But I saw no blood sign that morning, and the moose seemed to have gotten the better of the fight. At the end of it he plunged away into thick alder brush. I saw his tracks, moving more slowly now, as he climbed through a low saddle, going north in the shallow, unbroken snow. The three wolves trotted east toward Banner Creek.

8What might have been silence, an unwritten page, an absence, spoke to me as clearly as if I had been there to see it. I have imagined a man who might live as the coldest scholar on earth, who followed each clue in the snow, writing a book as he went. It would be the history of snow, the book of winter. A thousand-year text to be read by a people hunting these hills in a distant time. Who was here, and who has gone? What were their names? What did they kill and eat? Whom did they leave behind?

CONTINUED

Reading Comprehension Questions

Choose the best meaning of each word in *italics*. Use context clues to make your choice.

Vocabulary in Context

1. "A wolverine, and the loping, toed-in track I followed uphill for two miles one spring morning, until it finally dropped away into another *watershed*, and I gave up following it." (paragraph 2)

   a. crisis
   b. shack
   c. turning point
   d. a drainage area

Vocabulary in Context

2. "Snow blows across the highway before me as I walk—little, wavering trails of it swept along like a people *dispersed*." (paragraph 3)

   a. scattered
   b. gathered
   c. ignored
   d. disregarded

Central Idea

3. Which of the following sentences states the central idea of the passage?

   a. "To one who lives in the snow and watches it day by day, it is a book to be read." (paragraph 1)
   b. "On a divide between two watersheds I came upon the scene of a battle between a moose and three wolves." (paragraph 4)
   c. "I felt that I knew these wolves." (paragraph 7)
   d. "I have imagined a man who might live as the coldest scholar on earth, who followed each clue in the snow, writing a book as he went." (paragraph 8)

Supporting Details

4. After examining the moose's tracks in the snow, the author states that the moose was

   a. frightened.
   b. confused.
   c. strong.
   d. large.

Transitions

5. "The snow was torn up, with chunks of frozen moss and broken sticks scattered about; here and there, swatches of moose hair." (paragraph 5)

   The relationship of ideas **within** this sentence is

   a. cause and effect.
   b. time order.
   c. space order.
   d. generalization-example.

Patterns of Organization

 **6.** Overall, the author combines which two patterns of organization?

a. cause and effect
b. classification-example
c. comparison/contrast
d. space and time order

Fact and Opinion

 **7.** "The moose was large and alone, almost certainly a bull." (paragraph 6)

This sentence is a statement of

a. fact.
b. opinion.
c. fact and opinion.

Tone and Purpose

 **8.** The overall tone and purpose of the author is

a. to inform the reader about a fight between a moose and wolves in the snow.
b. to entertain the reader with information learned by studying the snow.
c. to persuade the reader to love the snow.

Inferences

 **9.** The details of the passage imply that signs or patterns in the snow

a. lead to different views of truth.
b. point the way out of the wilderness.
c. are evidence of events that occur in nature.
d. tell the story of mankind.

Argument

 **10.** The following items contain a claim and a list of supports for that claim. Which sentence states the claim?

a. "The story was written plainly in the snow at my feet." (paragraph 4)
b. "The wolves had come in from the west, following an old trail from Salcha River, and had found the moose feeding in an open stretch of the overgrown road I was walking." (paragraph 4)
c. "The snow was torn up, with chunks of frozen moss and broken sticks scattered about; here and there, swatches of moose hair." (paragraph 5)
d. "A confusion of tracks in the trampled snow—the splayed, stabbing feet of the moose, the big, furred pads and spread toenails of the wolves." (paragraph 5)

CONTINUED

Mapping

Complete the following story web with information from the passage. *Wording may vary.*

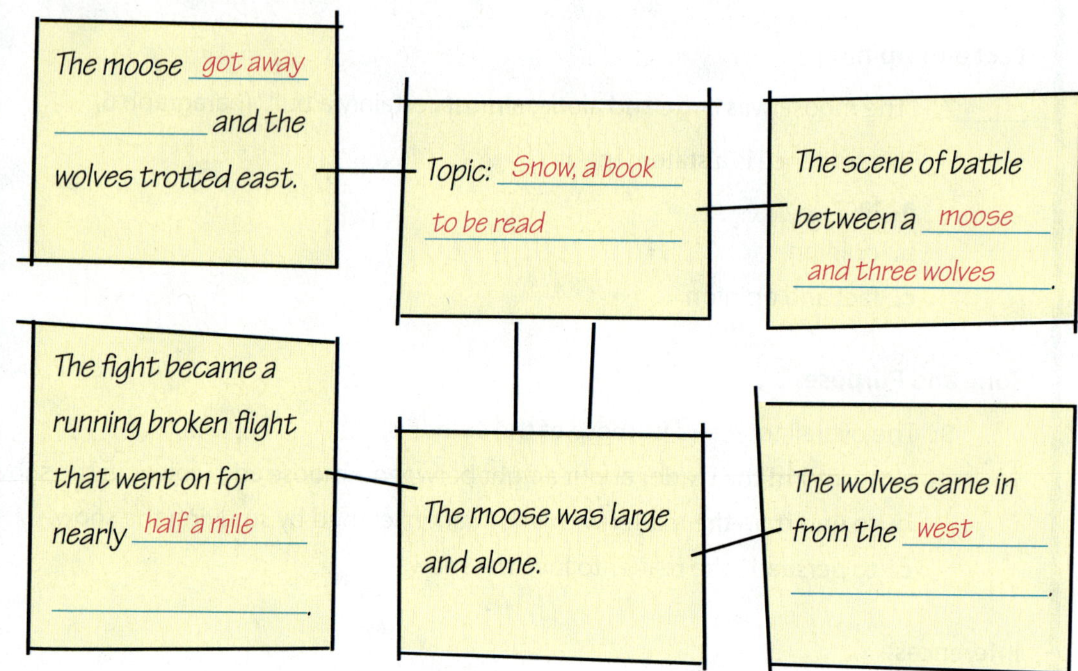

The moose got away and the wolves trotted east.
Topic: Snow, a book to be read
The scene of battle between a moose and three wolves.
The fight became a running broken flight that went on for nearly half a mile.
The moose was large and alone.
The wolves came in from the west.

After Reading Discussion Questions: Meaning, Structure, and Expression

1. **Main Idea:** Work as a group to write a summary that answers the following questions: What purpose did John Haines have for writing this essay? Who is his intended audience? What is the main idea of the essay?
2. **Relevant Details:** Haines states "To one who lives in the snow and watches it day by day, it is a book to be read." How does the incident with the moose support this point?
3. **Logical Order:** Paragraphs 1 through 3 and paragraph 8 focus on the snow, and paragraphs 4 through 7 tell about the wolves and the moose. Would the essay be just as effective if it began with the incident about the wolves and the moose and then made the point about snow? Why or why not?
4. **Effective Expression:** According to a *Washington Post Book World* review, "Haines is a poet who crafts each sentence piece by piece . . . slowly, carefully, each word examined meticulously for rightness before being slid into place." Identify three examples of Haines's use of words that you find particularly effective. Discuss the reasons for your selections.

What Do You Think?

1. Haines uses vivid sensory details in his descriptions of the snow, the wolves, and the moose to create strong visual images in his reader's mind. No doubt, he wrote what he had closely observed through experience. Use vivid sensory details to describe a place or event in nature that you have experienced. Choose details that make a point about the scene such as *nature soothes in times of trouble* or *nature teaches harsh lessons.*
2. Haines effectively describes the nature or temperament of the wolves and the moose based on their physical traits and behaviors. Write a description of a pet or animal that reveals its personality, temperament, or nature.

Effective Reading/Writing Scorecard

"Snow"

Skill	Number Correct	Points	Total
Vocabulary			
Vocabulary in Context (2 items)		x 5 =	
Comprehension			
Central Idea (1 item)		x 10 =	
Supporting Details (1 item)		x 10 =	
Transitions (1 item)		x 10 =	
Patterns of Organization (1 item)		x 10 =	
Fact and Opinion (1 item)		x 10 =	
Tone and Purpose (1 item)		x 10 =	
Inferences (1 item)		x 10 =	
Argument (1 item)		x 10 =	
Mapping (5 items)		x 2 =	
		Comprehension Score	

READING 2

Narration/Illustration

Latino Heritage Month: Who We Are . . . And Why We Celebrate?

1340L/13.6 GE/1125 words

LUIS J. RODRIGUEZ

Luis J. Rodriguez is the author of fourteen books of poetry, children's literature, fiction, and nonfiction, including the bestselling memoir, *Always Running: La Vida Loca, Gang Days in L.A.* He's cofounder of Tia Chucha's Centro Cultural and Bookstore, founder/editor of Tia Chucha Press, and cofounder of Barking Rooster Entertainment. His latest book is the sequel to *Always Running*, entitled *It Calls You Back: An Odyssey Through Love, Addiction, Revolutions, and Healing*. The following essay was posted online in *The Huffington Post*. In his essay, Rodriguez uses his own story to commemorate Latino Heritage Month.

Before Reading

Write a journal entry that responds to the question in Rodriguez's title: Who are Latinos? And why celebrate Latino Heritage Month?

Vocabulary

Before, during, and after reading the selection, annotate the text and write in your journal. Create a list of vocabulary words, along with their definitions. Give examples of their use from the selection you just read.

[1]I recently visited Orlando, Florida, home to more Puerto Ricans on the mainland other than New York City. I was there to spend time with my grandson Ricardo, who earlier this year graduated from high school with honors and is now into his first year of college. Ricardo is part of the Puerto Rican side of my family, wonderful law-abiding Christians, who worked hard and provided a loving home for my grandson when the world around him seemed bleak.

[2]For fifteen years, I lived in a mostly Puerto Rican community of Chicago, where Ricardo's mother grew up. Although I am Chicano, born on the Mexico-U.S. border, I've also lived among Mexican migrants, Central Americans, African Americans, Asians, Cuban Americans, and European Americans in Los Angeles, the San Francisco Bay Area, Miami, San Bernardino, and San Fernando. For years, I've spoken at and participated

in ceremonies in Native American reservations (a Navajo medicine man and his wife around ten years ago adopted my present wife). My other grandchildren are half German, half Scottish-Irish, and half Hungarian.

3My former wives and live-in girlfriends include a barrio-raised Chicana, an undocumented Mexican, a Mexican/Colombian, a poor white mother of two, and an African American. My own roots are with the **indigenous** Tarahumara (who call themselves Raramuri) of Chihuahua on my mother's side. My father—and you could see this on his face and in his hair—was native, Spanish, and African from the Mexican state of Guerrero.

4In fact, Ricardo's girlfriend is from Guyana, whose family was originally from India.

5To say the least, my extended family is complex and vibrant, made up of all skin colors, ethnicities, and languages . . . and as "American" as apple pie (or burritos, for that matter, since these were created on the U.S. side of that border).

6Purportedly I'm a Latino, although I rarely call myself this. I mean the original Latinos are Italians, right? Yet Italian Americans are not considered Latinos in this country. And so-called Latinos have origins in Native America, Africa, Europe, Asian, and a vast array of mixtures thereof. We are known as the largest "minority" group in the United States, yet we do not constitute one ethnic group or culture.

7Let me put it this way: Despite the umbrella of "Latino" above our heads, Puerto Ricans are not the same as Dominicans. And many Salvadorans I know don't want to be confused with being Mexican.

8Still, today we officially launch Latino **Heritage** Month, configured to run from September 15 to October 15, largely to coincide with the Independence Days of countries like Mexico, El Salvador, and others. Unofficially, of course, people who claim roots in Latino countries celebrate every day--they're also into the Fourth of July, Christmas, Martin Luther King Jr. Day, Hanukah, and Native American Sun Dance ceremonies. Regardless of their country of origin, these people are central to the American soul and deeply intertwined with the social fabric.

9Despite this Latinos seem to be a rumor in the country, a "middle people," neither black nor white, hardly in the popular culture, mostly shadows and shouts in the distance.

10Maybe what we celebrate is the complexities, the richness, the expansiveness of who we are. Maybe we celebrate that Latinos have bled and sweated for this country. Hundreds from the Dominican Republic, Colombia, Mexico, Ecuador, Argentina, and other Latin American countries died during the 9/11 attacks. People with Spanish or Portuguese surnames garnered more medals of honor during

CONTINUED

World War II and had a disproportionate number of casualties during the Vietnam War. The first known U.S. death from the Iraq War was a young man originally from Guatemala.

[11]Perhaps we celebrate that Latinos have worked in the auto plants of Detroit, steel mills of Chicago, cotton fields of Texas, textile centers of Massachusetts, and crop fields of California. That they are among the best in professional sports, and I'm not limiting this to soccer—they have been some of the world's best boxers, baseball players, football players, golfers, and tennis players.

[12]Let's celebrate that Latinos have been in the forefront of the organized labor movement and fought alongside African Americans against slavery and for Civil Rights. That they are among the oldest residents of the continent, as indigenous peoples from places like Mexico, Central America or Peru. And they are the majority of this country's most recent arrivals.

[13]Let's recognize that U.S. Latinos can be found among scientists, professors, doctors, politicians, and judges. That renowned actors, musicians, and writers include Carlos Santana, Ricky Martin, Jennifer Lopez, George Lopez, Danny Trejo, Celia Cruz, Oscar Hijuelos, Sandra Cisneros, Junot Diaz, Salma Hayek, Antonio Banderas, Los Lobos, Cheech Marin, Shakira, Javier Bardem, Penelope Cruz, Eva Mendes, and Bruno Mars.

[14]Our ancestors were former slaves and former slaveholders, peons and nobles, poets and conquistadors, African miners and native rebels. They include practitioners of the Flamenco and canto hondo with ties to the Roma people (so-called Gypsies) and the Arab/Muslim world, which once ruled Spain for close to 800 years. And so-called Latinos still use words, herbs, dance, and clothing from the wondrous civilizations of the Olmeca, Mexica (so-called Aztec), Maya, and Inca.

[15]The fact is Latino heritage is U.S. heritage. You wouldn't have such "American" phenomena as cowboys, guitars, rubber balls, gold mining, horses, corn, and even Jazz, Rock-and-Roll, and Hip Hop, without the contribution of Latinos. And besides the hundreds of Spanish words that now grace the English language (lariat, rodeo, buckaroo, adios, cafeteria, hasta la vista, baby), there are also indigenous words that English can't do without . . . chocolate, ocelot, coyote, tomato, avocado, maize, and barbecue, among others.

[16]Unfortunately, as we contemplate what Latino Heritage means, we have to be reminded that Latinos have been among the most scapegoated during the current financial crisis. States have established more laws against brown-skinned undocumented migrants while Arizona is trying to outlaw teachings on Mexican/Ethnic history and culture. They are also among the poorest, least healthy, and most neglected

Americans. Spanish-surnamed people are now the majority in the federal prison system and the largest single group in state penitentiaries of California, New Mexico, and Texas. And they are concentrated among this country's homeless and drug-addicted populations.

[17]So while all Americans have much to celebrate in Latino heritage, like most Americans we also have a long way to go.

[18]Whatever one thinks of Latinos, one thing is for sure: They have given much to this country, and have much more to give. I'm convinced any revolutionary changes in the economy, politics, technology, cultural life, social equity and justice must have Latinos (regardless of race, background, religion, social class, or political strain) at the heart of them. They are integral to the past, present, and future of this country.

[19]And this is a beautiful thing, baby.

Reading Comprehension Questions

Choose the best meaning of each word in *italics*. Use context clues to make your choice.

Vocabulary in Context

 **1.** "My own roots are with the *indigenous* Tarahumara (who call themselves Raramuri) of Chihuahua on my mother's side." (paragraph 3)

a. foreign
b. native
c. known
d. growing

Vocabulary in Context

 **2.** "Still, today we officially launch Latino *Heritage* Month . . ." (paragraph 8)

a. culture
b. admiration
c. wealth
d. revolution

CONTINUED

Central Idea

3. Which of the following sentences states the central idea of the passage?

a. "I recently visited Orlando, Florida, home to more Puerto Ricans on the mainland other than New York City." (paragraph 1)

b. "Still, today, we officially launch Latino Heritage Month, configured to run from September 15 to October 15, largely to coincide with the Independence Days of countries like Mexico, El Salvador, and others." (paragraph 8)

c. "Despite this Latinos seem to be a rumor in the country, a 'middle' people, hardly in the culture, mostly shadows and shouts in the distance." (paragraph 9)

d. "Whatever one thinks of Latinos, one thing is for sure: They have given much to this country, and have much more to give." (paragraph 18)

Supporting Details

4. In the article, the author asks, "the original Latinos are…?"

a. Native American.
b. Asian.
c. Italian.
d. Mexican.

Transitions

5. "For fifteen years, I lived in a mostly Puerto Rican community of Chicago, where Ricardo's mother grew up." (paragraph 2)

The relationship of ideas **within** this sentence is

a. cause and effect.
b. time order.
c. comparison/contrast.
d. generalization-example.

Patterns of Organization

6. The overall pattern of organization of the selection is

a. cause and effect.
b. time order.
c. comparison/contrast.
d. generalization-example.

Fact and Opinion

7. "The fact is Latino heritage is U.S. heritage." (paragraph 15)

This sentence is a statement of

a. fact.
b. opinion.
c. fact and opinion.

Tone and Purpose

c **8.** The overall tone and purpose of the author is

a. to inform the public about Latino Heritage Month.

b. to entertain the public with interesting details about the author's personal experiences as a Latino.

c. to persuade the public to celebrate Latino heritage.

Inferences

c **9.** Based on the details in this passage, we can infer that

a. everyone understands the significance of Latino heritage.

b. Latinos are a unified group.

c. many different ethnic groups are identified as Latino.

d. Latinos have only lived on this continent recently as this country's most recent arrivals.

Argument

d **10.** The following items from paragraph 16 contain a claim and a list of supports for that claim. Which sentence states the claim?

a. "States have established more laws against brown-skinned undocumented migrants while Arizona is trying to outlaw teachings on Mexican/Ethnic history and culture."

b. "They are also among the poorest, least healthy, and most neglected Americans."

c. "Spanish-surnamed people are now the majority in the federal prison system and the largest single group in state penitentiaries of California, New Mexico, and Texas."

d. "So while all Americans have much to celebrate in Latino heritages, like most Americans we also have a long way to go."

Summarizing

Complete the following summary with information from the passage. *Wording may vary.*

In his article "Latino Heritage Month: Who We Are . . . And Why We Celebrate?" Luis L. Rodriguez *first narrates his own background to show the* diversity *of Latino heritage. He then traces the Latino*

CONTINUED

contribution to this country as citizens, soldiers, workers, civil rights activists, artists, and athletes. Rodriguez also recognizes some of the challenges faced by Latinos in this country as undocumented immigrants, as the poor, as the majority in federal and California State prisons, as the homeless, and the drug addicted. No matter what people think of Latinos, he concludes, they are "integral to the past, present, and future of this country."

After Reading Questions: Meaning, Structure, and Expression

1. **Main Idea:** Work as a group to write a summary that answers the following questions: What purpose did Rodriguez have for writing this piece? Who is his intended audience? What is the main idea of the essay? What is the significance of the title of the piece?
2. **Relevant Details:** Reread the details in paragraphs 1 through 7. What is the significance of these details? How do these details relate to the main point Rodriguez is making? Would the essay be as effective if these details were deleted? Why or why not?
3. **Logical Order:** Rodriguez does not mention his topic "Latino Heritage Month" until paragraph 8, and then he doesn't state his central point until much later in the essay. Where in the essay does Rodriguez state his central point? Do you think the essay would be more effective if he had stated his topic and central point earlier? Why or why not?
4. **Effective Expression:** How would you describe the overall tone Rodriguez uses throughout his essay—admiring, critical, factual, proud, or some other attitude? Does his tone change at certain points? Identify and explain Rodriguez's tone. Support your explanation with examples from the essay.

What Do You Think?

1. In paragraph 13, Rodriguez recognizes several "renowned actors, musicians, and writers" who have made significant contributions to American culture. Assume one of these people will be a special guest speaker on your campus during Latino Heritage Month (choose a Latino listed in paragraph 13, or you may choose another Latino not mentioned). You have been asked to introduce this person to the audience. Write a brief biography that narrates the major contributions the special guest speaker has made to American culture.

2. "Latino Heritage Month: Who We Are . . . And Why We Celebrate?" relays Rodriguez's story of Latino heritage. By narrating his family's origin and the contributions of Latinos to American culture, he celebrates Latino heritage. Write a narrative that celebrates or honors your family or cultural heritage.

Effective Reading/Writing Scorecard

"Latino Heritage Month"

Skill	Number Correct	Points	Total
Vocabulary			
Vocabulary in Context (2 items)		x 5 =	
Comprehension			
Central Idea (1 item)		x 10 =	
Supporting Details (1 item)		x 10 =	
Transitions (1 item)		x 10 =	
Patterns of Organization (1 item)		x 10 =	
Fact and Opinion (1 item)		x 10 =	
Tone and Purpose (1 item)		x 10 =	
Inferences (1 item)		x 10 =	
Argument (1 item)		x 10 =	
Summarizing (5 items)		x 2 =	
		Comprehension Score	

READING 3
Process

Camping Out 1100L/7.0 GE/1504 words

ERNEST HEMINGWAY

Ernest Hemingway (1899–1961) was born in Oak Park, Illinois, and started his career as a writer in a newspaper office in Kansas City at the age of seventeen. He went on to win the Nobel Prize in Literature in 1954 "for his mastery of the art of narrative, most recently demonstrated in *The Old Man and the Sea*, and for the influence that he has exerted on contemporary style." Hemingway was an avid sportsman who wrote mainly about men who were soldiers, bullfighters, fishermen, and hunters. He created heroes of action who faced danger and tragedy stoically, without complaint, with "grace under pressure." The following article first appeared in the newspaper *Toronto Daily Star* in 1920.

Before Reading

Write a journal entry about an outdoor activity such as camping, hunting, fishing, or canoeing. If you do not like these types of activities, explain why. If you do like one or more of these outdoor activities, choose one and describe how you go about enjoying the experience. How do you prepare for the activity? What challenges do you face and how do you overcome them?

Vocabulary

Before, during, and after reading the selection, annotate the text and write in your journal. Create a list of vocabulary words, along with their definitions. Give examples of their use from the selection you just read.

1 Thousands of people will go into the bush this summer to cut the high cost of living. A man who gets his two weeks' salary while he is on vacation should be able to put those two weeks in fishing and camping and be able to save one week's salary clear. He ought to be able to sleep comfortably every night, to eat well every day and to return to the city rested and in good condition.

2 But if he goes into the woods with a frying pan, an ignorance of black flies and mosquitoes, and a great and abiding lack of knowledge about cookery, the chances are that his return will be very different. He will come back with enough mosquito bites to make the back of his neck look like a relief map of the Caucasus. His digestion will be wrecked after a valiant battle to **assimilate** half-cooked or charred grub. And he won't have had a decent night's sleep while he has been gone.

[3]He will solemnly raise his right hand and inform you that he has joined the grand army of never-agains. The call of the wild may be all right, but it's a dog's life. He's heard the call of the tame with both ears. Waiter, bring him an order of milk toast. In the first place he overlooked the insects. Black flies, no-see-ums, deer flies, gnats and mosquitoes were instituted by the devil to force people to live in cities where he could get at them better. If it weren't for them everybody would live in the bush and he would be out of work. It was a rather successful invention.

[4]But there are lots of dopes that will counteract the pests. The simplest perhaps is oil of citronella. Two bits' worth of this purchased at any pharmacist's will be enough to last for two weeks in the worst fly and mosquito-ridden country.

[5]Rub a little on the back of your neck, your forehead and your wrists before you start fishing, and the blacks and skeeters will shun you. The odor of citronella is not offensive to people. It smells like gun oil. But the bugs do hate it.

[6]Oil of pennyroyal and eucalyptol are also much hated by mosquitoes, and with citronella they form the basis for many proprietary preparations. But it is cheaper and better to buy the straight citronella. Put a little on the mosquito netting that covers the front of your pup tent or canoe tent at night, and you won't be bothered.

[7]To be really rested and get any benefit out of a vacation a man must get a good night's sleep every night. The first **requisite** for this is to have plenty of cover. It is twice as cold as you expect it will be in the bush four nights out of five, and a good plan is to take just double the bedding that you think you will need. An old quilt that you can wrap up in is as warm as two blankets.

[8]Nearly all outdoor writers rhapsodize over the browse bed. It is all right for the man who knows how to make one and has plenty of time. But in a succession of one-night camps on a canoe trip all you need is level ground for your tent floor and you will sleep all right if you have plenty of covers under you. Take twice as much cover as you think that you will need, and then put two-thirds of it under you. You will sleep warm and get your rest.

[9]When it is clear weather you don't need to pitch your tent if you are only stopping for the night. Drive four stakes at the head of your made-up bed and drape your mosquito bar over that, then you can sleep like a log and laugh at the mosquitoes.

[10]Outside of insects and bum sleeping the rock that wrecks most camping trips is cooking. The average tyro's idea of cooking is to fry everything and fry it good and plenty. Now, a frying pan is a most necessary thing to any trip, but you also need the old stew kettle and the folding reflector baker.

[11]A pan of fried trout can't be bettered and they don't cost any more than ever. But there is a good and bad way of frying them.

[12]The beginner puts his trout and his bacon in and over a brightly burning fire; the bacon curls up and dries into a dry tasteless cinder and the trout is burned outside while it is still raw inside. He eats them and it is all right if he is only out for the day and going home to a good meal at night. But if he is going to face more trout and bacon the next morning and other equally well-cooked dishes for the remainder of two weeks he is on the pathway to nervous dyspepsia.

CONTINUED

[13]The proper way is to cook over coals. Have several cans of Crisco or Cotosuet or one of the vegetable shortenings along that are as good as lard and excellent for all kinds of shortening. Put the bacon in and when it is about half cooked lay the trout in the hot grease, dipping them in corn meal first. Then put the bacon on top of the trout and it will baste them as it slowly cooks.

[14]The coffee can be boiling at the same time and in a smaller skillet pancakes being made that are satisfying the other campers while they are waiting for the trout.

[15]With the prepared pancake flours you take a cupful of pancake flour and add a cup of water. Mix the water and flour and as soon as the lumps are out it is ready for cooking. Have the skillet hot and keep it well greased. Drop the batter in and as soon as it is done on one side loosen it in the skillet and flip it over. Apple butter, syrup or cinnamon and sugar go well with the cakes.

[16]While the crowd have taken the edge from their appetites with flapjacks the trout have been cooked and they and the bacon are ready to serve. The trout are crisp outside and firm and pink inside and the bacon is well done—but not too done. If there is anything better than that combination the writer has yet to taste it in a lifetime devoted largely and studiously to eating.

[17]The stew kettle will cook your dried apricots when they have resumed their predried plumpness after a night of soaking, it will serve to concoct a mulligan in, and it will cook macaroni. When you are not using it, it should be boiling water for the dishes.

[18]In the baker, mere man comes into his own, for he can make a pie that to his bush appetite will have it all over the product that mother used to make, like a tent. Men have always believed that there was something mysterious and difficult about making a pie. Here is a great secret. There is nothing to it. We've been kidded for years. Any man of average office intelligence can make at least as good a pie as his wife.

[19]All there is to a pie is a cup and a half of flour, one-half teaspoonful of salt, one-half cup of lard and cold water. That will make pie crust that will bring tears of joy into your camping partner's eyes.

[20]Mix the salt with the flour, work the lard into the flour, make it up into a good workmanlike dough with cold water. Spread some flour on the back of a box or something flat, and pat the dough around a while. Then roll it out with whatever kind of round bottle you prefer. Put a little more lard on the surface of the sheet of dough and then slosh a little flour on and roll it up and then roll it out again with the bottle.

[21]Cut out a piece of the rolled out dough big enough to line a pie tin. I like the kind with holes in the bottom. Then put in your dried apples that have soaked all night and been sweetened, or your apricots, or your blueberries, and then take another sheet of the dough and drape it gracefully over the top, soldering it down at the edges with your fingers. Cut a couple of slits in the top dough sheet and prick it a few times with a fork in an artistic manner.

[22]Put it in the baker with a good slow fire for forty-five minutes and then take it out and if your pals are Frenchmen they will kiss you. The penalty for knowing how to cook is that the others will make you do all the cooking.

[23]It is all right to talk about roughing it in the woods. But the real woodsman is the man who can be really comfortable in the bush.

Hemingway, Ernest. "Camping Out." *Toronto Daily Star* on June 26, 1920.

Reading Comprehension Questions

Choose the best meaning of each word in *italics*. Use context clues to make your choice.

Vocabulary in Context

1. "His indigestion will be wrecked after a valiant battle to *assimilate* half-cooked or charred grub." (paragraph 2)
   - **a.** absorb
   - **b.** expel
   - **c.** understand
   - **d.** taste

Vocabulary in Context

2. "The first *requisite* for this is to have plenty of cover." (paragraph 7)
   - **a.** thought
   - **b.** option
   - **c.** condition
   - **d.** wish

Central Idea

3. Which of the following sentences states the central idea of the passage?
   - **a.** "Thousands of people will go into the bush this summer to cut the high cost of living." (paragraph 1)
   - **b.** "A man who gets his two week's salary while he is on vacation should be able to put those two weeks in fishing and camping and be able to save one week's salary clear." (paragraph 1)
   - **c.** "He ought to be able to sleep comfortably every night, to eat well every day, and to return to the city rested and in good condition." (paragraph 1)
   - **d.** "But the real woodsman is the man who can be really comfortable in the bush." (paragraph 23)

CONTINUED

READING SELECTION 3 *CONTINUED*

Supporting Details

 **4.** According to Hemingway, what is the simplest solution to counteract pests?

a. oil of citronella
b. oil of pennyroyal
c. lard
d. eucalyptol

Transitions

 **5.** "Drive four stakes at the head of your made-up bed and drape your mosquito bar over that, then you can sleep like a log and laugh at the mosquitoes." (paragraph 10)

The relationship of ideas **within** this sentence is

a. time order.
b. cause and effect.
c. comparison/contrast.
d. generalization-example.

Patterns of Organization

 **6.** The main pattern of organization Hemingway used is

a. cause and effect.
b. classification.
c. comparison/contrast.
d. time order.

Fact and Opinion

 **7.** Overall, to make his point, Hemingway uses

a. facts.
b. opinions.
c. facts and opinions.

Tone and Purpose

 **8.** The tone of paragraph 3 is

a. patient.
b. neutral.
c. admiring.
d. disgusted.

Inferences

b **9.** Based on the details in the passage, we can infer that Hemingway's main audience is

a. the general public.
b. men who want to be real woodsmen.
c. women who want to know how to camp out.
d. couples who like to camp out together.

Argument

 **10.** Which of the following sentences from paragraph 8 states a counterclaim?

a. "Nearly all outdoor writers rhapsodize over the browse bed."
b. "It is all right for the man who knows how to make one and has plenty of time."

c. "But in a succession of one-night camps on a canoe trip all you need is level ground for your tent floor and you will sleep all right if you have plenty of covers under you."

d. "You will sleep warm and get your rest."

Mapping

Complete the following flow chart with information from the passage. *Wording may vary.*

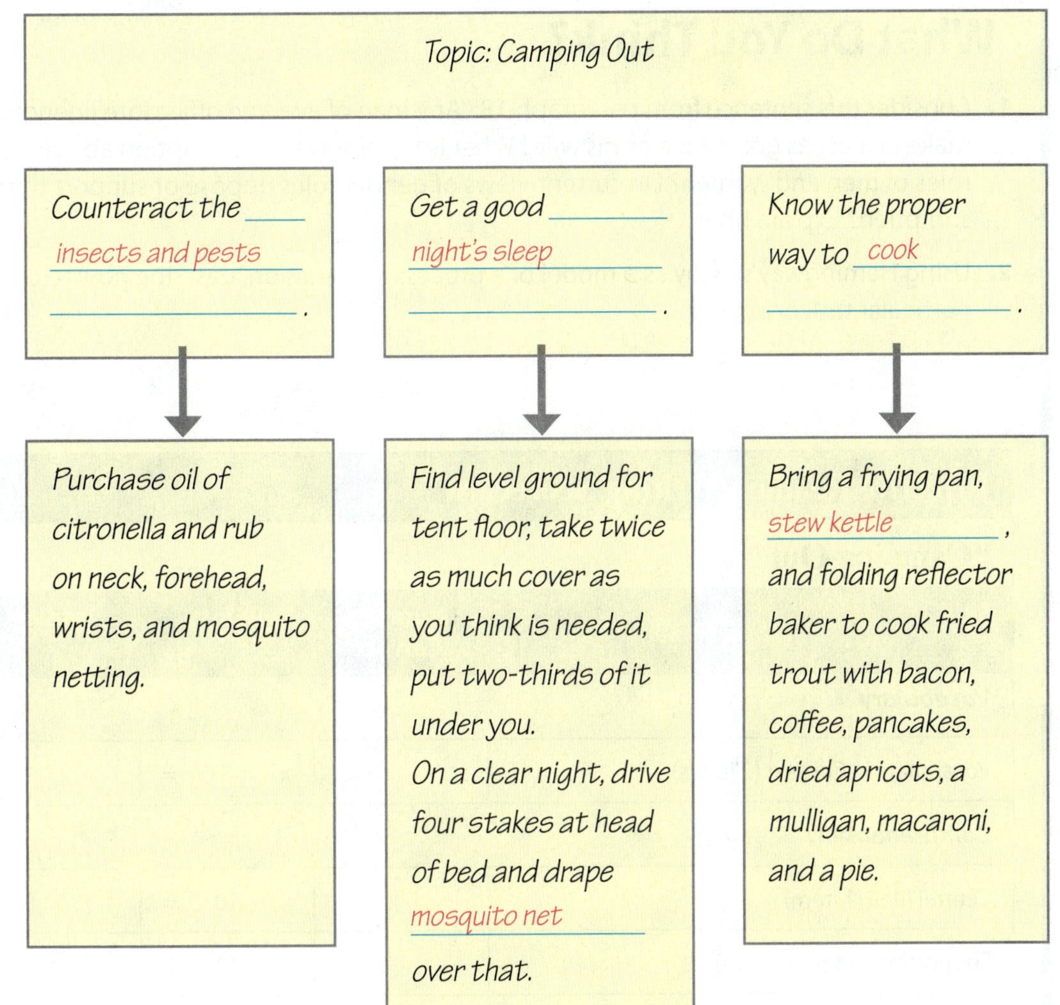

Topic: Camping Out
Counteract the insects and pests.
Get a good night's sleep.
Know the proper way to cook.
Purchase oil of citronella and rub on neck, forehead, wrists, and mosquito netting.
Find level ground for tent floor, take twice as much cover as you think is needed, put two-thirds of it under you. On a clear night, drive four stakes at head of bed and drape mosquito net over that.
Bring a frying pan, stew kettle, and folding reflector baker to cook fried trout with bacon, coffee, pancakes, dried apricots, a mulligan, macaroni, and a pie.

After Reading Questions: Meaning, Structure, and Expression

1. **Main Idea:** Work as a group to write a summary that answers the following questions: What purpose did Hemingway have for writing this piece? Who is the intended audience? What is the main idea of the essay? What is the significance of the title of the piece?

2. **Relevant Details:** Hemingway identifies three major ways to enjoy camping. What are his three methods to ensure an enjoyable camping experience? Do you agree that these three phases are the keys to being "really comfortable in the bush"? For example, reread paragraphs 17 through 22. Which phase of camping does this section discuss? Why does Hemingway spend so much time on this part of the camping process?

CONTINUED

3. **Logical Order:** The main organizational pattern for this essay is process—the steps to take to enjoy camping. However, paragraphs 1 and 2 contrast the unskilled and skilled camper. Why did Hemingway choose to begin his essay with this contrast? Is it effective or would the essay be more effective if it were left out? Explain your thinking.
4. **Effective Expression:** This essay is often praised for Hemingway's use of humor. Identify instances in the essay that are humorous. Explain why the examples you chose are amusing. Do you think this piece is as amusing today as it was in 1920? Why or why not?

What Do You Think?

1. Consider this sentence from paragraph 18: "Any man of average office intelligence can make at least as good a pie as his wife." What is Hemingway's assumption about the roles of men and women? Do current views of gender roles oppose or support this assumption? Explain how.
2. Using Hemingway's essay as a model of a process explanation, describe how to do a particular task or activity.

Effective Reading/Writing Scorecard

"Camping Out"

Skill	Number Correct	Points	Total
Vocabulary			
Vocabulary in Context (2 items)		x 5 =	
Comprehension			
Central Idea (1 item)		x 10 =	
Supporting Details (1 item)		x 10 =	
Transitions (1 item)		x 10 =	
Patterns of Organization (1 item)		x 10 =	
Fact and Opinion (1 item)		x 10 =	
Tone and Purpose (1 item)		x 10 =	
Inferences (1 item)		x 10 =	
Argument (1 item)		x 10 =	
Mapping (5 items)		x 2 =	
		Comprehension Score	

READING 4
Illustration

Don't Call Me a Hot Tamale 1240L/10.3 GE/1004 words

JUDITH ORTIZ COFER

Born in 1952 in Puerto Rico and raised in Paterson, New Jersey, Judith Ortiz Cofer is an acclaimed poet, novelist, and essayist. Her writings explore the experiences of being a minority as a Hispanic woman. She is currently the Regents' and Franklin Professor of English and Creative Writing at the University of Georgia.

Before Reading

Write a journal entry about your experiences with stereotypes. Have you ever been stereotyped? Describe the incident. What are some common stereotypes in our culture? How are these stereotypes harmful?

Vocabulary

Before, during, and after reading the selection, annotate the text and write in your journal. Create a list of vocabulary words, along with their definitions. Give examples of their use from the selection you just read.

[1]On a bus to London from Oxford University, where I was earning some graduate credits one summer, a young man, obviously fresh from a pub, approached my seat. With both hands over his heart, he went down on his knees in the aisle and broke into an Irish tenor's rendition of "Maria" from *West Side Story.* I was not amused. "Maria" had followed me to London, reminding me of a prime fact of my life: You can leave the island of Puerto Rico, master the English language, and travel as far as you can, but if you're a Latina, especially one who so clearly belongs to Rita Moreno's gene pool, the island travels with you.

[2]Growing up in New Jersey and wanting most of all to belong, I lived in two completely different worlds. My parents designed our life as a **microcosm** of their *casas* on the island—we spoke in Spanish, ate Puerto Rican food bought at the *bodega,* and practiced strict Catholicism complete with Sunday mass in Spanish.

[3]I was kept under tight surveillance by my parents, since my virtue and modesty were, by their cultural equation, the same as their honor. As teenagers, my friends and I were lectured constantly on how to behave as proper *señoritas.* But it was a conflicting message we received, since our Puerto Rican mothers also encouraged us to look and act like women by dressing us in clothes our Anglo schoolmates and their mothers found too "mature" and flashy. I often felt humiliated when I

CONTINUED

appeared at an American friend's birthday party wearing a dress more suitable for a semiformal. At Puerto Rican festivities, neither the music nor the colors we wore could be too loud.

[4]I remember Career Day in high school, when our teachers told us to come dressed as if for a job interview. That morning, I agonized in front of my closet, trying to figure out what a "career girl" would wear, because the only model I had was Marlo Thomas on TV. To me and my Puerto Rican girlfriends, dressing up meant wearing our mother's ornate jewelry and clothing.

[5]At school that day, the teachers assailed us for wearing "everything at once"—meaning too much jewelry and too many accessories. And it was painfully obvious that the other students in their tailored skirts and silk blouses thought we were hopeless and vulgar. The way they looked at us was a taste of the cultural clash that awaited us in the real world, where prospective employers and men on the street would often misinterpret our tight skirts and bright colors as a come-on.

[6]It is custom, not chromosomes, that leads us to choose scarlet over pale pink. Our mothers had grown up on a tropical island where the natural environment was a riot of primary colors, where showing your skin was one way to keep cool as well as to look sexy. On the island, women felt freer to dress and move provocatively since they were protected by the traditions and laws of a Spanish/Catholic system of morality and machismo, the main rule of which was: *You may look at my sister, but if you touch her I will kill you.* The extended family and church structure provided them with a circle of safety on the island; if a man "wronged" a girl, everyone would close in to save her family honor.

[7]Off-island, signals often get mixed. When a Puerto Rican girl who is dressed in her idea of what is attractive meets a man from the mainstream culture who has been trained to react to certain types of clothing as a sexual signal, a clash is likely to take place. She is seen as a Hot Tamale, a sexual firebrand. I learned this lesson at my first formal dance when my date leaned over and painfully planted a sloppy, overeager kiss on my mouth. When I didn't respond with sufficient passion, he said in a resentful tone: "I thought you Latin girls were supposed to mature early." It was only the first time I would feel like a fruit or vegetable—I was supposed to *ripen,* not just grow into womanhood like other girls.

[8]These stereotypes, though rarer, still surface in my life. I recently stayed at a classy metropolitan hotel. After having dinner with a friend, I was returning to my room when a middle-aged man in a tuxedo stepped directly into my path. With his champagne glass extended toward me, he exclaimed, "Evita!"

[9]Blocking my way, he bellowed the song "Don't Cry for Me, Argentina." Playing to the gathering crowd, he began to sing loudly a ditty to the tune of "La Bamba"—except the lyrics were about a girl named Maria whose exploits all rhymed with her name and gonorrhea.

[10]I knew that this same man—probably a corporate executive, even worldly by most standards—would never have **regaled** a white woman with a dirty song in public. But to him, I was just a character in his universe of "others," all cartoons.

[11]Still, I am one of the lucky ones. There are thousands of Latinas without the privilege of the education that my parents gave me. For them every day is a struggle

against the misconceptions perpetuated by the myth of the Latina as whore, domestic worker or criminal.

[12]Rather than fight these pervasive stereotypes, I try to replace them with a more interesting set of realities. I travel around the U.S. reading from my books of poetry and my novel. With the stories I tell, the dreams and fears I examine in my work, I try to get my audience past the particulars of my skin color, my accent or my clothes.

[13]I once wrote a poem in which I called Latinas "God's brown daughters." It is really a prayer, of sorts, for communication and respect. In it, Latin women pray "in Spanish to an Anglo God / with a Jewish heritage," and they are "fervently hoping / that if not omnipotent, / at least He be bilingual."

Reading Comprehension Questions

Choose the best meaning of each word in *italics*. Use context clues to make your choice.

Vocabulary in Context

1. "My parents designed our lives as a *microcosm* of their casas on the island—we spoke in Spanish, ate Puerto Rican food bought at the bodega, and practiced strict Catholicism complete with Sunday mass in Spanish." (paragraph 2)

a. large copy
b. small copy
c. society
d. memory

Vocabulary in Context

2. "I knew that this same man—probably a corporate executive, even worldly by most standards—would never have *regaled* a white woman with a dirty song in public." (paragraph 10)

a. bored
b. complimented
c. trapped
d. entertained

Implied Central Idea

3. Which of the following sentences states the implied central idea of the passage?

a. The author became a writer to overcome the prejudice she faced as a Latina.
b. Latinas live in two completely different worlds.
c. Many Latinas struggle against misconceptions based on negative stereotypes.
d. Puerto Rican girls receive conflicting messages from their mothers.

CONTINUED

Supporting Details

4. The author uses "Maria," "Rita Moreno's gene pool," and "Evita" as details that illustrate

a. successful women.

b. stereotypes of Latino women.

c. female Latino entertainers.

d. beautiful women.

Transitions

5. "The extended family and church structure provided them with a circle of safety on the island: if a man 'wronged' a girl, everyone would close in to save her family honor." (paragraph 6)

The relationship of ideas **within** this sentence is

a. cause and effect.

b. time order.

c. comparison/contrast.

d. generalization-example.

Patterns of Organization

6. The overall pattern of organization used by the author is

a. cause and effect.

b. space order.

c. comparison/contrast.

d. generalization-example.

Fact and Opinion

7. "She is seen as a Hot Tamale, a sexual firebrand." (paragraph 7)

This sentence is a statement of

a. fact.

b. opinion.

c. fact and opinion.

Tone and Purpose

8. The overall tone and purpose of the author is

a. to inform the public by raising awareness about the stereotypes Latinas struggle against in mainstream America.

b. to entertain the public with interesting details about the author's personal experiences as a Latina in America.

c. to persuade the public to fight the stereotypes of Latinas that pervade America.

Inferences

9. Based on the details in the passage, many of the mainstream stereotypes of Latinas are based on

a. skin color.

b. religion.

c. dress.

d. language.

Argument

a **10.** The following items contain a claim and a list of supports for that claim from paragraph 6. Which sentence states the claim?

a. "It is custom, not chromosomes, that leads us to choose scarlet over pale pink."

b. "Our mothers had grown up on a tropical island where the natural environment was a riot of primary colors, where showing your skin was one way to keep cool as well as to look sexy."

c. "On the island, women felt freer to dress and move provocatively since they were protected by the traditions and laws of a Spanish/Catholic system of morality and machismo, the main rule of which was: You may look at my sister, but if you touch her I will kill you."

d. "The extended family and church structure provided them with a circle of safety on the island; if a man 'wronged' a girl, everyone would close in to save her family honor."

Outlining

Complete the following outline with information from the passage. *Wording may vary.*

Don't Call Me a Hot Tamale

I. During graduate school, the "Maria" incident

II. Growing up in New Jersey

A. Living in two different worlds

B. Life as a microcosm of casas on the island

C. Career Day in high school

III. It is custom, not chromosomes

IV. Off-island, mixed signals

V. Recently, the "Evita" incident

VI. Replacing stereotypes with more interesting realities

CONTINUED

After Reading Discussion Questions: Meaning, Structure, and Expression

1. **Main Idea:** Work as a group to write a summary that answers the following questions: What purpose did Judith Ortiz Cofer have for writing this essay? Who is her intended audience? What is the main idea of the essay? What is the significance of the title?
2. **Relevant Details:** Cofer relies mostly on personal experience to make her point about stereotypes based on race or gender. Does she provide enough details to make her point convincingly? Would the use of facts or expert opinions strengthen her point? Why or why not?
3. **Logical Order:** Cofer opens her essay with an example from her personal life. Is this an effective opening for the essay? Why or why not? Compare the introduction of the essay to the conclusion. How does the conclusion relate to the introduction? Is this an effective conclusion? Why or why not? What other ways could Cofer have opened or closed her essay?
4. **Effective Expression:** Based on Judith Ortiz Cofer's choice of words, how would you describe the tone of this essay? Is it angry, embarrassed, disappointed, confrontational, or candid, or does it communicate some other attitude about stereotypes? Identify three expressions that illustrate the tone of the piece. Explain the reasons for your selections.

What Do You Think?

1. Cofer makes a connection between culture and fashion. According to her description, Hispanic fashion for women is "flashy," "mature," and "sexy" with "ornate jewelry" and "tight skirts and bright colors." Write an essay in which you illustrate how fashion represents a particular culture. For example, illustrate fashion in the Hip-Hop culture.
2. Cofer's essay illustrates the stereotypes she faces as a Hispanic woman. Identify and describe a stereotype that you or someone you know has encountered. For example, what are some stereotypes that elderly people face?

Effective Reading/Writing Scorecard			
"Don't Call Me a Hot Tamale"			
Skill	**Number Correct**	**Points**	**Total**
Vocabulary			
Vocabulary in Context (2 items)		x 5 =	
Comprehension			
Implied Central Idea (1 item)		x 10 =	
Supporting Details (1 item)		x 10 =	
Transitions (1 item)		x 10 =	
Patterns of Organization (1 item)		x 10 =	
Fact and Opinion (1 item)		x 10 =	
Tone and Purpose (1 item)		x 10 =	
Inferences (1 item)		x 10 =	
Argument (1 item)		x 10 =	
Outlining (5 items)		x 2 =	
		Comprehension Score	

READING 5

Example

Football's Bloodiest Secret

1260L/9.9 GE/1417 words

BUZZ BISSINGER

H. G. "Buzz" Bissinger is among the nation's most honored and distinguished writers. A native of New York City, Bissinger is the winner of the Pulitzer Prize, the Livingston Award, the American Bar Association Silver Gavel Award, and the National Headliners Award, among others. He is the author of three highly acclaimed nonfiction books: *Friday Night Lights, A Prayer for the City*, and *Three Nights in August*. Bissinger's short nonfiction pieces have appeared in a number of top U.S. magazines, including *Vanity Fair, Sports Illustrated*, and *The New York Times Magazine*. The following article was first posted in *The Daily Beast,* an online news site.

CONTINUED

Before Reading

Write a journal entry about sports in America. Do you think sports such as hockey, football, and basketball are too violent? Why or why not?

Vocabulary

Before, during, and after reading the selection, annotate the text and write in your journal. Create a list of vocabulary words, along with their definitions. Give examples of their use from the selection you just read.

[1]Many miles have passed in my life since I did the research for *Friday Night Lights* 21 years ago. At a certain point, an author should simply forget and move on. But the book continues to sell and the television show of the same name premiered its fourth season this week on DirecTV. The power of what I saw and what I heard still gets to me, and of all the interviews I did, the one that lingers the most took place in the living room of my rented ranch house in the dusty isolation of Odessa, Texas.

[2]The man I interviewed was named Brad Allen. He was the former head of the high school booster club I was writing about, and I wanted to get some observations on why high school football had become so dominant in the culture of Odessa. I thought he would refer to the usual pop-psychology suspects—the town's hermetic location in West Texas, the lack of anything substantive to do except work and drink, the paucity of good strip clubs, the boom-and-bust cycle of the oil field economy where nothing was ever certain.

[3]Today at the age of 21, one player lives with his parents, spends most of his time in a wheelchair, and struggles with short-term memory.

[4]The conversation started that way. But then it veered toward the experience of his own son, Phillip. Allen was the first to admit that Phillip was not a gifted athlete, but what he lacked in skill he made up for in toughness. To prove the point, Allen told the story of when Phillip broke his arm at the beginning of a high school football game. Rather than come out, Phillip continued to play. It was only at half time, when his arm had swelled so badly that his forearm pads had to be cut off of his body, that he reluctantly went to the hospital.

[5]Allen said he was not proud of the incident, but he told the story freely. What it signified was obvious: the **machismo** inherent to youth sports that parents crave. Football. Soccer. Baseball. Basketball. Hockey. The sport doesn't matter. The gender doesn't matter. What matters most is the vicarious thrill dad and mom get from their sons and daughters showing fearlessness and the absorption of agony in a tradition linking back to the

war heroes of Sparta. No amount of studies and medical warnings are going to fully extinguish the attitude that playing hurt is all part of the price.

6Yesterday, the House Judiciary Committee began hearings on the issue of brain injuries suffered in pro football. It followed a recent study commissioned by the National Football League showing that memory-related diseases have ostensibly occurred in pro players at a rate far exceeding that of the national population—19 times the normal rate for men ages 30 to 49. It was only through the superb work of *New York Times* reporter Alan Schwarz that the issue rose to the forefront at all. And almost as soon as the study was released, NFL officials tried to discredit it as inaccurate.

7Mark Hyman, an expert on injuries in youth sports, feels that any awareness of the problem, regardless of the NFL's utterly self-protective stance, is a good thing. Because of the intense public pressure, there is the real possibility of changes not simply at the pro level, but all the way down the line to high school and pre-high school sports. But if past history is prologue, which it usually is (see successful conquests of Afghanistan) the changes will still be at the edges. The macho culture of sports is just too deeply embedded to be fully eradicated.

8In his book *Until it Hurts*, Hyman points out that 3.5 million children under the age of 15 needed medical treatment for sport injuries each year, nearly half of which were the result of simple overuse. "Over the last 75 years, adults have staged a hostile takeover of kids' sports," he wrote. "The quest to turn children into tomorrow's superstar athletes has often led adults to push them beyond physical and emotional limits." Backs go out and young athletes continue to compete until somebody finally realizes that the ailment isn't some strain but a herniated disk and a stress fracture. High school football players have gotten concussions, been declared ready to play the following week, then suffered a far more serious second concussion.

9In Odessa, a player once lost a testicle after no one bothered to thoroughly examine a groin injury he had received. It wasn't until the testicle swelled to the size of a grapefruit that he went to the emergency room. By then it was too late—the testicle had to be removed. In another instance during the Texas high school football playoffs, where all sanity goes on **hiatus**, an Odessa player was already suffering from a painful hip. Since he was a star going both ways, the answer was to inject him with painkillers before the game and at halftime. A hole developed, which had actually been caused by a breaking of a band of cartilage at the front of his hip joint. It had also become infected, and the player after the season had to go the hospital for six months for treatments, including scraping out the infected tissue and iodine baths.

CONTINUED

10"We go insane worrying if our kids pedal down the driveway on their bikes without a helmet," says Hyman, but then allow them to clobber each other on the field until they're seriously hurt. The NFL has actually worked to build a better protective helmet. But the pace of innovation is still too slow, according to Hyman, because looking sleek and assassin-like is more important than staving off a head injury. In hockey, former NHL great Mark Messier teamed up with a sports-equipment maker to create a helmet that cuts down on blows to the brain by 26 percent, says Hyman. The number of NHL players who are using it this season? Eight—because they don't like the shape. Were substantial changes being made at the pro level, they would probably trickle down to college, high school, and youth teams. But they're not, even though 10 to 20 percent of teen hockey players suffer a concussion each year.

11Young athletes are far more vulnerable to head injuries than older ones. Just ask Cody Lehe, who in the typical tradition of football suffered a concussion in a helmet-to-helmet hit during a game. He complained of headaches the following week, but he was able return to practice on the basis of a brain scan. He suddenly collapsed the next game after a relatively mild hit to the helmet. He suffered what doctors described as a "second-impact concussion," according to a story by Dann Denny of the *Herald-Times* of Bloomington, Indiana. Lehe's second concussion took place before the symptoms of the first one had subsided, and his brain swelled rapidly. He was in a coma for three weeks. Today at the age of 21, he lives with his parents, spends most of his time in a wheelchair, and struggles with short-term memory.

12Youth sports will continue to be the most vulnerable—Pop Warner football leagues, travelling soccer and basketball leagues. None of these teams routinely have a doctor or a professional trainer as part of the staff. It is a coach who will generally make the call, and don't be fooled: these coaches, woefully inexperienced, still want to win every bit as badly as their brethren in the high school, college, and pro ranks. Which means if an injury occurs, the seriousness of which cannot be immediately gauged, the coach will tell the player to shrug it off and stop being a pussy. He will undoubtedly invoke some idiotic Knute Rockne aphorism—"When the going gets tough, the tough get going!"—and parents will be right behind them, pulling their sons and daughters back into the game and implying they are weaklings if they complain. Serious injuries will continue to go undiscovered, and even when they are, too many kids will be pushed to return too soon. Some of these injuries will be excruciatingly painful down the road, some of them will be so debilitating as to ruin careers, and a few of them will even be fatal.

[13]Because that's what too many sports are in America, whatever the age level—violent, dedicated solely to winning regardless of risk, and irresponsibly dangerous. Which is just the way we like it.

Reading Comprehension Questions

Choose the best meaning of each word in *italics*. Use context clues to make your choice.

Vocabulary in Context

1. "What it signified was obvious: the *machismo* inherent to youth sports that parents crave." (paragraph 5)

a. caution
b. manliness
c. maturity
d. humility

Vocabulary in Context

2. "In another instance during the Texas high school football playoffs, where all sanity goes on *hiatus*, an Odessa player was already suffering from a painful hip." (paragraph 9)

a. break
b. without stopping
c. in order
d. show

Central Idea

3. Which of the following sentences states the central idea of the passage?

a. "The power of what I saw and what I heard still gets to me, and of all the interviews I did, the one that lingers the most took place in the living room of my rented ranch house in the dusty isolation of Odessa, Texas." (paragraph 1)
b. "The sport doesn't matter." (paragraph 5)
c. "The macho culture of sports is just too deeply embedded to be fully eradicated." (paragraph 7)
d. "Youth sports will continue to be the most vulnerable—Pop Warner football leagues, travelling soccer and basketball leagues." (paragraph 12)

CONTINUED

Supporting Details

 **4.** According to the passage, Brad Allen is

a. an injured player confined to a wheelchair and struggling with short-term memory.

b. the former head of the high school booster club in Odessa, Texas.

c. an expert on injuries in youth sports and author of the book *Until it Hurts*.

d. a *New York Times* reporter.

Transitions

 **5.** "Young athletes are far more vulnerable to head injuries than older ones. Just ask Cody Lehe, who in the typical tradition of football suffered a concussion in a helmet-to-helmet hit during a game." (paragraph 11)

The relationship of ideas **between** these sentences is

a. cause and effect.

b. time order.

c. comparison/contrast.

d. generalization-example.

Patterns of Organization

 **6.** The overall pattern of organization used by the author is

a. cause and effect.

b. classification.

c. comparison/contrast.

d. generalization-example.

Fact and Opinion

 **7.** "What matters most is the vicarious thrill dad and mom get from their sons and daughters showing fearlessness and the absorption of agony in a tradition linking back to the war heroes of Sparta." (paragraph 5)

This sentence is a statement of

a. fact.

b. opinion.

c. fact and opinion.

Tone and Purpose

 **8.** The overall tone and purpose of the author is

a. to inform the public about the violent culture and dangers of youth sports.

b. to entertain the public with vivid details about violence in youth sports.

c. to persuade the public to change the violent culture of youth sports.

Inferences

 **9.** Based on the details in essay, we can infer that

a. the parents of players are concerned about dangers of youth sports.

b. only males are vulnerable to the dangers of youth sports.

c. youth sports teams should have a doctor or professional trainer as part of the staff.

d. most youth who play sports suffer severe injuries.

Argument

c **10.** Which of the following sentences from paragraph 7 states a counterclaim?

a. "Mark Hyman, an expert on injuries in youth sports, feels that any awareness of the problem, regardless of the NFL's utterly self-protective stance, is a good thing."

b. "Because of the intense public pressure, there is the real possibility of changes not simply at the pro level, but all the way down the line to high school and pre-high school sports."

c. "But if past history is prologue, which it usually is (see successful conquests of Afghanistan) the changes will still be at the edges."

Outlining

Complete the following outline with information from the passage. *Wording may vary.*

Football's Bloodiest Secret

I. The interview with Brad Allen in Odessa, Texas

II. The macho culture of sports

A. The study commissioned by the National Football League

B. Mark Hyman, an expert on injuries in youth sports and author of Until it Hurts

III. Illustrations of players injured in youth sports in Odessa, Texas

IV. The slow pace of innovation in sports safety

V. The vulnerability of young athletes and youth sport

After Reading Questions: Meaning, Structure, and Expression

1. **Main Idea:** Work as a group to write a summary that answers the following questions: What purpose did Bissinger have for writing this piece? Who is the intended audience? What is the main idea of the essay? What is the significance of the title of the piece?

CONTINUED

2. **Relevant Details:** Some of the details in this essay are very graphic, such as the illustration given in paragraph 9. Why did Bissinger include this disturbing example? Do you think the essay would be more or less effective if these details were left out? Explain your thinking.
3. **Logical Order:** Paragraphs 3 and 11 refer to the experiences of Cody Lehe. Why did Bissinger wait until paragraph 11 to tell Lehe's full story?
4. **Effective Expression:** Based on Bissinger's choice of words, would you describe the main tone of this essay as objective, sarcastic, or alarmed? Give and explain examples to support your thoughts about the essay's tone.

What Do You Think?

1. Reread the last paragraph in the essay. Write a response to Bissinger that agrees or disagrees with his concluding view. Assume you will post your response on the *Daily Beast* comments.
2. Assume you are the parent or coach of a football player. Write an essay that takes a stand for or against the violence in the game. Suggest an action that should be taken to preserve the game as it is or change it to make it less violent.

Effective Reading/Writing Scorecard

"Football's Bloodiest Secret"

Skill	Number Correct	Points	Total
Vocabulary			
Vocabulary in Context (2 items)		x 5 =	
Comprehension			
Central Idea (1 item)		x 10 =	
Supporting Details (1 item)		x 10 =	
Transitions (1 item)		x 10 =	
Patterns of Organization (1 item)		x 10 =	
Fact and Opinion (1 item)		x 10 =	
Tone and Purpose (1 item)		x 10 =	
Inferences (1 item)		x 10 =	
Argument (1 item)		x 10 =	
Outlining (5 items)		x 2 =	
		Comprehension Score	

READING 6

Comparison/Contrast

The Talk of the Sandbox; How Johnny and Suzy's Playground Chatter Prepares Them for Life at the Office 1010L/12.0 GE/1996 words

DEBORAH TANNEN

Deborah Tannen is best known as the author of *You Just Don't Understand*, which was on the *New York Times* bestseller list for nearly four years, including eight months as #1, and has been translated into 30 languages. Professor Tannen serves on the linguistics department faculty at Georgetown University. She has published twenty-one books and over 100 articles, and is the recipient of five honorary doctorates. The following article first appeared in the "Outlook" section of the *Washington Post.*

Before Reading

Write a journal entry about the differences between men and women. For example, do men and women differ in the ways they fight, apologize, compete, or learn? How so?

Vocabulary

Before, during, and after reading the selection, annotate the text and write in your journal. Create a list of vocabulary words, along with their definitions. Give examples of their use from the selection you just read.

1Bob Hoover of the Pittsburgh *Post-Gazette* was interviewing me when he remarked that after years of coaching boys' softball teams, he was now coaching girls and they were very different. I immediately whipped out my yellow pad and began interviewing him—and discovered that his observations about how girls and boys play softball parallel mine about how women and men talk at work.

2Hoover told me that boys' teams always had one or two stars whom the other boys treated with deference. So when he started coaching a girls' team, he began by looking for the leader. He couldn't find one. "The girls who are better athletes don't lord it over the others," he said. "You get the feeling that everyone's the same." When a girl got the ball, she didn't try to throw it all the way home as a strong-armed boy would; instead, she'd throw it to another team member, so they all became better catchers and throwers. He went on, "If a girl makes an error, she's not in the doghouse for a long time, as a boy would be."

CONTINUED

[3]"But wait," I interrupted. "I've heard that when girls make a mistake at sports, they often say 'I'm sorry,' whereas boys don't."

[4]That's true, he said, but then the girl forgets it—and so do her teammates. "For boys, sports is a performance art. They're concerned with how they look." When they make an error, they sulk because they've let their teammates down. Girls want to win, but if they lose, they're still all in it together—so the mistake isn't as dreadful for the individual or the team.

[5]What Hoover described in these youngsters were the seeds of behavior I have observed among women and men at work.

[6]The girls who are the best athletes don't "lord it over" the others—just the ethic I found among women in positions of authority. Women managers frequently told me they were good managers because they did not act in an **authoritarian** manner. They said they did not flaunt their power, or behave as though they were better than their subordinates. Similarly, linguist Elisabeth Kuhn found that women professors in her study informed students of course requirements as if they had magically appeared on the syllabus ("There are two papers. The first paper, ah, let's see, is due. . . . It's back here [referring to the syllabus] at the beginning"), whereas the men professors made it clear that they had set the requirements ("I have two midterms and a final").

[7]A woman manager might say to her secretary, "Could you do me a favor and type this letter right away?" knowing that her secretary is going to type the letter. But her male boss, on hearing this, might conclude she doesn't feel she deserves the authority she has, just as a boys' coach might think the star athlete doesn't realize how good he is if he doesn't expect his teammates to treat him with deference.

[8]I was especially delighted by Hoover's observation that, although girls are more likely to say, "I'm sorry," they are actually far less sorry when they make a mistake than boys who don't say it, but are "in the doghouse" for a long time. This dramatizes the ritual nature of many women's apologies. How often is a woman who is "always apologizing" seen as weak and lacking in confidence? In fact, for many women, saying "I'm sorry" often doesn't mean "I apologize." It means "I'm sorry that happened."

[9]Like many of the rituals common among women, it's a way of speaking that takes into account the other person's point of view. It can even be an automatic conversational smoother. For example, you left your pad in someone's office; you knock on the door and say, "Excuse me, I left my pad on your desk," and the person whose office it is might reply, "Oh, I'm sorry. Here it is." She knows it is not her fault that you left your pad on her desk; she's just letting you know it's okay.

[10]Finally, I was intrigued by Hoover's remark that boys regard sports as "a performance art" and worry about "how they look." There, perhaps, is the rub, the key to why so many women feel they don't get credit for what they do. From childhood, many boys learn something that is very adaptive to the workplace: Raises and promotions are based on "performance" evaluations and these depend, in large measure, on how you appear in other people's eyes. In other words, you have to worry not only about getting your job done but also about getting credit for what you do.

[11]Getting credit often depends on the way you talk. For example, a woman told me she was given a poor evaluation because her supervisor felt she knew less than her male peers. Her boss, it turned out, reached this conclusion because the woman

asked more questions: She was seeking information without regard to how her queries would make her look.

[12]The same principle applies to apologizing. Whereas some women seem to be taking undeserved blame by saying "I'm sorry," some men seem to evade deserved blame. I observed this when a man disconnected a conference call by accidentally elbowing the speaker-phone. When his secretary re-connected the call, I expected him to say, "I'm sorry; I knocked the phone by mistake." Instead he said, "Hey, what happened?! One minute you were there, the next minute you were gone!" Annoying as this might be, there are certainly instances in which people improve their fortunes by covering up mistakes. If Hoover's observations about girls' and boys' athletic styles are fascinating, it is even more revealing to see actual transcripts of children at play and how they mirror the adult workplace. Amy Sheldon, a linguist at the University of Minnesota who studies children talking at play in a day care center, compared the conflicts of pre-school girls and boys. She found that boys who fought with one another tended to pursue their own goal. Girls tended to balance their own interests with those of the other girls through complex verbal negotiations.

[13]Look how different the negotiations were:

[14]Two boys fought over a toy telephone: Tony had it; Charlie wanted it. Tony was sitting on a foam chair with the base of the phone in his lap and the receiver lying beside him. Charlie picked up the receiver, and Tony protested, "No, that's my phone!" He grabbed the telephone cord and tried to pull the receiver away from Charlie, saying, "No, that—uh, it's on MY couch. It's on MY couch, Charlie. It's on MY couch. It's on MY couch." It seems he had only one point to make, so he made it repeatedly as he used physical force to get the phone back.

[15]Charlie ignored Tony and held onto the receiver. Tony then got off the couch, set the phone base on the floor and tried to keep possession of it by overturning the chair on top of it. Charlie managed to push the chair off, get the telephone and win the fight.

[16]This might seem like a typical kids' fight until you compare it with a fight Sheldon videotaped among girls. Here the contested objects were toy medical instruments: Elaine had them; Arlene wanted them. But she didn't just grab for them; she argued her case. Elaine, in turn, balanced her own desire to keep them with Arlene's desire to get them. Elaine lost ground gradually, by compromising.

[17]Arlene began not by grabbing but by asking and giving a reason: "Can I have that, that thing? I'm going to take my baby's temperature." Elaine was agreeable, but cautious: "You can use it—you can use my temperature. Just make sure you can't use anything else unless you can ask." Arlene did just that; she asked for the toy syringe: "May I?" Elaine at first resisted, but gave a reason: "No, I'm gonna need to use the shot in a couple of minutes." Arlene reached for the syringe anyway, explaining in a "beseeching" tone, "But I—I need this though."

[18]Elaine capitulated, but again tried to set limits: "Okay, just use it once." She even gave Arlene permission to give "just a couple of shots."

[19]Arlene then pressed her advantage, and became possessive of her property: "Now don't touch the baby until I get back, because it IS MY BABY! I'll check her ears, okay?" (Even when being demanding, she asked for agreement: "okay?")

[20]Elaine tried to regain some rights through compromise: "Well, let's pretend it's another day, that we have to look in her ears together." Elaine also tried another approach

CONTINUED

that would give Arlene something she wanted: "I'll have to shot her after, after, after you listen—after you look in her ears," suggested Elaine. Arlene, however, was adamant: "Now don't shot her at all!" What happened next will sound familiar to anyone who has ever been a little girl or overheard one. Elaine could no longer abide Arlene's selfish behavior and applied the ultimate sanction: "Well, then, you can't come to my birthday!" Arlene uttered the predictable retort: "I don't want to come to your birthday!"

21The boys and girls followed different rituals for fighting. Each boy went after what he wanted; they slugged it out; one won. But the girls enacted a complex **negotiation**, trying to get what they wanted while taking into account what the other wanted.

22Here is an example of how women and men at work used comparable strategies.

23Maureen and Harold, two managers at a medium-size company, were assigned to hire a human-resources coordinator for their division. Each favored a different candidate, and both felt strongly about their preferences. They traded arguments for some time, neither convincing the other. Then Harold said that hiring the candidate Maureen wanted would make him so uncomfortable that he would have to consider resigning. Maureen respected Harold. What's more, she liked him and considered him a friend. So she said what seemed to her the only thing she could say under the circumstances: "Well, I certainly don't want you to feel uncomfortable here. You're one of the pillars of the place." Harold's choice was hired.

24What was crucial was not Maureen's and Harold's individual styles in isolation but how they played in concert with each other's style. Harold's threat to quit ensured his triumph—when used with someone for whom it was a trump card. If he had been arguing with someone who regarded this threat as simply another move in the negotiation rather than a non-negotiable expression of deep feelings, the result might have been different. For example, had she said, "That's ridiculous; of course you're not going to quit!" or matched it ("Well, I'd be tempted to quit if we hired your guy"), the decision might well have gone the other way.

25Like the girls at play, Maureen was balancing her perspective with those of her colleague and expected him to do the same. Harold was simply going for what he wanted and trusted Maureen to do likewise.

26This is not to say that all women and all men, or all boys and girls, behave any one way. Many factors influence our styles, including regional and ethnic backgrounds, family experience and individual personality. But gender is a key factor, and understanding its influence can help clarify what happens when we talk.

27Understanding the ritual nature of communication gives you the flexibility to consider different approaches if you're not happy with the reaction you're getting. Someone who tends to avoid expressing disagreement might learn to play "devil's advocate" without taking it as a personal attack. Someone who tends to avoid admitting fault might find it is effective to say "I'm sorry"—that the loss of face is outweighed by a gain in credibility.

28There is no one way of talking that will always work best. But understanding how conversational rituals work allows individuals to have more control over their own lives.

Reading Comprehension Questions

Choose the best meaning of each word in *italics*. Use context clues to make your choice.

Vocabulary in Context

1. "'Women managers frequently told me they were good managers because they did not act in an *authoritarian* manner.' (paragraph 6)

   a. irritating **c.** weak
   b. demanding **d.** friendly

Vocabulary in Context

2. "But the girls enacted a complex *negotiation*, trying to get what they wanted while taking into account what the other wanted." (paragraph 21)

   a. quarrel **c.** bargain
   b. scam **d.** story

Central Idea

3. Which of the following sentences states the central idea of paragraphs 1–11?

   a. "Bob Hoover of the Pittsburgh *Post-Gazette* was interviewing me when he remarked that after years of coaching boys' softball teams, he was now coaching girls and they were very different." (paragraph 1)
   b. "What Hoover described in these youngsters were the seeds of behavior I have observed among women and men at work." (paragraph 5)
   c. "Finally, I was intrigued by Hoover's remark that boys regard sports as 'a performance art' and worry about 'how they look.'" (paragraph 10)
   d. "Getting credit often depends on the way you talk." (paragraph 11)

Supporting Details

4. According to the passage, boys' teams always had one or two stars whom the other boys

   a. teased. **c.** competed against.
   b. envied. **d.** treated with deference.

Transitions

5. "Whereas some women seem to be taking undeserved blame by saying 'I'm sorry,' some men seem to evade deserved blame." (paragraph 12)

   The relationship of ideas **within** this sentence is

   a. cause and effect. **c.** comparison/contrast.
   b. time order. **d.** generalization-example.

CONTINUED

Patterns of Organization

 **6.** The overall pattern of organization of the passage is

a. cause and effect.
b. time order.
c. comparison/contrast.
d. generalization-example.

Fact and Opinion

 **7.** "Two boys fought over a toy telephone: Tony had it; Charlie wanted it." (paragraph 14)

This sentence is a statement of

a. fact.
b. opinion.
c. fact and opinion.

Tone and Purpose

 **8.** The overall tone and purpose of the author is

a. to inform the public about the difference between the ways men and women communicate.
b. to entertain the public with interesting details about how men and women differ in their communication styles.
c. to persuade the public to understand the importance of gender in communication styles.

Inferences

 **9.** Based on the details in the passage, we can infer that

a. men and women always disagree.
b. women are better communicators than men.
c. communication patterns develop early in life.
d. communication patterns cannot change.

Argument

 **10.** The following items from paragraph 11 contain a claim and list of supports for that claim. Which sentence states the claim?

a. "Getting credit often depends on the way you talk."
b. "For example, a woman told me she was given a poor evaluation because her supervisor felt she knew less than her male peers."
c. "Her boss, it turned out, reached this conclusion because the woman asked more questions."
d. "She was seeking information without regard to how her queries would make her look."

Mapping

Complete the following concept map with information from the passage. *Wording may vary.*

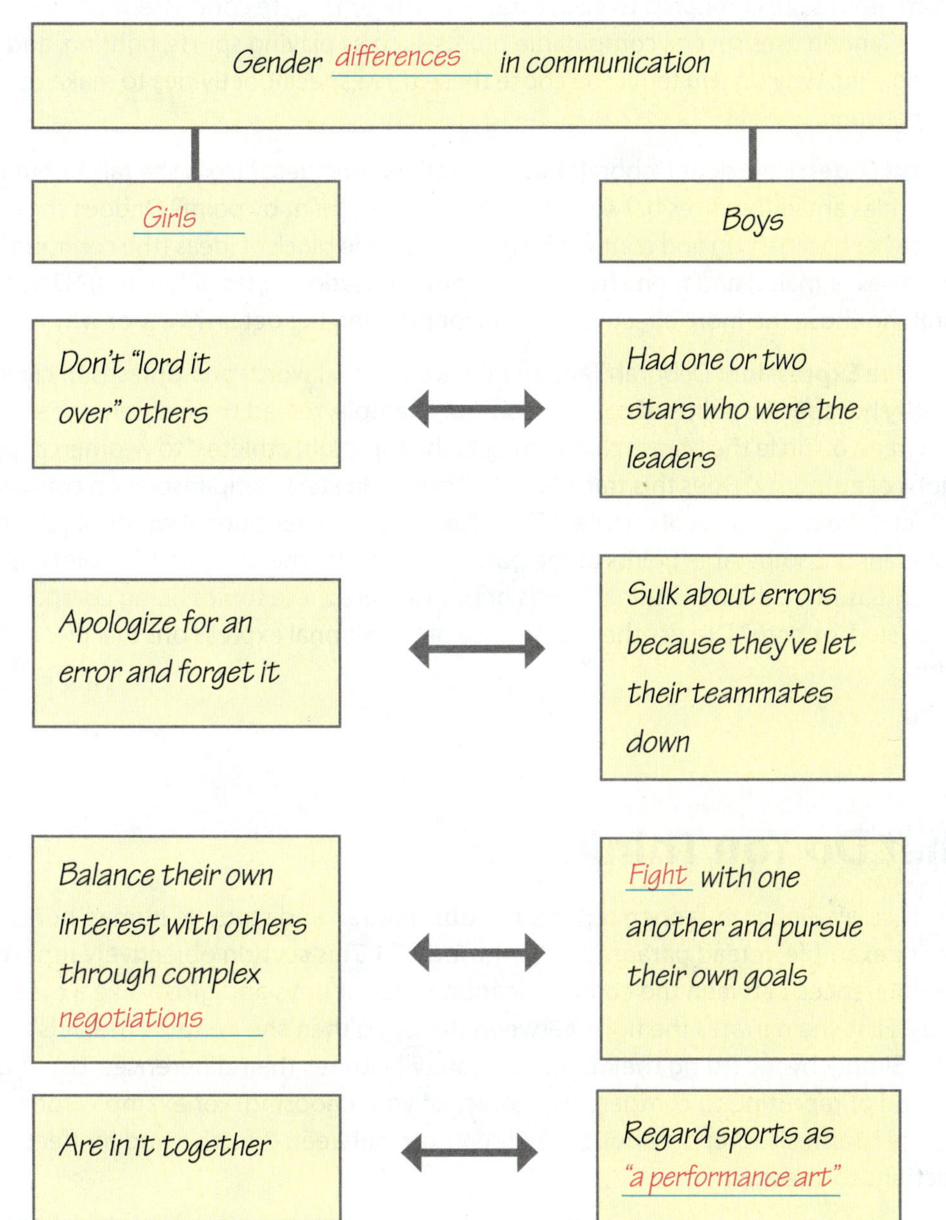
Gender differences in communication
Girls
Boys
Don't "lord it over" others
Had one or two stars who were the leaders
Apologize for an error and forget it
Sulk about errors because they've let their teammates down
Balance their own interest with others through complex negotiations
Fight with one another and pursue their own goals
Are in it together
Regard sports as "a performance art"

After Reading Discussion Questions: Meaning, Structure, and Expression

1. **Main Idea:** Work as a group to write a summary that answers the following questions: What purpose did Deborah Tannen have for writing this essay? Who is the intended audience? What is the main idea of the essay?

CONTINUED

2. **Relevant Details:** The details of this passage explain the similarities and differences in the conversation styles of four groups of people. What are those four groups? Which groups are compared to each other? Which groups are contrasted with each other? Tannen uses several comparable points such as playing sports, fighting, and apologizing. Why do you think she chose these three specific activities to make her comparisons?

3. **Logical Order:** How does Deborah Tannen organize her ideas? Does she talk about the similarities and differences between men and women point by point? Or does she organize her comparison and contrast by presenting one block of ideas (the communication styles of males) and then another (the communication styles of females)? Do you think she chose the more effective method for ordering her details? Why or why not?

4. **Effective Expression:** Deborah Tannen uses transitional words and phrases to clearly identify her specific points of comparison. For example, reread the first sentence in paragraph 6. Circle the phrase that connects the topic "girl athletes" to "women in positions of authority." Does this transitional phrase indicate a comparison or a contrast between the two groups of females? Find two additional transitional words or phrases that identify comparable points in the passage. What are the comparable points or topics? Based on the transitional words or phrases, are these topics being compared, contrasted, or both? Discuss the importance of transitional expressions in a piece of writing.

What Do You Think?

1. In this essay, Deborah Tannen reports her observation and study of human behavior. For example, reread paragraphs 13 through 28. This section objectively reports the differences between the communication styles of boys and girls—like a case study. First she narrates the fight between the boys; then she narrates the girls' fight. Simply by recording their behaviors, she illustrates their differences. Use this method of reporting to compare two topics of your choosing. For example, for a college health class report about the differences between effective and ineffective reactions to stress.

2. Deborah Tannen illustrates the differences between males and females by comparing and contrasting their communication styles as children and adults. What other differences between men and women have you observed? For example, do men and women prefer different types of movies, sports, books, cars? Do they differ in the way they act in their roles as parents, siblings, children, or friends? Write an essay using your own set of comparable points that discusses other important differences between men and women. Choose an audience and writing situation such as the following: an academic paper for a social science class or an article for the college newspaper.

Effective Reading/Writing Scorecard

"The Talk of the Sandbox"

Skill	Number Correct	Points	Total
Vocabulary			
Vocabulary in Context (2 items)		x 5 =	
Comprehension			
Central Idea (1 item)		x 10 =	
Supporting Details (1 item)		x 10 =	
Transitions (1 item)		x 10 =	
Patterns of Organization (1 item)		x 10 =	
Fact and Opinion (1 item)		x 10 =	
Tone and Purpose (1 item)		x 10 =	
Inferences (1 item)		x 10 =	
Argument (1 item)		x 10 =	
Mapping (5 items)		x 2 =	
		Comprehension Score	

READING 7

Definition

What is Poverty? 790L/4.4 GE/1959 words

JO GOODWIN-PARKER

The following selection was published in 1971 in George Henderson's *America's Other Children: Public Schools Outside Suburbs*, by the University of Oklahoma Press. The author specifically requests the right to her privacy and offers no additional information about herself for public use. In her essay, a personal testimony about living in poverty, she speaks directly to the reader.

CONTINUED

Before Reading

Write a journal entry about your response to poverty. How would you define poverty? Why are people poor? How does society react to the poor? Do you think our government does enough to help poor people? What can be done to fight poverty?

Vocabulary

Before, during, and after reading the selection, annotate the text and write in your journal. Create a list of vocabulary words, along with their definitions. Give examples of their use from the selection you just read.

[1]You ask me what is poverty? Listen to me. Here I am, dirty, smelly, and with no "proper" underwear on and with the stench of my rotting teeth near you. I will tell you. Listen to me. Listen without pity. I cannot use your pity. Listen with understanding. Put yourself in my dirty, worn out, ill-fitting shoes, and hear me.

[2]Poverty is getting up every morning from a dirt- and illness-stained mattress. The sheets have long since been used for diapers. Poverty is living in a smell that never leaves. This is a smell of urine, sour milk, and spoiling food sometimes joined with the strong smell of long-cooked onions. Onions are cheap. If you have smelled this smell, you did not know how it came. It is the smell of the outdoor privy. It is the smell of young children who cannot walk the long dark way in the night. It is the smell of the mattresses where years of "accidents" have happened. It is the smell of the milk which has gone sour because the refrigerator long has not worked, and it costs money to get it fixed. It is the smell of rotting garbage. I could bury it, but where is the shovel? Shovels cost money.

[3]Poverty is being tired. I have always been tired. They told me at the hospital when the last baby came that I had chronic anemia caused from poor diet, a bad case of worms, and that I needed a corrective operation. I listened politely—the poor are always polite. The poor always listen. They don't say that there is no money for iron pills, or better food, or worm medicine. The idea of an operation is frightening and costs so much that, if I had dared, I would have laughed. Who takes care of my children? Recovery from an operation takes a long time. I have three children. When I left them with "Granny" the last time I had a job, I came home to find the baby covered with fly specks, and a diaper that had not been changed since I left. When the dried diaper came off, bits of my baby's flesh came with it. My other child was playing with a sharp bit of

broken glass, and my oldest was playing alone at the edge of a lake. I made twenty-two dollars a week, and a good nursery school costs twenty dollars a week for three children. I quit my job.

[4]Poverty is dirt. You can say in your clean clothes coming from your clean house, "Anybody can be clean." Let me explain about housekeeping with no money. For breakfast I give my children grits with no oleo or cornbread without eggs and oleo. This does not use up many dishes. What dishes there are, I wash in cold water and with no soap. Even the cheapest soap has to be saved for the baby's diapers. Look at my hands, so cracked and red. Once I saved for two months to buy a jar of Vaseline for my hands and the baby's diaper rash. When I had saved enough, I went to buy it and the price had gone up two cents. The baby and I suffered on. I have to decide every day if I can bear to put my cracked sore hands into the cold water and strong soap. But you ask, why not hot water? Fuel costs money. If you have a wood fire it costs money. If you burn electricity, it costs money. Hot water is a luxury. I do not have luxuries. I know you will be surprised when I tell you how young I am. I look so much older. My back has been bent over the wash tubs every day for so long, I cannot remember when I ever did anything else. Every night I wash every stitch my school age child has on and just hope her clothes will be dry by morning.

[5]Poverty is staying up all night on cold nights to watch the fire knowing one spark on the newspaper covering the walls means your sleeping child dies in flames. In summer poverty is watching gnats and flies devour your baby's tears when he cries. The screens are torn and you pay so little rent you know they will never be fixed. Poverty means insects in your food, in your nose, in your eyes, and crawling over you when you sleep. Poverty is hoping it never rains because diapers won't dry when it rains and soon you are using newspapers. Poverty is seeing your children forever with runny noses. Paper handkerchiefs cost money and all your rags you need for other things. Even more costly are antihistamines. Poverty is cooking without food and cleaning without soap.

[6]Poverty is asking for help. Have you ever had to ask for help, knowing your children will suffer unless you get it? Think about asking for a loan from a relative, if this is the only way you can imagine asking for help. I will tell you how it feels. You find out where the office is that you are supposed to visit. You circle that block four or five times. Thinking of your children, you go in. Everyone is very busy. Finally, someone comes out and you tell her that you need help. That never is the person you need to see. You go see another person, and after spilling the whole shame of your poverty all over the desk between you, you find that this

CONTINUED

isn't the right office after all—you must repeat the whole process, and it never is any easier at the next place.

[7]You have asked for help, and after all it has a cost. You are again told to wait. You are told why, but you don't really hear because of the red cloud of shame and the rising cloud of despair.

[8]Poverty is remembering. It is remembering quitting school in junior high because "nice" children had been so cruel about my clothes and my smell. The attendance officer came. My mother told him I was pregnant. I wasn't, but she thought that I could get a job and help out. I had jobs off and on, but never long enough to learn anything. Mostly I remember being married. I was so young then. I am still young. For a time, we had all the things you have. There was a little house in another town, with hot water and everything. Then my husband lost his job. There was unemployment insurance for a while and what few jobs I could get. Soon, all our nice things were repossessed and we moved back here. I was pregnant then. This house didn't look so bad when we first moved in. Every week it gets worse. Nothing is ever fixed. We now had no money. There were a few odd jobs for my husband, but everything went for food then, as it does now. I don't know how we lived through three years and three babies, but we did. I'll tell you something, after the last baby I destroyed my marriage. It had been a good one, but could you keep on bringing children in this dirt? Did you ever think how much it costs for any kind of birth control? I knew my husband was leaving the day he left, but there were no goodbye between us. I hope he has been able to climb out of this mess somewhere. He never could hope with us to drag him down.

[9]That's when I asked for help. When I got it, you know how much it was? It was, and is, seventy-eight dollars a month for the four of us; that is all I ever can get. Now you know why there is no soap, no needles and thread, no hot water, no aspirin, no worm medicine, no hand cream, no shampoo. None of these things forever and ever and ever. So that you can see clearly, I pay twenty dollars a month rent, and most of the rest goes for food. For grits and cornmeal, and rice and milk and beans. I try my best to use only the minimum electricity. If I use more, there is that much less for food.

[10]Poverty is looking into a black future. Your children won't play with my boys. They will turn to other boys who steal to get what they want. I can already see them behind the bars of their prison instead of behind the bars of my poverty. Or they will turn to the freedom of alcohol or drugs, and find themselves enslaved. And my daughter? At best, there is for her a life like mine.

[11]But you say to me, there are schools. Yes, there are schools. My children have no extra books, no magazines, no extra pencils, or crayons, or paper and most important of all, they do not have health. They have worms, they have infections, they have pink-eye all summer. They do not sleep well on the floor, or with me in my one bed. They do not suffer from hunger, my seventy-eight dollars keeps us alive, but they do suffer from malnutrition. Oh yes, I do remember what I was taught about health in school. It doesn't do much good.

[12]In some places there is a surplus **commodities** program. Not here. The country said it cost too much. There is a school lunch program. But I have two children who will already be damaged by the time they get to school.

[13]But, you say to me, there are health clinics. Yes, there are health clinics and they are in the towns. I live out here eight miles from town. I can walk that far (even if it is sixteen miles both ways), but can my little children? My neighbor will take me when he goes; but he expects to get paid, one way or another. I bet you know my neighbor. He is that large man who spends his time at the gas station, the barbershop, and the corner store complaining about the government spending money on the **immoral** mothers of illegitimate children.

[14]Poverty is an acid that drips on pride until all pride is worn away. Poverty is a chisel that chips on honor until honor is worn away. Some of you say that you would do something in my situation, and maybe you would, for the first week or the first month, but for year after year after year?

[15]Even the poor can dream. A dream of a time when there is money. Money for the right kinds of food, for worm medicine, for iron pills, for toothbrushes, for hand cream, for a hammer and nails and a bit of screening, for a shovel, for a bit of paint, for some sheeting, for needles and thread. Money to pay in money for a trip to town. And, oh, money for hot water and money for soap. A dream of when asking for help does not eat away the last bit of pride. When the office you visit is as nice as the offices of other governmental agencies, when there are enough workers to help you quickly, when workers do not quit in defeat and despair. When you have to tell your story to only one person, and that person can send you for other help and you don't have to prove your poverty over and over and over again.

[16]I have come out of my despair to tell you this. Remember I did not come from another place or another time. Others like me are all around you. Look at us with an angry heart, anger that will help.

CONTINUED

Reading Comprehension Questions

Choose the best meaning of each word in *italics*. Use context clues to make your choice.

Vocabulary in Context

 1. "'In some places there is a surplus *commodities* program." (paragraph 12)

a. interests
b. favors
c. monies
d. products

Vocabulary in Context

 2. "He is that large man who spends his time at the gas station, the barbershop, and the corner store complaining about the government spending money on the *immoral* mothers of illegitimate children." (paragraph 13)

a. corrupt
b. honest
c. noble
d. misunderstood

Implied Central Idea

 3. Which of the following sentences states the implied central idea of the passage?

a. Poverty cannot be overcome.
b. Poverty is the lack of health, the inability to meet basic needs, and the loss of human dignity.
c. Poverty is a difficult lifestyle.
d. Poverty is a problem that harms women and children and must be addressed by society.

Supporting Details

 4. The author saved money for two months to buy

a. worm medicine.
b. diapers.
c. a jar of Vaseline.
d. a hammer, nails, and a bit of screen.

Transitions

 5. "Poverty is remembering. It is remembering quitting school in junior high because 'nice' children had been so cruel about my clothes and my smell." (paragraph 8)

The relationship of ideas **between** these sentences is

a. cause and effect.
b. classification.
c. comparison/contrast.
d. definition-example.

Patterns of Organization

6. "I try my best to use only the minimum electricity. If I use more, there is that much less for food." (paragraph 9)

The relationship of ideas **between** these sentences is

a. cause and effect.
b. classification
c. comparison/contrast.
d. definition and example.

Fact and Opinion

7. "Poverty is an acid that drips on pride until all pride is worn away." (paragraph 14)

This sentence is a statement of

a. fact.
b. opinion.
c. fact and opinion.

Tone and Purpose

8. The overall tone and purpose of the author is

a. to inform the public about poverty.
b. to entertain the public with interesting details about the author's experiences with poverty.
c. to persuade the public to help those who suffer in poverty.

Inferences

9. Based on the details in the passage, we can infer that poverty

a. can be overcome.
b. is the result of poor choices people make.
c. is a cycle that can last for generations.
d. programs offer adequate assistance to the poor.

Argument

10. The following items from paragraph 10 contain a claim and a list of supports for that claim. Which sentence states the claim?

a. "Poverty is looking into a black future."
b. "Your children won't play with my boys."
c. "They will turn to other boys who steal to get what they want."
d. "I can already see them behind the bars of their prison instead of behind the bars of my poverty."

CONTINUED

Outlining

Complete the following outline with information from the passage. *Wording may vary.*

What is Poverty?

I. *Poverty is living in a smell that never leaves.*

II. *Poverty is being tired.*

III. *Poverty is dirt.*

IV. *Poverty is asking for help.*

V. *Poverty is remembering.*

VI. *Poverty is looking into a black future.*

VII. *Even the poor can dream.*

VIII. *Look at us with an angry heart, anger that will help.*

After Reading Discussion Questions: Meaning, Structure, and Expression

1. **Main Idea:** Work as a group to write a summary that answers the following questions: What purpose did Jo Goodwin-Parker have for writing this essay? Who is her intended audience? What is the main idea of the essay?
2. **Relevant Details:** Parker offers her own life experiences to define poverty. Does she provide enough details to make her point convincingly? Would the use of facts or expert opinions strengthen her point? Why or why not?
3. **Logical Order:** Parker defines poverty with a series of statements that begin with "Poverty is." Summarize her definition of poverty using these seven statements. Do you agree with the order in which she presents these statements? Why or why not?
4. **Effective Expression:** Based on Parker's choice of words, how would you describe the tone of this essay? Is it angry, embarrassed, disappointed, reflective, sad, or optimistic, or does it communicate some other attitude about poverty? Identify three expressions that illustrate the tone of the piece. Explain the reasons for your selections.

What Do You Think?

1. Often, people do not understand what they have not experienced. Parker defines poverty for people who have never experienced it. In the last sentence in the first paragraph, she commands her readers to step into her shoes so they can learn from her experiences. Assume the view of one who understands an issue such as depression, addiction, or prejudice based on experience. Write an essay that defines the issue so that someone who has not experienced it can better understand the problem.
2. In her essay, Parker defines the problem of poverty, but she does not offer a solution, other than to say "look at us with an angry heart, anger that will help." What kind of anger will help this situation? Respond to Parker by writing an essay that defines this kind of anger. Consider using a phrase like "Anger that will help is" to reply to specific points she raises in her essay.

Effective Reading/Writing Scorecard

"What is Poverty?"

Skill	Number Correct	Points	Total
Vocabulary			
Vocabulary in Context (2 items)		x 5 =	
Comprehension			
Implied Central Idea (1 item)		x 10 =	
Supporting Details (1 item)		x 10 =	
Transitions (1 item)		x 10 =	
Patterns of Organization (1 item)		x 10 =	
Fact and Opinion (1 item)		x 10 =	
Tone and Purpose (1 item)		x 10 =	
Inferences (1 item)		x 10 =	
Argument (1 item)		x 10 =	
Outlining (5 items)		x 2 =	
		Comprehension Score	

READING 8

Cause and Effect

1109L/9.4 GE/1026 words

Why We Crave Horror Movies

STEPHEN KING

Stephen King, born in Portland, Maine in 1947, has been writing full time since the 1973 publication of his novel *Carrie*. He has since published over 40 books and has become one of the world's most successful writers.

Before Reading

Write a journal entry about your reaction to horror movies. Do you enjoy horror movies? Why or why not? Why do you think horror movies are so popular? Do graphically violent horror movies have a harmful effect on society? Explain your reasons.

Vocabulary

Before, during, and after reading the selection, annotate the text and write in your journal. Create a list of vocabulary words, along with their definitions. Give examples of their use from the selection you just read.

[1]I think that we're all mentally ill: those of us outside the asylums only hide it a little better—and maybe not all that much better, after all. We've all known people who talk to themselves, people who sometimes squinch their faces into horrible grimaces when they believe no one is watching, people who have some hysterical fear—of snakes, the dark, the tight place, the long drop . . . and, of course, those final worms and grubs that are waiting so patiently underground.

[2]When we pay our four or five bucks and seat ourselves at tenth-row center in a theater showing a horror movie, we are daring the nightmare.

[3]Why? Some of the reasons are simple and obvious. To show that we can, that we are not afraid, that we can ride this roller coaster. Which is not to say that a really good horror movie may not surprise a scream out of us at some point, the way we may scream when the roller coaster twists through a complete 360 or plows through a lake at the bottom of the drop. And horror movies, like roller coasters, have always been the special province of the young; by the time one turns 40 or 50, one's appetite for double twists or 360-degree loops may be considerably depleted.

[4]We also go to re-establish our feelings of essential normality; the horror movie is innately conservative, even reactionary. Freda Jackson as the horrible melting woman in *Die, Monster, Die!* confirms for us that no matter how far we may be removed from the beauty of a Robert Redford or a Diana Ross, we are still light-years from true ugliness.

[5]And we go to have fun.

[6]Ah, but this is where the ground starts to slope away, isn't it? Because this is a very peculiar sort of fun indeed. The fun comes from seeing others menaced—sometimes killed. One critic has suggested that if pro football has become the **voyeur's** version of combat, then the horror film has become the modern version of the public lynching.

[7]It is true that the mythic, "fairytale" horror film intends to take away the shades of gray. . . . It urges us to put away our more civilized and adult **penchant** for analysis and to become children again, seeing things in pure blacks and whites. It may be that horror movies provide psychic relief on this level because this invitation to lapse into simplicity, irrationality and even outright madness is extended so rarely. We are told we may allow our emotions a free rein . . . or no rein at all.

[8]If we are all insane, then sanity becomes a matter of degree. If your insanity leads you to carve up women like Jack the Ripper or the Cleveland Torso Murderer, we clap you away in the funny farm (but neither of those two amateur-night surgeons was ever caught, heh-heh-heh); if, on the other hand your insanity leads you only to talk to yourself when you're under stress or to pick your nose on the morning bus, then you are left alone to go about your business . . . though it is doubtful that you will ever be invited to the best parties.

[9]The potential lyncher is in almost all of us (excluding saints, past and present; but then, most saints have been crazy in their own ways), and every now and then, he has to be let loose to scream and roll around in the grass. Our emotions and our fears form their own body, and we recognize that it demands its own exercise to maintain proper muscle tone. Certain of these emotional muscles are accepted—even exalted—in civilized society; they are, of course, the emotions that tend to maintain the status quo of civilization itself. Love, friendship, loyalty, kindness—these are all the emotions that we applaud, emotions that have been immortalized in the couplets of Hallmark cards. . . .

[10]When we exhibit these emotions, society showers us with positive reinforcement; we learn this even before we get out of diapers. When, as children, we hug our rotten little puke of a sister and give her a kiss, all the aunts and uncles smile and twit and cry, "Isn't he the sweetest little thing?" Such coveted treats as chocolate-covered graham crackers often follow. But if we deliberately slam the rotten little puke of a sister's fingers in the door, sanctions follow—angry remonstrance from parents, aunts and uncles; instead of a chocolate-covered graham cracker, a spanking.

[11]But anticivilization emotions don't go away, and they demand periodic exercise. We have such "sick" jokes as, "What's the difference between a truckload of bowling balls and a truckload of dead babies?" (You can't unload a truckload of bowling balls with a pitchfork . . . a joke, by the way, that I heard originally from a ten-year-old.) Such a joke may surprise a laugh or a grin out of us even as we recoil, a possibility that confirms the thesis: If we share a brotherhood of man, then we also share an insanity of man. None of which is intended as a defense of either the sick joke or insanity but merely as an explanation of why the best horror films, like the best fairy tales, manage to be reactionary, anarchistic, and revolutionary all at the same time.

CONTINUED

[12]The mythic horror movie, like the sick joke, has a dirty job to do. It deliberately appeals to all that is worst in us. It is morbidity unchained, our most base instincts let free, our nastiest fantasies realized . . . and it all happens, fittingly enough, in the dark. For those reasons, good liberals often shy away from horror films. For myself, I like to see the most aggressive of them—*Dawn of the Dead,* for instance—as lifting a trap door in the civilized forebrain and throwing a basket of raw meat to the hungry alligators swimming around in that subterranean river beneath.

[13]Why bother? Because it keeps them from getting out, man. It keeps them down there and me up here. It was Lennon and McCartney who said that all you need is love, and I would agree with that.

[14]As long as you keep the gators fed.

Reading Comprehension Questions

Choose the best meaning of each word in *italics*. Use context clues to make your choice.

Vocabulary in Context

1. "One critic has suggested that if pro football has become the *voyeur's* version of combat, then the horror film has become the modern version of the public lynching." (paragraph 6)

a. actor's
b. watcher's
c. person's
d. soldier's

Vocabulary in Context

2. "It urges us to put away our more civilized and adult *penchant* for analysis and become children again, seeing things in pure blacks and whites." (paragraph 7)

a. dislike
b. horror
c. desire
d. strength

Central Idea

3. Which of the following sentences states the central idea of the passage?

a. "Some of the reasons are simple and obvious." (paragraph 3)

b. "It may be that horror movies provide psychic relief on this level because this invitation to lapse into simplicity, irrationality, and even outright madness is extended so rarely." (paragraph 7)

c. "If we are all insane, then sanity becomes a matter of degree." (paragraph 8)

d. "The mythic horror movie, like the sick joke, has a dirty job to do." (paragraph 12)

Supporting Details

 **4.** Who told Stephen King the "sick" joke about bowling balls?

a. a critic
b. a fan
c. a ten-year-old
d. Lennon and McCartney

Transitions

 **5.** "For those reasons, good liberals often shy away from horror films." (paragraph 12)

The relationship of ideas **within** this sentence is

a. cause and effect.
b. time order.
c. comparison/contrast.
d. generalization-example.

Patterns of Organization

 **6.** The overall pattern of organization of the passage is

a. cause and effect.
b. time order.
c. comparison/contrast.
d. generalization-example.

Fact and Opinion

 **7.** "Freda Jackson as the horrible melting woman in *Die, Monster, Die!* confirms for us that no matter how far we may be removed from the beauty of a Robert Redford or a Diana Ross, we are still light-years from true ugliness." (paragraph 4)

This sentence is a statement of

a. fact.
b. opinion.
c. fact and opinion.

Tone and Purpose

 **8.** The overall tone and purpose of the author is

a. to inform the public about why we crave horror movies.
b. to entertain the public with the author's personal views about why we crave horror movies.
c. to persuade the public to appreciate and watch horror movies.

Inferences

 **9.** Based on the details in the passage, we can infer that horror movies

a. are harmful to our mental health.
b. allow a healthy expression of anticivilization emotions.
c. lead to an increase in crime.
d. deepen our ability to express love, friendship, loyalty, and kindness.

CONTINUED

Argument

b **10.** The following sentence from paragraph 13 is

"It was Lennon and McCartney who said that all you need is love, and I would agree with that." (paragraph 13)

a. a claim.
b. a counterclaim.
c. an irrelevant detail.
d. a factual support.

Mapping

Complete the following concept map with information from the passage. *Wording may vary.*

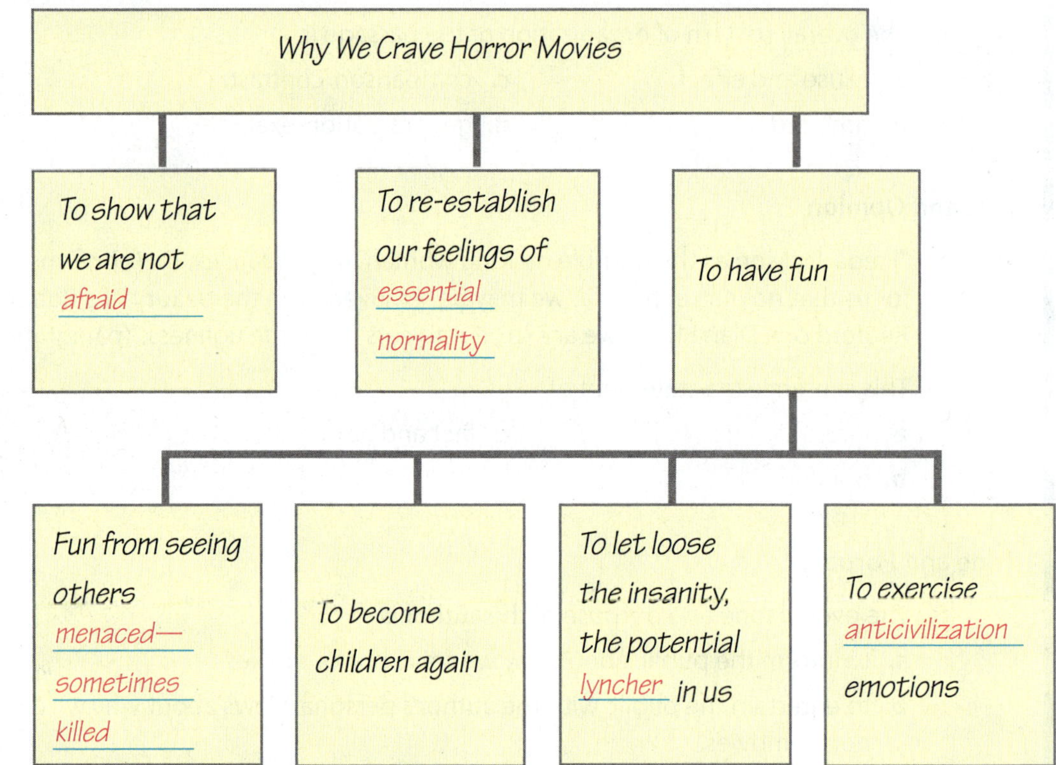

After Reading Discussion Questions: Meaning, Structure, and Expression

1. **Main Idea:** Work as a group to write a summary that answers the following questions: What purpose did Stephen King have for writing this essay? Who is his intended audience? What is the essay's main idea?
2. **Relevant Details:** In paragraphs 10 and 11, King uses children as examples to support his point. Why do you think he uses these examples? Do you think these examples are typical of most children? Do you agree that these examples effectively support his point? Why or why not?
3. **Logical Order:** King declares his thesis in paragraph 11. Locate his thesis statement. Why do you think King waited until this late in the essay to state his thesis? Reread his introduction. What is his opening point? Why do you think he opened his essay with

this idea? How would the impact of the essay change if King had stated his thesis in the opening paragraph?

4. **Effective Expression:** To make his point, King appeals to our senses and prior experiences with references to roller coasters, Jack the Ripper, lynching, and alligators. Discuss how each of these images supports his point.

What Do You Think?

1. King offers reasons that explain the positive effects of horror movies. However, many disagree with this view and see the violence in horror movies as a negative factor in our society. Assume you are the editor of your college's student newspaper. Write an essay that explains the negative impact of horror movies.
2. King claims that we are "all mentally ill" and that horror movies appeal to the "worst in us." However, many believe that humans are basically good. The famous American essayist Emerson once encouraged us "to look into yourselves and do good because you are good." Assume you are taking a college sociology class. Write an essay that illustrates the goodness and positive impact of human nature. Consider, for example, the reasons for and effects of Habitat for Humanity or other charities or volunteer organizations.

Effective Reading and Writing Scorecard

"Why We Crave Horror Movies"

Skill	Number Correct	Points	Total
Vocabulary			
Vocabulary in Context (2 items)		x 5 =	
Comprehension			
Central Idea (1 item)		x 10 =	
Supporting Details (1 item)		x 10 =	
Transitions (1 item)		x 10 =	
Patterns of Organization (1 item)		x 10 =	
Fact and Opinion (1 item)		x 10 =	
Tone and Purpose (1 item)		x 10 =	
Inferences (1 item)		x 10 =	
Argument (1 item)		x 10 =	
Mapping (5 items)		x 2 =	
		Comprehension Score	

READING 9

Argument

I am Adam Lanza's Mother 930L/6.6 GE/1455 words

LIZA LONG

On December 14, 2012, 20-year old Adam Lanza fatally shot twenty children and six adults and wounded two at Sandy Hook Elementary School in New Town, Connecticut. Before driving to the school, Lanza had killed his mother Nancy at their home. As first responders arrived at the school, Lanza committed suicide. The tragedy ignited a national discussion on violence and gun control in America. Liza Long, a writer based in Boise and single mother of four, one of whom is a special needs child, posted the following article in her blog *The Anarchist Soccer Mom*. The article was also published at *The Blue Review*, a web-based journal from the Boise State University College of Social Sciences and Public Affairs. Immediately, Long's article with its focus on mental illness went viral on the web and received over 1 million Facebook likes.

Before Reading

Write a journal entry about your reaction to school shootings. Why do you think they occur? What should society do to protect the public from shootings at schools, malls, and other public places?

Vocabulary

Before, during, and after reading the selection, annotate the text and write in your journal. Create a list of vocabulary words, along with their definitions. Give examples of their use from the selection you just read.

1 Three days before 20 year-old Adam Lanza killed his mother, then opened fire on a classroom full of Connecticut kindergartners, my 13-year old son Michael (name changed) missed his bus because he was wearing the wrong color pants.

2 "I can wear these pants," he said, his tone increasingly **belligerent**, the black-hole pupils of his eyes swallowing the blue irises.

3 "They are navy blue," I told him. "Your school's dress code says black or khaki pants only."

4 "They told me I could wear these," he insisted. "You're a stupid bitch. I can wear whatever pants I want to. This is America. I have rights!"

5"You can't wear whatever pants you want to," I said, my tone **affable**, reasonable. "And you definitely cannot call me a stupid bitch. You're grounded from electronics for the rest of the day. Now get in the car, and I will take you to school."

6I live with a son who is mentally ill. I love my son. But he terrifies me.

7A few weeks ago, Michael pulled a knife and threatened to kill me and then himself after I asked him to return his overdue library books. His 7 and 9 year old siblings knew the safety plan—they ran to the car and locked the doors before I even asked them to. I managed to get the knife from Michael, then methodically collected all the sharp objects in the house into a single Tupperware container that now travels with me. Through it all, he continued to scream insults at me and threaten to kill or hurt me.

8That conflict ended with three burly police officers and a paramedic wrestling my son onto a gurney for an expensive ambulance ride to the local emergency room. The mental hospital didn't have any beds that day, and Michael calmed down nicely in the ER, so they sent us home with a prescription for Zyprexa and a follow-up visit with a local pediatric psychiatrist.

9We still don't know what's wrong with Michael. Autism spectrum, ADHD, Oppositional Defiant or Intermittent Explosive Disorder have all been tossed around at various meetings with probation officers and social workers and counselors and teachers and school administrators. He's been on a slew of antipsychotic and mood altering pharmaceuticals, a Russian novel of behavioral plans. Nothing seems to work.

10At the start of seventh grade, Michael was accepted to an accelerated program for highly gifted math and science students. His IQ is off the charts. When he's in a good mood, he will gladly bend your ear on subjects ranging from Greek mythology to the differences between Einsteinian and Newtonian physics to Doctor Who. He's in a good mood most of the time. But when he's not, watch out. And it's impossible to predict what will set him off.

11Several weeks into his new junior high school, Michael began exhibiting increasingly odd and threatening behaviors at school. We decided to transfer him to the district's most restrictive behavioral program, a contained school environment where children who can't function in normal classrooms can access their right to free public babysitting from 7:30-1:50 Monday through Friday until they turn 18.

12The morning of the pants incident, Michael continued to argue with me on the drive. He would occasionally apologize and seem remorseful. Right before we turned into his school parking lot, he said, "Look, Mom, I'm really sorry. Can I have video games back today?"

13"No way," I told him. "You cannot act the way you acted this morning and think you can get your electronic privileges back that quickly."

14 His face turned cold, and his eyes were full of calculated rage. "Then I'm going to kill myself," he said. "I'm going to jump out of this car right now and kill myself."

15 That was it. After the knife incident, I told him that if he ever said those words again, I would take him straight to the mental hospital, no ifs, ands, or buts. I did not respond, except to pull the car into the opposite lane, turning left instead of right.

16 "Where are you taking me?" he said, suddenly worried. "Where are we going?"

CONTINUED

[17]"You know where we are going," I replied.

[18]"No! You can't do that to me! You're sending me to hell! You're sending me straight to hell!"

[19]I pulled up in front of the hospital, frantically waiving for one of the clinicians who happened to be standing outside. "Call the police," I said. "Hurry."

[20]Michael was in a full-blown fit by then, screaming and hitting. I hugged him close so he couldn't escape from the car. He bit me several times and repeatedly jabbed his elbows into my rib cage. I'm still stronger than he is, but I won't be for much longer.

[21]The police came quickly and carried my son screaming and kicking into the bowels of the hospital. I started to shake, and tears filled my eyes as I filled out the paperwork—"Were there any difficulties with . . . at what age did your child . . . were there any problems with . . . has your child ever experienced . . . does your child have . . ."

[22]At least we have health insurance now. I recently accepted a position with a local college, giving up my freelance career because when you have a kid like this, you need benefits. You'll do anything for benefits. No individual insurance plan will cover this kind of thing.

[23]For days, my son insisted that I was lying—that I made the whole thing up so that I could get rid of him. The first day, when I called to check up on him, he said, "I hate you. And I'm going to get my revenge as soon as I get out of here."

[24]By day three, he was my calm, sweet boy again, all apologies and promises to get better. I've heard those promises for years. I don't believe them anymore.

[25]On the intake form, under the question, "What are your expectations for treatment?" I wrote, "I need help."

[26]And I do. This problem is too big for me to handle on my own. Sometimes there are no good options. So you just pray for grace and trust that in hindsight, it will all make sense. I am sharing this story because I am Adam Lanza's mother. I am Dylan Klebold's and Eric Harris's mother. I am James Holmes's mother. I am Jared Loughner's mother. I am Seung-Hui Cho's mother. And these boys—and their mothers—need help. In the wake of another horrific national tragedy, it's easy to talk about guns. But it's time to talk about mental illness.

[27]According to Mother Jones, since 1982, 61 mass murders involving firearms have occurred throughout the country. Of these, 43 of the killers were white males, and only one was a woman. Mother Jones focused on whether the killers obtained their guns legally (most did). But this highly visible sign of mental illness should lead us to consider how many people in the U.S. live in fear, like I do.

[28]When I asked my son's social worker about my options, he said that the only thing I could do was to get Michael charged with a crime. "If he's back in the system, they'll create a paper trail," he said. "That's the only way you're ever going to get anything done. No one will pay attention to you unless you've got charges."

[29]I don't believe my son belongs in jail. The chaotic environment exacerbates Michael's sensitivity to sensory stimuli and doesn't deal with the underlying pathology. But it seems like the United States is using prison as the solution of choice for mentally ill people. According to Human Rights Watch, the number of mentally ill inmates in U.S. prisons quadrupled from 2000 to 2006, and it continues to rise—in

fact, the rate of inmate mental illness is five times greater (56 percent) than in the non-incarcerated population.

[30]With state-run treatment centers and hospitals shuttered, prison is now the last resort for the mentally ill—Rikers Island, the LA County Jail and Cook County Jail in Illinois housed the nation's largest treatment centers in 2011.

[31]No one wants to send a 13-year old genius who loves Harry Potter and his snuggle animal collection to jail. But our society, with its stigma on mental illness and its broken healthcare system, does not provide us with other options. Then another tortured soul shoots up a fast food restaurant. A mall. A kindergarten classroom. And we wring our hands and say, "Something must be done."

[32]I agree that something must be done. It's time for a meaningful, nation-wide conversation about mental health. That's the only way our nation can ever truly heal.

[33]God help me. God help Michael. God help us all.

Reading Comprehension Questions

Choose the best meaning of each word in *italics*. Use context clues to make your choice.

Vocabulary in Context

1. "I can wear these pants,' he said, his tone increasingly *belligerent*, the black-hole pupils of his eyes swallowing the blue irises." (paragraph 2)

a. humble
b. engaged
c. hostile
d. friendly

Vocabulary in Context

2. "You can't wear whatever pants you want to,' I said, my tone *affable*, reasonable." (paragraph 5)

a. cold
b. friendly
c. angry
d. fearful

Central Idea

3. Which of the following sentences states the central idea of the passage?

a. "Three days before 20 year-old Adam Lanza killed his mother, then opened fire on a classroom full of Connecticut kindergarteners, my 13-year old son Michael (name changed) missed his school bus because he was wearing the wrong color pants." (paragraph 1)

CONTINUED

b. "I live with a son who is mentally ill." (paragraph 6)

c. "We still don't know what is wrong with Michael." (paragraph 9)

d. "It's time for a meaningful, nation-wide conversation about mental health." (paragraph 32)

Supporting Details

 **4.** According to the passage, Michael pulled a knife and threatened to kill his mother and himself because

a. he had on the wrong color pants.

b. his mother asked him to return library books.

c. his mother grounded him from using electronics for the day.

d. his mother threatened to take him to a mental hospital.

Transitions

 **5.** "By day three, he was my calm, sweet boy again, all apologies and promises to get better." (paragraph 24)

The relationship of ideas **within** this sentence is

a. cause and effect.
b. time order.
c. comparison/contrast.
d. generalization-example.

Transitions

 **6.** "I love my son. But he terrifies me." (paragraph 6)

The relationship of ideas **between** these sentences is

a. cause and effect.
b. time order.
c. comparison/contrast.
d. generalization-example.

Fact and Opinion

 **7.** "With state-run treatment centers and hospitals shuttered, prison is now the last resort for the mentally ill—Rikers Island, the LA County Jail and Cook County Jail in Illinois housed the nation's largest treatment centers in 2011." (paragraph 30)

This sentence is a statement of

a. fact.
b. opinion.
c. fact and opinion.

Tone and Purpose

 **8.** The overall tone and purpose of the author is

a. to inform the public about her mentally ill son Michael.

b. to entertain the public with interesting details about the author's experiences with her son Michael.

c. to persuade the public to address the need for improved mental health care in this country.

Inferences

a **9.** Based on the details in paragraphs 29 and 30, we can infer that

a. there exists a strong link between mental health and crime.

b. all prison inmates are mentally ill.

c. prison is the best place to receive mental health care.

d. mentally ill people always commit crimes.

Argument

d **10.** The following items from paragraph 27 contain a claim and a list of supports for that claim. Which sentence states the claim?

a. "According to Mother Jones, since 1982, 61 mass murders involving firearms have occurred throughout the country."

b. "Of these, 43 of the killers were white males, and one was a woman."

c. "Mother Jones focused on whether the killers obtained their guns legally (most did)."

d. "But this highly visible sign of mental illness should lead us to consider how many people in the U.S. live in fear, like I do."

Mapping

Complete the following story web with information from the passage. *Wording may vary.*

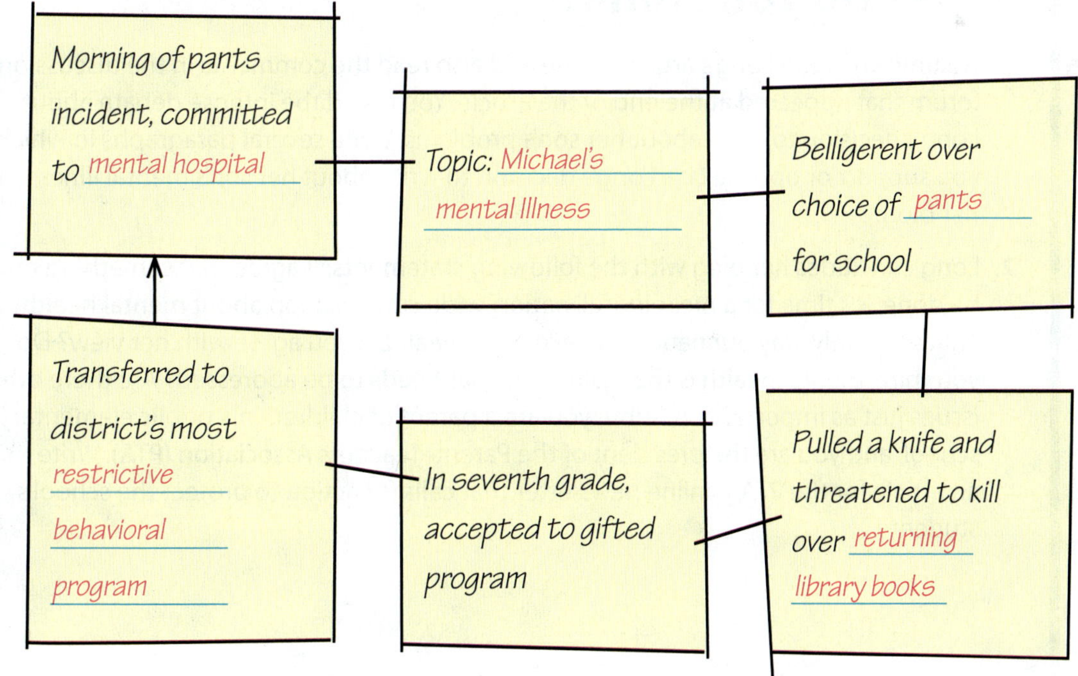

CONTINUED

After Reading Discussion Questions: Meaning, Structure, and Expression

1. **Main Idea:** Work as a group to write a summary that answers the following questions: What purpose did Liza Long have for writing this essay? Who is her intended audience? What is the essay's main idea?
2. **Relevant Details:** While many praised Liza Long as brave for focusing much needed attention on mental illness, others accused her of exploiting a tragedy for personal fame. Her critics claim she shared too much personal and damaging information about her son. One critic, Sarah Kendzior, pointed out that Long did little to protect her son's identity and damaged his reputation by promoting him as a future mass murderer. Do you think Liza Long was brave to publish her struggles and worries as a mother of a mentally ill child? Or do you agree with critics who accuse her of damaging her son's reputation?
3. **Logical Order:** Long begins her blog with a recent incident in her son's life. Then she moves back and forth in time from earlier experiences to the recent incident. Do you find her flow of ideas clear and easy to follow or confusing? Explain your thoughts.
4. **Effective Expression:** How would you describe Liza Long's attitude toward her son? What tone does she use as she discusses him? Why does she have this attitude or take this tone toward her son? Give examples.

What Do You Think?

1. Assume you read Long's article online and also read the comments in the discussion forum that appeared at the end of the article. You noted the intense debate about Long's decision to write about her son's problems. Write several paragraphs in which you support or oppose Liza Long's decision to write about her son's mental illness in her blog.
2. Long concludes her blog with the following statements: "I agree that something must be done. It's time for a meaningful, nation-wide conversation about mental health. That's the only way our nation can ever truly heal." Do you agree with her view? Do you think mental health is the main issue that needs to be addressed? Are there other issues just as important? Assume you are a parent of children in a public elementary school, and you are the president of the Parent–Teachers Association (PTA). Write an article for the PTA's online newsletter that calls for action to protect the school's students.

Effective Reading/Writing Scorecard

"I am Adam Lanza's Mother"

Skill	Number Correct	Points	Total
Vocabulary			
Vocabulary in Context (2 items)		x 5 =	
Comprehension			
Central Idea (1 item)		x 10 =	
Supporting Details (1 item)		x 10 =	
Transitions (2 items)		x 10 =	
Fact and Opinion (1 item)		x 10 =	
Tone and Purpose (1 item)		x 10 =	
Inferences (1 item)		x 10 =	
Argument (1 item)		x 10 =	
Mapping (5 items)		x 2 =	
		Comprehension Score	

Photo Credits

2: Solphoto/Shutterstock; 3 top: Lucky Business/Shutterstock; 3 middle: Pressmaster/Shutterstock; 3 bottom: Comstock Images/Getty Images; 4: Diego Cervo/Fotolia; 8: Sebastian Kaulitzki/Shutterstock; 11: Dvarg/Fotolia; 16 top: Wavebreak Media Ltd/Alamy; 16 middle: Blend Images/Alamy; 16 bottom: Nikolay Mamluke/Getty Images; 18: Wavebreak Media Ltd/Getty Images; 19 top left: Hurst Photo/Fotolia; 19 top right: Robert Kneschke/Fotolia; 19 bottom left: Blend Images/Shutterstock; 19 bottom right: SCPhotos / Alamy; 23: Purestock/Getty Images; 30: Wavebreak Media Ltd/Shutterstock; 31 left: Dwaschnig/Shutterstock; 31 middle: Blaj Gabriel/Shutterstock; 31 right: Rido/Shutterstock; 36: Frank and Helena/AGE Fotostock; 37: Ariel Skelley/AGE Fotostock; 49 and 51: Gina Sanders/Fotolia; 54: Cobalt/Fotolia; 62: Wavebreak Media Ltd/Shutterstock; 72: Purestock/Getty Images; 73 top: Image Source Plus/Alamy; 73 middle: Alex Skopje/Shutterstock; 73 bottom: Ragma Images/Shutterstock; 116: © DreamWorks/Courtesy Everett Collection; 122: Paul Vasarhelyi/Shutterstock; 123 top: Chris Ryan/Getty Images; 123 middle: Goodluz/Shutterstock; 123 bottom: Hill Street Studios/Blend Images/Corbis; 125 left: Tammy Hanratty/Corbis; 125 right: Tim Robbins/Mint Images/Corbis; 128 top left: Darrin Henry/Shutterstock; 128 top right: Corbis; 128 bottom left: Moodboard/Corbis; 128 bottom right: Bettmann/Corbis; 133: Radius Images/Corbis; 141 top: Eddie Gerald/Alamy; 141 middle: Visions of America/SuperStock; 141 bottom: Joe Stevens/Retna Ltd./Corbis; 162: Chromatika Multimedia/Shutterstock; 163 left: Troy House/Corbis; 163 middle: Kristy-Anne Glubish/Design Pics/Corbis; 163 right: Nathan Griffith/Corbis; 166 top: Cultura/Marcel Weber/Getty Images; 163 middle: Jeff Greenberg/PhotoEdit; 163 bottom: Bill Varie/Corbis; 168 top: Danita Delimont/Alamy; 168 bottom: Gene Blevins/LA Daily News/Corbis; 169 top: Florian Kopp/imagebro/AGE Fotostock; 169 middle top: Bob Krist/Corbis; 169 middle bottom: Susan MacLeod/Alamy; 169 bottom: Image Source/Corbis; 196: Arena Creative/Shutterstock; 197 top: Wave Break Media/Shutterstock; 197 middle: Monkey Business Images/Shutterstock; 197 bottom: Monkey Business Images/Shutterstock; 200: Sebastian Duda/Shutterstock; 205 left: Matthew Benoit/Shutterstock; 205 middle: Photographee/Shutterstock; 205 right: Jinga/Shutterstock; 210: Zoran Zeremski/Shutterstock; 227: Janos Levente/Shutterstock; 232: Burben/Shutterstock; 233 left: Diego Cervo/Shutterstock; 233 middle: R Snapshot Photos/Shutterstock; 233 right: Bike Rider London/Shutterstock; 249 left and right: Anton Oparin/Alamy; 251 left: Oleg Mikhaylov/Shutterstock; 251 right: John Panella/Shutterstock; 268 left: Pixellover RM 9/Alamy; 268 right: Pressmaster/Shutterstock; 269 top: Avana/Getty Images; 269 middle: Stock Connection Distribution/Alamy; 269 bottom: Jamie Kingham/Cultura/Corbis; 280 top left: Picture Net/Corbis; 280 top right: Wavebreak Media Ltd/Veer/Corbis; 280 bottom left: Hero Images/Corbis; 280 bottom right: Sonja Pacho/Corbis; 298 top left: Tracy Hornbrook/Dreamstime; 298 top middle: Jodi Jacobson/Getty Images; 298 top right: Craig McCausland/Getty Images; 298 lower top: Disc Pictures/AsiaPix/Corbis; 298 lower middle: Mediscan/Corbis; 298 lower bottom: Radius Images/Corbis; 314: Melis/Shutterstock; 315 top, middle, bottom: Tyler Olson/Shutterstock; 317 top left: Wire Image/Getty Images; 317 top middle: Mike Blake/Reuters/Corbis; 317 top right: Frank Polich/Reuters/Corbis; 317 bottom left: Joe Stevens/Retna Ltd./Corbis; 317 bottom right: Alex Wong/Pool/Corbis; 319 all: Russell Sadur/DK Images; 338: Everett Collection Historical/Alamy; 358: Shalunts/Shutterstock; 364: Umahtete/Shutterstock; 365 left: John Atashian/Corbis; 365 middle: Jessica Rinaldi/Corbis; 365 right: Chad Batka/Corbis; 368: Daizuoxin/Shuttestock; 369: Martin Rietze/Moodboard/Corbis; 376: Mast3r/Shutterstock; 385: Migclick/Shutterstock; 393: Image Source/Corbis; 398: Syda Productions/Shutterstock; 399 top: Tammy Hanratty/Corbis; 399 middle: Ken Seet/Corbis; 399 bottom: Studio Annika/Getty Images; 417: Ollyy/Shutterstock; 427: Tim Pannell/Corbis; 434: Shutterstock; 438: Brownie Harris/Corbis; 442 left: 145/Martin Carlsson/Ocean/Corbis; 442 right: Erwin Rachbauer/Imagebroker/Corbis; 443 top left: Gary Cameron/Reuters/Corbis; 443 top right: Ma Dan/Xinhua Press/Corbis; 443 middle left: Izmocars/Izmo/Corbis; 443 middle right: Izmocars/Izmo/Corbis; 443 bottom left: Richard Baker/In Pictures/Corbis; 443 bottom right: Stuart O'Sullivan/Corbis; 458 top: Meena/Shutterstock; 458 bottom: Whisson/Jordan/Corbis; 468: The Gallery Collection/Corbis; 472: Maradonna/Shutterstock; 476: George Diebold/Getty Images; 477 left: Blazej Lyjak/Shutterstock; 477 top right: Iko/Shuttestock; 477 middle right: Monkey Business Images/Shutterstock; 477 bottom right: Stock/360/Getty Images; 502: Guentermanaus/Shutterstock; 507: Egorich/Shutterstock; 512: Teeranop/Shutterstock; 513 top left: Snehit/Shutterstock; 513 top right: John Kwan/Shutterstock; 513 bottom left: Alex Skopje/Shutterstock; 513 bottom right: Dusit/Shutterstock; 520: Jimmy Margulies/Cagle Cartoons, Inc.; 537: Belushi/Shutterstock; 543 top: Mark Bowden/Getty Images; 543 bottom: Astro Boi/Fotolia; 544: Shutterstock; 548: ABB Photo/Shutterstock; 554: Tim Pannell/Corbis; 555 top: Alan Schein Photography/Corbis; 555 top middle left: Benelux/Corbis; 555 middle right: James Leynse/Corbis; 555 bottom middle left: Lisa B./Corbis; 555 bottom right: Monalyn Gracia/Corbis; 555 bottom left: Ariel Skelley/Corbis; 559: Cagle Cartoons; 565: National Fluid Milk Processor Promotion Board; 585: Lauri Patterson/Getty Images; 591: Paul Vasarhelyi/Shutterstock; 595: Ethan Daniels/Shutterstock; 596: Bike Rider London/Shutterstock; 597 left: Walter Lockwood/Alamy; 597 middle: Leah-Anne Thompson/Shutterstock; 597 right: Monkey Business Images/Shutterstock; 602: Dive Hive/Shutterstock; 618: NOAA; 625: Nick White/Image Source/Corbis; 686: 68/Ocean/Corbis

Text Credits

Aronson, Elliot, Wilson, Timothy D., and Akert, Robin M., *Social Psychology*, 8th ed., © 2013. Reprinted and Electronically reproduced by permission of Pearson Education, Inc., Upper Saddle River, New Jersey.

Audesirk, Gerald, Audesirk, Teresa, and Byers, Bruce E., *Biology: Life on Earth*, 9th ed., © 2011. Reprinted and Electronically reproduced by permission of Pearson Education, inc., Upper Saddle River, New Jersey.

Bade, Robin, and Parkin, Michael, *Foundations of Economics*, 6th ed., © 2013. Reprinted and Electronically reproduced by permission of Pearson Education, Inc., Upper Saddle River, New Jersey.

Bittinger, Marvin A., and Beecher, Judith A., *Introductory and Intermediate Algebra: Combined Approach*. Pearson Education.

Brownell, Judi, *Listening: Attitudes, Principles, and Skills*. Pearson Education.

Carl, John, *Think Sociology*. Pearson Education.

Carnes, Mark, and Garraty, John, *The American Nation: A History of the United States*. Pearson Education.

Ciccarellil, Saundra K., and White, J. Noland, *Psychology*, 4th ed., © 2015. Reprinted and Electronically reproduced by permission of Pearson Education, Inc., Upper Saddle River, New Jersey.

Daytona State College. Screenshot of Daytona State College Library Services, http://www.daytonastate.edu/library/. Reprinted by permission of Daytona State College.

DeVito, Joseph A., *Essentials of Human Communication*, 4th ed., © 2002. Reprinted and Electronically reproduced by permission of Pearson Education, Inc., Upper Saddle River, New Jersey.

DeVito, Joseph A. *The Essentials of Public Speaking,* 4th ed. Pearson Education.

DeVito, Joseph A., *Human Communication: The Basic Course*, 12th ed., © 2012. Reprinted and Electronically reproduced by permission of Pearson Education, Inc., Upper Saddle River, New Jersey.

DeVito, Joseph A. *The Interpersonal Communication Book*, 12th ed., © 2009. Reprinted and Electronically reproduced by permission of Pearson Education, Inc., Upper Saddle River, New Jersey.

DeVito, Joseph A. *Interpersonal Messages: Communication* and Relationship Skills, 2nd ed., © 2011. Pearson Education.

DiYanni, Robert, and Hoy, Pat C., *The Scribner Handbook for Writers*, Pearson Education.

Donatelle, Rebecca J., Access to Health, 13th ed., © 2014. Reprinted and Electronically reproduced by permission of Pearson Education, Inc., Upper Saddle River, New Jersey.

Donatelle, Rebecca J., *Health: The Basics, Green Edition*, 9th ed., © 2011. Reprinted and Electronically reproduced by permission of Pearson Education, Inc., Upper Saddle River, New Jersey.

Donatelle, Rebecca J., and Ketcham, Patricia, *Access to Health*, 12th ed., © 2012. Reprinted and Electronically reproduced by permission of Pearson Education, Inc., Upper Saddle River, New Jersey.

Ebert, Ronald J., and Griffin, Ricky W., *Business Essentials*, 8th ed., Pearson.

Eshleman, J. Ross, and Bulcroft, Richard, *The Family*. Pearson Education.

Evans, Alan, Martin, Kendall, and Poatsy, Mary Anne, *Technology in Action, Introductory Version*, 7th ed., © 2011. Reprinted and Electronically reproduced by permission of Pearson Education, Inc., Upper Saddle River, New Jersey.

Gerrig, Richard J., and Zimbardo, Philip G., *Psychology and Life*, 19th ed., © 2010. Reprinted and Electronically reproduced by permission of Pearson Education, Inc., Upper Saddle River, New Jersey.

Gianetti, Louis D., *Understanding Movies*, Pearson Education.

Henslin, James M., *Essentials of Sociology: A Down-to-Earth Approach*, 8th ed., © 2009. Reprinted and Electronically reproduced by permission of Pearson Education, Inc., Upper Saddle River, New Jersey.

Henslin, James M., *Essentials of Sociology: A Down-to-Earth Approach*, 9th ed., © 2011. Reprinted and Electronically reproduced by permission of Pearson Education, Inc., Upper Saddle River, New Jersey.

Henslin, James M., *Sociology: A Down-to-Earth Approach*, 10th ed., © 2010. Reprinted and Electronically reproduced by permission of Pearson Education, Inc., Upper Saddle River, New Jersey.

Hopson, Janet L., Donatelle, Rebecca J., and Littrell, Tanya R., *Get Fit, Stay Well!* Pearson Education.

Kennedy, X. J., and Gioia, Dana, *Literature: An Introduction to Fiction, Poetry, and Drama*, 8th ed., © 2002. Reprinted and Electronically reproduced by permission of Pearson Education, Inc., Upper Saddle River, New Jersey.

Kennedy, X. J., and Gioia, Dana, *Literature: An Introduction to Fiction, Poetry, Drama, and Writing*. © 2009. Reprinted and Electronically reproduced by permission of Pearson Education, Inc., Upper Saddle River, New Jersey.

Kosslyn, Stephen M., and Rosenberg, Robin S., *Psychology: The Brain, the Person, the World*, 1st ed., © 2001. Reprinted and Electronically reproduced by permission of Pearson Education, Inc., Upper Saddle River, New Jersey.

Lutgens, Frederick K., Tarbuck, Edward J., and Tasa, Dennis G., *Foundations of Earth Science*, 6th ed., © 2011. Reprinted and Electronically reproduced by permission of Pearson Education, Inc., Upper Saddle River, New Jersey.

Marieb, Elaine N., *Essentials of Human Anatomy & Physiology*, 9th ed., © 2009. Reproduced and Electronically reproduced by permission of Pearson Education, Inc., Upper Saddle River, New Jersey.

Martin, James Kirby, Roberts, Randy J., Mintz, Steven, McMurry, Linda O., and Jones, James H., *America and It's Peoples: Vol 1 to 1877*, Pearson Education.

McGuigan, F. J., *Encyclopedia of Stress*. Pearson Education.

Novak, Mark, *Issues in Aging*. Pearson Education.

Powers, Scott K., Dodd, Stephen L., and Jackson, Erica M., *Total Fitness & Wellness*, 6th ed., © 2014. Reprinted and Electronically reproduced by permission of Pearson Education, Inc., Upper Saddle River, New Jersey.

Pruitt, B. E., and Stein, Jane J., *Healthstyles: Decisions for Living Well*, 2nd ed., © 1999. Reprinted and Electronically reproduced by permission of Pearson Education, Inc., Upper Saddle River, New Jersey.

Rutledge, Kim, "The Great Garbage Patch." *National Geographic Education*.

Schmalleger, Frank, *Criminal Justice Today: An Introductory Text for the 21st Century*, Pearson.

Schwartz, Mary Ann A., and Scott, Barbara Marliene, *Marriage and Families: Diversity and Change*, 6th ed. Pearson Education.

Smith, Robert Leo, and Smith, Thomas M., *Elements of Ecology*, 4th ed. Pearson Education.

Smith, Thomas M., and Smith Robert Leo, *Elements of Ecology*, 8th ed. Pearson Education.

Solomon, Michael, et al., *Better Business*, 3rd ed., © 2014. Pearson Education.

Sterns, Peter N., Adas, Michael, Schwartz, Stuart B., and Gilbert, Mark J., *World Civilization: The Global Experience*, 6th ed., Longman, 2011.

Strayer, David L., Drews, Frank A., and Crouch, Dennis J., *A Comparison of the Cell Phone Driver and the Drunk Driver* from HUMAN FACTORS. Used by permission of SAGE Publications via CCC.

Tannen, Deborah, *You Just Don't Understand*. Copyright © by Deborah Tannen. Reprinted by permission of HarperCollins Publishers.

Teenshealth.org. "Bullying is a Big Problem." Teenshealth.org. Nemours Foundation.

U.S. Federal Bureau of Investigation, "Consumers Beware."

Van Syckle, Barbara, and Tietje, Brian, Anybody's Business, 1st ed., © 2010. Reproduced and Electronically Reproduced by permission of Pearson Education, Inc., Upper Saddle River, New Jersey.

Walker, John R., *Introduction to Hospitality*, 6th ed. Pearson Education.

Walker, John R., *Introduction to Hospitality Management*, 3rd ed., © 2010. Reprinted and Electronically reproduced by permission of Pearson Education, Inc., Upper Saddle River, New Jersey.

Wood, Samuel E., Wood, Ellen Green, and Boyd, Denise G., *Mastering the World of Psychology*, 3rd ed., © 2008. Reprinted and Electronically reproduced by permission of Pearson Education, Inc., Upper Saddle River, New Jersey.

Index

D

E

P

T